Routledge Handbook of Development Ethics

The *Routledge Handbook of Development Ethics* provides readers with insight into the central questions of development ethics, the main approaches to answering them, and areas for future research. Over the past seventy years, it has been argued and increasingly accepted that worthwhile development cannot be reduced to economic growth. Rather, a number of other goals must be realised:

- Enhancement of people's well-being
- Equitable sharing in benefits of development
- Empowerment to participate freely in development
- Environmental sustainability
- Promotion of human rights
- Promotion of cultural freedom, consistent with human rights
- Responsible conduct, including integrity over corruption

Agreement that these are essential goals has also been accompanied by disagreements about how to conceptualize or apply them in different cases or contexts. Using these seven goals as an organizing principle, this *Handbook* presents different approaches to achieving each one, drawing on academic literature, policy documents and practitioner experience.

This international and multidisciplinary *Handbook* will be of great interest to development policymakers and program workers, and students and scholars in development studies, public policy, international studies, applied ethics and other related disciplines.

Jay Drydyk is Professor of Philosophy at Carleton University, Ottawa, Canada. He is Past President of the International Development Ethics Association and a Fellow of the Human Development and Capability Association.

Lori Keleher is Associate Professor of Philosophy at New Mexico State University, USA. She serves on the board of the International Development Ethics Association, as well as on the Executive Council and as a Fellow for the Human Development and Capability Association.

"Jay Drydyk and Lori Keleher have done a stellar job in bringing leading scholars in development ethics together for this *Handbook of Development Ethics*. The chapters in this handbook make it clear that development is not just about economic growth, but in the first place about wellbeing, justice, empowerment, the environment, human rights, cultural freedoms, and taking responsibilities. This handbook will become an essential resource for any student or teacher of development ethics. And it should be interesting for anyone who wants to think systematically about what matters when moving towards a better world for all."

Ingrid Robeyns, Chair in Ethics of Institutions, Department of Philosophy and Religious Studies, Utrecht University, Netherlands

"The three quarters of a century after the second world war has seen dramatic improvements, on average, in life expectancy, educational achievements, and income in parts of the world where these were lowest. The 'on average' qualification is of course important—some have benefited much more than others, and significant numbers have been immiserized. What are the basic ethical principles according to which one would assess the gains for some against the losses for others in health, education and income? Are these the only dimensions along which changes are to be measured and assessed? And in any case, can such consequentialist perspectives capture the essence of ethical dilemmas in development? These questions do not make for easy answers, and there is lively debate among scholars on development ethics, animated by ground level political expressions, sometimes violent, of huge discontent among those 'being developed'. This excellent volume brings together leading analysts to chart the terrain and lay the foundations for further systematic debate and exploration. It will become a go-to reference for those working on normative assessment of the development process."

Ravi Kanbur, T.H. Lee Professor of World Affairs, International Professor of Applied Economics and Management, and Professor of Economics at Cornell University, USA

"This book is an extraordinary conversation among diverse ethical values that in the process revises each one of them. Like in a symphony, where the color and sound of an instrument is perceived differently when joined by others, the seven values organizing this handbook interact as living creatures. The orchestra is in place; and it is worth listening to it like a unified piece. It is much more than a handbook."

Javier M. Iguiniz-Echeverria, Professor Emeritus, Pontifical Catholic University of Peru, Executive Secretary of the National Accord of Peru, President of the Institute for Human Development in Latin America

Routledge Handbook of Development Ethics

Edited by Jay Drydyk and Lori Keleher

First published 2019
by Routledge

2 Park Square, Milton Park, Abingdon, Oxfordshire OX14 4RN
52 Vanderbilt Avenue, New York, NY 10017

Routledge is an imprint of the Taylor & Francis Group, an informa business

First issued in paperback 2020

British Library Cataloguing-in-Publication Data
A catalogue record for this book is available from the British Library

Library of Congress Cataloging-in-Publication Data
Names: Drydyk, Jay, editor. | Keleher, Lori, editor.
Title: Routledge handbook of development ethics / edited by Jay Drydyk and Lori Keleher.
Other titles: Handbook of development ethics
Description: Abingdon, Oxon ; New York, NY : Routledge, 2018. | Includes bibliographical references and index.
Identifiers: LCCN 2018009994 (print) | LCCN 2018025386 (ebook) | ISBN 9781315626796 (eBook) | ISBN 9781138647909 (hardback)
Subjects: LCSH: Economic development—Moral and ethical aspects. | Economic development—Social aspects. | Social ethics. | Human rights.
Classification: LCC HD75 (ebook) | LCC HD75 .R679 2018 (print) | DDC 174/.4—dc23
LC record available at https://lccn.loc.gov/2018009994

ISBN: 978-1-138-64790-9 (hbk)
ISBN: 978-0-367-62945-8 (pbk)

DOI: 10.4324/9781315626796

Contents

Figures and tables

Figures

Tables

Notes on contributors

Alejandra Boni is Professor at the Universitat Politècnica de València, Spain, and Deputy Director of the INGENIO Research Institute (CSIC-UPV). She is Honorary Professor at the University of the Free State, South Africa, and Vice-President of the International Development Ethics Association. Her research analyzes educational processes using the capability approach and development education. She is co-author of *Universities and Global Human Development: Theoretical and Empirical Insights for Social Change*, published by Routledge in 2016.

Jérôme Ballet is Senior Lecturer in economics at the University of Versailles and Senior Research Fellow at the C3ED (Economics and Ethics Center for Environment and Development). He is the editor of the online journal *Ethics and Economics* and has published several books and articles on ethics and economics. He is on the advisory board of the International Development Ethics Association.

Benedict S. B. Chan is currently Assistant Professor in the Department of Religion and Philosophy and Research Fellow at the Centre of Applied Ethics at Hong Kong Baptist University. He received his PhD in the Philosophy Department at the University of Maryland, College Park. His areas of research specialization include social and political philosophy, applied ethics and moral philosophy, and comparative philosophy (Chinese and Western). He has published in academic journals such as *Dao: A Journal of Comparative Philosophy*, *Global Policy*, *International Journal of Chinese Comparative Philosophy of Medicine*, and *Journal of Bioethical Inquiry*.

Flavio Comim is Associate Professor at Ramon Llull University in Barcelona and an Affiliated Lecturer in Land Economy and Development Studies at the University of Cambridge as well as a Visiting Fellow at St. Edmund's College. He has worked as Senior Economist for UNDP and as a consultant for UNEP, FAO, WHO, and UNESCO. He coordinated the 2014 Panama Human Development Report on *Children and the Youth in Panama* and the 2010 Brazil Human Development Report on *Human Values*. He has co-edited three books on the capability approach.

Andrew Crabtree is Adjunct Associate Professor at Copenhagen Business School where he holds a course on poverty, sustainability, and the private sector. His publications include work on ethics, the capability approach, sustainability and unsustainability, sustainability indicators, climate change, disasters, and mental health. He has advanced a conceptualization of sustainable development as being an increase in *legitimate freedoms:* Freedoms that cannot be reasonably rejected.

Julian Culp is Assistant Professor in Philosophy at the American University of Paris (France). He has written his dissertation and habilitation in Philosophy at Goethe University Frankfurt

(Germany) and held postdoctoral fellowships at the universities of Toronto (Canada) and Louvain (Belgium). He is the author of *Global Justice and Development* (Palgrave Macmillan, 2014) and is currently working on a book entitled *Transnational Democratic Education*. He also serves as co-editor of *Global Justice: Theory Practice Rhetoric*.

Séverine Deneulin is Associate Professor in International Development at the University of Bath, UK, and, in 2017–2018, she was a Visiting Fellow at the Kellogg Institute for International Studies at the University of Notre Dame, Indiana, USA. Her research interests are social ethics and the interaction between religion, social justice, and environmental concerns. She holds a DPhil in Development Studies from Oxford University, UK.

Nigel Dower is Honorary Senior Lecturer in Philosophy and Associate at the Centre for Global Development at the University of Aberdeen where he taught for thirty-seven years, with an interruption to teach for three years in Zimbabwe. His main research interests are in the ethics and philosophy of development, environment, and international relations. He is the author of *World Poverty – Challenge and Response* (1983), *World Ethics – the New Agenda* (1998, 2nd ed. 2007), *An Introduction to Global Citizenship* (2003), and *The Ethics of War and Peace* (2009) as well as co-editor of *Global Citizenship – a Critical Reader* (with John Williams, 2002). He was the second president of the International Development Ethics Association (IDEA).

Stephen L. Esquith is Professor of Philosophy and Dean of the Residential College in the Arts and Humanities at Michigan State University. He is the author of *The Political Responsibilities of Everyday Bystanders* (Pennsylvania State University Press, 2010). Since 2004 he has been working on several peace-building projects in Mali, currently a collaborative project with the Malian Institut pour l'Education Populaire funded by the MSU Alliance for African Partnership.

Oscar Garza-Vázquez is Associate Professor in Economics at Universidad de las Américas Puebla, México. His areas of research include development ethics, the intersection between welfare economics and theories of justice from the perspective of the capability approach, and the practical relevance of these theories to design and evaluate social policies. He received his PhD in International Development from the Department of Social and Policy Sciences at the University of Bath, UK.

Rebecca Gutwald is Academic Director (PhD programmes) at the Munich School of Philosophy, Germany. Her main areas of research are political philosophy, the capability approach, and the normative foundations of social justice. Currently, she is working on a book on the concept of resilience in development and the capability approach.

Louise Haagh is a Reader in the Politics Department of the University of York. Previously, she obtained her doctorate from St. Antony's College, Oxford University, and held a British Academy Postdoctoral Research Fellowship at St. Antony's. She researches problems relating to the democratization of human development, comparative welfare states, economic justice, modalities of institutional change, and social transformation in middle-income and mature economies.

Sirkku K. Hellsten was a Senior Researcher at the Nordic Africa Institute. She worked as a Professor of Philosophy at the University of Dar es Salaam, Tanzania, and held a permanent affiliation with the University of Helsinki as a Docent of Social and Moral Philosophy. She has worked as Counsellor for Economics, Governance, and Human Rights at the Finnish Embassies in Maputo,

Mozambique, and Nairobi, Kenya. She has published extensively on issues related to development ethics, social justice, human rights, governance, and African political economy. She was a member of the advisory board of the International Development Ethics Association and a Lead Editor of the *Journal of Global Ethics*. Dr. Hellsten passed away shortly before this volume was published.

Yuvraj Joshi is a human rights lawyer and scholar. His main areas of research are in constitutional and comparative law, gender, sexual and reproductive rights, affirmative action, transitional justice, and critical perspectives on human rights.

Asmita Kabra is Professor and Dean at the School of Human Ecology, Ambedkar University, Delhi, India. She teaches, researches, and writes on conservation, human displacement, and agrarian livelihoods using perspectives from critical agrarian studies, political economy, and political ecology. She has also been engaged for two decades with development practice in the fields of rural livelihood, school education, participatory conservation, and social impact assessment of development/conservation projects.

Serene J. Khader is a moral and political philosopher working primarily on feminist issues in global justice. Khader is the author of *Adaptive Preferences and Women's Empowerment* (2011) and she is at work on a book titled *Decolonizing Universalism in Transnational Feminist Ethics* (Oxford University Press). She holds the Jay Newman Chair in Philosophy of Culture, Brooklyn College, and is an Associate Professor of Philosophy and Women's and Gender Studies at the CUNY Graduate Center.

Kouamékan J. M. Koffi holds a PhD in Economics and a Master's degree in Development Sociology. A Researcher at the Ivoirian Center for Economic and Social Research (CIRES) and at the Mixed Unit of International Resilience Research (UMI 236 Résiliences – IRD/CIRES), his research focuses on the social sustainability of development, the ethics of development, and resilience. He has published several papers on natural resource management in sub-Saharan Africa. Concerning the analysis of resilience and its socio-economic implications, he was the guest editor of the special issue "Resilience and Societies" published in the 2014 issue of *Ethics and Economics*.

Christine M. Koggel is Professor of Philosophy at Carleton University in Ottawa and Professor Emerita of Philosophy at Bryn Mawr College, Pennsylvania. Her main areas of research and teaching are in moral and political philosophy with specific interests in development ethics, feminism, and relational theory. She has authored, edited, and co-edited more than fifteen books, collections, and special issues and has numerous publications in journals and edited collections. She has held offices with the Canadian Society for Women in Philosophy, the International Development Ethics Association, and the American Philosophical Association.

Stacy J. Kosko is Assistant Research Professor and Associate Director of the Minor in International Development and Conflict Management (MIDCM) in the Department of Government and Politics at the University of Maryland (USA). She holds a PhD in Public Policy and Development Studies from the University of Maryland and an MS in Foreign Service and International Conflict Management from Georgetown University, with a certificate in Refugee and Humanitarian Emergencies. Her research focus is on development ethics, human rights, and severely marginalized populations. She spent the 2017–2018 academic year as a Fulbright Scholar in Moldova. With Lori Keleher, she is the co-editor of *Agency and Democracy in Development Ethics: Essays in Honor of David A. Crocker* (Cambridge University Press, 2018).

Alice Kouadio, born Odounfa, is an engineer of statistical work; a doctor of economics; a researcher at the Faculty of Economics and Development at the Alassane Ouattara University in Bouaké, Republic of Côte d'Ivoire; and a founding member of the UMI Résilience "International Joint Research Unit on Resilience," co-chaired by the Ivory Coast Center for Economic and Social Research (CIRES) and the International Research Institute for Development (IRD). She also chairs the NGO "Study Group on Education in Africa – Côte d'Ivoire Section (GRETAF-CI). Her research themes relate to the living conditions of the household, inequalities in access to education, and the setting up of observatories on resilience.

Anna Malavisi is Assistant Professor in the Department of Philosophy and Humanistic Studies at Western Connecticut State University. She has a PhD in Philosophy from Michigan State University. Her dissertation, "Global Development and Its Discontents: Rethinking the Theory and Practice," is a critical analysis of global development from an ethical and feminist epistemology perspective. Her interests include practical and global ethics, feminist philosophy/epistemology, social and political thought, and the philosophy of violence. She has a Master of Health and International Development degree and has worked for sixteen years in Latin America in the NGO sector in areas of development practice and management.

Stephen P. Marks is the François-Xavier Bagnoud Professor of Health and Human Rights at the Harvard T.H. Chan School of Public Health, where he directs the Program on Human Rights in Development. With degrees in law and international relations from Stanford and several universities in France, as well as the Syrian Arab Republic, he has worked for the United States Senate, the International Institute of Human Rights (Strasbourg), UNESCO (Paris), the Ford Foundation (New York), and UN peacekeeping operations. His publications focus on development, biotechnology, mass atrocities, terrorism, cultural rights, tobacco control, access to medicines, human rights education, neuroscience, and the right to health.

Katherine Marshall is Senior Fellow at Georgetown University's Berkley Center for Religion, Peace, and World Affairs and Professor of the Practice of Development, Religion, and Conflict, School of Foreign Service. She heads the World Faiths Development Dialogue (WFDD), an NGO that bridges gulfs separating worlds of development and humanitarian affairs and religion. She spent some thirty-five years at the World Bank in varied operational positions, working in Africa, Latin America, and East Asia. Her most recent books include *Global Institutions of Religion: Ancient Movers, Modern Shakers* (Routledge, 2013) and, with Susan Hayward co-editor, *Women, Religion, and Peacebuilding: Illuminating the Unseen* (US Institute of Peace, 2015).

Roger Merino is Research Professor of Public Policy and Legal Theory at the Universidad del Pacífico (Lima, Peru). He was Visiting Scholar at the Harvard Law School's Institute for Global Law and Policy in 2016. He received a PhD in Social and Policy Sciences and a Master's degree with distinction in Globalization and International Policy at the University of Bath (UK). Roger's research agenda includes critical approaches to law and policy, development studies, political ecology, indigenous rights, and social and economic rights. He has published in *Oxford Development Studies*, *Extractive Industries and Society*, and other international journals.

Shashi Motilal is Professor of Philosophy in the Department of Philosophy, University of Delhi, India. She obtained her PhD from SUNY, Buffalo, USA, and has been Visiting Faculty at the University of Akron, Ohio, USA, and Carleton University, Ontario, Canada. She has several publications in national and international journals including three books in the areas of ethics, applied ethics, human rights, gender, and environment. Her research interests also include Indian ethics, philosophy of language, meta-ethics, and normative theory and public policy.

Milena Nikolova is Assistant Professor in the Department of Global Economics and Management at the University of Groningen and a Nonresident Fellow at the Brookings Institution. Her research focuses on a variety of topics related to subjective well-being, migration, transition economies, nonprofits and civil society, international development, labor issues, and institutions.

Eric Palmer is Professor of Philosophy at Allegheny College in Pennsylvania, USA. He is co-editor of *Journal of Global Ethics* and President of the International Development Ethics Association. His writing extends beyond these areas to globalization, to business ethics, and to the history and philosophy of science and culture.

Alain Piveteau is Researcher at the French National Research Institute for Sustainable Development (IRD) in the area of economy. He had for several years carried out research on "assisted development" and local economic development in sub-Saharan Africa, particularly about the role of NGOs and of decentralization (Burkina Faso and Senegal). His work examines social and political conditions of economic transformation in developing countries. His current researches on Morocco include relations between industrialization, innovation, and development, and focuses on emerging capitalisms. He is the author of books, articles, and chapters dealing with the evaluation problem in processes of development, public politics, and globalization.

Prakriti Prajapati is Research Associate at the Energy and Resources Institute, New Delhi, India. She has an MSc degree in Environmental Economics from TERI School of Advanced Studies, Delhi, and a BA with honors in Economics from Lady Shri Ram College for Women, University of Delhi, India. She has served as Guest Faculty in Professional Ethics and Social Responsibility at the Indian Institute of Technology, Delhi. She was previously a Researcher at Indian Institute of Management, Ahmedabad, India, and Ashoka Trust for Research in Ecology and the Environment, Bengaluru, India. Her research interests include philosophy of development, languages of valuation, environmental justice, political ecology of food–water–energy nexus, and biocentrism.

Matthew R.G. Regan is researching a dissertation on democracy and culture in Southeast Asia, focusing on the "Asian values" debate. He holds a BA in History and an MA in modern European History from the Catholic University of America in Washington, D.C., where his research focused on the history of the biological and social sciences and European interpretations of Asian thought and culture. His research interests include the ethics of global development, sustainable development, and Buddhist philosophy.

Karie Cross Riddle is Postdoctoral Fellow in Peace Studies and Political Science at the University of Notre Dame. She has conducted field research with women's peacebuilding groups in Manipur, India, and advocated against child labor in Nepal with the Advocacy Project and BASE-Nepal. Her research focuses on feminist political theory, especially critical approaches to liberal theory, and the conceptualization of broad topics related to global justice, such as peace, justice, and development. Karie is one of the co-coordinators of the Ethics and Development Thematic Group at the Human Development and Capability Association.

Laura Rodríguez is a researcher working on post-mining transitions in the Andean region. She holds an MSc in Political Science and an MA in Development Studies. After working in the public sector in Latin America as a policy advisor, she has been dedicated to implementing action-research methodologies to advance empirical knowledge while coordinating various development projects on human rights, agriculture, indigenous peoples, and food sovereignty.

Eric Rougier is Professor of Economics at the University of Bordeaux (France) and Researcher in GREThA (CNRS 5113). His work examines economic transformation in developing countries with specific focus being put on productive modernization, institutional change, and distributional issues. He has published various pieces of research linking these issues in the case of middle-income countries in general, and of Middle East and North African economies in particular. He has also animated collective research on emerging countries' varieties of capitalisms and middle classes.

Byaruhanga Rukooko Archangel is currently Associate Professor at the Department of Philosophy, Makerere University, Kampala, Uganda. He is currently teaching evolution of international human rights, implementation of ethics and integrity in Uganda, history of philosophy, and media and human rights. He is also currently and thematically researching on homosexuality and his book *Cultures at Crossroads: Homosexuality and Human Tights in Uganda* came out 2017. He also earlier published various articles on the right to food and taught epistemology, social political philosophy, and African philosophy. He is a former Dean of the Faculty of Arts at Makerere University.

Chloe Schwenke is the Interim Executive Director of the Association of Writers and Writing Programs. She previously served as Senior Researcher and Director of the Global Program on Violence, Rights and Inclusion at the International Center for Research on Women; as Vice-President for Global Programs at Freedom House; and earlier still (as a political appointee during the Obama administration) in the dual role of Senior Advisor on Human Rights for Africa and Senior Advisor on LGBT issues at the US Agency for International Development. Her publications include *Reclaiming Value in International Development* (2008) and *Self-ish: A Transgender Awakening* (2018). She is on the executive board of the International Development Ethics Association, and the advisory board of World Learning.

Mitu Sengupta is Associate Professor in the Department of Politics and Public Administration at Ryerson University, Toronto, Canada. She has a PhD in Political Science. She has published widely on Indian market liberalization and development, on labor and migration in India, and on the politics of sporting events and film. Her recent work focuses on normative concerns in international development and international relations, including universal development goals and fair climate change and trade agreements. She is interested, in particular, in India's interventions in these global arenas, and their relationship with domestic normative debates and social movement discourses.

Mario Solís is Professor and Director of the Graduate Program in Philosophy at the University of Costa Rica (UCR) where he teaches moral and political philosophy. He received his PhD at the University of Essex, UK. He has served as a visiting researcher at the Uppsala University, Sweden, and a Visiting Research Associate at UCL, London. His interests include global justice, human rights, and moral and political philosophy. He is the author of *Justicia Situacional: Racionalidad, Normatividad y Teoría Crítica Latinoamericanista* (Situational Justice:

Rationality, Normativity and Latin American Critical Theory) (2016). He is a member of the International Development Ethics Association's executive board; of the Research Committee of the Instituto de Investigaciones Filosóficas, UCR; and of the Asociación Latinoamericana de Filosofía Analítica.

Frances Stewart is Emeritus Professor of Development Economics, University of Oxford. She was Director of the Oxford Department of International Development (1993–2003) and the Centre for Research on Inequality, Human Security, and Ethnicity (2003–2010). She has an honorary doctorate from the University of Sussex and received the Leontief Prize for Advancing the Frontiers of Economic Thought from Tufts in 2013. Her prime recent research interests are horizontal inequalities, conflict, and human development. Among many publications, she is leading author of *Horizontal Inequalities and Conflict: Understanding Group Violence in Multiethnic Societies* (2016) and *Advancing Human Development: Theory and Practice* (with Gustav Ranis and Emma Samman, 2018).

Paul B. Thompson holds the W.K. Kellogg Chair in Agricultural, Food, and Community Ethics at Michigan State University, where he serves on the faculty in the departments of Philosophy, Community Sustainability and Agricultural, Food and Resource Economics. Thompson is the author or co-author of over two hundred scholarly articles. His book *From Field to Fork: Food Ethics for Everyone* (2015) won the Book of the Year Award from the North American Society for Social Philosophy. His book *The Spirit of the Soil: Agriculture and Environmental Ethics* was published in an updated second edition in 2017.

Sridhar Venkatapuram is Senior Lecturer of Global Health and Philosophy in the Department of Global Health and Social Medicine at King's College London. His research and expertise are in global/public health, human rights, ethics, and political philosophy. He aims to bridge normative reasoning, particularly about social justice, with relevant natural and social sciences related to human health. He is the author of *Health Justice: An Argument from the Capabilities Approach.*

Polly Vizard is Associate Professorial Research Fellow and Associate Director of the Centre for Analysis of Social Exclusion at the London School of Economics. Her research focuses on multidimensional poverty and inequality, the analysis of deprivation and distributional outcomes using social surveys and administrative data, social and public policy, social indicators, Sen's capability framework, human rights–based approaches, and equality and human rights monitoring. She is currently Principal Investigator on the CASE research programme Social Policies and Distributional Outcomes in a Changing Britain, which runs from October 2017 to October 2020.

Johannes M. Waldmueller is currently Research Professor in the Department of Political Science and International Relations at the Universidad de Las Américas (UDLA), Quito; Member of the Doctoral Committee in the Faculty of Administration at the Escuela Politécnica Nacional; and Vice-President of Kompreno International. This research association, with offices in Geneva, Sao Paolo, and Ouagadougou, focuses on bridging theory and practice of sustainable development, human rights, and disaster prevention in the global South. His research and publications are concerned with development indicators, interculturality, non-Western approaches to development alternatives, urban–rural transformations, South–South cooperation, and multiple vulnerabilities in disaster mitigation.

Krushil Watene is Senior Lecturer in Philosophy at Massey University in New Zealand. Previously, she was Research Fellow at the James Henare Maori Research Centre at the University of Auckland. Her research interests include contemporary moral and political philosophy, indigenous philosophies, Maori philosophies, and development ethics. She has published widely on the capability approach, Maori and indigenous philosophies, and justice. She is co-editor of *Theorizing Justice*, published by Rowman and Littlefield International, and co-author of *The Capability Approach and Indigenous Peoples*, forthcoming with Routledge.

Merridy Wilson-Strydom is an Associate Professor in the SARCHI Chair in Higher Education and Human Development (HEHD) Research Programme at the University of the Free State, Bloemfontein South Africa. Her work centers on social justice in and through higher education, with a particular focus on inequalities in the contexts of university access and undergraduate education. Merridy has published widely in the fields of higher education and human development/capability approach and is currently a co-researcher on a large-scale ESRC-DfID-funded project (2017–2020) on inclusive higher education learning outcomes (understood as capabilities) for rural and township youth in South Africa.

Acknowledgements

One lovely afternoon in 2008, the editors sat together enjoying cool drinks and New Delhi sunshine. They mused that it would be nice to edit a book together. Now, ten years and several ideas later, that Delhi daydream is a reality.

This particular book represents the state of development ethics thought and research at the present time. The field would not have reached this state were it not for a network of people who, by interacting with and supporting each other's thought and research, have nurtured the discussion of development ethics for the past thirty-five years. We want to begin by acknowledging them – including many who are not named in this list of acknowledgements.

Denis Goulet inspired everyone who knew him to take development ethics seriously, and one of us had the pleasure of having some conversations with him in the back of a bus on a development ethics field trip in Honduras. David Crocker had a longer association with Denis, which began in collaborating with E. Roy Ramirez, Luis Camacho (contributing especially on issues of technology, consumption, and sustainable development), and others in Costa Rica to organize the first workshop on development ethics and to found the International Development Ethics Association. In its early days, this association (IDEA) was more a network than an association, yet it succeeded in drawing development researchers and practitioners together every few years for international conferences on several different continents. We would like to acknowledge the participants but especially the organizers of these conferences that kept this discussion of development ethics alive, notably David Crocker, Ken Aman, Ramon Romero, Cristián Parker, Nigel Dower, Peter Penz, Deane Curtin, K. Rajaratna, Byaruhanga Rukooko Archangel, Chloe Schwenke, Adela Cortina, Christine Koggel, Jay Drydyk, Mario Solís, Anna Malavisi, Lori Keleher, Jérôme Ballet, and Stacy Kosko. We are likewise grateful to the presidents of IDEA who have nurtured and grown the organization: David Crocker, Nigel Dower, Jay Drydyk, Asuncion St. Clair, and Eric Palmer.

We would like to acknowledge the founders, leaders, and many wonderful active members (who are too many to name) of a parallel network for the capability approach, organized as the Human Development and Capabilities Association (HDCA), which has overlapped with IDEA considerably, sharing people, ideas, and projects like this one.

Jean-Luc Dubois's work in sustaining a smaller parallel network of development researchers in France and the French-speaking countries of Africa, whose members have promoted development ethics both within IDEA and within HDCA, also deserves acknowledgement.

Each of us owes a special debt to David Crocker. One of us was recruited into development ethics by Dave while partaking with Nigel Dower in roasted goat, ugali, and Tusker beer at a roadside stand outside Nairobi during the 1991 World Congress of Philosophy. The other co-editor appreciates his supervision for her doctoral thesis, his mentorship, and, above all, his friendship.

The book itself owes much to the help of many people. It has directly benefited from the insights and intellect of our many extraordinary contributors. Ana Reynolds and Holly Longair assisted with various administrative and editorial tasks. Arielle Stirling was especially generous with her time and talent, not only in editing, but more importantly in sharing her insights about how to make many of the chapters more accessible to readers who are new to development ethics.

Our special thanks go to Helena Hurd, Leila Walker, and the rest of the supportive team at Routledge who were always quick and clear with helpful responses to our many questions and whose patience never failed. In the final stages of production we benefitted immensely from the powerful proofreading of Marie Lynne Grandbois and the skilled indexing of Christu John. We are also grateful to Khanam Virjee, the former Routledge editor who encouraged us to begin this project.

We appreciate the support we have received from our colleagues at New Mexico State University and Carleton University.

Finally, we are most grateful for the support of our friends and family throughout the process of working on this book. Lori is especially grateful to her wonderful daughters, Katherine and Samantha, for their patience and encouragement.

1

Introduction

What is development ethics?

Jay Drydyk and Lori Keleher

When we tell people that we work in development ethics, they typically understand us only well enough to be puzzled. They think they understand 'ethics'. They think they understand 'development'. But 'development ethics' – what is that? *Our* question, after hearing this so often, is why 'development ethics' seems so perplexing to so many people. The answer, we think, is relatively simple and yet reveals much about the concept of development ethics. So it is a good starting point for this book.

We pursue that question in the next section. Three further questions are taken up in subsequent sections. First, what are the values or goals that distinguish development that is worthwhile from that which is undesirable? Along which dimensions is some development comparable to others, as better or worse? Here we introduce the seven broad values around which this *Handbook* is organized: well-being, equality, agency and empowerment, environmental sustainability, human rights, cultural freedom, and responsibility. Second, why is it important for development decisions and processes to be ethically justifiable? Does their legitimacy depend on public justifiability? Third, the foregoing demonstrates how open and inclusive development ethics is to people working in development practice as well as to people in many different academic disciplines. Since both of the editors are philosophers by profession, we want to complete this introduction by discussing the particular contributions that our fellow philosophers are well suited to make, if they would like to join the development ethics team.

Judgment and justification

Consider the following comments made in later chapters of this book:

> The paradigm of development as economic growth has been particularly pernicious in generating and entrenching inequalities within and across borders and specifically with respect to gender.
>
> *(Chapter 11, p. 117)*

DOI: 10.4324/9781315626796-1

> Governments and funding agencies, on the other hand, cling to vague expressions like 'meaningful consultation', leaving the details of how these are actualised largely to project proponents. Thus while national and international policy guidelines are firm and clear about unacceptable outcomes, they are slack and opaque about unacceptable exclusion of stakeholders from decision-making.
>
> *(Chapter 19 p. 203)*

> Indigenous tribal communities in valleys continue to suffer from the trauma of displacement, including the hardships and treacheries of resettlement and the ongoing struggle for justice; international funding agencies support the expansion of projects that aim to provide for aspiring urban sections of society, regardless of the environmental and cultural cost to marginalized communities.
>
> *(Chapter 33, p. 377)*

> After independence, the French-speaking countries of Africa were propelled towards a model of development that was greatly influenced by the colonial period. This institutional legacy, which is evidenced by France's continued leverage, has left a trail of political cronyism and corruption.
>
> *(Chapter 36, p. 398)*

These comments about models, projects, or processes of socio-economic development include critical assessments. They raise issues about practices of development – from individual projects to entire strategies. The thrust of criticism is not just that these practices were ineffective but that they reflect badly on the agents and institutions that chose them *because these were the wrong things to do.* The criticism is that, on the great spectrum from doing the right thing towards the many wrong things to do, these practices are closer to the wrong end. Since this right–wrong spectrum is the domain of ethical judgment, these judgments about development practices belong to development ethics.

If we think of development ethics in this way – as recognizing wrongdoing in development practices – then discussions of development ethics are perhaps more widespread than we would otherwise think. Discussing development ethics, in this sense, is reminiscent of speaking in prose, according to Moliere's M. Jourdain: 'Good heavens. For more than forty years I have been speaking prose without knowing it' (Moliere 1671, act 2, scene 4; Ratcliffe 2017). So, too, many likely have been discussing development ethics without knowing it.

Why then does 'development ethics' seem so puzzling? The reason, we suggest, is that development ethics also has another domain: it is not just about judgments; it is also about their justification. Passing judgments is easy. But if we are interested in knowing about the right conduct (here, the right ways of conducting development) then we should also be seeking the right judgments, and so we will demand justifications for these judgments. So development ethics involves seeking and giving justifications for judgments about the right and wrong ways of conducting development. This may account for some of the puzzlement: the space of judgment seems familiar, but the space of justification may not. People may recognize that ethics involves ethical judgments, and they may also recognize ethical judgments that can be made about development, but the business of justifying those judgments may seem daunting. In other words, there is a divide between judgment and justification. As Des Gasper explains: first development ethics must identify 'ethical concerns about development experiences and policies', but from there it must go on to examine 'major valuative concepts and theories used to guide, interpret or critique those experiences and actions' (Gasper 2004, xii). Crossing this divide takes a further step that may seem unfamiliar and uncomfortable.

Whereas development thinkers and practitioners have approached this divide from one end, philosophers have approached it from the other. That is to say, when philosophers discuss applied ethics, they are often better informed about evaluative theories and concepts than they are about the practices that need to be evaluated. David Crocker was first asked to teach development ethics at a time when neither he nor anyone else knew what this might entail. As a philosopher, his initial response was to reach for well-known applications of evaluative theories and concepts related to practices that seemed to be relevant to development, particularly the arguments about duties of famine relief that were made prominent in the 1970s by Peter Singer. (Parallel arguments were drawn later from different ethical theories, notably the Kantian arguments by Onora O'Neill (1986, 1993; Aiken and LaFollette 1977).)

There can be much uncertainty on both sides of this divide. On one side, people with strong, clear judgments about the wrong things to do for development may be less certain about how to justify these judgments. On the other side of the divide, people who know enough about moral theories and concepts to evaluate nearly anything may be less certain of what the actual issues are in development practice. Crocker noticed this early on. For example, he noticed that the way in which Singer had framed the issue of international aid was incomplete, being oblivious to 'how national development was conceived and what developing nations were already doing (or failing to do) to bring about good or better development', giving too little attention to the agency of the people that aid was meant to benefit, and failing to recognize 'deeper, more structural problems, such as maldistribution of wealth and power' (Crocker 2008, 8–9).

Crocker responded by working both sides of this divide and promoting interaction across it. In the 1980s he drew upon the thinking of Denis Goulet, whose approach to values and justification was more anthropological than philosophical (Gasper 2011; Goulet 1971, 1995, 2006), and the thinking of Costa Rican philosophers Luis Camacho and E. Roy Rodriguez (Crocker 2008, 12). After, Crocker and his Costa Rican colleagues organized a Development Ethics Working Group in 1984 and held the first conference of the International Development Ethics Association in 1987 (IDEA 2017). Since then, many others joined this effort – including the co-editors of this book. IDEA has held ten international conferences and numerous smaller workshops on five continents on a wide range of themes, including economic crises; alternative development models; development needs, capabilities, and rights; environmental sustainability; dependency; globalization; corruption; global justice; and gender justice (IDEA 2017).

For the question of what development ethics is, this gives a good first answer: development ethics is 'working both sides of the divide' between ethical justifications and ethical judgments about development practices.

While this characterization is correct as far as it goes, it neglects two other important dimensions. One is that the term 'development' itself is often used normatively. Hence we should not just look to external moral theories and concepts for guidance; we should also consider what people mean by 'development' when they advocate for development as a social goal. What is meant when people use 'development' as a standard for evaluating how well or badly a society, its government, or its leaders are doing? The other neglected dimension is political. Governments direct much development activity and even private sector development takes place within legal and regulatory frameworks. Either way, some exercise of power is involved. If this exercise of power is not justifiable, then its legitimacy is open to question. Insofar as development ethics targets ethical justifiability, it bears on political legitimacy.

Acknowledging these two further dimensions of development ethics is one of the hallmarks of this book. Each has its own rationale. The first dimension expands the space of justification to include more people's values – the values that are implicit when people demand development as a social goal. The justificatory space, then, is not just for philosophers. While philosophers have much to contribute to this space, it is not their fiefdom. The second dimension answers a particular kind of political skepticism about ethics. 'You say that our development strategy is not ethically acceptable? So what? You can't make an omelet without breaking eggs.' The short answer is: if your omelet-making is not justifiable to those for whom, by whom, and with whom the omelet is made, then your claim to be a legitimate chef may vanish. Both points deserve to be discussed less metaphorically, more analytically, and this is what we will begin to do in the next two sections.

Normative dimensions: goals and values of worthwhile development

Even narrowly conceived as 'economic development', the concept of development has, since the middle of the twentieth century, undergone remarkable change. Currently, economic growth is only one part of its meaning according to a recent account, which defines 'economic development' as 'the process in which an economy grows or changes and becomes more advanced, especially when both economic and social conditions are improved' ('Economic development' 2017). As the term was used in the 1950s, the definition could have been reduced to the first part, ' . . . the economy grows', as a measure of 'improvements in material well-being' (Okun and Richardson 1961, 230). Restricting the concept of development to growth, even in the 1950s, seems implausible to some, like economist Jacob Viner, who found it 'a paradox to claim that country is achieving economic progress as long as the extent of . . . poverty has not lessened. . . .' And yet, at the time, Viner feared that including poverty reduction as part of the meaning of 'economic development' would entail 'separating myself from the whole body of literature in this field' (Viner 1952, 126–127). Nevertheless, over the next twenty years this restriction could not hold out, and indeed by the 1970s poverty reduction had been incorporated into the dominant conception of development in the major institutions.

This was just one way in which the conception of development came to be expanded in this period, from mere growth to a richer conception of human development (Gasper 2004). Our question is, why did this change the concept of *development*? To say that the concept of development had to change in order to recognize the importance of poverty reduction is not sufficient as an explanation. What was wrong with calling for development (meaning growth) *plus* poverty reduction? Why was it necessary to think of development *as including* poverty reduction? The only plausible explanation acknowledges that 'development' had a normative connotation, the connotation of 'improvement' noted in the contemporary dictionary definition from which I began. If 'development' implies valuable social change, then it makes sense to feel uneasy about including, as development, a process of growth that fails to reduce poverty. We hear the same unease in Dudley Seers's famous 1969 address on 'The Meaning of Development', when he says, 'One cannot really say that there has been development for the world as a whole, when the benefits of technical progress have accrued to minorities which were already relatively rich' (Seers 1969, 6).

Denis Goulet identified this normative connotation and based his call for development ethics upon it. As early as 1960 he stressed the importance of distinguishing between kinds of economic and social change that are worthy of being pursued as social goals, which sometimes he called 'authentic human development', and those undesirable kinds which he sometimes called 'false development' (Goulet 2006, 5) or 'anti-development' (Goulet 2006, 45). This terminology echoes and amplifies the normative connotation of the term 'development'.

Goulet's great legacy to development ethics is the idea, on which he expanded in his 1971 book *The Cruel Choice*, that this distinction between 'authentic development' and 'false development' or 'anti-development' or 'maldevelopment' is an ethical, value-based distinction:

> Ancient barbarisms were characterized by the triumph of might over right. Today's false development, which assigns supremacy to mere economic might, would lead to a new form of barbarism, on which is all the more dangerous because it hides behind the mask of progress and civilization. Today's world is at a crossroads: either it will leave behind the ancient impasses bred of privilege and of limited solidarities, or it will get bogged down in new patterns of violent servitudes. If the world is to succeed in its development efforts, it needs to discover, to promote, and to propose an ethics which takes full account of the requirements of authentic development.
>
> *(Goulet 2006, 4)*

This has enormous implications for where we locate discussions of development ethics. First, ethics is not isolated from politics or power, not disengaged from the messy world of conflict, privilege, solidarities, and servitudes. This entanglement of power, politics, public reason, and legitimacy with development ethics is discussed at greater length in the next section. Second, ethics is not confined to applying ethical theories to development practices. Rather, development ethics must also include discussions of what 'development' must be, in order to satisfy the normative connotation of the word – to be 'authentic' development, as Goulet called it. Development ethics is part of the discussion defining what else 'development' must mean (besides economic growth) in order to be the kind of worthwhile change that satisfies its normative meaning.

From this perspective the numbers of development ethics discussions are multiplied many times over, even if the discussants do not recognize themselves as 'development ethicists'. More prose.

These discussions were treated in a systematic way as discussions of development ethics by Des Gasper in his 2004 book *The Ethics of Development: From Economism to Human Development*. Ideas of 'human development' insist that development must enhance people's well-being, it must be equitable, and it must be empowering, and it must be environmentally sustainable. Mahbub ul Haq, who is widely recognized as one of the founders of the human development approach, included these four values among the 'pillars of human development' (Haq 1995). In addition to these four, Jay Drydyk's 'Development Ethics Framework' of 2011 identified three more values that have been relied upon to distinguish worthwhile development from undesirable maldevelopment: human rights, cultural freedom, and integrity (Penz et al. 2011, Chapter 6).

This *Handbook* is structured by those seven values. Some of the contributors refer to them as 'ethical goals' of development, and this may provoke questions about exactly *whose* goals these are. The answer is that they have been discovered, in wide-ranging public discussion of how 'development' can go wrong, as values that distinguish development that is worthwhile and justifiable from other processes of economic growth and social change that may be called 'development' in some quarters but do not live up to the normative connotations of the term. Rather than 'goals' it may be less misleading to refer to these values as dimensions in which development can be better or worse, succeeding or failing to meet justifiable normative expectations.

Why then do we need several chapters on each one? The reason is that these broad values are usefully vague: we can agree on them in general terms while disagreeing on exactly what each of them entails and requires. For example, we may agree that development is worthwhile to the degree that it enhances people's well-being, yet disagree about how 'well-being' should be understood: should we understand it in terms of wealth and income, satisfaction of preferences, basic needs, capabilities to live well, or subjective satisfaction? It is here that some of the most important discussions of development ethics occur, for which our prior agreement that development enhances well-being only sets the stage.

If we can know, even approximately, the goals and dimensions of worthwhile development, this knowledge will yield many consequences not only for particular development projects but also for the legitimacy of the governmental, institutional, and corporate policies and practices that support these projects.

A memorable example is provided by the Kariba dam project, built 1955–59, across the Zambezi River. The main beneficiaries of this project were electricity consumers, copper mines, and other industries that could enjoy greater supply and lower prices for electricity. Some 57,000 Tonga people, who relied primarily on agriculture for their livelihood, were displaced and resettled onto replacement land that was of poor quality and would not support their customary farming methods. Food production fell, a famine occurred in the period following resettlement, and the Tonga ceased to be self-sufficient in food production for decades to come. Resettlement of the Tonga on different sites divided by the Zambezi River led to their isolation from each other, especially when the river became a boundary between the independent states of Zambia and Zimbabwe. Some resettled groups melted into host communities, losing their language and Tonga identity. (For references see Drydyk 2015.)

Consider this in light of the value dimensions of development. Displacement and resettlement harmed the Tongas' well-being, not least in terms of food security. While *their* well-being was diminished, electrical power consumers (from industries to urban dwellers) benefited. So this project had a negative impact on well-being and equity alike. While some consultations were held and some concessions were granted, these were not convincing to many of the villagers, who resisted and were evicted and resettled by force. The colonial denial of human rights made this possible. Finally, the project had a negative cultural impact: merging with host populations, some resettled Tonga lost their language and culture; thus their cultural freedom was also diminished. Well-being, equity, empowerment, human rights, and cultural freedom are five dimensions in which development can go well or badly, and in all of them this project was impressively bad – 'maldevelopment five times over' (Drydyk 2015, 101).

Public reason and political legitimacy

The ethical risks of maldevelopment may also entail political risks. To see this, we should consider what basis or grounding the values of worthwhile development have. If they are grounded by public reasoning, and if the exercise of power depends on public justifiability for its legitimacy, then the political risks of maldevelopment may be considerable.

The idea of public reason, though much debated, is much less difficult to understand than it might seem. Earlier in this chapter we drew attention to two spaces in which ethical discussion occurs. In one, we make judgments about which practices are right and which are wrong. In the other, we discuss whether those judgments are justified. Various ideas can come up in such a discussion. Is this practice helpful or harmful? What if everyone did that? Is this what a good person would do? Does it respect others' dignity, autonomy, reason, or rights? How does it impact people's relationships or community? Now consider a subsection within this space, limited to discussions of how to exercise power. Minimally these are discussions of state power, from how to organize and limit it constitutionally, to legislation, to policy and program choices. It could be objected: these are not purely ethical choices; politics is not reducible to ethics. While we might accept this, we would add that it is not possible to segregate ethical considerations (concerning what are the right and wrong things to do) from other political considerations. 'Public reason' refers to this space, where justifications are sought for choosing among different options for exercising state power, and 'public reasoning' refers to the kinds of discussions appropriate to this space.

'Public reason' is most often discussed in relation to state power, although this may be too restrictive. Arguably, corporations exercise power when the choices they make asymmetrically affect the choices that others have. Whether this exercise of power is legitimate surely requires justification. The exercise of power along gender and racial lines is distinguished by its unjustifiability, for though history is littered with attempted justifications, these have never stood the tests of reason. There are limits to the justifiable power that parents can exercise over their children. Whether religious power relations are justifiable – even among believers themselves, as well as in connection with state power – has long been controversial. Our view is that the limits and legitimacy of all such exercises of power are in principle subject to evaluation by public reason, though this is probably a minority view among philosophers at the present time (Quong 2018).

For any practice that we need to evaluate, we may find that different evaluations follow from different normative ideas. Suppose a developer proposes to evict riverside villages in order to build a bridge across a dangerous river crossing. Cost-benefit analysis and some forms of utilitarianism might condone evicting the villagers for this purpose while many other views would answer, 'not so fast'. These critical views could include Kantian opposition to treating the villagers as mere means; concern for the villagers' security of tenure as an element of their human right to adequate housing; Buddhist compassion; the Golden Rule; and, of course, Christians might ask, 'What would Jesus do?' None of these perspectives can be dismissed out of hand, because they all give reliable answers to other moral questions. Moreover, different people are more familiar and confident with some of these ideas than with others – for example, some people are Kantians, others are Buddhists – and it would seem wrong to deny them use of the particular moral tools in which they have the greatest confidence. This 'fact of pluralism' presents a dilemma for public reason. If public reason is open to many normative ideas that do not always agree, how can we avoid stalemate and settle on a single evaluation? On the other hand, it would seem arbitrary to achieve agreement by excluding some of these ideas from consideration, since they are in other cases reliable.

This dilemma also confronts development ethics. Why? As we observed earlier, development ethics must include not only ethical judgments about right and wrong development practices, but also justifications for those judgments. Since development practices involve exercise of power, these justifications fall within public reason. More particularly, the values that distinguish worthwhile development from undesirable maldevelopment were discovered through public reasoning about the failures of development strategies adopted by governments and international development institutions. If the fact of pluralism poses problems for public reason, it also poses problems for development ethics.

These problems are real and prevalent enough that we should not expect a decisive answer from public reason on every question of development policy; there will be stalemates. Yet public reason can also be remarkably robust. Disputes about human rights are a stunning example, which is also significant for development ethics insofar as worthwhile development entails progress in realizing human rights. Human rights movements have become adept and experienced at motivating human rights protections in ways that draw upon the particular ethical traditions of each region. From time to time political actors have pitted human rights against regional traditions to claim that development in their regions must be unfettered by human rights. And yet this claim is not so plausible when people experience the reality of being unprotected against states and development strategies that do not respect human rights. What enables public reason to be conclusive, despite the fact of pluralism? According to John Rawls (1999), we must restrict ourselves in public reasoning to giving only reasons that our fellow citizens can accept, based on purely political ideas that are not tied to comprehensive doctrines; Amartya Sen opposes this restriction and opts for an 'open impartiality' in which all voices are heard and yet everyone's good is given equal consideration, as would be done by the 'impartial spectator' famously discussed by Adam Smith (Sen 2009, Chapters 5–6, 114–152); Charles Taylor (1999) adds that people who evaluate the same practices from different normative perspectives should at least appreciate each other's perspectives. This is not a debate we can settle here. Still, we can frame the question optimistically. Despite the fact of pluralism, public reason can and does seem to remain conclusive about matters as important and sometimes controversial as human rights protections. So why should public reason be any less conclusive and robust about the boundaries of worthwhile development?

Does development ethics carry any political weight? We believe that it can, *especially if it is grounded in public reason*. This claim is based on the idea that political legitimacy is conditional on public reason. A weak version of this idea can be found in Kant's famous article, 'What Is Enlightenment?', which concludes that it would be prudent for monarchs to allow public reasoning rather than to censor it (Kant 1996 [1784]). This may have been the strongest endorsement of public reason that Kant could sneak past the Prussian censors in 1784, but as the public sphere bulked larger over the next 250 years, so did ideas that heeding public reason is a necessary condition for political legitimacy in some way or other.

In what way it is necessary remains a matter of debate. In a remarkable passage in *Political Liberalism*, John Rawls links it both to the structure of political power and to its exercise. Starting from the premise that political power is fundamentally the combined power of citizens, exercised collectively, he explores what it could mean for each to have 'an equal share in the coercive political power that citizens exercise collectively over one another' (Rawls 1993, 217). Two things are required, he finds. First, the allocation of power must be constitutional, structured in a way that is acceptably conducive to fair political give-and-take among citizens ('reasonable') consistent with citizens' life priorities ('rational') as they understand them (Rawls 1993, 217). This, he says, is 'the liberal principle of legitimacy', to which he immediately adds a second requirement, that 'since the exercise of power itself must be legitimate, the ideal of citizenship imposes . . . the duty of civility . . . to be able to explain to one another . . . how the principles and policies they advocate and vote for can be supported by the political values of public reason' *(Rawls 1993, 217)*.

As we noted earlier in this section, in Rawls's model of public reason shared conclusions are to be reached only from shared values that are purely political, meant for application only in political life, rather than comprehensive ideas meant to hold throughout life, in every dimension. We also noted that this is only one conception of public reason, as there are others that involve converging on shared conclusions based on diverse values. Can we also put these wider conceptions of public reasoning forward as a necessary condition for political legitimacy? Rather than starting from an ideal, Rainer Forst begins by considering what we mean justice to avoid, and with this in mind he argues that the core concept of justice is that social life should be free of all forms of arbitrary rule or domination (Forst 2012, 189). 'Arbitrariness' can be defined (again, negatively) by a process of justification that screens out unacceptable claims of privilege (Forst 2012, 194). 'Justice means first and foremost that the social relations within this system can be justified; the fundamental equality is the justificatory equality of individuals' (Forst 2012, 194). Forst adopts a 'strong reading' of political legitimacy that ties it to this conception of justice, and, hence, to justificatory equality in public reason (Forst 2014, 213). Note that this requires not merely that some particular structure or exercise of power *could be* justified fairly, but that those over whom this power is exercised have the power to *make it so*. 'Power, understood as the effective "justificatory power" of individuals, is the highest good of social justice: . . . the "discursive" power to provide and to demand justifications, and to challenge false legitimations' (Forst 2012, 196).

The upshot is that development decisions that defy public reason are themselves lacking in legitimacy and count against the legitimacy of the constitutional or institutional arrangements that authorize them. In this way ethical risks are risks to political legitimacy.

Does development ethics have any particular political identity? Can we locate it anywhere in particular on a political spectrum? Politics embracing the values of worthwhile development would call for improving well-being, reducing inequality, empowering people to engage in their own development decision-making, realizing human rights and cultural freedoms, promoting environmental sustainability, and eliminating corruption. We can locate this more precisely as a political orientation if we divide the political spectrum into four segments, in relation to economic growth and corporate power. For this purpose we can define 'corporate power' simply and uncontroversially in the following way: many of the business decisions that corporations *make* asymmetrically determine the choices that human beings *have* – for example, in the way that investment decisions affect people's employment options. The politics at one end of the political spectrum calls for preserving and enhancing ('freeing up') corporate power in ways that promote economic growth and for limiting corporate power only as necessary to protect economic growth and public security. At the opposite end we would locate a post-development politics that views capitalist economic growth processes as tyrannical and seeks to detach communities from them. Development ethics is not particularly conducive to politics of these two types: it holds that other values may warrant regulation of corporate power, but rather than opposing growth per se, it holds processes of development and growth accountable to those values. (Nevertheless we cover post-development thinking in Chapter 4 of this *Handbook* because it is an important perspective that must be given due consideration.) Between these two extremes we might identify two other segments. In one we might place the various strands of counter-hegemonic politics aiming to reverse what they perceive as subordination of the people and their democratic self-rule to corporate power. In the other segment we might place reformist politics aiming to regulate corporate power so that such a radical role reversal is not necessary. Development ethics can be conducive to counter-hegemonic as well as reformist politics and does not make any *a priori* choice between them. By the same token, development ethics would hold both reformist and counter-hegemonic politics accountable to the values of worthwhile development.

Going forward

The earliest contributions to development ethics discussed in this introduction date more than fifty years back, to 1960. At present, development ethics is not just a dream or demand, as it was for Denis Goulet in 1960, but an actual ongoing set of discussions, research, political interventions, and policy initiatives. So the best question to ask about its future is: what forms of cooperation are required to continue this work best? In particular, we want to conclude this introduction by considering helpful forms of *cooperation* between philosophers, other academics, and practitioners.

In part, we frame the question in this way because the contributions of philosophers to development ethics has been understated so far in this introduction. We did so intentionally, so as to stress the inclusive nature of development ethics – that it is *not* the exclusive domain of philosophers. Nevertheless, philosophers do have special contributions to make, and this introduction would be incomplete if we did not mention them.

We can begin reflexively by pointing out that the account of development ethics that we have given in this introduction is actually quite philosophical in character. Just as many may have been speaking prose and doing development ethics without knowing it, in this chapter we have already been doing philosophy, perhaps without the readers knowing that they were engaged in a philosophical exercise, as we analyzed the concept of development, arguing that 'development' has a normative connotation that requires looking beyond (but not without) moral theories. We then made arguments on whether and how development ethics is grounded in public reason and derived implications concerning the legitimacy of the policies, institutions, and power relations in which development is carried out.

To continue in this vein, then, what are some other kinds of philosophical work that might contribute to the further development of development ethics? It may be useful to distinguish between three different domains in which this work may be done.

Meta-ethics considers higher order questions about the nature and scope of argumentation and knowledge about normative (moral and political) claims and judgments. As Anna Malavisi shows in Chapter 5, numerous topics and trends in epistemology have direct and important applications to development ethics: social epistemology, feminist epistemology, epistemologies of ignorance, and the concept of epistemic injustice. Conversely, moral epistemology has much to learn from development ethics.

Applied or practical ethics considers more specific issues or realms of human action in a way that generates subject-specific guidelines or positions on specific questions: for example, the realm of medical ethics, or the specific question of whether or not physician-assisted suicide is morally permissible. Conventionally, especially in introductory teaching of applied ethics, an attempt is made to reach conclusions about these issues from principles that have been articulated in *normative ethics*. One example is Immanuel Kant's humanity formula, that we ought never treat humanity whether in ourselves or another person merely as a means, but always as an end. Another is Jeremy Bentham's utility principle that we ought to approve or disapprove of every action according to the tendency it appears to have to augment or diminish the happiness of the party whose interest is in question. In addition, different sub-fields of applied ethics (such as bioethics, environmental ethics, business ethics) may have principles and concepts that apply to their issues and practices specifically, as for example patient autonomy and doing no harm apply in medical ethics.

Social philosophy and global ethics discuss theories of justice, whether and how they are applicable globally as well as socially, and other ethical principles that may apply when cross-border interactions raise ethical issues. Greater awareness of issues specific to development would clearly enrich discussions of these theories and principles, and, conversely, high-level principles can also shed new light on particular development issues.

Personal or integral ethics (Keleher 2017, 2018) is the domain in which we as individuals must consider the moral dimensions of our particular actions as an individual part of the various realms of life in which we participate and how we might integrate choices made in various spheres of our lives, including commitments, duties, relationships, abilities, and resources. For example:

> . . . consider Samantha, an agro-economist who works for a large development firm whose work undermines sustainability. Samantha personally believes that sustainability ought to

> be a high priority, especially in development interventions. How does she reconcile this belief with her work at the firm? She has used the established channels to suggest changes, but finds that people in authority simply dismiss her. She suspects that these dismissals are at least in part because she is a woman and the people in authority at her firm are all men. Quitting her job would mean losing the health plan that pays for her expensive medications, and would compromise her ability to provide for her three children.
>
> *(Keleher 2018)*

In this domain we deal not only with actors and actions, but with webs of relationships and responsibilities – often conflicting responsibilities. Philosophical attention has been given to this domain by approaches including relational theory (see Chapter 11 and Koggel 2002 and 2012), care ethics (Tong and Williams 2016), and virtue ethics (Hursthouse and Pettigrove 2016).

This *Handbook* demonstrates how robust development ethics *research* has become. However, the scope of *teaching* and *grassroots discussion* of development ethics remains very limited, especially when compared with fields of applied ethics such as environmental ethics, business ethics, or bioethics. Outside universities, scope for discussion of development ethics is equally limited, if not worse. As Chloe Schwenke observes in Chapter 30, there are few ongoing venues in development organizations or institutions in which the people who work on development policies, programs, and projects can discuss emerging ethical issues as they experience them. Moreover, the ways in work is structured and directed in these organizations and institutions leaves little space and time for that discussion.

Different fields of applied ethics offer different models of how to further extend the field of development ethics beyond academia. We suggest the following steps. Development and anti-poverty organizations like the United States Agency for International Development (USAID), OXFAM, the World Bank, and others, ought to have designated positions for development ethicists who are trained and hold degrees in development ethics, similar to the positions hospitals and large medical organizations have for medical ethicists. In addition to designated development ethics positions, and in smaller organizations where it is not possible to designate an entire position to development ethics, qualified development ethicists should be brought in to consult and train others on specific topics whenever applicable. Moreover, qualifications in development ethics should be recognized as advantageous and listed as desiderata for a wider range of positions held throughout development agencies. Finally, associations, including the International Development Ethics Association (IDEA), ought to be more widely recognized as providing valuable opportunities for interdisciplinary discussions among scholars and practitioners.

Within academia, philosophy departments and interdisciplinary programs ought to give greater recognition to development ethics by regularly teaching courses and offering specializations in development ethics. After all, billions of people throughout the world live below the poverty line, and given that all nations struggle with issues of inequality, limited resources, and sustainability, there are good reasons to hold that all nations are developing nations. Likewise, development scholars outside of philosophy who have been implicitly speaking in the 'prose' of ethics and critical thinking would do well to directly engage and explicitly recognize the value of philosophical insights and tools in development work. Development ethics courses ought to be offered in programs for public policy, development economics, peace studies, and so on. Scholars and theoreticians within university ought to seek to establish working relationships with development practitioners.

Clearly, much remains to be done. Readers who would like to join this effort are invited to contact either the co-editors, or the authors of particular chapters, or the International Development Ethics Association via its website.

References

Aiken, W. and LaFollette, H. (1977) *World Hunger and Moral Obligation*. Prentice-Hall, Englewood Cliffs NJ.

Crocker, D.A. (2008) *Ethics of Global Development: Agency, Capability, and Deliberative Democracy*. Cambridge University Press, Cambridge and New York.

Drydyk, J. (2015) The Centrality of Empowerment in Development-Induced Displacement and Resettlement: An Ethical Perspective. In Satiroglu, I. and Choi, N. eds., *Development-Induced Displacement and Resettlement: New Perspectives on Persisting Problems*. Routledge, Abingdon and New York, 97–110.

Forst, R. (2012) *The Right to Justification; Elements of a Constructivist Theory of Justice*. Columbia University Press, New York.

Forst, R. (2014) *Justice, Democracy and the Right to Justification*. Bloomsbury Academic, New York.

Gasper, D. (2004) *Ethics of Development: From Economism to Human Development*. Edinburgh University Press, Edinburgh.

Gasper, D. (2011) Goulet, Denis. In Chatterjee, D. ed., *Encyclopedia of Global Justice*. Springer Science+Business, New York, 457–459.

Goulet, D. (1971) *The Cruel Choice*. Atheneum, New York.

Goulet, D. (1995) *Development Ethics: A Guide to Theory and Practice*. Apex Press, New York, and Zed Books, London.

Goulet, D. (2006) *Development Ethics at Work: Explorations 1960–2002*. Routledge, New York and London.

Haq, M. (1995) *Reflections on Human Development*. Oxford University Press, New York.

History of IDEA. International Development Ethics Association (IDEA). https://developmentethics.org/about-2/. Accessed 18 December 2017.

Hursthouse, R. and Pettigrove, G. (2016) Virtue Ethics. In Zalta, E.N. ed., *The Stanford Encyclopedia of Philosophy*. https://plato.stanford.edu/archives/win2016/entries/ethics-virtue/.

Kant, I. (1996 [1784]) An Answer to the Question, "What Is Enlightenment?" In Gregor, M.J. ed., *Immanuel Kant: Practical Philosophy*. Cambridge University Press, Cambridge, 11–22.

Keleher, Lori. (2017) Toward an Integral Human Development Ethics. *Veritas: Revista de Filosofía y Teología* 37: 19–34.

Keleher, Lori. (2018) Why Development Needs Philosophy. In Keleher, Lori and Kosko, Stacy J. eds., *Agency and Democracy in Development Ethics*. Cambridge University Press, Cambridge.

Koggel, C. (2002) Equality Analysis in a Global Context: A Relational Approach. *Canadian Journal of Philosophy: Supplementary Volume: Feminist Moral Philosophy* 28: 247–272.

Koggel, Christine M. (2012) A Relational Approach to Equality: New Developments and Applications. In Downie, J. and Llewellyn, J. eds., *Being Relational: Reflections on Relational Theory and Health Law*. UBC Press, Vancouver, 63–88.

Moliere (Jean-Baptiste Poquelin). *Le Bourgeois Gentilhomme*, 1671.

Okun, B. and Richardson, R.W. (1961) Economic Development: Concepts and Meaning. In Okun, B. and Richardson, R.W. eds., *Studies in Economic Development*. Holt, Rinehart and Winston, New York, 230–237.

O'Neill, O. (1986) *Faces of Hunger: An Essay on Poverty, Justice, and Development*. Allen & Unwin, New York.

O'Neill, O. (1993) Ending World Hunger. In Regan, T. ed., *Matters of Life and Death: New Introductory Essays in Moral Philosophy*. McGraw-Hill, New York, 235–277.

Penz, P., Drydyk, J. and Bose, P.S. (2011) *Displacement by Development: Ethics, Rights and Responsibilities*. Cambridge University Press, Cambridge and New York.

Quong, J. (2018) Public Reason. In Zalta, E. ed., *The Stanford Encyclopedia of Philosophy*. https://plato.stanford.edu/archives/spr2018/entries/public-reason/.

Ratcliffe, Susan, ed. (2017) *Oxford Essential Quotations*. 5th ed. Oxford University Press, Oxford.

Rawls, J. (1993) *Political Liberalism*. Columbia University Press, New York.

Rawls, J. (1999) The Idea of Public Reason Revisited. In Rawls, J. ed., *The Law of Peoples, With "The Idea of Public Reason Revisited"*. Cambridge University Press, Cambridge, MA, 129–180.

Seers, D. (1969) The Meaning of Development. https://www.ids.ac.uk/files/dmfile/themeaningofdevelopment.pdf.

Sen, A. (2009) *The Idea of Justice*. Harvard University Press, Cambridge MA.

Taylor, C. (1999) Conditions of an Unforced Consensus on Human Rights. In Bauer, J. and Bell, D. eds., *East Asian Challenge for Human Rights*. Cambridge University Press, Cambridge, 124–144.

Tong, R. and Williams, N. (2016) Care Focussed Feminist Approaches to Ethics, section 2 of "Feminist Ethics". In Zalta, E.N. ed., *The Stanford Encyclopedia of Philosophy*. https://plato.stanford.edu/archives/win2016/entries/feminism-ethics/.

Viner, J. (1952) *International Trade and Economic Development: Lectures Delivered at the National University of Brazil*. Free Press, Glencoe IL.

Part I
Contexts

The nature and scope of development ethics may be made clearer by comparing and contrasting it with related fields and schools of theory and practice. We begin by considering how development ethics stands in relation to global ethics. Then two historically influential schools of thought are considered: integral human development and post-development (or 'anti-development'). The final chapter, on epistemology, raises issues for development ethics that also confront other forms of knowledge and discussion that have strong implications for policy and practice.

Is development ethics a branch of global ethics? How much do they actually have in common? Nigel Dower understands global ethics as the search for a global ethic, a set of values and norms that are applicable to human beings everywhere. Should development ethics be universalistic in this sense? Against relativism, Dower argues that development ethics requires culturally sensitive universalism – willing to accept shared norms coming from diverse sources – combined with global responsibility.

As Lori Keleher explains, the integral human development perspective, which originated in Catholic social teaching, conceives of development as authentic insofar as it enables every person to live a life that is 'more human'. Before these ideas became Church doctrine, they had been developed by French development theorist and practitioner Louis-Joseph Lebret. Similar ideas can be found in the thinking of Denis Goulet, who studied with Lebret, and they can also be seen as precursors to other human-centered multidimensional approaches to development, such as the human development approach or the capability approach (which is discussed in Chapter 7).

As Mitu Sengupta shows, post-development (or anti-development) thinkers challenge the distinction between worthwhile development and maldevelopment, arguing that the concept of development is a neo-colonial construction perpetuating the social and economic domination both nationally and internationally. Thus they contend that the entire concept should be rejected, not reformed; rather than alternative forms *of* development, we should seek alternatives *to* development. As Sengupta shows, this view has also met with significant criticism.

Anna Malavisi demonstrates the importance of recent trends in social epistemology for development ethics. Citing the case of neglected tropical diseases, she shows how inadequate conceptions of knowledge and knowledge production can contribute to maldevelopment. Risks of *epistemic injustice* should be of central concern to development ethicists, Malavisi argues. This injustice can take two forms: groups that are dominated or marginalized suffer *testimonial injustice* when their knowledge is diminished and discounted; they may also suffer *hermeneutical injustice* when their means of self-understanding are excluded from the public sphere.

DOI: 10.4324/9781315626796-2

2

Global ethics

Development ethics as global ethics

Nigel Dower

On the face of it development ethics and global ethics appear to be two rather different areas of enquiry. Development ethics is concerned with the means and ends of development, and is concerned both with sound models of development based on ethical principles and with critiquing ethically what is done in the name of development in terms of the wrong goals and/or the wrong ways of pursuing them. The focus of development is on what happens within some particular nation-state or other unit like a region. Global ethics is enquiry into the nature, extent and justification of norms and values that are in some sense universal, including norms to do with global or trans-boundary responsibilities not to harm and to some extent to help humans anywhere in the world, and focuses on the external relations between nation-states and different people and social groups in the world (see Dower 2007).

There are in fact five logical possibilities concerning how the two fields are related. That is, the relationships can be seen as one of five kinds: identity, non-overlap, partial overlap, the subsumption of development ethics within a wider field of global ethics or the subsumption of global ethics within a wider field of development ethics. These are presented here as logical possibilities. How far thinkers do explicitly locate or have any interest in locating what they are doing is a secondary question. In any case in terms of how people understand what they are doing (the phenomenology, as it were, of their engagement in the discourses), they may be doing global ethics, doing development ethics, doing environmental ethics, doing peacebuilding ethics or doing any or all of these things at the same time, particularly if causal or conceptual connections are recognised, e.g. between development and peace or between development and environment. My main concern is with logical possibilities, depending on how development ethics and global ethics are defined.

The subsumption of global ethics within a wider field of development ethics, whilst a logical possibility, seems rather implausible given the much wider range of concerns covered by global ethics, both in terms of content (issues) and level of focus on global/international relations. The identity thesis may seem implausible for the same reason, though given certain ways of understanding each, one could argue that they cover much of the same content, albeit approached from two different starting points/sets of interests motivating them.

The non-overlap thesis would be that development ethics may be seen as a field in which, whatever the appropriate norms are for a given country or group's development, they are

DOI: 10.4324/9781315626796-3

specific to that country or group and are not universal at all (a relativist claim), and in regard to trans-boundary responsibilities, these are either disputed (a communitarian claim) or seen as belonging to a field other than development ethics (with, for instance, the ethics of aid being seen as a distinct field). The non-overlap thesis might either be a claim that there is no such thing as a global ethic – either universal values and norms or trans-boundary duties – or a claim that the contents of global ethics is limited, which does not include the specific issues of development ethics.

Fourth, development ethics and global ethics may be seen as overlapping fields, because some but not all development ethics issues are indeed global ethics issues, and some but not all global ethics issues are development ethics issues. In this approach, whilst some ethical issues in development are certainly universal – to do with the core elements of human well-being or to do with the trans-boundary duty not to harm others or to help them – others are not. Some norms and values may be specific to particular development contexts, and some universal values, understood in a very general form, may need expressing in culturally specific or sensitive ways in order to be appropriate to development, and the ethical issues do not transfer across all development contexts. Conversely, whilst a large part of global ethics is indeed concerned with universal values and norms that are appropriate for a general model of sound development and with trans-boundary obligations as they affect development anywhere in the world, there are other significant areas of global ethics which are quite different. These are to do with, for example, environmental protection or climate change mitigation and adaptation, for instance, or the promotion of peace and the promotion and protection of human rights quite generally.

To avoid misunderstanding here, on most accounts of development, certainly ones in which ethics is central, development policies include protecting the environment, promoting human rights and building peace, both because they are background conditions and because they are intrinsically valuable elements of good development. But the focus of much global ethics discourse may be different in that, first, it looks at these issues at an international level (global governance and international laws and institutions), and, second, concern for the environment, human rights and peace are not exhausted by their relevance to development. (For the rich variety of areas in which global ethics issues are discussed, see in particular the *Journal of Global Ethics*.)

Fifth, development ethics might be seen as a field within global ethics. If it is thought that, notwithstanding views to the contrary, exactly the same norms and values really should apply to development anywhere (so differences of practice are down to issues of efficacious means, not different values), and global ethics is about universal values and norms generally, then the norms and values of development are the norms and values of global ethics (and development ethics is just a field of application of these norms and values). And if as part of development ethics we have the framework of global responsibility both to help humans anywhere to flourish and to have less suffering (aid, personal and official) and to avoid (or minimise) harming others anywhere e.g. through avoiding unfair trade practices or reducing one's contribution to hardship caused by climate change, then that discussion is merely part of the wider field of our global responsibilities towards one another.

This subsumption position involves several possibilities. If development ethics involves core ethical elements claimed to be valid for all development and includes the ethics of the international/global framework within which development is facilitated or impeded, then it is clearly included in the domain of global ethics. This inclusion claim may be resisted: if it is claimed that some core ethical issues in development are uniquely particular to that society's development and not universal, and global ethics is conceived as only being about universal values (and maybe criticised or rejected for its implicitly imperialistic or homogenising tendencies), then development ethics is at least in part a separate domain. But again, if global ethics is seen as *acknowledging* culturally diverse expressions of core universal values and also some cultural values specific to particular cultures, and as *endorsing/promoting* (as part of what it is about) global responsibility to show *respect for* such cultural diversity, then a development ethic that stresses such forms of diversity is after all part of global ethics.

It is this position I wish to defend, alongside the chapter's analytic purpose of exploring different understandings of the relationship. That is, I shall defend a form of global ethics which postulates culturally sensitive universal values and norms, which both allows for different forms of expression in different societies and at the same time retains a framework of trans-boundary responsibility towards humans anywhere. Whilst the actual expression of that diversity in terms of particular development contexts may be specific to those contexts (or applicable to other like contexts), the global ethics is itself inclusive of and welcoming to this diversity, and it can be seen as within the approach of that form of global ethics.

In the rest of this chapter I first trace the historical context of how global ethics and development ethics developed and then intersected with each other. I then examine global ethics and various areas and issues, followed by a similar examination of development ethics. Finally I return to an examination of the relationship between the two.

Historical context

Historically, development ethics arose out of explicitly critical discussions about the assumptions behind the standard models of development in the UN development decades from the 60s onwards, where the main alternatives were economic growth, that is, increasing a country's Gross National Product (GNP), and growth with equity, that is, increasing GNP but with an eye towards fair distribution through various forms of state intervention. Discussions about the ethics of aid were not cast in explicitly 'global ethics' terms, but were essentially about establishing responsibility, whether of individuals or official aid. Consider for instance Peter Singer's influential article 'Famine, Affluence and Morality' that argued that the wealthy should do a great deal to help famine and poverty alleviation, on the principle 'If it is in our power to prevent something very bad from happening, without sacrificing anything of comparable moral importance, we ought to do it' (Singer 1972, 231). These issues were largely about *why* we should give aid and *how much*, rather than about the appropriateness of the aid itself. (To be sure there were critiques of aid but that was about how effective it was, not whether it was based on wrong models of development.) The various areas of ethical concern which eventually coalesced under general labels such as international ethics, world ethics or global ethics were on the whole largely independent areas of ethical reflection, whether it was about nuclear weapons, increasing concern about environmental destruction, world health issues, human rights violations or the issue of military intervention.

By the 90s two parallel processes were occurring. There was increasingly sophisticated critical reflection on the assumptions underlying development as economic growth (e.g. in the work of the International Development Ethics Association (IDEA)) and recognition that the ethics of aid was as much about the right kinds of aid as about the 'why' of aid, thus linking ethical reflection about development with the international context. IDEA was formed in 1987, and brought together philosophers, social scientists and development practitioners, and this organisation helped to embody institutionally the new discipline of development ethics. But there had been, some time before and also continuing independently alongside IDEA, ethical reflection about development in writers like Paul Streeten and Frances Stewart (basic needs; e.g. Streeten 1981; Stewart 1985), Amartya Sen (capabilities approach; e.g. Sen 1999) and Mahbub ul Haq (human development; e.g. Haq 1996). Denis Goulet had also written extensively about authentic development (e.g. Goulet 1977, 1995), and was associated with the formation of IDEA for which he was an inspirational figure. (Goulet himself had been inspired by the writings of Louis-Joseph Lebret, a French thinker working in the 50s and 60s on value questions raised by development; e.g. Lebret 1961.)

One response to the growth model of development was the rejection of the values implicit in this as 'western' or 'colonialist' and thus an affirmation of the cultural relativity of values implicit in authentic development, and a rejection of a universal ethic that was seen as tied to the western project (e.g. Sachs 1992).

There was also an increasing recognition of the inter-relatedness of different global issues, particularly over development and environment, and this led to wide acceptance of the concept of 'sustainable development', and over development and security, and this led to broadening security to include environmental security and human security, all seen as having global relevance. The problems of development came to be seen by many as not problems for poorer countries alone but problems for all countries, partly because of the environmental consequences of high growth in richer countries. Global ethics as a field in which all these issues could be discussed together emerged and is still developing.

Globalisation, which also both as an idea and a process gained momentum in the 90s onward, was an aspect of the increasing inter-relatedness of all these issues (Scholte 2000; Tomlinson 1999). But that in turn contributed to the sceptical turn in which many rejected what they saw as the 'homogenising' tendencies of globalisation, with a return to emphasising local culturally diverse values and rejection of the global ethics perspective (see Robertson 1992), and parallel to this (and one might say part of it) are different approaches to the ethical basis of development, whether it should be universal, universal in a contextually sensitive way (Nussbaum 1988) or relativist in character (Sachs 1992).

Another development which illustrates the convergence of concerns in development ethics and concerns in global ethics is the increasing acceptance in the last twenty years or so of the idea of global citizenship (though in fact, as explained later, it is a return to ideas of an earlier era). Global citizenship is closely linked to the idea of a global ethic. Whilst it is possible for someone to accept a global ethic but not the idea of global citizenship (as either conceptually incoherent or empirically inapplicable or as unhelpful), usually the two go together (see Dower 2003; see also Carter 2001 and O'Byrne 2003). A global citizen accepts a global ethic in the sense of a claim about the universal ethical standing of all human beings and in the sense of claiming we all have a global responsibility towards one another, combined usually with a commitment to self to make a difference globally. Global citizenship may be expressed in a number of ways, especially in connection with supporting appropriate aid, engaging in fair trade, living sustainably or promoting peace. What is often now called 'global learning' in schools in countries like the UK is about global citizenship (see e.g. Stride). This is more generally about sustainability and the many dimensions of the seventeen 'Sustainable Development Goals' (SDGs), but also particularly about what is called development education, that is, getting pupils to be both knowledgeable about and care about what happens in poorer countries and how what people do in richer countries by way of aid and trade – fair or unfair – impacts on that.

Global ethics

Global ethics is a more complex field than my sketch has so far indicated. Global ethics is a field of enquiry into the character of ethical relations between people across the world. Here I am assuming a sense to the word 'ethics' which is common amongst academics, namely that ethics is (note the singular verb despite the plural-looking noun) an *activity* of thinking about ethical issues, usually critically and systematically. It covers the relations between people as individuals as well as relations between corporate bodies such as nation-states or business companies. Global ethics as an enquiry is often focused on the nature, extent and justification of ethical values and norms that make up what may be called a 'global ethic', generally understood as a set of universal values and norms including some norms to do with trans-boundary responsibilities. Someone who is doing global ethics at the level of normative ethics (or world ethics as it used sometimes to be called (Dower 1998, 2007)) is usually comparing different normative theories such as Kantianism and Utilitarianism in relation to global relations generally or to some particular global issues such as war and peace, development issues, climate change or health issues, and defending one of them.

In this normative sense of global ethics, where positions on substantive value issues including transboundary responsibilities are taken and argued for, there are at least two foci of interest. First, general claims are made about what countries, corporations, NGOs and bodies ought to do or ought to promote, and also about what other individuals ought to do. But usually anyone doing global ethics is also making decisions about what he or she should do in order to express their acceptance of their global ethic – give aid, buy fair trade goods, cut their carbon emissions, protest against war and so on.

However there are at least two other approaches possible under the general label of global ethics. Second, someone interested in global ethics could be interested in more abstract meta-ethical or theoretical issues about the nature of a global ethic, for instance, about what makes such an ethic possible in the face of diverse ethical approaches amongst individuals and between cultures. He could even take a sceptical view about the possibility of a global ethic, by questioning in general the universality of values or questioning in particular the idea of significant obligations between different societies and states. Third, a more descriptive social scientific approach is possible, where either the global ethicist attempts to map different ethical approaches across the world (much as someone studying world religions is interested in the diversity of religions across the world), or documents the extent to which human relations are now informed by various globally shared ethics and/or converging on one such shared ethic or another, that is, with an interest in what may be called the 'globalisation of ethics' (as distinct from the 'ethics of globalisation' which is the ethical critique of aspects of what goes on in the world under the label globalisation; for the latter see Singer 2002; for the former see Dower 2003).

Although the main focus of the chapter is on global ethics in the first sense – the idea of different theories of global ethics and how they are applied to global issues – the concerns raised under the other ideas of global ethics will from time to time feature in the discussion, not least because they are all inter-related.

There are at least three main sources of interest in global ethics in the modern world. First, there is the historically long trajectory of interest in the idea of a universal ethic that is found in at least some of the ethical thought of all the major religious traditions. One source of this in the Western world was the thinking of the Stoics in the Graeco-Roman world. Their vision of cosmopolitanism (being a citizen of the world/universe) was of all humanity living in one large moral community in which a common moral law, discerned by reason, was acknowledged (see Brown and Kleingeld 2006 for an overview of cosmopolitanism). This kind of thinking was reflected later in the Catholic idea of the natural law applicable to all human beings – that is, the moral law is accessible to all peoples – through writers like De Vitoria and Suarez in the 16th century (see e.g. De Vitoria 1991; Suarez 1866). In the 17th century Grotius developed the idea of universal moral law, but in a more secular form, and used it in his pivotal theory of international relations (e.g. Grotius 1925). In the 18th century the explicit idea of cosmopolitanism was again brought out, particularly in the writing of Kant (e.g. Kant 1970). This dimension is part of a theological and philosophical tradition. (For modern discussions of cosmopolitanism, see Pogge 2000, 2002; Tan 2004; Brock 2009; Van Hooft and Vanderkerckhove 2010.)

Second, it has become increasingly apparent, especially since the Second World War, how many of the problems that we face are global problems, that is, problems are caused in one country by the actions of other countries or corporate bodies such as transnational companies, and solutions to common problems require co-operation and co-ordination between countries. Here a global ethic of collective responsibility is clearly reinforced by, and sometimes justified by appeals to, collective self-interest, since it is in everyone's interest that the co-operation occurs (see for instance CGC 1995). Global ethics arguments are not always like this: arguments for humanitarian assistance often have little link with any interests of the donor.

Third, with increasing information and communications across the world – the globalisation of knowledge and community – people are more aware of their global inter-connectedness, their identities being more formed by relations across the world, not merely local relations, and there is greater recognition of common values, but equally of how much values differ (Scholte 2000). These all become important aspects of how the world is experienced.

What then is a global ethic? There are two ways of approaching this question (see Dower 2007). First, one can think of it as an ethic accepted by an individual or a group which has a certain global *content*. It is that individual's or group's ethical view of the world. This view is likely to have two main elements: first, some set of values and norms that are believed to be universally valid, that is, applicable to human beings anywhere; second, some view about our obligations or responsibilities, again seen as universally valid, towards people anywhere in the world, for instance that the wealthy of one country have some obligations to help alleviate extreme poverty in other countries, or that anyone avoids harming others even indirectly, e.g. by cutting down on one's carbon emissions as a way of reducing one's negative impact on others in the world. Various ethical theories, some of which will be mentioned later, drawn from philosophy and theology, present and defend a global ethic in this sense. (For various views on global ethics generally, see also Van Hooft 2009; Kutchings 2010; Widdows 2011.)

Second, we can think of an ethic as global in the sense of being *globally accepted*, that is, that there is a set of values and norms that is accepted by people all over the world – perhaps by people for instance who share a particular religious faith, or by the community worldwide of international diplomats (or people in business companies). In this sense there could be a number of different versions of a global ethic (or 'global ethic-s' in the plural). What is of interest to some is whether there is a core set of values that can be said to be actually universally shared (or at least nearly universally shared since there are always some ethical odd balls). This could then be seen as *the* global ethic that is almost universally shared.

An example of this last idea is the *Declaration towards a Global Ethic* of the World Parliament of Religions in 1993, which sought to articulate the common moral core to all the major religions – reflecting the approach of one of its key advocates, namely Hans Küng (Küng and Kuschel 1993). Küng was a Swiss theologian who developed a world ethic of global responsibility based on dialogue (Küng 1990). Bhikhu Parekh presented the idea of a global ethic as one which is both consented to and assented to – consented to through the process of inter-cultural dialogue, and at the same time assented to because each person or group has their own reasons – philosophical, theological, drawn from cultural narratives – for assenting to it (Parekh 2005, 27). Linked to this is the distinction that can be drawn between a global ethic as a set of values and norms understood as detached from the person's particular philosophical, theological or cultural sources, and a global ethic as a set of values and norms embedded in one's source story/world view. This is the difference between what I have called a global ethic and a global ethic+ (see

Dower 2007, 2009, 65–67). Obviously the possibility of a shared global ethic across the world is much greater if we take the former sense than if we take the latter sense. Indeed if people wish to defend their global ethic as a global ethic+, the possibility of conflict (even violent conflict) is great. The relevance of these ideas to development will become apparent later on (see also Kim 1999).

Development ethics

The emergence of development ethics as a self-conscious area of enquiry is very recent – roughly thirty years old – but in fact the issues of development ethics have been around for centuries. Reflection on various value issues explicitly connected to development and aid had been around for some while before, in the writings of, for instance, Lebret, Goulet, Sen, Singer, Streeten and ul Haq, as noted earlier. Indeed more broadly philosophers and thinkers generally have raised the fundamental questions about human well-being and about how societies to create a good society should be organised from Plato and Aristotle to Marx and Mill. These two sets of questions remain at the heart of development ethics.

I give two definitions from Goulet and Crocker. Denis Goulet, characterised it as 'work on ethical and value questions posed by development theory, planning and practice' (Goulet 1977, 5) and David Crocker, a more recent leading advocate of the field of enquiry, has called it the ethics of 'development theory/practice' (Crocker 1991, 71–73; see also Crocker 2008). Both these definitions bring out that development ethics is both about general ethical principles underlying development and about the practice of development and how ethical dilemmas are faced in concrete situations. Both thinkers bring out that development ethics is about the ends and the means of development – what is to be pursued and how it is to be pursued.

There is a key conceptual point here: development is a process of socio-economic-political change which takes place in a country (locality, region etc. – whatever one's focus of interest). We should note that it is not merely economic change that is relevant to the improvement of peoples' well-being. Social and political factors are important, as is apparent in many countries struggling with issues of governance and corruption. (For a wide definition, see United Nations 1986.) Development does not merely happen: it is something which is to some extent pursued by governments and other agencies such as NGOs at all levels – locally, regionally, nationally and internationally. If development is pursued, then there are either explicitly or implicitly certain values involved. As Aristotle in the 4th century BCE said: 'Every action or pursuit aims at the good' (Aristotle 1908, 1). If development is something pursued, it is intended, and if it is intended, then it may be chosen from amongst alternative paths. So development ethics naturally involves the consideration of alternative paths or models for development.

A development ethicist may focus on endorsing one conception of development, but she may also focus on criticising other conceptions of development, for instance those actually assumed by what governments do 'in the name of development' which may be seen as 'maldevelopment'. As such, it becomes the object of critical assessment by others: 'how well are the values pursued?', and 'are they the right values?', etc. Development ethics arises out of this critical stance.

We should note that I have called development ethics an area of enquiry. As such, ethics in this sense is to be contrasted, like the global ethic/ethics distinction, with 'a development ethic', where an ethic is a set of values and norms accepted by a person or a group. These values and norms which inform the way development is pursued may be accepted as a result of more or less critical reflection by at least some of those who have these values and norms. What development ethics does is to look at the values and norms involved in development, often comparing different approaches and seeking a justification for what seems the right approach. Such thinking can be done monologically by the thinker thinking through things for herself, hopefully in response to what others say or have said in discussions and in writings; but it can also be done dialogically through extensive dialogue and interaction between people of different approaches, especially from different cultural backgrounds.

Of interest here are two levels of questions: first internal questions about the nature of development itself, as it occurs or ought to occur within a country or other unit of development and second the external framework in which this occurs. This is the international or global framework of other states, international organisations, business corporations and global civil society. The internal questions are questions like: what are the values that development as a process, usually taken to involve economic growth, should be directed to promoting? How should we define the human well-being that development promotes? How should the benefits of development be distributed? What procedural values (like democratic participation) should inform development? The external framework includes questions like: why ought rich countries and/or rich individuals give aid to help very poor people and/or countries? What is an acceptable basis for international trade and investment? Should crippling debt in very poor countries be cancelled? The two levels – internal and external – are connected in various ways. There is an obvious way, which I shall elaborate more fully later, in which the external framework impacts on how development is pursued in poorer countries.

The internal questions about the kind of development which is pursued or ought to be pursued arise in richer countries too. Though (by definition) richer countries are more economically advanced than poorer countries, it does not follow that richer countries are 'fully' developed, or that they ought to be emulated by poorer countries, or that there are not a lot of complex moral issues about how development should be pursued and understood within them. This is partly to do with internal social and political failings. It is partly to do with environmental constraints that either do or should limit or determine what is done. But it is partly about how such countries should pursue their own development in the face of legitimate expectations of poorer countries to escape extreme poverty and to do better economically. Thus what should happen globally (in international political and economic relations) vis-à-vis development for poor countries may affect what should be done in rich countries. We should not forget that the definition of development ethics is quite general and in principle includes development issues in all countries. The fact that development ethics issues arise for all countries already suggests the plausibility of seeing a close link between development ethics and global ethics. Let us now explore this relationship more fully.

Connections between global ethics and development ethics

We will look at the connection between global ethics and development ethics in two stages: first, the idea of global ethics in respect to universal values and norms, and second in respect to trans-boundary responsibilities.

If we look at the aspect of global ethics concerned with universal values and norms, we can see that the same issues concerning how they are understood and how they are justified apply equally to development ethics. Let us consider this in regard to two approaches to global ethics: first, the acceptance of some first order normative theory, second, the idea of a set of norms and values widely accepted from a variety of theoretical sources. If one is, for instance, a Kantian in respect to basic ethical principles and one's understanding of human well-being in terms of the proper exercise of agency, this applies equally to one's understanding of a global ethic which will be applied to all manner of subject matter (war and peace, the environment etc.) as it does to one's understanding of what norms ought to underlie development or one's understanding of the key role of agency in development (O'Neill 1986). It would not make sense to be a Kantian in respect to other areas of global interest but not a Kantian in respect to development. If one is a utilitarian, one's general view about how global issues should be assessed will have to do with maximising utilities however understood (like preference satisfaction), but equally one's view of what makes for good development will be shaped by such considerations. If one is a libertarian, one will have certain views about the centrality of freedom especially economic freedom in one's account of development, but by the same token other global issues will be assessed from the same perspective. The same will go for a human rights approach. If one advocates human rights these are by definition universal rights applicable to all people, and are relevant to one's conception of development as being or including the progressive realisation of human rights.

One might think that there is one exception to this parallelism of theoretical justification – namely the capabilities approach of Sen, Nussbaum and others (Sen 1999; Nussbaum 2000), since this approach is, insofar as it is applied to ethics, almost exclusively applied to development ethics. However, appearances are deceptive. The conception of human well-being that lies at the heart of the approach – the exercise of fully developed capabilities or freedoms – is generally presented as a universal model of development not one that only applies to certain societies, or at least one in which unequal capability is a frame that captures inequalities that matter in any society. It therefore meets the criterion of being a global ethic as a set of values and norms applicable to all.

On the other hand, if one thinks of a global ethic as a set of values and norms shared widely where there is a diverse range of sources (philosophical, theological), then the same parallelism can be detected. No claim that there is as a matter of fact widely, though not universally, shared values and norms can be made without acknowledging the diversity of sources. But the same goes for development ethics. Any claim about what values as a matter of fact underlie a widely accepted view of a proper model of development would not make much sense unless it is also accepted that a wide variety of theories support these core values (theories that derive not just from different philosophies but from diverse religious and cultural traditions).

Here I am echoing Parekh's analysis of a global ethics having two aspects – consent and assent. The value of his analysis survives the recognition that probably there is no single widely shared global ethic, rather a number of them where different 'global ethics' are each shared by people with a range of different source stories. The consensuses of international diplomats, of business people and of many NGOs may be different consensuses, but they are consensuses shared by individuals and groups with different source stories and world views. If we value consensus where it is possible (the consent element), we still need to value the 'assent' aspect of people's and groups' acceptance and to understand that the acceptance of first order normative theories, some of which I mentioned earlier, remains important. Just because we value agreement, we do not give up intellectual integrity. But my point is that exactly the same applies to development ethics as well. No doubt there are different consensuses about the core values in development – consider for instance the difference between the 'Washington consensus', the UNDP consensus as reflected in the Human Development Reports from 1991 onwards and the consensus of many non-governmental organisations (NGOs) within the field of development – but where there are consensuses, the theories or source stories for each party may well be different.

The acknowledgement of the consent/assent duality in both global ethics thinking and development ethics thinking provides a way of tackling the relativist challenge. A relativist challenge is that there is as a matter of fact disagreement not only about norms and values but also, even more, in the different theories individuals and groups have for supporting their 'ethic'. The fact that there is diversity does not of course mean that some theories (philosophical or theological) aren't more reasonable or nearer the truth than others, but the distinction between a global ethic and a global ethics+ (and in parallel a development ethic and a development ethic+) helps to defuse the impact of the relativist challenge. This is because there being shared norms and values across people and groups from all over the world completely cuts across the relativist claim that norms are embedded in and relative to particular cultures. The point is that there are different sets of shared norms between people and groups from all over the world – a point that does not depend on whether one accepts or rejects assessments of 'truth'/reasonableness.

However there is an aspect of the relativist challenge which is important and should affect our understanding of universally applicable norms and values, whether in global ethics generally or development ethics in particular. The criticism that purported universal values and norms simply reflect the projection of the dominant values of certain parts of the world can be met, as I noted at the beginning, by recognising that these norms and values should be understood in very general abstract terms which allow for a significant degree of interpretation in different cultural contexts. There is, it must be acknowledged, a tension in most of these source stories such as Kantianism and Human Rights (and even the Capabilities Approach) in that they can be presented in a highly specific way which is a projection of the specific cultural norms, but they can also be presented in ways that do not do this and allow for latitude of interpretation. It should be noted that to the extent that the global ethic account as opposed to the global ethic+ account is accepted and that a consensus of shared values derived from various sources is accepted, the importance of flexibility is underlined. This applies both to global ethics in general and to development ethics in particular.

If we turn to the trans-boundary aspect of a global ethics, namely global responsibility and the assessment of global/international relations, the same subsumption of development ethics within it can be shown. This admittedly requires one to assume a broad account of the scope of development ethics to include the global framework within which the development of any given country or unit occurs. That global framework covers many things, from aid policies through trade policies, tackling tax havens, the damaging effect of certain intellectual property regimes, to the whole design and functioning of international institutions, including the UN. If one asks the key question 'what actions and policies need to be pursued by other governments, by persons and corporate agencies in other countries and by international institutions to enable the goal of genuine development to be achieved within particular counties (whether poor or rich)?', the ethical principles used to answer this question are none other than the ethical principles which would need to be invoked in tackling other global challenges in global ethics. Again, the familiar ethical sources such as Kantianism, utilitarianism and human rights theories apply to the international framework for development in just the same way as they do to the wide range of other global ethics issues. The same is true of social justice theories such as Rawls', as applied rather meekly by Rawls himself (Rawls 1999) and more robustly by Beitz and Pogge to global relations (Beitz 1979; Pogge 1989). Even in the case of the Capabilities Approach, which does not have a well-developed account of global responsibility of its own, it assumes a backing from ethical theory that there is the international obligation to take actions and shape policies so that the enabling conditions for development and expression of capabilities can be best realised everywhere. These are only a few theories. Others, such as those drawn from specific religious traditions or from ecological foundations have the same feature: if they posit universal values and norms, they also posit global responsibility and the ethical critique of trans-boundary and international relations in regard to both development and other domains of concern.

Typically, someone doing global ethics may have a primary focus, be it for instance, development, environmental policy, war and peace, peacebuilding, or for that matter governance issues or global health issues. Whether he or she thinks these are all in various ways causally and/or conceptually deeply connected, as I would argue they are, or more discreet domains, the fact remains that most global issues are complex and involve consequences in many of these domains.

So from a global ethics perspective, even if one thought of development in rather limited terms e.g. about economic growth and distribution, what comes out of global ethical deliberation may be somewhat different from what might be thought to come out, if one simply focused on the global implications of development issues narrowly so conceived. But that is to be expected, if the development ethics ethical framework is subsumed under the wider global ethics framework. Global justice, for instance, isn't merely economic justice, climate justice (Harris 2009), more broadly environmental justice or international (i.e. inter-state) justice or justice in any other specific domain of global interest, it is all of these appropriately integrated (see Caney 2005).

The significance of the global ethics framework of global responsibility applied to development ethics or more generally can be underscored by pointing out the pitfalls of adopting a sceptical view of universal values from a relativist point of view. Relativists are prone to point out the effects of the colonial imposition of their values on other cultures as being unjust. But relativism actually is in danger of throwing out the baby with the bathwater, since it loses any purchase on the claim that what is done to another culture is unjust: the claim of injustice, if it is an appeal to anyone, presupposes some other universal theory of justice (see e.g. Apel 1992). One advantage of meeting relativism with a culturally sensitive universalism is that it allows us to have a theory of global responsibility with which to criticise what countries and companies do in many parts of the world, whether this is do with development, warmongering, environmental exploitation or whatever.

Conclusion

The recognition of a culturally sensitive universalism combined with global responsibility, the willingness to accept shared norms coming from diverse sources, the recognition that ethical challenges of development are best seen as nested within the framework of global ethics, the casting of global ethical issues in the language of global justice, and the recognition that in addition to our local and national identities we are all global citizens with shared responsibility for what happens anywhere in respect to development, environmental protection, peace and respect for human rights generally, all seem to me to be things that will be increasingly accepted as the ethical issues about development and global relations continue to be debated.

References

Apel, K.-O. (1992) The Moral Imperative. *Unesco Courier* July/August.

Aristotle (1908 [350 BCE]) *Nicomachean Ethics*, many editions, Ross, W.D. trans., Clarendon Press, Oxford.

Beitz, C.R. (1979) *Political Theory and International Relations*. Princeton University Press, Princeton, NJ.

Brock, G. (2009) *Global Justice: A Cosmopolitan Account*. Oxford University Press, Oxford.

Brown, E. and Kleingeld, P. (2006) Cosmopolitanism. *Stanford Encyclopedia of Philosophy*. http://plato.stanford.edu/entries/cosmopolitanism/, 2006. Accessed 10 March 2013.

Caney, S. (2005) *Justice Beyond Borders: A Global Political Theory*. Oxford University Press, Oxford.

Carter, A. (2001) *The Political Theory of Global Citizenship*. Routledge, London.

Commission of Global Governance (1995) *Our Global Neighbourhood*. Oxford University Press, Oxford.

Crocker, D. (1991) Towards a Development Ethic. *World Development* 19: 5.

Crocker, D. (2008) *Ethics of Global Development: Agency, Capability, and Deliberative Democracy*. Cambridge University Press, Cambridge.

De Vitoria, F. (1991) *Political Writings*. Cambridge University Press, Cambridge.

Dower, N. (1998) *World Ethics – the New Agenda* (2nd ed. 2007). Edinburgh University Press, Edinburgh.

Dower, N. (2003a) The Ethics of Globalisation or the Globalisation of Ethics? The Relevance of the Question for Global Governance. In *Perspectives on Global Governance – Theoretical Orientations – Ethics – Global Orders*. Academy of Finland.

Dower, N. (2003b) *Introduction to Global Citizenship*. Edinburgh University Press, Edinburgh.
Dower, N. (2009) *Ethics of War and Peace*. Polity Press, Cambridge.
Goulet, D. (1977) *The Uncertain Promise*. Overseas Development Council, Washington, DC.
Goulet, D. (1995) *Development Ethics: Theory and Practice*. Zed Books, London.
Grotius, H. (1925 [1625]) *De Iure Belli ac Pacis (On the Law of War and Peace)*. Kelsey, F.W. trans. Clarendon Press, Oxford.
Haq, M. ul (1996) *Reflections on Human Development*. Oxford University Press, Oxford.
Harris, P. (2009) *World Ethics and Climate Change*. Edinburgh University Press, Edinburgh.
Hutchings, K. (2010) *Global Ethics: An Introduction*. Polity Press, Cambridge. *Journal of Global Ethics*, www.tandfonline.com/toc/rjge20/current. Accessed 27 April 2017.
Kant, I. (1970 [1784]) *The Idea of a Universal History with a Cosmopolitan Intent*, Reiss, H. trans. *Kant's Political Writings*. Cambridge University Press, Cambridge.
Kim, Y. (1999) *A Common Framework for the Ethics of the 21st Century*. UNESCO, Paris.
Küng, H. (1990) *Global Responsibility – In Search of a New World Ethic*. SCM Press, London.
Küng, H. and Kuschel, K.-J. (1993) *A Global Ethic: The Declaration of the Parliament of World Religions*. SCM Press, London.
Lebret, L.-J. (1961) *Concrete Dynamics of Development*. Les Editions Oevrieres, Paris.
Nussbaum, M. (2000) *Women and Development*. Cambridge University Press, Cambridge.
Nussbaum, M.C. (1988) Non-Relative Virtues: An Aristotelian Approach. *Midwest Studies in Philosophy* 13(1): 32–53.
O'Byrne, D. (2003) *The Dimensions of Global Citizenship: Political Identity Beyond the Nation-State*. Taylor & Francis, New York.
O'Neill, O. (1986) *Faces of Hunger*. Allen and Unwin, London.
Parekh, B. (2005) Principles of a Global Ethic. In Eade, J. and O'Byne, D. eds., *Global Ethics and Civil Society*. Ashgate, Aldershot.
Pogge, T.W. (1989) *Realizing Rawls*. Cornell University Press, New York.
Pogge, T.W. ed. (2000) *Global Justice*. Clarendon Press, Oxford.
Pogge, T.W. (2002) *World Poverty and Human Rights: Cosmopolitan Responsibilities and Reforms*. Cambridge University Press, Cambridge.
Rawls, J. (1999) *The Law of Peoples*. Harvard University Press, Cambridge MA.
Robertson, R. (1992) *Globalization: Social Theory and Global Culture* (published in association with *Theory, Culture & Society*). Sage, London.
Sachs, W. ed. (1992) *The Development Dictionary*. Zed Books, London.
Scholte, J.A. (2000) *Globalization: A Critical Introduction*. Palgrave, Basingstoke.
Sen, A. (1999) *Development as Freedom*. Oxford University Press, Oxford.
Singer, P. (1972) Famine, Affluence and Morality. *Philosophy & Public Affairs* I: 229–243, and, extended, "Rich and Poor" In Singer, P. (1979) *Practical Ethics*. Cambridge University Press, Cambridge.
Singer, P. (2002) *One World – The Ethics of Globalisation*. Yale University Press, London.
Stewart, F. (1985) *Basic Needs in Developing Countries*. Johns Hopkins University Press, Baltimore, MD.
Streeten, P. (1981) *First Things First: Meeting Basic Human Needs in the Developing Countries* (published for the World Bank). Oxford University Press, New York.
Stride. www.stridemagazine.org.uk/ Accessed 27 April 2017.
Suarez, F. (1866 [1597]) Disputationes Metaphysicae. In Berton Voils, C. ed., *Opera Omnia*. Vives, Paris, 25–26.
Tan, K.-Ch (2004) *Justice without Borders: Cosmopolitanism, Nationalism, and Patriotism*. Cambridge University Press, Cambridge.
Tomlinson, J. (1999) *Globalisation and Culture*. University of Chicago Press, Chicago.
United Nations (1986) *Declaration on the Right to Development* Resolution 41/128.
Van Hooft, S. and Vanderkerckhove, W. eds. (2010) *Questioning Cosmopolitanism*. Springer, London.
Van Hooft, S. (2009) *Cosmopolitanism: A Philosophy for Global Ethics*. Acumen, Durham, UK.
Widdows, H. (2011) *Global Ethics: An Introduction*. Acumen, Durham, UK.

3

Integral human development

Development of every person and of the whole person

Lori Keleher

Integral human development is a human-centered development perspective that originated from Catholic social teaching. The perspective holds that authentic development is development that makes every person "more human." Although it is seldom named in the literature, integral human development has had considerable influence on notions of authentic development, and in turn, development ethics. In this short chapter, I provide a brief explanation of the origins and implications of the conceptual foundations of integral human development both within and beyond the Catholic Church. I argue that integral human development offers a truly radical participatory approach to human development. I briefly raise and respond to some concerns about agency, civic liberty, and integral human development's connection to the Catholic Church. I conclude with a short explanation of integral human development in practice.

Lebret and the origins and implications of integral human development

The first place we see the phrase "integral human development" is in Pope Paul VI's very influential 1967 encyclical *Populorum Progresio*, or the *Development of Peoples*. But much of the thought found in this encyclical, and therefore the conceptual foundations of integral human development, can be traced back even earlier to the work of French economist, social activist and Dominican priest Louis-Joseph Lebret. Lebret's work with sea fisheries in France in the 1930s and decades of work in grass roots mobilization in Latin America, led him to the realization that the traditional economic schemes that focus only on growth and wealth accumulation were inadequate to address human needs. In response, Lebret introduced the significant idea of *human economy*, which goes beyond the mere "integration of the human element into the social sciences" to be "an economy whose very functioning . . . would be favourable to human development" which offers "the greatest possible number of people, a fully human life" (Lebret 1954). Lebret's understanding of a fully human life was grounded in human dignity and involves cultural, economic, political, social and spiritual dimensions.

This idea that development must be human centered, and that to be human is to be much more than a consumer or human capital in an economic system, is both at the heart of integral human development and a central feature of authentic development for contemporary

DOI: 10.4324/9781315626796-4

development ethicists. Denis Goulet, who was Lebret's student and is often called the "father" of development ethics (Dower 2008, 184; Wilber et al. 2010), reflects this understanding as he writes: "Societies are more human, or more developed, not when men and women '*have* more' but when they are enabled to '*be* more.' The main criterion of development is not increased production or material well being but qualitative human enrichment" (1995, 6–7).

In his lifetime, Lebret worked with scholars, politicians, religious, fishermen, farmers and many others to promote integrated human-centered development across several continents. He gave several very visible and influential talks, for example, at the United Nations in 1964 (Cosmao 1970; Chamedes 2015), and established at least two significant organizations *Economie et humanisme* (1941) and IRFED, the *Institut international de recherche et de formation en vue du développement harmonisé* or the International Institute of Research and Training toward Integrating Development (1958) (Chamedes 2015). Yet, there remains a sense in which *integral human development* was not actually brought into being until after Lebret's death (in 1966) with the dissemination of *Populorum Progresio* (1967), for which Lebret was the principle investigator. This encyclical is considered to be the foundational document of integral human development. It has inspired subsequent Popes to write encyclicals that consider integral human development in the context of their times (Pope John Paul II's *Sollicitudo Rei Socialis*, 1987, and Pope Benedict XVI's *Caritas in Veritate*, 2007), and grounds what the international development aid organization Catholic Relief Services calls the *Integral Human Development Concept and Framework* (Heinrich 2009), which strives to put the theory of integral human development into practice.

Promoting the good of every person and of the whole person

Populorum Progresio explains the sense in which truly authentic human development must be *integral*. "Development cannot be limited to mere economic growth. In order to be authentic, it must be complete: integral, that is, it has to promote the good of every person and of the whole person" (14). Thus, authentic development must be *integral* in at least two ways. First, authentic development must be the development of the whole person, not just the narrowly understood development of economic growth or monetary income. A person's truly human needs in such realms as health, learning, emotional, social and political interaction, spiritual life, creativity and self-determination are also essential concerns from the integral human development perspective. Although the approach is human centered, its realm of concern is not limited to human persons but also involves non-human animals and the environment (Heinrich 2009; Francis 2015, 2017). This is not unlike other human-centered, multidimensional approaches to development, for example, the capability approach (see Chapter 7 in this *Handbook*).

The second way in which integral human development is integral is less discussed yet more radical. It is the idea that authentic development is the development of *every* person. On this view, "every person" does not mean every person below a certain threshold of income, well-being, or functioning. Integral human development is concerned with the development of *every single person*, whether they are marginalized peasants, powerful elites, or someone in between. The philosophical underpinnings of integral human development hold that truly authentic development requires not only that the poor be relieved of poverty but also that *every* person – rich or poor – stands together with others in a relationship of solidarity as members of the human family.

The idea that development involves the rich giving up wealth so that others may have a better standard of living is by itself not unfamiliar within the literature of development or of distributive justice. John Rawls (2009), Martha Nussbaum (2009, 2011), Amartya Sen (1981) and many others, have argued this point. What is so radical about integral human development is that on this view development is never simply a process in which monetary or other "sacrifices" by the rich are used to aid the poor. Within integral human development standing in relationships of solidarity enriches *all* who participate regardless of their initial holdings or wealth. Thus, the poor *and the rich* are beneficiaries of authentic development.

The position that *every* person benefits from participation in authentic development is inevitable when we recall that integral human development is concerned with development of the *whole person* in such a way that enables people to *be* more human where *being* more is distinct from *having* more. When this notion is taken seriously, it follows that economic and material resources are not the only benefits that emerge during authentic development. When we add to this idea that standing in relationships of solidarity with others is an inherently human and a humanizing process, it becomes clear that *all* people who engage in processes of authentic human development are made more human and, therefore, benefit from their engagement in the process. It is in this way that integral human development is concerned with the complete development of every person.

This understanding of development radically shifts the development paradigm away from one in which aid, charity, or service, flows one way: from the rich "givers" to the poor "beneficiaries" or "takers." Instead, within the integral human development perspective, authentic development integrates each and every person in a humanizing process of standing in relationships of solidarity as we strive together towards promoting the common good. The recognition of the human dignity of each and every person is both the means and the end of this process.

This humanizing process has been called the *human ascent* (Lebret 1954, 1955, 1959; Goulet 1971, 1995, 1997, 2006). It is the transformation of human values toward recognition of universal human dignity and a commitment to promoting the common good in all spheres of life. Human ascent – not the redistribution of wealth – is the primary goal of integral human development. This is because, according to integral human development, a failure to recognize and respect universal human dignity is the real cause of poverty. As damaging as they are, inequalities of wealth and power are mere symptoms of this problem. If we address the symptoms without addressing the cause, other damaging symptoms will emerge. Thus, only through authentic human ascent can we achieve authentic human development.

Human ascent is grounded in an understanding that every human has inherently valuable and inalienable human dignity and all have it equally (whether or not that dignity is being recognized and respected). If we accept this understanding, then we recognize that we are equal bearers of *the same* human dignity as every other human being. Within integral human development, this recognition of our personal and equal human dignity leads both to (1) an understanding that each one of us is deserving of all that is required for human flourishing, and to (2) an attitude of solidarity. According to John Paul II this attitude of solidarity is not merely a "feeling of vague compassion or shallow distress," but a "firm and persevering determination to commit oneself to the common good . . . the good of all and each individual" (1987, 38). Attitudes of solidarity lead to relationships of solidarity, which are the foundations of *more human* societies in which those who have greater share of the goods and power are ready to share all they possess with the disadvantaged, while the disadvantaged claim their legitimate rights and do what they can to promote the common good (*ibid.*, 39). Thus, by striving to promote the good of every person and of the whole person, integral human development brings about the qualitative human enrichment that Goulet and other development ethicists identify as authentic development.

Some concerns

Some may worry that the inherently social notions of "solidarity" and "common good" entailed by integral human development undermine agency. Human ascent requires promoting authentic agency. We cannot mandate that people adopt the attitudes and social virtues involved in authentic respect for human dignity and solidarity. Moreover, from the integral human development perspective, each person has a legitimate and equal claim to all that is required for human flourishing and is never a merely passive recipient of aid. All are encouraged to act as agents who take up the shared task of promoting the common good. The common good is not an aggregate of the good of all members of society; the deprivation of some cannot be offset by luxuries enjoyed by others. Instead, the common good reflects the good of the whole person (including agency) and *every* person and the relationships they share.

Although integral human development seeks to promote agency, it may do so by re-thinking institutional liberties with regards to wealth accumulation. As Lebret told the United Nations in 1964:

> We must explore new ways which would respect basic liberties as much as possible, while subjecting them to strict disciplines which are indispensable at the international level in order to stop the growing disparity in standards of living between privileged peoples and peoples scientifically and technically less developed.

He suggests that

> the distribution of goods produced by all may be carried out in such a manner that all those who do not yet enjoy a dignified standard of life, or those who . . . cannot hope to escape extreme poverty, may have their essential needs satisfied and reach a level of living that is consistent with human dignity.
>
> *(Lebret, as cited by Cosmao 1970, 66)*

The upshot is that institutionalized liberties must be respected as much as possible but may be limited so that every person can achieve a standard of living consistent with human dignity. So, although we cannot mandate authentic human ascent, we can and should structure institutions in a way that are most likely to promote the development of the whole person consistent with human dignity.

A related concern one might have about integral human development is its connection to the corpus of Catholic theology. There are historical and logical reasons to believe that integral human development follows from Catholic social teaching. (Indeed, Benedict XVI says *all* the work of the Church is engaged in promoting integral human development (2007, 11).) However, the connection does not necessarily go the other way: one can adopt the integral human development perspective without practicing Catholicism, or any other religion. (Ludovic Bertina (2013) purports to show that integral human development *cannot* be fully captured by non-religious development theory, but as I read it, the article shows only that it has not been so captured by certain non-religious organizations.)

John Paul II affirms this position as he expresses his hope that "men and women without an explicit faith would be convinced that the obstacles to integral development are not only economic, but rest on more profound attitudes which human beings can make into absolute values" and that "whether or not they are inspired by a religious faith" people will work to promote "the full development 'of the whole individual and of all people'" (1987, 37). Thus, one need not be Catholic, or religious, to engage the integral human development perspective, even if one does need "profound attitudes" about human dignity and solidarity.

Moreover, respecting religious liberty is an essential part of the perspective. Paul VI characterizes integral human development as "building a world where every man, no matter his race, religion or nationality can live a fully human life" (1967, 47). John Paul II proclaims: "People or nations too have a right to their own full development. . . . Not even the need for development can be used as an excuse for imposing on others one's way of life or own religious belief" (1987, 32). Thus, it is abundantly clear that one need not be Catholic or even religious to participate in integral human development. Finally, it must be noted that integral human development and both Catholic social teaching are both living traditions that grow and change.

Yet, there are many specific and nuanced version of this general concern that seeks to establish *exactly* how Catholic thought is, or should be, reflected in the necessary "profound attitudes" of integral human development. Many of these questions have the form "Is X consistent with human dignity?" Discussion of such specific questions is beyond the scope of this chapter. But perhaps it is enough to say that such a discussion would closely resemble other discussions about human dignity in a development context among *and beyond* Catholic scholars in that it would include various positions. Integral human development is not limited to Catholics, so there is no reason to think that discussions of human dignity would or should be so limited. (For more on religion and development see Marshall's Chapter 28 in this *Handbook*. For more on the relationship between largely secular development ethics and traditionally Catholic integral human development, see Keleher, 2017.)

Operationalizing integral human development

Catholic Relief Services is an international humanitarian agency that is grounded in and guided by integral human development (Catholic Relief Services 2007, 2011; Heinrich et al. 2009). Accordingly, they embrace the "IHD Concept" which "promotes the good of every person and the whole person; it is cultural, economic, political, social and spiritual" and the "IHD process" which "enables individuals and communities to protect and expand the choices they have to improve their lives, meet their basic human needs, free themselves from oppression and realize their full human potential" (Heinrich 2009, 52). The organization's vision is that the people "increasingly realize their full human potential in solidarity with others and in the context of a just and peaceful society that respects the dignity of every person and the integrity of creation" (*ibid.*). To this end, the organization has developed several tools including the Integral Human Development framework, which is a diagrammatic representation designed to help people think about situations in a holistic way that promotes integral human development (*ibid.*, 4–8).

References

Benedict XVI (2007) *Encyclical Letter: Caritas in Veritate*. Vatican City, http://w2.vatican.va/content/benedict-xvi/en/encyclicals/documents/hf_ben-xvi_enc_20090629_caritas-in-veritate.html.

Bertina, L. (2013) The Catholic Doctrine of "Integral Human Development" and Its Influence on the International Development Community. In *International Development Policy: Religion and Development*. Palgrave Macmillan, London, 115–127.

Catholic Relief Services (2007) *Strategy Document IHD Narrative and Results Framework*. CRS, Baltimore, MD.

Catholic Relief Services (2011) *Institutional Strengthening Guide*. CRS, Baltimore, MD. https://www.crs.org/sites/default/files/tools-research/institutional-strengthening.pdf.

Chamedes, G. (2015) The Catholic Origins of Economic Development after World War II. *French Politics, Culture & Society* 33(2): 55–75.

Cosmao, V. (1970) Louis-Joseph Lebret, OP 1897–1966: From Social Action to the Struggle for Development. *New Blackfriars* 51(597): 62–68.

Dower, N. (2008) The Nature and Scope of Development Ethics. *Journal of Global Ethics* 10(2): 249–262.

Francis (2015) *Encyclical Letter: Laudato Si*. Vatican City, http://w2.vatican.va/content/francesco/en/encyclicals/documents/papa-francesco_20150524_enciclica-laudato-si.html

Francis (2017) Audience with the Participants in the Convention Organized by the Dicastery for Promoting Integral Human Development on the Fiftieth Anniversary of "Populorum Progressio."

Goulet, D. (1971) *The Cruel Choice: A New Concept in the Theory of Development*. Atheneum, New York.

Goulet, D. (1995) *Development Ethics: A Guide to Theory and Practice*. Zed Books, London.

Goulet, D. (1997) Development Ethics: A New Discipline. *International Journal of Social Economics* 24(11): 1160–1171.

Goulet, D. (2006) *Development Ethics at Work: Explorations – 1960–2002*. Routledge, Abingdon and New York.

Heinrich, G., Leege, D. and Miller, C. (2009) *A User's Guide to Integral Human Development (IHD): Practical Guidance for CRS Staff and Partners*. Catholic Relief Services, Baltimore, MD.

John Paul II. (1987) *Encyclical Letter: Sollicitudo Rei Socialis*.

Keleher, L. (2017) Toward an Integral Human Development Ethics. *Veritas: Revista de Filosofía y Teología* 37: 19–34.

Lebret, Louis-Joseph (1954) Économie et Humanisme No. 89. Revue for the Economie and Humanism Society.

Lebret, Louis-Joseph (1955) *Human Ascent*. First Publishers Association Chicago Illinois.

Lebret, Louis-Joseph (1959) *Manifeste pour une civilisation solidaire*. Éditions Économie et Humanisme, Calurie.

Nussbaum, M.C. (2009) *Frontiers of Justice: Disability, Nationality, Species Membership*. Harvard University Press, Cambridge MA.

Nussbaum, M.C. (2011) *Creating Capabilities*. Harvard University Press, Cambridge MA.

Paul VI (1967) *Encyclical Letter: Populorum progressio*. Vatican City, http://w2.vatican.va/content/paul-vi/en/encyclicals/documents/hf_p-vi_enc_26031967_populorum.html.

Rawls, J. (2009) *A Theory of Justice*. Harvard University Press, Cambridge MA.

Sen, A. (1981) *Poverty and Famines: An Essay on Entitlement and Deprivation*. Oxford University Press, Oxford.

Wilber, C.K., Dutt, A.K. and Hesburgh, T.M. (2010) *New Directions in Development Ethics: Essays in Honor of Denis Goulet*. University of Notre Dame Press, Notre Dame, IN.

4

Post-development

No development is good development

Mitu Sengupta

Post-development, as an identifiable school of thought, emerged in the second half of the1980s, chiefly out of criticism of how the concept of 'development' had been theorized and translated into practice in the early post–World War II period. Post-development's startling claim, which set it apart from other critical perspectives aiming at the same target, was that the concept of 'development' could not be reformed and, thus, should be rejected. A key proponent, Gustavo Esteva, put it bluntly: "The time has come to recognize development itself as a malignant myth . . . a huge, irresponsible experiment that, in the experience of a world-majority, failed miserably" (1985, 78). A collective volume regarded as representative of the post-development position began with this provocative claim: "The last forty years is coming to an end. The time is ripe to write its obituary" (Sachs 1992, 1). Post-development's interest, according to another major advocate, is not in "development alternatives," but in "alternatives to development" (Escobar 1995, 215). Indeed, over the years, post-development's campaign to expunge the concept of 'development' from our minds and vocabularies has persisted. Aram Ziai, a contemporary post-development theorist argues, for instance, that there are better indigenous concepts, such as 'Ubuntu' and 'haq,' and also no reason why "development aid" cannot just be called "global social policy" (2013, 134).

In this chapter, I assess the principal arguments upon which post-development's rejectionist position is built. Post-development, it is suggested, emphasizes many concerns that are relevant to development ethics, such as how 'progress' is defined by established development discourses, and who loses and who gains as a result of development programs and policy (for a succinct account of concerns raised by development ethics, the field of inquiry, see Gasper 2016, 860). Readers are cautioned, nonetheless, towards the worrying political implications of some aspects of post-development thought.

Core claims

It should be acknowledged, from the outset, that the scholars associated with the post-development perspective emphasize a diverse range of concerns and often disagree. Their many areas of agreement derive from what they share: an intellectual heritage in post-structuralism, the philosophy of Michel Foucault (on this, see Escobar 1984; Storey 2000), and post-colonialism (see Simon 2006).

DOI: 10.4324/9781315626796-5

The starting point, for post-development, is that language does not neutrally reflect our identities and social relations but, rather, that it plays an active role in creating and changing our world. The concept of 'development' is regarded as an example of how language is used to construct reality, and how the "specific way in which it does so has consequences" (Ziai 2013, 125). We have come to assume, argues Ziai, that "there is such a thing as development," and as a result, a diverse and rich universe of social, economic, political, and cultural phenomena has come to be construed, simplistically, as "manifestations of development and underdevelopment" (2013, 126).

Post-development's argument is that social problems are not only misdiagnosed by established development discourses, they are presented in an ahistorical and deliberately apolitical ('depoliticized') light that ultimately serves the interests of powerful people and institutions. Problems that have roots in asymmetrical power relations and other inequalities at the national or international level – and that may require struggles for justice to resolve – are represented as in need of the 'solution' of 'development.' In the classic post-development text, *Rule of Experts*, Mitchell (2002) explains, for example, how USAID self-servingly explained Egypt's increasing dependence on imported grain as an outcome of the country's high population growth and lack of arable land. The 'solution' proposed by USAID was "more than three billion dollars' worth of Egyptian grain purchases from the United States between 1975 and 1988, making Egypt the world's largest importer of subsidized grain" (*ibid.*, 2002, 216). In Mitchell's alternative account of Egypt's food crisis, the root of the problem lay in changing consumption patterns among the Egyptian upper classes, which led to the diversion of scarce resources from producing grains for human consumption to producing animal feed. In another classic text, *Anti-Politics Machine*, Ferguson (1994) provides a fascinating analysis of how poverty in Lesotho was explained in apolitical terms by various development agencies (for an extended discussion of Mitchell 2002 and Ferguson 1994, see Sahle 2009). For post-development critics, development theory's depoliticizing drive is only reinforced by the institutional interests of development organizations, which have a mandate to avoid being 'political.' Ziai (2013) points out that it is much easier to obtain funding from these organizations for irrigation and electrification projects than for struggles for justice by landless peasants and other marginalized populations.

Another important dimension of the post-development critique is that 'development' is an ethnocentric concept that is deeply rooted in Western ideas about human progress. In fact, not only is development conceptualized as a set of normatively positive processes that everyone is destined to follow, it is seen to have taken place in some geographical areas, but not in others. Development theory is given the charge of explaining why countries in Asia, Africa, and the rest of the 'backward' world is lagging behind the more 'mature' West, which is constructed as an ideal model, and in generating policies to help them 'catch up.' The notion that countries in the North might also require improvement is rarely accepted, and nor is it acknowledged that not every person will accept that the "highly individualized consumer societies based on competition, infinite human needs, and unimpaired exploitation of nature constitutes the best of all possible worlds" (Ziai 2013, 128). Post-development's ethnocentrism charge is levelled not only at modernization theory and other classical approaches to development, but also at critical approaches, such as Marxism and dependency theory, which are viewed, ultimately, as prisoners of their own epistemological roots in Western, Enlightenment philosophies (on this, see Kapoor 2008). Latouche (1993) finds fault even with the concept of 'alternative development' (as articulated by Hettne 1990) for proposing a unilinear development path that amounts, ultimately, to "the Westernization of the world" (1993, 161).

The "emergence of expert knowledges" (Escobar 2007, 19) is another core concern for post-development. With its emphasis on forcing technical solutions onto political problems – the imposition of science as power (see Nandy 1988) – development discourse has engendered the belief that positive social change can be achieved through interventions based on expert knowledge "possessed by a privileged group that acts as a trustee for the common good" (Ziai 2013, 125). There is an assumption that experts "know better what the people need than the people themselves" and that development interventions based on expert knowledge are "not in need of legitimation by the people affected by these interventions" (Ziai 2013, 130). Proponents of post-development point out that development experts are typically not local, do not speak local languages, and spend little time in the societies for which they prescribe change. Their focus, rather, is on top-down transfers of capital, technology, and knowledge from the global North to the South. While Western experts remain in demand following decolonization, the "mantle of trusteeship," as Ziai puts it (*ibid.*), has been gradually shifted onto national elites, who are also out of touch with the local and vernacular. The reification of expert knowledge, post-development critics further argue, has led to the "exclusion of the knowledges, voices and concerns of those whom, paradoxically, development was supposed to serve: the poor of Asia, Africa and Latin America" (Escobar 2007, 20). Such exclusions are not only authoritarian and morally objectionable, but the disconnect between external expert and ground reality has meant that development simply does not work, producing "a long list of white elephants, failed projects and disastrous consequences" (Ziai 2013, 131).

It is, indeed, a core claim of the post-development school that the concept of development, with its ingrained notions of European superiority and racism towards non-European people, is not an accidental invention. Rather, it is means for the West to reassert its moral and cultural superiority in a world where colonialism is wrongly assumed to have ended. Development, it is argued, is not a natural, disembodied, value-neutral project. It signals the continuation of the colonial project of 'civilizing' the savage 'other' under a "non-offensive-sounding rubric" (Sahle 2009, 69), and is a tool for the West's "economic and geopolitical expansion" in order to supplement a "dying and obsolete colonialism" and "recapture new ground" (Rahnema and Bawtree 1997, 379). The argument that development, as both idea and "vast institutional apparatus" (Escobar 2007, 19), is representative of our 'colonial present' is woven through most representative post-development texts, and thus illuminates post-development's foundations in the post-colonial thought of Said (1979), Bhabha (1994), Hall (1997), and others. 'Development' is a purposeful project, which is why it should be purposefully overthrown.

But will discarding 'development' leave us lurching in the darkness? Rahnema suggests that the "end of development should not be seen as an end to the search for new possibilities of change," but that "it should only mean that the binary, the mechanistic, the reductionist, the inhumane and the ultimately self-destructive approach to change is over" (2000, 319). Post-development scholars argue for the primacy of the "local and the place-based" (Escobar 2007, 19) and "radical democracy" (Lummis 1996), and envision social movements and grassroots mobilizations as the basis for transitioning into a new, 'post-development' period (Esteva and Prakash 1998; Rahnema and Bawtree 1997; Rist 1997). Other, more specific, advice includes cultivating a critical stance towards established scientific discourses (Escobar 1995, 215) and "to give salience to the forms of knowledge produced by those who are supposed to be the 'objects' of development so that they can become subjects in their own right" (Escobar 2007, 21).

Salient criticisms

Post-development has received criticism from a wide spectrum of sources, including post-development itself (such as Ziai 2004), and other critical perspectives inspired by Marxism, neo-Marxism, postcolonialism and feminism, that share many of post-development's reservations about mainstream development approaches (such as Munck 2012; Storey 2000; Kiely 1999; Corbridge 1998). Of the countless objections to post-development, two salient clusters are reviewed below, one to do with post-development's characterization of development discourse, and the other, with its articulation of alternatives.

In relation to post-development's characterization of 'development,' the argument is that, although the post-development school denounces development theory for rendering an over-generalized and essentialized view of the world, it bases its critique on precisely such an over-generalized and essentialized view of development theory; one that is blind to the myriad ways in which theorizing about development has changed over the years, and to the rising diversity among development institutions. Development theory has progressed well beyond the heavy emphasis on economic growth and industrialization of its early years, Pieterse (1998) points out, writing in the late 1990s. Concepts such as basic needs, participation, sustainability, and endogenous development are "no longer controversial" and have "long been adopted in mainstream development" (*ibid.*, 348–349). Post-development is also faulted for failing to recognize that not all practical applications of 'development' are the same, and that development programs can be creatively resisted, transformed, and reformulated by local cultures, leading to hybrid outcomes that defy clear categorization (see Nustad 2001).

Post-development is criticized, moreover, for holding 'development' responsible for poverty and other social ills that, in many cases, existed prior to it (and thus could not have been caused by it), and for "demonising industrial modernity" (Ziai 2004, 1048). It is pointed out that many social movements and local organizations in the global South have made clear demands for "access to development" (Pieterse 1998, 363), human rights, and other so-called 'Western' inventions, and that development has produced man unambiguous positives, such as rising life expectancies. For millions of people in the world, the affluence and democratic values associated with the West are desirable, and it is 'self-righteous,' Corbridge suggests, to belittle their aspirations and preach that "only the simple life is a good life" and that "we can all live like the Mahatma, or would want to" (1998, 139). Post-development, from this angle, is a paternalistic and cynical perspective, primarily developed by self-indulgent intellectuals in the North, who misuse the "bulky historical category 'the West'" (Pieterse 1998, 365) and arrogantly assume that those who want development must lack agency (also see Cowen and Shenton 1996).

Another biting criticism is that post-development presents an essentialized and romanticized vision of non-Western societies and 'local culture' that overlooks various forms of domination and injustice that arise in these contexts. Nanda (1999, 7), for example, warns against "the anti-modernist and patriarchal values of the traditional elites." Beyond this, critics argue, the very notion that the 'local' can be isolated from the 'global' does not correlate easily with people's lived experiences. Since identity formation in the global South has been influenced by hundreds of years of complex, supra-local processes including colonialism, nationalism and globalization, clumsy binaries tend to lose meaning. Post-development "seems devoid of the devious ways that knowledge has been 'worlded' by the forces of globalization such that local ideas become hybrid," Sylvester suggests (1999, 709). Post-development is also charged with being overly invested in exposing the workings of power, and not enough in tendering practical solutions to everyday problems faced by disadvantaged people, the 'subaltern' of the world. "It rarely asks 'Can the subaltern eat?' and, if not, why not?" says Munck (2012, 87). The "trend" in many post-development sources is to "stop at critique," notes Pieterse, and "[w]hat this means is an endorsement of the status quo" (1998, 365). The few 'alternatives' suggested by post-development, furthermore, put too much stock in the transformational capacities of social movements and advocate "an openness in politics" that is "so open-ended and vague that it effectively washes its hands of politics" (Kiely 1999, 46).

One might be inclined to argue, in the face of such scathing criticisms, that it is the post-development critique, rather than the development as an idea, that ought to be expelled from our lexicons. Yet criticism aimed at post-development has not always been fair (see Escobar 2000).

Prominent post-development scholars, including Escobar, have been careful to warn against "assuming the existence of pure . . . vernacular societies, free of domination" (1995, 188). Moreover, a critical perspective need not come up with a clear blueprint of an alternative society in order to be considered valuable. There is reason, furthermore, to be admiring of post-development's fierce, uncompromising stance, and the possibility of radical social transformation that it intimates. After all, despite the rise of progressive concepts, such as basic needs, capabilities, and human rights, the classical paradigm of development – with its espousal of economic growth, industrialization, and capital, technology, and expert knowledge transfers from the North to the South – remains influential, even dominant. Post-development surely deserves applause for pushing boundaries beyond typical reformist measures, and for taking the question of racism seriously. Finally, post-development is as complex and changing as any major theoretical perspective, and the temptation to caricature it should be resisted. Ziai (2013) distinguishes, for example, between a first generation 'neo-populist' stream, and a 'sceptical' second generation, with which he identifies himself as well as others like Rist (1997). Many standard criticisms of post-development apply to the neo-populists, says Ziai, but not to the sceptics, who resist romanticizing a specific (simple) way of life, and argue, instead, that there are "numerous ways of living a 'good life,' and it is up to each society to invent its own" (Rist 1997, 241 cited in Ziai 2013, 128).

Having said this, many criticisms of post-development do hold merit, and detract from its otherwise astute analysis of the value questions and choices implied in processes of development. One problem is post-development's lingering insensitivity to the risk of domination in local contexts. While we may accept that post-development's second-generation sceptics are not given to issuing romanticized prescriptions for the 'good life' (Ziai 2013), their suggestion that "each society will invent its own" pathway is by no means unproblematic. In the absence of universal criteria, how will this be determined? Whose voice will bear authority? Will the oppressed and marginalized be heard? Such questions are not answered clearly. In our intricately interconnected world, post-development's dogged endorsement of endogenous development is problematic for another reason. Even if it were possible to realize fair forms of wholly 'bottom-up' development, it would probably not be advisable to shift power and considerations of justice so definitively to the local level. As Pogge (2008), Brock (2008), and other theorists of global justice argue, the world's poor and disadvantaged people are profoundly affected by global institutions, rules, and processes, which often work against them. National and international organizations must be accorded not only the moral responsibility, but also the capacity, to resist harmful global forces. This brings us to carefully consider post-development's other dogged claim, namely, that the concept of 'development' should be abandoned (even 'second-generation' sceptics, such as Ziai, call for it). Without doubt, development is a loaded, imperfect term. Yet it is a concept understood by people in power; the much-reviled "vast institutional apparatus" (as Escobar 2007, 19, puts it) of the Bretton Woods institutions, the UN system, and the national planning and development agencies of states. In our non-ideal world, it is perhaps the only instantly recognizable word that fixes attention on how economic benefits and burdens are distributed across societies, both locally and globally. Ejecting it might well have negative ramifications for proponents of distributive justice.

References

Bhabha, H. (1994) *The Location of Culture*. Routledge, London.

Brock, G. (2008) Taxation and Global Justice: Closing the Gap between Theory and Practice. *Journal of Social Philosophy* 39(2): 161–184.

Corbridge, S. (1998) Beneath the Pavement Only Soil: The Poverty of Post-Development. *Journal of Development Studies* 34(6): 138–148.

Cowen, M. and Shenton, R.W. (1996) *Doctrines of Development.* Taylor & Francis, London.
Escobar, A. (1984) Discourse and Power in Development: Michel Foucault and the Relevance of His Work to the Third World. *Alternatives* 10(3): 377–400.
Escobar, A. (1995) *Encountering Development: The Making and Unmaking of the Third World.* Princeton University Press, Princeton.
Escobar, A. (2000) Beyond the Search for a Paradigm? Post-Development and Beyond. *Development* 43(4): 11–14.
Escobar, A. (2007) "Post-Development" as Concept and Social Practice. In Ziai, A. ed., *Exploring Post-Development: Theory and Practice, Problems and Perspectives.* Routledge, London, 18–31.
Esteva, G. (1985) Development: Metaphor, Myth, Threat. *Development: Seeds of Change* 3: 78–79.
Esteva, G. and Prakash, M.S. (1998) *Grassroots Post-Modernism: Remaking the Soil of Cultures.* Zed Books, London.
Ferguson, J. (1994) *The Anti-Politics Machine: Development, Depoliticization and Bureaucratic Power in Lesotho.* University of Minnesota Press, Minneapolis.
Gasper, D. (2016) Development Ethics. In ten Have, H. ed., *Encyclopedia of Global Bioethics.* Springer, New York, 860–868.
Hall, S. (1997) Introduction. In Hall, S. ed., *Representation: Cultural Representation and Signifying Practices.* The Open University, London.
Hettne, B. (1990) *Development Theory and the Three Worlds: Towards an International Political Economy of Development.* Longman Scientific & Technical, New York.
Kapoor, I. (2008) *The Postcolonial Politics of Development.* Routledge, London.
Kiely, R. (1999) The Last Refuge of the Noble Savage? A Critical Assessment of Post-Development Theory. *The European Journal of Development Research* 11(1): 30–55.
Latouche, S. (1993) *In the Wake of the Affluent Society: An Exploration of Post-development.* Zed Books, London.
Lummis, C.D. (1996) *Radical Democracy.* Cornell University Press, Ithaca.
Mitchell, T. (2002) *Rule of Experts: Egypt, Technopolitics, Modernity.* University of California Press, Berkeley.
Munck, R. (2012) Marxism and Development: A Search for Relevance. In Johnson, M. ed., *The Legacy of Marxism: Contemporary Challenges, Conflicts, and Developments.* Continuum, London.
Nanda, M. (1999) Who Needs Post-Development? Discourses of Difference, Green Revolution, and Agrarian Populism in India. *Journal of Developing Societies* 15(1): 5–31.
Nandy, A. ed. (1988) *Science, Hegemony and Violence.* Oxford University Press, New Delhi.
Nustad, K.G. (2001) Development: The Devil We Know? *Third World Quarterly* 22(4): 479–489.
Pieterse, J.N. (1998) My Paradigm or Yours? Alternative Development, Post-Development, Reflexive Development. *Development and Change* 29(2): 343–373.
Pogge, T.W. (2008) *World Poverty and Human Rights.* Polity Press, Cambridge.
Rahnema, M. (2000) Towards Post Development. In Corbridge, S. ed., *Development: Critical Concepts in the Social Sciences, Vol V (Identities, Representations, Alternatives).* Routledge, London, 304–331.
Rahnema, M. and Bawtree, V. (1997) *The Post-Development Reader.* Zed Books, London.
Rist, G. (1997) *The History of Development: From Western Origins to Global Faith.* Zed Books, London.
Sachs, W. (1992) *The Development Dictionary: A Guide to Knowledge as Power.* Zed Books, London.
Sahle, E.N. (2009) Post-Development and Alternatives to Development. In Haslam, P.A., Schafer, J. and Beaudet, P. eds., *Introduction to International Development: Approaches, Actors, and Issues.* Oxford University Press, Don Mills, 68–85.
Said, E. (1979) *Orientalism.* Vintage Books, New York.
Simon, D. (2006) Separated by Common Ground? Bringing (Post)Development and (Post)Colonialism Together. *The Geographical Journal* 172(1): 10–21.
Storey, A. (2000) Post-Development Theory: Romanticism and Pontius Pilate Politics. *Development* 43(4): 40–46.
Sylvester, C. (1999) Development Studies and Postcolonial Studies: Disparate Tales of the "Third World". *Third World Quarterly* 20(4): 703–721.
Ziai, A. (2004) The Ambivalence of Post-Development: Between Reactionary Populism and Radical Democracy. *Third World Quarterly* 25(6): 1045–1060.
Ziai, A. (2013) The Discourse of "Development" and Why the Concept Should Be Abandoned. *Development in Practice* 23(1): 123–136.

5

Epistemology

Epistemic injustice and distortion in development theory and practice

Anna Malavisi

One of the fundamental problems of development theory and practice is grounded in the limitations of theoretical discussions of knowledge, and how this knowledge is then applied in the practice. Development depends on knowledge. Understanding what development is relies on knowledge; decisions about development policies and programs are based on a certain knowledge; often the knowledge of some can be deemed to have a higher epistemic authority and, hence, credibility than the knowledge of others. However, there is also an increasing awareness that the persistence of certain types of knowledge can actually lead to harm and injustice. Therefore, having some understanding about the importance of context, the situatedness of knowers, the value of experience, but also, how this influences one's judgment are crucial for understanding the challenges that arise in development. This chapter is an analysis of the notion of knowledge as understood within development, but also, how epistemology plays a role in development ethics. Epistemology is an area within the discipline of philosophy that is defined as the theory of knowledge. It is concerned primarily with the production of knowledge and, in particular, justified true belief. Who does one believe? How do our beliefs come about? Epistemology as the study of knowledge attempts to provide answers to these questions.

In this chapter the focus is on the value of epistemology for the pursuit of worthwhile development, as distinct from maldevelopment (see Chapter 1, Introduction, in this *Handbook*). For this type of development to occur, some understanding is needed of the problems and challenges that currently thwart development that often leads to maldevelopment. The first section discusses how epistemology, particularly critical theories of epistemology such as social epistemology, feminist epistemology, epistemologies of ignorance, and alternative epistemologies are relevant for development ethics. Next, epistemology and development are discussed, based on the premise that a fundamental problem of development theory and practice is rooted in epistemology. In the following section I discuss some of the epistemic challenges that arise in development, theoretically and practically. The concept of epistemic injustice is introduced, and an analysis given on how the theory and practice of global development is epistemically unjust. Finally, some thoughts are offered on how to mitigate epistemic injustices, broadly construed, as a component of development ethics, and possible future research areas are suggested.

DOI: 10.4324/9781315626796-6

Epistemology

There are multiple ways to think about knowledge, such as knowing how to ride a bicycle or knowing your aunt who lives in New York. Traditional epistemology is primarily concerned with propositional knowledge, usually denoted by the formula S *knows that* p. A proposition is a declarative statement that describes a putative fact, or a state of something. An everyday understanding would be the following: Bianca *knows that* the sun will rise tomorrow. Additionally, the concern is with the epistemology of knowledge production, which differs from the sociology of knowledge which is the empirical study of how social conditions affect knowledge production. The epistemology of knowledge production emphasizes the normative role, 'seeking not only to describe our current social practices of knowledge production, but also to understand how we ought to know and how we can improve our knowledge practices' (Grasswick 2013; Coady 2012).

Epistemology is also recognized for being ahistorical and abstract, and focused on the individual. Along with this, there has been a division of epistemology and the ethico-political which as Lorraine Code (2014) writes, obstructs any opportunity for the need of epistemic responsibility, defined as 'the responsibility to know well in order to advocate honorably' (7). Fortunately, many philosophers have begun to consider other ideas within the realm of epistemology that challenges its traditional structure. Social epistemology, feminist epistemology, and epistemologies of ignorance are just some of these. In social epistemology, the emphasis is on understanding knowledge through the investigation of social interactions, both individual and institutional. The belief is that the 'human epistemic situation . . . is largely shaped by social relationships and institutions' (Goldman and Blanchard 2016).

'Traditional epistemology' tends to ignore the status of knowers or their capacity as situated knowers. For feminist epistemologists there is a need to challenge and question these ideas, but also to expand and offer new thoughts on the theory of knowledge. Therefore, feminist epistemology moves beyond a critical analysis, it is instrumental in reframing the puzzling aspects of knowledge within a different framework (Alcoff and Potter 1993). One of the main threads in feminist epistemology calls for a strong objectivity. Sandra Harding is best recognized for this in her work on standpoint epistemology and the importance of starting from the everyday lives of people to achieve objectivity. Her claims on standpoint methodology have challenged scientists and science to break with sexist and androcentric assumptions, and have provoked much discussion among those not so eager to listen (Harding 1993). Another notable aspect is the importance of understanding where knowers are situated in the world. A standpoint from a dominant paradigm will result in a weak form of objectivity since 'the standpoint of this group is epistemically limited with respect to the standpoint of various marginalized groups' (Alcoff and Potter 1993, 6).

Knowledge seen through the eyes of 'traditional epistemology' is in fact not representative of knowledge deemed general or human. The analysis of knowledge by epistemologists excludes crucial aspects, which are concrete and unique of our physical and social worlds. With this in view, epistemologies of ignorance have also surfaced. Epistemologies of ignorance depart from the premise that just as understanding knowledge is important, understanding ignorance is equally so. Epistemologies of ignorance examine the complex nature of ignorance: its different forms, its production and continuity and its role in the practice of knowledge (Sullivan and Tuana 2007). Ignorance may be conceived as a lack of knowledge, but this is not its only form. Sometimes, as Charles Mills argues, ignorance, and particularly white ignorance is a form caused by structural features entrenched within our society that foment power and domination (Mills

2007). This type of analysis results in an urgent attempt to contest the 'whiteness' of epistemology by demanding that race and other social categories become visible. Other critiques that challenge traditional or Western epistemology include decolonial ones, which I discuss in the next section.

The need for other epistemologies

Boaventura de Sousa Santos, in his critique of Western thought, argues that what has happened over the years as a result of the dominant science paradigm can be considered, among other things, a suppression of knowledge which he calls 'a form of epistemicide' (2008, xix). This is a dimension that is often missed or blatantly ignored, due to the epistemological way the global north has imposed a capitalist and imperial order on the global south. There is an urgent need to supplant the dominant monocultural paradigm in science with other epistemologies or what Santos calls *ecology of knowledges*. In his words,

> The ecology of knowledges is an invitation to the promotion of non-relativistic dialogues among knowledges, granting 'equality of opportunities' to the different kinds of knowledge engaged in ever broader epistemological disputes aimed both at maximizing their respective contributions to build a more democratic and just society and at decolonizing knowledge and power.
>
> *(2008, xx)*

This does not mean that we completely reject Western thought, rather the idea is that we need to make the knowledges of others visible. We cannot rely only on Western thought or consider it as a universal truth (Santos 2008).

Current scientific knowledge presents a specific worldview, yet it has been conceived as representing a universal reality and explanation. This eliminates any possibility of an alternative or even complementary articulation of knowledges and is redolent of colonialism and relations of inequality. (See Mills 1997.) The type of knowledge inherent to modern science is supposedly rational and highly rigorous. Science today continues to put forward this form of knowledge as the only true, reliable, and accurate one. In contrast, common sense knowledge, which can be classified as 'the knowledge that we, as individual or collective subjects, create and use to give meaning to our practices, but which science insists on considering irrelevant, illusory and false,' is not even taken into account (Santos 2007, 15). Claims by climate change deniers could be put forward as a way to support this notion, in that, these people reject science in this instance. This is not a good thing. However, my response would be that the knowledge climate change deniers make their claims on is not a legitimate nor substantive form of knowledge. The argument here is not that the science is not true, but it has limitations, such as ignoring social and political contexts.

There are two underlying premises of non-traditional epistemologies. The first is that a Western understanding of the world is not broad enough. The second is based on the notion that the diversity witnessed in the world, such as diversity in being, thinking, feeling and knowing is in fact infinite. How we perceive time, life, existence, and death throughout the world is not accommodated by just one epistemology, nor other theories developed in the north. Epistemologies from the west (or the north), therefore, limit, undermine, and blatantly ignore other ways of seeing, thinking, and knowing (Santos 2007; Mignolo 2011). In the next section I discuss the particular relevance epistemology has for development and development ethics.

Epistemology and development

There *is* an epistemology of development based on a certain epistemology embedded within a particular social imaginary that excludes other epistemologies, such as those from poorer countries or of those living in less-advantaged situations. The dimension of power within an epistemic landscape is not often discussed, but it could be argued that this is where the power begins. The ethical aspects of epistemic conduct are also rarely considered. Global development programs and policies devised within large multilateral institutions such as the World Bank, UN, and others are epistemically dependent on types of knowledge that have led to injustices. (See Chapter 4, Post-Development, in this *Handbook*.) Consider for example, Neglected Tropical Diseases (NTDs). These provide a clear case of the way that epistemic issues are relevant for development ethics. NTDs are a group of seventeen diseases that blight the lives of more than a billion people worldwide. The manner in which NTDs are addressed is based on a certain type of knowledge. This type of knowledge has proven to be inadequate and inappropriate, and only highlights the need to broaden the way we think about global development today.

The type of knowledge required for development is consistent with the critical types of epistemology mentioned earlier. The scope of knowledge needs to be expanded to include not only propositional knowledge, *knowing that*, but also other forms of knowledge such as experiential knowledge and *knowing how*. It lies in the notion that just as theory cannot be separated from practice, knowledge cannot be separated from values. Intrinsic to knowledge in this context is experience, what one has lived and is living. How many global development policies are designed from the schema of propositional knowledge, '*S* knows that *p*', and how many times is this form of knowledge inappropriate and inaccurate? Our knowledge claims always derive from a social context of situatedness, and failure to recognize this or interrogate the implications of this by those in dominant positions provides distorted forms of knowledge (Harding 2004).

Development ethicists are skeptical about the type of knowledge produced within global institutions such as the World Bank or the International Monetary Fund, often revered as the only source for expert knowledge on development. For many of these experts, their certainty of truth is based on neo-liberal and capitalist foundations entrenched in patriarchal hegemonies (St. Clair 2007). The consequences of this are many: the production of knowledge is confined to the professionals of these institutions. The type of knowledge evident that is credited and legitimized by each one of them, however, is divorced from the reality of poorer people in less advantaged countries. Attempts have been made to include the voices of the oppressed. The World Bank study *Voices of the Poor* is a phenomenal piece of work that provides a rich insight into the lives of the poor, however, when it comes to the decision-making, poor people are not at the table (Narayan-Parker 2000).

In a study conducted in Bolivia analyzing the relationship between northern non-government organizations (NNGOs) and southern non-government organizations (SNGOs), comments by members of SNGOs in relation to NNGOs said the following: 'they come here without really knowing the context and we have to comply with their requirements'. One respondent said, 'a type of north – south confrontation takes place: those who control and those who depend; they give the funds but maintain their distance creating a power relation. This force generates an attitude of superiority and arrogance where decisions are made for SNGOs by NNGOs when it doesn't really correspond to them.' She went on to say that the development paradigms NNGOs advocate are from the north; 'we could have different conceptions of development but they do not even ask us' (Malavisi 2010, 49). These are examples of epistemic injustice, which is discussed in the next section.

Epistemic injustice

For the remainder of this chapter I focus only on critical theories of epistemology since it is those that are most relevant for development and development ethics. These critical theories depart from the non-ideal, in other words, the reality on the ground: the cultural and doxastic differences, the diverse worldviews, distinct experiences, and others. A relatively new concept that has emerged within feminist epistemology within the last decade is epistemic justice. (Feminist epistemology is not confined to thinking about epistemic issues based only on gender and sexuality but also considers other social categories such as race, culture, religion, etc.) This concept, I argue, is extremely relevant for development ethics, because it enables one to understand that the injustices and inequalities that persist in global development are not only attributable to social, political, and economic factors but also epistemological. By focusing on epistemic justice I do not intend to argue that this is the only way to address epistemic issues. To expand on this area and include other ideas such as epistemologies of ignorance requires more room than I have here.

Miranda Fricker in her book *Epistemic Injustice* approaches the idea of epistemic justice from its inverse, injustice (2007). By analyzing the epistemic injustices it enables us to understand what these injustices are, how these are produced, what the obstacles are and how we can move forward. Fricker's aim is to expose some of our moral and epistemic assumptions (which, of course, have socio-cultural and political implications) that influence how we constitute what is knowledge. Her analysis focuses on the situatedness of knowers, and many critics of Fricker's work have offered further insights crucial for understanding epistemic justice (Anderson 2012; Dotson 2012; Medina 2012; Mason 2011).

The impetus for Fricker is the impoverishment of epistemology by the absence of a theoretical framework that reveals ethical and political aspects of epistemic conduct (Fricker 2007). Her work reveals the ethical dimension of epistemic practice. According to Fricker, 'The world is "structured" by the powerful to the detriment of the powerless, there is another species of oppression at work, one that has not been registered in mainstream epistemology: epistemic oppression' (1999, 191). Oppression can be understood in various ways: political, economic, social, sexual, and others. The concern here is with oppression as a result of epistemic domination and marginalization.

Fricker introduces two forms of epistemic injustice: testimonial injustice and hermeneutical injustice. Testimonial injustice takes place when a hearer gives a diminished level of credibility to what someone has said due to prejudice (Fricker 2007). Jose Medina claims that in some cases the level of credibility can be excessive, when a speaker earns more credibility such as in the case of a white, male teacher (Medina 2011). Hence the dysfunction based on prejudice can be of two types. It can be a credibility excess when the speaker earns more credibility or credibility deficit when the speaker earns less credibility. A significant characteristic of testimonial injustice, being the most pernicious, is that it is systematic. It is termed as systematic since it is not produced by a single form of prejudice. Rather, it is embedded within the diverse dimensions of a social structure. Therefore testimonial injustice has political, economic, cultural, and social connotations. This systematic testimonial injustice is upheld by a prejudice closely linked to social identity which Fricker calls *identity prejudice*. An example of testimonial injustice is portrayed in *To Kill a Mockingbird*: in the court house where Tom Robinson, a black man, is charged with the rape of Mayella Ewell, a white girl. The jury based their decision on a belief entrenched within a systemic racial prejudice, that Tom's story was just a lie.

The second form of epistemic injustice is hermeneutical injustice. Hermeneutical injustice provides a description of how power relations and privilege influence interpretations and understandings which are socially embedded. As a collective occurrence of social understanding, disadvantaged groups are hermeneutically marginalized often without the awareness of the individual. Hermeneutical injustice is reflective of the social situation of individuals and groups within society, like groups based on gender, race, and other minorities. It is difficult (but not impossible) to detect. However, since hidden within this social context is the way efforts of interpretation are usually based on our own interests – 'we try hardest to understand those things it serves us to understand' (Fricker 2007, 152). Thus, what we see happening is how hegemonic and dominant forces oppress the social experience of many resulting in a hermeneutical marginalization which excludes them from participating in certain practices (Fricker 2007). An example of hermeneutical injustice is the way development is often lauded as the solution to eliminating global poverty. A certain social understanding and interpretation is given to it by those who hold the power, those who devise and control the global economic order.

As a way to mitigate or prevent testimonial and hermeneutical injustice, Fricker offers the virtues of justice which rely on the need for a type of epistemic conduct. Fricker differentiates between two forms of virtues: intellectual and ethical. Although Fricker acknowledges that the problem of epistemic injustice is structural in nature, her solution to address epistemic injustice in the way of intellectual virtues is based in the individual. In regard to testimonial justice, there is a need for credibility judgments, which incorporate the responsibilities we have as hearers on the need to cultivate a testimonial sensibility. What this requires is a critical openness but also critical reflexiveness. Of course, when the socially situated context lends itself to credibility excess and credibility deficit, how then, can we begin to break down these social constructs? This is where Fricker's account does not completely respond to this conundrum.

Since epistemic injustice is primarily a structural problem, its solutions must also be structural. While not completely discounting the value of cultivating individual epistemic virtues, Elizabeth Anderson considers that relying on individuals may be necessary but not sufficient. She argues that just as Rawls claims that a virtue of social institutions is distributive justice, the same could be said for epistemic justice. It needs to take place at the level of institutions. She calls for a type of epistemic democracy (Anderson 2012). An understanding of this is crucial for development professionals. It leads to the realization that to address epistemic injustice work needs to be done at both levels: individual and institutional.

A second challenge to Fricker's account is concerned with forms of testimonial injustice which are structural. Anderson discusses how in the field of social psychology cognitive biases are understood as a form of prejudice. 'Cognitive biases tend to be deeply entrenched in our minds, and operate automatically, unconsciously, and more rapidly than conscious thought' (2012, 167). Even people with the best intentions of avoiding discriminatory thoughts or conduct, being unaware of their views cannot easily control them. Therefore, in thinking about how to counteract these it is not enough to only consider identity prejudice as the only way that credibility can be denied. Anderson considers three causes, all structural in nature, that pose the same threat as prejudice but are group-based. These are the differential access to markers of credibility; ethnocentrism and the 'shared reality bias' (2012, 169). A credibility marker is an assessment of someone based on their education and level of expertise. The use of credibility markers is commonplace: for example, in situations where educated judgments are required, the level of education and certain expertise of groups will account as credibility markers. There is intrinsic value to this. However, in societies where groups are deprived of access to a decent standard of education, they are completely excluded from any form of participation for their lack of credibility. This, according to Anderson, must also be considered as a testimonial injustice.

The second structural cause is ethnocentrism, where the testimonial account of some groups is discounted primarily due to the bias towards groups of which one is a member. A higher level of credence can be given to an in-group member over someone outside the group. Hence, credibility excess can also be considered a testimonial injustice. The third cause is the shared reality bias. According to Anderson, this is the way groups that interact on a regular basis have a convergence of perspectives and share judgments. This is not always pernicious, rather it can build solidarity and cooperation. However, as Anderson poignantly says, 'the shared reality bias will tend to insulate members of advantaged groups from the perspectives of the systematically disadvantaged' (2012, 170). All three causes demonstrate the way structural injustices play a significant role in the realization of testimonial and hermeneutical injustice, the causes of which cannot be limited only to prejudice and will not be resolved by individual epistemic virtues.

For some philosophers, Fricker's hermeneutical marginalization does not emphasize the role power plays in obscuring hermeneutical resources of marginalization. The epistemic agency of a knower is compromised through situated ignorance. Situatedness determines both one's epistemic boundaries and one's boundaries of ignorance. Kristie Dotson argues that epistemic frameworks both obscure and illuminate epistemic differences. We can recognize these differences but we don't, due to willful hermeneutical ignorance (Pohlhaus 2011; Dotson 2012). In the next sections I apply an understanding of epistemic injustice to the theory and practice of global development.

Epistemic challenges in development: theoretical and practical issues

The epistemic injustice in global development begins with its concept. Development as we know it today emerged from Harry Truman in his inaugural address of 1949. That's not to say that development was not conceived of prior to this, but this event marks the stage for the beginning of a process that has become a mega-industry over the span of nearly 70 years (Esteva 1992).

The first development theories assessed the 'development' of nations in terms of an increase in national income. Therefore development was conceptualized only as economic growth. Gross Domestic Product (GDP) was the measure for growth, and for more than 40 years GDP was considered the only indicator worthy as a measurement of development. The higher the GDP of a country, the 'less poor' were its people. However, it became obvious that relying on GDP was insufficient for assessing the impact of development. Understanding development as economic growth greatly influenced the *project* of development, how development was then translated into operative plans. Development became synonymous with economic growth, so programs and projects reflected this. Fortunately, thinking about development has changed over the years, with the introduction of human development and other approaches (Baru and Haq 1998; Streeten 1984). Although these approaches may appear as more reasonable attempts to address global poverty and disparities, they are still entrenched within a knowledge paradigm dominated by Western thought and ideology (Mignolo 2008; Santos 2008; for further discussion on the models of development, see Chapter 18 in this *Handbook*, on education).

The practice of development incorporates many stakeholders: multilateral agencies, national governments, corporations, international and national NGOs, and community-based organizations. Epistemic injustice occurs at different levels: between multilateral agencies and national governments in the case of structural adjustment programs; national governments as bilateral donors to other governments or NGOs; between international NGOs and national NGOs; and between any of these former entities and community-based organizations.

Testimonial injustice is pervasive in development. It happens all the time in the field and in the offices of national and international development organizations. Credibility deficit occurs between indigenous communities and local and international NGOs. Poor, illiterate indigenous women are credited less than development professionals working within a national or international NGO. On the other hand, credibility excess is showered on those working in international NGOs, especially if they are foreigners. It also happens when the knowledge of indigenous peoples is not credited or valued (but mostly ignored) by corporations or international agencies. Prejudicial stereotypes are a significant cause of testimonial injustice.

Testimonial injustice is also evident when development professionals visit poorer countries for a few days and believe they *understand* the situation of the other, and therefore base their decisions on this experience. So, rather than development professionals believing they know what it is like for a mother whose children go to bed hungry every night, or who has to walk miles every day to fetch two pails of water; or even bury her children due to malnutrition, would it not be better to accept that there are some experiences we will never know? (Tuana 2006). Chagas disease, which is a Neglected Tropical Disease (NTD), is an example of a form of testimonial injustice more akin to Anderson's understanding of testimonial injustice for its structural nature. Many of these NTDs have been around for thousands of years. Not surprisingly, NTDs are found in poor countries, among the poorer and most vulnerable sectors of that country (Hotez 2008).

As previously discussed, the three causes of testimonial injustice Elizabeth Anderson discusses are: credibility markers, ethnocentrism, and the shared reality bias. Credibility markers in the case of Chagas disease designate credible knowers as the scientists who research Chagas and the pharmaceutical companies which produce and distribute the drugs for the treatment of the disease. First, this provides only one type of knowledge, and, second, provides a very narrow understanding of the problem of Chagas disease. A principal cause that has contributed to the perpetuation of NTDs is the way they have been confined to a medical problem, ignoring the social, political, economic, and cultural factors. Only the expertise of these medical researchers is sought. The second cause of testimonial injustice is ethnocentrism. It is of no coincidence that NTDs are primarily found in the poorer countries in the world, yet, most decisions about the global health programs are made in the richer countries: decisions that are based on the perspectives and knowledge of those in richer countries about the lives and problems of those in different cultures. The third cause is the shared reality bias, where the perspectives of a certain group such as the international community are insulated from those who are systematically disadvantaged. This, as Anderson says need not be pernicious, in some cases it can foster solidarity and cooperation. But in this case it is pernicious. It becomes evident at congresses, conferences, meetings, and so forth. It is where international players such as those who work for multilateral and bilateral agencies, international NGOs, and others share their perspectives and biases converge. NTDs are an example of hermeneutical injustice for the way they reflect how power relations and privilege such as those exercised by large multilateral agencies such as the WB, UN, and the WHO dictate global health problems. The social experience of the *campesinos* living with Chagas is obscured from the collective understanding of those making the decisions.

What this means is that pharmaceutical companies spend very little of their research and development budgets on NTDs, and global development and health policies tend to reflect global trends rather than the needs of particular, individual countries. Chagas disease as an example of an NTD reflects the social disparities and inequities in the world since it really affects only poorer sectors of the society. Understanding epistemic injustice, as a critical theory of epistemology can bring to light that to be able to address NTDs effectively we must also address poverty. To understand the persistence of NTDs requires a deeper analysis of the existence of poverty.

Working towards epistemic justice as a component of development ethics

The path to epistemic justice entails addressing epistemic injustice. To begin, we need to make visible pluralist forms of knowledge such as those evident in other development actors such as social movements. So, the strengthening and empowering of social movements is a plausible move which would also include addressing testimonial and hermeneutical injustices within these groups. This will require some form of awareness-raising and education at all levels: social movements, NGOs (national and international), bilateral and multilateral institutions, governments, and corporations. Second, if we acknowledge that an underlying problem of epistemic injustice is structural, then this will require a structural solution: institutional reforms at a global level. How can these reforms be motivated in the face of competing political and national interests?

Anderson does provide us with some ideas on how to address these structural injustices. First, at the scale of individuals and institutions, epistemic virtue is a requirement. This epistemic virtue can be understood as one's obligation and responsibility to not *know well* but to know within an ethical framework which allows one to identify epistemic actions that are both harmful and wrongful. One structural remedy is group integration. This necessarily needs to become an epistemic virtue of institutions. In the case of development practice, this would demand the equal hermeneutical participation of all. To avoid the use and exploitation of credibility markers, an understanding needs to take place among all concerned about what this actually means, why and how it happens. This shared inquiry can lead to the production of a shared reality. Ethnocentrism can be addressed by an increased understanding and awareness of those with the most propensities to commit ethnocentric acts. This is difficult given that, 'Reflection which lies at the core of testimonial justice is cognitively taxing and impossible to keep up in an environment that demands rapid responses' (Anderson 2012, 168). But on a more positive note, there are steps to be taken by those in more powerful situations that can begin the process. According to Gail Pohlhaus, 'The dominantly situated knower cannot step outside of her situatedness in order to experience the world as others do; however, she can learn to use epistemic resources developed from the experiences of marginalized knowers' (2011, 7). We learn to use these epistemic resources from listening, from learning from and with marginalized knowers, and with epistemic humility.

The focus needs to be on mitigating epistemic injustice, and this can be facilitated by considering such a topic as a component of development ethics. This emphasizes the importance of understanding some of the theoretical foundations of epistemology, particularly critical theories of epistemology. This can be done at the university level; including it as a component of a development ethics approach for development professionals as part of professional development or other forms of training. This also implies the bringing together of ethical and epistemic issues, a way of thinking that denotes epistemic injustice as an ethical problem. The coupling of ethical and epistemic perspectives is evident in the areas of public health and climate science. Global development is also an area worthy of this. Further research should be done in this area (Katikireddi and Valles 2015; Tuana 2013).

Conclusion

Our globalized world is calling out for change. This call is coming from the social movements scattered all over the globe, north and south. Strong objectivity, situated knowledge, testimonial and hermeneutical justice, the epistemology of ignorance and alternative epistemologies are all sub-themes developed in critical theories of epistemology that greatly help in understanding the injustices taking place at a global level, particularly in the practice of global development. It seems that this process also demands the inclusion of voices of those who need to be represented, those who are the oppressed, the dominated, and the marginalized. In an increasingly interdependent and interrelational world pluralist epistemologies should be the norm rather than the exception.

Critical theories of epistemology provide a more in-depth analysis of the social imbalances evident in our society. In particular, the work of feminist epistemologists brings forth the importance of an ethical dimension in knowledge. And the epistemologies of ignorance are becoming an increasingly important area for the way analysis links oppression and knowledge production; the way conceptions and assumptions can foster white privilege but also white ignorance. Both of these areas can provide a substantive contribution to the theory and practice of global development. And since the problem is also structural, this requires change at a higher, more complex and complicated level. A first step towards change here is rooted in epistemic issues, and particularly, the epistemology of knowledge production, the need for a greater understanding of what we ought to know, and how we should develop better knowledge practices.

References

Alcoff, L. and Potter, E. eds. (1993) *Feminist Epistemologies*. Routledge, New York.

Anderson, E. (2012) Epistemic Justice as a Virtue of Social Institutions. *Social Epistemology* 26(2): 163–173.

Baru, S. and Haq, M. (1998) Human Development: A Tribute. *Economic and Political Weekly* 33(5): 2275–2279.

Coady, D. (2012) *What to Believe Now*. Wiley Blackwell, Oxford.

Code, L. (2014) *Epistemic Responsibility*. Brown University Press, Hanover.

Dotson, K. (2012) A Cautionary Tale: On Limiting Epistemic Oppression. *Frontiers* 33: 124–147.

Esteva, G. (1992) Development. In Sachs, W. ed., *The Development Dictionary*. Zed Book, London.

Fricker, M. (1999) Epistemic Oppression and Epistemic Privilege. *Canadian Journal of Philosophy Supplementary* 25/25: 191–210.

Fricker, M. (2007) *Epistemic Injustice: Power and the Ethics of Knowing*. Oxford University Press, Oxford.

Goldman, A. and Blanchard, T. (2016) Social Epistemology. In Zalta, E. ed., *The Stanford Encyclopedia of Philosophy*. https://plato.stanford.edu/archives/win2016/entries/epistemology-social/.

Grasswick, H. (2013) Feminist Social Epistemology. In Zalta, E. ed., *The Stanford Encyclopedia of Philosophy*. http://plato.stanford.edu/archives/spr2013/entries/feminist-social-epistemology/.

Harding, S. (1993) Rethinking Standpoint Epistemology: What Is Strong Objectivity? In Alcoff, L. and Potter, E. eds., *Feminist Epistemologies*. Routledge, New York.

Harding, S. (2004) *The Feminist Standpoint Theory Reader: Intellectual and Political Controversies*. Routledge, New York.

Hotez, P.J. (2008) *Forgotten People, Forgotten Disease*. ASM Press, Washington.

Katikireddi, S.V. and Valles, S.A. (2015) Coupled Ethical–Epistemic Analysis of Public Health Research and Practice: Categorizing Variables to Improve Population Health and Equity. *American Journal of Public Health* 105(1): e36–e42.

Malavisi, A. (2010) A Critical Analysis of the Relationship between Southern Non-government Organizations and Northern Non-government Organizations in Bolivia. *Journal of Global Ethics* 6(1): 45–56.

Mason, R. (2011) Two Kinds of Unknowing. *Hypatia* 26(2): 294–307.

Medina, J. (2011) The Relevance of Credibility Excess in a Proportional View of Epistemic Injustice: Differential Epistemic Authority and the Social Imaginary. *Social Epistemology: A Journal of Knowledge, Culture and Policy* 25(1): 15–35.

Medina, J. (2012) Hermeneutical Injustice and Polyphonic Contextualism: Social Silences and Shared Hermeneutical Responsibilities. *Social Epistemology: A Journal of Knowledge, Culture and Policy* 26(2): 201–220.

Mignolo, W.D. (2008) The Geopolitics of Knowledge and the Colonial Difference. In Moraña, M., Dussel D.D. and Jáuregui, C.A. eds., *Coloniality at Large: Latin America and the Postcolonial Debate*. Duke University Press, Durham, 225–258.

Mignolo, W.D. (2011) *The Darker Side of Western Modernity*. Duke University Press, Durham.

Mills, C. (1997) *The Racial Contract*. Cornell University Press, Ithaca.

Mills, C. (2007) White Ignorance. In Sullivan, S. and Tuana, N. eds., *Race and Epistemologies of Ignorance*. SUNY Press, Albany.

Narayan-Parker, D. (2000) *Can Anyone Hear Us?* Published by Oxford University Press for the World Bank, New York.

Penz, P., Drydyk, J. and Bose, P. (2011) *Displacement by Development: Ethics, Rights and Responsibilities*. Cambridge University Press, New York.

Pohlhaus, G. (2011) Relational Knowing and Epistemic Injustice: Toward a Theory of Willful Hermeneutical Ignorance. *Hypatia* 1127(4): 715–735.

Santos, B. ed. (2007) *Cognitive Justice in a Global World: Prudent Knowledge for a Decent Life*. Lexington Books, New York.

Santos, B. ed. (2008) *Another Knowledge Is Possible: Beyond Northern Epistemologies*. Verso, London.

St. Clair, A. (2007) A Methodologically Pragmatist Approach to Development Ethics. *Journal of Global Ethics* 3(2): 143–164.

Streeten, P. (1984) *Basic Needs: Some Unsettled Questions*. Office of Women in International Development, Michigan State University, Lansing.

Sullivan, S. and Tuana, N. (2007) *Race and Epistemologies of Ignorance*. SUNY Press, Albany.

Tuana, N. (2006) The Speculum of Ignorance: The Women's Health Movement and Epistemologies of Ignorance. *Hypatia* 21: 1–19.

Tuana, N. (2013) Embedding Philosophers in the Practices of Science Bringing Humanities to the Sciences. *Synthese* 190: 1955–1973.

Part II
Well-being

Economic growth in a region may or may not enhance people's well-being, and this observation animated much critical discussion of development in the 1960s. Calls for 'putting people first' drew attention initially to human needs, but even this was surpassed by the radical and thoroughgoing reconceptualizations of well-being and development introduced by the human development approach, as expressed in the Human Development Index and Human Development Reports, and by the capability approach. These critical perspectives shared important core beliefs: well-being is not reducible to income or wealth, we can better capture changes in well-being in non-monetary measures, and enhanced well-being is essential to worthwhile development.

Yet well-being can be conceptualized in different ways, as Rebecca Gutwald shows in the lead chapter. After tracing the origins of well-being as a concept in development, she presents the central theoretical approaches to well-being, in which, she argues, the discussion of human needs should be included. The chapter concludes with three issues for further research in development ethics: securing well-being over time, the social dimensions of well-being, and the interconnectedness of elements of well-being.

Following this, Oscar Garza-Vázquez and Séverine Deneulin introduce the capability approach and the key authors who have shaped this normative conceptual framework. This chapter offers a comprehensive view of the main differences and advantages of the capability approach over other approaches to well-being, equity, and other dimensions of "worthwhile development." They conclude by highlighting some controversies within the capability approach and important new directions.

If objective measures of well-being, apart from GDP, are necessary for worthwhile development, does it follow that subjective measures of happiness or life satisfaction are unimportant? This is a fallacy, according to Milena Nikolova, who shows why and how subjective measures of well-being are also important for assessing good development. These measures, which pertain either to feelings of happiness or assessments of satisfaction with one's life, are not simply noise but rather reflect meaningful information about perceived quality of life. Hence they are relevant to assessing development, despite their risks and limitations.

DOI: 10.4324/9781315626796-7

Severe and chronic deprivation can cause people to abandon all hope and desire for things they wanted as parts of a good life, leaving them with 'adaptive preferences' instead. As Serene Khader argues, development that increases life-satisfaction only by deflating what people want and hope for should not be mistaken for worthwhile development. Khader addresses problems of defining "adaptive preference" and considers whether it is paternalistic not to accept people's judgments of their own life satisfaction at face value.

6

Well-being

Happiness, desires, goods, and needs

Rebecca Gutwald

Well-being is important for all of us: we want to be well, we want to feel well, we want to do well. Most certainly, we do not want to live a life of misery and harm. Given this universal fact of life, one may wonder why development does not focus mainly on the research of well-being. The main reason is that it is difficult to capture the full meaning of the term beyond this minimal claim. One approach that has gained popularity in development research during the 1970s invoked the idea of (basic) human need to explain what is 'needed' for human lives to go at least marginally well. Framing well-being along the lines of human needs has the advantage of having an intuitive appeal: like all living creatures, human beings *need* things to survive, things like nutrition, fluids, security. Hence, an account of human needs could prove helpful in spelling out the idea of well-being.

This chapter should help readers to navigate through the diverse conceptualizations of well-being and human needs in the context of development ethics. It rests on the assumption that the notion of human needs can be used to spell out the idea of human well-being. In the first section, I cover the origins of well-being as a concept in development. Then, in the next section, I present the most prominent conceptual approaches to well-being in philosophy and development ethics. In due course, I discuss the most crucial objections, based on which it will be established, why a hybrid theory that is interpreted holistically is the most plausible interpretation of well-being. In a third section human needs discourse is introduced, and I sketch out a human needs approach to well-being. In the conclusion, I point out the most pressing open questions that remain for further research.

Well-being in philosophy and development: a conceptual history

As Des Gasper notes in his article on conceptualizing well-being, the rise of well-being research in development was "rather little, rather late" (Gasper 2007, 48). Until the mid-1990s, it was not common to find entries on well-being in textbooks and encyclopedias. The concept of *quality of life* has been around since the 1970s, e.g. with the *Physical Quality of Life Index* (PQLI) that sociologist David Morris developed (Morris 1980), but it did not have much impact on development. It gained traction during the 1990s, when the United Nations Development Program

DOI: 10.4324/9781315626796-8

(UNDP) put it at the center of development, instead of focusing on standard of living measured by income.

The interest in well-being grew out of the dissatisfaction of some development economists with the gross domestic product (GDP) and income as a measurement of progress. GDP does not tell us enough about how people in a country or globally are doing, i.e. about how happy they are, whether they realize their potential or how they themselves view their lives (Qizilbash 1996). Therefore, development ethicists have looked for new conceptions of development and progress that take human beings and their lives more seriously.

So, well-being is a relatively recent idea in development research, but an old one in philosophy. Ancient philosophers often speak of happiness, but it must be noted that this means more than merely feeling happy or lacking pain. Following classic Aristotelian philosophy, happiness can be conceived of more broadly as the right training and exercise of human faculties such as reasoning, forming social relationships or attaining knowledge. Some contemporary approaches in ethics use this concept of 'eudaimonia' to describe what is intrinsically good for a person, such as that of James Griffin (1988), John Finnis (2011), Fred Feldman (2004) or Roger Crisp (2017). Eudaimonists characterize well-being in an objective way, i.e. as containing several valuable elements.

This raises the central question, that is, how people's own views about their life matter, in particular if they are contrary to the ideal that is proposed. Brad Hooker (2015) proposes a counterfactual test to find out whether an element of human life is important for well-being: we imagine two possible lives for someone as similar as possible except that one contains element X while the other lacks X. We ask which of these lives is more beneficial for the person. Intuitively, a life in which someone is content or even happy seems better than one in which somebody is not satisfied.

In philosophy, there have been several ways to account for the subjective perspective on well-being. Traditional utilitarians base ethical and political evaluations of good action and society on judgements about welfare. Jeremy Bentham (1996 [1798]) claimed that pleasure was the relevant unit of utility. Vice versa, people should avoid pain. Well-being is thus evaluated along what has been called the 'hedonic calculus': pleasure and pain, it is assumed, can be measured according to their intensity, duration and extent. On this basis, these utilitarians claim that goods and services need to be measured according to the ways they increase pleasure and reduce pain.

Bentham's purely hedonistic account has been criticized by his successor John Stuart Mill (1989 [1851]), who called it "swine philosophy" that does not consider the genuine qualities and faculties that make us human. Mill argued that certain pleasures have more quality than others, such as those that involve higher human faculties like reading and studying (Mill 1998 [1863]). Another objection to Bentham's ideas was that it is unclear how one should measure feelings of pleasure. As I shall discuss in the next section, modern hedonists still face these kinds of criticism.

Wanting to avoid the problem of 'counting' pleasures, mainstream welfare economists focused on people's desires measuring well-being. People are assumed to be rational choosers who maximize their own utility (Gasper 2004). Economists further assume that people's preferences can be imputed to their choices. Well-being has been equated with (or rather, reduced to) preference fulfilment. The most prominent way to measure these choices is by looking at consumption and the means to it, i.e. income. However, people who have significant income may be well-off but may still lack well-being, because they are deprived in other dimensions of life, e.g. by disability or social discrimination (Sen 1999). Also, as we shall discuss later, preference fulfilment may be contrary to well-being for other reasons. Choice and income are thus an unsatisfactory representation of human well-being in modern development research.

In psychology, a considerable body of investigation focuses on *subjective well-being* (Gasper 2004; see also Chapter 8 of this *Handbook*). Researchers in positive psychology tried to measure well-being based on a person's own self-reported life satisfaction (Diener et al. 1999; Diener 2000). Others explored more objective factors such as the resources that contribute to well-being and health. Abraham Maslow was also one of the first researchers to suggest spelling out well-being by drawing on a theory of human needs (Maslow 2013b [1962]), which will be discussed later in this chapter.

Looking at the short conceptual history just presented, we see that philosophy has laid the groundwork for several distinctions that are still relevant in other sciences such as economics and psychology. The ideas found in modern well-being research, e.g. the fundamental distinction between subjective and objective, originate from traditional philosophical theories. Philosophy, as a discipline of reflection and conceptual clarification, can also further contribute to sharpen the conceptualization of well-being as a basis for empirical investigation and interdisciplinary discourse, since – simply put – all researchers as well as people working in practice must use concepts. In what follows, we will turn to the most fundamental philosophical distinctions in the discussion of well-being, which are helpful to classify the nature of well-being.

Well-being: clarification and classification

Derek Parfit conceives of well-being as "what makes life go best" (Parfit 1986, 13). He has developed a categorization to characterize the main three theoretical approaches to well-being. The reason why this distinction is still so prominent in philosophical discussion of the theme seems to be that all three characterizations capture a crucial part of well-being but are missing out on others. I will use Parfit's distinction as a starting point to identify the most central elements of well-being. On this basis, I will argue that modern conceptualizations of well-being must transcend Parfit's scheme in order to be plausible. Therefore, I will introduce hybrid theories as a fourth category.

Hedonism

Following Bentham, hedonists claim that what makes a life go well is the right balance of pleasure and pain (since the absence of pain is a minimal form of pleasure). Roger Crisp (2017) distinguishes between *substantive* and *explanatory* hedonism. The former will give us an answer to the question what well-being consists in, while the latter tells us why pleasure is good – which is very often tautologically explained by pointing out that pleasure feels good. Hedonism has ancient roots in Platonic dialogues, mainly Protagoras and Meno, which explored what is good for people (Plato 2005 [C4 BCE]). Let us apply Hooker's test once again here to gauge how pleasure is important for well-being: imagine two lives for someone that are as much alike as possible, but one contains a larger amount of innocent pleasure than the other. Intuitively we would say that the life with more innocent pleasure would be better.

However, transferring this idea to development proves to be problematic. Let us assume that we provide two persons with material resources, e.g. food or housing. One of them experiences pleasure while the other does not. Does this mean we have benefitted one person, but not the other? Surely most people would say that there is an objective value in the material goods that is beneficial for human well-being no matter how the beneficiary takes pleasure in them. Also, it can be difficult to identify pleasure as such. Bentham claimed that pleasure is a sensation that has duration and intensity. However, pleasures in human life can be very diverse. The positive feelings we get from reading a book are very different from the ones that we get from sexual activity or from eating truffles. It is almost impossible to find feelings that these experiences have in common (Crisp 2017), let alone measure it in a reliable way.

Aside from these problems there are three objections against hedonism that are problematic from a normative perspective. First, the evaluative implications of hedonism are dubious. As we have seen, Mill has already objected that simple hedonism is too crude, because it puts all pleasures on a par. Simple hedonism seems to be a quite misguided basis for measuring well-being and progress in policy, since it would imply that giving people intense pleasures (e.g. partying) takes precedence over pursuits that elicit less excitement, e.g. a healthy life or education. We would therefore need a more sophisticated normative framework for deciding which pleasures are valuable, and which of these should be promoted. However, this leads us astray from the main hedonist idea, since we are introducing other normative considerations than pleasure.

A second and more serious objection can be formulated around Robert Nozick's *experience machine* (Nozick 2013): imagine you are plugged in a machine all your life which would give you experiences of whatever kind, e.g. writing a novel, getting the Nobel prize for it, becoming rich, having a beautiful family etc. Would plugging in be beneficial for a person's well-being? If we say yes, are people not obliged to plug in? Something seems very wrong in claiming that people should prefer artificial instead of real-world experiences. As Hannah Arendt put it (2013 [1958]), human life is constituted by activity: labor, work and action. We take part in the world by engaging with it in these three ways – plugging into an experience machine thus takes away something fundamentally human from our well-being. In development, we do not simply want to make people's lives feel better. Rather, we want them to enable them to live genuinely human lives. Hence, creating the equivalent of an experience machine in development would be an equally misguided suggestion.

The third objection may be the most problematic for development. Hedonist theories are vulnerable to bias and adaptive responses. People who are deprived or oppressed will often acquiesce to oppression and violence (Khader 2011; see Chapter 9 of this *Handbook*). In addition, psychology research shows that pleasure and other subjective sensations are highly conditional on so-called framing-effects as well as other forms of implicit bias (Kahneman and Tversky 2000). Framing means that people's attitude towards an object or activity, and thus their pleasure, will vary how these are presented (e.g. in advertisement). Pleasure and many emotional responses may easily be distorted or perverted which makes hedonism as the sole basis of well-being research questionable. However, people's subjective perspective should not be ruled out, which is why some theorists have turned to desire theory.

Desire theories

The subjective account that has become most prominent in welfare economics is *desire theory*, which has just been briefly described. In its most prominent form, *revealed preference theory* (Samuelson 1948), people's desires are imputed from what they choose. Whatever people choose is what they prefer – and what they prefer is what contributes to their well-being. This model allows for a ranking of preferences and the development of "utility functions" which economists can use to assess standards of living, e.g. using money as the standard (Gasper 2004).

The main reason for its popularity is that preferences are simple to measure. The simplest version of this account is a *present desire theory*, which assumes that people are well off if their present preferences are met. However, the most obvious objection to this theory is that some present desires may be detrimental to well-being in the longer run. If I, for instance, have an overwhelming desire for jumping out of the window because I am frustrated at work, I will certainly harm my well-being in the long run. Nevertheless, it is what I prefer to do right now, and thus, the presumption goes, it is what I should rationally choose. Many desires are of this kind, e.g. desires for drugs, unhealthy food or very risky behaviour.

A more sophisticated desire theory seems to be better to rule out desires that harm a person's well-being, e.g. by demanding that only people's fully informed preferences count or only those that they would have were they fully rational (Scanlon 1993; Gasper 2004). This is called *informed desire theory*, which would amount to full information from birth to lead the best life one would desire were one fully informed about all the (nonevaluative) facts. However, imagine a life that seems devoid of all meaningful pursuits. John Rawls (1971) has described the case of the grass-counter: imagine a brilliant Harvard mathematician who prefers to spend her life counting grass on the lawns of Harvard despite being informed of all other options. If she is free from mental illness, informed desire theorists would have to accept that she is well. However, her life seems devoid of real meaning.

Another objection is that full information, even if it were available, would not keep some people from the distortions or adaptations that have already been mentioned. Hence, desire theories also create similar problems as hedonist accounts for development. On the grounds of informed desire theory, we have no reason to criticize people's desires even if they are distorted or biased. Hence, basing the conceptualization of well-being on subjective standards alone proves to be difficult. It seems that some kind of objective standard is needed that guides evaluations about which desires are conducive to well-being and which are not. This move, however, leads us astray from subjective theories altogether, and points towards objective accounts.

Objective list theories

The term objective *list* theory is misleading. Neither do all objective accounts embrace lists (e.g. Sen's capability approach does not; Sen 1999) nor are all lists objective (for instance, hedonism may produce a list of pleasures that are conducive to well-being). Following Scanlon (1993), Gasper suggests renaming them 'substantive good conceptions' (Gasper 2004). Very often these accounts are defined by a process of elimination, i.e. being theories that refer neither merely to pleasures nor to desire-satisfaction. More precisely, we must distinguish between the substantive good conceptions that are purely objective and those theories that combine subjective and objective elements, which should more aptly be labelled 'hybrid theories' (Woodard 2015). I will discuss those in the next section.

Many objective conceptions refer to the Aristotelian idea of that "what in isolation makes life desirable" (Aristotle 2002 [C4 BCE] 1097b15), i.e. intrinsic values that human beings pursue for their own sake, not because they have other goals. The result are theories of eudaimonia, which have been mentioned above. Traditional eudaimonic theories develop a complex idea of the "highest good" (ibid. 1095a) that spans the whole of human life. Some of these theories are perfectionist and naturalist, since their objective is to perfect human nature (Hurka 1996). Thus, if acquiring knowledge, friendship or reproduction is part of human nature, these items go on the list of good that human beings should attain to live well. Other theories may be eudaimonic, such as Martha Nussbaum's account of central human capabilities (Nussbaum 2001), without being perfectionist. Nussbaum emphasizes that the items on the list do not have to be fully realized to live a life that is reasonably good. Only a certain threshold must be reached.

Many objective list theories like Nussbaum's are pluralist in claiming that there are multiple constituents of well-being (Woodard 2015). In contrast to this, hedonism is a monist theory, because well-being is reduced to one element. Pluralism is a plausible view, because, as we have seen, there are many ways to be well, e.g. long-term or short-term, intense pleasure or quiet contemplation. Sabina Alkire, for instance, surveys 39 lists of proposed fundamental irreducible aspects of well-being, all of which make convincing claims about well-being (Alkire 2002). Pluralist theories certainly have the potential to capture these items better, since they can incorporate both subjective and objective elements of different kinds. Hence, it makes sense to construct lists in a pluralist way.

Establishing a list of substantive goods entails several difficulties. The first is how we decide what goes on the list. Aristotle developed a substantial view on the ends of human life, which ultimately amounted to prioritizing a life of contemplation over other lifestyles (Aristotle 2002 [C4 BCE] 1172a16–1172b8). In a modern pluralist society, and in development, where we encounter even more variation in lifestyles because of cultural differences, we need to make more room for considerable variation. This does not only create problems for determining the content of the list, but also for choosing the methodology. Nussbaum claims that her list represents the result of "years of cross-cultural discussion" (Nussbaum 2001, 76) and that the input of other voices has shaped the list a lot. She also claims that the items on the lists can be changed or even deleted (Nussbaum 2006). However, ultimately her list rests on philosophical justification, i.e. reflective judgement and intuition.

Ingrid Robeyns (2005) points out though that this does not make the selection process clear, since Nussbaum neither specifies a procedure nor criteria for legitimacy. This makes the legitimacy of the list dubious and raises suspicions of elitism. Robeyns (2005) examines several methods, which include more democratic, localized ways and methods of social sciences for coming up with a list. The research on participatory methodologies can be useful here to refine methodology in order to come up with lists and principles that reflect the perspective of the people that are affected (White and Pettit 2007). However, if we go down this route, we again include subjective perspectives on well-being.

It must be noted that objective lists do not have to entail elitism, even though paternalism is certainly a concern (Deneulin 2002). Nussbaum puts practical reason on the list and only wants to promote capabilities, not functionings. Hence, people can still decide whether to exercise the capabilities that are offered. Nussbaum also formulates the items on the list deliberately general to make room for specification in the relevant context. In addition, we need to distinguish between conceptualization and implementation: just because we know what (perfect) well-being may be, it does not mean that we have to force people into it. John Stuart Mill, for instance, held a very perfectionist position about well-being while prohibiting government to get too involved, since having an undisturbed private sphere is an integral part of human individuality (Mill 1989 [1851]; Feinberg 1986).

Many substantive good accounts are not objective in the strict sense. They make considerable room for freedom and autonomy. For instance, practical reason has an "architectonic" (Nussbaum 2001, 82) role on Nussbaum's list, and capabilities are closely connected to the idea of human freedom and opportunities for meaningful choice. These considerations raise the issue in what way freedom and autonomy are part of the well-being discourse. Thinking back to Hooker's test mentioned above, we can say that a life with more autonomy seems to be better than one with less. It thus seems that an objective account cannot fully capture the idea of well-being, since a person's own perspective on her life should also be a basic element in a conceptualization of well-being. Constructing a hybrid account might be a worthwhile strategy to pursue.

Hybrid theories of well-being

In his recent work, Christopher Woodard (2015) has distinguished between different ways of constructing hybrid theories. Hybrid theories must be distinguished from pluralist accounts, since the former claim that there are multiple *conditions* for something to be a constituent of well-being, while pluralists say well-being has multiple constituents. The two can, but do not have to be combined. As Woodard notes, advocates of hybrid theories hope that hybrid accounts possess the positive traits of the traditional theories, combining them in more plausible ways. However, cross-breeding may not always be successful. The offspring may not only inherit the positive traits of their parents, but also their faults.

Woodard identifies two ways of joining subjective and objective elements of well-being into one theory. One is the joint necessity model, which claims that an element is a constituent of an individual's well-being if and only if (a) she subjectively engages with that element and (b) the element is objectively good. Shelly Kagan (1994, 2009) has proposed an account of this kind in claiming that being well-off means that there is objective good in one's life which one also takes adequate pleasure in. In a different manner, Joseph Raz (1988) argues that well-being consists in satisfaction of desires for the good, i.e. success in pursuing worthwhile goals. Goals mean "projects, plans, relationships, ambitions, commitments, and the like" (ibid., 291).

Raz is one of the few theorists that incorporate aspects of time, relationships and long-term pursuits, which is a dimension of well-being that is underrepresented on most accounts. Certain projects or pursuits may take some time and positive evaluation may not always immediately be present. If I, for example, aspire to be a chef in a three-star restaurant I will have to work long hours every day, whether I find pleasure in this activity or not. Much of the experience may be unpleasant, and my positive evaluation may be years away from slaving long hours in the kitchen. However, I will stick to the plan, because I have decided to follow a long-term plan. In mainstream well-being research, the importance of long-term projects of people is, if ever, only addressed indirectly, e.g. in putting elements like education, meaningful work or family on the list. Only a few philosophers discuss the role of long-term plans, coherence of a life plan and meaningfulness, and most of this work is in ethics or in theory of action (Bratman 1999; Nida-Rümelin 2000; Kauppinen 2012). It remains unclear, what this means for a measurement of well-being in development. One question would be, for instance, whether we should prioritize people's longer-term goals over their short-term desires.

Thinking about long-term goals and life plans raises an even more fundamental concern for hybrid theories with joint necessity. Hybrid theories of joint necessity claim that desires for harmful things or distortions do not have to be included in well-being simply because they are desired. So, it seems that they rule out desires for harmful things and activities. However, people may choose actions and even lifestyles which harm their well-being severely, but which may be ethically admirable and highly meaningful for that person. Hence, they may be part of their overall well-being in life. Nelson Mandela has suffered tremendously for 27 years in prison, because his bodily and psychological well-being and thus several items on the list were significantly harmed. Yet, he accepted these hardships to fight for what he perceived was right, namely the end of apartheid in South Africa. The question is whether hybrid theories, or any account of well-being, can assess cases like these adequately.

The characterization of joint necessity has been criticized by Woodard (2015) on other grounds. We can say that somebody's well-being increases even though only one of the two conditions just mentioned is fulfilled, say (a). Imagine somebody has an increment of passive pleasure from something trivial, e.g. a drink every night. Would we not say that her well-being was made somewhat better by this worthless pleasure? Likewise, we may say that well-being is enhanced by the possession of objectively good things, even though they are not enjoyed (Sarch 2012). As we have seen, distortion and adaptation may cause a failure to appreciate valuable elements of well-being. Thus, like purely objective theories they face the problem of justifying their account without becoming elitist or illegitimate.

Given this clustering of issues, Woodard suggests a second interpretation of hybrid theories, namely *holism*. He refers once again to Parfit who suggested that the value of a whole depends in a more complex way on its parts than the joint necessity model suggests. Some aspects of a person's life may, taken by themselves, not contribute much to her well-being, but may do so, if some other conditions are fulfilled. We may, for instance, appreciate a piece of abstract art only slightly in the beginning, but more when we know about its meaning and history. Likewise, Mandela's suffering in prison and his goals of fighting apartheid and achieving equality are linked in more complex ways. This view does not demand necessity but allows for a more flexible and more complex connection between the elements of well-being. Since human well-being is diverse and multifaceted, holism has the potential of painting a richer and more adequate picture of it.

Another advantage of holism lies in its considerations of dependencies between major determinants of well-being. Gasper has pointed out that many aspects are correlated with others, e.g. evidence shows that the presence of objective aspects such as health, family, employment often has a strong positive correlation with subjective well-being (Gasper 2004). Also, we may explain why some measures of well-being, e.g. income, are not a good indicator of overall well-being. For instance, the so-called Easterlin paradox indicates that, at some point, the increase in income does not correlate with an increase in self-reported well-being.

Pluralist, hybrid accounts that are interpreted holistically present a way of conceptualizing well-being that does justice to the richness and diversity of the idea. Many accounts of well-being can be interpreted in this way. Some recent theories of human needs can be interpreted in a holistic manner. In general, the idea of human needs can be viewed as a way of capturing well-being which is intuitively and universally appealing: after all, all human beings need certain things like water, food or shelter. In the subsequent part I therefore examine *human needs theory* as an approach to conceptualizing well-being in development.

Human needs and development

The rise of needs theory has also been a rather recent phenomenon in development, parallel with the emergence of development ethics. We can identify two waves of needs theory. The first rise of human needs theory in development can be dated back to the 1970s, when the World Bank espoused a policy priority to *basic* needs, mainly interpreted as material needs. The approach lost popularity after two decades, since it proved rather difficult to pin down what basic needs really are and to determine who should decide which needs matter. Hence the first wave lacked conceptual clarity and political appeal (Gasper 2004). The second wave of needs theories that rose in the early 1990s tried to avoid these problems by laying out their concepts clearly and considering the respective policy implications.

The origins of human needs theory: basic needs

As Paul Streeten writes, the discussion of needs in development was stimulated by the adaption of a recommendation for a basic needs strategy by the World Employment Conference of the *International Labour Organisation* (ILO) in 1976 (Streeten 1981). Also, we can interpret the *Millennium Development Goals* as a form of commitment to basic needs theory (Gasper 2007). The purpose of the basic needs approach in development was to remove mass deprivation, a concern that has always been central to development. Basic needs theory seemed to be a viable alternative to growth theories then, since the latter were largely unsuccessful in ending deprivation. Also, the intuitive appeal of needs theory made it attractive for many researchers and policy makers. The core claim of the approach is deceptively simple: certain elements of human life (nutrition, health, education) are essential for full labor utilization and progress in a country.

The early conceptualization of basic needs focused on basic material needs such as food, clothing, shelter, water, and sanitation. The concept of needs that was used was thus that of normative necessity: needs are those elements of human life that people need to avoid serious harm or even death (Doyal and Gough 1991). Needs that have no direct link to human survival, e.g. psychological and social needs such as education, family, social recognition, were often viewed as subordinate. So the model was built around the first and possibly second stage of the theory of human needs that was developed by psychologist Abraham Maslow's (2013b [1962]). His 'pyramid of needs' contained five stages of need in a strict hierarchy was used by some economists to spell out the idea of growth (Diener and Diener 1995). The physiological needs just mentioned constitute the foundation of the pyramid, while the psychological, social and personal elements of human life, mainly self-actualization, form the final stages which can only be realised when the lower stages are reached.

Another theory of basic human needs was presented by one of the pioneers of development ethics, Louis-Joseph Lebret. He identified three categories of needs (Goulet 2006):

(1) Essential subsistence needs (food, clothing, health care etc.)
(2) Needs related to comfort and facilities that make life easier (transportation, leisure etc.)
(3) Needs related to human fulfilment (relationships, social intercourse etc.)

Denis Goulet (2006) stated that "clear policy suggestions" follow from this (ibid., 57), because he assumed a clear hierarchy: the fulfilment of (1) is a priority over (2) and (3). However, Maslow's and Lebret's accounts have one major problem, namely the assumption of a strict hierarchy, which can be questioned empirically. Studies indicated that self-actualisation and social needs are important to people even if many of the basic needs are not fulfilled (Wahba and Bridwell 1976). Early basic needs theorists also overlooked the adaptation of needs to the situation and the cultural context as well as the fundamental role of evolutionary needs such as mating, reproducing and parenting.

Basic needs theory fell from grace in the late 1980s (Gasper 2007). In addition to the problems just mentioned, Gasper notes that early basic needs accounts in development lacked conceptual clarity as well as technical and political language that could have made the approach more accessible to mainstream economics and politics. Yet, the idea of needs retained its general plausibility and was revived two decades later in development ethics and theories of global justice.

Second-wave theories of human needs

The second wave of needs theory avoids many mistakes of the first wave through more careful conceptualization. For instance, advocates of these recent needs theories distinguish between several diverse modes of needs. Also, they aim to appeal to politics by incorporating information from social sciences and evaluating policy options (Brock 2009). Second-wave needs theory can be found in the works of Peter Penz (1986), David Braybrooke (1987), Len Doyal and Ian Gough (1991) as well as Manfred Max-Neef (1992). Most recently, Gillian Brock (1998, 2009) has developed a version of needs theory for tackling problems of global justice. In what follows, I consider Doyal and Gough's and Brock's accounts, since they present the most complete normative conceptualization to needs theory.

Doyal and Gough define needs as "preconditions for participation in any form of life" (Doyal and Gough 1991, 69), i.e. what a human being needs to be a functioning member of society. They thus take needs as a normative category of goals that are universalizable. The most basic human needs are the following two main normative preconditions: first, staying alive by avoiding harm, and, second, having mental competence to deliberate and choose. In other words: health and autonomy are the normative pillars of Doyal's and Gough's theory. They also specify a level of needs that is quite diverse and has complex linkages: instrumentally valuable "intermediate needs" ("universal satisfier characteristics", as they also call them). They connect these two basic needs with others to enable autonomy, e.g. the need for commodities or security. Thus Doyal and Gough develop a long and complex basic list of how needs can be met, mainly by providing housing, clean water, safe birth control, care, work etc. In fact, they make room for several lists to be assembled according to the context and purpose. Chains of instrumental needs can be quite intricate and long (Gasper 2007). Doyal and Gough thus make room for diversity, which reflects the complexity of well-being. They also avoid the imposition of a strict hierarchy of needs, which has proven too simplistic.

Doyal and Gough's account is a pluralist, hybrid theory in combining two irreducible elements of well-being, which are objective (health) and subjective (autonomy). It is also holistic, since it does not follow the joint-necessity-model, because they do not demand that people evaluate the elements on the list or any of the preconditions positively. Their account leaves room for autonomy to override physical or mental needs (as in the example of Nelson Mandela mentioned earlier). Basic needs can thus be satisfied in a more complex way, e.g. by fulfilling several different intermediate needs. They also shift the focus of theorizing from individual life to functioning as a society member, which integrates the often-neglected Aristotelian idea that human beings are essentially social animals. Strictly speaking, they thus introduce a third criterion of well-being and needs: social relatedness.

Based on Doyal's and Gough's account and considerations by Daniel Braybrooke, Gillian Brock (1998, 2009) has developed an approach to human needs in global justice theory. Satisfying needs is the first key goal of global social justice. The second key goal is the protection of basic human liberties, and the political and social arrangements for those who are unable to meet their needs on their own. It is worth pointing out that Brock's account is sufficientarian: she identifies what a decent human life requires, not, as perfectionists would do, what the ultimate goal of life should be.

Brock claims that "meeting needs is essential to our ability to function as human agents" (2009, 65). The main precondition of agency, Brock states, is that people are able to meet their own needs. She derives the content of the five focal needs by what human agency requires:

(1) a certain amount of physical and psychological health
(2) sufficient security to be able to act
(3) a sufficient understanding of the options one is choosing among
(4) a certain amount of autonomy
(5) decent social relations with at least some others.

Brock notes that some of the needs she identifies are more complex than others but stays vague about what that means for each of these categories. For instance, physical health seems to be less complex than autonomy; which is one of the most problematic notions of political philosophy. Also, Brock does not state how the concept relates to the basic liberties and the other elements of this list. The relationship and the dependencies between choice, well-being and needs are indeed quite difficult to capture. Even though Brock bases her account on Doyal and Gough's approach to human needs, she does not adopt their distinction between basic and intermediate needs. Brock's account is more convincing, however, in giving social relatedness a central role as an element of well-being. The same goes for the issue of social security to which I will come back in the final section. Combining Brock's approach with Doyal's and Gough's more sophisticated distinction between levels of need could thus provide us with a more holistic perspective on human needs as a theory of well-being.

A fundamental objection to the modern theories just introduced is whether they can still be called genuine theories of *need*, since the concept of needs these theories use becomes very similar to other ideas in development such as capability (which Brock (2009) also admits). Hence, we may wonder, whether a more sophisticated needs approach is a version of another theory of well-being such as the capability approach or vice versa. Another objection can be formulated in an opposite way: even though needs theories may have evolved, they may still miss out important concerns in development, mainly the interconnectivity of needs, their security and their openness to change. So, a central question for theories of human needs – and for any account of well-being – will be whether they can meet the future challenges of development or whether they have reached their ultimate limits.

Outlook: new challenges in well-being research

The principal goal of this chapter has been to familiarize readers with the diverse and most prominent accounts of well-being. The theory of human needs was presented as one version of these. Well-being and needs can be interpreted very diversely, despite the intuitively simple appeal that they have for most people. Hybrid, holistic theories of well-being and needs seem to capture the diversity and complexity of the idea reasonably well. The resulting theories are more adequately grounded in people's experience of their own well-being, which is rich and multifaceted.

However, there are three themes that have emerged during the previous discussion, which development ethicists should investigate in more detail. First, theories of well-being and need do not pay enough attention to the questions of time and security. As Gasper (2005, 2007) has shown, human security is a fundamental concern for development, which has been promoted by the UNDP since 1994. The main point of security is that people should be safe against risks like disease, lack of food, natural disasters etc. Conceptualizations and policies of well-being and needs often focus on getting people to a certain threshold of well-being and needs fulfilment. Less thought is given to how we make sure that people will stay there. Jonathan Wolff and Avner de-Shalit have made a similar point in their work on disadvantage: what matters for people is not only their well-being at any particular point in time but also their prospects of sustaining that level throughout their lives (Wolff and de-Shalit 2007). We have to take into account how to keep people at a certain level of well-being through different phases of their lives and in diverse circumstances. This requires a considerable amount of flexibility in a theoretical account. For instance, certain phases of human life like very young or old age, in which human beings have significant needs and demand more care by society than in other phases.

This brings me to a second point. Most of the accounts presented are individualistic, even though some modern theories of need acknowledge that a major goal is to enable people to participate in society. However, many questions remain as to what social relatedness means for many of the other elements of well-being. Social connections have a deep influence on many elements of well-being or rather needs. Not only are many needs negatively influenced by a lack of relatedness (e.g. health, work), but social connection is also instrumental in many different ways: social collectives can take on tasks of care and support for vulnerable people in society and thus create structures for fulfilling needs. What we also must ask, especially in development, is whether some social collectives (including indigenous peoples) have special communal needs that should be reflected in conceptualization and policy. Hence, the individualist focus of a theory of well-being and needs may have to be expanded.

A third, related point is the interconnectedness of the elements of well-being. The theories just presented have given us a good overview over the elements of well-being and needs. As I have noted in discussing hybrid theories of well-being, some aspects of objective well-being like health, family or employment typically have significant influence on someone's subjective well-being. Also, as Wolff and de-Shalit (2007) point out, disadvantage is usually clustered. Certain deprivations like homelessness have a cumulative impact on many dimensions of human life and may thus impact many basic needs. Correspondingly, certain elements of well-being which seem instrumental and intermediate, like education, provide the fundament for many others, e.g. employment, income, even health. Hence, a worthwhile investigation would be how we can identify the corrosive and pivotal elements of well-being, since they would provide effective entry points for policy.

We must address well-being and needs therefore not only as static conceptualizations that can be neatly broken down into several components, as it sometimes seems when lists of well-being are presented. Rather we must recognize the interconnectedness and the contextuality of these elements – as well as the challenge to sustain well-being. Well-being thus remains one of the most difficult concepts to grasp in development, since it demands a rich, flexible and complex conceptualization. Thus, it may be more difficult to measure and operationalize, but we may be closer to what we want in development: understanding and changing people's actual lives for the better.

References

Alkire, S. (2002) Dimensions of Human Development. *World Development* 30(2): 181–205.

Arendt, H. (2013 [1958]) *The Human Condition: Second Edition*. University of Chicago Press, Chicago.

Aristotle, Rowe C.J. trans. and Broadie, S. commentator ([C4 BCE] 2002) *Nicomachean Ethics*. Oxford University Press, Oxford.

Bentham, J. (1996 [1798]) *The Collected Works of Jeremy Bentham: An Introduction to the Principles of Morals and Legislation*. Clarendon Press, Oxford.

Bratman, M.E. (1999) *Intention, Plans, and Practical Reason*. Cambridge University Press, Cambridge.

Braybrooke, D. (1987) *Meeting Needs*. Princeton University Press, Princeton.

Brock, G. (1998) *Necessary Goods: Our Responsibilities to Meet Others' Needs*. Rowman & Littlefield, Lanham, MD.

Brock, G. (2009) *Global Justice: A Cosmopolitan Account*. Oxford University Press, Oxford.

Crisp, R. (2017) Well-Being. In Zalta, E.N. ed. *The Stanford Encyclopedia of Philosophy* (Fall 2017). https://plato.stanford.edu/archives/fall2017/entries/well-being/. Accessed 27 December 2017.

Deneulin, S. (2002) Perfectionism, Paternalism and Liberalism in Sen and Nussbaum's Capability Approach. *Review of Political Economy* 14(4): 497–518.

Diener, E. (2000) Subjective Well-being: The Science of Happiness and a Proposal for a National Index. *The American Psychologist* 55(1): 34–43.

Diener, E., Suh, E.M., Lucas, R.E. and Smith, H.L. (1999) Subjective Well-being: Three Decades of Progress. *Psychological Bulletin* 125(2): 276–302.

Diener, E.D. and Diener, C. (1995) The Wealth of Nations Revisited: Income and Quality of Life. *Social Indicators Research* 36(3): 275–286.

Doyal, L. and Gough, I. (1991) *A Theory of Human Need*. Palgrave Macmillan, London.

Feinberg, J. (1986) *Harm to Self*. Oxford University Press, Oxford.

Feldman, F. (2004) *Pleasure and the Good Life: Concerning the Nature, Varieties, and Plausibility of Hedonism*. Clarendon Press, Oxford.

Finnis, J. (2011) *Natural Law and Natural Rights*. Oxford University Press, Oxford.

Gasper, D. (2004) Human Well-being: Concepts and Conceptualizations. Discussion Paper 2004/006. Helsinki: UNU-WIDER. www.wider.unu.edu/publication/human-well-being. Accessed 27 December 2017.

Gasper, D. (2005) Securing Humanity: Situating "Human Security" as Concept and Discourse. *Journal of Human Development* 6(2): 221–245.

Gasper, D. (2007) Conceptualising Human Needs and Wellbeing. In Gough, I. and MacGregor, J.A. eds., *Wellbeing in Developing Countries – From Theory to Research*. Cambridge University Press, Cambridge, 47–70.

Goulet, D. (2006) *Development Ethics at Work: Explorations – 1960–2002*. Routledge, Abingdon and New York.

Griffin, J. (1988) *Well-being: Its Meaning, Measurement, and Moral Importance*. Clarendon Press, Oxford.

Hooker, B. (2015) The Elements of Well-Being. *Journal of Practical Ethics* 3(1): 15–35.

Hurka, T. (1996) *Perfectionism*. Oxford University Press, Oxford.

Kagan, S. (1994) Me and My Life. *Proceedings of the Aristotelian Society* 94: 309–324.

Kagan, S. (2009) Well-Being as Enjoying the Good. *Philosophical Perspectives* 23(1): 253–272.

Kahneman, D. and Tversky, A. (2000) *Choices, Values, and Frames*. Cambridge University Press, Cambridge.

Kauppinen, A. (2012) Meaningfulness and Time. *Philosophy and Phenomenological Research* 84(2): 345–377.

Khader, S.J. (2011) *Adaptive Preferences and Women's Empowerment*. Oxford University Press, Oxford.

Morris, D. (1980) The Physical Quality of Life Index (PQLI). *Development Digest* 1: 95–109.

Nida-Rümelin, J. (2000) Rationality: Coherence and Structure. In *Rationality, Rules, and Structure*. Springer, Dordrecht, 1–16.

Nozick, R. (2013) *Anarchy, State, and Utopia*. Hachette UK, London.

Maslow, A.H. (2013b [1962]) *Toward a Psychology of Being*. Simon and Schuster, New York.

Max-Neef, M. (1992) *From the Outside Looking: Experiences in Barefoot Economics*. Zed Books, London.

Mill, J.S. (1989 [1851]) *J. S. Mill: "On Liberty" and Other Writings*. Cambridge University Press, Cambridge.

Mill, J.S. (1998 [1863]) *Utilitarianism*. Oxford University Press, Oxford.

Nussbaum, M.C. (2001) *Women and Human Development: The Capabilities Approach*. Cambridge University Press, Cambridge.

Nussbaum, M.C. (2006) *Frontiers of Justice: Disability, Nationality, Species Membership*. Belknap Press, Cambridge, MA.

Parfit, D. (1986) *Reasons and Persons*. Oxford University Press, Oxford.

Penz, G.P. (1986) *Consumer Sovereignty and Human Interests*. Cambridge University Press, Cambridge.

Plato (2005 [C4 BCE]) *Protagoras and Meno*. Penguin UK, London.

Qizilbash, M. (1996) Capabilities, Well-being and Human Development: A Survey. *Journal of Development Studies* 33(2): 143–162.

Rawls, J. (1971) *A Theory of Justice*. Harvard University Press, Cambridge MA.

Raz, J. (1988) *The Morality of Freedom*. Clarendon Press, Oxford.

Robeyns, I. (2005) Selecting Capabilities for Quality of Life Measurement. *Social Indicators Research* 74(1): 191–215.

Samuelson, P.A. (1948) Consumption Theory in Terms of Revealed Preference. *Economica* 15(60): 243–253.

Sarch, A.F. (2012) Multi-Component Theories of Well-being and Their Structure. *Pacific Philosophical Quarterly* 93(4): 439–471.

Scanlon, T. (1993) Value, Desire, and Quality of Life. In Nussbaum, M. and Sen, A. eds., *The Quality of Life*. Oxford University Press, Oxford, 185–201.

Sen, A. (1999) *Commodities and Capabilities*. Oxford University Press India, New Delhi.

Streeten, P. (1981) *First Things First: Meeting Basic Human Needs in the Developing Countries*. Oxford University Press, Oxford.

Wahba, M.A. and Bridwell, L.G. (1976) Maslow Reconsidered: A Review of Research on the Need Hierarchy Theory. *Organizational Behavior and Human Performance* 15(2): 212–240.

White, S. and Pettit, J. (2007) Participatory Approaches and the Measurement of Human Well-being. In *Human Well-Being*. Palgrave Macmillan, London, 240–267.

Wolff, J. and de-Shalit, A. (2007) *Disadvantage*. Oxford University Press, Oxford.

Woodard, C. (2015) Hybrid Theories. In Fletcher, G. ed., *The Routledge Handbook of Philosophy of Well-Being*. Routledge, Abingdon and New York, 161–174.

7

The capability approach

Ethics and socio-economic development

Oscar Garza-Vázquez and Séverine Deneulin

Development ethics begins from the position that development processes always involve ethical judgments and normative valuations (Crocker 1991, 2008; Goulet 1980, 1997). It is concerned with 'the project of rethinking and redefining "development"' (Qizilbash 1996) in order to distinguish between 'worthwhile development and undesirable maldevelopment' (Drydyk 2016). Because ethical judgements are concerned about what *should* be done and which corresponding actions to take, laying bare and discussing *what* counts as development and *how* it can be assessed is key to designing, evaluating, and legitimising public policies. In this chapter, we offer an overview of the capability approach, one of the most important conceptual frameworks that has contributed to this ethical debate. We discuss why a capability view of development provides the most compelling ethical framework to date for dealing with the practical and normative questions that development processes raise. We present the approach as an interdisciplinary evaluative framework which views concerns for well-being, equity, rights, agency and participation, freedom, and justice as central to the theory and practice of development.

We start by setting the empirical ground for our theoretical discussion. We present a concrete policy case, namely recent labour reforms in Mexico, to illustrate why ethical judgements matter for people's lives. In the second section, we introduce the capability approach and the key authors who have shaped this normative conceptual framework. We then identify the main differences and advantages of the capability approach over other evaluative perspectives used in development policy such as subjective approaches or resource-based approaches. In the third section, we discuss some implications of the capability approach for development ethics and other dimensions of 'worthwhile development'. We conclude by highlighting some controversies within the capability approach and important new directions.

Development policy and why we need development ethics

Throughout history, development, broadly conceived as 'good' social change, has always been a contested concept both in theory and in practice. How it has been interpreted has shaped our shared social reality and continues to do so in the present. The example of labour policy in Mexico illustrates how interpretation matters, and how any policy, whether social, economic, political, cultural, or environmental, reflects certain values which embody

DOI: 10.4324/9781315626796-9

a specific understanding of what a society is aiming for and of the ways used to move towards that aim.

The current Mexican President, Enrique Peña Nieto, enacted after his election a series of legal and economic reforms known as 'Moving Mexico' (*Mover a México*, in Spanish), in order to promote development in the country. Among these reforms were amendments to labour laws that aimed at promoting competitiveness, flexibility of labour markets and making job hiring easier. Following these reforms, several economic and financial organisations such as the OECD, Standard & Poor's (S&P), and the Mexican Business Coordinating Council expressed their support due to the expected positive impact of these 'modern' labour practices on economic growth, investment, and productivity (e.g. see Cruz 2012; Hernández 2012). This position was also shared by the Mexican Association for Human Resources Management (AMEDIRH) which expressed its support in the following words: "The way to create jobs in modern society is [through] companies. So we must be clear that the law that best protects workers, is one that protects the companies where they work" (Borda 2012; authors' translation).

Yet, these reforms were met with strong resistance in the country due to their associated social costs. In general, the labour reforms were perceived to be in opposition to the historical labour rights that have been won since the Mexican Revolution of 1910. For instance, the labour reform threatened workers' rights to seniority, social security and pension benefits (Art. 39-F), labour stability, and redundancy payments. As a result of the reforms, corporations are now able to dismiss employees 'without [involving] any responsibility for the employer', that is, without any compensation to the employee (Art. 35, 39-A). Meanwhile, the reforms formalised outsourcing employment (Art. 13) (Bensusán 2013).

These two contrasting positions reflect the fact that there are different visions about what is of ultimate value for different people and the appropriateness of the means to achieve these visions. While for some the main concern was that of increasing productivity and competitiveness of the country in order to promote economic growth, others emphasised the necessity of protecting the conditions of workers and their employment stability. Similar conflicts between different understandings of what is of value to people and questions about how these can be settled are ubiquitous in development practice. How can we, as a society, assess whether a social, political, or economic reform such as the Mexican labour reform is actually conducive to successful and desirable development?

For too long these ethical decisions have been based on a narrow understanding of development in which social progress and human well-being are associated to the amount of material prosperity a nation produces. From this perspective, the objective of development policies is to enhance economic growth. Meanwhile the relevance of any other social or environmental concerns is seen only as instrumentally important for the end of expanding the economy. As a result, the study and practice of development risks being reduced to a 'technical examination of how to mobilize resources and people most efficiently and fashion the institutional arrangements best suited to growth' (Goulet 1997, 1160). The approval of the labour reforms in Mexico in 2012 shows that this framework continues to be dominant in policy-making in countries such as Mexico.

In recent decades, however, the understanding of development as economic growth and its ability to respond to the challenges that societies face today has been questioned, for material expansion does not necessarily translate in increased well-being of its members. In fact, this narrow view of development can make things worse by justifying unnecessary and undesirable social inequalities, as well as human and environmental harm. Ultimately, the current runaway climate and global inequalities ask us to reflect about what development ought to be so that it could be considered 'worthwhile' as opposed to 'undesirable' (see Penz et al. 2011).

It is precisely in this context of ethical reflection about the ends and means of development that 'the capability approach' provides the most compelling evaluative framework to promote 'worthwhile development' to date.

The capability approach

Nobel Prize–winning economist Amartya Sen introduced what is now known as 'the capability approach' in the late 1970s (e.g. see Sen 1980, 1985, 1988). It has been expanded by him (e.g. see Sen 1990, 1992, 1993, 1999a, 1999c, 2009), by philosopher Martha Nussbaum (e.g. see Nussbaum and Sen 1993; Nussbaum 2000, 2006, 2011a), and by a variety of scholars (for overviews of the capability approach see, for example, Alkire 2005; Deneulin 2009, 2014a, 2014b; Crocker 1992, 2006, 2008; Qizilbash 1996; Robeyns 2005a, 2006, 2011, 2016). As it will be clear later, the capability approach has been developed in different ways and for different purposes. In this chapter, we take Sen's writings as basis and highlight some different interpretations among its key authors.

The capability approach makes two fundamental normative assertions. First, the human being and his or her quality of life ought to be at the centre of any assessment of society or social life. A second assertion is that people's quality of life is better appraised by focusing on their capabilities, and not on the incomes or resources they possess. In other words, the capability approach can be seen as a broad normative proposition that development, well-being, and justice concerns, such as poverty and inequality, must be assessed in relation to people's capabilities (Sen 1980, 1992, 1999a, 1999c, 2009). Indeed, the initial motivation behind the capability approach was that of providing a better space for appraising well-being in comparison to alternative spaces such as the commodities/resources or utility/happiness spaces (Sen 2017), as we will examine further later in the chapter.

The statement that the focus of assessment of society and social life ought to be on people's capabilities means that what really matters is paying attention to the kind of life that people are able to live, what they are able or not able to *do* and *be* given their incomes, resources and the social arrangements in which their life unfolds. From this perspective, the ultimate objective of moral concern is the real freedom a person enjoys to achieve valuable *doings* and *beings* such as being well fed, being educated, or enjoying social relationships of quality, participating in social life, living in a secure and non-polluted environment, and so on. The notion of capability then is composed of two distinct but complementary aspects: the actual *beings* and *doings* that a person may value, and the *freedom* to choose between these. While the actual achievement of the various *doings* and *beings* a person may value are called 'functionings' (e.g. being well fed), the actual freedom to achieve them would be the corresponding capability (e.g. being able to be well fed) (see Sen 1999a, 75). In short, capability is the 'actual freedom of choice a person has over alternative lives [i.e. functionings] that he or she can lead' (Sen 1990, 114).

Even though both the actual achievement of *doing* and *being* (i.e. functionings) as well as the actual freedom to achieve them (i.e. capabilities) are constituents of living well (Sen 1985), the capability approach maintains that it is fundamentally the notion of capability which provides a more appropriate space for judging people's quality of life than income, commodities, or the utility space, although both capabilities and functionings belong to the same evaluative space, and different contexts will give more priority on the latter than the former (Sen 1980, 1985, 1992, 2017).

The critique of the capability approach to evaluations in the utility space is that they evaluate social life on the basis of people's mental states such as happiness or life satisfaction as assessments of quality of life, which may not be sensitive enough to other non-mental deprivations and can be easily distorted. For instance, people who live in situations of extreme deprivation may adapt to their circumstances and be content with the little they have (Nussbaum 2000; Sen 1992, 1993, 1999a). This phenomenon of adaptation is known in the literature as 'adaptive preferences' (see, among others, Clark 2012; Khader 2011). Meanwhile other people might be well-off but feel dissatisfied if they do not get expensive luxuries they would love to own, yet this does not necessarily mean they are worse off than those who have adapted to their circumstances but are not able to be well nourished and live in minimal proper conditions. Hence, equality in subjective evaluations can subsist with disparities in other important spaces such as needs (Sen 1992).

The capability approach is also a critique of the evaluation of social life based on information related to income or resources. The problem with income or resource measures of wellbeing is that they focus on the *means* to, and not the freedom to achieve well-being itself. Focusing the evaluation of social life in the space of income or resources does not pay attention to people's different abilities to convert such means into valuable ends. The ability to convert income or resources into actual *doing* and *being*, such as spending time with friends at night, will vary across people if, for example, a society imposes more restriction to women than to men. Similarly, even if two individuals possess the same amount of resources their freedom to move from one place to another may vary due to a personal disability.

The capability approach then, would insist that both information about subjective evaluations and resources fail to acknowledge and account for people's diversity (i.e. that people are different in diverse ways). On the one hand, subjective evaluations fail to recognise that people value various things and for distinct reasons besides happiness, on the other, a focus on resources fails to recognise that 'equality in holdings of primary goods or resources can go hand in hand with serious inequalities in actual freedoms enjoyed by different persons' (Sen 1990, 115).

For this reason, the capability approach affirms that focusing on what people are actually able to *do* and *be* offers a better metric to development and justice. This does not mean that a capability-based assessment regards income, resources, and other goods as unimportant. Rather, it emphasises that income and resources are only instrumentally important to achieve valuable states of being. As Robeyns (2005a, 100) writes: 'all the means of well-being, like the availability of commodities, social institutions, and so forth, are important, but the capability approach presses the point that they are not the ultimate ends of well-being'. Similarly, the capability approach would not deny the importance of subjective states, but it would argue that being happy is only one of the many things someone may have reason to value *being* and *doing* and therefore an exclusive focus on happiness or life satisfaction is inadequate. As Sen notes, the functionings that people can value are plural and may 'vary from such elementary things as being adequately nourished, being in good health . . . to more complex achievements such as being happy, having self-respect, taking part in the life of the community, and so on.' (Sen 1992, 39; see also Sen 1993, 31, 36–37). In this way, the capability approach makes a clear normative distinction between the ends and the means of social, political, and economic policies. It claims that if development is about enhancing people' well-being then development must be concerned with the expansion of people's capabilities, i.e. the expansion of 'the real freedoms that people enjoy' (Sen 1999a, 3).

To return to our example, the concepts of capability and functionings provide us with an alternative conceptual framework to assess the labour reforms in Mexico. From a capability-centred understanding of development, one would judge this labour policy on the basis of the extent to which it serves the end of enabling people to achieve *doings* and *beings* that they might have reason to value. Besides considering their income-enhancing features, one could also ask whether the reforms provide greater opportunities to be in a fulfilling and stable job, whether they enhance workers' skills, their self-respect, whether they allow workers to spend more time with their family and friends, or to live in better housing conditions, etc. From a capability perspective, those things matter because they are intrinsically valuable for living well, regardless of whether they contribute to productivity and economic growth. In fact, even if the Mexican labour reforms were to be actually conducive to higher levels of national income (including workers' income), there could still be good reasons to contest them because they may further exploitative, unsafe, unstable, and discriminating conditions, which do not facilitate people's freedom to live well.

So far, we have established that the capability metric provides a more adequate space for evaluating society and social life if we are concerned with people's quality of life, and that this assessment involves a plurality of things that people may value *doing* and *being*. Sen, however, does not indicate which capabilities should enter the evaluation as constitutive of living well. Rather, he presents the approach as intentionally open-ended and indeterminate (Sen 1993, 48–49, 1999a, 253–254). He opts for limiting the notion of capability as a space for comparative assessment and advocates for an agency-oriented approach to identify capabilities people 'have reason to value' (Sen 1992, 81) through public discussion. The relevant capabilities would vary not only according to the context but also for different 'practical purpose[s]' (Sen 2004a, 79). This idea is made more explicit in his *Idea of Justice* (Sen 2009) where he uses the capability metric for comparative assessments of justice but insists in an agency-view of individuals who engage in public deliberation to select, weight, and make comparative evaluations. In contrast, Nussbaum has developed the approach as a 'partial theory of justice' in which she defends a list of ten central capabilities (see Nussbaum 2000, 2003, 2006, 2011a). There are other areas in which Nussbaum's and Sen's versions of the approach differ. Overviews of the capability approach including similarities and differences in Sen's and Nussbaum's writings can be found in the work of David Crocker (2008, particularly Chapters 4, 5, 6) and Ingrid Robeyns (2005a, 2006, 2011); see also Nussbaum (2011a), Robeyns (2016), and Sen (2004a, 2009).

Despite its incompleteness and it being subject to different interpretations, the rather simple, and yet radical, ideas of the capability approach have provided the theoretical tools underlying new alternative measures for assessing progress. We can note here the pioneering role of the Human Development Index to assess development or progress differently, taking people as the real wealth of nations (see the annual Human Development Reports, and the many regional and national human development reports which have developed alternative measures of progress at a regional and national level, see hdr.undp.org). For, when assessing social life what counts as progress or 'success' would depend on how it is measured, whether we measure it in terms of economic growth performance or in capability expansion. For example, Drèze and Sen (2013) have illustrated in their study on India that despite high economic growth rates over the last decade, the ability of children to be well nourished has not expanded. The capability approach has also played an important role in developing measures of poverty by emphasising the multidimensionality of capability deprivations that people experience (Alkire et al. 2015). Several national governments are using alternative measures of poverty and have shifted from relying solely on income-related information to information about how well people are doing in several dimensions of quality of life. (See the Multidimensionality Poverty Peer Network, www.mppn.org.) India again, as other countries, appears as showing a contrasting performance if poverty is measured in the income space or capability space (see www.ophi.org.uk).

While these examples are already salient contributions of the capability approach to development concerns, one should not restrict its relevance solely to the space of capability-evaluation. The capability approach and its key concepts of capabilities, functionings and agency, has made significant contributions to ongoing debates within development ethics regarding equality, participation, agency, sustainability, and human rights, among others.

The capability approach and topical issues in development ethics

One of the fundamental positions of development ethics is that positive social change must avoid those forms of development that deepen social inequalities. Here, the capability approach emphasises that those inequalities that matter are those in the space of capability, e.g. inequality in the ability to be healthy, to participate in society or to have one's voice heard by those who make decisions. Still one could ask which distributive criteria should inform our concern for inequality.

Although his 'Equality of What?' (Sen 1980) question seems to suggest equality of capabilities as policy goal, his account of comparative justice refutes settling the question dogmatically and favours leaving the answer to the question open-ended (Sen 2009, 2017). He would insist instead on public deliberation to settle this question by weighting equality concerns in relation to other important considerations such as human rights or efficiency (Sen 2009). Nussbaum, in contrast, whose approach remains closer to the demands of a theory of justice, proposes a distributive rule, i.e. that a just social arrangement is one in which everyone is above a certain threshold of her list of central human capabilities (Nussbaum 2000, 2006, 2011a).

Another contribution of the capability approach to a central topic of development ethics is with regard to agency and participation (what Sen would call the 'process aspect' of freedom, in contrast to the 'opportunity aspect' contained in the concept of capabilities). As Crocker (2008) writes:

> If countries are to progress towards the goal of authentic development, it will be largely because of critical discussion among and collective participation by citizens themselves, especially those worst off (p. 90) . . . when done well, international development ethics requires global dialogue and democratic deliberation in a variety of venues – from small villages, through development-planning ministries, to the World Bank.
>
> *(95)*

Importantly, worthwhile development involves more than simply asking for people's opinions, or engaging people superficially in a project just for ticking the externally imposed participation box. Rather, it requires seeing people as agents of change themselves. Sen defines agency as 'someone who acts and brings about change, and whose achievements can be judged in terms of her own values and objectives' (1999a, 19); or as the person's freedom 'to do and achieve . . . whatever goals or values he or she regards as important' (Sen 1985, 203). Agency freedom is thus the counterpart of the notion of capability (i.e. well-being, freedom) and both are constituents of development (Sen 1985). In *Development as Freedom*, Sen (1999a) stresses that freedom is the ultimate end of development as well as the primary means to achieve it.

Therefore, instead of participation loosely defined, it is agency which promotes worthwhile development. In this context, some have defined the concept of empowerment as 'expansion of agency' (Alkire 2006; Ibrahim and Alkire 2007; Penz et al. 2011). However, some have contested reducing the concept of empowerment to agency alone (see Chapter 16, Empowerment, in this *Handbook*). Others have extended Sen's notion of agency to propose an 'agency-oriented' deliberative version of democracy to 'freedom-enhancing development' (Crocker 2008, 2; Crocker and Robeyns 2009; Keleher 2014; see also Chapter 17, Agency, in this *Handbook*).

It is not only the well-being freedoms and agency freedoms of current generations, but also that of future generations that are of concern for development ethics. Worthwhile development must be also sustainable development. Here too, the conceptual framework of the capability approach can make some contributions to this ongoing debate of intergenerational justice.

While there is no single definition of sustainability that is accepted by all, the definition proposed by the Brundtland Commission Report *Our Common Future* has been the most widely used. This report defined sustainable development as 'development that meets the needs of the present without compromising the ability of future generations to meet their own needs' (WCED 1987, 8). The capability approach would agree with the general terms of this definition and its implications but it insists that it is capabilities that should be sustained for the present and future generations (Anand and Sen 2000; Sen 2013). According to Sen, this provides a broader understanding of humanity and accounts for the process aspect of freedom by respecting people's agency (see also Holland 2014 for an analysis of environmental policy from a capability perspective). Sen (2009, 250) writes:

> Certainly, people do have needs, but they also have values and, in particular, cherish their ability to reason, appraise, choose, participate and act. Seeing people only in terms of their needs may give us a rather meagre view of humanity . . . Our reason for valuing particular opportunities need not always lie in their contribution to our living standards, or more generally to our own interests.

From this freedom-based perspective, 'sustainable development is essentially about sustainable human development in terms of enhancing [human freedoms] of present and future generations' (Anand 2014, 126). Also, from a more philosophical position, some scholars have examined the possibility of extending Sen's capability approach into an intergenerational theory of justice (e.g. Crabtree 2013; Gutwald et al. 2014). Similarly, Nussbaum has proposed different ways in which her capabilities approach can incorporate intergenerational justice not only for humans but also for non-human animals (Nussbaum 2000, 2003, 2006).

Despite these merits of a capability perspective to sustainable development, however, some advocate for going beyond what it is primarily an anthropocentric understanding of sustainable development. (See Chapter 22, Buen Vivir and the Rights of Nature, in this *Handbook*). We shall return to this issue in the fourth section.

Another important area of concern for development ethics is that of human rights (see Chapter 23, Human Rights, in this *Handbook*). Many of the previously mentioned values that make development a desirable enterprise such as well-being, equality, and sustainability could be pursued by coercion and violation of human rights such as rights to freedom of culture or religion. This is why worthwhile development sees both development and the promotion of human rights as belonging to the same project (Burchardt and Vizard 2011; Drydyk 2011; Nussbaum 1997, 2011b; Sen 2004a, 2005; Vizard et al. 2011). This has been ratified by the UN Declaration of the Right to Development (1986) which states that each individual is 'entitled to participate in, contribute to, and enjoy economic, social, cultural and political development, in which all human rights and fundamental freedoms can be fully realized' (see Chapter 24, The Right to Development, in this *Handbook*).

Sen and Nussbaum, as well as other scholars working with the capability approach have been influential voices in human rights debates. Sen (1997, 1999a, 231–248), for example, has debunked the belief that "Asian values" (if it is possible to group their cultural diversity within one single group of values) are traditionally less embracing of freedom and civil and political rights than so-called Western values (see Chapter 34, East Asia, in this *Handbook*). Sen also refutes the idea that authoritarian regimes that suppress civil and political rights could offer a better route to achieve well-being or equality. Human rights have intrinsic value and are irreducible to each other. From a capability perspective, destroying for example the cultural heritage of a group of people to promote employment opportunities is not 'worthwhile development', neither is ensuring education and health for all while at the same time undermining freedom of expression or putting political opponents in prison.

Critical issues and new directions

We have illustrated in the previous section the highly influential character of the capability approach to enrich current debates within development ethics, but differences of interpretations and contestation within the approach remain. Among the unresolved questions are: Which capabilities are relevant for the evaluation of states of affairs, and how is this decision made? How can we measure and operationalise the notion of capabilities? To what extent is the capability approach a theory of justice? What kind of individualism does the capability approach endorse, and is it sufficiently broad? Is the capability approach solely an evaluative framework or is it also action-oriented?

The capabilities that people have 'reason to value'

The issue of 'list vs. non-list' has been widely discussed in the literature (e.g. see Crocker 2008; Nussbaum 2000, 2003; Robeyns 2005b, 2006, 2011; Sen 2004a), therefore we shall concentrate on a related but different issue. One could argue that Sen's emphasis on agency, empowerment, and public participation is a better fit to the values of development ethics. A 'totally fixed' list is problematic since it 'den[ies] the possibility of fruitful public participation on what should be included and why'. Sen compellingly defends his position against a 'predetermined canonical list of capabilities' (Sen 2004a, 77–78 both quotes) in favour of treating people as ends in themselves and as agents to choose the capabilities that *people have reason to value*. In this way, agency freedom via public discussion and well-being freedom (i.e. capabilities) go hand by hand in the development process.

While agreeing with the latter, there is still the issue of the indeterminacy about how 'the capabilities that people have reason to choose and value' should be understood. Alkire (2015, 14), for example, recognises that there is uncertainty about whether it implies '(a) things people value; (b) things people have reason to value; or (c) things people both value and have reason to value'. Yet, this question cannot be but crucial to development ethics, especially in real contexts of large social inequalities, power imbalances, discrimination, and marginalisation. To illustrate, let us go back to our initial example of the labour reforms in Mexico. Considering the high levels of social and income inequality (CONEVAL 2013), corruption, discrimination, and marginalisation (CONAPRED 2011a, 2011b), along with the fact that only 8.8% of the Mexican labour force are associated to a labour union (Martínez 2013), which is itself co-opted by leading political parties (Obregón 2013), one could question the outcome of 'public' deliberation in such conditions. If it turns out that after due 'public' reasoning, the Mexican people value more the capability of flexible employment with one of the lowest wages in Latin America as opposed to the capability for decent and stable employment, could one separate such outcome from the unjust situation in which it takes place – a situation characterised by a long history of colonialist mind-set of exploitation and marginalisation that has left poor people with little choice other than being contented and thankful for even having the chance to be employed? (see also Sen 2017, 177).

It is in this sense that some capability scholars worry that, with its emphasis on individual capabilities and individual agency, the capability approach may overlook the far reaching impact of social structures and social influences (e.g. marketing towards a consumerist life) on people's own expression of agency and on the objectives they value (e.g. Deneulin 2008, 2011; Deneulin et al. 2006; Evans 2002; Gore 1997; Stewart and Deneulin 2002). It would indeed be problematic if the capabilities that people end up valuing are the result of entrenched unjust social contexts, manipulation, or else.

Sen is certainly aware of the pervasiveness of social influences on individuals, as we will discuss in the next section, on *ethical individualism*, yet he would still insist that it is through 'more [and inclusive] public engagement' (Sen 2009, 245) that people's sequestered reason can be 'partly or wholly overcome in ways that take us to a less confined view' (Sen 2009, 170). And indeed, Sen's forceful and coherent support for democracy and agency as means to overcome injustice and prejudices provides a strong argument (see Alkire 2006; Crocker 2008; Drèze and Sen 2013; Sen 1999a, 1999b). It is people themselves who ought to decide via open public discussion which capabilities are relevant in their own contextual realities. This is why Alkire (2015) concludes that the capability approach is neither based on people´s preferences *only* (option 'a'), nor in preference-independent approaches such as externally imposed lists and weights between the plural capabilities (option 'b'), but rather it endorses option 'c'. That is, in line with Sen's emphasis on the intrinsic, instrumental, and the constructive role in shaping the values of society, 'the capability approach aims at expanding the intersection of what people value *and* have reason to value – not just one category or the other' (Alkire 2015, 15; emphasis in original).

The problem is that Sen gives little guidance about what would make a public discussion acceptable, how such public discussion can take place in specific social realities, or what kind of actions would improve it. Some scholars have proposed different ways to fill this gap. For instance, Crocker (2006, 2008) has taken Sen's writings on agency and public participation into a more complete model of deliberative democracy. In addition, others have developed alternative criteria/methods for selecting relevant capabilities (e.g. Alkire 2002; Anderson 1999; Robeyns 2003a, 2005b; see also Robeyns 2006, 2011 for other references). Notwithstanding these *theoretical* proposals, the challenge for development ethicists to deal with these issues in *practice* remains. In doing so, it might be worth bearing in mind Sen's (1999b) sharp thought: '[a] country does not have to be deemed fit *for* democracy; rather, it has to become fit *through* democracy' (p. 3; emphasis in original).

Ethical individualism

A major area of dispute in the capability approach relates to the kind of individualism that the capability approach espouses, *ethical individualism*. Ethical individualism claims that in the assessment of social life, 'individuals, and only individuals, are the ultimate units of moral concern' (Robeyns 2008, 90; emphasis in original – see also Robeyns 2005a, 107). From this perspective, all economic, social, and political institutions, as well as formal and informal norms ought to be assessed in relation to their contribution to people's freedom to live well. It is important to remark, nonetheless, that 'a commitment to ethical individualism is not incompatible with an account of personhood that recognises the connections between people, their social relations and their social embedment' (Robeyns 2008, 91; 2005a, 108).

According to Robeyns, Sen's capability approach advances this ethical position. This is why Sen is able to recognise the influence of social phenomena in people's 'thinking, choosing, and doing' (Sen 2009, 245); that 'individual freedom is quintessentially a social product' (Sen 1999a, 31, xi–xii, 297); and that the notion of capability 'provides a perspective in which institutional assessment can [and should] systematically occur' (Sen 1999a, 142; see also Robeyns 2005a), and yet insist that the role of these social aspects 'can be sensibly evaluated in the light of their contributions to [people's] freedom' (Sen 1999a, 142).

Some scholars find Sen's ethical individualism troublesome. At risk of simplification, they advance two main points: (1) that the nature and existence of social structures and collectivities lie beyond – even if bounded by – individual's actions and properties; and (2) that the sum of these social relations embodied in cultural and political practices are necessary to fully understand and promote people's functionings and capabilities (e.g. see Alkire 2008; Deneulin 2014b, 2008, 2006; Deneulin and McGregor 2010; Gore 1997; Hill 2003; Robeyns 2005a, 2008; Sen 2002; Stewart 2013). For example, a society in which corruption is institutionalised at all levels may force an honest person to be corrupt even if she detests corruption and values an honest life herself. Yet, this is imposed on her by a corrupt structure that she can neither change nor escape it (see Deneulin et al. 2006, 6–7). Consequently, they argue for including institutions and groups, or what is sometimes referred to as collective capabilities (Evans 2002; Ibrahim 2006; Stewart 2005) or social competences (Stewart 2013), as an *intrinsic* aspect of the evaluation of states of affairs along with individual freedoms.

There are at least two explanations for Sen's reluctance to embrace these critiques of ethical individualism. First, ethical individualism avoids overlooking inequalities between individuals within a group, collectivity, or community (Alkire 2008). For instance, Robeyns (2008) argues that ethical individualism serves better feminist concerns within the family in so far as it focuses on the well-being of each member and not on the family as collective unit, which may hide the oppression to some of its members – usually women. Second, to the extent that including collective units in the moral assessment of state affairs may involve demarcating between *good* and *bad* structures, this position might be at odds with agency freedom in the sense of seeing people 'as being actively involved in shaping their own destiny' (Sen 1999a, 53). Implicit in Sen's writings is the idea that there is no reason to discard in advance the possibility of very different social arrangements providing the conditions that enable people to live well in terms of the capabilities 'people have reason to value', which may as well vary from context to context.

For this reason Alkire (2008, 40), along with Sen and Robeyns, concludes 'that ultimately the capability approach must focus on individual' capabilities for evaluative purposes. However, this position can only be presented as a partial resolution given the different interpretations of the approach. Of particular relevance here is the valuation of nature, and whether non-human life has value only if it furthers individual capabilities, a point which shall be discussed further on in the chapter.

Evaluative and action-oriented framework

To be of relevance for people's actual lives, a capability-based understanding of development needs to be translated into concrete policies or actions to expand people's capabilities. In this respect, Alkire (2008) suggests that another (perhaps more fruitful) way to understand the previous arguments against Sen's ethical individualism is in terms of the kind of guidance that the capability approach is likely to provide for policy. She argues that the focus is therefore on the '*prospective application* of the capability approach' which, in contrast to the 'evaluative' role, is concerned with advancing capabilities and the 'policies, activities, and recommendations . . . most likely to' promote this goal (Alkire 2008, 30; emphasis in original).

Again, this position is contested. Critics of ethical individualism argue that one cannot separate the evaluative from the prospective role, for the purpose of evaluation is ultimately to feed policy recommendations. Hence, they argue that it is precisely due to the exclusive focus on individual freedoms that the capability approach might fail to examine adequately, and thus bring into question, the social structures which are partly responsible for the kind of lives that people are able to lead. Let us illustrate with an example of the reality that many indigenous people experience in Latin America.

In Mexico, indigenous people have fewer opportunities for education, health, good quality jobs, and for participation in public, and their physical appearance, the way they dress and talk is a constant target for shame and humiliation (e.g. CONAPRED 2011a, 2011b; see PNUD 2010). While the capability approach as an evaluative framework might be apt to account for all of these forms of unfreedoms (Pereira 2013; Robeyns 2003b), the problem would be the way in which these situations are conceptualised solely in terms of individual deprivations. This interpretation runs the risk of disregarding the underlying social structures and social mechanisms that generate (*ex-ante*) such unjust outcomes in the first place, thus leaving them outside of the political action needed to redress such situation. This concern is echoed by others who analyse the capability approach from a critical perspective and who emphasise the importance of a relational approach to international development (e.g. Hickey 2014; Koggel 2013; see also Robeyns 2003b).

Robeyns (2005a, 2008) argues that the capability approach does allow for the systematic analysis of structural and social phenomena since these are factors that partly determine what someone can *do* and *be*. Therefore, capability expansion will most likely involve structural, social, and institutional amendments according to the issue at hand (Drèze and Sen 2002, 2013; Robeyns 2005a).

It remains, nonetheless, an open challenge to deal with, and find ways to orient policy in such a way that the translation of the capability approach into practice does not brush away structural features. One solution may be the one proposed by Alkire (2008) which requires being explicit about the distinct uses of the capability approach, and the need to complement it with other social or explanatory theories for the sake of prospective analysis (Robeyns 2005a). Alternatively, one of the authors of this chapter wonders whether replacing the word 'individualism' – which may cause some confusion and objection – for 'personalism' could be a strategic solution to this debate. Using 'ethical *personalism*' might better capture the interplay between the uniqueness of human beings who are part of social relations and groups that make up that unicity. This position, however, would have to show that it can accommodate both collective and individual information as units of moral concerns without the risk of hiding the heterogeneities of individuals within such relationships and/or the oppression of individual members.

Beyond an anthropocentric perspective?

The environmental situation of the world and the value that different models of development attach to nature also pose a challenge to the ethical individualism of the capability approach. The depletion of nature through extractive industries in Latin America, climate change, ocean acidification, floods, and other environmental concerns are already having disastrous impacts on people's lives (especially the poor), other species, and whole ecosystems (see Chapter 20, Sustainability and Climate Change, in this *Handbook*). It is not surprising therefore that there is an urgent call for an alternative development model to the one that leads to these undesirable expressions of 'development' (see chapter 22, Buen Vivir and the Rights of Nature, in this *Handbook*). In this respect, as noted previously, the capability approach can enrich our understanding of sustainable development by emphasising that it is the 'generalized capacity to create wellbeing', which present generations are 'obligated to leave behind' (Anand and Sen 2000, 2035).

While several scholars recognise the relevance of the contribution of the capability approach within the sustainability debate (e.g. see Anand 2014; Bockstael and Watene 2016; Ballet et al. 2013; Holland 2008a; Scholtes 2010), others question whether it is indeed sufficient to deal with the broader environmental concerns (e.g. see Bockstael and Watene 2016, Merino 2016; Watene 2016). The main issue at stake is that the capability approach tends to value the natural world in so far as it contributes to people's freedom (e.g. Anand and Sen 2000; Holland 2014,

2008a, 2008b; Sen 2013), or if it threatens human security (Gasper 2013). From this perspective, nature does not have any intrinsic worth, rather its value is contingent on people's well-being and agency (in Sen's version of the approach) or on the dignity of humans and non-human animals (in Nussbaum's version of the approach) (see Watene 2016). The problem, critics argue, is that this position leaves nature vulnerable since it is conceptualised in terms of resources that can be exploited, appropriated and substituted (Anand and Sen 2000, 2035). This position and valuation of nature contrast with many indigenous perspectives that see nature and people as interdependent, and thus conceptualise development as living well together in harmony with one another and in harmony with the natural world (Merino 2016; Watene 2016). As such, Watene (2016) concludes that the ethical individualism of the approach may exclude certain world views such as the Māori.

Sen has been quite explicit about his anthropocentric view of nature. However, he has also been equally emphatic in defending the relevance of agency and public reasoning for dealing with such problem (see Scholtes 2010 and the references cited there).

> It is not so much that humanity is trying to sustain the natural world, but rather that humanity is trying to sustain itself. It is us that will have to 'go' unless we can put the world around us in reasonable order. The precariousness of nature is *our* peril, *our* fragility. There is, however, also another side of this relationship. The quandary of unsustainability may be our predicament, but the task of solving it is ours as well. The nature of the problem, its fuller appreciation and the ways and means of solving it all belong to us – humanity as a whole.
>
> *(Sen 2013, 6–7; emphasis in original)*

Indeed, Sen's notion of agency aims to capture the fact that we can value and pursue ends which are not necessarily connected to our well-being. Hence, Sen's position is less restrictive as it first appears. His emphasis on agency leaves open the possibility for accommodating different perspectives on, and different ways to deal with, nature. One could, for example, 'judge that we ought to do what we can to ensure the preservation of some threatened animal species, say, spotted owls' even if our well-being might be completely 'unaffected by the presence or absence of spotted owls' (Sen 2004b, 10–11). The point is – Sen would say – that whether we need to attach intrinsic or instrumental value to nature is a matter of public debate, for there are contrasting views about the place of nature between individuals even within the *buen vivir* movement (Merino 2016) let alone across different societies. Moreover, there are other scholars who find in the capability approach a better framework to deal with the environment from the perspective of justice (e.g. Holland 2014, 2008a, 2008b), especially when one goes beyond 'the relationship between [Wo]Man and Nature' to also include 'the relationships between human beings mediated by nature' (Ballet et al. 2013, 31).

There is no doubt, however, that there is a lot of scope for future research and (as Watene suggests) intercultural dialogue in order to develop better ways to deal with what is one of the most significant challenges to date, not only to development ethics, but to the future of humankind. Hence, as Sen would suggest, more public discussion should be directed to this fundamental subject, as no human life is possible without a well-functioning environment for it to function.

Conclusion

In this chapter we have argued that the capability approach, by putting human lives and their quality of life as the ultimate end of development processes, provides a promising conceptual framework to displace the mind-set that reduces development to economic growth. We have used Mexican labour reform law to illustrate these arguments. However, there are some important questions left which will have to find some resolution for the capability approach to make a difference for the way policy decisions are taken and the kind of decisions that are made. Of particular concern is whether the capability approach is helpful in resisting the reproduction of unjust structures when people can no longer identify the injustice or when the injustice has been so normalised that is seen as 'just' or part of what a 'good' society is about, and fit to stop the reproduction of a development model based on the instrumental use of nature to human ends alone.

A central feature of the capability approach is the centrality of reasoning processes, and perhaps this is its major contribution to development ethics, beyond offering an evaluative framework to judge societies from the perspective of what people are able to *do* and *be*. Sen (2009, 451) sees the 'ability to reason' as a fundamental human feature, and we would add that this ability is also linked to the ability to give sense and meaning to the kind of person one is and to what one does. A conceptual framework based on questioning and reasoning about the meanings and ultimate ends of one's actions cannot but be an antidote to the ever-expanding instrumental reason and the alienation of human life from its purpose of living an examined life and living it well.

References

Alkire, S. (2002) *Valuing Freedoms: Sen's Capability Approach and Poverty Reduction.* Oxford University Press, Oxford.

Alkire, S. (2005) Why the Capability Approach? *Journal of Human Development* 6(1): 115–135.

Alkire, S. (2006) Structural Injustice and Democratic Practice. In Deneulin, S., Nebel, M. and Sagovsky, N. eds., *Transforming Unjust Structures.* Springer, Dordrecht.

Alkire, S. (2008) Using the Capability Approach: Prospective and Evaluative Analyses. In Comim, F., Qizilbash, M. and Alkire, S. eds., *The Capability Approach: Concepts, Measures and Applications.* Cambridge University Press, Cambridge.

Alkire, S. (2015) The Capability Approach and Well-being Measurement for Public Policy. *OPHI Working Paper* No. 94.

Alkire, S., Foster, J., Seth, S., Santos, M.E., Roche, J.M. and Ballon, P. (2015) *Multidimensional Poverty Measurement and Analysis.* Oxford University Press, Oxford.

Anand, P.B. (2014) Sustainability and the Capability Approach: From Theory to Practice? In Tiwari, M. and Ibrahim, S. eds., *The Capability Approach: From Theory to Practice.* Palgrave Macmillan, Basingstoke.

Anand, S. and Sen, A. (2000) Human Development and Economic Sustainability. *World Development* 28(12): 2029–2049.

Anderson, E.S. (1999) What Is the Point of Equality? *Ethics* 109(2): 287–337. http://doi.org/10.1086/233897.

Ballet, J., Koffi, J. and Pelenc, J. (2013) Environment, Justice and the Capability Approach. *Ecological Economics* 8528–8534. doi:10.1016/j.ecolecon.2012.10.010.

Bensusán, G. (2013) Reforma laboral, desarrollo incluyente e igualdad en México. *Serie estudios y perspectivas CEPAL* 143: 67.

Bockstael, E. and Watene, K. (2016) Indigenous Peoples and the Capability Approach. *Oxford Development Studies* 44(3): 265–270.

Borda, P. (2012) Boletín de prensa: Reforma Laboral. http://amedirh.com.mx/publicaciones/noticias/item/boletin-de-prensa. Accessed 31 August 2016.

Burchardt, T. and Vizard, P. (2011) "Operationalizing" the Capability Approach as a Basis for Equality and Human Rights Monitoring in Twenty-First-Century Britain. *Journal of Human Development and Capabilities* 12(1): 91–119.

Clark, D. ed. (2012) *Adaptation, Poverty and Development.* Palgrave Macmillan, Basingstoke.

CONAPRED (2011a) *National Survey on Discrimination in Mexico.* México: Conapred.

CONAPRED (2011b) *Documento informativo sobre Discriminación Racial en México*. Conapred, México.
CONEVAL (2013) *Resultados de la medición de pobreza 2012*. CONEVAL, México.
Crabtree, A. (2013) Sustainable Development: Does the Capability Approach have Anything to Offer? *Journal of Human Development and Capabilities* 14(1): 40–57.
Crocker, D. (1991) Toward Development Ethics. *World Development* 19(5): 457–483.
Crocker, D. (1992) Functioning and Capability: The Foundations of Sen's and Nussbaum's Development Ethic. *Political Theory* 20(4), 584–612.
Crocker, D. (2006) Sen and Deliberative Democracy. In Kaufman, A. ed., *Capabilities Equality: Basic Issues and Problems*. Routledge, New York.
Crocker, D. (2008) *Ethics of Global Development : Agency, Capability, and Deliberative Democracy*. Cambridge University Press, Cambridge.
Crocker, D. and Robeyns, I. (2009) Capability and Agency. In Morris, C. ed., *Amartya Sen*. Cambridge University Press, Cambridge.
Cruz, J.C. (2012) Reforma laboral haría de México "un país atractivo": Standard & Poor's *Proceso*. www.proceso.com.mx/320937/reforma-laboral-haria-de-mexico-un-pais-atractivo-standard-poors. Accessed 22 August 2016.
Deneulin, S. (2006) "Necessary thickening": Ricoeur's Ethic of Justice as a Complement to Sen's Capability Approach. In Deneulin, S., Nebel, M. and Sagovsky, N. eds., *Transforming Unjust Structures*. Springer, Dordrecht.
Deneulin, S. (2008) Beyond Individual Freedom and Agency: Structures of Living Together. In Comim, F., Qizilbash, M. and Alkire, S. eds., *The Capability Approach: Concepts, Measures and Applications*. Cambridge University Press, Cambridge.
Deneulin, S. ed. (2009) *An Introduction to the Human Development and Capability Approach*. Earthscan/IDRC, London.
Deneulin, S. (2011) Development and the Limits of Amartya Sen's The Idea of Justice. *Third World Quarterly* 32(4): 787–797. http://doi.org/10.1080/01436597.2011.567008.
Deneulin, S. (2014a) *Wellbeing, Justice and Development Ethics*. Routledge, London.
Deneulin, S. (2014b) Constructing New Policy Narratives: The Capability Approach as Normative Language. In Cornia, G.A. and Stewart, F. eds., *Towards Human Development*, Oxford University Press, Oxford. http://opus.bath.ac.uk/31885/.
Deneulin, S. and McGregor, J.A. (2010) The Capability Approach and the Politics of a Social Conception of Wellbeing. *European Journal of Social Theory* 13(4): 501–520. http://doi.org/10.1177/1368431010382762.
Deneulin, S., Nebel, M. and Sagovsky, N. eds. (2006) *Transforming Unjust Structures: The Capability Approach*. Springer, Dordrecht.
Drèze, J. and Sen, A. (2002) Democratic Practice and Social Inequality in India. *Journal of Asian and African Studies* 37(2): 6–37.
Drèze, J. and Sen, A. (2013) *An Uncertain Glory: India and its Contradictions*. Allen Lane, London.
Drydyk, J. (2011) Responsible Pluralism, Capabilities, and Human Rights. *Journal of Human Development* 12(1): 39–61.
Drydyk, J. (2016) Ethical Issues in Development. In Grugel, J. and Hammett, D. eds., *The Palgrave Handbook of International Development*. Palgrave Macmillan, Basingstoke.
Evans, P. (2002) Collective Capabilities, Culture and Amartya Sen's Development as Freedom. *Studies in Comparative International Development* 37(2): 54–60.
Gasper, D. (2013) Climate Change and the Language of Human Security. *Ethics, Policy, and Environment* 16(1): 56–78.
Gore, C. (1997) Irreducibly Social Goods and the Informational Basis of Amartya Sen's Capability Approach. *Journal of International Development* 9(2): 235–250.
Goulet, D. (1980) Development Experts: The One-eyed Giants. *World Development* 8: 481–489.
Goulet, D. (1997) Development Ethics: A New Discipline. *International Journal of Social Economics* 24(11): 1160–1171.
Gutwald, R., Leßmann, O., Masson, T. and Rauschmayer, F. (2014) A Capability Approach to Intergenerational Justice? *Journal of Human Development and Capabilities* 15(4): 355–368.

Hernández, M. (2012) ¿Reforma laboral?. *El Economista*. http://eleconomista.com.mx/finanzas-publicas/2012/09/30/reforma-laboral. Accessed 22 August 2016.

Hickey, S. (2014) Relocating Social Protection Within a Radical Project of Social Justice. *European Journal of Development Research* 26(3): 322–337. http://doi.org/10.1057/ejdr.2014.9.

Hill, M. (2003) Development as Empowerment. *Feminist Economics* 9(2–3): 117–135. http://doi.org/10.1080/1354570022000077962.

Holland, B. (2008a) Ecology and the Limits of Justice. *Journal of Human Development* 9(3): 401–425.

Holland, B. (2008b) Justice and the Environment in Nussbaum's "Capabilities Approach". *Political Research Quarterly* 61(2): 319–332.

Holland, B. (2014) *Allocating the Earth*. Oxford University Press, Oxford.

Ibrahim, S. (2006) From Individual to Collective Capabilities. *Journal of Human Development* 7(3): 397–416.

Ibrahim, S. and Alkire, S. (2007) Agency and Empowerment. *Oxford Development Studies* 35(4): 379–403.

Keleher, L. (2014) Sen and Nussbaum: Agency and Capability Expansion. *Ethics and Economics* 1(2): 54–70.

Khader, S. (2011) *Adaptive Preferences and Women's Empowerment*. Oxford University Press, Oxford.

Koggel, C. (2013) Is the Capability Approach a Sufficient Challenge to Distributive Accounts of Global justice? *Journal of Global Ethics* 9(2): 145–157. http://doi.org/10.1080/17449626.2013.818458.

Martínez, M. (2013) La tasa de sindicalización va a la baja en México. *Economista*. http://eleconomista.com.mx/industrias/2013/10/28/tasa-sindicalizacion-va-baja-mexico.

Merino, R. (2016) An Alternative to "Alternative Development"?: Buen Vivir and Human Development in Andean Countries. *Oxford Development Studies* 44(3): 271–286.

Nussbaum, M. (1997) Capabilities and Human Rights. *Fordham Law Review* 66(2): 273–300.

Nussbaum, M. (2000) *Women and Human Development*. Cambridge University Press, Cambridge.

Nussbaum, M. (2003) Capabilities as Fundamental Entitlements. *Feminist Economics* 9(2–3): 33–59. http://doi.org/10.1080/1354570022000077926.

Nussbaum, M. (2006) *Frontiers of Justice*. Harvard University Press, Cambridge, MA.

Nussbaum, M. (2011a) *Creating Capabilities: The Human Development Approach*. Harvard University Press, Cambridge, MA.

Nussbaum, M. (2011b) Capabilities, Entitlements, Rights. *Journal of Human Development and Capabilities* 12(1): 23–37.

Nussbaum, M. and Sen, A. eds. (1993) *The Quality of Life*. Oxford Clarendon Press, Oxford.

Obregón, C. (2013) *México: Un país desarrollado*. México: Pensamiento Universitario Iberoamericano.

Penz, P., Drydyk, J. and Bose, P. (2011) *Displacement by Development: Ethics, Rights and Responsibilities*. Cambridge University Press, Cambridge.

Pereira, G. (2013) *Elements of a Critical Theory of Justice*. Palgrave Macmillan, Basingstoke.

PNUD (2010) *Informe sobre desarrollo humano de los pueblos indígenas en México*. Programa de las Naciones Unidas para el Desarrollo, México.

Qizilbash, M. (1996) Ethical Development. *World Development* 24(7): 1209–1221. http://doi.org/10.1016/0305-750X(96)00030-7.

Robeyns, I. (2003a) Sen's Capability Approach and Gender Inequality. *Feminist Economics* 9(2/3): 61–93.

Robeyns, I. (2003b) Is Nancy Fraser's Critique of Theories of Distributive Justice Justified? *Constellations* 10(4): 538–554. http://doi.org/10.1046/j.1351-0487.2003.00352.x.

Robeyns, I. (2005a) The Capability Approach: A Theoretical Survey. *Journal of Human Development*, 6(1): 93–117. http://doi.org/10.1080/146498805200034266.

Robeyns, I. (2005b) Selecting Capabilities for Quality of Life Measurement. *Social Indicators Research* 74(1): 191–215.

Robeyns, I. (2006) The Capability Approach in Practice. *Journal of Political Philosophy* 14(3): 351–376. http://doi.org/10.1111/j.1467-9760.2006.00263.x.

Robeyns, I. (2008) Sen's Capability Approach and Feminist Concerns. In Comim, F., Qizilbash, M. and Alkire, S. eds., *The Capability Approach: Concepts, Measures and Applications*. Cambridge University Press, Cambridge.

Robeyns, I. (2011) The Capability Approach. In Zalta, E.N. ed., *The Stanford Encyclopedia of Philosophy* (Summer 2011). http://plato.stanford.edu/archives/sum2011/entries/capability-approach/.

Robeyns, I. (2016) Capabilitarianism. *Journal of Human Development and Capabilities* 17(3): 397–414. http://doi.org/10.1080/19452829.2016.1145631.

Scholtes, F. (2010) Whose Sustainability? Environmental Domination and Sen's Capability Approach. *Oxford Development Studies* 38(3): 289–307. doi:10.1080/13600818.2010.505683.

Sen, A. (1980) Equality of What? *The Tanner Lecture on Human Values* I: 197–220.

Sen, A. (1985) Well-Being, Agency and Freedom. *The Journal of Philosophy* 82(4): 169–221. http://doi.org/10.2307/2026184.

Sen, A. (1988) The Concept of Development. *Handbook of Development Economics* 1: 9–26. http://doi.org/10.1016/S1573-4471(88)01004-6.

Sen, A. (1990) Justice: Means versus Freedoms. *Philosophy and Public Affairs* 19(2): 111–121.

Sen, A. (1992) *Inequality Re-examined.* Oxford Clarendon Press, Oxford.

Sen, A. (1993) Capability and Well-being. In Nussbaum, M. and Sen, A. eds., *The Quality of Life.* Clarendon Press, Oxford, 30–53.

Sen, A. (1997) Human Rights and Asian Values. *The New Republic* 217(2–3): 33–40.

Sen, A. (1999a) *Development as Freedom.* Anchor Books, New York.

Sen, A. (1999b) Democracy as a Universal Value. *Journal of Democracy* 10(3): 3–17.

Sen, A. (1999c) *Commodities and Capabilities.* Oxford University Press, Oxford.

Sen, A. (2002) Response to Commentaries. *Studies in Comparative International Development* 37(2): 78–86. http://doi.org/10.1007/BF02686264.

Sen, A. (2004a) Capabilities, Lists, and Public Reason. *Feminist Economics*, 10(3): 77–80. http://doi.org/10.1080/1354570042000315163.

Sen, A. (2004b) Why We Should Preserve the Spotted Owl? *London Review of Books* 5 February, 26(3): 10–11.

Sen, A. (2005) Human Rights and Capabilities. *Journal of Human Development* 6(2): 151–166.

Sen, A. (2009) *The Idea of Justice.* Allen Lane, London.

Sen, A. (2013) The Ends and Means of Sustainability. *Journal of Human Development* 14(1): 6–20.

Sen, A. (2017) *Collective Choice and Social Welfare.* Allen Lane, London.

Stewart, F. (2005) Groups and Capabilities. *Journal of Human Development* 6(2): 185–204.

Stewart, F. (2013) *Capabilities and Human Development: Beyond the Individual* (SSRN Scholarly Paper No. ID 2344469). Rochester, NY: UNDP.

Stewart, F. and Deneulin, S. (2002) Amartya Sen's Contribution to Development Thinking. *Studies in Comparative International Development* 37(2): 61–70.

Vizard, P., Fakuda-Parr, S. and Elson, D. (2011) Introduction: The Capability Approach and Human Rights. *Journal of Human Development and Capabilities* 12(1): 1–22.

Watene, K. (2016) Valuing Nature: Māori Philosophy and the Capability Approach. *Oxford Development Studies* 44(3): 287–296.

World Commission on Environment and Development (WCED) (1987), *Our Common Future*, http://www.un-documents.net/our-common-future.pdf.

8

Happiness

Using subjective well-being metrics to gauge development

Milena Nikolova

Economists and policy makers often define and gauge human progress and well-being in terms of gross domestic product (GDP). Nonetheless, this measure – encompassing the value of goods and services produced in an economy – reflects economic activity, which is not synonymous with well-being. Moreover, viewing human progress solely in terms of income and wealth may fail to distinguish between worthwhile development and undesirable maldevelopment. High GDP levels and economic growth could entail the provision of public goods, universal healthcare, childcare, and a clean environment, which enable quality of life for all. Nevertheless, economic progress could be coupled with oppression, discrimination against women and minorities, eroded civic capital, and the empowerment of corrupt elites, which would constitute maldevelopment.

Objective well-being measures thus provide valuable information about means and actual circumstances. However, given that development is multifaceted, these measures alone are insufficient to judge human progress. The subjective well-being approach complements our understanding of development by introducing the idea that how people perceive and evaluate their circumstances is just as important as the circumstances themselves (OECD 2011). Given that subjective well-being measures are self-reported (i.e. measured via surveys as explained below), individuals can judge and assess their circumstances on their own. The subjective well-being approach is thus democratic and non-paternalistic (Binder 2014).

In addition, "good development" entails not just high achievements in terms of objective conditions but also a worthwhile process through which these conditions were achieved. As such, subjective well-being measures can reflect how people assess and experience the development process. For example, while economic growth may signal improving economic well-being, the evidence from Latin America and elsewhere shows that people in faster-growing economies are on average less happy than those with slower growth rates (controlling for income levels) (Lora and Chaparro 2008). Graham and Lora (2009) call this the "paradox of unhappy growth", explaining that it arises because rapid economic growth often brings instability in people's lives, which income measures fail to reflect. Focusing on growth alone may thus obscure its frustrating aspects such as rising job insecurity or inequality (Graham 2009).

Finally, several countries – such as Morocco, Australia, Britain, Canada, France, Italy, and New Zealand – are now collecting subjective well-being measures as part of their national statistics

DOI: 10.4324/9781315626796-10

(Durand and Smith 2013). Bhutan has replaced Gross National Product with gross national happiness as a measure of progress. Despite the momentum and the great promise that subjective well-being measures could offer in terms of broadening the basis upon which we judge human progress, development scholars need to carefully consider the challenges before trusting and using such measures.

What is subjective well-being and (how) can it be measured?

Subjective well-being measures are usually based upon self-reported evaluations collected via nationally representative surveys conducted with thousands of individuals across countries and over time (Graham 2011b). Such surveys also gather information on income, employment, health and socio-demographic characteristics such as age, education, and gender, among others. In some cases, panel surveys follow the same individuals within a country over time and ask the same questions each year. This allows researchers to adjust subjective well-being scores for factors related to personality and individual response styles. For example, optimistic people may naturally score higher on well-being questions, while pessimists may repeatedly report low life evaluations. Using panel data and statistical techniques allows researchers to eliminate the influences of such (time-constant) personality traits on self-reported well-being scores.

Subjective well-being has both hedonic (i.e. *affective*) and cognitive (i.e., *evaluative*) dimensions. Along with "good moods" and feelings of joy, happiness is an example of positive hedonic well-being. Negative hedonic well-being includes experiences of stress, anger, sadness or worry. Hedonic well-being measures are reflections of experiences *at a particular point in time* and can be measured using either *experiential* or *survey* methods. For example, with the Experience Sampling Method (ESM), respondents are contacted several times a day via a beeper or another signaling device and asked questions about their activities, surroundings, and emotions. Developed as a response to the intrusive and labor-intensive ESM data collection method, the Day Reconstruction Method (DRM) asks people to reflect in a diary what happened at different episodes during the previous day (Kahneman et al. 2004). Nevertheless, the DRM answers may be subject to recall bias, as respondents may not remember what they did or how they felt during the day. In large-scale surveys, hedonic well-being is measured with a short series of questions asking respondents how they felt during the previous day. For example, global surveys such as the Gallup World Poll ask interviewees whether or not they experienced a lot of happiness or smiled a lot or whether they felt depressed, worried, angry or stressed the day before.

In contrast, evaluative well-being is an overall reflection on one's life. This dimension is typically measured using general life satisfaction questions or the Cantril ladder of life questions, whereby respondents rate their current life on an 11-point scale, where 0 represents their worst possible life and 10 corresponds to the best possible life that they can imagine for themselves. Judging one's satisfaction with life as a whole requires a thorough evaluation of one's circumstances, both past and present. These measures usually reflect people's capabilities, means, and long-term opportunities (Graham and Nikolova 2015). By contrast, hedonic experiences indicate emotions and moods triggered by pleasant and unpleasant daily experiences such as sitting in a traffic jam, having a cold, meeting with friends or watching a funny movie.

Despite being correlated, the two subjective well-being dimensions are distinct. Specifically, responses to these two questions can vary across individuals and countries, depending on objective circumstances. For instance, a high-achieving Ivy-League school graduate working on Wall Street could have higher-than-average life satisfaction but also higher-than-average stress levels and low levels of daily happiness due to long working hours and many daily sacrifices on the personal front. At the same time, a destitute person with bleak life prospects may report average smiling and joy experiences but low satisfaction with life as a whole due to a lack of opportunities and capabilities. Part of the explanation for this surprising finding rests upon hedonic adaptation (see Chapter 9), whereby people in deprived circumstances learn how to make their lives more tolerable and pleasurable by focusing on what they have, e.g. children, friends or social networks. For example, using Latin American data, Graham and Lora (2009) show that respondents with more material means tend to place a greater emphasis on work and health aspects when assessing their well-being levels. By contrast, the poor tend to focus on friends and social networks, which likely help them to get through the day and make it more pleasurable in the hedonic sense.

Hedonic and evaluative well-being have different determinants. For example, income and opportunities tend to be much more important for evaluative rather than hedonic well-being (Graham and Nikolova 2015). Smiling and learning something interesting the day before are among the key determinants of hedonic happiness (Graham and Nikolova 2015). Furthermore, progress and development can increase some subjective well-being dimensions but worsen others. For instance, access to information and communications technology (ICT) can reduce information and communication costs or enable respondents to conduct financial transactions or connect with relatives abroad, which can improve life satisfaction and happiness. Nonetheless, ICT access may also lead to stress and anger, especially among respondents who previously lacked such access (Graham and Nikolova 2013). By providing information, technology such as cell phones or TV and Internet also raise the expectations and frustration among the poor.

A third subjective well-being dimension, eudaimonic well-being, is related to the Aristotelian concept of happiness as meaning and purpose in life. Research is still in progress to better understand how to measure and interpret this dimension. As Graham (2011b) notes, Aristotle likely thought of this concept not in terms of what people *say* about their lives but rather how they *live* their lives. White and Dolan (2009) used the DRM described earlier to study eudaimonia, finding that activities that are pleasurable are not necessarily meaningful. For example, spending time with children can be rewarding but not pleasurable, while watching TV can be pleasurable but not meaningful (White and Dolan 2009). Graham and Nikolova (2015) find that *belief in hard work* is the most important determinant of eudaimonic well-being, which they measure using a Gallup World Poll question on whether respondents have meaning and purpose in life.

Are subjective well-being measures simply noise?

Empirical social scientists – and economists in particular – are cautious about what people say and focus instead on what people do, i.e. their revealed preferences. Their rationale is that "talk is cheap" and respondents can untruthfully answer survey questionnaires, which suggests that self-reported accounts cannot be trusted. Critics also highlight that the understanding of happiness can differ from person to person or across countries and cultures. Moreover, one's own understanding of happiness can also change over time. Therefore, critics insist that happiness scores cannot be validly and reliably compared across individuals, time, and countries.

Nonetheless, subjective well-being questions are never open-ended but rather are given a bounded scale. For example, a typical life satisfaction question asks: "Overall, how satisfied are you with your life as a whole these days?", with possible answers ranging from 0 "completely dissatisfied" to 10 "completely satisfied." Thus, respondents' answers are anchored to their own judgment of how their lives are going. Arguably, unlike with income questions, respondents have no incentives to lie to subjective well-being inquiries, which is reflected in the high response rates to these questions. Many of the other criticisms related to comparability such as disagreement about definitions, differences in how people answer questions, and the role of culture (see Stewart 2014) have already been addressed (OECD 2013; Exton et al. 2015). Forty years of work among psychologists and economists, including by Nobel Prize laureates Daniel Kahneman and Angus Deaton, has shown that subjective well-being measures capture the underlying concepts, are valid and reliable, as well as comparable across people, countries, and over time (Krueger and Schkade 2008; Exton et al. 2015; Helliwell and Barrington-Leigh 2010; OECD 2011).

In short, subjective well-being measures are not simply noise but rather reflect meaningful information about perceived quality of life. Given their subjective nature, these measures cannot be directly validated, although they have been indirectly validated by being tested for plausible correlations with other variables (DiTella and MacCulloch 2006). For example, if they were simply noise, these measures would be (statistically) unrelated to life events and circumstances such as unemployment, marriage or death of a family member; nonetheless, cross-sectional and longitudinal studies find that they are. Other indirect validations show that subjective well-being scores correlate with the frequency of "genuine" Duchene smiles, biological markers such as brain activity and cortisol, as well as ratings made by friends and partners (OECD 2011). Of course, no measurement of any variable – objective or subjective – can be completely error-free and as such subjective well-being indicators are imperfect. Certain response modes (e.g. phone vs. in-person interviews), temporary moods, and the presence of others during the interview can distort the answers to subjective well-being questions (Conti and Pudney 2011; Dolan and Kavetsos 2012; Krueger and Schkade 2008). Limits to validity also include one-off events affecting a large number of respondents such as day-of-the week effects and different circumstantial events such as interviewer effects, which should dissipate in large samples, however (OECD 2013).

Subjective well-being measures can allow a broader perspective of the consequences of complex development phenomena such as migration, growth, economic and democratic transitions, or increased access to information technology. Happiness economists estimate regressions from which they can discern the relative importance for subjective well-being of factors such as income, employment conditions, education and health, which are important policy variables (Graham and Nikolova 2015; Tay and Diener 2011). The subjective well-being approach is especially relevant for assessing the welfare consequences of institutional arrangements that individuals cannot change, such as inequality, macroeconomic volatility, political systems or migration policies. These arrangements are external from the individual perspective, whereby a person cannot express revealed preferences for them (aside from protesting or migrating in certain cases) (Graham 2011b). However, life satisfaction answers and institutional- or macro-level data allow researchers to statistically assess the welfare implications of the latter. As such, subjective well-being measures can be informative about how individuals value different aspects of development, and especially features that they are powerless to change.

Adaptation and Sen's critique of happiness

One of the strongest critiques against using subjective well-being in the development policy arena is the problem of *hedonic adaptation* (see Chapter 9). As mentioned earlier, people living in deprived circumstances may adjust to what they consider possible. Furthermore, one can also be dissatisfied with a relatively good life by adapting to a high standard of living or changing the comparison group (Stiglitz et al. 2009). Carol Graham's "happy peasants and frustrated achiever" paradox is one such example (2009, 255). While poor individuals are on average less happy than rich individuals within a country, very poor people often report being relatively happy, while wealthy individuals report lower subjective well-being and higher-than-average frustration with their economic situation. The paradox could be partly explained by the fact that poor people adapt their expectations downwards, while richer or more upwardly mobile respondents have ever-increasing expectations (Graham 2009).

Moreover, people in different countries have varying norms of what is acceptable and tolerable. For example, Latin America is the world's happiest region in terms of hedonic well-being, despite also being a high-violence, -crime and -corruption region, whereby crime and corruption are detrimental to subjective well-being. Therefore, how can it be the case that Latin Americans are so happy? Research shows that if crime and violence are high, they become the norm and people adapt to them (Graham 2011a). In such circumstances, people who become the victims of crime and corruption are less likely to feel victimized and experience less moral conflict if they have to engage themselves in such activities.

In a similar vein, Amartya Sen provides one of the sharpest critiques of the happiness economics approach, which relates to adaptation. According to what Crocker calls the "small mercies" argument, people may be seriously deprived but quite happy if they do not expect much from life and accept the "small mercies" that appear in their lives (Crocker 2008, 127; Crocker 1992, 601). In other words, Sen's main argument against using happiness as a measure of human progress is the fact that by lowering expectations and suppressing suffering in the name of survival, a deprived person such as the "hopeless beggar", the dominated wife or those working in precarious conditions may still be well off in terms of a "mental metric of utility." Thus, according to this critique, the happiness approach would fail to reflect the true degree of deprivation (Sen 1987, 45–46, 2003, 45).

One response to this critique refers to the difference between hedonic and evaluative well-being explained earlier: while a person may adapt their daily experiences to an unfavorable situation, the data suggest that they rarely evaluate a deprived life as the best possible life. The evidence from around the world demonstrates that a destitute person may report to be happy while also indicating low life satisfaction (Helliwell et al. 2013).

While individual adaptation can be a mechanism that allows people to cope with and recover from unfavorable situations, collectively, it can lead to bad equilibria (Graham 2011b). For example, people could adapt to corruption, poor health standards and undemocratic institutions and learn to be happy. In such circumstances, dysfunctional institutions become the norm, which makes reform less likely to occur. This example demonstrates that in such situations, subjective well-being measures alone can neither constitute good development nor be a good measure of it. Complementing the subjective well-being perspective with objective measures or assessing people's actual capacities to pursue the kinds of lives they have reasons to value would be advisable.

In short, adaptation is a double-edged sword for those willing to incorporate subjective well-being metrics in development theory and practice. On the one hand, understanding differences in the capacity to adapt broadens our understanding of well-being and the nuances of the development processes. On the other hand, adaptation presents one of the major challenges of using subjective well-being measures as a guide to policy (Graham 2011b). If the information provided by subjective well-being is mis-used or abused, malevolent governments may adopt policies to encourage adaptation to precarious conditions rather than addressing deprivation (Stewart 2014). For example, as Stewart (2014) argues, policies that help the poor deal with mental health issues arising from living in poverty may encourage adaptation to deprivation rather than promoting development or reducing poverty. These critiques are valid and important and warn against the danger of using subjective well-being measures as the sole indicators of progress. Worthwhile development should thus be gauged based on both objective conditions and subjective assessments of these conditions.

Indeed, while adaptation presents a challenge to happiness economics, one way around the small mercies argument is to use hedonic and evaluative measures side-by-side – and the different and at times contradictory information that these metrics yield both within and across individuals and countries – to gain a fuller understanding of the human condition. Nevertheless, just like emphasizing objective measures of progress can conceal sides of maldevelopment such as frustration and dissatisfaction with institutions, putting forward subjective well-being measures to argue that "things are going well" is just as misguided and arguably unethical. Unchanging or rising subjective well-being measures amidst worsening health, education, and crime indicators should not be interpreted as "things going well" but rather as a sign of concern and government failure. To be informative, subjective well-being measures should thus be used fairly and be balanced against objective conditions.

The Easterlin Paradox

A central debate in the subjective well-being literature – with important implications for development ethics – concerns the relationship between income (growth) and happiness. Within a country, the rich are happier than the poor. Likewise, at any point in time, rich countries are happier than poor ones. Therefore, *at a particular point in time*, the relationship between income and happiness is positive. However, looking at the relationship over time, as countries become richer, it appears that they do not get happier. This is the Easterlin Paradox: while cross-sectionally (i.e. at a particular point in time), income and happiness are positively correlated, as countries become richer *over time*, the relationship does not hold.

There are two main explanations for this paradox, namely, social comparisons and adaptation (Clark 2016). According to the social comparisons explanation, individuals compare their income to that earned by a peer group (e.g. neighbors, colleagues, classmates). While own-income increases are positively associated with happiness, as the reference group income rises, own happiness falls. The two effects cancel each other out, leading to the result that income is unassociated with happiness over time. The second explanation refers to a within-person comparison, i.e. the person compares their current and past income. Complete adaptation entails that higher income will initially lead to higher happiness, although after some time, the individual fully adapts to this higher income and happiness returns to its pre-income increase levels (Clark 2016).

While scholars agree on the evidence and the positive relationship between income and happiness at a given point in time, the disagreement concerns the over-time relationship. Depending on the data and methodology, some studies find that rising income leads to rising happiness, which contradicts the Easterlin Paradox. Indeed, while several recent papers have tried to challenge the Easterlin Paradox (Stevenson and Wolfers 2008; Sacks et al. 2012; Diener et al. 2013; Veenhoven and Vergunst 2014), Easterlin (2016) has re-affirmed the paradox, noting that the divergent findings are due to methodology, including the length of the time series, the choice of the countries included in the analyses, question wording, and survey peculiarities.

A modified version of the paradox, which is also subject to debate, is that income only improves happiness until basic needs are met (Veenhoven 1991; Clark et al. 2008). Once basic needs are met, income is unrelated to happiness because other factors become relatively more important. Several studies have empirically challenged this explanation, showing that – if anything – the relationship between income and happiness may be stronger in richer rather than poorer countries (Deaton 2008; Stevenson and Wolfers 2013). This could be the case because wealthier people are better able to take advantage of income as a means of achieving happiness (Graham 2009).

What do these debates imply for development theory and practice? On the one hand, if there is indeed no over-time relationship between happiness and income and if income does not matter for happiness after basic needs are met, then income has limited informational value as a quality of life measure. On the other hand, income cannot be ignored as high-income economies also score high on other markers of a good society, such as freedom of choice, functioning labor markets, and public goods (Graham 2011b).

Policy implications and future directions

As argued throughout this chapter, subjective well-being should not be the sole measure of development. Yet, arguments to the contrary exist. For example, Richard Layard proposes that life satisfaction should be the only relevant measure of human well-being. He claims that society needs a single overarching well-being measure, whereby life satisfaction is the obvious candidate as it depends on satisfaction with policy-relevant domains such as health, education, family and work, among others (Layard 2009). While subjective well-being outcomes may advise development policy, these measures have several limitations and can best serve as a complement to rather than as a replacement of progress indicators in the policy arena.

First, from a normative perspective, subjective well-being cannot be the only well-being measure because people may be happy by engaging in immoral or unlawful behavior. According to this critique, not only rising income, better education or health can lead to higher well-being (Duncan 2010); for instance, a gang member could report to be happy, while obviously engaging in criminal behavior and hurting others. This criticism is usually addressed by noting that policy makers and development experts need a range of objective and subjective metrics including several subjective well-being dimensions to credibly assess welfare.

Second, hedonic adaptation remains an unresolved challenge. If people adapt to negative circumstances, well-being scores would not reflect the negative welfare consequences of sub-par institutions or policies, leading policy makers and development experts to think that no action is necessary (Graham 2011b; Binder 2014). Looking across different subjective well-being dimensions and interpreting the data correctly are pivotal steps towards overcoming this problem.

Third, while unhappiness may point to destitution and a lack of economic progress, a related yet open-ended question is whether some unhappiness and frustration accompany the development process, at least in the short run (Graham and Nikolova 2015; Graham 2011b). It may also be the case that individuals trade off hedonic happiness in the present to achieve better life evaluation in the future. To understand this process and the associated trade-offs, the same individuals need to be followed over time.

Finally, while subjective well-being indicators are democratic, using them as the only measure of human progress makes them subject to misuse and misrepresentation by politicians. One can also imagine citizens being constantly polled about their well-being and thus being reduced to passive "metric stations" automatically submitting subjective well-being answers, which is inimical to democracy (Frey and Stutzer 2010).

As argued throughout this chapter, human well-being is multidimensional, and different life events or development processes have complex consequences that cannot be captured by a single tell-all metric. Data on a range of objective measures such as income, health, education, consumption, and employment and subjective indicators such as happiness, job satisfaction, life satisfaction, and negative emotions can provide a more comprehensive view of the human condition and serve as a better policy guide. Accordingly, having well-trained researchers who can correctly and credibly assess the data using theory, robust empirical methods, and a range of metrics as a guide will be an essential part of informing development theory and practice in the future.

Acknowledgments

The author would like to thank the editors and two anonymous reviewers for valuable critiques. In addition, the author is grateful to Carol Graham, Boris Nikolaev, Olga Popova, and Tom Ivlevs for helpful comments, corrections, and suggestions. The author also thanks Margard Ody for help locating relevant studies, Daria Golokhvastova for research assistance, and Richard Forsythe for copyediting support. All errors are the author's.

References

Binder, M. (2014) Subjective Well-being Capabilities: Bridging the Gap between the Capability Approach and Subjective Well-being Research. *Journal of Happiness Studies* 15(5): 1197–1217.

Clark, A.E. (2016) Adaptation and the Easterlin Paradox. *Advances in Happiness Research*. Springer, 75–94.

Clark, A.E., Frijters, P. and Shields, M.A. (2008) Relative Income, Happiness, and Utility: An Explanation for the Easterlin Paradox and Other Puzzles. *Journal of Economic Literature* 46(1): 95–144.

Conti, G. and Pudney, S. (2011) Survey Design and the Analysis of Satisfaction. *Review of Economics and Statistics* 93(3): 1087–1093.

Crocker, D.A. (1992) Functioning and Capability: The Foundations of Sen's and Nussbaum's Development Ethic. *Political Theory* 20(4): 584–612.

Crocker, D.A. (2008) *Ethics of Global Development: Agency, Capability, and Deliberative Democracy*. Cambridge University Press, Cambridge.

Deaton, A. (2008) Income, Health, and Well-Being around the World: Evidence from the Gallup World Poll. *The Journal of Economic Perspectives* 22(2): 53–72.

Diener, E., Tay, L. and Oishi, S. (2013) Rising Income and the Subjective Well-being of Nations. *Journal of Personality and Social Psychology* 104(2): 267–276.

DiTella, R. and MacCulloch, R. (2006) Some Uses of Happiness Data in economics. *The Journal of Economic Perspectives* 20(1): 25–46.

Dolan, P. and Kavetsos, G. (2012) Happy Talk: Mode of Administration Effects on Subjective Well-Being. *Centre for Economic Performance Discussion Paper No 1159*, 1–17.

Duncan, G. (2010) Should Happiness-Maximization be the Goal of Government? *Journal of Happiness Studies* 11(2): 163–178.

Durand, M. and Smith, C. (2013) The OECD Approach to Measuring Subjective Well-being. In: Helliwell, J., Layard, R. and Sachs, J. eds., *World Happiness Report*. UN Sustainable Development Solutions Network, New York, 112–137.

Easterlin, R.A. (2016) Paradox Lost? *IZA DP No. 9676*.

Exton, C., Smith, C. and Vandendriessche, D. (2015) Comparing Happiness across the World. *OECD Statistics Directorate Working Paper No. 62*.

Frey, B.S. and Stutzer, A. (2010) Happiness and Public Choice. *Public Choice* 144(3–4): 557–573.

Graham, C. (2009) *Happiness Around the World: The Paradox of Happy Peasants and Miserable Millionaires*. Oxford University Press, Oxford.

Graham, C. (2011a) Adaptation Amidst Prosperity and Adversity: Insights from Happiness Studies from around the World. *The World Bank Research Observer* 26(1): 105–137.

Graham, C. (2011b) *Pursuit of Happiness: An Economy of Well-Being*. Brookings Institution Press, Washington, DC.

Graham, C. and Lora, E., eds. (2009) *Paradox and Perception: Measuring Quality of Life in Latin America*. Brookings Institution Press, Washington, DC.

Graham, C. and Nikolova, M. (2013) Does Access to Information Technology Make People Happier? Insights from Well-Being Surveys from around the World. *The Journal of Socio-Economics* 44(0): 126–139.

Graham, C. and Nikolova, M. (2015) Bentham or Aristotle in the Development Process? An Empirical Investigation of Capabilities and Subjective Well-Being. *World Development* 68: 163–179.

Helliwell, J.F. and Barrington-Leigh, C.P. (2010) Viewpoint: Measuring and Understanding Subjective Well-Being. *Canadian Journal of Economics* 43(3): 729–753.

Helliwell, J.F., Layard, R. and Sachs, J.D. (2013) Introduction. In Helliwell, J.F., Layard, R. and Sachs, J. eds., *World Happiness Report 2013*. UN Sustainable Development Solutions Network, New York, 2–7.

Kahneman, D. et al. (2004) A Survey Method for Characterizing Daily Life Experience: The Day Reconstruction Method. *Science* 306(5702): 1776–1780.

Krueger, A.B. and Schkade, D.A. (2008) The Reliability of Subjective Well-being Measures. *Journal of Public Economics* 92(8/9): 1833–1845.

Layard, R. (2009) Why Subjective Well-being Should be the Measure of Progress. In *OECD World Forum: Charting Progress, Building Visions, Improving Life*, 27–30 October 2009. Busan, Korea.

Lora, E.A. and Chaparro, J.C. (2008) The Conflictive Relationship Between Satisfaction and Income. *Inter-American Development Bank*, Working Paper 642.

OECD (2011) *How's Life?: Measuring Well-being*. Organisation for Economic Cooperation and Development, OECD Publishing. http://dx.doi.org/10.1787/9789264121164-en.

OECD (2013) *OECD Guidelines on Measuring Subjective Well-Being*. OECD Publishing, Paris.

Sacks, D.W., Stevenson, B. and Wolfers, J. (2012) The New Stylized Facts about Income and Subjective Well-being. *Emotion* 12(6): 1181–1187.

Sen, A. (1987) *On Ethics and Economics*. Blackwell Publishing, London.

Sen, A. (2003) Development as Capability Expansion. *Readings in Human Development*, 3–16.

Stevenson, B. and Wolfers, J. (2008) Economic Growth and Subjective Well-Being: Reassessing the Easterlin Paradox. *Brookings Papers on Economic Activity*, 1–102.

Stevenson, B. and Wolfers, J. (2013) Subjective Well-being and Income: Is there Any Evidence of Satiation? *The American Economic Review* 103(3): 598–604.

Stewart, F. (2014) Against Happiness: A Critical Appraisal of the Use of Measures of Happiness for Evaluating Progress in development. *Journal of Human Development and Capabilities 15*(4): 293–307.

Stiglitz, J., Sen, A. and Fitoussi, J.-P. (2009) The Measurement of Economic Performance and Social Progress revisited. *Reflections and Overview. Commission on the Measurement of Economic Performance and Social Progress*, Paris.

Tay, L. and Diener, E. (2011) Needs and Subjective Well-being around the World. *Journal of Personality and Social Psychology* 101(2): 354–365.

Veenhoven, R. (1991) Is Happiness relative? *Social Indicators Research* 24(1): 1–34.

Veenhoven, R. and Vergunst, F. (2014) The Easterlin Illusion: Economic Growth Does Go with Greater Happiness. *International Journal of Happiness and Development* 1(4): 311–343.

White, M.P. and Dolan, P. (2009) Accounting for the Richness of Daily Activities. *Psychological Science* 20(8): 1000–1008.

9

Adaptive preferences

Accounting for deflated expectations

Serene J. Khader

A woman sees no reason to protest the fact that she is paid less than a man for doing more difficult work (Nussbaum 2001, 113). A person living in poverty describes themselves as happy, contented by life's "small mercies" (Sen 1988, 45). A victim of domestic violence sees beatings as beneficial to wives who are unruly (see Jakobsen 2014). Attitudes, desires, and behaviors like these have come to be known in development ethics as "adaptive preferences." Development policies that sought to fulfill women's desires to be beaten or treated the happiness of the poor as reason to ignore poverty or inequality seem intuitively like instances of "maldevelopment" (see Drydyk 2011 and the introduction to this *Handbook*).

Adaptive preferences (APs) present difficulties for all approaches to development that take people's existing attitudes, behaviors, and desires to provide valuable information about what is good for them. Since the capability approach measures well-being in terms of access to valuable beings and doings, and since utilitarian (also called "welfarist") approaches have, in contrast, emphasized desire-satisfaction, APs have played a prominent role in arguments in favor of the capability approach (Sen 1988; Sen 1990; Nussbaum 2001; Robeyns 2003; Qizilbash 2012). Taking APs seriously is compatible with approaches to development besides the capability approach; what matters is that the relevant approaches do not define the good exclusively in terms of fulfilling existing wants. But adaptive preferences are not merely theoretical test cases for conversations about how to measure development. Real people's desires and behavior often seem shaped by deprivation, so adaptive preferences pose practical development challenges. Two important debates concern a) how adaptive preferences should be defined and b) whether a preoccupation with them might support unjustified paternalism, especially in cross-cultural contexts. These debates, which I will discuss here, overlap on the question of whether and how it is possible to demonstrate respect for people while questioning their preferences.

Defining adaptive preferences

Jon Elster coined the term "adaptive preference" to describe "sour grapes," the phenomenon wherein a person downgrades a previously valued option because it is no longer available (Elster 1987). However, as Martha Nussbaum argues, the term is now used more broadly in development ethics to include a broad range of attitudes and behaviors that seem causally related to lack of options

DOI: 10.4324/9781315626796-11

(Nussbaum 2001, 139). Development ethicists generally take the presence of adaptive preferences to be a bad thing; they are harmful or constitute evidence of harm. It is thus important to distinguish the term "adaptive preference" from the term "adaptation." As David A. Clark argues, the term "adaptation" is sometimes used positively to refer to the resilience with which individuals and communities respond to challenges such as poverty climate change (Clark 2012; see also Whyte 2013).

Why question adaptive preferences: autonomy or well-being

It seems objectionable for development interventions to promote and fulfill adaptive preferences, and a definition of the concept should help us see why. The reason cannot be that they are adapted to social conditions, since all or most preferences have this character (Nussbaum 2001; Khader 2011). One may play the oud rather than the sitar because of where one was born, or switch from baseball to swimming because one moves near a lake, but these cases do not raise the same worries as that of say, a poor person who does not aspire to a secondary education. Nor can APs simply be socially caused reductions in desire. Policies that encourage driving a cheaper car to pay taxes that fund education seem politically justifiable, for example.

The debate about what makes APs a target for questioning and transformation by development interventions focuses on whether to characterize them as deficits in autonomy or well-being.

Autonomous preferences are those that genuinely "belong to" an agent in the sense of reflecting her values or being endorsed by her. On procedural accounts, we cannot determine whether a preference is autonomous on the basis of its content; it is a person's attitude toward it that matters. Many philosophers have taken procedural autonomy deficiency as a defining characteristic of adaptive preferences (Colburn 2011; Friedman 2006; Elster 1987; Teschl and Comim 2005; Christman 2014) and development theorists, those who argue that people with APs lack choices (Kabeer 1999; Nagar 2003), can be read as committed to a similar view (Khader 2009).

Understanding adaptive preferences as deserving special political attention because they are nonautonomous has the advantage of seeming compatible with respect for persons, and openness to a variety of ways of life. If they are preferences that people do not really want to have, we need not worry that questioning adaptive preferences involves telling people what is good for them or forcing them to live according to that ideal. If, for example, someone has never reflected on prevailing gender norms, her acceptance of domestic violence may seem to manifest uncritical acceptance of social norms rather than a considered view about how to live her life. However, understanding adaptive preferences as necessarily unreflective seems inaccurate and to encourage disregarding the perspectives of the oppressed and deprived. As I have argued elsewhere, preferences to perpetuate one's oppression or deprivation are often very reflective and endorsed as part of life plans (Khader 2011, 2012). Additionally many preferences that are not procedurally autonomous, such as unreflectively eating strawberries instead of yogurt, seem unproblematic.

A competing account of why adaptive preferences are worthy of special moral and political attention characterizes them relative to a conception of flourishing, or well-being. I advocate such an account, arguing that adaptive preferences are preferences that are incompatible with basic flourishing, formed under conditions where basic flourishing was unavailable, and that an agent would reverse upon exposure to improved conditions (Khader 2011, 2012). Though it may seem that this account requires ignoring or overriding people's desires, it need not. Employing conception of flourishing that is minimal, vague, and arrived at by cross-cultural deliberation allows criticism of adaptive preferences without suggesting a one-size-fits all solution. Further, the idea that development should promote flourishing is compatible with restricting the means for promoting it by, for example, prohibiting coercion (Raz 1988).

A third type of approach builds a conception of flourishing into autonomy and suggests that adaptive preferences are nonautonomous. Martha Nussbaum sometimes seems to offer such an account, claiming that autonomy is available only when a person has access to a full list of functionings (Nussbaum 1999, 50; see also Stoljar 2000; MacKenzie 2008; Stoljar 2014). Though such substantive autonomy accounts promise to capture preferences that intuitively seem adaptive, they risk disrespecting people with APs in similar ways to procedural accounts; they suggest people with APs are unreflective. To solve this problem, Rosa Terlazzo (Terlazzo 2016) suggests we should see autonomy as requiring the presence of certain options but no particular choice among those options and Catriona MacKenzie suggests we distinguish lacks self-direction autonomy from lacks of self-governance autonomy (Mackenzie 2015).

Related concepts

The concept of AP overlaps with some other important concepts. Internalized oppression and false consciousness are concepts arising from the observation that deprived people's existing desires, attitudes, and behaviors can get in the way of ending their deprivation (Babbitt 1993; Bartky 1990; Collins 2000). Most definitions of adaptive preferences include internalized oppressive beliefs but also include other attitudes and behaviors. Unlike false consciousness, however, the concept of adaptive preference does not suggest that people who have them are dupes; adaptive preferences may be what Amartya Sen would call "positionally objective," views that any rational person would develop given similar social positioning and life experiences (Sen 2009, 157–164).

Some suggest that adaptive preferences should be defined as limited aspirations. Some subset of adaptive preferences fit this description, but understanding adaptive preferences as aspiration deficits may suggest that it is the presence or absence of, rather than the character of, aspirations that AP interventions should be concerned about. As Tanya Burchardt notes (Burchardt 2009), aspirations are shaped by our social contexts, and sometimes in ways that are harmful (see also Conradie and Robeyns 2013). The aspiration to be a "good wife" who does not deserve a beating is still an aspiration. Additionally, to avoid suggesting that it is always good for people to desire more than what they have, a view of APs as aspiration limitations needs to say something about what people should aspire to.

Agency is the ability to influence the world in ways that are chosen to be "congruent with one's values" (Alkire 2008, 455). If agency is understood value-neutrally, in a way that measures its presence relative to what a person values rather than what some external conception holds they should value, many paradigmatic cases of adaptive preference do not involve agency deficits (Khader 2015, 359–361). A woman who accepts domestic violence because she has taken the goal of not being an unruly wife does not experience a lack of agency; not challenging the goals of unjust social structures may help an oppressed person achieve well-being within the constraints of that structure (Khader 2014; see also Bruckner 2009; Kosko 2012; George 2015). Attempts to argue that adaptive preferences are agency deficits can try to solve this problem by defining agency as the pursuit of well-being (see Kabeer 1999). These end up roughly identical to the well-being accounts described earlier but with the added undesirable implication that deprivation-perpetuating preferences that exist under bad conditions cannot be self-interested.

More helpful ways of understanding the relationship between adaptive preferences and agency do not take lack of agency to be a defining feature of adaptive preference. Instead, one may argue that a goal of AP interventions is to form flourishing-compatible preferences that also enhance agency and autonomy (Olsaretti 2005; Khader 2011). On this type of view, interventions should emphasize strategies that promote flourishing but that are capable of being approved and recognized by people with APs and are arrived at through engagement with agent's existing perspectives. Additionally, a specific type of agency – the ability to affect public life and participate in public deliberation – may be particularly important in overcoming APs (Kabeer 2011; Sen 2004, 1999; Alkire 2006; Nussbaum 1999; Khader 2016; Crocker 2008). Since APs exist because of social and political conditions that favor the rich and powerful, enhancing the political agency of people with adaptive preferences can help them scrutinize and overcome adaptive preferences, as well as promote change of the conditions that cause adaptive preferences to form.

Paternalism concerns

Paternalism involves treating a person as though they are not the best judge of their own interests. Development approaches that see adaptive preferences as a problem inevitably face paternalism charges; the idea of adaptive preference requires the view that people's own beliefs and behaviors can undermine their well-being. I discuss some paternalism-related worries later in the chapter and suggest some ways adaptive preference theorists might respond.

Do adaptive preferences exist?

Adaptive preference cases have played an important role in justifying theories about what ethical development is. Yet philosophers notoriously rely on improbable examples. If preferences do not actually exist in the form they are imagined, then a development ethics focused on responding to them risks focusing on the wrong phenomena – or worse, risks causing misunderstandings of people's psyches or the conditions of their lives. A body of theory, especially in postcolonial feminism, claims that theorists exaggerate or misrepresent the problem of adaptive preference (see Baber 2007; Jaggar 2005; Jaggar 2006; Agarwal 1997; Narayan 2002; Khader 2011, 2012; Clark 2012; Neff 2014). For instance, Bina Agarwal (1997) famously argues that what Amartya Sen saw as South Asian women internalizing the belief that they deserved less food than men actually involved their accessing food covertly. In Agarwal's example, women who seemed to accept the belief that women were entitled to lesser or worse food than men were actually doing their best to ensure the favor of their husbands on whom their well-being depended. The women also sometimes ate in secret or feigned spirit possession to access off-limits foods. The risks of misunderstanding and worsening the lives of deprived people seems endemic to development, especially because of power inequalities between theorists and practitioners on one hand, and intended development beneficiaries, on the other.

Disrespect concerns

One worry underlying the controversy about whether adaptive preferences exist simply reminds us of the importance of treating oppressed and deprived people as agents whose decisions about their lives deserve to be respected. Uma Narayan argues that Western feminists tend to see "other" women as "dupes of patriarchy" who are "engulfed" by oppressive views of themselves (Narayan 2002). It seems condescending to treat people who seem to have adaptive preferences as generally possessed of defective moral and psychological capacities (Baber 2007; Begon 2014). A theory of adaptive preference may respond to this concern, first by rejecting the idea that adaptive preferences are usually deficits in the type of autonomy that authorizes one to make one's own life decisions (Khader 2011). A second type of response is to see adaptive preferences as capable of coexisting with healthy values and reject the view that people's entire selves become co-opted by oppression and deprivation (see Meyers 2002; Lugones 2003; Khader 2011). Adaptive preferences may be divided into sub-types that do not involve complete adaptation, such as those caused by selective value distortion and those wherein an agent is making tradeoffs forced by circumstances outside of her control (Khader 2013). Once it is acknowledged that most people with adaptive preferences maintain rational capacities, a theory of adaptive preference can also argue that oppressed and deprived people must be consulted and deliberated with about attempts to improve their lives (Khader 2011).

Culture concerns

Alison Jaggar notes that most adaptive preference theorists live in the North and most of those theorized about life in the global South (Jaggar 2005). This raises questions about whether what looks like adaptive preference is really just morally unproblematic cultural difference. This concern need not be relativist, since it is possible to believe some practices should be eradicated or transformed without believing all of them should (see Tamale 2005). One way a theory of adaptive preference can avoid ethnocentrism is by recognizing the presence of flourishing-promoting values in all cultures and by attempting to identify adaptive preferences from some cross-culturally agreed upon standpoint (Khader 2011; Nussbaum 2001). For instance, the values embedded in the notion of human rights, though they continue to be controversial, can no longer be thought of as the values of a specific culture. Additionally, a theory of adaptive preference need not assume that replicating Northern and Western practices is the solution. Knowing that something is an adaptive preference involves knowing what is wrong with the preference, but not necessarily which thick, specific preferences should replace it (Khader 2011: 136–171). It may thus be possible to attempt to transform APs without a particular idea of what they should be transformed into. For example, ending severe female genital cutting may be done by creating new, culturally embedded, coming-of-age rituals rather than doing away with such rituals altogether (James 1998; Wanawake 2007). However, avoiding ethnocentrism also depends heavily on the ability of development theorists and practitioners to hear those who are not like them (Jaggar 2006; Chambers 1994), and it is important for those working with marginalized and "othered" populations to cultivate the relevant skills (Khader 2010; Kapoor 2002; Gujit and Shah 1998; Young 1997).

Ineffectiveness concerns

Interventions based on a paternalistic fantasy of adaptive preference are also likely to have harmful effects. Such ineffective or misplaced interventions are likely in two types of cases: a) where those intervening lack the contextual knowledge required to understand the well-being effects of existing preferences (Charusheela 2008) or b) cases where people with suspected adaptive preferences are doing the best they can to promote their well-being but face limitations that are out of their control (Ackerly 2000; Agarwal 1997; Narayan 2002; Tobin 2009; Khader 2011). Both situations are involved in Agarwal's example discussed earlier. According to her, those who see women as accepting a lesser claim on food a) miss women's clandestine food consumption through secret picnics, feigning spirit possession, etc., and b) ignore the fact that being a "good wife" is the best path to food security in a society where their access to many goods depends on male patronage. If these women were also critical of gender inequality, a development intervention designed to, say, increase their self-esteem, would be of little use.

To respond to such worries, a theory of adaptive preference must acknowledge the significant barriers to understanding why another person appears to participate in her own oppression and deprivation. Practitioners engaged in adaptive preference interventions must have rich knowledge of the contexts in which they intervene. It is difficult to see how they can gain adequate knowledge without attention to the first-person perspectives of suspected adaptive preference bearers, so oppressed and deprived people should be involved in diagnosing their own suspected adaptive preferences and deciding what is to be done about them (Khader 2011; Conradie and Robeyns 2013). Strategies for change that people with adaptive preferences participate in crafting are particularly likely to be effective in improving their lives.

Adaptive preference theories might also do well to assume that people do not usually desire what is bad for them (Khader 2012). What looks like devaluing of a functioning may be weighing one valuable functioning against another because it is impossible to achieve both (Khader 2011; Ackerly 2000), so development ethicists should be cautious about "psychologizing the structural" and assuming that adaptive preferences are caused by defects in people rather than defects in the world (Khader 2011, 55–58; see also Begon 2014). Rather than valuing subordination for its own sake, Agarwal's women weigh long-term food security (and other goods associated with kinship) over household bargaining power and short-term access to food. The options of the oppressed and deprived are shaped by forces out of their control in ways that make it difficult to simply read what they really value of their behaviors. Development practitioners should thus not assume that psychological interventions are always the most effective solution.

Future directions

Oppression and deprivation often reproduce themselves through the attitudes, beliefs, and behaviors of those who are subject to them. Development ethicists cannot ignore this fact, but they must theorize about adaptive preferences in ways that avoid treating deprived individuals and communities as objects of disrespect. To do so, we must refuse to assume that all preferences that are unfamiliar to theorists and development practitioners as adaptive and take seriously the fact that people who participate in their deprivation are often rational autonomous agents. Much work remains to be done to prevent theorizing about adaptive preferences from reproducing the real-world inequalities to which it attempts to respond. Work about the ways in which advantage and luxury distort the preferences of the powerful would be helpful in this regard. Many questions about the relationship between adaptive preferences and agency also remain unanswered; we lack a conceptual apparatus that clearly explains the types of agency expansion that would benefit people with adaptive preferences – at least one that does not inadvertently entail distorting and condescending views about people with adaptive preferences. To take seriously the challenges raised by critics, it is important for adaptive preference theorists to engage with empirical literature about the actual reasons people become complicit in their deprivation and the challenges practitioners face to understanding these reasons.

References

Ackerly, B. (2000) *Political Theory and Feminist Social Criticism*. Cambridge University Press, Cambridge.

Agarwal, B. (1997) Bargaining and Gender Relations: Within and Beyond the Household. *Feminist Economics* 3(1): 1–51.

Alkire, S. (2006) Public Debate and Value Construction in Sen's Approach. In Kaufman, A. ed., *Capabilities Equality: Basic Issues and Problems*. Routledge, New York, 133–150.

Alkire, S. (2008) Concepts and Measures of Agency. In *Arguments for A Better World*. Oxford University Press, Oxford, 455–474.

Babbitt, S. (1993) Feminism and Objective Interests: The Role of Transformation experiences in Rational Deliberation. In Potter, L.A.E. ed., *Feminist Epistemologies*. Routledge, New York, 245–265.

Baber, H.E. (2007) Adaptive Preference. *Social Theory and Practice* 33(1 (January)): 105–126.
Bartky, S. (1990) *Femininity and Domination: Studies in the Phenomenology of Oppression*. Routledge, New York.
Begon, J. (2014) What Are Adaptive Preferences? *Journal of Applied Philosophy* 32(3): 241–257.
Bruckner, D. (2009) In Defense of Adaptive Preferences. *Philosophical Studies* 142(3): 307–324.
Burchardt, T. (2009) Agency Goals, Adaptation, and Capability Sets. *Journal of Human Development and Capabilities* 10(1).
Chambers, R. (1994) All Power Deceived. *IDS Bulletin* 25(2).
Charusheela, S. (2008) Social Analysis and the Capabilities Approach. *Cambridge Journal of Economics* 33(6): 1–18.
Christman, J. (2014) Coping or Oppression: Autonomy and Adaptation to Circumstance. In Veltman, A. and Piper, M. eds., *Autonomy, Oppression, and Gender*. Oxford University Press, New York, 201–227.
Clark, D.A. (2012) Adaptation and Development – Issues, Evidence, and Policy Relevance. In Clark, D.A. ed., *Adaptation, Poverty, and Development*. Palgrave, London.
Colburn, B. (2011) Autonomy and Adaptive Preferences. *Utilitas* 23(1): 52–71.
Collins, P.H. (2000) *Black Feminist Thought*. Routledge, New York.
Conradie, I. and Robeyns, I. (2013) Aspirations and Human Development Interventions. *Journal of Human Development and Capabilities* 14(4): 559–580.
Crocker, D. (2008) *Ethics of Global Development: Agency, Capability, and Deliberative Democracy*. Cambridge University Press, Cambridge.
Drydyk, J. (2011) Development Ethics. In Chatterjee, D. and Drydyk, J. eds., *Encyclopedia of Global Justice*. Springer, New York.
Elster, J. (1987) *Sour Grapes: Studies in the Subversion of Rationality*. Cambridge University Press, Cambridge.
Friedman, M. (2006) *Autonomy, Gender, Politics*. Clarendon Press, New York.
George, A. (2015) Explicating the Capability Approach through the Voices of the Poor. *Journal of Human Development and Capabilities* 16(1): 33–46.
Gujit, I. and Shah M.K., eds. (1998) *The Myth of Community: Gender Issues in Participatory Development* Stylus. London.
Jaggar, A. (2005) Saving Amina: Global Justice for Women and Intercultural Dialogue. *Ethics and International Affairs* 19(Fall): 55–75.
Jaggar, A. (2006) Reasoning About Well Being: Nussbaum's Methods of Justifying the Capabilities Approach. *The Journal of Political Philosophy* 14(3): 301–322.
Jakobsen, H. (2014) What's Gendered about Gender-Based Violence: An Empirically Grounded Theoretical Exploration from Tanzania. *Gender and Society* 28(4): 537–561.
James, S.M. (1998) Shades of Othering: Reflections on Female Circumcision/Female Genital Mutilation. *Signs* 23(2): 1031–1048.
Kabeer, N. (1999) Resources, Agency, Achievements: Reflections on the Measurement of Women's Empowerment. *Development and Change* 30(3): 435–464.
Kabeer, N. (2011) Between Affiliation and Autonomy: Navigating Pathways of Women's Empowerment and Gender Justice in Rural Bangladesh. *Development and Change* 42(2): 499–528.
Kapoor, I. (2002) The Devil's in the Theory. *Third-World Quarterly* 23(1): 101–117.
Khader, S. (2012) Must Theorizing About Adaptive Preferences Deny Women's Agency. *Journal of Applied Philosophy* 29(4): 302–317.
Khader, S.J. (2009) Adaptive Preferences and Procedural Autonomy. *Journal of Human Development and Capabilities* 10(2): 169–187.
Khader, S.J. (2010) Beyond Inadvertent Ventriloquism: Caring Virtues for Participatory Development. *Hypatia* 25(1): 742–761.
Khader, S.J. (2011) *Adaptive Preferences and Women's Empowerment*. Oxford University Press, Oxford.
Khader, S.J. (2013) Identifying Adaptive Preferences in Practice: Lessons from Postcolonial Feminisms. *Journal of Global Ethics* 9(3): 311–327.
Khader, S.J. (2014) Empowerment Through Self-Subordination: Microcredit and Women's Self Respect. In Meyers, D. ed., *Poverty, Agency, and Human Rights*. Oxford University Press, New York, 223–249.

Khader, S.J. (2015) Development Ethics, Gender Complementarianism, and Intrahousehold Inequality. *Hypatia* 30(2): 352–369.

Khader, S.J. (2016) Beyond Autonomy Fetishism: Affiliation with Autonomy in Women's Empowerment. *Journal of Human Development and Capabilities* 17(1): 125–139.

Kosko, S.J. (2012) Adapting to Feasible Means or Ends. *Journal of Human Development and Capabilities* 13(3): 415–450.

Lugones, M. (2003) Structure/Anti-Structure and Agency Under Oppression. *Pilgrimages/Peregrinajes* Rowman and Littlefield, Lanham MD.

MacKenzie, C. (2008) Relational Autonomy, Normative Authority and Perfectionism. *Journal of Social Philosophy* 39: 512–533.

Mackenzie, C. (2015) Responding to the Agency Dilemma: Autonomy, Adaptive Preferences, and Internalized Oppression. *Personal Autonomy and Social Oppression* 48–68.

Meyers, D. (2002) *Gender and the Mirror*. Oxford University Press, New York.

Nagar, R.a.S.R. (2003) Women, NGOs, and the Paradoxes of Empowerment and Disempowerment. *Antipode* XXX: 1–13.

Narayan, U. (2002) Minds of Their Own: Choices, Autonomy, Cultural Practices, and Other Women. In Boulder, L.M.A.a.C.E.W. ed., *A Mind of One's Own: Feminist Essays on Reason and Objectivity*. Westview, Boulder.

Neff, D. (2014) Adaptation, Poverty, and Well-being: Evidence from South India. In Clark, D.A. ed., *Adaptation, Poverty, and Development*. Palgrave, London, 137–157.

Nussbaum, M.C. (1999) *Sex and Social Justice*. Oxford University Press, Oxford.

Nussbaum, M.C. (2001) *Women and Human Development: The Capabilities Approach*. Cambridge University Press, Cambridge.

Olsaretti, S. (2005) Endorsement and Freedom in Amartya Sen's Capability Approach. *Economics and Philosophy* 21: 89–108.

Qizilbash, M. (2012) Utilitarianism, Adaptation, and Paternalism. In Clark, D.A. ed., *Poverty, Adaptation, and Development*. Palgrave, London, 35–60.

Raz, J. (1988) *The Morality of Freedom*. Clarendon Press, Oxford.

Robeyns, I. (2003) Sen's Capability Approach and Gender Inequality. *Feminist Economics*.

Sen, A. (1988) *On Ethics and Economics*. Blackwell, Malden MA.

Sen, A. (1990) Gender and Cooperative Conflicts. in Tinker, I. ed., *Persistent Inequalities: Women and World Development*. Oxford University Press, Oxford.

Sen, A. (1999) *Development as Freedom*. Knopf, New York.

Sen, A. (2004) Capabilities Lists and Public Reason. *Feminist Economics* 10: 77–80.

Sen, A. (2009) *The Idea of Justice*. Harvard University Press, Cambridge.

Stoljar, N. (2000) Autonomy and the Feminist Intuition. In Stoljar, C.M.a.N. ed., *Relational Autonomy: Feminist Perspectives on Autonomy, Agency, and the Social Self*. Oxford University Press, Oxford.

Stoljar, N. (2014) Autonomy and Adaptive Preference Formation. In Veltman, A. and Piper, M. eds., *Autonomy, Oppression, and Gender*. Oxford University Press, New York.

Tamale, S. (2005) Eroticism, Sexuality, and Women's Secrets Among the Baganda. *Feminist Africa* 9–34.

Terlazzo, R. (2016) Conceptualizing Adaptive Preferences Respectfully: An Indirectly Substantive Account. *Journal of Political Philosophy* 24(2): 206–226.

Teschl, M. and Comim, F. (2005) Adaptive Preferences and Capabilities: Some Preliminary Conceptual Explorations *Review of Social Economy* LXIII(2): 230–246.

Tobin, T. (2009) Using Rights to Counter Gender-Specific Wrongs. *Human Rights Review* 10: 521–530.

Wanawake, M.Y. (2007) FGM – Advocacy Strategy for the Eradication of Female Genital Mutilation in Kenya. Taver Network Solutions 2000.

Whyte, K. (2013) Indigenous Women, Climate Change Impacts, and Collective Action. *Hypatia* 29(3).

Young, I.M. (1997) *Intersecting Voices: Dilemmas of Gender, Political Philosophy and Policy*. Princeton University Press, Princeton.

Part III
Social and global justice

There is a broad consensus that worthwhile development must be "equitable." Minimally, this identifies unequal development (which creates or expands inequalities) as maldevelopment. A stronger version might require worthwhile development to reduce unjust inequalities; development that reproduces social and global inequalities rather than reducing them would fail to meet this higher standard. It is often unequal development that is excluded when "development" is used with a normative meaning. Okun and Richardson once commented that Kuwait is a country "which has an exceedingly high level of per capita income but which, by no stretch of the imagination, can be considered a developed country." Their reason: the per capita income was inflated by oil royalties that were captured by the royal family, whereas "almost the entire population lives in poverty" (Okun and Richardson 1961, 233). In a similar vein, Dudley Seers argued in his well-known "Meaning of Development" address that

> One cannot really say that there has been development for the world as a whole, when the benefits of technical progress have accrued to minorities which were already relatively rich, whether we are speaking of minorities within nations or the minority of nations which are rich.
>
> *(Seers 1969, 6)*

Nevertheless, there is rich disagreement about exactly what social and global justice require. In addition, the specific inequalities to which particular groups are subjected (e.g., women, indigenous peoples, minorities, and children) should arguably be understood in their specificity.

In the past, theorists of social and global justice have not always been well informed about development, and development theorists, captivated by the concept of growth, were not well informed about liberal-egalitarian theories of social and global justice. Julian Culp discusses some ways in which these two solitudes have been broken down to allow for more dialogue between them. Further attacks on these barriers were led by feminist critiques of gender injustice in development (see also Chapter 11 in this *Handbook*), human rights demands (see also Chapter 24, The Right to Development), and demands for environmental (and intergenerational) sustainability (see also Chapter 20 in this *Handbook*). The barriers are broken down most

DOI: 10.4324/9781315626796-12

decisively by the capability approach, which achieves a kind of "dialectical enrichment" between theories of development and theories of justice.

In her chapter on gender inequalities, Christine Koggel discusses interactions between development frameworks and feminist frameworks for addressing gender inequalities, adding a further interaction with feminist movements. Koggel begins by focusing on the conceptual shift from women to gender and shows that, while this shift was driven initially by Western feminist theorists, further critical insights emerged from women's movements and activism in a global context. In a concluding section she discusses contemporary work on gender inequalities and what remains to be done to understand and address them in theory and in practice.

Drawing from the South Pacific as well as Latin America, Krushil Watene and Roger Merino discuss the particular requirements of worthwhile development for Indigenous peoples. They argue that Indigenous people's self-determination, which is acknowledged in international law, is essential, and this entails institutional transformation consistent with the creation of cultural, economic, political, and environmental conditions that nourish the well-being of Indigenous communities. They show how decolonization and Indigenous philosophies are vital to these goals.

Frances Stewart discusses horizontal inequalities between groups of people, as distinct from vertical inequalities among individuals. These are important first because they have a critical bearing on individual capabilities and, second, because large horizontal inequalities are almost invariably unjust. Stewart also shows how horizontal inequalities relate to the other goals of worthwhile development.

No one would deny that worthwhile development requires proper attention to childhood. However, as Flavio Comim argues, this is not simply a matter of child *welfare*. It is also a far-reaching matter of *justice*, because the inequalities and injustices that a person faces later in life can be heavily influenced by the kind of childhood the person experienced. Poverty and underdevelopment cannot only frustrate families' capacity to meet their children's material and educational needs but can also undermine parenting practices in other ways, impacting the children's emotional and developmental needs. Sequences of negative consequences can form intergenerational chains of transmission for poverty and inequality.

Similarly, Sridhar Venkatapuram argues that while health is an important component of well-being, health outcomes in development can also raise questions about social justice. Recent research on the determinants of health shows that health outcomes are profoundly affected by social hierarchies. As Venkatapuram argues, by showing that health is affected by all basic social institutions, not just the health care system, this research in effect challenges many distributivist assumptions in Anglo-American theories of social justice. The chapter presents some basic findings of social epidemiology and implications for theories of justice, as well as future directions.

References

Okun, B. and Richardson, R.W. (1961) Economic Development: Concepts and Meaning. In Okun, B. and Richardson, R.W. eds., *Studies in Economic Development*. Holt, Rinehart and Winston, New York, 230–237.

Seers, D. (1969) The Meaning of Development. *International Development Review* 11(4): 2–6.

10

Social and global justice

Models of development and theories of justice

Julian Culp

Ever since the publication of John Rawls's *A Theory of Justice* (1971) moral and political philosophers have engaged intensively in discussing various kinds and aspects of liberal-egalitarian theories of justice (cf. Arneson 2006 for an overview). Some participants of this debate have extended Rawls's ideas and articulated liberal-egalitarian theories of justice that claim worldwide rather than merely domestic validity (Beitz 1979; Pogge 1989, 1994; Gosepath 2001; Moellendorf 2002; Tan 2004; Caney 2005). This wide-ranging and subtle theorizing of justice has had a considerable impact on development ethics. The aim of this chapter is to explore in some depth one particular way in which this impact has unfolded: it critically reconstructs how liberal-egalitarian theories of justice have shaped normative understandings of social development.

But before explaining how theories of social and global justice have left a mark on this area of development ethics, I begin by clarifying the similar meanings of justice and development as well as the difference between theories of social and global justice. In the following section I recall that an economic growth–based understanding of development has dominated several development conceptions in the 20th century and highlight that economic growth is an aggregative indicator that stands in tension with the idea of individual rights that is part and parcel of liberal theories of justice. Then, in the next section, I illustrate how feminist, human rights, and sustainability have offered alternatives to the economic growth–based development understanding. In the following section I show how basic needs and capabilities approaches have fundamentally criticized this development understanding. While these approaches have already drawn upon several intuitions that are central to liberal-egalitarian theories of justice, they have not conceptually tied together theories of justice and development. But in the next section I present Martha Nussbaum's justice-based development understanding, which has at last drawn an explicit and clear connection between justice and development. In addition, in this section I also point at additional ways in which such a connection could be made. Given the similarity of the meanings of justice and development it appears curious – at least in retrospect – how long it has taken until normative theorists have systematically interwoven their understandings of justice and development.

It should not come as a surprise, however, that the concept of development is linked to that of justice. As Denis Goulet has argued, it is important to distinguish between *worthwhile development* on the one hand and *undesirable maldevelopment* on the other. But in order to draw such a

DOI: 10.4324/9781315626796-13

distinction, it is necessary to employ a normative concept such as justice for determining under which conditions it is appropriate to speak of worthwhile rather than of undesirable (mal) development. Indeed, several sections of this *Handbook* analyze alternative ways of drawing on concepts such as well-being, empowerment, environmental sustainability and human rights that can be employed to demarcate the boundaries between worthwhile development and undesirable maldevelopment.

The plurality of these concepts raises the further question of how to think of development when the specific ways in which these various normative concepts substantiate the meaning of development give rise to conflicting claims. Many theorists of justice follow Rawls's (1971, 5) dictum that "justice is the first virtue of social institutions" and maintain that justice is the decisive concept for distinguishing worthwhile development from undesirable maldevelopment. But, of course, other normative theorists contest that claim. Thus development ethicists do not only engage in discussions regarding which theory of social or global justice is best for conceiving development, but also debate as to which normative concept – justice, well-being, empowerment, etc. – should be used for specifying one's understanding of development.

The similar meanings of justice and development

Social justice is an "essentially contested concept" (Gallie 1956), in that there is a shared core meaning of justice, but disagreement about how to understand it best. Following Rawls (1971, 5), social justice's core meaning is that "no arbitrary distinctions are made between persons in the assigning of basic rights and duties." Various *conceptions* of social justice interpret and determine differently what it means to avoid such arbitrary distinctions (Hart 1961, 155–159). Accordingly, various theories of social justice interpret the core meaning of justice in a distinct manner. In particular, they differ regarding the *content* and *scope* of justice. The content of a conception of social justice that its principles express refers to the *metric* and *rules* it deems valid (cf. Anderson 2010). The metric of social justice determines the type of justice-relevant goods by reference to which demands of social justice are made. Candidates include utility – that is, the experience of pleasure or its opposite – resources and opportunities. The rules of social justice specify how these goods are to be distributed. For example, an egalitarian rule holds that everyone should have an equal amount of the justice-relevant goods, whereas a sufficientarian rule requires merely that all should have enough thereof. Justice-relevant goods might be monetary resources such as income and wealth, effective opportunities or capabilities to do certain things or enjoy certain states of being, or specific legal rights that confer upon the rights-holder a particular standing. The scope of social justice means the reach of the population to which a certain content of justice applies. It can be limited to a city, a state or a continent, or span the entire world.

For my purposes here, theories of *social justice* differ from theories of *global social justice* (henceforth global justice) regarding their understanding of the scope of non-sufficientarian principles. Different from theories of global justice, theories of social justice restrict the scope of such principles to the boundaries of states. Non-sufficientarian principles are comparative and determine persons' rights to certain goods relative to how much others possess of these goods. Some theorists of social justice (Blake 2001; Brock 2009; Miller 2007) – so-called *weak statists* – recognize that justice requires the fulfillment of sufficientarian principles of justice everywhere. They demand, for example, that all individuals globally should enjoy sufficient autonomy, that is, a decent range of choices (Blake 2001). *Strong statists*, by contrast, deny that any requirements of justice apply outside the state (Nagel 2005). But all statist theorists agree that comparative, non-sufficientarian principles of justice are only valid inside the state. (On the distinction between weak and strong statism, see Cohen and Sabel 2006, 150.) Theorists of global justice do not limit the scope of comparative, non-sufficientarian principles of justice in this manner. *Globalists* (Beitz 1979; Pogge 1989; Moellendorf 2002; Tan 2004) hold that certain egalitarian principles of justice are valid among all individuals globally, and *internationalists* (Rawls 1999; Pettit 2010; Culp 2014) maintain that inter-state relations should be governed by comparative principles. Whereas globalists believe that principles of global justice should regulate the arrangements of a global society of individuals, the internationalists hold that such principles should regulate a society of states.

In these ways theories of social and global justice offer critical standards that they express in terms of social arrangements that would be either more just or perfectly just. As I show in this chapter, these theories thus assume a critical function that is analogous to normative theories of development. For these latter theories also provide critical standards on the basis of which it is possible to scrutinize social arrangements regarding their degree of development. Rather surprisingly, however, relatively few normative development theories are informed by theories of justice. Consequently the normative ideas inherent in the various kinds of theories of justice have not been fully explored in the normative literature on development so far. Thus there is still further room for theorists of justice and development ethicists to engage in a fruitful academic dialogue. In the Conclusion I predict that this dialogue is most likely to continue in the future, as concerns of intergenerational and climate justice have recently garnered substantial attention from both kinds of normative theorists.

There is a variety of theories of social development – or theories of development, for short – and it is important to distinguish between their normative and descriptive features (cf. Sen 1988; Greig et al. 2007, 240–242; Hopper 2012, 3). The difference between these two sorts of features refers to whether these theories make normative claims about how social affairs *should* develop or empirical claims about how such affairs *actually* develop. These two sorts of features stem from two corresponding usages of the term 'development.' In its descriptive use this term simply means 'transition,' 'changeover,' 'trend,' or 'change.' Following this usage, theories of development aim at determining the most decisive explanatory factors that account for such a transition or changeover. In its normative use, by contrast, development refers to a "worthwhile development" (Goulet), a "desired alternative" (Goulet 1995, 1), a "good change" (Chambers 1997, vi), or a transition "from a less human to a more human phase" (Lebret 1960, cited in Goulet 1995, 6). The core meaning of this usage is thus that of social progress. Accordingly the *Human Development Report 2010* (UNDP 2010, 11) claims that its normative conception of human development "is the best way of thinking about human progress."

So theorists of development conceptions discuss, first, the normative criteria relative to which social progress should be measured or, put differently, the normative ends that constitute development. Second, they offer competing accounts of the means by which development should be achieved. That is, they involve alternative social-scientific ideas regarding the instruments that are conducive for realizing the normative ends of development. In this way normative theorists of development pursue aims that are similar to those of theorists of social and global justice. This is because by offering accounts of worthwhile development or social progress, normative theorists of development, like theorists of justice, outline a social ideal or provide a normative source of critique of existing social arrangements. For in the same way in which theorists of justice ask what ideally just arrangements would entail and what would effectively reduce injustice today, normative theorists of development consider what should be the ultimate goal of social change and criticize actual social conditions for reflecting an insufficiently developed or progressive state of affairs.

Despite these similarities between the aims and critical functions of the normative usage of the two concepts, however, it has taken a considerable amount of time before scholars have undertaken efforts to inform normative theories of development on the basis of theories of justice. One central reason for this is that throughout most of the second half of the 20th century development theorists have taken for granted that the normative end of development is economic growth (Rodan-Rosenstein 1943; Nurkse 1953; Myrdal 1957). Indeed, this view of development has come under fierce attack in the 1960s. Nevertheless economic growth has continued to be used as sole indicator of development throughout most of the second half of the 20th century. Consequently these theorists disagreed primarily regarding their explanations as to which kind of factors would be key for spurring economic growth, and thereby neglected normative discussions. In the next section, development theories that have posited economic growth as the end of development are summarized. The two sections that follow this illustrate how feminist, basic needs and capabilities approaches to development have already questioned this economic growth-based understanding of development, before I explain, in a further section, how theories of social and global justice have been used to systematically conceptualize anew the understanding of development.

Development as economic growth: modernization theory, dependency theory, and the 'Washington Consensus'

The two most influential development conceptions that emerged in the beginning of the second half of the 20th century were modernization and dependency theory. Both of these theories understand development primarily as that kind of social change that generates a greater production of goods and services, that is, economic growth (cf. Greig et al. 2007, 73). They also share one commonality regarding the means of development, as they attribute a major role to the state in leading the development process. Yet dependency and modernization theories nevertheless differ quite radically in their analysis of the factors that the state should try to influence. Modernization theory stresses the *endogenous* cultural, infrastructural, and technological prerequisites for economic growth (Rostow 1960; Inkeles 1966). Dependency theory by contrast emphasizes growth-relevant *exogenous* factors such as the terms of trade among states (Cardoso and Faletto 1979; Frank 1975). The so-called Washington Consensus, which emerged in the 1980s, agrees with these two initial theories that economic growth is the normative end of development (Williamson 1990; Krueger 1990; Krugman 1995; cf. also Rapley 2007, ch. 4; Fukuda-Parr 2011). The novelty of the Washington Consensus concerns its view on the means of development, as it claims that market mechanisms that are maximally unrestrained from government intervention are optimal for economic growth. Furthermore, like modernization theory, the Washington Consensus emphasizes the importance of an endogenous transformation of the economic, legal, and political framework so as to facilitate a stable environment for entrepreneurial activity. Yet in addition, like dependency theory, it also recognizes the relevance of exogenous factors such as trade relations. But different from dependency theorists that favors import substitution policies, it holds that free trade is economically most beneficial.

Feminist, human rights, and sustainability approaches to development

Several novel approaches to development arose due to frustrations associated with development policies that had economic growth as their target. These frustrations reached their climax in the 1980s, which is often referred to as a 'lost decade,' because economic growth has been very slow during that period (UNDP 1997, ch. 1). But rather than attempting to find better means for spurring such growth, these novel approaches propose alternative ends of development. They consist of loose clusters of ideas concerning gender justice, human rights and intergenerational justice, which are regarded as key considerations for conceiving worthwhile development. While these approaches widen the view on possible ends of development, they do not yet represent elaborate theories of justice-based development.

Concerns of gender justice and women's empowerment had started entering development thinking from the 1970s onwards. Studies of scholars such as Boserup (1970) and Deere (1976) show that women in many cases facilitate the introduction of wage labor through non-remunerated care work and small-scale subsistence farming. This work not only renders women especially vulnerable; it is also associated with low degrees of social esteem, relative to the higher degrees of social esteem associated with the wage labor carried out by men. This feminist approach to development thinking laid the basis for the 1976–1985 United Nations (UN) Decade for Women and found an even more articulate expression in the 1985 Nairobi Women's Conference. It also gained further international recognition at the 1993 UN General Assembly on the Elimination of Violence Against Women, the 1993 Vienna Human Rights Conference and the 1995 Beijing Women's Conference.

Under the heading of Women in Development (WID) feminist concerns have been integrated or mainstreamed in development policy and discourse by several international organizations such as UNDP. However, this process unfolded slowly and did not lead to immediate success. Thus the World Bank (2001, 1) observed that "[g]ender discrimination remains pervasive in many dimensions of life – worldwide. This is so despite considerable advances in gender equality in recent decades." The concerns of WID focused on educating and training women in ways that would allow them to access wage labor in formal markets. Feminist scholars such as Tinker (1990) argued that this would benefit not only women but also economic development.

Other feminist development scholars (Elson and Pearson 1981) criticized this economistic orientation and emphasized that the productive male laborer should not be taken as the ideal that women should try to emulate. In addition, feminist scholars (Sen and Grown 1987) associated with the international network Development Alternatives with Women for a New Era (DAWN) emphasized women's distinct knowledge that should be harnessed for more gender-sensitive development policies. Based on a similar kind of standpoint epistemology, so-called ecofeminists have argued that women would be especially well placed to address environmental problems (Mies and Shiva 1993). Their argument to that effect has been that environmental problems arise from patriarchal norms that regulate the capitalist economic order and which rely on a dichotomy between culture and nature that is environmentally harmful.

More recently, feminist scholars such as Khader (2014) have interrogated the nexus between income and women's agency. Khader (2014, 225) argues that successful poverty-reducing interventions may "leave gender inequality intact," contrary to the widely held assumption that income increases correlate positively with women's empowerment. When, for example, women accept being viewed as collateral from a microcredit agency, they might wind up supporting patriarchal norms *while* improving their incomes.

Remarkably, up until the mid-1980s development conceptions have not been shaped by international legal human rights, although the UN has called for the international recognition of these rights ever since the adoptions of the 1948 Universal Declaration of Human Rights, the 1976 International Covenant of Civil and Political Rights, and the 1976 International Covenant on Social and Economic Rights. One reason for this is that during the Cold War the U.S. and many of its allies aimed at marginalizing the idea that socio-economic human rights could possibly be as important as civil and political rights (Greig et al. 2007, 66–68). This resulted in a paradoxical situation in which, as David Forsythe (1997, 335) remarked aptly, "the United

Nations – in a fundamental contradiction – endorsed democracy but did not endorse democratic development."

This situation came to an end in 1986 with the adoption of the Declaration on the Right to Development (cf. UN 1986). In this declaration the UN (Art. 1) articulated clearly that persons and peoples are "entitled to participate in, contribute to, and enjoy economic, social, cultural and political development, in which all human rights and freedoms can be fully realized." Hence this "Development Declaration" pointed towards a novel development approach that demands the fulfillment of human rights. Later on this approach was further refined at the 1993 World Conference on Human Rights, the 1995 Fourth World Conference on Women and the 1995 World Summit for Social Development (cf. Hamm 2001, 1007). But although human rights are a central concern of several theories of justice, such theories of justice have not been employed for supporting the normative case for a theoretically more refined human rights-based understanding of development. It is important to note, however, that some normative theorists have emphasized that not only negative duties of non-interference but also positive duties correlate with at least some rights such as the right to subsistence (Shue 1980; Nickel 2005). The recognition of such positive duties allows arguing that if the international community wants to take such rights seriously, then it must actively support certain states' social and economic development.

Considerations of sustainability were eventually taken up in the formulation of the ends of development in the influential publication *Our Common Future* (United Nations World Commission on Environment and Development 1987). Published in 1987 by the World Commission on Environment and Development (ibid., para. 27), it calls for sustainable development that "meets the needs of the present without compromising the ability of future generations to meet their own needs." While this understanding of sustainable development draws attention to the natural conditions necessary for fulfilling human needs, it is resolutely anthropocentric, as it does not demand preserving nature as an intrinsic end. The anthropocentrism of the idea of sustainable development is also evident in the Rio-Declaration that resulted from the 1992 UN Conference on Environment and Development (1992, principle 1): "Human beings are at the center of concern for sustainable development." Thus the value added by the conception of sustainable development is not that of the intrinsic moral value of nature, but rather the recognition of concerns of intergenerational justice. However, this conception also did not rely on any particular theory of intergenerational justice.

Development as freedom: basic needs and capabilities

Another important impulse for normative development theorizing was the basic needs approach. From the early 1970s onwards this approach found considerable support from many practitioners working at international and non-governmental development organizations (McNamara 1973; Dag Hammarskjold Foundation 1974, 1975; International Labor Organization (ILO) 1976). This approach did not only put into question the economic growth–based development conception; it also sparked normative discussions that were crucial for formulating a sophisticated conception of human development, which was the first to be thoroughly informed by theories of justice.

The core idea of the basic needs approach is that development requires the fulfillment of all persons' basic needs. Amartya Sen (1984, 513–515) argued that this approach primarily calls for the provision of a certain bundle of goods such as nutrition, shelter, clean drinking water, and basic sanitation. In that way the basic needs approach is treated merely as an account of certain goods that are morally especially important. This neglects, however, that for many scholars of the basic needs approach the normative intuition behind this approach is more sophisticated.

These scholars argue that the fulfillment of basic needs matters in order to be able to choose among a decent range of options (Streeten and Burki 1978; Streeten 1981, 1984). Paul Streeten (1981, 21), for one, clarified that "the basic needs concept is a reminder that the objective of the development effort is to provide all human beings with the opportunity for a full life." Moreover, Doyal and Gough (1991) conceive the fulfillment of basic needs as necessary conditions for functioning in one's society and for avoiding severe harm (cf. also Gasper 2007). Thereby the basic needs approach offers the criticism that the materialism inherent in the idea that development simply means economic growth and highlights the moral importance of human freedom.

Ever since the 1980s Sen and Nussbaum have refined certain aspects of this approach much further and have thereby offered an even more subtle critique of the dominant conception of economic growth-based development. They have articulated a conception of development as freedom, which is also known as the human development conception. Similar to the basic needs approach, it argues that goods and services are only means but not the ends of development. Sen (1984, 10) expressed this idea pointedly as follows:

> [W]hile goods [. . .] are valuable, they are not valuable in themselves. Their value rests on what they can do for people, or rather, what people can do with these goods [. . .]. This question is an important one to emphasize because 'commodity fetishism' . . . is such a widespread phenomenon, and the important role that the exchange of commodities plays in modern societies tends to sustain that fetishism.

Sen and Nussbaum defend the idea that the end of development is to expand human freedoms (Sen 1989, 1999; Nussbaum 1992, 2000, 2011; cf. also Robeyns 2005, 2011). Sen (1997) and Nussbaum (1992) conceive these freedoms as effective opportunities to do certain things and to enjoy certain states of affairs. They call these freedoms 'capabilities.' In technical parlance, 'capabilities' refer to the effective freedoms to realize so-called functionings, which represent the various 'beings' and 'doings' that an individual may experience or exercise. So the real opportunity to be healthy or ride a bicycle is a capability. And the various combinations of functionings that an individual has the effective opportunity to choose constitute her capability set (Sen 1991, ch. 3). Different from the basic needs approach, however, the conception of development as freedom does not view solely those capabilities that one possess when one's basic needs are met as being of normative importance. This conception is broader and also asks bringing into view persons' other capabilities as "informational base" (Sen 1999, 55) when assessing development.

Using capabilities as such an informational base for measuring development, Sen and Nusssbaum criticize further that the availability of goods and services is a poor indicator for estimating development (Sen 1997 sect. 3; 1984, 510–511; 1991, 28–30, 36–38; 1999, 70–71; Nussbaum 2000, 60–61; 2011, 47–50, 56–58). For persons' 'conversion rates' that determine which and how many capabilities persons have relative to the goods that they possess can differ quite substantially. Depending on persons' internal features such as their metabolic rates and external features such as their political system, two persons' capabilities can vary greatly even if they possess the same amount and kinds of goods. That means that even if the economic growth–based development conception would regard material goods solely as a means rather than the end of development, it would still remain unsatisfactory.

Sen and Nussbaum's wide-ranging research on this topic has effectively discredited the economic growth–based development conception within scholarly circles. In addition, it also had a lasting impact on the way in which the international community measures development, because it has inspired the publication of the *Human Development Reports* from 1990 onwards (cf. Fukuda-Parr 2011, 126; McNeill 2007, 8). Emphasizing the importance of human freedom rather than goods, the first report (UNDP 1990, 9) states: "People are the real wealth of a nation."

Nevertheless there are also important differences in the way in which Sen and Nussbaum employ the capabilities approach. Sen – at least by and large – restricts himself to emphasizing the need for an appropriate informational base for measuring development. Thus he (1999, 33–34; cf. Nussbaum 2003, 33–36) is unwilling to argue in favor of a certain kind of moral hierarchy among alternative realizations of different sets of capabilities. Beitz (1986) criticized this aspect of Sen's work early on as it renders his work not particularly helpful for determining which particular course of action or policy should be chosen. Nussbaum, by contrast, defends a much more action guiding capability-based theory of justice as the basis for her conception of human development. Hence Nussbaum's conception of human development is directly informed by a particular conception of justice, which is why it is her work that reflects most clearly the impact of theories of justice on the normative conceptualization of development.

Justice-based development: outcome-oriented and democratic approaches

Nussbaum's theories of development and justice illustrate that due to the similar aims of theories of justice and development they can mutually inform each other in illuminating ways. In fact, this kind of 'dialectical enrichment' between theories of development and justice marked the very beginning of the capabilities approach to human development. Sen (1997) coined the term 'capability' in his 1979 "Equality of What?" Tanner Lecture on Human Value, in which he engaged with liberal theorists of justice who debated how to understand the basic demand that all persons ought to be treated equally. Sen argued that equality should be conceived in terms of equality among capability sets, rather than in terms of an equal amount of resources, or in terms of equality in the marginal utility deriving from the prevalent distribution of resources. In that way Sen's concern with the normative importance of capabilities stemmed from his engagement with discussions about the proper metric of justice, which in turn inspired Sen's conceptualization of development. But Sen has not used the capabilities approach to work out a full-fledged conception of justice, as he concentrates on defending an idea rather than a theory of justice (cf. Sen 2009). This idea consists of ranking alternative states of affairs rather than developing the principles of a perfectly just institutional order in the way in which Rawls (1971) has done this in his work.

Nussbaum, by contrast, articulates a distinct capabilities-based theory of justice. More specifically, she articulates and defends a partial theory of justice, which determines solely certain basic requirements of justice, but does not claim to represent all requirements of justice (cf. Nussbaum 2011, 63). Nussbaum (2003, 40; 2006, 75–79, 159–160, 292; 2011, 31) articulates her conception of justice by asking what is involved in leading a life worthy of human dignity, and by framing her answer in terms of which capabilities are of such central importance "that their removal makes a life not worthy of human dignity." She (2000, 72) substantiates what she means by human dignity as follows: "[The] core idea is that of the human being [. . .] who shapes his or her own life in cooperation and reciprocity with others, rather than being passively shaped or pushed around by the world in the manner of a 'flock' or 'herd' animal."

On that basis Nussbaum (2011, 33) defends her list of ten central capabilities as those that are necessary elements of a minimally flourishing life worthy of human dignity. These ten central capabilities are life; bodily health; bodily integrity; sense, imagination and thought; emotions; practical reason; affiliation; contact with other species; play; and control over one's environment (cf. Nussbaum 2011, 33–34). Nussbaum maintains that they should be fulfilled in every society and protected by constitutional means. Thereby she sets out a clear moral hierarchy among different capabilities. The ten central capabilities enjoy lexicographical priority and all must be realized fully for recognition of human dignity to be secured. They are not substitutable; the insufficient fulfillment of one cannot be compensated by a greater realization of another.

Nussbaum qualifies her understanding of the importance of these ten central capabilities by arguing that these express distinctively *political* demands of basic justice. As such, they are compatible with a plurality of competing yet reasonable understandings of what a good life consists. With this qualification Nussbaum (2000, 76–77; 2003, 42–43; 2006, 79, 297; 2011, 19) takes up a key insight of Rawls's *Political Liberalism* (1993). Therein Rawls (1993, 56–57) argues that "the burdens of judgment" make it the case that within free institutions the free exercise of reason renders this plurality a permanent feature of the social world. These burdens of judgment include that people make different experiences throughout their lives, that they differ on which empirical information they deem relevant for practical judgment, and that they have to rely on interpretations of moral and political concepts that are underspecified. Therefore one can only defend a *political* conception of justice that, in contrast to a *comprehensive* conception, is not based on a full-fledged or perfectionist account of the good life. This means, first, that the domain of a conception of justice should be restricted to questions of fundamental justice or constitutional essentials of social arrangements. That is, neither should a political conception of justice deal with all facets of the human experience, such as, for example, life after death; nor should it defend a particular view regarding what perfectly just social arrangements would involve. Second, the validity claim and the corresponding type of justification of a political conception is that of reasonableness and public justification, whereas those of a comprehensive conception are, respectively, truth and non-public justification. Accordingly, a theorist of justice must defend an account of the conditions under which a reasonable public justification is possible, rather than aiming at defending the true conception of justice on the basis of philosophical arguments alone.

Nussbaum's way of articulating a particular kind of capabilities-based conception of justice not only advances the theorization of justice by offering a subtle justification of the metric of justice, but also contributes to a more thorough understanding of development. Since Nussbaum's political conception of justice informs her normative development conception, the latter benefits from all of the normative ideas that are part of the former. For one, this development conception makes use of and substantiates a particular idea of human dignity. In addition, it clearly restricts the validity of its normative claims to the realm of political relations that are characterized by a lasting disagreement regarding the question of what a good human life involves. Consequently, Nussbaum's justice-based political conception of human development stands out within the normative literature on development, as its philosophical resources are much richer than those of any other such conceptions.

Nevertheless Nussbaum's theory of development and justice is also subject to severe criticism by development ethicists who follow Nussbaum's lead in devising a justice-based conception of development. In particular, those normative theorists (Crocker 2008, ch. 8; Culp 2014, ch. 7; cf. Claasen 2011) who endorse a democratic understanding of justice put into question the outcome-orientation of Nussbaum's capabilities theory, as they believe that it downplays excessively the importance of the philosophical and political question: Who is to decide what counts as a fundamental claim of basic justice? (cf. Forst 2014, ch. 2) *Pace* Nussbaum, they hold that reasonably democratic procedures should determine which capabilities should count as so fundamental that they require constitutional protection. Accordingly, while they accept that those capabilities that are necessary for engaging in democratic procedures can be justified abstractly by philosophical argument, they deny that the moral importance of any other capability can be justified in this manner. Similarly, Sen (2009, ch. 15) also emphasizes the importance of public deliberation for determining which capabilities should be realized in a particular social and political context (cf. also Drydyk 2005). Yet Sen fails to draw the conclusion that democracy-enabling capabilities enjoy special importance vis-à-vis other capabilities. He (1999, 33–34, 55) insists that his contribution consists merely in conceptualizing capabilities as the proper informational base for making comparative assessments.

What is more, Nussbaum's conception belongs to the *weak statist* theories of social justice, because it does not recognize any non-sufficientarian, comparative principles of justice beyond the state. Accordingly, her corresponding conception of development fails to account for the core idea of theories of global justice that comparative principles of justice should regulate a global society of individuals or a global society of states. In response, some internationalists (Culp, chs. 5 and 6) have argued that the notion of development should not be restricted to the global realization of certain kinds of sufficientarian principles. Globalists, however, so far have not used their ideal of global interpersonal equality to infuse normative debates about how to conceive development.

Conclusion

In this chapter I have explored how theories of justice have shaped normative understandings of development. It revealed that these theories have influenced normative debates about development predominantly through Nussbaum's work, as well as through the work of her critics who favor procedural and internationalist approaches. The dialogue between theorists of justice and development ethicists is likely to continue and will perhaps become even more intense in the near future. The reason for this is that concerns of intergenerational justice have infused the Sustainable Development Goals, which constitute the recently adopted political framework for promoting development and which place great emphasis on environmental protection. This framework raises several moral problems such as how to weigh the goals' relative moral importance and how to conceive the moral responsibility for realizing them. Since moral and political philosophers have recently offered intriguing accounts of intergenerational and, in relation to that, climate justice (Heath 2013; Gosseries and González 2016; Moellendorf 2014; Shue 2014), they are in a good position to continue their conversation with development ethicists. Another important part of this conservation is the importance of principles of social, global, and intergenerational justice vis-à-vis values like well-being – in general and in the case of particular practical conflicts.

References

Anderson, E. (2010) Justifying the Capabilities Approach to Justice. In Brighouse, E. and Robeyns, I. eds., *Measuring Justice*. Cambridge University Press, Cambridge, 81–100.

Arneson, R. (2006) Justice after Rawls. In Dryzek, J., Honig, B. and Anne, P. eds., *Oxford Handbook of Political Theory*. Oxford University Press, Oxford, 111–126.

Beitz, C. (1986) Review of Amartya Sen's *Resources, Values, and Development*. *Economics and Philosophy* 2: 282–291.

Beitz, C. (1979) *Political Theory and International Relations*. Princeton University Press, Princeton.

Blake, M. (2001) Distributive Justice, State Coercion, and Autonomy. *Philosophy and Public Affairs* 30: 257–296.

Boserup, E. (1970) *Women's Role in Economic Development*. Allen and Unwin, London.

Brock, G. (2009) *Global Justice*. Oxford University Press, New York.

Caney, S. (2005) *Justice beyond Borders*. Oxford University Press, Oxford.

Cardoso, F. and Faletto, E. (1979) *Dependency and Development in Latin America*. University of California Press, Berkeley.

Chambers, R. (1997) *Whose Reality Counts? Putting the Last First*. Intermediate Technology Publications, London.

Claasen, R. (2011) Making Capability Lists: Philosophy versus Democracy. *Political Studies* 59: 491–508.

Cohen, J. and Sabel, C. (2006) Extra rempublicam nulla justitia? *Philosophy and Public Affairs* 34: 147–175.

Crocker, D. (2008) *Ethics of Global development: Agency, Capability and Deliberative Democracy*. Cambridge University Press, Cambridge.

Culp, J. (2014) *Global Justice and Development*. Palgrave Macmillan, Basingstoke and New York.

Culp, J. (2015) Development. In Moellendorf, D. and Widdows, H. eds., *The Handbook of Global Ethics*. Routledge, London and New York, 170–181.

Culp, J. (2016) Toward Another Development Practice. In Barcelos, P. and de Angelis, G. eds., *International Development and Humanitarian Aid*. Edinburgh University Press, Edinburgh, 79–107.

Dag Hammarskjold Foundation (1974) Cocoyoc Declaration. *Development Dialogue* 2: 88–96.

Dag Hammarskjold Foundation (1975) What Now? Another Development. *Development Dialogue* 1–2: 1–129.

Deere, C. (1976) Rural Women's Subsistence Production in the Capitalist Periphery. *Review of Radical Political Economy* 8: 9–17.

Doyal, L. and Gough, I. (1991) *A Theory of Human Need*. Macmillan, London.

Drydyk, J. (2005) When is Development More Democratic? *Journal of Human Development and Capabilities* 6: 247–67.

Elson, D. and Pearson, P. (1981) "Nimble fingers make cheap workers": An Analysis of Women's Employment in Third World Export Manufacturing. *Feminist Review* 7: 87–107.

Forsythe, D. (1997) The United Nations, Human Rights, and Development. *Human Rights Quarterly* 19: 334–349.

Forst, R. (2014) *Justification and Critique*. Polity Press, Cambridge.

Frank, A. (1975) *Capitalist Underdevelopment*. Oxford University Press, Oxford.

Fukuda-Parr, S. (2011) Theory and Policy in International Development. *International Studies Review* 13: 122–132.

Gallie, W.B. (1956) Essentially Contested Concepts. *Proceedings of the Aristotelian Society* 56: 167–198.

Gasper, D. (2007) Conceptualising Human Needs and Well-being. In Gough, I. and MacGregor, J.A. eds., *Wellbeing in Developing Countries: New Approaches and Research Strategies*. Cambridge University Press, Cambridge, 47–70.

Gosepath, S. (2001) The Global Scope of Justice. *Metaphilosophy* 32: 135–159.

Gosseries, A. and González, I. eds. (2016) *Institutions for Future Generations*. Oxford University Press, Oxford.

Goulet, D. (1995) *Development Ethics*. The Apex Press, New York.

Greig, A., Hulme, D. and Turner, M. (2007) *Challenging Global Inequality*. Palgrave Macmillan, Basingstoke and New York.

Hamm, B. (2001) A Human rights approach to Development. *Human Rights Quarterly* 23: 1005–1031.

Hart, H.L.A (1961) *The Concept of Law*. Clarendon Press, Oxford.

Heath, J. (2013) The Structure of Intergenerational Cooperation. *Philosophy & Public Affairs* 41: 31–66.

Hopper, P. (2012) *Understanding Development*. Polity Press, Cambridge.

Inkeles, A. (1966) The Modernization of Man. In Weiner, M. ed., *Modernization*. Basic Books, New York, 151–166.

International Labour Organisation (1976) *Employment, Growth and Basic Needs*. International Labour Organisation, Geneva.

Khader, S. (2014) Empowerment through Self-subordination? Microcredit and Women's Agency. In Meyers, D.T. ed., *Poverty, Agency, and Human Rights*. Oxford University Press, Oxford, 223–248.

Krueger, A. (1990) Government Failures in development. *Journal of Economic Perspectives* 4: 9–23.

Krugman, P. (1995) Dutch Tulips and Emerging Markets. *Foreign Affairs* 74: 28–44.

Lebret, L. (1960) Editorial. *Développement et Civilisations* 1: n.p.

McNamara, R. (1973) *Address to the Board of Governors*. World Bank, Washington, DC.
McNeill, D. (2007) Human Development: The Power of the Idea. *Journal of Human Development* 8: 5–22.
Mies, M. and Shiva, V. (1993) *Ecofeminism*. Zed Books, London.
Miller, D. (2007) *National Responsibility and Global Justice*. Oxford University Press, Oxford.
Moellendorf, D. (2002) *Cosmopolitan Justice*. Westview Press, Boulder.
Moellendorf, D. (2014) *The Moral Challenge of Dangerous Climate Change*. Cambridge University Press, Cambridge.
Myrdal, G. (1957) *Economic Theory and Under-developed Regions*. Duckworth, London.
Nagel, T. (2005) The Problem of Global Justice. *Philosophy and Public Affairs* 33(2): 113–47.
Nickel, J. (2005) Poverty and Rights. *The Philosophical Quarterly* 55: 385–402.
Nurkse, R. (1953) *Problems of Capital Formation in Underdeveloped Countries*. Oxford University Press, New York.
Nussbaum, M. (1992) Human Functioning and Social Justice: In Defense of Aristotelian Essentialism. *Political Theory* 20: 202–246.
Nussbaum, M. (2000) *Women and Human Development*. Cambridge University Press, Cambridge.
Nussbaum, M. (2003) Capabilities as Fundamental entitlements: Sen and Social Justice. *Feminist Economics* 9: 33–59.
Nussbaum, M. (2006) *Frontiers of Justice*. Harvard University Press, Cambridge, MA.
Nussbaum, M. (2011) *Creating Capabilities*. Harvard University Press, Cambridge, MA.
Pettit, P. (2010) A Republican Law of Peoples. *European Journal of Political Theory* 9: 70–94.
Pogge, T. (1989) *Realizing Rawls*. Cornell University Press, Ithaca.
Pogge, T. (1994) An Egalitarian Law of Peoples. *Philosophy and Public Affairs* 23: 195–224.
Rahnema, M. (2010) Poverty. In Sachs, W. ed., *The Development Dictionary*, 2nd ed. Zed Books, London, 158–176.
Rapley, J. (2007) *Understanding Development*, 2nd ed. Lynne Rienner, Boulder, CO.
Rawls, J. (1971) *A Theory of Justice*. Harvard University Press, Cambridge, MA.
Rawls, J. (1993) *Political Liberalism* Columbia University Press, New York.
Rawls, J. (1999) *The Law of Peoples*. Harvard University Press, Cambridge, MA.
Robeyns, I. (2005) The Capability Approach: A Theoretical Survey. *Journal of Human Development* 6: 93–117.
Robeyns, I. (2011) The Capability Approach. In Zalta, E. ed., *The Stanford Encyclopedia of Philosophy* http://plato.stanford.edu/ (home page).
Rodan-Rosenstein, P. (1943) Problems of Industrialization of Eastern and South-eastern Europe. *Economic Journal* 53: 202–211.
Rostow, W. (1960) *Stages in Economic Development*. Cambridge University Press, Cambridge.
Sangiovanni, A. (2007) Global Justice, Reciprocity, and the State. *Philosophy and Public Affairs* 35: 3–39.
Sen, A. (1984) Goods and People. In Sen, A. ed., *Resources, Values and Development*. Basil Blackwell, Oxford, 509–532.
Sen, A. (1988) The Concept of development. In Chenery, H. and Srinivasan, T.N. eds., *Handbook of Development Economics. Vol. 1*. Elsevier, North Holland, 157–180.
Sen, A. (1989) Human Development as Capability Expansion. In Fukuda-Parr, S. and Shiva Kumar, A.K. eds., *Readings on Human Development: Concepts, Measures, and Policies for a Development Paradigm*. Oxford University Press, New York, 3–16.
Sen, A. (1991) *Inequality Reexamined*. Oxford University Press, Oxford.
Sen, A. (1997[1980]) Equality of What? In Sen, A. ed., *Choice, Welfare and Measurement*. Harvard University Press, Cambridge, MA, 353–372.
Sen, A. (1999) *Development as Freedom*. Oxford University Press, New York.
Sen, A. (2009) *The Idea of Justice*. Allen and Unwin, London.
Sen, G. and Grown, C. (1987) *Development, Crises, and Alternative Visions*. Monthly Review Press, New York.
Shue, H. (1980) *Basic Rights: Subsistence, Affluence, and U.S. Foreign Policy*. Princeton University Press, Princeton.
Shue, H. (2014) *Climate Justice: Vulnerability and Protection*. Oxford University Press, Oxford.

Streeten, P. (1981) *First Things First: Meeting Basic Human Needs in the Developing Countries*. World Bank, Washington, DC.

Streeten, P. (1984) Basic Needs: Some Unsettled Questions. *World Development* 12: 973–978.

Streeten, P. and Burki, S. (1978) Basic Needs: Some Issues. *World Development* 6: 411–421.

Tan, K.C. (2004) *Justice without Borders*. Cambridge University Press, Cambridge.

Tinker, I. (1990) *Persistent Inequalities: Women and World Development*. Oxford University Press, New York.

United Nations (1986) *Declaration on the Right to Development*. U.N. Doc. A/Res/41/925/Annex. www2.ohchr.org/english/law/pdf/rtd.pdf.

United Nations Conference on Environment and Development (1992) *The Rio Declaration on Environment and Development*. www.unesco.org/education/information/nfsunesco/pdf/RIO_E.PDF.

United Nations Development Programme (1990) *Human Development Report*. Oxford University Press, New York.

United Nations Development Programme (1997) *Human Development Report*. Oxford University Press, New York.

United Nations Development Programme (2010) *Human Development Report*. Oxford University Press, New York.

United Nations World Commission on Environment and Development (1987) *Our Common Future*. www.un-documents.net/wced-ocf.htm.

Williamson, J. (1990) What Washington means by Policy Reform. In Williamson, J. ed., *Latin American Adjustment: How Much Has Happened?* Institute for International Economic, Washington, DC, 7–20.

World Bank (2001) *Engendering Development. Enhancing Development Through Gender Equality in Rights, Resources, and Voice*. Oxford University Press, Oxford.

11

Gender

Feminist insights on inequality in development

Christine M. Koggel

In its original and (so-called) descriptive sense, development has been aligned with goals of economic growth and allied processes of industrialization, modernization, technological advances, and market structures. These are goals and processes that are also associated with the Western tradition and liberal theory more generally and are, therefore, norms about what constitutes development that are not merely descriptive. In the context of post-World War II, development described how countries outside North America and Europe (many of them former colonies) were to be transformed from what their colonizers judged as backward, primitive, and underdeveloped into advanced, modern, and developed nations. This understanding of development dominated the discourse in the 1950s, 1960s, and into the 1970s and reflected beliefs that governments in North America and Western Europe had a legitimate role to play in implementing development projects designed to improve the lives and living conditions of those in "underdeveloped" or "developing" countries. Alongside this understanding of development were projects and policies directing countries away from traditional agricultural based societies (precisely the sort of societies that tended to display different gender roles, duties, and activities) toward industry, manufacture, and technology. This background is important for understanding the role that development theory and policy has played in assuming particular gender roles and norms and entrenching gender inequalities in a range of areas and domains across the globe.

Development ethics has challenged and broadened the study of development by revealing the underlying normative assumptions that tend to reflect Western values and promote liberal strategies for what counts as progress toward development. Development ethics does so by exploring answers to a number of questions about what constitutes appropriate or worthwhile development (Goulet 1995). What is assumed when countries and peoples are judged as in need of development? What effects do development projects and policies accepted by theorists, international bodies, and governments have on people and the lives they can lead? Who decides what policies and programs are to be implemented and where? What can be learned from a history of failed development projects and policies that have done more harm than good for those affected? What sorts of principles can allow us to make fair judgments about what policies or processes result in worthwhile development instead of maldevelopment? And, most importantly for purposes of this chapter, what implications emerge for understanding the role of gender in development and for addressing gender inequalities?

 DOI: 10.4324/9781315626796-14

This *Handbook* is structured to explore seven guiding principles that have been taken as central to development ethics: well-being, social and global justice, empowerment and agency, environmental sustainability, human rights, cultural freedom, and integrity and responsibility. It is fair to say that "gender inequalities" describe the situation with respect to achieving the goals and objectives of each of the principles. Amartya Sen makes this point about women's inequalities in connection with the principle of empowerment and agency:

> [t]he extensive reach of women's agency is one of the more neglected areas of development studies, and most urgently in need of correction. Nothing, arguably, is as important today in the political economy of development as an adequate recognition of political, economic and social participation and leadership of women.
>
> *(Sen 1999, 109)*

The quotation also highlights another important point: theories about what equality means or about the source of inequalities connect with policies that are advocated to alleviate or remove those inequalities.

Sen defends a complex account of inequalities as interconnected and shaped in and through particular processes and contexts. As covered elsewhere in this volume, his is a version of the capabilities approach that examines the freedoms that people have to be and to do – in both the subjective sense of what an agent wants to do and be and in the objective sense of being able to choose in ways that enable an agent to live well. This is but a quick snapshot of Sen's complex account of inequalities as centred on the importance of removing unfreedoms – to participate in social, political, and economic processes and to have a say in how one shapes and plans one's own life. Accounts of equality by libertarians (equality as satisfied when no one is barred from having equal liberty rights and freedoms) and by Rawlsians (inequalities in the distribution of goods are permitted if they benefit the least well off) are liberal versions of equality that are less complex than that defended by Sen. It is fair to say that liberal theories of equality shape the background against which development has been conceptualized and policy has been implemented. How one theorizes about equality has a direct bearing on the solutions one proposes by way of alleviating inequalities. Nowhere are the effects of this more evident than when one describes inequalities experienced by those who are disadvantaged by race, gender, class, ethnicity, age, nationality, ability, and so on.

The paradigm of development as economic growth has been particularly pernicious in generating and entrenching inequalities within and across borders and specifically with respect to gender. The history of development reveals a litany of projects and policies that are now recognized as initiated from a Eurocentric perspective and emerging from histories of colonialism. One cannot examine frameworks for theorizing about gender inequalities in development policy and practice without referencing the important work by feminist, race, postcolonial, and other theorists that examine, test, and challenge traditional and mainstream liberal accounts of both development and gender. An insight central to feminist theory and movements is that theory that has been based mainly on the experiences of males or on beliefs, structures, and practices in specific societies embed norms and assumptions held by dominant groups and thereby reflect skewed and partial perspectives on lives and on what matters or should matter to people. Correcting for biases and uncovering and testing these assumptions means incorporating/listening to/taking seriously the lived and everyday experiences of those who have been excluded from theorizing, knowledge building, and the design and implementation of policy. This work by feminist and other theorists and by women's movements around the world has resulted in shifts to how gender is conceptualized and theorized in development theory and policy.

In this chapter, therefore, my examination of gender inequalities will need to examine the intersections of theory and practice on all sides of the debates in development ethics and in feminist theory and movements. The chapter begins with an examination of theoretical frameworks in the development literature that have been used to address gender inequalities and then moves to a discussion of feminist theoretical frameworks that were relevant to and interacted with debates on development theory and policy. Then I discuss the significant moves by Western feminist theory from conceptual analyses of women to gender, and then to how these theories and frameworks were first challenged from within feminism itself and then by women's movements and activism in a global context. The concluding section discusses contemporary work on gender inequalities and on what remains to be done to understand and address them in theory and in practice. A core idea to keep in mind is that much of what has happened in development theory and practice started with and is a response to the power wielded by North American and Western European countries in a colonial and postcolonial context that shaped judgments and beliefs about which countries and peoples needed to become developed and how. It is also important to keep in mind that gender inequalities have emerged from and are perpetuated in and through development theories and processes that assumed and then utilized gender norms delineating women's proper roles, duties, and activities. Finally, it is important to note that debates within Western feminist theory and movements about whose voices and perspectives were invisible or being ignored would be important to shaping contemporary feminist theories and movements that call for taking seriously the voices and perspectives of all women.

Historical background: development frameworks and gender inequalities

Development theories, movements, and policies happen in specific historical contexts in which they evolve and change as conditions and circumstances change and as challenges are presented. The specific attention given to gender inequalities is fairly recent in that development initiatives by economists and colonial powers in the 1930s tended to ignore women altogether in the march to install Western technology, institutions, and values in countries and societies considered to be "backward" and "primitive." The 1940s and 1950s witnessed the growth of activities by development planners whose goal was to "modernize" colonies all over the globe. The failures of these modernization projects began to emerge in movements by countries to decolonize and gain independence from colonial powers. Yet the rejection of modernization was not the outcome for all countries resisting colonialism. In this time period as well, the U.S. emerged as the hegemonic power and became the model for countries pursuing modernization. This model was adopted by many newly independent countries that followed the U.S. in thinking that modernization, industrialization, and technology were key features of how to become and be judged as developed – or at least developing.

The emergence of attention to gender in development can be linked to development policies implemented by international institutions and national governments that tended to mirror those found in liberal societies (and liberal feminist theory) more generally. The strategy was to work within and reform the development as economic growth paradigm by bringing women *into* development. The Women in Development (WID) approach tended to accept the discourse and assumptions of development as economic growth and modernization and had the objective of including women in economic processes such as being employed outside the home, earning an income, and contributing to the economic growth of their countries (Collier 1988; Joekes 1990; Weekes-Vagliani 1985). The WID approach worked within the paradigm of economic growth by measuring development as progress being made in adopting Western technologies, institutions, and values – and now including women in these development processes. WID resulted in improvements to women's access to education, training, property, credit, and employment – all within the framework of allowing women into processes that once ignored or excluded them and of giving them opportunities that men had been given. WID thinking and goals are still evident in policies that support the liberal feminist idea that women can gain equality merely by participating in political and economic activities and leaving the private sphere activities of reproductive and domestic labour behind – to be done by other women or on top of their paid work outside the home.

WID had its detractors – in feminist theories and in movements led by women in developing countries (Buviniç 1986; Benería 2003a; Parpart et al. 2000). The Commission on the Status of Women (CSW) was set up in 1947, two years after the formation of the United Nations, and tasked with monitoring United Nations' activities on behalf of women through its human rights framework. By the end of the 1950s and into the 1960s women of newly independent countries became more involved in United Nations' organizations and programs – raising development-oriented issues that were outside the purview of what was perceived as the UN's limited human rights framework. This involvement led to a review of the First Development Decade of the 1960s, a review that revealed the cracks in a WID based set of policies that works with assumptions that Western technologies, institutions, and modernization hold the answers and that indigenous populations and indigenous knowledge could and should be denigrated, ignored, and rejected. During this time period as well, women's grassroots movements increasingly removed themselves from WID programs and efforts and worked independently and strategically in meeting their practical needs and in promoting issues and strategies relevant to their lives and experiences of caring for families and communities. Their removal from the activities of WID reflected a rejection of the very framework of Western modernization and values that treated women as mere instruments, or human capital, in the unquestioned goal of economic growth. Rejected as well was the WID approach that paid little to no attention to the impact of the global on the local and national as well as of the impact of race and class on women's lives (Mohanty 1988; Alexander and Mohanty 1997; Mies 1989). More complex analyses and theories were needed to show how these factors shaped women's lives and impacted them differently in specific contexts, histories, structures, and practices. These insights and critiques continue to be important to contemporary postcolonial and third-world feminisms that I examine in more detail in the section "Women's Movements and Third World Feminism."

Ester Boserup's *Women's Role in Economic Development*, published in 1970, was instrumental in raising the profile of the perspectives of women in developing countries (Boserup 1970). Her work was influential in providing evidence from Africa, Asia, the Caribbean, and Latin America that showed the disruptive effects of colonialism, modernization, and the increasingly global market economy on the sexual division of labour in countries that displayed norms of men's and women's roles and activities different from those in North/developed countries. Her research showed that projects of economic development in these countries drew men away from production based on family labour and gave them almost exclusive access to economic, social, and political resources, access that women already had before these development interventions. In other words, modernization and industrialization strategies had worsened the lives of women and the poor – at least in some "developing" countries.

Boserup's research gave support to the argument that the economic survival of "developing" countries depended on reversing this trend of ignoring women's lives and experiences by more fully integrating them into development processes on their own terms. Her research also coincided with the resurgence of movements for civil rights in Western countries and the push to extend rights to people within countries as well as globally. The key idea behind these critiques of development theory and policy is that *both* women and men need to be lifted from poverty and that *both* women and men need to contribute to and benefit from development processes and policies. But integration did not mean merely adding women to development. Instead it meant that differences in the norms, beliefs, values, and structures of countries and societies needed to be acknowledged as significant for assessing what sorts of development projects and policies were appropriate if women's experiences were to be taken seriously and their lives improved.

The period post Boserup marked the beginning of the change from WID strategies to ones that focused on Women and Development (WAD) and then Gender and Development (GAD) (Jackson and Pearson 1998; Parpart et al. 2000; Razavi and Miller 1995). The change signalled a move beyond, even if in a limited way, an individualist focus on lifting women by giving them access to economic opportunities to a community-oriented focus that paid some attention to how relationships and roles were being shaped and reshaped in and through development projects and policies that assumed that men were the main actors in social, economic, and political processes. WAD allowed recognition of the distinctiveness of women's knowledge, women's work, and women's aspirations and responsibilities. As noted above, awareness of the experiences and lives of women in different parts of the world suggests that the sexual division of labour in our society may not be the norm elsewhere and that norms can be changed. WAD could acknowledge the fact that women are the mainstay of agricultural production in many countries – and that this has been overlooked and marginalized in many development projects and policies. Gender norms are entrenched and they are "sticky" (Petesch 2012). The idea that the subordination of women was based on biological or sociological factors that were natural or universal began to give way – at least in work by feminist theorists and by those involved in women's movements (Jaggar 2009a). Relations between women and men can change – even as factors such as globalization, race, ethnicity, class, age, sexual orientation, ability, nationality, and so on influence and shape those relations. As I will go on to show, Boserup's insights into the sexual division of labour have not been fully incorporated – not even in WAD initiatives that emerged from her work.

In *African Women and Development: A History*, Margaret Snyder and Mary Tadesse describe WAD as emerging from an understanding of women and development as a concept and movement with the long-term goal of achieving the well-being of communities of men, women, and children. It was meant to be responsive to women's needs, a responsiveness that is reflected in acknowledging and knowing about women's local movements, groups, and networks. Snyder and Tadesse take WAD to have incorporated the following ideas: (1) "development" understood in accordance with the International Development Strategy for the Second Development Decade is meant "to bring about sustained improvements in the well-being of the individual and to bestow benefits on all"; (2) women comprise more than half of the human population and resources and need to be central to the economic and social well-being of societies – development goals cannot be fully reached without their participation; (3) the goals of women's equality and of worthwhile development need to be integrally connected in that one cannot be achieved without the other; (4) women must have "both the legal right and access to existing means for the improvement of oneself and of society" (1995, 6).

WAD and other initiatives led by women's grassroots organizing throughout the world resulted in the United Nations declaration of International Women's Year in 1975, which was launched by the First International Women's Conference in Mexico City. The conference was marked by the presence of networks of women's groups from nearly all countries in the world and had the theme, "Equality, Development, and Peace." The goals achieved at this conference included extending its work into the United Nations Decade for Women, 1976–85. This time period also witnessed the emergence of United Nations based groups such as the United Nations Fund for Women and the International Training and Research Centre for Women as well as of international institutions, non-governmental organizations, national commissions, and global networks of women centred groups – all of which contributed to the recognition of women and development as an internationally significant set of concepts and issues.

While WAD was an important corrective to WID's focus on male-dominated roles and strategies as the answer to addressing gender inequalities, there have been objections raised against WAD as well. WAD's transformative potential and advantage can be found in the fact that it is women led and organized. But this advantage turns to a disadvantage when such organizing and networking tends to be ignored or made invisible by mainstream and powerful organizations and programs. The WAD approach has also been criticized for universalizing the experiences of women and for downplaying the differences among women with respect to factors such as race, gender, caste, class, ethnicity, and nationality (as discussed in the section that follows). These criticisms emerged at the same time as the face and approach of development thinking and programs began to change. International financial institutions such as the International Monetary Fund (IMF) and the World Bank drew attention to the importance of providing basic human needs for all by addressing and alleviating poverty. Thus were born new ways of improving women's access to income through such efforts as micro-credit and the creation of small-scale income generating projects – designed to better fit women's lives than were the WID based programs. These programs designed to generate income for women continue to be subjected to criticism for failing to improve women's lives in many parts of the world (Karim 2011).

These and other efforts by international institutions were largely thwarted in the 1990s by economic crises in countries throughout the world that resulted in policies and programs that intensified processes of globalization through increased creation of and competition in global markets. So began the goal of addressing these crises by restructuring failed economies. With attention to the assumed positive role that powerful countries and transnational corporations could play, international financial institutions played a key role in implementing structural adjustment programs (SAPs) that tied loans to a country's efforts to increase their market productivity and efficiency and to decrease their spending on social programs such as education, health care, and welfare policies. SAPs reflected the resurgence of liberal development thinking and its assumptions about the virtues of economic growth and prosperity. SAPs also increased the mobility of labour and of capital as countries struggling to improve economic growth and efficiency sent their citizens abroad for work and wages or attempted to attract transnational and multinational corporations to set up factories in third world countries with cheap labour costs (Fussell 2000; Kabeer 2004; Koggel 2003).

These programs and policies had particularly pernicious effects with respect to increasing inequalities in women's lives in several ways: social programs such as education and healthcare had been and continue to be important means by which to meet basic needs and improve conditions for women, families, and communities; women were recruited into jobs that were insecure, low-skilled, low-paying, had poor working conditions, and still required the double-shift work of reproductive and household labour (the results of which were reflected in a feminization of the labour force and of poverty); male citizens from the South migrated to urban centres or to other countries in the North to get jobs and left women to care for themselves and their families; and women from various countries in the South were recruited into and paid to do the work of caring for children and doing housework for rich people in the North (Weir 2005; Benería 2008). All of these conditions have contributed to what has sometimes been referred to as "transnational cycles of gendered vulnerabilities" (Jaggar 2009b) or "global chains of dependency and interdependency" (Weir 2005). Few women in either the North or South had their lives improved through restructuring processes rooted in processes of economic globalization. In fact, many more women became worse off (Parpart et al. 2002; Salazar-Parreñas 2001).

To summarize: both WID and WAD were affected and changed by global and economic forces that undermined their mandates and their effectiveness. Some feminists and development theorists had been skeptical all along that either approach could address the fundamental factors that structure and maintain women's inequalities. While these responses could have opened the door to examining the role of gender norms themselves (as I will go on to show), the skepticism about WID and WAD initially arose through questioning the very use of the concept "women." The criticism would emerge from within Western feminist theory, be incorporated into development theory and practice, and be further questioned and challenged by women in grassroots movements in the South and by third-world and postcolonial feminists.

Feminist theoretical frameworks and movements

Feminists have played a critical role in uncovering norms at play in development policies and challenging the discourse and policies that entrench gender norms and keep gender inequalities in place or fail to recognize let alone remove them. Although there is a large and diverse range of feminist theories, feminists can be said to agree that inequalities/oppression/injustices/subordination/discrimination continue to exist and feminists are united in their commitment to addressing and alleviating these inequalities/oppression/injustices/subordination/discrimination. Where they differ is on issues of conceptual analysis (which concepts are favored and how to describe the phenomena) and on the sources or causes of the inequalities/oppression/injustices/subordination/discrimination and so on. The framework issues of how to describe and explain the phenomena tend to be linked to normative issues of how to address, alleviate, or remove the inequalities/oppression/injustices/subordination/discrimination and so on. These features of differences among feminist theorists can be illustrated by returning to a discussion of the paradigm of economic growth and modernization that continues to dominate the literature on development. Here, the cause of women's inequality is taken to be women's unequal access to economic, social, and political opportunities and participation. Recommendations for removing these inequalities tend to be ones that promote equality of opportunity by removing discriminatory laws (formal equality) and/or addressing discriminatory biases and practices (informal equality). Policies that allow women to compete for the same opportunities as men – for jobs, workplace conditions, political offices, and so on and as reflected in WID-based programs – are then promoted as programs and policies that can address inequalities.

The WID approach has also been associated with liberal feminism. As is well-known in critiques of early liberal feminism (e.g., Friedan 1963), this approach has been challenged by women of color in the U.S. as reflecting a narrow set of experiences and interests; that of white, middle-class women in their homes and excluded from public and political sphere activities. African American women, already needing to be in the workplace but in low-paying service jobs and domestic work, were legitimately critical of an approach that failed to describe their experiences or capture what might be needed to alleviate the oppression and inequalities they experienced. The experiences of women of color, non-heterosexual, poor, and single women revealed a different set of inequalities: of not being able to care for their own children because they were holding jobs that had them care for the children of privileged women, or of not having or wanting men on whom to depend, or of experiencing racial or class-based discrimination in the jobs that they occupied. The critique of mainstream feminism as paying little to no attention to differences among women on the basis of factors such as race, ethnicity, class, nationality, sexual orientation, religion, and so on is evident in the work of feminists of color such as bell hooks who in commenting on the feminist argument that women want rights equal to men asks "which men do women want to be equal to?" (hooks 1984, 28). That the answer to this question is all too obvious reveals the assumed norm of white middle-class heterosexual males who reside in rich and powerful countries and against whom others are judged and measured.

This challenge would turn out to play a central role in the development of feminist approaches and critiques within Western feminism generally and, more specifically, within U.S. feminist theory and movement. Work by lesbian feminists and feminists of color such as Audre Lorde (1984), bell hooks (1984, 1988), Patricia Hill Collins (1990), Gloria Anzaldúa (1987) and Cherríe Moraga and Anzaldúa (1981) were important for retaining the importance of describing women's experiences while challenging accounts by white feminists of what constituted those experiences and women's oppression more generally. The onus was now on feminists to show that their descriptions of inequalities or injustices were sensitive to differences in women's experiences and that the policies they were prepared to advocate could address the wide range of inequalities and kinds of discrimination experienced by a variety of women affected by factors other than gender.

As will be discussed later, global, postcolonial, and third-world feminists would expand this critique of falsely generalizing and universalizing women's experiences of oppression. They would develop accounts that put global relations of power at the forefront of the descriptive and normative components of feminist theory and movement (Narayan 1997; Narayan and Harding 2000; Alexander and Mohanty 1997). They would uncover biases in feminisms dominated and contained within the U.S. and not evident or common in women's experiences across history, time, and cultures or present in locations outside the U.S. (Mohanty 1988).

What has emerged from these critiques by race, class, postcolonial, and third-world feminists is a call to acknowledge and incorporate the experiences and knowledge of diverse women – both within countries and across the globe. Taking into account diverse experiences of kinds of inequalities/oppression/injustices/subordination/discrimination and so on would turn out to be the catalyst for changing and expanding feminist theory by incorporating issues of intersecting factors of race, class, ethnicity, ability, age, sexual identity and orientation, nationality, and so on. Intersectionality holds that descriptions of women's inequalities and injustices need to be placed within a complex network of intersecting kinds of oppression (Crenshaw 1991). Women are not only women; gender intersects with one or more factors of race, class, ethnicity, disability, sexual orientation, age, nationality, and so on and in ways that call for attending to the specificity of those experiences and for advocating policies that are effective in removing the particular inequalities and injustices experienced by women at the intersection of multiple kinds of oppression. If feminism's objective is to understand and end women's oppression, then intersectionality explains that interlocking kinds of oppression call for a multi-pronged and integrated approach of describing oppression of all kinds and of dismantling domination in all its forms. As Elizabeth Spelman writes, "no woman is subject to any form of oppression simply because she is a woman; which forms of oppression she is subject to depend on what 'kind' of woman she is" (Spelman 1998, 52). Another important change and expansion to Western feminist theory would also be demanded by feminists calling for accounts of how gender inequalities manifest differently in particular contexts and countries with colonial histories and pasts and through the overarching context of economic globalization that shapes the lives and experiences of members of oppressed groups around the world (Koggel 2002). What is made evident is that development theory and policy has had to be sensitive to a range of feminist theories and critiques of development itself.

This is but a snapshot of the kinds of feminist theory (more later) emerging from a set of critiques within feminism itself (Koggel 2011). The upshot is that the fields of both development ethics and feminist theory have had to change in response to charges of universalizing what humans are and need and of assuming the norms of Western/North/liberal thinking. These norms have reflected assumptions about lives, experiences, beliefs, structures, and practices that have led to policies and processes that have treated people in the non-Western/South countries as victims/patients of development processes rather than as agents who control and ought to control the paths of their own lives and futures. Lessons about what this means for development theory and practice and for feminist theory and movement are still being learned. As with the liberal paradigm of development as involving processes of economic growth, modernization, industrialization, and technological advances that has been challenged so too has the liberal paradigm of feminist theory as equality of opportunity to do, be, and compete for what white, able-bodied, heterosexual, middle-class men been challenged. In both cases, what is revealed are the ways in which processes, projects, and policies have adversely affected the lives of those outside the norm – whether one theorizes about inequalities familiar to one's own context or country or of inequalities less familiar and well-known but evident in contexts and countries very different from one's own.

From "women" to "gender" in feminist theory and development policies and practices

The previous two sections described changes to the research agendas, discourse, theories, and frameworks in feminist theory and in development projects and policies with respect to understanding and addressing inequalities experienced by women within and across borders. The changes in both domains of development policy and feminist theorizing resulted in another shift, one that replaced the concept of "women" with that of "gender." The adoption of "gender" emerged from the important distinction feminists drew between "sex" (the biological component of what constitutes being male versus being female) and "gender" (the sociological and socialization features of roles and duties assigned to males versus those assigned to females). The distinction between sex and gender was crucial to feminist theory in claims that the biological was distinct and could be disconnected from social and economic roles assigned to males (those associated with masculinity) and to females (those associated with femininity). Associating "sex" with the biological suggests that it is fixed and not subject to change. "Gender" captures the turn by feminists to what is socially constructed and subject to change. The distinction itself was examined and sometimes challenged by feminist and other theorists (Antony 1998; Jaggar 1983; Nicholson 1994). Discussions of the distinction between "sex" and "gender" (at least in most feminist theory and in academic circles) has been set aside in favor of the widely used and accepted concept "gender."

"Gender" is now taken to capture the complexities of women's oppression/subordination, the interconnectedness of the sociological and the biological, and the idea that inequalities are the result of structures and practices rather than biological features. The language of gender is also reflected in the shift from talking about "women's inequalities" (suggesting essentialist notions of what all women have in common) to "gender inequalities" (suggesting that there is no set of experiences shared by all women and that a strict dichotomy of male/female is belied by a spectrum of sexes and genders) (Fausto-Sterling 1993a, 1993b, 2000, 2003). This clarification of the now widely accepted use of gender explains how terminology that was once accepted in development projects and policies is shaped by these sorts of attempts to better understand and address kinds of inequalities. In contemporary feminist theory, gender designates an analytical social category that interacts with other social factors such as race, ethnicity, class, nationality, age, and so on to shape and influence the experiences of group members differentially impacted by a range of factors in particular contexts.

It may seem that the widespread acceptance of gender (as preferred over women or sex) is a Western feminist preoccupation, as sometimes mirrored in discussions about what to call academic departments. As Joan Scott points out,

> in its simplest usage, "gender" is a synonym for "women." Any number of books and articles whose subject is women's history have in the past few years substituted "gender" for "women" in their titles. In some cases this usage . . . is about political acceptability in the field. In these instances, the use of "gender" is meant to denote scholarly seriousness of work, for "gender" has a more neutral and objective sound than does "women."
>
> *(Scott 1989, 16)*

Following this trend of using "gender" was the move to replace Women in Development" (WID) and Women and Development (WAD) with Gender and Development (GAD) or even Gender concerns in Development (GCID).

The GAD approach synthesized the analysis of Western socialist feminism that emphasized Marxist materiality and material conditions (Eisenstein 1978; Hartsock 2004; Holmstrom 2002; Martin 1986) with the radical feminist analysis of patriarchy as a system and structure shaping all lives (Daly 1978; Firestone 1970; Koedt et al. 1973; Morgan 1970). The resulting analysis theorizes that patriarchy plays out in the material conditions of political economies that shape and affect women's status, roles, duties, and activities at all levels – local, regional, national, and global. GAD reflects a two-pronged approach of examining women's material conditions and class position as well as the patriarchal structures, beliefs, and practices that maintain and entrench women's inequalities/oppression/injustices/subordination/discrimination and so on. In other words, material and economic conditions are shaped by patriarchal structures and together the two shape and entrench norms and practices defining gender roles, duties, and activities in particular societies. Gender norms can be said to shape and define what women can be and do – and what women can be and do is in turn affected by structures, beliefs, practices, and policies at local, regional, national, and global levels. Because gender norms are taken for granted, they are sometimes invisible and not easily recognized as sources for inequalities. And because they are taken for granted, they are entrenched and difficult to address or dislodge.

The GAD approach can be viewed as shifting the focus to the role of institutions and structures. The model of development as lifting women out of poverty and improving their lives by having them enter male dominated domains of social, economic, and political institutions relied on assumptions about the interests, projects, and goals that women needed to pursue. With GAD the focus shifts from individual women to the relationships between women and men that themselves shape women's interests, projects, and goals, and which in turn determine their status, roles, and positions in particular societies. In the development context, these insights from radical and socialist feminists resulted in a clear and more accurate account of the ways in which relationships shape lives, are not immutable, and can be subject to change. Examining the networks of relationships in which people are situated can help explain how power and oppression operate to shape specific experiences, lives, and contexts (Koggel 2012, 2013). The message is that gender does not reflect the natural order of things but is socially constructed in and through relationships of power that shape what are taken to be appropriate patterns of behavior for men and women.

An analysis of GAD's account of the interconnections and intersections of gender, race, and class opened the door to deeper and more complex feminist analyses of oppression as affected by a broad range of factors: gender, race, class, colonial history, culture, nationality, economic globalization, the international economic order, and so on. Paying attention to how development policies and practices themselves shape relationships, affect women's and men's lives differently, and are dynamic and changeable also signified GAD's recognition of women as agents and not simply as patients or recipients of development policies and practices. Yet criticisms would continue to be raised by women from the South and by third-world and postcolonial feminists who challenged the hegemony and power of Western feminism and movement (Mohanty 1988).

Women's movements and third world feminism: challenges from the South

The first thing to note is that women in countries and contexts less privileged than those working in academic circles have raised a legitimate fear that the academic debate about the use of "gender" instead of "women" means that women will once again become less visible. Women involved in grassroots movements in the South have pointed out that all research fields in development theory and policy, whether of WID, WAD, GAD, GCID, feminist theory, gender studies, or women's studies, need to be grounded in women's movements and the experiences and struggles of women working together to achieve equality and justice in everyday lives and contexts. One of these influential grassroots organizations is Development Alternatives with Women for a New Era (DAWN). DAWN emerged from the 1985 Nairobi international NGO forum that happened parallel to the official World Conference on Women. More than 15,000 women activists from around the world rallied to call for an approach to women's development that acknowledged the importance of global and gender inequalities. DAWN, and other women-centred organizations and NGOs, drew attention to women's unique contributions to national and global development, contributions that reached beyond viewing women as mere instruments for advancing the goals and processes of achieving economic growth.

As noted earlier, this call to pay attention to the activism, struggle, and solidarity of women in movements around the world is central to what it means to gain knowledge of the experiences and lives of those who suffer from poverty, oppression, inequalities, and injustices of various kinds in particular contexts. This approach also challenges feminist scholars and academics to revise theory that ignores or fails to accommodate the concrete details of lives and experiences of women from around the world. Chandra Mohanty's "Under Western Eyes: Feminist Scholarship and Colonial Discourses" is important not only for revealing the power and influence of Western feminism in the global context, but also for uncovering tendencies in Western feminist theory and methodology that result in women in third-world countries being depicted as a homogeneous group, all of whom are perceived to be suffering injustices and inequalities similar to but much worse than those suffered by women in Western countries. Without proper descriptions of the "historically specific material reality of groups of women," argues Mohanty, third-world women tend to be depicted as a monolith, all of whom are mere passive victims of male violence or of an entrenched sexual division of labour (Mohanty 1988). Not only does this deny agency to third-world women, who have always been and continue to be active in understanding and responding to oppression as it manifests itself in their specific contexts, but it privileges Western feminist normative accounts of what can or ought to be done to "help" third-world women.

Mohanty's account and others by third-world feminists such as Uma Narayan in her critique of Western accounts of women and feminism in India (Narayan 1997) reject overarching or monocausal explanations, but still insist that descriptions and explanations of inequality, injustice, oppression, or discrimination can and need to be given. Paying attention to how kinds of oppression interlock and are then reflected in and perpetuated by economic, political, legal, and cultural conditions shaped by particular histories and contexts does not mean giving up on explanations. Instead, it calls for fine tuning the descriptive components so that more accurate accounts of women's lives can be provided. With more accurate descriptions in hand, the idea is that more effective strategies can then be devised for removing oppression, inequality, injustice, and discrimination as it manifests itself in particular contexts and in the lives of women in those contexts. Using insights from Maria Mies's careful analysis of the concept of "sexual division of labor" (Mies 1982), Mohanty writes: "if such concepts are assumed to be universally applicable, the resultant homogenization of class, race, religious and daily material practices of women in the third word can create a false sense of the commonality of oppressions, interests, and struggles between and amongst women globally" (Mohanty 1988, 76–77).

Taking the broad range of different lives and experiences into account cannot help but strengthen the links between feminist theory and practice. To keep these lessons in the forefront, especially when we are theorizing about people in so-called "developing" countries, is to treat people as agents, to give credibility and value to lives and livelihoods different from that which is familiar and dominant in Western/liberal societies, and to open up possibilities for questioning Western ways of being that are detrimental to people, countries, women's lives, and the environment. This work by women's movements in the South as well by third-world and postcolonial theorists attends to the actual experiences, lives, and needs (created and maintained by the global order) and focuses on the practical and strategic interests of meeting needs and empowering women (Molyneux 1988; Holmstrom 2002). This work thereby creates openings for analyzing which policies, organizations, structures, and practices at the local, national, and global levels actually work to meet immediate needs and at the same time result in changes to structures of power and oppression.

However, what happens in women's movements and in challenges to Western feminist theory or approaches to development is not necessarily reflected in the development theory and practice that is still dominated by the paradigm of economic growth. This has tended to mean that the language and policy of WID and WAD are still in place and operational. Yet pressure from the areas outlined in this section has meant that these far-reaching critiques by women's movements in the South and by third-world and postcolonial feminists have had some influence in development theory and practice designed to remove gender inequalities. This is evident in the *World Development Report (WDR)*, the annual flagship publication of the World Bank, that devoted its 2012 report to its first-time examination of the theme *Gender Equality and Development*. In the next and final section, I will explore some of the contents of the *WDR 2012* to highlight both what has been accomplished in contemporary understandings of development theory and practice and where approaches to understanding and removing gender inequalities still need work.

The *World Development Report 2012* and future directions for gender equality and development

WDR 2012 is explicit about borrowing the notion of the centrality of freedom to an account of development from Sen's version of the capabilities approach: "Following Amartya Sen, we see development as a process of expanding freedoms equally for all people" (*WDR 2012*, 3). Chapter 1, "A Wave of Progress" details the ways in which women's lives have changed for the better with large and fast gains in the second half of the 20th century. The report admits that progress has been slow and limited for some women in some domains and then goes on to identify four areas where gender gaps are most significant "and where growth alone cannot solve the issues": (1) reducing excess female mortality and closing the education gaps where they remain; (2) improving access to economic opportunities for women; (3) increasing women's voice and agency in the household and in society; and (4) limiting the reproduction of gender inequality across generations (*WDR 2012*, abstract). It would seem that (1), (2), and (3) connect with mainstream development policies and projects designed to enhance women's agency and well-being freedoms by including them in social, economic, and political spheres and activities. Sen, for example, tends to endorse the usual set of liberal strategies and policies (Koggel 2003, 2013, 2018):

> empirical work in recent years has brought out very clearly how the relative respect and regard for women's well-being is strongly influenced by such variables as women's ability to earn an independent income, to find employment outside the home, to have ownership rights and to have literacy and be educated participants in decisions within and outside the family. Indeed, even the survival disadvantage of women compared with men in developing countries seems to go down sharply – and may even get eliminated – as progress is made in these agency aspects.
>
> *(191)*

Yet the *WDR 2012*'s discussion of (4) would seem to go beyond the dominant liberal paradigm in recognizing the force of gender norms that create, perpetuate, and entrench inequalities:

> Perhaps the "stickiest" aspect of gender outcomes is the way patterns of gender inequality are reproduced over time. Part of this persistence is rooted in slow-moving social norms and how they affect what happens in the household. . . . Norms may be learned in the household, but they are often reinforced by market signals and institutions, which are gender biased in many aspects. For example, gender differences in the responsibility for house and care work, as just discussed, are rooted in gender roles but strengthened by discrimination in labour markets and by a lack of child-care services.
>
> *(21)*

The report also recognizes that effective solutions very much depend on context specific factors of social and political structures, histories, traditions, and practices:

> Gender disparities persist for multiple reasons: there may be a single institutional or policy "fix" that is difficult and easily blocked; there may be multiple reinforcing constraints in markets, formal institutions, and households that combine to block progress; or they may be deeply rooted in gender roles or social norms that evolve very slowly. Effective policy design requires a good understanding of which of these situations prevails in a particular context, and of where and what the binding constraints are.
>
> *(37)*

Finally, the report appears to acknowledge that there is more to addressing gender inequalities than improving access to markets – at least in some contexts:

> The reproduction of specific gender inequalities across generations gives rise to "gender inequality traps," which are likely to most affect the poor and excluded in society. Women's lack of political voice means that the market and institutional failures feeding gender inequality are unlikely to be corrected. Income growth alone does little to address the processes that underlie these persistent gaps.
>
> *(WDR 2012, 32)*

While the report shows promise in its recognition that gender norms generate inequalities that are hard to dislodge, it falls back on assuming (rather than interrogating) that the unpaid work of caring for dependents can legitimately and justly limit access to paid work. It does not acknowledge or explain that unpaid reproductive and caring work *is* work that is vital to the functioning of any economy (Robinson 2006; Schutte 2002). Nor does it explain that market structures assume and accept the formal and informal rules and practices that value male labour in the marketplace and devalue female labour that involves caring activities and responsibilities for meeting the needs of others (Robinson 1999). As Marilyn Waring has argued, these and other activities done by women simply do not count as work (Waring 1999). The *WDR 2012* instead takes women's work outside the home to have instrumental value in improving the efficiencies of market structures and increasing economic growth. The report contains two assumptions – both of which are problematic. First, perceiving women's work outside the home as contributing to economic growth sets the task as needing to undermine gender norms that keep them in the home – and have them engage in activities of meeting the needs of others. Second, getting them out of the home is perceived as challenging gender norms that devalue caring for others at the same time as it is assumed that this work will nevertheless get done (Fraser 1997; Koggel 2018).

In a review of the *WDR 2012*, Shahra Razavi explains that

> if we see labour markets for what they are: social institutions that operate on the basis of social norms and power inequalities, then it is not too difficult to understand why patriarchal and racialized strategies are deployed to create hierarchical structures that further the effective control and exploitation of the workforce.
>
> *(Razavi 2011, 5)*

Razavi picks up on the report's assumption that market mechanisms will enhance agency and well-being freedoms. She points out, however, that market structures also deploy and exploit gender, race, class, ethnicity, nationality, and so on to maximize profits and growth. As noted earlier, these are insights central to postcolonial and third-world feminisms. To this can be added that patriarchal and racialized strategies are not only deployed to control and exploit the workforce; they are also deployed to reduce the effectiveness of strategies for enhancing agency and well-being freedoms for those left in the home or dependent on others to meet their needs. Again, the assumption and expectation is that women's agency is enhanced when they leave behind what they do and who they are in the home.

The report seems to come close to recognizing this failing when it acknowledges, "Important challenges remain in working conditions for those outside formal employment" only to have this followed by recommending strategies of including social clauses, codes of conduct, and the ILO's "decent work" approach (*WDR 2012*, 267). No mention is made of how sticky gender norms assume women's necessary but unpaid and devalued work of meeting the needs of others and that this is often exploited rather than addressed through policies endorsing greater participation in economic and political structures. The one place where the report acknowledges that "gender differences in care responsibilities can prevent women from seizing new agricultural and wage opportunities in the export sector," it bemoans women's inability to find other female members in the household to take on these "household duties" instead of calling for the provision of childcare programs to better meet the demands of the important work of caring for and meeting the needs of others (*WDR 2012*, 269). As Razavi points out, "*WDR 2012* counsels against provision of 'subsidies to new childcare programs' if 'fairly cheap alternatives already exist' (*WDR 2012*, 297) – again there seems to be no . . . concern about the working conditions of the workers providing the service" (Razavi 2011, 7).

Even in its acknowledgement of the "stickiness" of gender norms and the connections between these norms and women's lack of power and voice, the report fails to identify needs and responsibilities to others in and through networks of relationships in which people's needs and their very possibilities for effective agency can be created, worsened, or undermined (Koggel 2008, 2013; Drydyk 2013). These shortcomings highlight how oppressive relationships and institutional structures shape the very policies designed to improve women's lives. Because an examination of the broad network of relationships in which all agents are embedded is absent, it can be said that the World Bank report's focus is too exclusively on individuals who fit the dominant picture of agents engaged in market activities (Koggel 2008, 2013). An examination of the full range of who agents are and what they can do and be challenges our understanding of the kinds of gender inequalities that remain even as policies designed to challenge them result in some gains for women in places around the world (Razavi and Staab 2010; Benería 2003b, 2008).

The upshot with respect to development theory and practice is that the insights from contemporary feminist theory and women's movements that I have examined in this chapter provide the needed critical lens through which to understand how concepts, frameworks, public debate, and policies embed norms that are taken-for-granted and kept in place. This is especially true with respect to gender inequalities where sticky gender norms manifest differently with respect to factors such as race, class, ethnicity, nationality, age, and so on and these factors in turn are shaped and affected by colonial histories, postcolonial contexts, and the forces of economic globalization (Mohanty 1997; Fussell 2000; Benería 2003a; Koggel 2003). These sticky gender norms leave questions about inequalities generated by and entrenched through reproductive and domestic labour unanswered – or the assumption is that gender norms that entrench inequalities in these domains will be addressed or removed through policies that open up opportunities for women in the public sphere. Thinking ahead to work that remains in theorizing and the making of policy, these tricky, complex, and sticky issues to do with gender inequalities have yet to be incorporated into development theory and policy or into feminist theory itself.

A deeper and broader analysis of gender inequalities needs to attend to work done by women that is unpaid, devalued, not counted as work, or relegated to insecure, informal, low-skilled, and low paying jobs. To list examples of a wide range of factors affecting and shaping inequalities: some women do unpaid work in the home; some do both unpaid work in the home as well as waged and unpaid work outside the home; some work outside the home and employ other women to work in the home; some are recruited to take unskilled, low pay work under poor working conditions; some travel from poor countries to care for children in rich countries; some "choose" or are forced into no-exit options as sex workers or as domestic servants or even as wives. In all cases, gender inequalities are affected by factors such as race, class, ethnicity, age, ability, and so on. And a range of inequalities are further complicated and magnified in a global context in which women are vulnerable to forces of economic globalization that keep them in particular kinds of jobs or exploit them for profit. As has been argued in this chapter, development projects and policies that have adopted or continue to adopt goals of modernizing and bringing countries in the South/Third World into the structures of economic globalization tend to perpetuate rather than alleviate gender inequalities in countries and societies around the world.

References

Alexander, M.J. and Mohanty, C. eds. (1997) *Feminist Genealogies, Colonial Legacies, Democratic Futures*. Routledge, New York.

Antony, L. (1998) "Human nature" and Its Role in Feminist Theory. In Kourany, J. ed., *Philosophy in a Feminist Voice*. Princeton University Press, New Haven.

Anzaldúa, G. (1987) *Borderlands. La Frontera: The New Mestiza.* Aunt Lute Books, San Francisco.
Benería, L. (2003a) *Gender, Development, and Globalization: Economics as if all People Mattered.* Routledge, New York.
Benería, L. (2003b) Paid and Unpaid Labour: Meanings and Debates. In *Gender, Development and Globalization: Economics as if all People Mattered.* Routledge, London, 131–160.
Benería, L. (2008) The Crisis of Care, International Migration, and Public Policy. *Feminist Economics* 14(3): 1–21.
Boserup, E. (1970) *Women's Role in Economic Development.* Allen & Unwin, London.
Buviniç, M. (1986) Projects for Women in the Third World: Explaining their Misbehavior. *World Development* 14(5): 653–664.
Collier, P. (1988) *Women in Development: Defining the Issues.* World Bank, Washington.
Collins, P.H. (1990) *Black Feminist Thought: Knowledge, Consciousness, and the Politics of Empowerment.* Unwin Hyman, Boston.
Crenshaw, K. (1991) Mapping the Margins: Intersectionality, Identity Politics, and Violence against Women of Color. *Stanford Law Review* 43(6): 1241–1299.
Daly, M. (1978) *Gyn/Ecology: The Metaethics of Radical Feminism.* Beacon Press, Boston.
Drydyk, J. (2013) Empowerment, Agency, and Power. *Journal of Global Ethics* 9(3): 249–262.
Eisenstein, Z. (1978) *Capitalist Patriarchy and the Case for Socialist Feminism.* Monthly Review Press, New York.
Fausto-Sterling, A. (1993a) *Myths of Gender: Biological Theories about Women and Men.* Basic Books, New York.
Fausto-Sterling, A. (1993b) The Five Sexes: Why Male and Female are Not Enough. *The Sciences* 33: 20–24.
Fausto-Sterling, A. (2000) *Sexing the Body.* Basic Books, New York.
Fausto-Sterling, A. (2003) The Problem with Sex/Gender and Nature/Nurture. In Williams, S.J. Birke, L. and Bendelow, G.A. eds., *Debating Biology: Sociological Reflections on Health, Medicine and Society.* Routledge, New York.
Firestone, S. (1970) *The Dialectic of Sex: The Case for Feminist Revolution.* William Morrow and Company.
Fraser, N. (1997) *Justice Interruptus: Critical Reflections on the 'Postsocialist' Condition.* Routledge, New York.
Friedan, B. (1963) *The Feminine Mystique* Norton, New York.
Fussell, E. (2000) Making Labor Flexible: The Recomposition of Tijuana's Maquiladora Female Labor Force. *Feminist Economics* 6: 59–79.
Goulet, D. (1995) *Development Ethics: A Guide to Theory and Practice.* Apex Press, New York.
Hartsock, N. (2004) The Feminist Standpoint: Developing the Ground for a Specifically Feminist Historical Materialism. In Harding, S. *The Feminist Standpoint Theory Reader: Intellectual and Political Controversies.* Routledge, New York, 35–54.
Holmstrom, N. ed. (2002) *The Socialist Feminist Project: A Contemporary Reader in Theory and Politics* Monthly Press, New York.
hooks, b. (1984) *Feminist Theory: From Margin to Center.* South End Press, Boston.
hooks, b. (1988) *Talking Back: Thinking Feminist, Thinking Black.* Between the Lines, Toronto.
Jackson, C. and Pearson, R. eds. (1998) *Feminist Visions of Development: Gender Analysis and Policy.* Routledge, London.
Jaggar, A. (1983) Human Biology in Feminist Theory: Sexual Equality Reconsidered. In Gould, C. ed., *Beyond Domination: New Perspectives on Women and Philosophy.* Rowman & Littlefield, Lanham.
Jaggar A. (2009a) The Philosophical Challenges of Global Gender Justice. *Philosophical Topics: Gender and Global Justice* 37(2): 1–15.
Jaggar, A. (2009b) Transnational Cycles of Gendered Vulnerability: A Prologue to a Theory of Global Gender Justice. *Philosophical Topics. Gender and Global Justice* 37(2): 33–52.
Joekes, S.P. (1990) Excerpts on Women in Development: International Development strategy for the Third United Nations Development Decade. In *Women in the World Economy: An INSTRAW Study.* Oxford University Press, Oxford.
Kabeer, N. (2004) Globalization, Labor Standards, and Women's Rights: Dilemmas of Collective (In)action in an Interdependent World. *Feminist Economics* 10(1): 3–35.
Karim, L. (2011) *Microfinance and its Discontents: Women in Debt in Bangladesh.* University of Minnesota Press, Minneapolis.

Koedt, A. Levine, A. and Rapone, A. eds. (1973) *Radical Feminism.* Times Books, New York.

Koggel, C. (2002) Equality Analysis in a Global Context: A Relational Approach. *Canadian Journal of Philosophy Supplementary Volume: Feminist Moral Philosophy* 28: 247–272.

Koggel, C. (2003) Globalization and Women's Paid Work: Expanding Freedom? *Feminist Economics, Special Issue on the Ideas and Work of Amartya Sen* 9(2–3): 163–183.

Koggel, C. (2008) Agency and Empowerment: Embodied Realities in a Globalized World. In Campbell, S. Maynell, L. and Sherwin, S. eds., *Embodiment and Agency.* Pennsylvania State University Press, Philadelphia, 250–268.

Koggel, C. (2011) Global Feminism. In Garfield, K. ed., *Oxford Handbook of World Philosophy.* Oxford University Press, Oxford.

Koggel, C. (2012) A Relational Approach to Equality: New Developments and Applications. In Downie, J. and Llewellyn, J. eds., *Being Relational: Reflections on Relational Theory and Health Law.* UBC Press, Vancouver, 63–88.

Koggel, C. (2013) A Critical Analysis of Recent Work on Empowerment: Implications for Gender. *Journal of Global Ethics* 9(3): 263–275.

Koggel, C. (2018) Expanding Agency: Conceptual, Explanatory, and Normative Implications. In Keleher, L. and Kosko, S. eds., *Agency, Democracy, and Participation in Global Development.* Cambridge University Press (forthcoming).

Lorde, A. (1984) *Sister Outsider: Essays and Speeches.* The Crossing Press, Freedom CA.

Martin, G. (1986) *Socialist Feminism: The First Decade, 1966–76.* Freedom Socialist Publications, Seattle.

Mies, M. (1982) The Dynamics of the sexual division of labor and integration of rural women into the world market. In Benería, L. ed., *Women and Development: The Sexual Division of Labor in Rural Societies.* Praeger, New York, 1–28.

Mies, M. (1989) *Patriarchy and Accumulation on a World Scale.* Zed Press, London.

Mohanty, C. (1988) Under Western Eyes: Feminist Scholarship and Colonial Discourses. *Feminist Review* 30: 61–88.

Mohanty, C. (1997) Women Workers and Capitalist Scripts: Ideologies of Domination, Common Interests, and the Politics of Solidarity. In Alexander, J. and Mohanty, C. eds., *Feminist Genealogies, Colonial Legacies, Democratic Futures.* Routledge, New York, 3–29.

Molyneux, M. (1988) The Politics of Abortion in Nicaragua: Revolutionary Pragmatism – Or Feminism in the Realm of Necessity? *The Feminist Review* 29: 114–132.

Moraga, C. and Anzaldúa, G. eds. (1981) *This Bridge Called My Back: Writings by Radical Women of Color.* Kitchen Table, Women of Color Press, New York.

Morgan, R. ed. (1970) *Sisterhood Is Powerful: An Anthology of Writings from the Women's Liberation Movement.* Random House, New York.

Narayan, U. (1997) *Dislocating Cultures: Identities, Traditions, and Third World Feminism.* Routledge, New York.

Narayan, U. and Harding, S. eds. (2000) *Decentering the Center: Philosophy for a Multicultural, Postcolonial, and Feminist World.* Indiana University Press, Bloomington.

Nicholson, L. (1994) Interpreting Gender. *Signs* 20: 79–105.

Parpart, J.L., Connelly, M.P. and Barriteau, V.E. eds. (2000) *Theoretical Perspectives on Gender and Development.* International Development Research Centre, Ottawa.

Parpart, J.L., Rai, S.M. and Staudt, K. eds. (2002) *Rethinking Empowerment: Gender and Development in a Global/Local World.* Routledge, London.

Petesch, P. (2012) Unlocking Pathways to Women's Empowerment and Gender Equality: The Good, the Bad, and the Sticky. *Ethics and Social Welfare* 6(3).

Razavi, S. (2011) *World Development Report 2012, Gender Equality and Development: An Opportunity both Welcome and Missed (an Extended Commentary).* United Nations Research Institute for Social Development.

Razavi, S. and Miller, C. (1995) From WID to GAD: Conceptual shifts in the Women and Development Discourse. United Nations Research Institute Occasional Paper series, United Nations Research Institute for Social Development.

Razavi, S. and Staab, S. (2010) Underpaid and Overworked: A Cross-national Perspective on Care Workers. *International Labour Review* 149(4): 407–422.

Robinson, F. (1999) *Globalizing Care: Ethics, Feminist Theory and International Relations*. Westview Press, Boulder.

Robinson, F. (2006) Beyond Labour Rights: The Ethics of Care and Women's Work in the Global Economy. *International Feminist Journal of Politics* 8(3): 321–342.

Salazar-Parreñas, R. (2001) *Servants of Globalization: Women, Migration and Domestic Work*. Stanford University Press, Palo Alto.

Schutte, O. (2002) Dependency Work, women, and the Global Economy. In Kittay, E.F. and Feder, E.K. eds., *The Subject of Care: Feminist Perspectives on Dependency*. Rowman & Littlefield, Lanham, 138–158.

Scott, J.W. (1989) Gender: A Useful Category of Historical analysis. In Rao, A. ed., *Women's Studies International: Nairobi and Beyond*. Feminist Press at City University of New York, New York.

Sen, A. (1999) *Development as Freedom*. Anchor Books, New York.

Spelman, E. (1998) *The Inessential Woman*. Beacon Press, Boston.

Synder, M. and Talesse, M. (1996) *African Women and Development: A History*. Zed Books, London.

Waring, M. (1999) *Counting for Nothing: What Men Value and What Women are Worth*. University of Toronto Press, Toronto.

Weekes-Vagliani, W. (1985) *The Integration of Women in Development Projects*. OECD Publishing, Washington.

Weir, A. (2005) The Global Universal Caregiver: Imaging Women's Liberation in the New Millennium. *Constellations* 12(3): 308–330.

World Bank (2011) *World Development Report 2012: Gender Equality and Development*. World Bank, Washington.

12

Indigenous peoples

Self-determination, decolonization, and indigenous philosophies

Krushil Watene and Roger Merino

Drawing from the South Pacific and Latin America, this chapter explores how development for and by indigenous peoples can be enabled, and reflects on how this bears on our ideas about the ends and means of development. We begin by introducing self-determination as it is discussed within international law and the United Nations Declaration on the Rights of Indigenous Peoples (UNDRIP). We note that self-determination entails institutional transformation consistent with the creation of (cultural, economic, political, and environmental) conditions conducive to enabling its pursuit and realization. We further observe that, while the details of such institutional transformation depend on specific contexts and histories, it nonetheless entails transformation that nourishes the well-being of indigenous communities. We find that 1) decolonization and 2) indigenous philosophies are vital to these goals. We conclude by outlining how the opportunities and challenges for achieving self-determination for indigenous peoples transform how development ethicists should think about, and undertake to design and implement, well-being and development ideas today.

Self-determination

The notion of indigenous self-determination has a rich genealogy that begins with the imperial history of colonization. Some important milestones in the conceptual narrative were the discussions around the decolonization of Africa. Around World War I, self-determination became the subject of a powerful political discourse from which notions of statehood were derived. When the United Nations (UN) was created, 'the self-determination of peoples' was included in the founding principles of the UN Charter. In 1960, the UN General Assembly adopted the Declaration on the Granting of Independence to Colonial Countries and Peoples, referring to self-determination in relation to formal colonial rule (UN 1960; Meuhlebach 2003). The 'peoples' in this declaration were colonized peoples dominated by foreign powers. For them, self-determination meant independence from the colonial authority. Deriving statehood from self-determination was, however, problematic. Although all states claimed international political recognition and sovereignty, inside many 'postcolonial' states lived different indigenous nations. For this reason, international scholars differentiated between 'external self-determination' and 'internal self-determination' (Fromherz 2008; Dodds 1998). The former refers to a situation in

DOI: 10.4324/9781315626796-15

which a specific nation has the right to be an independent republic in front of the international community, and the latter refers to a situation in which different nations coexist within a specific state and maintain some degree of political autonomy under a unitary legal and political framework (Merino 2017).

When international legal instruments and most scholars refer to indigenous self-determination they are referring to 'internal self-determination' as the right to maintain their ancestral territory and their specific cultural and social norms as peoples within a specific state (Errico 2007). This version of self-determination was recognized in the International Covenant on Economic, Social and Cultural Rights and the International Covenant on Civil and Political Rights, adopted by the UN General Assembly in 1966. Most significantly, these are the sources of Article 3 of the UNDRIP of 2007, which recognizes the 'right of self-determination', while respecting the principle of political unity of the sovereign state (Merino 2017). The UNDRIP outlines minimum standards 'for the survival, dignity and well-being of the indigenous peoples of the world' (UNPFII 2007). The declaration includes protections from assimilation, discrimination, and forced removals from traditionally owned lands (Articles 8, 9, 26). The declaration includes rights to self-government, to participate in, and consent to, any decisions which affect them, and to control (and have returned) traditionally owned lands and natural resources (Articles 4, 19, 32, 26). The rights entitle indigenous peoples to 'freely determine their political status and freely pursue their economic, social and cultural development' (UNPFII 2007).

For James Anaya (2004, 105), achieving self-determination requires two things. The 'substantive aspect' of self-determination requires that the 'governing institutional order be substantially the creation of processes guided by the will of the people, or peoples, governed', and also requires that peoples be able to 'live and develop freely on a continuous basis' (105). Here self-determination applies to how society is designed, to the role peoples (as individuals and collectives) have in its creation, and to the freedom of those peoples within it. All peoples should play a part in shaping the structure of society, and they ought to be able to develop and redevelop within it. Secondly, indigenous peoples' self-determination 'gives rise to remedies that tear at the legacies of empire, discrimination, oppression of democratic participation, and cultural suffocation' (107). This 'remedial aspect' of indigenous self-determination is (Anaya tells us) not based solely on correcting historical wrongs, but on remedying 'a particular set of vulnerabilities' that are understood in terms of 'disparities of economic and political power rooted in history' (107). Implementing self-determination here requires, at the very least, some thinking along dimensions of: non-discrimination, cultural integrity, control over land and resources, social welfare and development, as well as self-government. Achieving self-determination requires that we rethink social and political structures, and that issues of power are taken on board. This calls for institutional transformation at the levels of governance, policy, and law.

There are, of course, different perspectives on the degree of institutional transformations that states must undertake to recognize indigenous self-determination. Some argue for the deepening of the multicultural state that recognizes minority rights (Kymlicka 1995) and social inclusion (Van Cott 2006). Other scholars propose a more profound structural change that reshapes the state architecture towards the creation of a federal state with multiple nations (Tully 1995), or a plurinational state (Santos 2007). Yet others still propose state independence for indigenous peoples (Churchill 2002). The most appropriate state form depends on the historical trajectory and political context of each indigenous nation. In all cases, however, institutional transformation is centrally concerned with providing space for indigenous peoples to articulate, pursue, and realize lives that they value in their own ways and for their own reasons. Self-determination is about what indigenous peoples are (individually and collectively) able to do and be. This requires that indigenous peoples are able to create conditions in which they can flourish in the ways valuable to them.

In this light, development by and for indigenous peoples is centrally about self-determination. Indigenous development is development that is undertaken by indigenous peoples in ways consistent with their values, needs, and aspirations. Indigenous peoples are sceptical of development initiatives that presume to speak on their behalf, and they are sceptical of development policies and programs designed in terms of priorities imposed on them. If indigenous development is development for and by indigenous peoples themselves, then it is shaped by, at least, two interdependent movements, both of which remain critical to institutional and indigenous community transformation. In what follows, we show that 1) decolonization and 2) the revitalization of indigenous knowledges are movements that remain central to creating the conditions in which indigenous peoples are able to articulate, pursue, and realize their own development needs and goals.

Decolonization

Not all indigenous communities have been subject to European colonization. Indeed, many indigenous communities remain subjected to oppression within their homelands – lacking recognition and the rights required for protecting their ways of life. The Adivasis of India are one such example of an indigenous community lacking the rights guaranteed by the UNDRIP not by European colonization per se, but by the government of India.

Nevertheless, European colonization has ushered in the destruction of many indigenous communities. In Aotearoa, New Zealand, colonization systematically undermined the structural bones of the Māori world. Ideas about property ownership framed policies and land tenure systems that reconfigured the relationships Māori were able to have with ancestral lands, opening the way for widespread land dispossession (Kawharu 1989, 1997; Williams 2007; Mutu 2012). Disconnection from lands and natural resources impacted on the functioning of Māori kin-communities – breaking down relationships and community (Taskforce 2010; Watene 2016a, 2016b; Smith 1999; Waitangi Tribunal 2011a, 2011b). This would be exacerbated by policies preventing the Māori language from being spoken in schools (Hohepa 2014), and the migration away from ancestral 'marae' communities in search of the stability and opportunities available in urban centres (Tapsell 2014). Today, less than 6% of New Zealand's total land area remains under collective ownership (Kingi 2008). The majority of tribal descendants live outside of their tribal areas (Statistics New Zealand 2014). Around 20% of Māori speak the Māori language (Statistics New Zealand 2014).

Rectification and reconciliation processes often deepen oppression. For instance, the Treaty of Waitangi claims processes and settlements attempt to provide space and opportunities for Māori communities to give voice to and to be fairly compensated for historical injustices. Te Tiriti o Waitangi (written *Te Tiriti* in Te Reo Māori, the Māori language) is a formal agreement, made in the interests of peace and friendship between Māori chiefs and the British Crown in 1840 (Waitangi Tribunal 2011a, 2011b; Mutu 2013; Walker 2004; Kawharu 1989). Te Tiriti affirmed, and committed to upholding, the mana, tino rangatiratanga, and tikanga of Māori – recognizing the system of laws that had existed prior to the arrival of colonial settlers (Mutu 2013). For representatives of the British Crown, however, the Treaty of Waitangi ('The Treaty' being its title in English) detailed the cessation of sovereignty by Māori over Aotearoa, New Zealand, to Queen Victoria. Assumptions underpinning The Treaty – assumptions regarding state sovereignty, authority, ownership – silenced, oppressed, and marginalized the Māori ways of knowing, being, and doing affirmed and protected by Te Tiriti (Matiu and Mutu 2003; Mutu 2013, 2012; Jackson 1992).

Māori activists and scholars have long held that the settlement process continues to undermine the values and identities of Māori tribal communities, leading to increased cultural poverty and cultural disconnection (Kawharu 2013; Mutu 2013; Poata-Smith 2004). According to Margaret Kawharu (2013):

> While being 'claimants' reinforces, embraces and strengthens the notion of a Māori identity, it undermines, systematizes, and limits being Māori as well. That the terms are determined by the Crown is in itself a result of patterns of interaction shaped by a legal, adversarial settlement process and an iniquitous colonial past.
>
> *(Kawharu 2013, 51)*

Similarly, according to Margaret Mutu (2013):

> The process is not about settling claims at all. Nor is it about giving Māori many millions of dollars in compensation. Rather it is a unilaterally Crown-determined policy which aims to legally extinguish all historic Māori claims against the Crown as cheaply and as expeditiously as possible. The whole process is deeply racist, dishonest and yet another gross violation of Te Tiriti o Waitangi. These claims most often involve hundreds of thousands of acres of lands and other resources and gross atrocities perpetrated against Māori.
>
> *(Mutu 2013, 8)*

As both Kawharu and Mutu demonstrate, for many of the hapū (kin-communities) who have been part of this process, it is a contemporary example of colonial oppression in the way that it prioritizes the objectives of the Crown and continues to redefine Māori communities. The ability of Māori communities to pursue and realize lives they value is bound up with the extent to which Māori are able to define themselves (UNPFII 2007).

A central problem is that within many colonial-settler states, indigenous peoples have never been recognized as 'sovereign nations', but rather as 'indigenous communities' with property rights instead of territorial rights. In Latin America, for example, after colonization, the political and economic elites built the new countries under European patterns according to which the state was an attempt to formally express a relatively homogeneous social collective (a 'nation'). Within such a framework, indigenous peoples have to be either included within these new nation-states (denying their different social, political, and economic arrangements) or excluded from them (which meant in some contexts the legal and material elimination of these peoples). In the new state model 'indigenous nations' were unacceptable.

This political tension continues today. For instance, when most Latin American constitutions recognize the right of self-determination or autonomy for indigenous peoples, they actually refer to the right of each indigenous community to govern itself within a specific space legally protected with property entitlements. There is no recognition of the self-determination of a whole indigenous nation with territorial rights, only the recognition of specific communities of individuals 'included' in the political and economic logic of the nation-state. For example, the Peruvian state has legally recognized Amazonian indigenous peoples not as proper nations but as autonomous natives communities (thus, for instance, the Awajun people is divided into more than 200 natives communities). This creates a situation in which the state does not recognize a whole indigenous territorial governance but selectively delimits an extractive frontier for managing natural resources that would pertain to the 'nation-state' (Merino 2015). Thus, by recognizing specific plots through property entitlements, huge extension of the territory, which includes the forest, rivers, and mountains, are left 'free', and as such are used for mining, oil, or agribusiness exploitation.

This paradox responds to the colonial denial of two key aspects of indigenous law and politics: 1) the denial of their territories and 2) the denial of their character as nations. Within the context of the dominant liberal theory, indigenous peoples must be integrated, included, assimilated, or accommodated within the liberal framework as ethnic minorities with proprietary entitlements, so they can 'participate' in the benefits of 'development'. This comes at the cost of viewing indigenous peoples as nations with territorial rights, and who are able to fully pursue their own models of development.

The colonizing project was based on the idea of progress and civilization. The aim was the expansion of colonial interests, and the eradication of indigenous cultures. The starting point for colonial-settler interactions was an image of indigenous peoples as savage, backward, and inferior. The laws, values, beliefs, and languages of the colonizers were deemed to be superior. Indigenous beliefs and values were abused, ignored, oppressed, and outlawed. Treaties between settlers and indigenous communities, where they were made, were never honoured. From here, it is straightforward to see that decolonization is centrally about a continuing political struggle. It is also straightforward to see that decolonization requires the courage to call into question these long-standing systems and power structures, and to challenge myths that serve to subjugate indigenous communities (Smith 1999; Jackson 1992; Whyte 2016a, 2016b, 2017; Mikaere 2011). Decolonization requires that development ethicists reflect on their own ideas and practises, and that they be courageous enough to face the possibility of their own explicit and internalized biases. Oppression and domination persist both in the structures which govern our lives and in the beliefs, ideas, values, and activities that we ascribe to and undertake ourselves, particularly as researchers and practitioners.

As development scholars and practitioners, we know that knowledge can be oppressive and empowering. Development researchers, in this context, hold privileged positions. How researchers conceptualize the ends and means of development, and how researchers undertake to 'improve people's lives' are shaped by ideas about well-being and about how it is best secured and enhanced. What we measure and how we measure 'development' determines the information from which policies and programmes are designed. Knowledge, principal among the colonizing tools, lies at the heart of decolonization. Indigenous research that contributes to decolonization challenges mainstream thinking and undertakes to reframe, redesign, and rethink our assumptions about research and development (Mikaere 2011; Smith 1999; Mutu 2012; Walker 2004; Ruru 2014; Whyte 2013, 2016a, 2016b, 2017; Kawharu 2000). This research privileges indigenous knowledges, reconnects indigenous communities with themselves, and transforms, rather than conforms to, existing systems.

We all have a role to play in decolonization, in creating space for critically engaging with mainstream assumptions about development (Merino 2016; Watene and Yap 2015). In such a way, we all have a role to play in creating space in which indigenous peoples can begin to plan for their future, and to reclaim and reimagine their places in this world. Creating space to articulate and pursue indigenous systems of governance, political systems, and legal systems, are central to indigenous development, itself grounded in indigenous philosophies. Decolonization is central to and intimately bound up with the revitalization of indigenous philosophies. Decolonization is central to conversations about the appropriate application of these philosophies to the development challenges and opportunities faced by indigenous communities today.

Indigenous philosophies

Indigenous philosophies are diverse bodies of knowledge within which indigenous worlds were framed prior to European colonization, and which have come to also include deep knowledge of the (ongoing) experiences of colonization (Smith et al. 2016; Turner 2006; Marsden 2003; Whyte 2016a, 2017; Mead 2003). These philosophies chart ideas about time and space, reality, being, knowledge, beauty, well-being, right and wrong, and justice (among many other things) (Smith et al. 2016; Marsden 2003). The philosophies have travelled across geographical spaces, and are woven through multiple generations of lived experiences within diverse (social, political, cultural, economic, and natural) environments (Smith et al. 2016; Whyte 2013). Indigenous philosophies find expression in oral histories, narratives, ceremonies, social and political organizations, the natural environment, astronomy, and in art forms such as weaving, carving, architecture, music, and dance (Smith et al. 2016; Marsden 2003; Royal 2009; Waitangi Tribunal 2011a, 2011b; Sadler 2007; Walker, 2004).

'Mātauranga Māori' is the term used to describe the body of knowledge that Polynesian ancestors brought with them across to Aotearoa, New Zealand. Today it includes the knowledge gathered during early life in Aotearoa, as well as the (ongoing) experiences of colonial-settler relations (Smith et al. 2016; Royal 2009). Relationships and connections lay at the heart of Mātauranga (Marsden 2003; Royal 2009). The Māori world weaves together people, land, and natural resources. From a relational perspective, identity and well-being are shaped by, and bound up with, our (physical and spiritual) connections (Kawharu 2000; Marsden 2003). From a relational perspective, worthwhile development would strengthen, enable, expand, and protect these relationships in their combined cultural, social, environmental, and economic forms. Alongside relationships, creativity and innovation shape the history and development of Māori worldviews. Both of these virtues ground the Pacific Ocean voyages, the development of Māori knowledge, and the embedding of that knowledge in the landscapes of Aotearoa, New Zealand.

Similarly, *buen vivir* is rooted in Andean indigenous cosmologies, particularly from the Quechua and Aymara indigenous peoples of the Andes of Bolivia, Ecuador, and Peru. *Buen vivir* (good life), or *vivir bien* (living well), is the Spanish translation of the Quechua and Aymara words *sumac kawsay* and *suma qamaña*. The notion is built on the principles of reciprocity, complementarity, and relationality in human interactions and in relation to the cycles of nature (Altman 2013; Blaser et al. 2010; Kauffman and Martin 2014; Vanhulst and Beling 2014; Villalba 2013). Such a view implies a profound respect of the differences (and an emphasis on the complementarities) among human beings and between human beings and the natural environment.

This particular view on human relations and the natural environment is shared by indigenous peoples throughout the Amazon. The Amazon rainforest includes territory belonging to nine countries: Brazil, Peru, Colombia, Venezuela, Ecuador, Bolivia, Guyana, Suriname, and French Guiana. According to the last census, somewhere between 42 and 45 million indigenous people represent an estimated 8% to 12% of the total Latin American population (ECLAC 2014; World Bank 2015; IWGIA 2017). They belong to the almost 600 indigenous peoples of the continent, many of whom inhabit the territories of Mexico, Peru, Guatemala, Bolivia, and Ecuador (IWGIA 2017). In Bolivia and Guatemala, indigenous people are the majority, whereas in Mexico, Ecuador, and Peru they are between 10% and 40% of the population (Van Cott 2006).

Given the similarities between different indigenous cosmologies from the Andes and the Amazon, it is possible to understand how the concept of *buen vivir* has now been translated into the language and discourses of the Awajun (as Tajimat Pujut) and Ashaninka (as Kametsa Asaike), two Amazonian indigenous peoples in Peru who use the term as a political platform for their agenda of self-determination and territorial rights (Merino 2016). It is also important to mention that similar notions exist among other indigenous peoples in Latin America: Ñandereko (Guarani), Shiir waras (Ashuar) and Küme Mongen (Mapuche). All these indigenous concepts broadly converge on the idea of living in plenitude, in a state of permanent respect, harmony and balance between the individual, society, and the cycles of nature (Altmann 2013; Blaser et al. 2010; Kauffman and Martin 2014; Vanhulst and Beling 2014).

According to Descola (2004), unlike Western dualism between humans and non-humans, Amazonian cosmologies – as with most indigenous worldviews from Latin America and elsewhere – classify a scale of beings in which the differences between human beings, plants and animals are of degrees and not of nature. Such worldviews are not of the dominant species over the others, but one of a kind of transcendental ecosystem conscious of the totality of interactions developed on its basis. Looking specifically to the Awajun, Green (2009) finds that the people, certain animals, plants, and meteorological phenomena are all considered agents (human), given specific circumstances, and that they have souls or wakan. Similarly, Viveiros de Castro (2004) found that for Amazonian peoples "the original common condition of both humans and animals is not animality but, rather, humanity" (465). Amazonian narratives tell how animals, which perform key symbolic roles, lost the qualities inherited or retained by humans. From there, personhood and 'perspectivity' are matters of degree and context rather than features of particular species.

Within a relational account of development, the natural environment and non-human animals are connected to each other and to human beings. All human beings, non-human animals and the natural world have a common origin, history, and future. Our lives are not merely made possible, or enriched, by the natural environment but rather are bound up with, and inseparable from, the natural world. Our human lives are only one part of a story that includes and weaves all things in the natural world together (Marsden 2003). On this view, lands, oceans, mountains, and rivers *connect* us (Hau'ofa 1995). What follows from this starting point is a view of development that takes the destruction of the natural environment to violate these relationships, and the values that mediate them.

Indigenous knowledges are capturing the imaginations of people all over the world. In varying degrees, indigenous knowledges are beginning to frame development policy also. For instance, mātauranga has become central to a range of government policy and tribal development strategies in Aotearoa, New Zealand (Watene et al. 2017). Similarly, *buen vivir* has become a political signifier able to express the aspirations of many indigenous peoples (Merino 2016). *Buen vivir* has become a key concept for understanding the current political transformations in state structures in Latin America. Many language revitalization programmes, health models, environmental policies, as well as approaches to law and justice are grounded in the worldviews of indigenous peoples.

Māori health models such as Te Whare Tapa Wha frame health and well-being around physical, spiritual, family, and psychological dimensions (Durie 1998). These holistic and community-based understandings of health reframe the delivery of health services and health policy. In particular, these approaches place relationships between people, and between people and the natural environment, to be as significant for health and well-being as physical determinants (Watene et al. 2017). Similarly, Te Urewera Act 2014 has transformed conservation law in Aotearoa New Zealand by recognizing the deep connection that the people of Tuhoe have with Te Urewera, describing Te Urewera as: 'ancient and enduring, a fortress of nature, alive with history; its scenery [. . .] abundant with mystery, adventure, and remote beauty' and as having 'an identity in and of itself, inspiring people to commit to its care' (quoted in Ruru 2014).

The influential 'Kaupapa Māori' approach serves to decolonize the research methodologies that have come to dominate and underpin development research in Aotearoa New Zealand and elsewhere (Smith 1999; Pihama 2001). By challenging the power structures inherent in development research, such as the place of community in research, Kaupapa Māori has served to create space for new ways of thinking about the role of research for articulating well-being and development (Smith and Reid 2000). Kaupapa Māori has been pivotal in challenging top-down research agendas and the legitimacy of research-informed policies that serve to benefit indigenous peoples. These approaches illustrate the interdependence of decolonization and the revitalization of indigenous knowledges. They demonstrate the transformative and decolonizing force of indigenous research methodologies and indigenous knowledges themselves.

In Latin America, policy developments can be divided into 1) multicultural policies and 2) self-determination policies. Multicultural policies are based on the constitutional reforms and new constitutions enacted in Latin America in the 1990s which seek to include indigenous peoples within the state. These included the constitutions of Brazil (1988), Colombia (1991), Paraguay (1992), Peru (1993), Guatemala (1993), Bolivia (1995), Ecuador (1998), and Venezuela (1999). Significant constitutional reforms were undertaken by Mexico (1992) and Argentina (1994). Some scholars contend that these policies have been positive (see for instance Van Cott 2006). This is based on the contention that it is at least positive that there are some constitutional rights for indigenous peoples, such as collective land rights, the recognition of customary law and language rights, and in some cases some degree of autonomy for indigenous peoples (control over a territorial space and the recognition of indigenous systems of justice). According to this view, these policies express 'a friendly liquidation of the past' in overcoming centuries of discrimination, exploitation, and marginalization (Van Cott 2006). Such a view takes these policies to have been beneficial because they provide a basis for the articulation of indigenous demands in the formal political system.

Such an approach to policy is widespread. The approach seeks to include indigenous peoples within existing policy frameworks and assumes that limited recognition of rights satisfies government requirements to accommodate indigenous peoples. Such a view can also be traced to the claim that current political systems are well-suited to the needs and aspirations of indigenous peoples. For instance, some scholars hold that, although most indigenous organizations criticize neoliberalism and globalization, their economic claims can be satisfied by a capitalist welfare state. Thus, indigenous peoples could seek some degree of political and administrative autonomy and economic redistribution through state social programs (for example, access to credit, market assistance, and agricultural subsidies) in order to compete within the capitalist economic model. Such a view seeks to make room within the established state system for indigenous economic aspirations.

Not all scholars agree. Indeed, some scholars contend that political elites admit some indigenous rights in order to avoid more radical demands. In line with this view, indigenous participation in the political system and in policymaking is highly symbolic because political elites only accept a limited number of claims (Horton 2006). Multicultural policy in this light becomes an instrument to ensure the power of neoliberal governments rather than expressing a real commitment to indigenous peoples (Sieder 2011). For instance, Latin American elites promote cultural rights with very rigid conceptual and political boundaries and only insofar as they do not constitute challenges to the foundations of the economic development model (Hale 2005). Indigenous activism occupies a space allowed for political and economic elites (they become *indios permitidos* – allowed Indians). Indigenous peoples obtain some important achievements related to their cultural recognition but they lose the possibility of articulating other fundamental claims.

In contrast, self-determination policies are aimed at transforming the state. These policies are the most important expressions of the implementation of indigenous cosmologies in development today. These policies (inspired by *Buen vivir* in Latin American) have been expressed in the current political constitutions of Bolivia and Ecuador. The Ecuadorian Constitution regulates the 'rights of *Buen vivir*', including many social rights (nutrition, environment, water, education, housing, health) and recognizes collective indigenous rights and the rights of "Mother Earth"

(Articles 71, 72). This constitutes an epistemic-political event which contradicts the modern political assumption whereby nature is an inert object to be appropriated (Escobar 2010). The Constitution also regulates a section named 'regimen of *Buen vivir*', which focuses on the fostering of inclusion and equity, as well as the conservation of biodiversity. In this new configuration, economic development is just a means to achieve *buen vivir* (Gudynas 2011).

In Bolivia, *buen vivir* is the ethical and political foundation of plurinationality, a new state form that recognizes the different nations forming the Bolivian state (Larrea 2010). The Constitution of 1994 acknowledged the multi-ethnic and pluricultural character of Bolivian society, providing some special rights to the indigenous population and a general framework for recognizing some degree of autonomy to indigenous communities. Thus, legal reforms of decentralization allowed that those areas with large numbers of indigenous people become indigenous municipal districts organized according to their own customs, but still subject to top-down state decision-making (Galindo 2010). The new Constitution goes beyond this framework by providing a plurinational character to legislative, judicial, and executive government branches. Thus, Bolivia has moved from a multicultural state which recognizes the social and political rights of indigenous peoples to participate in the unitarian liberal state towards a plurinational state in which indigenous peoples are conceived as 'nations' (Galindo 2010).

Given these gains, the institutionalization of *buen vivir* has received global attention and has been viewed with optimism by intellectuals and social organizations for expressing an alternative to capitalist development (Kauffman and Martin 2014). The reality, however, is that *buen vivir* implementation has so far been theoretically contentious. For example, in spite of the innovations so far, the two constitutions continue to allow the exploitation of indigenous land on behalf of 'national interests', and do not recognize the right of indigenous peoples to provide *consent* before approving legal and administrative norms that can affect their collective rights. Moreover, in the development plans of Ecuador and Bolivia there are contradictory conceptions regarding the role of economic growth in well-being, and remain rooted in conventional views of development, such as economic development and (to some extent) human development (Radcliffe 2012; Merino 2016). This has led to deep contradictions between official pronouncements and actual governmental practices (Escobar 2010; Radcliffe 2012). For example, governments continue to promote mining activities in the Amazon and in ecological areas which are meant to be protected. This is the case even though both governments also supported the Universal Declaration of the Rights of Mother Earth (2010) with strong ecological discourses. The difficultly lies in the way in which the financing of social programs continues to be based on the appropriation of nature and the exportation of minerals and hydrocarbons (Gudynas 2011).

In this context, *buen vivir* has become a political discourse used by both ecological critical intellectuals and state officials (Guardiola and García-Quero 2014; Vanhulst 2015; Villalba 2013). Ecological critical scholars defend a conservationist perspective of *buen vivir*. While this is grounded in indigenous thinking, the use of different postmodern approaches, such as post-development, renders the position ambiguous (Bretón et al. 2014; Hidalgo-Capitán 2014). On the other hand, state officials understand *buen vivir* in general as human well-being that must be achieved by the exploitation of the natural resources available for economic redistribution or '*buen vivir* socialism' (Bretón 2013). For them, ecological or indigenous perspectives of *buen vivir* essentialize indigenous peoples and are unable to propose real changes to the neoliberal model (Bretón 2013; Sánchez 2011). The indigenous notion of *buen vivir* is different from these two perspectives. Indigenous movements seek to reappropriate and reconnect it to their own demands for self-determination and territoriality (Merino 2016). For indigenous peoples *buen vivir* is not merely an 'invented tradition' (Bretón 2013), but rather a reconstruction of ideas rooted in traditional indigenous thinking (Vanhulst 2015; Altmann 2013). Thus, through *buen vivir*, indigenous peoples aim to establish a platform to articulate new conceptions, institutions, and practices (Vanhulst and Beling 2014) that have the potential to transform the way development has been implemented in the region.

The existence and well-being of all peoples is tied to the ability to recount and take inspiration from their knowledges, histories, narratives, and values as they shape and reshape their places in the world. Being able to speak or to learn indigenous languages, to participate in ceremonies, to engage in and learn about art forms, native food, and environmental knowledges are vital to indigenous well-being. Indigenous knowledges play a central role both in revitalizing indigenous communities themselves and in transforming – and ultimately decolonizing – the structures that frame the unjust terms by which we live together. While our examples show that the revitalization of indigenous knowledges provide us with opportunities to seek out new development pathways, one of the real challenges that we face is a lack of willingness to look beyond our current development ideas and practices. Often indigenous policies are framed within existing systems. This, in part, gives rise to a further challenge of ensuring that indigenous knowledges are not hijacked by governments and activists in ways that misunderstand and therefore downplay their importance. A general challenge that the revitalization of indigenous knowledges face is how to revitalize knowledges in ways that protect them from continuing appropriation. These challenges are, of course, challenges to self-determination. Self-determination is about being able to reframe the grounds upon which development thinking rests, to decolonize existing development thinking and to revitalize indigenous conceptions of development. Unsurprisingly, then, self-determination remains vital, and yet – so far – elusive.

Conclusion

How can indigenous development be enabled? Self-determination lies at the heart of development for and by indigenous peoples. Achieving self-determination requires both the transformation of governance and law, as well as space to enable indigenous peoples to articulate, pursue, and realize lives they value. Self-determination entails transformation that nourishes the collective well-being of indigenous peoples. How does this transform our ideas about the ends and means of development? At least two movements remain central to enabling indigenous self-determination and thus indigenous development. Decolonization is required to challenge and ultimately 'remove the shackles' of colonial oppression (Mutu 2012). Additionally, decolonization is fundamental for the revitalization of indigenous knowledges which in turn is fundamental for reimagining how development is conceived, designed, and implemented. While there have been gains for indigenous peoples in pursuing self-determination, challenges remain. Most important among them are the need to ensure that development initiatives that seek to mitigate the effects of colonization are not themselves oppressive. Further, that indigenous knowledges are not hijacked by government officials, environmental activists, development scholars, and policymakers.

How can development ethicists support indigenous development? Indigenous peoples lay down the challenge for development to include the voices and knowledges of local communities. To acknowledge the activism and scholarship that exists, and to acknowledge the expertise within indigenous communities. Indigenous development asks: How can we seek to give voice to development ideas and narratives that remain on the margins? How can we begin to engage with local indigenous knowledges and community priorities in ways that do not reinforce oppression? What is required for indigenous communities to be able to speak for themselves? Development ethicists can play a significant role in answering these and many other questions. They can do this by recognizing the need for listening, the co-creation of knowledge, and by acknowledging the limits of their own abilities. They can do this by recognizing that their roles (if any) are supplementary or marginal, and that the ultimate aim should be to render that role unnecessary. As small first few steps at least, development ethicists can play a significant role simply by recognizing that development thinking and practice is framed by assumptions about the relevance of their own ideas and roles in the development process. Often these assumptions, despite their good intentions, are misguided. Indigenous communities are well-equipped to articulate, pursue, and realize their own needs and aspirations. Indigenous communities simply need the space to be able to do so.

Acknowledgments

This research was supported by National Science Challenge, Our Land and Water Funding (Mauri Whenua Ora), as well as a Royal Society of New Zealand Faststart Grant (Exploring Social Justice Concepts).

References

Altmann, P. (2013) Good Life as a Social Movement Proposal for Natural Resource Use: The Indigenous Movement in Ecuador. *Consilience: The Journal of Sustainable Development* 10: 59–71.

Anaya, J. (2004) *Indigenous Peoples and International Law*. Oxford University Press, Oxford.

Blaser, M., Costa, R., McGregor, D. and Coleman, W. (2010) Reconfiguring the Web of Life: Indigenous Peoples, Relationality, and Globalization. In Blaser, M., de Costa, R., McGregor, D. and Coleman, W.D. eds., *Indigenous Peoples and Autonomy: Insights for a Global Age*. UBC Press, Vancouver 3–26.

Bretón, V. (2013) Etnicidad, desarrollo y "Buen Vivir": Reflexiones críticas en perspectiva histórica [Ethnicity, Development and "Buen vivir". Critical Reflections in Historical Perspective]. *Revista Europea de Estudios Latinoamericanos y del Caribe* 95: 71–95.

Bretón, V., Cortez, D. and García, F. (2014) En busca del sumak Kawsay. Presentación del Dossier. [Looking for Sumak Kawsay (Living well)] *Íconos, Revista de Ciencias Sociales* 48: 9–24.

Churchill, W. (2002) *Struggle for the Land: Native North American Resistance to Genocide, Ecocide, and Colonization*. City Lights Books, San Francisco.

Descola, P. (2004) Las cosmologías indígenas de la Amazonía. In Surralles and Hierro, Garcia eds., *Tierra Adentro: Territorio indígena y percepción del entorno*. IWGIA, Copenhagen.

Dodds, S. (1998) Justice and Indigenous Land Rights. *Inquiry: An Interdisciplinary Journal of Philosophy* 41(2): 187.

Durie, M. (1998) *Whaiora: Māori Health Development*. Oxford University Press, Auckland.

Economic Commission for Latin American and the Caribbean – ECLAC (2014) *Guaranteeing Indigenous People's Rights in Latin America. Progress in the past decade and remaining challenges*. United Nations: Santiago de Chile.

Errico, S. (2007) The Draft UN Declaration on the Rights of Indigenous Peoples: An Overview. *Human Rights Law Review* 7(4): 741.

Escobar, A. (2010) Latin America at a Crossroads: Alternative Modernizations, Post-liberalism, or Post-development? *Cultural Studies* 24(1): 1–65.

Fromherz, C.J. (2008) Indigenous Peoples' Courts: Egalitarian Juridical Pluralism, Self-Determination, and the United National Declaration on the Rights of Indigenous Peoples. *University of Pennsylvania Law Review* 156(5).

Galindo, J. (2010) Cultural Diversity in Bolivia: From liberal interculturalism to indigenous modernity. In Janssens, M. ed., *The Sustainability of Cultural Diversity: Nations, Cities and Organizations*. Edward Elgar, Cheltenham and Northampton, MA.

Greene, S. (2009) *Customizing Indigeneity: Paths to a Visionary Politics in Peru*. Stanford University Press, Stanford.

Guardiola, J. and García-Quero, F. 2014. Buen Vivir (living well) in Ecuador: Community and environmental satisfaction without household material prosperity? *Ecological Economics* 107: 177–184.

Gudynas, E. (2011) Buen Vivir: Today's Tomorrow. *Development* 54(4): 441–447.

Hale, C. (2005) Neoliberal Multiculturalism: The Remaking of Cultural Rights and Racial Dominance in Central America. *Political and Legal Anthropology Review* 28(1): 10–28.

Hau'ofa, E. (1995) Our Sea of Islands, A New Oceania. In *Rediscovering Our Sea of Islands, Suva, Fiji*. The University of the South Pacific, 2–16.

Hidalgo-Capitán, A. (2014) Seis debates abiertos sobre el sumak kawsay [Six Open Debates on Sumak Kawsay (Living Well)]. *Íconos. Revista de Ciencias Sociales* 48: 25–40.

Hohepa, M. (2014) Te Reo Māori and Schooling. In Kawharu, M. ed., *Maranga Mai! Te Reo and Marae in Crisis?* Auckland University Press, Auckland, 103–127.

Horton, L. (2006) Contesting State Multiculturalisms: Indigenous Land Struggles in Eastern Panama. *Journal of Latin American Studies* 38(4): 829–858.

International Work Group for Indigenous Affairs – IWGIA (2017) *The Indigenous World 2017*. IWGIA: Copenhagen.

Jackson, M. (1992) The Colonisation of Māori Philosophy. In Oddie, G. and Perrett, R. eds., *Justice, Ethics, and New Zealand Society*. Oxford University Press, Auckland.

Kauffman, C. and Martin, P. (2014) Scaling up Buen Vivir: Globalizing Local Environmental Governance from Ecuador. *Global Environmental Politics* 14: 40–58.

Kawharu, I.H. (1989) Mana and the Crown: A Marae at Orakei. In Kawharu, I.H. ed., *Waitangi: Maori and Pakeha Perspectives of the Treaty of Waitangi*. Oxford University Press, Auckland, 211–233.

Kawharu, I.H. (1997) *Maori Land Tenure: Studies of a Changing Institution*. Clarendon Press, Oxford.

Kawharu, M. (2000) Kaitiakitanga: A Maori Anthropological Perspective of the Maori Socioenvironmental Ethic of Resource Management. *Journal of the Polynesian Society* 110(4) 349–370.

Kawharu, M. (2013) Whakapapa and Metamorphosisi. *Sites: A Journal of Social Anthropology and Cultural Studies* 10(1).

Kingi, T. (2008) Maori Landownership and Land Management in New Zealand. In *AusAID, Making Land Work Volume Two, Case Studies on Customary Land and Development in the Pacific*. AusAID, Canberra, 129–152.

Kymlicka, W. (1995) *Multicultural Citizenship: A Liberal Theory of Minority Rights*. Clarendon Press, Oxford.

Larrea, A. (2010) La disputa de sentidos por el buen vivir como proceso contrahegemónico. In *Los nuevos retos de América Latina: socialismo y Sumak Sawsay*. Senplades, Quito.

Marsden Rev. Māori (2003) *The Woven Universe: Selected Writings of Rev. Māori Marsden*. Estate of Rev. Māori Marsden.

Matiu, McCully and Mutu, M. (2003) *Te Whanau Moana: Nga Kaupapa me nga Tikanga: Customs and Protocols*. Reed, Auckland.

Mead, H.M. (2003) *Tikanga Maori: Living by Maori Values*. Huia, Wellington.

Merino, R. (2015) The Politics of Extractive Governance: Indigenous Peoples and Socio-environmental Conflicts in Peru. *Extractives industries and the Society* 28(1): 85–92.

Merino, R. (2016) An Alternative to "alternative development"?: Buen Vivir and Human Development in Andean Countries. *Oxford Development Studies* 44(3): 271–286.

Merino, R. (2017) Law and Politics of Indigenous Self-determination: The Meaning of the Right to Prior Consultation. In Watson, I. ed., *Indigenous Peoples as Subjects of International Law*. Routledge, London, 120–140.

Mikaere, Ani (2011) *Colonising Myths, Māori Realities: He Rukuruku Whakaaro*, Huia Publishers and Te Wananga o Raukawa, Wellington.

Muehlebach, A. (2003) What Self in Self-Determination? Notes from the Frontiers of Transnational Indigenous Activism. *Identities: Global Studies in Culture and Power* 10(2): 241.

Mutu, M.S. (2012) Custom Law and the Advent of New Pākehā Settlers: Tuku Whenua Allocation of Resource Use Rights. In Keenan, D. ed., *Huia Histories of Māori: Ngā Tāhuhu Kōrero*. Huia Publishers, Wellington, 93–108.

Mutu, M.S. (2013) Te Tiriti o Waitangi in a Future Constitution: Removing the Shackles of Colonisation. 2013 Robson Lecture 22 April 2013. www.converge.org.nz/pma/shackles-of-colonisation.pdf. Accessed 29 May 2017.

Pihama, L. (2001) *Tihei mauri ora Honouring our voices: Mana wahine as kaupapa Maori Theoretical Framework*. Unpublished PhD, The University of Auckland, Auckland.

Poata-Smith, E. (2004) Ka tika a muri, ka tika a mua? Maori Protest Politics and the Treaty of Waitangi Settlement Process. In Spoonley, P., Macpherson, C. and Pearson, D. eds., *Tangata Tangata: The Changing Ethnic Contours of New Zealand*. Thomson/Dunmore Press, Australia.

Radcliffe, S. (2012) Development for a Postneoliberal era? Sumak Kawsay, Living Well and the Limits to Decolonisation in Ecuador. *Geoforum* 43: 240–249.

Royal, Te Ahukaramu Charles. (2009) Mātauranga Māori: Perspectives, Monograph Five of Te Kaimānga: Towards a New Vision for Mātauranga Māori. (online).

Ruru, J. (2014) Tūhoe-Crown Settlement – Te Urewera Act 2014. *Māori Law Review* October 2014. http://maorilawreview.co.nz/2014/10/tuhoe-crown-settlement-te-urewera-act-2014/.

Sadler, H. (2007) Mātauranga Māori (Māori Epistemology). *The International Journal of the Humanities* 4.

Sánchez, J. (2011) Discursos Retrovolucionarios [Re(tro)volutionary Discourses]: Sumak Kausay, derechos de la naturaleza y otros pachamamismos. *Ecuador Debate* 84: 31–50.

Santos, B.S. (2007) *Another Knowledge Is Possible: Beyond Northern Epistemologies*. Verso, London.

Sieder, R. (2011) "Emancipation" or "regulation"? Law, Globalization and Indigenous Peoples' Rights in Post-war Guatemala. *Economy and Society* 40(2): 239–265.

Smith, L.T. (1999) *Decolonizing Methodologies: Research and Indigenous Peoples*. Zed Books, London.

Smith, L.T., Maxwell, T.K.K., Puke, H. and Temara, P. (2016) Indigenous Knowledge, Methodology and Mayhem: What is the Role of Methodology in Producing Indigenous Insights? A Discussion from Mātauranga Māori. *Knowledge Cultures* 4(3): 131–156.

Smith, L.T. and Reid, P. (2000) Māori Research Development: Kaupapa Māori Principles and Practises, A Literature Review. Report prepared for Te Puni Kokiri. www.rangahau.co.nz/assets//SmithL/Maori_research.pdf.

Statistics New Zealand (2014) Te Kupenga 2013 (English) – Corrected. www.stats.govt.nz/ browse_for_stats/people_and_communities/Maori/TeKupen ga_HOTP13.aspx. Accessed 29 May 2017.

Tapsell, P. (2014) Tribal Marae: Crisis? What Crisis?. In Kawharu, M. ed., *Maranga Mai! Te Reo and Marae in Crisis?* Auckland University Press, Auckland, 35–64.

Taskforce on Whānau Centred Initiatives (2010) *Whānau Ora: Report of the Taskforce on Whānau-Centred Initiatives*. Report produced for Hon Tariana Turia, Minister for the Community and Voluntary Sector, Ministry of Social Development, Wellington. www.msd.govt.nz/documents/about-msd-and-our-work/publications-resources/planning-strategy/whanau-ora/whanau-ora-taskforce-report.pdf. Accessed 29 May 2017.

Tully, J. (1995) *Strange Multiplicity: Constitutionalism in an Age of Diversity*. Cambridge University Press, Cambridge.

Turner, D. (2006) *This is Not a Peace Pipe: Towards a Critical Indigenous Philosophy*. University of Toronto Press Scholarly Publishing Division.

United Nations (1960) *Declaration on the Granting of Independence to Colonial Countries and Peoples*. GA Res 1514/15, UN Doc A/RES/1514(15) (adopted 14 December 1960).

United Nations Permanent Forum for Indigenous Issues (2007) *United Nations Declaration on the Rights of Indigenous Peoples*. www.un.org/esa/socdev/unpfii/en/drip.html.

Van Cott, D. (2006) Multiculturalism versus Neoliberalism in Latin America. In Banting, K. and Kymlicka, W. eds., *Multiculturalism and the Welfare State: Recognition and Redistribution in Contemporary Democracies*. Oxford University Press, Oxford.

Vanhulst, J. (2015) El laberinto de los discursos del Buen vivir [The labyrinth of Buen vivir discourses]: entre Sumak Kawsay y Socialismo del siglo XXI. *Polis, Revista de la Universidad Bolivariana* 14(40): 1–21.

Vanhulst, J. and Beling, A.E. (2014) Buen Vivir: Emergent Discourse Within or Beyond Sustainable Development? *Ecological Economics* 101: 54–63. https://creativeecologies.ucsc.edu/wp-content/uploads/sites/196/2015/10/Vanhulst-Beling-Buen-Vivir.pdf.

Villalba, U. (2013) Buen Vivir vs Development: A Paradigm Shift in the Andes? *Third World Quarterly* 34: 1427–1442.

Viveiros de Castro, E. (2004) Exchanging Perspectives: The Transformation of Objects into Subjects in Amerindian Ontologies. *Common Knowledge* 10(3): 463–484.

Waitangi Tribunal (2011a) *Ko Aotearoa Tenei: Te Taumata Tuatahi (Wai 262)*. Legislation Direct, Wellington.

Waitangi Tribunal (2011b) *Ko Aotearoa Tenei: Te Taumata Tuarua (Wai 262)*. Legislation Direct, Wellington.

Walker, R. (2004) Ka Mau Tonu te Whawhai: The Struggle Continues. In *Ka Whawhai Tonu Matou: Struggle Without End*. Penguin, Auckland.

Watene, K. (2016a) Indigenous Peoples and Justice. In Watene, K. and Drydyk, K. eds., *Theorizing Justice: Critical Insights and Future Directions*. Rowman and Littlefield International.

Watene, K. (2016b) Valuing Nature: Māori Values and the Capability Approach. In *Oxford Development Studies (Special Issue: Indigenous Peoples and Human Development)*, published online 5 Jan 2016.

Watene, K., Rochford, T. and Tamariki, N. (2017) Whānau Ora: Transforming Health and Well-Being. In Chadwick, S. ed., *How Should We Live? Ethical Issues in Aotearoa New Zealand*. Massey University Press, Auckland.

Watene, K. and Yap, M. (2015) Culture and Sustainable Development: Indigenous Contributions. *Journal of Global Ethics* 11(1): 51–55.

Whyte, K.P. (2013) Justice Forward: Tribes, Climate Adaptation and Responsibility. Climatic Change 120: 517–530.

Whyte, K. (2016a) Indigenous Experience, Environmental Justice and Settler Colonialism. In Bannon, B. ed., *Nature and Experience: Phenomenology and the Environment*. Rowman & Littlefield, 157–174.

Whyte, K. (2016b) Indigeneity and U.S. Settler Colonialism. In Zack, N. ed., *Oxford Handbook of Philosophy and Race*. Oxford University Press, Oxford, 91–101.

Whyte, K. (2017) Our Ancestors' Dystopia Now: Indigenous Conservation and the Anthropocene. In Heise, U., Christensen, J. and Niemann, M. eds., *Routledge Companion to the Environmental Humanities*. Routledge, London, 206–215.Williams, D.V. (2007) Māori Social Identification and Colonial Extinguishments of Customary Rights. *New Zealand. Social Identities: Journal for the Study of Race, Nation and Culture* 13(6): 735–749.

World Bank (2015) *Indigenous Latin America in the Twenty-First Century*. Washington, DC: World Bank.

World People's Conference on Climate Change and the Rights of Mother Earth (2010) *Universal Declaration of the Rights of Mother Earth*. Cochabamba, Bolivia.

13

Horizontal inequalities

Individual capabilities and inequalities between groups

Frances Stewart

Horizontal inequalities are inequalities between *groups* of people, in multiple dimensions, in contrast to vertical inequality which is defined as inequality among individuals. Horizontal inequalities have critical bearing on individual capabilities, and also on broader issues related to the capability approach, including all the seven (non-growth) goals of development which form the focus of this book. However, perhaps, the most important reason for concern with horizontal inequalities is that large horizontal inequalities are almost invariably unjust. In this chapter I will first consider the relationship between horizontal inequalities and justice; second, how horizontal inequalities relate to individual capabilities; and third, how they relate to the other six goals.

Defining horizontal inequalities

People can be grouped in a very large number of ways, potentially leading to multiple horizontal inequalities. Only categorizations of salience for the particular society and the way people live are of wider interest, however. Which categories are salient varies across societies; gender and age are important to people in any society; other categorizations which are politically salient or affect people's sense of their (and others') identity and well-being in a fundamental way can include ethnicity, race, religion, and class. These categorizations are socially constructed, apply in some societies and not others, can change over time and may be fluid. Yet they are often of critical importance to people in particular contexts, especially where there is discrimination and large horizontal inequalities. Indeed, in such situations they can be a cause of political mobilization and violent conflict (Stewart 2008; Cederman, Weidmann et al. 2011).

Horizontal inequalities are multidimensional, with socio-economic, political and cultural dimensions. Each dimension covers several elements: the socio-economic dimension includes access to education, health and social networks, employment and asset ownership. The political dimension comprises group representation at different levels of government, including in the bureaucracy, the police and the army. The cultural dimension concerns respect for a group's language, and members' cultural and religious practices. The various dimensions and elements each affect people's well-being and their capabilities directly, as well as indirectly and instrumentally – for example by causing violence they can undermine people's security and livelihoods.

DOI: 10.4324/9781315626796-16

A question of justice

Intuitively, it would seem that significant horizontal inequalities in important dimensions are unjust. Why should one race, for example, own less land and other assets than another; be more educated; have lower incomes; be more likely to be killed by the police; be more likely to be imprisoned; face constraints on their ability to vote to a greater extent than other groups; have less representation in top political positions? Yet this is the position of blacks in the US vis-à-vis whites; or blacks in Brazil; or Somalis in Kenya; or Hutus in Rwanda; or Muslims in Europe and India; or women almost everywhere (Uven 2000; Hertz 2005; SID 2007; Stewart 2010; Osorio 2012; Shapiro, Meschede et al. 2013).

Turning to selected philosophical approaches to justice may be helpful if we wish to move beyond intuition. Rawls' social contract and economists' perspectives both provide justification for some vertical inequalities, or inequalities among individuals. Rawls regards inequality as unjust unless it improves the position of the poorest (known as 'maximin'), while economists, who generally avoid talking about justice explicitly, consider inequality instrumentally, as needed to maximize output. From both perspectives, some vertical inequality may be justified in order to provide incentives and reward effort, thus bringing about 'maximin' in a Rawlsian contract, or, taking an economist's perspective, for achieving a Pareto optimum or maximizing economic growth (Okun 1975; Rawls 2002). Given that some vertical inequality may reflect differential performance due to differences in individuals' effort which might not occur in its absence, to this extent the vertical inequality could be regarded as just, although the extent of just inequality, according to this reasoning, would be likely to be much less than that which is typically observed. Yet where large groups are concerned, this type of justification of inequality does not make sense since talent and effort can be assumed to be randomly distributed with broadly equal incidence across large groups. Hence incentive payments would be distributed equally across groups. Large inequalities among groups invariably suggest that some past (or current) inequality and discrimination is responsible, not incentive payments. Indeed, as soon as one gains familiarity with the situation in a particular context, this immediately becomes apparent. The history of slavery and discrimination lies behind horizontal inequalities in Brazil and the US; long-term patriarchical discrimination underlies today's inequalities between men and women; colonial policies of discrimination among ethnic groups explains much of the current ethnic inequalities in African countries; and so on. Even Nozick, whose philosophy justifies any outcome, however unequal, if it results from *legitimate* acquisition or transfer, argues that where assets are acquired illegitimately, by theft, fraud or slavery, the assets should be restored according to the principle of rectification (Nozick 1974). Theft, fraud or slavery are responsible for many of the horizontal inequalities we observe today and hence cannot be justified, even when adopting Nozick's approach to a just distribution.

'Luck egalitarianism', an approach adopted by some philosophers as the basis of a just distribution, also points to large horizontal inequalities as being unjust. According to luck egalitarianism a distribution is just if it reflects people's own decisions and efforts and is not due to circumstances outside their control (Cohen 1989; Anderson 1999; Kaufman 2004). Membership of the type of groups we are considering here is generally inherited rather than chosen. Therefore, according to luck egalitarianism, membership of a particular group as such should not affect just outcomes. Only if there are systematically different decisions and efforts across groups, freely chosen and not due to inherited circumstances, can group inequality be justified according to this approach.

In short, the intuitive view that large inequalities between major groups are unjust appears to have the support of some important philosophical approaches to defining a just distribution.

Horizontal inequalities and individual capabilities

Individual capabilities consist of all possible functionings, defined by Sen (Sen 1985), as all those things that an individual can do or be. People in poor groups find that their capabilities are heavily constrained, compared with members of richer groups, an important form of horizontal inequalities. Poor people, of course, in general have more limited capabilities than the rich, given their more limited resources. Horizontal inequalities, however, impose greater constraints for several reasons. First, overt discrimination makes it more difficult for children to advance in education, or for adults to get jobs, or loans. Second, this is compounded by asymmetrical social capital, since networks are much stronger within than between groups, and members of poor groups therefore have less promising networks from the perspective of advancing economically, socially or politically. A third reason is that where there are political horizontal inequalities (so that the deprived group is less well represented in powerful political positions) the participatory/political capabilities of the deprived group are subject to particularly severe constraints and it becomes unlikely that they will receive compensatory or even proportionate support from the state. Finally, inequality in cultural recognition is an inequality which affects individuals because of their group membership or identity; it can have direct negative effects on individuals' capabilities constraining them from practicing their chosen religion, language or customs, and also often handicaps them indirectly since economic opportunities may be constrained where a person's language is not recognized or used by the state. Thus in many respects, where there are large horizontal inequalities, members of deprived groups are in a worse capability position than deprived people in homogeneous societies, or ones where poverty is randomly distributed among the different groups. Of course, the other side of this coin is that richer groups are in an even stronger situation where horizontal inequalities are favorable to them than they would be if they lived in a homogeneous society or if riches were randomly distributed across groups.

The capability approach rarely confronts the issue of distribution directly (although Burchardt and Hick (2018) is an exception). But the heavy focus it has always taken on improving the position of the poorest suggests that the advantage of rich groups in no way compensates for the disadvantage of poor groups (Drèze and Sen 1989; Sen 1999). Moreover, the potential expansion of individual capabilities of the poor, associated with a reduction in inequality, are greater than the reduction in capabilities of the rich, certainly in terms of basic capabilities (having the capability to be well-nourished, educated, healthy) and arguably in terms of other capabilities. For example, 'having enough to eat' or 'being educated' are important basic capabilities. While these capabilities among people in poor groups are constrained so they do not have enough to eat and are not able to access education at a reasonable level, members of rich groups already have more than enough to eat and can access as much education as they want and their situation in this respect is not enhanced by the deprivations of poor groups and would not be changed by a reduction in inequality. Similar points can be made about other capabilities: for example, the capability to get from one place to another within a country can be met by public transport, a small car, a large car or a helicopter. The poor groups may have access to none of these, so their capability of movement is severely constrained; members of the rich group may be able to travel faster or in more comfort because of their position, but the basic capability of getting from one place to another could be met with much fewer resources.

Horizontal inequalities, consequently, impose severe constraints on the capabilities of members of poor groups, both at a point in time, and in terms of prospects of advancing over time (Stewart 2009). Political and cultural inequalities are of importance here, as well as economic inequalities. Intersecting inequalities are also relevant here: being both female and indigenous in Latin America, for example, frequently leads to the most limited capabilities (Barrón Ayllón

2005; Kabeer 2010). The fact that horizontal inequalities enable richer groups to have more extensive capabilities does not compensate for this impoverishment – not only because it is unjust, but also because the gains of rich groups, particularly in basic capabilities, are not proportionate to the losses of poor groups due to these inequalities.

Horizontal inequalities and the seven non-economic goals

Horizontal inequalities have direct bearing on each of the seven goals of worthwhile development discussed in this *Handbook*.

Enhancement of people's well-being, and equitable sharing in benefits

Well-being is a function of many elements, including an individual's family, social and societal circumstances, their personal disposition, the resources available to them, their security and autonomy, and their satisfaction with their status, which depends not just on their own position but also that of others. Horizontal inequalities have direct bearing on many of these elements. Members of poorer groups obviously suffer from fewer resources than richer groups and have poorer health, while political horizontal inequalities imply that they have limited autonomy. The existence of horizontal inequalities can also have a negative impact on people's perception of their well-being – as they value not only their own resources but identify with the situation of the group as a whole – indeed, considerable evidence has been produced on the negative psychological effects of racial inequality in relation to the position of US blacks (Brown, Williams et al. 1999), while studies of the determinants of 'happiness' have shown that the position of particular reference groups is one significant factor (Kingdon and Knight 2004; Graham and Felton 2006; Knight and Gunatilaka 2011). Akerlof and Kranton (2000) have argued, for this reason, that the well-being of the group to which the individual belongs should enter the utility function of an individual, in addition to the individual's own income. Inequality has been argued to worsen aggregate societal health outcomes as well as leading to poorer health for deprived people (or groups) (Wilkinson and Pickett 2006). Horizontal inequalities also reduce social cohesion and make violent conflict more likely, thereby reducing the security and well-being of people in rich groups as well as in poor (Langer, Stewart et al. 2017). Clearly, horizontal inequalities have a direct negative bearing on the well-being of individuals in poorer groups.

As far as equity is concerned, the earlier arguments concluding that horizontal inequalities are unjust imply that they are inequitable.

Empowerment to participate freely in development

Inequalities of any kind are disempowering, but horizontal inequalities are particularly disempowering. Implicit and explicit discrimination can prevent particular groups from full participation at local and national levels. An extreme example is that of scheduled castes and tribes in India, who are debarred from many activities. Disempowerment due to group membership is especially the case for those minority groups which are deprived of political power as well as being relatively impoverished economically. There are many examples, including: indigenous peoples in Latin America, the Ughers in China, Muslims in Myanmar, the Philippines and Thailand. However, where the poorer groups form a majority, they may dominate politics, particularly in a democratic system, despite lower economic status, and in such cases, economic horizontal inequalities alone may not lead to disempowerment. In Malaysia, for example, it is the richer Chinese that are politically weak, while the poorer Malays participate fully in politics and rate highly on cultural recognition.

Environmental sustainability

This is one of the most fundamental issues, since without it the well-being and capabilities of current generations will be at the expense of those of future generations. Justice across generations requires environmental sustainability in contemporary actions. Inequality is tied up with environmental sustainability in several ways (Boyce 1994; Stewart 2015; Raworth 2017). First, there is general agreement that the poorest people (and groups) tend to suffer most from environmental costs, even though they typically contribute least to them (Neumayer 2011; UNDP 2007–08; CDP 2009). Poorer people (and countries) are located in areas more affected by climate change – from 2000 to 2004, high-income countries faced just 1.5% of the risk of poor countries of being affected by natural disasters (UNDP 2007–08). Moreover, poorer people and groups within a country suffer proportionately more from environmental costs, partly because more people in poor countries are farmers, who are particularly badly affected and poor people have fewer protective mechanisms in place when disasters occur.

Whether greater inequality increases or reduces environmental costs, however, is much debated. On the one hand, it has been argued that 'Higher inequality, both between and within countries is associated with lower emissions at given average incomes' (Ravallion et al. 2000, 651). On the other hand, Boyce (2007, 7–8) concludes that 'societies with wider inequalities of wealth and power will tend to have more environmental harm'. Empirical work is ambiguous on which of these arguments is correct, with conclusions varying according to the particular pollutant and the methodology adopted (Torras and Boyce 1998; Mikkelson et al. 2007; Shafik 1994). But there are reasons for expecting more inequality to have a long-term indirect adverse impact on sustainability. This is because inequality among people and groups provides one of the most powerful motives for economic growth. Within a country, each group aims to catch up with the standards of richer groups – poorer groups aim to catch up richer groups; and richer groups aim to attain the standards observed in rich countries; and country economic policy is partly motivated by the objective of attaining the per capita income of richer countries. Despite powerful arguments for believing that growth should cease to be an objective at high incomes, given the costs it imposes and the limited benefits it confers, this has nowhere been accepted (Raworth 2017). Governments invariably aim to maximize economic growth in order to meet popular pressures for more incomes and more services coming from those seeking to catch-up, without having to confront the political challenge of realizing catch-up through redistribution. In contrast to the other goals considered, here vertical inequality is as relevant as horizontal.

In summary, failure to achieve environmental sustainability is likely to worsen both vertical and horizontal inequality; while inequality (of both types) tends to make the achievement of sustainability more difficult. Moreover, irrespective of these instrumental reasons, justice requires that our limited global resources be fairly distributed across people and groups. In 2010, the carbon emissions per head were 11,579 Kt tons in rich countries and 0.3 Kt tons in poor countries. With a global limit on the amount that can be emitted safely, justice clearly demands redistribution.

Promotion of human rights

The existence of significant horizontal inequalities generally implies that the human rights of some groups are impaired, particularly in poor societies: poor groups have limited access to health services, education of a reasonable quality or shelter – all important human rights. Political and cultural freedoms of some groups are also often constrained, implying that universal human rights are not realized. In richer societies, however, some human rights might be universal despite some social and economic horizontal inequalities since there is no commitment to equality in the human rights agreements. In general, nonetheless, full acceptance of a human rights approach to development would involve a significant reduction in horizontal inequalities almost everywhere.

Promotion of cultural freedom

Culture is a group characteristic and cultural freedom implies a lack of constraints on group practices unless these are justified by a strongly negative impact of some cultural practices on others. Restrictions on cultural freedom lie at the heart of horizontal inequalities in cultural status or recognition (Langer and Brown 2008). In Sri Lanka, for example, the Tamil language is not recognized in government business. In Turkey, until 1990, the Kurds were not allowed to use their language in public. In Tibet, there are severe restrictions on the practice of Buddhism. In Egypt, Christian churches are subject to restrictions and attack. In Europe, immigrant groups frequently face dress restrictions. These restrictions on cultural freedom constitute horizontal inequalities in cultural recognition.

Promotion of integrity over corruption

This is the one goal where a direct connection with horizontal inequalities is not apparent. But there are important indirect connections. In contemporary societies, corruption among politicians enables them to amass great fortunes. Where political horizontal inequalities exist, this leads to the further enrichment of the dominant political group. Those in power also tend to grant favors to their own group disproportionately, in terms of employment and investments, in order to gain and reward supporters. For example, evidence for Kenya, shows the regional distribution of investments favors the group in power (Cohen 1995; SID 2007; Stewart 2010). In Burundi, the region where the president came from received 50% of national investments and the province where most of the top politicians came from secured 16% of the total, 1980–1985 (Gaffney 2000). Thus where there are political horizontal inequalities, corruption tends to contribute to socio-economic horizontal inequalities and also to consolidate the political ones. A substantial reduction in corruption would undoubtedly make it much easier to reduce horizontal inequality.

Conclusion

Large horizontal inequalities present a severe barrier to the achievement of a just society, in which people's well-being, capabilities and human rights are realized. Horizontal inequalities predispose societies to violent conflict and are a clear indicator of inequity. The combination of re-enforcing economic, political and cultural inequalities make them particularly intractable. Yet in global dialogue – particularly in neo-liberal economics – they are invisible even though the importance of tackling vertical inequality is increasingly recognized (Piketty 2014; Milanović 2016). At a national level, where these inequalities are more clearly visible and felt, there is much more recognition, and in some cases effective counter action, showing that it is possible to devise and implement policies to reduce horizontal inequalities (Stewart et al. 2008).

Acknowledgments

I am grateful to the editors for helpful comments on an earlier draft.

References

Akerlof, G.A. and Kranton, R.e. (2000) Economics and Identity. *The Quarterly Journal of Economics* cxv(3): 715–753.

Anderson, E.S. (1999) What Is the Point of Equality?. *Ethics* 109(2): 287–337.

Barrón Ayllón, M. (2005) Horizontal Inequalities in Latin America: A Quantitative Comparison of Bolivia, Guatemala and Peru. *CRISE Working Paper*, Oxford Department of International Development, Oxford.

Boyce, J.K. (2007) Is Inequality Bad for the Environment? *Working Paper Series 135*. Political Economy Research Institute, Amherst.

Boyce, J.K. (1994) Inequality as a Cause of Environmental Degradation. *Ecological Economics* 11: 169–178.

Brown, T.N., Williams, D.R., Jackson, J.S., Neighbours, H., Sellers, S., Myriam, T. and Brown, K. (1999) Being Black and Feeling Blue: Mental Health Consequences of Racial Discrimination. *Race and Society* 2(2): 117–131.

Burchardt, T. and Hick, R. (2018) Inequality, Advantage and the Capability Approach. *Journal of Human Development and Capabilities* 19(1): 38–52.

CDP (2009) Achieving Just Development in an Age of Climate Change. *C. f. D. Policy*. United Nations, New York.

Cederman, L.E., Weidmann, N.B. and Gleditsch, K.S. (2011) Horizontal Inequalities and Ethno-nationalist Civil War: A Global Comparison. *American Political Science Review* 105(3) 478–495.

Cohen, G.A. (1989) On the Currency of Egalitarian Justice. *Ethics* 99: 906–944.

Cohen, J.M. (1995) Ethnicity, Foreign Aid and Economic Growth in Sub-Saharan Africa: The Case of Kenya. *Development Discussion Papers*, Harvard Institute for International Development, Cambridge, MA.

Drèze, J. and Sen, A.K. (1989) *Hunger and Public Action*. Clarendon Press, Oxford.

Gaffney, P.D. (2000) Burundi: The Long Sombre Shadow of Ethnic Instability. In Nafzier, E.W., Stewart, F. and Varynen, R. eds., *War, Hunger and Displacement: The Origins of Humanitarian Emergencies. Volume 2: Case Studies*, 2: 119–158.

Graham, C. and Felton, A. (2006) Does Inequality Matter to Individual Welfare: An Exploration based on Happiness Surveys in Latin America. *Journal of Economic Inequality* 4: 107–122.

Hertz, T. (2005) Rags, Riches and Race: The International Mobility of Black and White Families in the United States. In Bowles, S., Gintis, H. and Osborne Groves, M. eds., *Unequal Chances: Family Background and Economic Success*. Princeton University Press, Princeton, 165–191.

Kabeer, N. (2010) Can the MDGs Provide a Pathway to Social Justice. The Challenge of Intersecting Inequalities. Retrieved 27 April 2015.

Kaufman, A. (2004) Choice, Responsibility and Equality. *Political Studies* 52: 819–836.

Kingdon, G. and Knight, J. (2004) *Community Comparisons and Subjective Wellbeing in a Divided Society*. Centre for the Study of African Economies, Oxford.

Knight, J.B. and Gunatilaka, R. (2011) Does Economic Growth Raise Happiness in China? *Oxford Development Studies* 39(1): 1–24.

Langer, A. and Brown, G. (2008) Cultural Status Inequalities: An Important Dimension of Group Mobilization. In Stewart, F. ed., *Horizontal Inequalities and Conflict: Understanding Group Violence in Multiethnic Societies*. Palgrave, London, 41–53.

Langer, A., Stewart, F. and Smedts, K. (2017) Conceptualising and Measuring Social Cohesion in Africa: Towards a Perceptions-Based Index. *Social Indicators Research* 131(1): 321–343.

Mikkelson, G.M., Gonzalez, A. and Peterson, G.D. (2007) Economic Inequality Predicts Biodiversity Loss. *PloS ONE* 2(5).

Milanović, B. (2016) *Global Inequality : A New Approach for the Age of Globalization*. The Belknap Press of Harvard University Press, Cambridge.

Neumayer, E. (2011) Sustainability and Inequality in Human Development. *Human Development Research Paper*. UNDP, New York.

Nozick, R. (1974) *Anarchy, State, and Utopia*. Blackwell, Oxford.

Okun, A.M. (1975) *Equality and Efficiency : The Big Tradeoff*. Brookings Institution, Washington, DC.

Osorio, R.G. (2012) The Persistence of Black-white Income Differentials in Brazil. In Brown, G., Langer, A. and Stewart, F. eds., *Affirmative Action in Plural Societies*. Palgrave, London, 100–137.

Piketty, T. (2014) *Capital in the Twenty-First Century*. Belknap, Cambridge.

Ravallion, M., Heil, M. and Jalan, J. (2000) Carbon Emissions and Income Inequality. *Oxford Economic Papers* 52(4): 651–669.

Rawls, J. (2002) *A Theory of Justice*. Clarendon Press, Oxford.

Raworth, K. (2017) *Doughnut Economics: Seven Ways to Think Like a 21st-Century Economist*. Random House, London.

Sen, A.K. (1985) *Commodities and Capabilities*. North-Holland, Amsterdam.

Sen, A.K. (1999) *Development as Freedom (DAF)*. Oxford University Press, Oxford.

Shafik, N. (1994) Economic Development and Environmental Quality: An Econometric Analysis. *Oxford Economic Papers* 46: 147–162.

Shapiro, T., Meschede, T. and Osoro, S. (2013) The Roots of the Widening Racial Wealth Gap: Explaining the Black-White Economic Divide. *Research and Policy Brief*, Brandeis University Institute on Assets and Social Policy.

SID, S.f.I.D. (2007) *Readings on inequality in Kenya*. SID, Nairobi.

Stewart, F. ed. (2008) *Horizontal Inequalities and Conflict: Understanding Group Violence in Multiethnic Societies*. Palgrave, London.

Stewart, F. (2009) Horizontal Inequality: Two Types of Trap. *Journal of Human Development and Capabilities* 10(3): 315–340.

Stewart, F. (2010a) Global Aspects and Implications of Horizontal Inequalities: Inequalities Experienced by Muslims Worldwide. In Clapp, K. and Wilkinson, R. eds., *Global Governance, Poverty and Inequality*. Routledge, London, 265–294.

Stewart, F. (2010b) Horizontal Inequalities in Kenya and the Political Disturbances of 2008: Some Implications for Aid Policy. *Conflict, Security and Development* 10(1): 133–159.

Stewart, F. (2015) Sustainability and Inequality. *Development* 58(3 and 4).

Stewart, F., Brown, G. and Langer, A. (2008) Policies towards Horizontal Inequalities. In *Horizontal Inequalities and Conflict: Understanding Group Violence in Multiethnic Societies*. Palgrave, London, 301–326.

Torras, M. and Boyce, J.K. (1998) Income, Inequality and Pollution: A Reassment of the Environmental Kuznets Curve. *Ecological Economics* 25: 147–160.

UNDP (2007/2008) *Human Development Report 2007/8: Fighting Climate Change. Human Solidarity in a Divided World*. London, Palgrave Macmillan.

Uven, P. (2000) Rwanda: The Social Roots of Genocide. In Nafixiger, E.W., Stewart, F. and Vayrynen, R. eds., *War, Hunger and Displacement: The Origin of Humanitarian Emergencies, Vol. Two*. Oxford University Press, Oxford, 159–185.

Wilkinson, R.G. and Pickett, K.E. (2006) Income inequality and population health: a review and explanation of the evidence. *Social Science Medicine* 62(7): 1768–1784.

14

Children

Intergenerational transmission of poverty and inequality

Flavio Comim

Worthwhile development cannot happen without proper attention to childhood. Indeed, it is during childhood that individuals' cognitive and psycho-emotional skills are formed and what a person becomes in the future is shaped by the love, recognition and stimuli received (or not) during childhood. The forms of inequality and injustices that a person might face later in life can be heavily influenced by the kind of childhood the person experienced. And yet, it is remarkable to see how childhood has been ignored not only in leading development books, such as Ray (1998) and Todaro and Smith (2014) but also in Human Development Reports, without a global report being published to date on this issue (unlike for gender in 1995). Even outstanding development ethics books, such as Gasper (2004) and Vizard (2006), do not dedicate much attention to childhood as a development issue.

Childhood is not a single period; it is comprised of stages that are different depending on whether one is investigating children's biological, cognitive, emotional, social or moral development (Keenan and Evans 2009). This diversity of contexts and disciplines is vast and beyond the scope of this chapter, which focuses on three key findings of the research on 'children and development'. The first highlights the foundational role of childhood in shaping individuals' future opportunities. Indeed, quite frequently poverty, inequality or other development problems are discussed as if by a medical examiner carrying out an autopsy, since more often than not different analyses, policies and interventions cannot bring people back to (economic or social) life due to temporal irreversibilities. Conversely, a focus on child development means 'development-in-the-making' when there is still time for changing people's future trajectories. The second part of this chapter briefly explores the psycho-emotional dimensions in which children can develop, investigating several paths in which inequality can consolidate unfair differences among individuals. The third part discusses the role of families on reducing social inequalities and injustices and argues for a fuller inclusion of families into development policies.

The central message of this chapter is straightforward: childhood is a key development issue that should not be ignored; it is about processes that form and shape different skills that often produce unfair inequalities among distinct individuals. Development theories have not been serious enough about the significance of path dependences and time-irreversibilities that lock individuals in (deprived) lives that they cannot be changed without great effort (Baltes 1987). Often, development theories propose atemporal interventions as if, for instance, uneducated

DOI: 10.4324/9781315626796-17

adults could be educated with the same effectiveness as if they would have been educated during their childhood. Moreover, childhood interventions should extrapolate the remit of government policies involving children's families, schools and friends. Understanding the genesis of children's ethical reasoning is essential for thinking about development ethics and fairer human development policies.

Childhood and the roots of underdevelopment

Several development problems that affect the adult population such as chronic poverty, illiteracy, innumeracy, under-nutrition, obesity, heart problems, mental health, suicide and violent behaviour, to mention just a few, have their roots in the early years of childhood (Bradbury et al. 2001; Walker et al. 2007; Heckman 2008; Calvin et al. 2017 and Sonuga-Barke et al. 2017). There are at least three different ways in which this evidence can be understood from a development ethics perspective. First, the issue can be seen as a violation of fundamental entitlements, of any kind, including the emotional given that children should have the right to be loved, to use their senses and imagination in a 'truly human' way, to be able to play and laugh, etc. (Nussbaum 2011). Secondly, problems during childhood can be seen as a cause of future problems during adulthood; for example health, with plenty of evidence of this causal relation published in medical journals such as *The Lancet*, *Nature* or *British Medical Journal*. Thirdly, achievements during childhood can be seen as necessary but not sufficient conditions for achievements in adulthood. Thus, attending primary school is a necessary but not a sufficient condition for someone going to college; a healthy diet during childhood is a necessary but not a sufficient condition for good health in old age. The underlying principle in these three perspectives is the acknowledgement that what happens during childhood matters because there is an important timing aspect in the formation of individuals that brings a degree of irreversibility to individuals' lives. In other words, it can be argued that personal development that does not take place during childhood is not easy to achieve later in life.

Cognitive development starts in the womb. Foetuses have memories of their mother's voice and of pieces of music (Hepper 1992). During an infant's first year of life there is the development of his or her central nervous system (including the mesencephalon and the spinal cord, responsible for the regulation of basic functions such as sleeping, suction, breathing, digestion and head movements), and the brain doubles in size (Cole et al. 2005). Two-year-old toddlers have the same density of synapses as an adult brain. Interestingly enough, the number of synapses doubles again when children go from two to three years of age. This expansion of children's brain coincides with the development of key cognitive skills such as speaking, colour recognition and an effective use of memory (Goswami 1998). It is within the first three years that children's brains are considered 'plastic' or fully flexible and there is a window of opportunity for laying the foundations for future cognitive and non-cognitive capabilities (Dawson et al. 2000). Although there is no single approach to examine how intelligence is constructed from infancy into childhood (Fagan 2011), estimated correlation coefficients suggest that there is 0.36 correlation between infant learning and later IQ.

Cunha and Heckman (2007) put forward the concepts of 'critical' and 'sensitive' periods for the development of certain skills during childhood. Just as tentative benchmarks they argue that one's IQ stabilizes around 10 years of age and one's skill to speak a foreign language as a native speaker around 12 years of age. This does not mean that one's IQ is static but that the development of individuals' cognitive skills has a neurological basis, similarly to the development of one's pre-frontal cortex (responsible for the regulation of emotions) seems to stabilize when individuals are in their early 20s (Damasio 1994). The implication of this set of results that emerges from the neuroscience and child development literatures is that the foundations for individuals' human development are laid very early in life and that poverty and inequalities are crystalized much earlier than what has been considered by conventional development policies (Bradbury et al. 2001; Biggeri et al. 2011).

Love, recognition and development

Individuals' life trajectories are affected not only by what interferes with their brain and neuronal development but also with their psychological and emotional development during childhood. Several authors emphasize the importance of childhood on a person's human and moral development. Most notably for development ethics, John Rawls (1971) argued that individuals' sense of justice starts being shaped during childhood, in a stage that he named 'morality of authority'. Accordingly, children learn from their parents how to behave by respecting legitimate authority. Rawls notes that children lack the knowledge and understanding necessary for justifying moral actions. Parents follow their duties because they love their children and in due time children come to love their parents. As a result, children are assured of their worth as a person affirming their self-esteem. Later in life, individuals are exposed to a morality of association. As Rawls (1971: 468) writes "Our moral understanding increases as we move in the course of life through a sequence of positions", engaging into different forms of social cooperation. Once youngsters develop their capacity for fellow feeling and reciprocity they might arrive at more complex forms of morality defined by principles that are shaped by a conception of rights independent from contingencies. But when childhood is affected by familiar disruption and lack of love, negative implications can affect children's future emotional and social development with clear subsequent consequences on society's political life (Sroufe 1995).

It is during childhood that individuals are recognized as 'concrete creatures of need', as argued by Honneth (1995). It is also during this period that individuals form their personality and their sense of worth that is foundational for their identity and participation in the community. Similar to Rawls, for Honneth, love is the pillar of a person's status as worthy individuals that supports other forms of recognition by civil society and the State. The withdrawal of maternal care can lead to several disturbances in individuals' behaviour as children and adults (1995, 96). Love is then a first step towards societal forms of recognition and respect. Within this perspective, several 'development struggles' could be considered fights for recognition and equality (gender, indigenous, populations, labour rights, etc.) the roots of which can be found in the way that people are (or not) loved and considered, with on the one hand individuals with the strength to stand up against inequalities and on the other hand individuals that feeling unrecognized become the oppressors violating the rights of others. Cortina (1997, 163–164) notes that forms of violence during childhood and teenager years can be understood as struggles for recognition.

A loveless childhood is a development problem. It can affect individuals' future abilities to relate and to respect other individuals or the potential of entire societies to achieve common grounds and coordinate actions. When development problems affect parent-child relations much is at stake. The cultivation of emotions during childhood affects the sort of 'political emotions' that people develop as adults and how they commit or not to 'a larger common good', as argued by Nussbaum (2013).

The importance of families for development

Families are on the driving seat of much of what we call development. A certain obsession in development with governments' policies (see for instance, Meier and Stiglitz 2001) prevents a fair and due acknowledgement of the role of families towards the achievement of private and social goals. In their essence, families are networks of love and care. They define the type of experiences that everyone has early in life. They provide an initial distribution of goods and opportunities and shape inequality standards for people born into different families (Brighouse and Swift 2014). Families influence children's development not merely by what they say but by what they do. Families matter for the environment, values and stimuli that they provide to children (Layard et al. 2009).

Families have been classified according to their parenting styles and practices, which can be positive and negative. Positive practices entail i) parents' moral behaviour in practice: when children see their parents practising acts of compassion, generosity and empathy (Salvo et al. 2005); ii) suitable communication of positive feelings such as love, with hugs and kissing (Weber et al. 2003); iii) playing together that strengthens children's self-confidence and future resilience (Ginsburg 2007); iv) positive feedback: praise for good results (Eisenberg and Mussen 1989); and v) suitable discipline, helping children to understand the consequences of their acts (Grusec and Goodnow 1994).

On the other hand, negative parenting practices comprise i) negative communication between parents and children, with excessive criticisms and lack of praise (Rinaldi and Howe 2012); ii) lack of implementation of discipline, when parents introduce rules but do not enforce them (Comim 2011), iii) inconsistent punishment, according to parents' state of mind, causing confusion in children about what is right and wrong (Faber and Mazlish 2013); iv) negative monitoring with excessive control on children, favouring anxious and depressive behaviour (Salvo et al. 2005); v) physical and psychological abuse involving insults and humiliation, that affect children's self-esteem and social skills (Toth et al. 2011); and vi) use of coercion and shouting, physical violence and deprivation of affection as ways of imposing discipline, that are related to future aggressiveness and disobedience (Hoffman 1994).

When underdevelopment undermines parenting practices, there are sequences of potential negative consequences that are put in place that define an intergenerational chain of transmission of poverty and inequality. For instance, circumstances such as teenage pregnancy, single mothers, violent households, mothers' lower level of schooling or even households without access to public services, such as health and education, impact on several parental practices (Garbarino and Abramowitz 1992; Estrada and Nilsson 2004; Conger et al. 2010). Inequalities might be reproduced by simple demographic trends and customs and habits that characterise families' lives and practices. In order to break these intergenerational chains of inequality, public policies should embrace aspects so far considered 'exogenous' for belonging to a private sphere of individuals' lives (Brooks and Nussbaum 2015). This is not a trivial task. Parenting has been considered a private matter in liberal societies. If so, it follows that it should be protected against external interventions. But if parenting has also a public dimension (either because parenting is heterogeneous or because there are clear wrongs in parenting like trafficking, child brides, etc.) then several difficulties can challenge the liberal position. Thus, the debate about children and development stretches the limits of development ethics, raising issues about civility, common good, the role of education, political emotions and the limits of political liberalism. Issues about children and development are not just about child welfare but are long-lasting issues of social justice. If worthwhile development is about the future and about change, it cannot continue to turn its back on children.

References

Baltes, P.B. (1987) Theoretical Propositions of Life Span Developmental Psychology: On the Dynamics between Growth and Decline. *Developmental Psychology* 23: 611–626.

Biggeri, M., Ballet, J. and Comim, F. eds. (2011) *Children and the Capability Approach*. Palgrave Macmillan, Hampshire.

Bradbury, B., Jenkins, S. and Micklewright, J. (2001) *The Dynamics of Child Poverty in Industrialised Countries*. Cambridge University Press, Cambridge.

Brighouse, H. and Swift, A. (2014) *Family Values: The Ethics of Parent-child Relationships*. Princeton University Press, Princeton.

Brooks, T. and Nussbaum, M. eds. (2015) *Rawls's Political Liberalism*. Columbia University Press, New York.

Calvin, C., Batty, G., Der, G., Brett, C., Taylor, A., Pattie, A., Cukic, I. and Deary, I. (2017) Childhood Intelligence in Relation to Major Causes of Death in 68 Year Follow-up: Prospective Population Study. *British Medical Journal* 357(2708): 1–13.

Cole, M., Cole, S. and Lightfoot, C. (2005) *The Development of Children,* 5th ed., Worth Publishers, New York.

Comim, F. (2011) "Developing Children's Capabilities: The Role of Emotions and Parenting Style. In Biggeri, M., Ballet, J. and Comim, F. eds., *Children and the Capability Approach*. Palgrave Macmillan, Hampshire, 331–339.

Conger, R., Conger, K. and Martin, M. (2010) Socioeconomic Status, Family Processes and Individual Development. *Journal of Marriage and the Family* 72(3): 685–704.

Cunha, F. and Heckman, J. (2007) The Technology of Skill Formation. *American Economic Review* 97(2) 31–47.

Damasio, A. (1994) *Descartes' Error: Emotion, Reason and the Human Brain*. Putnam Publishing, New York.

Dawson, G., Ashm, S. and Carver, L. (2000) The Role of Early Experience in Shaping Behavioural and Brain Development and its Implications for Social Policy. *Development and Psychopathology* 12 695–712.

Eisenberg, N. and Mussen, P. (1989) *The Roots of Prosocial Behaviour in Children*. Cambridge University Press, Cambridge.

Estrada, F. and Nilsson, A. (2004) Exposure to Threatening and Violent Behaviour among Single Mothers: The Significance of Lifestyle, Neighbourhood and Welfare Situation. *British Journal of Criminology* 44(2): 168–187.

Faber, A. and Mazlish, E. (2013) *How to Talk So Kids Will Listen and Listen So Kids Will Talk*. Piccadilly Press London.

Fagan, J. (2011) Intelligence in Infancy. In Sternberg, R. and Kaufman, S. eds., *The Cambridge Handbook of Intelligence*. Cambridge University Press, Cambridge, 130–143.

Garbarino, J. and Abramowitz, R. (1992) The Ecology of Human Development. In Garbarino, J. ed., *Children and Families in the Social Environment*. Aldine de Gruyter, New York.

Gasper, D. (2004) *The Ethics of Development*. Edinburgh University Press, Edinburgh.

Ginsburg, K. (2007) The Importance of Play in Promoting Healthy Child Development and Maintaining Strong Parent-child Bonds. *Pediatrics* 119(1): 182–191.

Goswami, U. (1998) *Cognition in Children*. Taylor and Francis, London.

Grusec, J. and Goodnow, J. (1994) Impact of Parental Discipline Methods on the Child's Internationalization of Values: A Reconceptualization of Current Points of View. *Developmental Psychology* 30(1): 4–19.

Heckman, J. (2008) Schools, Skills and Synapses. *Economic Inquiry* 46(3): 289–324.

Hepper, P. (1992) Fetal Psychology: An Embryonic Science. In Nijhuis, J. ed., *Fetal Behaviour: Developmental and Perinatal Aspects*. Oxford University Press, Oxford, 129–156.

Hoffman, M. (1994) Discipline and Internalization. *Developmental Psychology* 30(1): 26–28.

Honneth, A. (1995) *The Struggle for Recognition*. Polity Press, London.

Keenan, T. and Evans, S. (2009) *An Introduction to Child Development*. Sage, London.

Layard, R., Dunne, J. and the panel of the Good Childhood Inquiry (2009). *A Good Childhood: Searching for Values in a Competitive Age*. Penguin Books, London.

Nussbaum, M. (2011) *Creating Capabilities: The Human Development Approach*. Belknap Press, Cambridge MA.

Nussbaum, M. (2013) *Political Emotions: Why Love Matters for Justice*. Belknap Press, Cambridge MA.

Meier, G. and Stiglitz, J. eds. (2001) *Frontiers of Development Economics: The Future in Perspective*. Oxford University Press and the World Bank, Oxford and Washington, DC.

Rawls, J. (1971) *A Theory of Justice*. Oxford University Press, Oxford.

Ray, D. (1998) *Development Economics*. Princeton University Press, Princeton.

Rinaldi, C. and Howe, N. (2012) Mothers and Fathers Parenting Styles and Associations with Toddlers Externalising, Internalising and Adaptive Behaviours. *Early Childhood Research Quarterly* 27(2): 266–273.

Salvo, C., Silvares, E. and Toni, P. (2005) Práticas educativas como forma de predição de problemas de comportamento e competência social. *Estudos de Psicologia* 22(2): 187–195.

Sonuga-Barke, E., Kennedy, M., Kumsta, R., Knights, N. Golm, D. Rutter, M. and others (2017) Child-to-Adult Neurodevelopmental and Mental Health Trajectories After Early Life Deprivation: The Young Adult Follow-up of the Longitudinal English and Romanian Adoptees Study. *The Lancet* 389(10078): 1539–1548.

Sroufe, L. (1995) *Emotional Development: The Organization of Emotional Life in the Early Years*. Cambridge University Press, Cambridge.

Todaro, M. and Smith, S. (2014) *Economic Development*. Pearson, New York.

Toth, S., Harris, L., Goodman, G. and Cicchetti, D. (2011) Influence of Violence and Aggression on Children's Psychological Development: Trauma, Attachment, and Memory. In Shaver, P. and Mikulincer, M. eds., *Human Aggression and Violence: Causes, Manifestations, and Consequences*. American Psychological Association, Washington, DC.

Vizard, P. (2006) *Poverty and Human Rights: Sen's "Capability Perspective" Explored*. Oxford University Press, Oxford.

Walker, S., Wachs, T., Gardner, J., Lozoff, B., Wasserman, G., Pollitt, E. and Carter, J. (2007) "Child Development: Risk Factors for Adverse Outcomes in Developing Countries. *The Lancet* 369(9556): 145–157.

Weber, L., Brandenburg, O. and Viezzer, A. (2003) A Relação entre o estilo parental e otimismo na criança. Psico-USF 8(1): 71–79.

15
Health
Social gradients and unjust health outcomes

Sridhar Venkatapuram

An understandable response to the millions of deaths due to AIDS, maternal mortality, or sudden epidemics such as Ebola in West Africa has been to focus discussion and social action on access to medicines and healthcare. In ethical discussions, the glaring differences in deaths to diseases that occur in richer countries versus poorer countries raises questions of global distributive justice, particularly about the distribution of healthcare goods and services, including the healthcare workforce. In this chapter I set out an alternative and growing discussion that expands the focus of justice on the causes and distribution of disease and mortality, rather than just on the inequality in access to their care and treatments. It is undeniable that healthcare goods and services are vitally important to human beings everywhere. At the same time, we are now beginning to appreciate much more that the causation and distribution of disease and mortality among individuals and social groups is determined by social conditions operating from the local to the global, and where they are located on the social hierarchy. While the distribution of valued and valuable goods such as income and wealth or healthcare goods and services is familiar in distributive justice debates in Anglo-American philosophy, the second and broader discussion on the social roots of health inequalities is less familiar and, indeed, deeply challenging to many theories of social ethics and justice.

The first section presents an influential 'health equity' argument that appears to have global applicability; however, its shortcomings lead us to seek guidance from philosophical theories of social and global justice. Yet recent epidemiological research seems to challenge fundamental aspects or assumptions of some leading theories of justice. The second section discusses the transformative research about the social determinants of health and health inequalities and its implications for social/global justice philosophy. The third section reviews recent philosophical debates on justice and global justice in light of social epidemiology. The fourth section concludes the chapter by identifying some future directions in this area.

Health equity

The phrases 'health equity' or 'global health equity' now frequently appear in scholarly literature, policy discussions and documents, as well as part of names of programmes and centers. Health equity seems to function as an umbrella term that captures both concern about the persistence

DOI: 10.4324/9781315626796-18

of preventable ill-health, and health inequalities across social groups in industrialized countries, as well as the concern about the persistent high prevalence of preventable mortality and impairments in low-income countries (Whitehead 1990; Evans, Whitehead et al. 2001; Braveman and Gruskin 2003; Braveman 2006). This is remarkable in one aspect because, historically, addressing health issues facing rich versus poor countries has been seen as requiring fundamentally different analytical paradigms and responses. Such dualist thinking was profoundly shaped by grand theories of demographic and epidemiological transitions of countries (Omran 1971; Preston 2007). For example, the burden of disease in a country was expected to transition from infectious diseases to chronic diseases as it became more economically developed. However, the emergence of new and resurgent infectious diseases in rich countries and chronic diseases in poor countries has meant that such dualistic theories have fallen out of favour for being inaccurate.

In any case, Margaret Whitehead initially developed a conception of 'health equity' for the World Health Organization's Europe office in the late 1980s. The success in applying her health equity concept to the broad diversity of countries and regions within the European community made it seem plausible to generalize it to all the countries in the world. The motivating idea behind Whitehead's conception of health equity is that certain ethical values compel social action to decrease 'health inequities' across social groups.

Whitehead starts from what seems a shared understanding – that not every death or all health impairments are necessarily morally troubling. In order to identify the subset of all health inequalities that qualify as *inequities* that require a social response as a matter of social ethics or justice, she identified three criteria in the form of a decision tree (Whitehead 1990). A health difference or inequality becomes a health inequity when it is deemed to be (a) avoidable, (b) unnecessary, and (c) unfair or unjust. A society is morally obligated to act to prevent and mitigate the set of health inequities that are identified as remaining after applying the three-tier filter (Whitehead 1990; Whitehead 1992; Evans et al. 2001).

One appealing aspect of this conception or framework for moral action is that it seems applicable anywhere in the world. However, the health equity criteria have a number of conceptual weaknesses. The most prominent weakness is the overarching ambiguity about whether the moral concern about health inequalities is only regarding the distribution patterns of health constraints – inequalities between social groups – or also includes other dimensions. That is, should we be morally troubled primarily about relative health inequalities between groups, or that some groups have really poor health, or that some groups are not achieving what they could – which is evidenced through a relative comparison with what other groups are achieving? And importantly, are we worried only about inter-group inequalities, or also inter-individual inequalities?

These ambiguities about whether our ethical evaluation of health inequalities should be driven foremost by the concern for equality or by the intrinsic or instrumental value of health, (priority), or both, and whether the ethical concern is for groups or individuals, or both, are not minor issues. It is crucially important to be clear from the beginning as the initial choices profoundly determine much of the ethical reasoning that follows (Parfit 1997; Murray et al. 1999; Braveman, Krieger et al. 2000; Gakidou et al. 2000; Braveman, Starfield et al. 2001). I have discussed elsewhere the many ambiguities about the three health equity principles in more detail (Venkatapuram and Marmot 2009; Venkatapuram 2011).

What is worth emphasizing here is that fairness and justice cannot be the last or lowest ranking criterion. The people experiencing health constraints that become classified as 'unavoidable' or 'necessary' by the first two steps are pushed outside the scope of justice. That means that no claims from fairness/justice are available to individuals who experience 'unavoidable' or 'necessary' impairments and mortality. Though Whitehead starts from seemingly uncontroversial points such as not all deaths are unjust, her health equity criteria lead us to conclusions that are hugely problematic. The social response to individuals who are vulnerable to or experience unavoidable impairments (i.e. genetic diseases) or necessary impairments or mortality (necessary for what?) ought not be silence. Treating them with equal concern and respect which is their due means that their claims cannot be postponed as being 'hard cases' or handled as a matter for charity rather than justice (Kittay 1997; Nussbaum 2006; Wasserman 2006). In fact, the notion that impairments and mortality of some individuals are 'necessary' requires extraordinary justification.

Even if we were to accept justice and fairness as the last and lowest level consideration, the three-tier criteria express no clear alliance or commitment to a particular conception or theory of justice or fairness. The health equity literature often refers to human rights, and oblique references to John Rawls' theory of social justice, and even to the capabilities approach developed by Amartya Sen and Martha Nussbaum (Ostlin and Diderichsen 2001; Peter and Evans 2001; Anand 2002; Braveman and Gruskin 2003). Interestingly, despite the use of human rights rhetoric by health equity advocates because of their global applicability, the three-pronged health equity view is actually unsympathetic to rights.

Given the parsimonious three principles, health equity advocates would have great difficulty navigating the conflicts between various rights, and unlikely to side with the individual in the classic conflict between individual rights and increasing overall social benefit. That is, decreasing the magnitude of health inequities overall in a population is likely to be given priority over respecting a particular individual's right to health or their other human rights. Nevertheless, despite the weaknesses and ambiguities in the health equity principles pointed out above, Whitehead's health equity principles' role in galvanizing greater attention to the normative dimensions of health inequalities is hugely praiseworthy. And, in fairness, the health equity principles do reflect the notion that 'ought implies can'. If we cannot prevent or treat a disease then we cannot be burdened with duties to prevent or treat. Indeed, without Whitehead's introduction to the dimensions of avoidability in terms of prevention and treatment, necessity, and fairness/justice, the discussions would likely still have been on distribution of healthcare. But there is clearly the need to reconcile the principles of equal treatment with that of 'ought implies can' with notions of rights and so forth. More robust philosophical arguments about health inequalities and especially those that place fairness and justice as primary values motivate engaging more deeply with philosophical theories about social/global justice. And yet, social epidemiology, the field that Whitehead helped develop, has been producing research that are fundamentally challenging to the theories of social and global justice.

Social and global determinants of health

Over the last four decades, epidemiologists have produced compelling evidence that health outcomes (e.g. life expectancy, mortality rates, obesity, and cognitive development) are distributed along a social gradient; each socio-economic class – defined by income, occupational grade, or educational attainment, et cetera – has worse health outcomes than the one above it (Macintyre 1997; Marmot et al. 1997; Kawachi et al. 2002). There is a health/illness gradient from top to bottom of the social hierarchy within societies, in every society. Research also shows that the steeper the socio-economic gradient (i.e. more social inequality), the lower overall health and well-being of the entire population; everyone in that society is worse off in the domain of health and many other domains than they could be otherwise (Deaton 2003; Wilkinson and Pickett 2009).

The remarkable findings on the social distribution patterns of ill-health have motivated numerous studies on the underlying causal determinants. The important thing to note here is that unlike studies which try to identify what causes a disease in one individual rather than others, these studies aim to identify what causes disease in certain individuals and in differing amounts in different social groups. The main hypothesis is that the causal factors are in the social conditions – the factors affecting social groups differently in different places on the social hierarchy. Where one stands on the social gradient determines the types and levels of harmful exposures and protective factors in pathways to ill-health and mortality.

The research has so far illuminated a whole range of social determinants (discrete exposures and pathways) to ill-health over the entire life cycle starting from the social conditions surrounding the mother while still in-utero to quality of social relationships in old age. To be clear, while availability of healthcare is crucial, other more influential causal determinants include such things as early infant care and stimulation, safe and secure employment, housing conditions, discrimination, self-respect, personal relationships, community cohesion, and income inequality (Marmot and Wilkinson 1999; Berkman and Kawachi 2000).

The important implication for social justice philosophy is that the causes of ill-health and mortality shift from the natural or personal domains to the social – the moral responsibility falls on social institutions. Furthermore, the scope of social justice is affected as these determinants operate at levels ranging from the micro such as material deprivations and individual level psychosocial mechanisms to the macro such as community cultures, national political regimes, and *global* processes affecting trade and respect for human rights. The possibility that extra-national, global determinants may have significant impact on the health and longevity of some individuals and social groups requires that the causal analysis as well as the ethical analysis has to start with a global scope from the beginning. That is, one can no longer assume that the causes are local, or that moral duties are primarily local, and then global. To put it another way, if one is directly causing disease and death to people far away, then one's duty to correct that harm far away is stronger than duties to fellow members of a local, social contract. The scope has to be global from the start because your harms and obligations will not be visible if you start local and build your ethical responsibilities outward and making them weaker as they get distant.

Inequality and social justice theory

The concern with equality and inequality more broadly has been a central theme in Anglo-American moral and political philosophy for most of the 20th century. While there is no self-evident logical relation between equality and social justice, a common starting point is that for any conception or theory of liberal social justice (a 'good society') to be plausible in the modern world, it has to treat human beings equally in some meaningful way (Kane 1996a, 1996b; Sen 1996). To put an even finer point on it, to be taken seriously, contemporary theories of social justice must not just express platitudes regarding the moral equality of persons but must treat individuals equally in some substantive way that is relevant to the theory (Sen 1982).

Such a starting point, however, does not identify in what *space* or *how* societies should treat individuals equally. There is also much disagreement about whether such a starting point means that every extant human being, as well as possible future human beings, must be treated equally in a meaningful way within the scope of a theory of social justice. In a seminal 1979 paper titled 'Equality of What', Amartya Sen interrogates the place of equality in different approaches to social justice including utilitarianism and other theories which distribute resources, such as that of John Rawls (Sen 1982). Sen argues that both kinds of approaches should be rejected by showing how their focal points of equality directly offend our moral intuitions, their implications in certain situations run counter to our moral intuitions, or they run counter to some other more basic moral principles. Sen then goes on to argue for 'basic capability equality'.

Since the 'equality of what' discussions set off in the 1980s, myriad targets of equality are presently being advanced including rights, welfare, advantage, resources, capabilities, opportunities for welfare, and mid-fare. And each of these focal points can be attached to a further myriad of distributive rules such as absolute equality, priority, sufficiency, maximization, optimization, and shortfall equity. Justice, targets or focal points of equality, and distribution rules go together. As Elizabeth Anderson states so nicely, theories of justice at their core have a metric (valued good) and a rule (distribution) (Anderson 2010).

Given the myriad of valued ethical goods and distribution rules, which inequalities are deemed to be unjust in the world will vary according to a chosen theory's focal point of equality (the what), and/or are a deviation from the correlative distribution rules – *how* things are distributed, and *to whom* they are distributed. It is also here, in the space of equality or in the distribution rules that the concern for health or for global justice is most directly fleshed out. Health or, indeed, healthcare, health utility, health capability, or some other variation is conceptualized and justified as a focal point of equality. And, how they are distributed, and to whom, determines whether the theory also has global scope – a global justice theory.

Theories of global justice

Best exemplified by John Rawls' theory, the most actively developed area of social justice philosophy in the Anglo-American tradition is based on the social contract tradition (Rawls 1971). Whether referring to peoples, societies or nation-states, philosophers such as Rawls and others who work in the social contract tradition conceive of individuals as having distinctly different rights and obligations within their societal/national borders versus outside. Taken to an extreme, a 'relational-statist' position contends that there are absolutely no moral rights and responsibilities to individuals or other entities outside one's own societal borders (Sangiovanni 2007). Justice does not exist in the space or relations between societies. At the other end of the spectrum, there is the extreme 'cosmopolitan' position which asserts that there exist the same moral rights and responsibilities between all individuals irrespective of societal borders (Singer 1972; Beitz 1988; Caney 2005). At this end of the spectrum, national borders simply have no moral significance. Global justice debates, as a result, are disputes over whether justice also applies outside the social contract, and if so, what does that entail?

Conclusion – future directions

The empirical research in social epidemiology thus extends the moral scope of the concern for health and health inequalities much wider than healthcare or even public health, and deep into the basic structures of domestic and indeed, global society. And many extant approaches to social justice, especially based on the social contract, are conceptually ill-equipped to evaluate the ethics of such a broad relationship between social and global arrangements and ill-health/health inequalities. The assumptions and theoretical structures erase much of the health injustices occurring in the world, or push these concerns outside the scope of justice.

While much of the global justice literature early in first decade of the 21st century was framed as 'what do we owe the global poor' or about the access to life saving medicines, the current and future directions of research in this area are about integrating the quickly evolving empirical research on social determinants of health within and across countries with normative reasoning about who has the duties or responsibilities to do what, where, when and how. Proving causal pathways between actors and harm across vast geographical spaces and time will require new kinds of empirical methodologies as well as more nuanced thinking about moral responsibilities and duties. For example, showing how increasing import tariffs affects the health of people in the exporting country will require novel statistical analyses as well as nuanced ethical reasoning about the associated moral duties.

Aside from these cases where actors are being linked to harm, there will likely be more arguments about moral duties where there is no link to causing harm. For example, Sen advocates for social action at the global level based on the ethical principle that where one has the power to prevent or mitigate injustice, one has sufficient reason to consider doing so. Sen terms this an 'obligation from effective power' (Sen 2009, 205–207). The capacity or agency to mitigate injustice is sufficient enough grounds to consider acting. It is similar and less stringent than Peter Singer's seminal altruism argument, but may radically differ regarding the target of action or goals (Singer 1972, 2004). There will likely be more arguments about such non-relational duties in the face of health injustices. Furthermore, there is likely to be significant research and argumentation about both the targets and distribution principles as people aim to guide real world actions addressing urgent health issues using different theories.

References

Anand, S. (2002) The Concern for Equity in Health. *Journal of Epidemiology and Community Health* 56(7): 485–487.

Anderson, E. (2010) Justifying the Capabilities Approach to Justice. In Brighouse, H. and Robeyns, I. eds., *Measuring Justice: Primary Goods and Capabilities*. University Press, Cambridge.

Beitz, C.R. (1988) Recent International Thought. *International Journal* 43(2): 183–204.

Berkman, L.F. and Kawachi, I.O. (2000) *Social Epidemiology*. Oxford University Press: New York.

Braveman, P. (2006) Health Disparities and Health Equity: Concepts and Measurement. *Annual Review of Public Health* 27: 167–194.

Braveman, P. and Gruskin, S. (2003) Defining Equity in Health. *Journal of Epidemiology Community Health* 57(4): 254–258.

Braveman, P., Krieger, N. and Lynch, J. (2000) Health Inequalities and Social Inequalities in Health *Bulletin of the World Health Organization* 78(2): 232–234; discussion 234–235.

Braveman, P., Starfield, B., Geiger, H.J. and Murray, C.J.L. (2001) World Health Report 2000: How it Removes Equity From the Agenda for Public Health Monitoring and Policy. *Bulletin of the World Health Organization* 323(7314): 678–681.

Caney, S. (2005) *Justice Beyond Borders: A Global Political Theory*. Oxford University Press, Oxford.

Deaton, A. (2003) Health, Inequality, and Economic Development. *Journal of Economic Literature* 41(1): 113–158.

Evans, T., Whitehead, M., Diderichsen, F., Bhuiya, A. and Wirth, M., eds. (2001) *Challenging Inequities in Health: From Ethics to Action*. Oxford University Press, Oxford and New York.

Gakidou, E., Murray, C.J.L. and Frenk, J. (2000) A Framework for Measuring Health Inequality. *Bulletin of the World Health Organization* 78: 42–54.

Kane, J. (1996a). Basal Inequalities – Reply. *Political Theory* 24(3): 401–406.

Kane, J. (1996b) Justice, Impartiality, and Equality: Why the Concept of Justice Does Not Presume Equality. *Political Theory* 24(3): 375–393.

Kawachi, I., Subramanian, S.V. and Almeida-Filho, N. (2002) A Glossary for Health Inequalities. *Journal of Epidemiology of Community Health* 56(9) 647–652.

Kittay, E. (1997) Human Dependency and Rawlsian Equality. In Meyers, D.T. ed., *Feminists Rethink the Self*. Westview Press, Boulder CO.

Macintyre, S. (1997) The Black Report and Beyond: What Are the Issues?. *Social Science Medicine* 44(6): 723–745.

Marmot, M., Ryff, C.D., Bumpass, L.L., Shipley, M. and Marks, N.F. (1997) Social Inequalities in Health: Next Questions and Converging Evidence. *Social Science Medicine* 44(6): 901–910.

Marmot, M.G. and Wilkinson, R.G. (1999) *Social Determinants of Health*. Oxford University Press, Oxford and New York.

Murray, C.J.L., Gakidou, E.E. and Frenk, J. (1999) Health Inequalities and Social Group Differences: What Should We Measure? *Bulletin of the World Health Organization* 77(7): 537–543.

Nussbaum, M.C. (2006) *Frontiers of Justice: Disability, Nationality, Species Membership.* The Belknap Press of Harvard University Press, Cambridge MA and London.

Omran, A.R. (1971) The Epidemiologic Transition: A Theory of the Epidemiology of Population Change. *The Milbank Quarterly* 49(4): 509–538.

Ostlin, P. and Diderichsen, F. (2001) Equity-oriented National Strategy for Public Health in Sweden. Policy Learning Curve Series, World Health Organization Europe.

Parfit, D. (1997) Equality and Priority. *Ratio* New Series 10(3): 202–221.

Peter, F. and Evans, T. (2001) *Ethical Dimensions of Health Equity: Challenging Inequities in Health: From Ethics to Action.* T. Evans, M. Whitehead, F. Diderichsen, A. Bhuiya and M. Wirth eds., Oxford University Press, Oxford [England]; New York, xvi, 348 p.

Preston, S.H. (2007) The Changing Relation Between Mortality and Level of Economic Development (Reprinted from Population Studies, vol. 29, July 1975). *International Journal of Epidemiology* 36(3): 484–490.

Rawls, J. (1971) *A Theory of Justice.* Harvard University Press, Cambridge, MA.

Sangiovanni, A. (2007) Global Justice, Reciprocity, and the State. *Philosophy and Public Affairs* 35(1): 3–39.

Sen, A. (1982) Equality of What? In Sen, A. ed., *Choice, Welfare, and Measurement.* Harvard University Press, Cambridge, MA, 353–369.

Sen, A. (1982) Liberty, Unanimity and Rights. In Sen, A. ed., *Choice, Welfare and Measurement.* Harvard University Press, Cambridge, MA, 291–326.

Sen, A. (1996) On the Status of Equality. *Political Theory* 24(3): 394–400.

Sen, A. (2009) *The Idea of Justice.* Allen Lane, London.

Singer, P. (1972) Famine, Affluence, and Morality. *Philosophy and Public Affairs* 1: 229–243.

Singer, P. (2004) *One World: The Ethics of Globalization.* Yale University Press, New Haven CT and London.

Venkatapuram, S. (2011) *Health Justice: An Argument from the Capabilities Approach.* Polity Press, Cambridge.

Venkatapuram, S. and Marmot, M. (2009) Epidemiology and Social Justice in Light of Social Determinants of Health. *Bioethics* 23(2): 78–89.

Wasserman, D. (2006) Disability, Capability, and Thresholds for Distributive Justice. In Kaufman, A. ed., *Capabilities Equality: Basic Issues and Problems.* Routledge, New York and London.

Whitehead, M. (1990) *The Concepts and Principles of Equity in Health,* 29 World Health Organization Regional Office for Europe, Copenhagen.

Whitehead, M. (1992) The Concepts and Principles of Equity and Health. *International Journal of Health Services* 22(3): 429–445.

Wilkinson, R.G. and Pickett, K. (2009) *The Spirit Level : Why More Equal Societies Almost Always Do Better.* Allen Lane, London.

Part IV
Empowerment and agency

Authentic development requires more than raising gross national product, or even increasing household incomes. It requires the empowerment of people, so that they are to an increasing extent able to act as agents with regard to the valuable decisions in their own lives. This is because being poor is more than simply not having enough money, it is not having enough opportunity and control over one's life to do and be what one values. Most development institutions use the language of 'empowerment' and 'agency' and at least claim to strive to empower people. Yet the extent to which empowerment programs actually result in empowering the poor is debated. Moreover, unlike gross national product, empowerment and agency are not precise and easy to define. The United Nations Development Program (UNDP) has a Gender Empowerment Measure (GEM), which seeks to determine what share of public sphere power women enjoy relative to men. The index reflects percentages of (1) seats held by women in National parliament, (2) women in economic decision-making positions, and (3) female income. But as helpful as it might be in some areas, it would be foolish to insist that the GEM provides a complete and accurate understanding of how a particular person's life is going.

It is clear that empowerment and agency are not categorical concepts, such that either you are an empowered agent or you are not. Instead, people can be more or less empowered or have more or less agency. Moreover, given that we each participate in various social, political and economic relationships, it is worth considering factors related to different types and dimensions of empowerment (for example: political empowerment, private sphere empowerment, gender empowerment, etc.) and agency (direct vs. indirect agency, process vs. outcome agency, individual vs. collective agency). Yet because many scholars and practitioners disagree about what exactly empowerment and agency are and how we as development ethicists might facilitate, cultivate, or prevent obstructing the empowerment of oppressed, vulnerable, and marginalized people, there is a great literature discussing the nature and scope of the social, political, and economic dimensions of these concepts as well as how empowerment and agency emerge. The first two chapters of this section explore this great literature on empowerment and agency. The third chapter looks at education as a means of promoting empowerment and agency, and the fourth chapter considers the disempowering impact of displacement by development.

Karie Cross Riddle surveys the current and most influential positions on empowerment within development ethics. She makes a compelling case that, although there are good insights

DOI: 10.4324/9781315626796-19

in the existing literature, development ethicists need to consider more voices from among feminist, post-colonial, indigenous, and ethnic/racial critics of Western ideals of democracy and justice, while at the same time being careful not to co-opt or ventriloquize these sources.

A closer look at agency and democratic participation in development is offered by Matt Regan. He focuses on the role that agency plays as "the expansion of social and individual freedoms" – both within international development in general and in David Crocker's agency-focused version of the capabilities approach in particular. Regan argues that democratic procedures ensure solutions that are more effective, robust, and humane than other approaches can offer.

Alejandra Boni and Merridy Wilson-Strydom reflect on how education is understood within different paradigms of development (liberal capitalist, marxist, post-colonial and post-development, liberal egalitarian and radical humanist approaches). The authors then use the capability approach (see Chapter 7) to analyze a particular case study in South African education. The authors argue that equality, diversity, and participation are essential to promote a worthwhile education that empowers students and benefits families and communities.

Finally, Asmita Kabra and Jay Drydyk draw attention to issues of empowerment and democratic agency that emerge as a result of displacement by development. Displacement by development occurs when projects conducted in the name of development deprive people access to land they used for their homes and livelihoods. Displacement and resettlement processes typically are disempowering for the displaced, not only because they lose access to territory, but also because they are often not given an effective voice in democratic deliberations on whether and how the displacing projects and their own resettlement are conducted.

16

Empowerment

Participatory development and the problem of cooptation

Karie Cross Riddle

In her insightful work *Black Feminist Thought*, Patricia Hill Collins argues that "self-definition is key to individual and group empowerment." Drawing upon her own experiences and the work of other black feminists, Collins develops a "black women's standpoint" which is *by* and *for* African-American women in the United States. This standpoint serves as an epistemological basis for "black women's empowerment and resistance" – resistance to interlocking oppressions of race, gender, and class. While others such as white women and African-American men are encouraged to ally with African-American women to support and disseminate black feminist thought, they cannot define it (Collins 1990, 34–35). Moreover, the content of black feminist thought comes from two levels of participation: living as black women and sharing experiences of intersectional discrimination and theorizing together about what those experiences of daily life mean (*ibid.*, 30). Thus, the self-definition that is so central to empowerment *depends upon* participation.

Collins' black feminist approach to empowerment and participation can serve as a useful guide for this review of the current literature on empowerment and participatory development. I therefore take black feminist thought and the writings of other feminists from the Global South as the starting point of our discussion, structuring the essay according to its content about lifting up previously marginalized voices. We will soon turn to the vast literature on different definitions and aspects of empowerment and participation, exploring works by well-known scholars of development such as Amartya Sen, Denis Goulet, Séverine Deneulin, David Crocker, Jay Drydyk, Naila Kabeer, and Serene Khader. However, given the topic at hand, I think it is important for the comparison and evaluation of these thinkers to occur in light of the insights coming from more marginalized voices.

I begin with a few insights from black feminist thought, quickly moving to more sustained engagement with feminists from the Global South who were directly concerned with development. Only after understanding empowerment and participation from their view, will we begin to engage with the work of well-known development ethicists, in sections on empowerment and participation. Each of these sections features my recommendations for fruitful future work. I conclude with connections between empowerment and participation and recommendations for decolonizing not only empowerment and participation themselves, but also the ways in which we theorize about them.

DOI: 10.4324/9781315626796-20

Views from the margins

According to black feminist thought, empowerment comes from marginalized people themselves; it is not something that can be bestowed upon them by those who hold more power. Second, black feminism springs from intersecting structural oppressions such as racism and sexism. The structural nature of oppression questions the understanding of power as something that can be held by some and transferred to others. Instead, power is a more systemic, diffuse relation that we can observe in small, every day interactions and social norms. Third, others outside of the marginalized group can play important roles as allies, although they should not have the privilege of defining the parameters for empowerment (*ibid.*, 28–29).

Collins' thoughts on empowerment, worked out in African-American women's life experiences and social movements of the 1960s through the 1980s, mirror much of the content of Gita Sen and Caren Grown's work *Development, Crises, and Alternative Visions: Third World Women's Perspectives*. This short volume serves as the manifesto of Development Alternatives with Women for a New Era (DAWN), a transnational women's group that formed in Bangalore, India, in 1984. DAWN responded to the harms associated with the World Bank's top-down, structural adjustment development policies, as well as the United Nations' attempts to address gender inequality merely by integrating women more fully into development. The feminists of DAWN – primarily women from the Global South, but including marginalized women and other allies from the Global North (such as African-American women) – demanded not just the integration of women into existing practices, but rather a transformation of those practices through women's empowerment and substantive participation (Sen and Grown 1987).

Credited with bringing the term empowerment to the field of international development, the women of DAWN call attention to the close links between means and ends (Calvès 2010, 735–749; Cronin-Furman et al. 2017). Sen and Grown note in their explanation of DAWN's methods:

> The nature of our vision of a better society is powerfully influenced by the methods adopted to achieve it. . . . To build a social order that is just, equitable, and life-affirming for all people, our methods must correspondingly be open and respectful of differences, and must try to break down hierarchies, power, and distrust.
>
> *(Sen and Grown 1987, 10)*

Such a social order would push back against the oppression of women in "economic, political, and cultural processes," through the substantive participation of the very women who experience subordination. The responsibility for transforming the social order does not rest solely on the shoulders of women, however. Those affiliated with DAWN are meant to organize and demand changes from "those in power," such as national governments and development agencies (*ibid.*, 22). In this vision, women's self-empowerment precipitates deeper structural changes in multiple arenas, including politics.

With the emergence of DAWN and the publication of *Development, Crises, and Alternative Visions* in 1987, new feminist studies on empowerment and development appeared rapidly (Batliwala 1993; Kabeer 1994). First seen as overly radical, the empowerment approach to development gained followers and hence credence with international actors, evolving from a marginalized concept to a politically correct idea that large organizations felt compelled to support. Early usage of the term on the international stage, at the International Conference on Population and Development (1994) and the Beijing World Conference on Women (1995), answered DAWN's call to target gendered power relations across economic and political structures. But by the time the United Nations Millennium Summit set women's empowerment as the third of eight Millennium Development Goals, the term had become ambiguous and had lost its critical edge (Calvès 2010, 742).

Many scholars argue that the once-radical nature of empowerment was essentially co-opted by large development institutions like the World Bank (Cornwall and Brock 2005; Kapoor 2005; Sardenberg 2008; Calvès 2010; Khader 2011; Cornwall and Fujita 2012). A closer look at the language and research methods associated with its much-lauded, multi-country study known as Consultation with the Poor reveals underlying assumptions about poor people and the policies that are intended to alleviate their poverty. Editors Deepa Narayan and Patti Petesch refer to "the poor" as "the true poverty experts." They argue that any policy targeting poverty, therefore, must rest upon "the experiences, priorities, reflections, and recommendations of poor children, women, and men" (2002, 2). Particularly in light of the harmful consequences of structural adjustment policies, leaders at the World Bank knew that their credibility rested upon asking "the poor" to assist in determining development policies. Thus, the Bank undertook an enormous consultation with these newly-discovered poverty experts, through participatory research methods in which "local people act as partners in problem identification, data collection, analysis, and follow-up action" (*ibid.*, 3).

The introduction to one of the Bank's publications based on the Consultation, *Voices of the Poor*, reveals, however, that the World Bank itself is still very much in control of development policy-making. In their foreword to the 2002 publication, Clare Short and James D. Wolfensohn write: "Poor people's descriptions of encounters with a range of institutions call out for all of *us* to rethink *our* strategies" (*ibid.*, xiii, emphasis mine). While the strategies may be newly-informed by poor people, they still belong to the World Bank. Moreover, the writers' description of "poor people," meant to express solidarity, betrays instead a damaging Othering. With apparent surprise, Short and Wolfensohn find common ground with the Bank's research subjects: "Poor people care about many of the same things all of *us* care about: happiness, family, children, livelihood, peace, security, safety, dignity, and respect" (*ibid.*). The "us" and "our" in these two quotations demonstrate that, participatory research aside, the poor are those who inform policies and then receive their effects, whereas the Bank's researchers are those who analyze the poor and then construct policies that address their needs.

Development scholars Andrea Cornwall and Mamoru Fujita refer to this process as "ventriloquizing 'the Poor.'" The authors visited some of the World Bank's original research sites, to better understand the local context of some of the quotations presented in *Voices of the Poor*. In a scathing critique, Cornwall and Fujita (2012) argue that the Consultation failed to use genuinely participatory methods. Participatory research should emphasize the research subjects' own categories, terms, and meanings, using these as the starting point for analysis and blurring the line between researcher and researched. The authors note that for the purposes of comparing the poor across twenty-three countries, however, World Bank researchers relied upon set lists of questions, involving terms and topics that have specific origins and narrative meanings.

Moreover, World Bank researchers had the ability to determine (in consultation with local groups) who "the poor" were, even when many of their respondents resisted labelling themselves or their neighbors as poor. Cornwall and Fujita also claim that when compiling their reports, researchers tended to de-textualize quotes, using them to justify the World Bank's neoliberal policies rather than to explain people's desires for more equitable political and social relations (Cornwall and Fujita 2012, 1758).

Through unfortunate processes like this, many scholars argue that the terms "empowerment" and "participatory development" have become nothing but moralizing window dressing for the same top-down policies that have long faced critique. The World Bank has learned to talk about its work with the language of empowerment, but Anne-Emmanuèle Calvès refers to its actions as "falsely consensual," while Cecelia Sardenberg views its approach as more "liberal" than "liberating" (Calvès 2010; Sardenberg 2008; Kapoor 2005).

Ilan Kapoor argues that development institutions try to "obscure their own participation in participation" through the empowerment of poor people. With one side of their mouths, they promote First World geopolitical interests, while the other spouts "a series of seemingly incontestable maxims: PD [participatory development] is naturally progressive, [and] community participation is inherently good. . . ." Empowerment and participatory development thus tend to allow large institutions to do top-down development "with a clear conscience," so long as they consult someone from the Global South (Kapoor 2005, 1206).

Clearly, empowerment and participatory development face a great deal of criticism. This raises two very important questions. First, should academics, practitioners, and members of the international community, whether from the Global South or North, give up on these terms, and their corresponding processes, in favor of something else? Second, if they are worth retaining, how can scholars and practitioners define and do them well?

If we return to my initial argument, that we should learn about empowerment and participation first from marginalized people, then we should heed feminists from the Global South. Many of those who initially supported projects like DAWN's now lament the turn that empowerment has taken, but they call for a reclamation of the term and its attendant processes such as participatory development (Calvès 2010, 748; Pereira 2008; Staudt et al. 2003). For example, writing in the Nigerian context, Charmaine Pereira argues:

> State agencies' adoption of terms developed in one context to mean something quite different in another context, go[es] beyond changes in meaning to involve differences in intent and political interests. . . . This terrain [development policy] is a key arena in which the struggle to reclaim feminism in the pursuit of social and economic justice in Nigeria has to be fought.
>
> *(2008, 49)*

Answering my first question with a resounding "no," Pereira suggests we must proceed to question two. How can we define and carry out processes of empowerment and participatory development well? I will take the two terms in turn, although many aspects of them are inter-related.

Empowerment

In a recent article on the concept of empowerment, Jay Drydyk (2013) observes that the term is widely contested. Citing Alkire and Ibrahim's work cataloging different iterations of the term, he notes thirty different definitions of empowerment within the field of human development (2007). How can we make sense of the proliferation of definitions and the conceptual fuzziness that they produce? Before returning to Drydyk's helpful understanding of empowerment and other recent, notable scholarship by Serene Khader and Naila Kabeer, I will first recount some of the early uses of the term by foundational scholars of human development such as Mahbub ul Haq, Amartya Sen, and Martha Nussbaum.

In his 1995 work *Reflections on Human Development*, Mahbub ul Haq describes the human development approach as "neither paternalistic nor based on charity." Instead, it "envisages full empowerment of the people," enabling them to make meaningful choices in political, social, cultural, and economic realms. He explicitly mentions empowering women and men so that they can interact as equals, and he does not shy away from promoting democratic politics (ul

Haq 1995, 19–20; referenced in Drydyk 2016, 59). Thus, much of his approach is in accord with feminist visions of empowerment from the Global South, which promote changing gendered power relations through transparent, democratic processes (Sen and Grown 1987).

Lori Keleher (2007) argues that Amartya Sen and Martha Nussbaum both make use of an implicit conceptualization of empowerment in their economic and philosophical approaches to human development. For Sen, empowerment appears in two forms: agency and capability-set expansion. Agency empowerment can assume two forms: the ability to achieve and actually achieving. Capability-set expansion, or a growing set of capabilities that a person has reason to value, implies more power to "decide about and achieve valuable functionings" (2014). Keleher notes that although Sen and Nussbaum treat agency and well-being very differently, their approaches to empowerment are remarkably compatible, providing practitioners with a cogent theoretical foundation for empowerment regardless of whose approach they choose (*ibid.*, 55). Whereas Sen promotes two aspects of empowerment through distinct concepts of agency and well-being, Nussbaum promotes it through a more general approach to human flourishing and human dignity, which requires a threshold level of certain capabilities for all. Expanding sets of capabilities such as practical reason and control over one's own environment, for Nussbaum, likewise represent enhanced agency. She therefore sees no need to distinguish between agency and well-being (*ibid.*, 67–68). But importantly for Keleher, Nussbaum's promotion of expanded capabilities matches Sen's, and both serve as representations of empowerment.

Ul Haq, Sen, and Nussbaum are some of the most influential scholars of human development, but they are not particularly known for their work on empowerment. To guide our current understanding and to move towards beneficial future research, I argue that we should pay close attention to insights coming from Kabeer, Khader, and Drydyk.

In her early work, Kabeer conceives of empowerment as a process of change, from lesser to greater levels. She divides it into three aspects, resources, agency, and achievements, with the first two comprising conditions for the third. Resources include material, human, and social aspects of life that can "enhance the ability to exercise choice" (Kabeer 1999, 437). Because this category includes social resources, it involves institutions and structures that exert power over people's lives, such as the market and a community's norms. Agency goes beyond "observable action" to include individuals' motivations, or their "power within." Such agency can take the commonly-understood form of decision-making, but also other forms such as bargaining, deception, resistance, and analysis. Kabeer notes that power is often exerted by an individual or institution, but it may also "operate in the absence of any explicit agency," as social norms and unwritten rules (e.g., what Pierre Bourdieu refers to as *doxa*) can have a large impact upon acceptable outcomes. This has much in common with Collins' understanding of power in *Black Feminist Thought*, explicated earlier. Finally, achievement represents greater levels of empowerment, whereas the failure to achieve one's goals (because of constraints, rather than laziness) exemplifies lesser levels, or disempowerment (Kabeer, 438; Bourdieu 1977, cited in Kabeer, 441). Kabeer notes that we ought to be primarily interested in inequalities in people's ability to choose, rather than in simple differences among the choices that they make (439).

Khader builds upon yet respectfully disagrees with some aspects of Kabeer's approach, in her well-regarded 2011 work *Adaptive Preferences and Women's Empowerment*. Tackling a problem that has long plagued the human capabilities approach, Khader offers ways to distinguish among preferences that reveal greater or lesser levels of empowerment, which she conceptualizes as a spectrum, rather than as a binary paired with disempowerment (178). Whereas Kabeer wishes to define empowerment in terms of "whether or not an achievement embodies meaningful choice," in addition to "whether [other choices] were *conceived* to be within the realms of possibility," she expresses some concerns with relating empowerment too closely to choice (Kabeer, 442). For example, it is difficult to distinguish between disempowerment and a real desire to avoid flourishing. Some who act against their interests may not do so because of a lack of real choices (Khader, 180). Moreover, available choices are not merely different from one another; some reflect good options for flourishing, while others would block flourishing. This leads Khader to argue that empowerment theorists should be primarily interested in uncovering the psychological processes that influence decisions that lead to apparent harm (*ibid.*, 181). Merely having available choices is not good enough for Khader; a woman's options must reflect genuine opportunities to flourish if she is to be considered empowered.

Khader's insistence upon relating empowerment to flourishing, comparable to Nusbaum's privileging of a (flexible) concept of human flourishing within the human capabilities approach, distinguishes her among theorists of empowerment. Applying her "deliberative perfectionist approach" to "inappropriately adaptive preferences (IAPs)," she argues that her understanding of empowerment helps development practitioners (or theorists, students, or others who might have a stake in promoting empowerment) to distinguish between preferences that are "just different" and those that reflect real disempowerment. Khader explains her own approach best, in this short passage:

> My own approach . . . begins from the assumption that some preferences – preferences inconsistent with basic flourishing – are particularly likely to be causally related to oppression or deprivation. This is what is *perfectionist* in my perfectionist definition of IAP. The idea is that people tend to seek their basic flourishing and that choices inconsistent are unlikely to persist when people have access to – and an understanding of – objectively better conditions. On my view, finding out whether a preference is the result of "difference" or disempowerment is emphatically *not* a matter of finding out whether it is the result of a choice. Rather, it is a matter of finding out what opportunities were available when the preference was formed and what opportunities are available now.
>
> *(184)*

Khader tries to leave a great deal of room for "epistemic uncertainty" in her approach, merely marking some preferences as "suspect" while others become "genuinely inappropriately adaptive" only after actual encounters with people who have suspect preferences (185). Khader readily acknowledges that Kabeer's use of Bourdieu's *doxa* provides a possible context for understanding self-harming choices as disempowering. In Kabeer's approach, being able to at least imagine different possibilities reflects a move from uncritical acceptance of daily life to a critical consciousness about various aspects of a society's norms and practices. The ability to conceive of alternatives, Kabeer notes, "has an obvious bearing on . . . functioning achievements as an aspect of empowerment" (441).

Khader maintains that her approach has two important advantages over Kabeer's, however. Her account can consider cases of self-harming behavior that might not be the product of uncritical acceptance of *doxa*. For example, young girls who are aware that it is possible to live well without genital cutting might choose it anyway (188). Furthermore, she argues that some choices that follow a society's *doxa* might not be disempowering. What if a given village's traditions include women and men making household decisions together, as equal partners? Is the non-critical acceptance of this tradition disempowering? (182, 189).

Despite Khader's important work on empowerment, she neglects the insights of participatory development to the detriment of her project. She directs her work towards development practitioners who likely hail from the Global North, trying to offer an ethical method for practitioners to identify and mitigate the effects of IAPs. Certainly, her approach promotes deliberation about such preferences, and she requires "actual encounters" with people in the field whose preferences might need to be changed. But some of Khader's language, particularly relating to these "actual encounters," implies that practitioners from the Global North are still the group that directs resources and controls the mechanisms that could improve the well-being of those in the Global South, *if* practitioners deem them deserving. Empowerment seems to be *given* by practitioners, rather than worked out by those who are trying to flourish. (This dynamic is something that Kabeer pays close attention to in her more recent work on women's empowerment, particularly as it is conceived of in the Millennium Development Goals. See Kabeer 2010.) The potential post-colonial dimensions of this relationship are troubling, particularly in the context of a work on empowerment. The participatory nature of development, and of empowerment itself, needs more emphasis in Khader's work.

Drydyk's approach to empowerment has much in common with Kabeer's and Khader's. For example, all three thinkers conceive of empowerment as a process of change, rather than a state to be attained. Moreover, they agree that it is a scalar concept, rather than a binary. Tracking with both black feminist thought and the women of DAWN, all of the authors also pay careful attention to empowerment's role in transforming gendered power relations (Drydyk 2013, 250–251; Khader 2011, 177–178; Kabeer 2010, 461). Drydyk's unique addition to the conversation lies in his helpful conception of empowerment in terms of three dimensions – power, well-being freedom, and agency – and particularly in his insistence upon exploring the interconnected nature of the three. Drydyk notes that capability theorists' contributions might be most effective if they theorize about "*how* and *under what conditions* agency can be an effective means – effective specifically in expanding people's substantive freedom to live in ways that they have reason to value" (2010, 260). This must go hand in hand with an explicitly relational approach that considers not only an individual's own improvement or slippage in agency, power, or well-being, but also how that individual is embedded in a group, and in turn, how that group is situated in a larger context. Empowerment is related to, for example, an individual's power to make decisions in her home, as well as to her status as a member of a minority or majority ethnic group in her state (Drydyk 2010, 256; see also Christine Koggel's helpful emphasis upon relationality in the context of power; Koggel 2013).

In my view, some of the most helpful insights from Drydyk, Kabeer, and Khader include an emphasis from both Drydyk and Kabeer upon exploring the particular *conditions* that may support or detract from empowerment; Khader's insistence upon using a conception of human flourishing in conjunction with empowerment; the understanding of all three that empowerment must be analyzed and promoted through relational and contextual means; and Kabeer's willingness to think of power as systemic and structural, not merely held and exercised by individuals. Future research on empowerment might most fruitfully explore questions such as: Under what political arrangements have members of X minority group in State Y best flourished, and has that flourishing been equal for men and women? Or: five years after the implementation of development initiative A, have vulnerable groups B and C maintained equitable access to resource D, and has that access translated into improved flourishing?

Despite the differences among the approaches to empowerment that I have laid out in this review, the authors agree (at least on the surface) on one important idea: empowerment and participation are closely linked. We will therefore examine the meaning and practice of participatory development, as it relates to empowering individuals to influence their own paths to well-being.

Participatory development

Development ethicists often ask: Who decides? Who designs development policies and implements them? Should those who hold the purse-strings make the decisions, or should it be those whose lives are most impacted by the policies? Any number of decisions, from which type of crop to introduce in a specific field to what sorts of structural adjustments may be best for a national economy, may be reached by different configurations of people. Development ethicists have long argued that higher quality participation by those experiencing the effects of policy leads to more ethical development. However, it can be difficult to measure and to evaluate quality participation. Such a task is both empirical and normative, and like the study of empowerment, the study of participation requires contextual cross-cultural understanding. For the sake of narrowing an extremely broad literature, I will focus on a few, key thinkers on participatory development, as I did with the concept of empowerment. Denis Goulet, Séverine Deneulin, and David Crocker collectively provide diverse and useful understandings of participatory development and its relationship to democracy.

Long before researchers at the World Bank considered concepts like empowerment and methods like local participation, Denis Goulet questioned the ethics of imposing development policies on groups in the Global South (Goulet 1971). Drydyk notes that Goulet's early promotion of participation was particularly "prescient" in one area – his consideration of people as agents, rather than as beneficiaries (Goulet, 123, 148, and 283 in Drydyk 2010, 355). Goulet's understanding of participation was grounded in Paulo Freire's pedagogical philosophy (1971), which promotes student participation in the creation of knowledge, rather than the mere transfer of knowledge from teacher to student. Referring to Freire as "the most important thinker on participation," Goulet borrows his question: Can those who were treated as objects become the "subjects of their own social destiny"? (Goulet 1989, 165). Put differently, can they exert agency to pursue their own well-being?

Goulet argues that the subjects of development *can* exert agency, and that in order for development to be ethical, they *should*. Promoting what he refers to as "authentic participation," he lays out a four-dimensional typology of participation that reveals its complexity. First, participation may be a goal or a means. Some who recognize its inherent value will employ participation even at the cost of efficiency or other values, while others use participation instrumentally, anticipating more effective results. Second, participation differs according to its arena of operation, whether in politics, education, health, or others. Third, participation may be generated by experts, top-down; by the affected population; or by a third party. Finally, the quality of participation varies greatly in relation to *when* participation of the affected population begins (*ibid.*, 166–167). Participation is most authentic, Goulet argues, when local, non-elites maintain decision-making power, freed from manipulation by outsiders (*ibid.*, 168).

Goulet's agency- and power-oriented approach clearly privileges one sort of political process over others – democracy. While it might be possible to implement narrowly economic development via top-down methods, it is difficult to promote truly human-centered development without some component of democratic participation (Drèze and Sen 2002, 377). Thus, Amartya Sen and other scholars of human development tend to champion democratic processes. In *Development as Freedom*, Sen relates democracy to human capabilities by promoting citizen participation in the selection, promotion, and weighting of capabilities. Rather than employing an intuition-based list of capabilities, as Nussbaum does, Sen relies upon local-level deliberation and public reason to determine which capabilities are appropriately supported by which communities. (Note that Nussbaum herself stresses that her list is not fixed-forever, and that it is the product of cross-cultural conversation. See Nussbaum 2000, 77.) For Sen (1999, 33, 78–79), such participation is a vital component of the expansion of substantive political freedom.

In their summary of Sen's thought on democracy, Séverine Deneulin and Lila Shahani (2009) point to its three potential uses for human development. First, it is intrinsically valuable. Participating in democratic political processes is one way of exercising agency, and it is a way of being that humans have reasons to value. Second, it has instrumental value, leading to good consequences in political, social, and economic realms. Finally, democracy has constructive value, as deliberative processes help to create values like tolerance and social equity. Deneulin notes elsewhere, however, some conceptual muddiness in Sen's work that elides an important distinction between democratic practice and participation. These two terms are not interchangeable; instead, democratic decision-making tends to be associated with the election of representatives who make political decisions, whereas participatory decision-making is comprised of the direct involvement of citizens. Deneulin advocates for maintaining this distinction, because

> participatory policy-making mechanisms which bypass the existing democratic political structures are often unable to transform the outcomes of decisions into actions because they fail to take into account the power structures involved in the existing political processes of decision-making.
>
> *(2006, 90)*

Participation, in Deneulin's mind, *must* take account of power. She and Shahani cite two recent books on participation that pay attention to the relationship between participatory development and pre-existing political structures. In *Participation: The New Tyranny?*, authors Bill Cooke and Uma Kothari warn against the tendency for participation to reinforce injustices if it occurs in the context of unjust power structures. Merely inviting citizens to have a say at the micro-level does little to address macro inequalities (Cooke and Kothari 2001, 13–14, cited in Deneulin and Shahani 2009, 190). Samuel Hickey and Giles Mohan offer a similar critique, as they emphasize the need for participatory processes to stretch from individual to institutional and structural levels, to be truly transformative (Hickey and Mohan 2004; cited in Deneulin and Shahani 2009, 190).

While Sen has certainly noted this dynamic in his work, his approach to participatory processes would benefit from distinguishing between democracy and participation and paying more explicit attention to the power dynamics that might disrupt equitable participation. Along with co-author Jean Drèze, Sen has noted that economic and political inequalities might prove insurmountable obstacles to ethical, inclusive participation (Drèze and Sen 2002, 9–10). However, they should likewise consider the less recognized interpersonal and personal dynamics, which make it more difficult for some to participate than others. For example, critical feminists Iris Marion Young and Brooke Ackerly have warned against confining deliberative democracy (one potential route forward for authentic participation) to certain criteria, such as calm, reasoned statements grounded in non-religious or non-emotional argumentation. They point out that such criteria often exclude women at a much greater rate than men (Young 2000; Ackerly 2000). Liberal feminist Bina Agarwal has also helpfully explored gender-based participatory exclusions that might take the form of social norms, community expectations, and even property ownership (Agarwal 2001, 1623–1648, cited in Crocker 2008, 342).

David Crocker's recent, careful work on the links between development and democracy approaches them from a different angle. Whereas Sen, Drèze, Deneulin, and Shahani tend to focus on productive complementarities between the two (as Crocker has also done throughout much of his career), Crocker helpfully warns against multiple factors that might impede their connection (Crocker 2006, 2008). (In the interest of keeping this review brief, I have not cited many of Crocker's well-known arguments connecting participatory methods to ethical development because he is much in agreement with the points that I raised coming from Goulet and Deneulin.) First, he insists that technical assistance can never be apolitical, despite claims to neutrality. Even development that is meant to be "strictly economic" can heighten political tensions, as aid creates asymmetrical advantages for different groups. Second, he notes that the "good governance" framework often associated with neoliberal economic reform is a thin enough conception of democracy to be compatible with strains of authoritarianism (Crocker 2017). (Crocker cites Levitsky and Way's "managed democracy" and "competitive authoritarianism" as examples. See Levitsky and Way 2010.) Simply holding elections does not necessarily challenge elites' hold on political power. Third, Crocker maintains that the idea of democracy ought to be expanded to include "social movements and democratic militants." To truly promote ethical participation, democratic processes must occur year-round (Crocker 2017, 296).

Finally, Crocker also calls attention to an understudied topic in development ethics – the relationship between corruption and maldevelopment. In Crocker's view, the neglect of this topic goes hand in hand with the desire of the World Bank and other development agencies to remain politically neutral. Rooting out corruption involves the evaluation of individuals and widespread political change. But in Crocker's view, ethical development requires targeting corrupt practices that, in Michael Johnston's words, "abuse public roles for private benefit" (Michael Johnston 2014, 9, cited in Crocker 2017, 298). The remedy for such practices is *more* and *deeper* democratization – essentially, better and more power-conscious participation by all who are impacted by development aid and policy-making. It is more difficult for elites to get away with corrupt activity if non-elites practice authentic participation at all steps of the decision-making process. Here, Goulet's typology of participation is useful. Decision-making power by non-elites is more effective if it begins earlier in the process (see Goulet 1989).

Gleaning the most important insights from Goulet, Deneulin, and Crocker, I argue that the study and practice of participatory development ought to address unjust power structures from the local to the global level, highlighting and rooting out corruption; treat participants as agents who can define their own development agendas; promote participation along all dimensions of Goulet's typology, paying special attention to the time at which participants are brought into decision-making processes; and employ some conception of human flourishing (that is flexible and accessible across cultures) to guide participation.

Linking empowerment to participatory development

Empowerment and participatory development share much in common. Both are often portrayed as purely economic and therefore politically neutral, but many scholars of both have vigorously refuted this notion. Empowerment and participation are both *political* endeavors, and they are most effective when development ethicists and those in charge of development policies consciously address, rather than brush aside, asymmetries of power and unjust economic, social, and political structures. This political view also maintains the distinction between participation and democratic politics, which in turn demands that participation extend from individual or village-level interventions to impact national and international political problems.

Because empowerment and participation are so closely linked, it also follows that participatory development would likewise benefit from the highly contextual and relational approach that I recommended for the study of empowerment. Such an approach does not assume that various measurements of participation are equally applicable across cultures, but instead would ask: under what conditions do participatory mechanisms lead to more ethically defensible outcomes?

Fruitful paths forward might come from genuinely participatory research into the process of participation itself. Those who have experienced deliberation over development policies or participatory budgeting processes could guide research into what does and does not work in participatory development. Many scholars have tried to examine the impacts of participation upon development policies, but how many have done so through the concepts, questions, and research designs of those who participate? In addition to conducting empirical work alongside marginalized people, I think that development ethicists should draw more directly from theories that come from the margins. Ethicists often turn to important political theorists like Aristotle, Kant, Smith, Marx, Rawls, Finnis, and Pogge, to name but a few. (I have in mind influential scholars of human development such as Alkire 2002; Nussbaum 2000; Sen 1999 and Crocker 2008.) Yet lesser-known theorists employing postcolonial, feminist, indigenous, and other critiques – many of which are intersectional in nature, accounting for how dynamics like racism, classism, misogyny, and other forms of discrimination intersect and transform one another – have a great deal to say about the imposition of norms upon marginalized communities. (Certainly, many ethicists adopt feminist and indigenous lenses. For example, see Koggel 2013; Kosko 2013; Tripp 2010.) Surely it is no accident that many of the best insights that I found among development ethicists share much in common with the work of Patricia Hill Collins and the women of DAWN. If development ethicists are concerned with the neo-colonial impact of development policies, they should likewise consider the extent to which their choice of philosophical resources colonizes ethical evaluation (see Mohanty 2003).

References

Ackerly, B. (2000) *Political Theory and Feminist Social Criticism*. Cambridge University Press, Cambridge.

Agarwal, B. (2001) Participatory Exclusions, Community Forestry, and Gender: An Analysis for South Asia and a Conceptual Framework. *World Development* 29(10): 1623–1648.

Alkire, S. (2002) *Valuing Freedoms: Sen's Capability Approach and Poverty Reduction*. Oxford University Press, Oxford.

Batliwala, S. (1993) *Women's Empowerment in South Asia: Concepts and Practices*. ASPBAE/FAO, New Delhi.

Bourdieu, P. (1977) *Outline of a Theory of Practice*. Cambridge University Press, Cambridge.

Calvès, A.-E. (2010) Empowerment: The History of a Key Concept in Contemporary Development Discourse. *Revue Tiers Monde* 200(4): 735–749.

Collins, P.H. (1990) *Black Feminist Thought*. Routledge, New York.

Cooke, B. and Uma Kothari, U. (2001) *Participation: The New Tyranny?* Zed Books, London and New York.

Cornwall, A. and Brock, K. (2005) Beyond Buzzwords: "Poverty Reduction," "Participation," and "Empowerment" in Development Policy. Programme Paper number 10, United Nations Research Institute for Social Development.

Cornwall, A. and Fujita, M. (2012) Ventriloquising "the Poor"? Of Voices, Choices and the Politics of "Participatory" Knowledge Production. *Third World Quarterly* 33(9): 1751–1765.

Crocker, D. (2006) Sen and Deliberative Democracy. In Kaufman, A. ed., *Capabilities Equality: Basic Issues and Problems*. Routledge, New York, 155–197.

Crocker, D. (2008) *Ethics of Global Development: Agency, Capability, and Deliberative Democracy*. Cambridge University Press, Cambridge.

Crocker, D. (2017) Confronting Inequality and Corruption: Agency, Empowerment, and Democratic Development. In Otto, H.-U., Pantazis, S., Ziegler, H. and Potsi, A. eds., *Human Development in Times of Crisis: Renegotiating Social Justice*. Palgrave MacMillan, New York, 291–302.

Cronin-Furman, K., Gowrinathan, N. and Zakaria, R. (2017) Emissaries of Empowerment. The City College of New York, September 2017. www.ccny.cuny.edu/file/emissaries-empowerment-2017pdf.

Deneulin, S. (2006) *The Capability Approach and the Praxis of Development*. Palgrave MacMillan, New York.

Deneulin, S. and Shahani, L. (2009) *An Introduction to the Human Development and Capability Approach: Freedom and Agency*. Earthscan and International Development Research Centre, Sterling VA, Ottawa ON, and London.

Drèze, J. and Sen, A. (2002) *India: Development and Participation*. Oxford University Press, New York.

Drydyk, J. (2010) Participation, Empowerment, and Democracy: Three Fickle Friends. In Wilber, C.K. and Dutt, A.K. eds., *New Directions in Development Ethics: Essays in Honor of Denis Goulet*. University of Notre Dame Press, Notre Dame IN.

Drydyk, J. (2013) Empowerment, Agency, and Power. *Journal of Global Ethics* 9(3): 249–262.

Drydyk, J. (2016) Ethical Issues in Development. In Grugel, J. and Hammett, D. eds., *The Palgrave Handbook of International Development*. Grugel, Jean and Hammett, Daniel eds., Palgrave MacMillan, London, 55–76.

Freire, P. (1971) *Pedagogy of the Oppressed,* trans MB Ramos. Herder and Herder, New York.

Goulet, D. (1971) *The Cruel Choice: A New Concept in the Theory of Development*. Atheneum, New York.

Goulet, D. (1989) Participation in Development: New Avenues. *World Development* 17(2): 165–178.

Haq, M. (1995) *Reflections on Human Development*. Oxford University Press, New York.

Hickey, S. and Mohan, G. (2004) *Participation, from Tyranny to Transformation? Exploring New Approaches to Participation in Development*. Zed Books, London and New York.

Ibrahim, S. and Alkire, S. (2007) Agency and Empowerment: A Proposal for Internationally Comparable Indicators. *Oxford Development Studies* 35(4): 380–403.

Johnston, M. (2014) *Corruption, Contention, and Reform: The Power of Deep Democratization*. Cambridge University Press, Cambridge.

Kabeer, N. (1994) *Reversed Realities: Gender Hierarchies in Development Thought*. Verso, London and New York.

Kabeer, N. (1999) Resources, Agency, Achievements: Reflections on the Measurement of Women's Empowerment. *Development and Change* 30(3): 435–464.

Kabeer, N. (2010) Gender Equality and Women's Empowerment: A Critical Analysis of the Third Millennium Development Goal 1. *Gender & Development* 13(1): 13–24.

Kapoor, I. (2005) Participatory Development, Complicity and Desire. *Third World Quarterly* 26(8): 1203–1220.

Keleher, L. (2007) Empowerment and Development. PhD, University of Maryland, College Park, MD. https://search.proquest.com/docview/304854386/abstract/EEEB9253110246C3PQ/2.

Keleher, L. (2014) Sen and Nussbaum: Agency and Capability-Expansion. *Ethics and Economics* 11(2): 54–70.

Khader, S. (2011) *Adaptive Preferences and Women's Empowerment*. Oxford University Press, Oxford.

Koggel, C. (2013) Is the Capability Approach a Sufficient Challenge to Distributive Accounts of Global Justice? *Journal of Global Ethics* 9(2): 145–157.

Kosko, S. (2013) Agency Vulnerability, Participation, and the Self-Determination of Indigenous Peoples *Journal of Global Ethics* 9(3): 293–310.

Levitsky, S. and Way, L. (2010) *Competitive Authoritarianism: Hybrid Regimes after the Cold War*. Cambridge University Press, Cambridge.

Mohanty, C. (2003) *Feminism without Borders: Decolonizing Theory, Practicing Solidarity*. Duke University Press, Durham, NC.

Narayan, D. and Petesch, P. eds. (2002) *Voices of the Poor: From Many Lands*. Oxford University Press and The World Bank, New York.

Nussbaum, M. (2000) *Women and Human Development*. Harvard University Press, Cambridge MA.

Pereira, C. (2008) Appropriating "Gender" and "Empowerment": The Resignification of Feminist Ideas in Nigeria's Neoliberal Reform Program. *IDS Bulletin* 39(6): 42–50.

Sardenberg, C.M.B. (2008) Liberal vs. Liberating Empowerment: A Latin American Feminist Perspective on Conceptualizing Women's Empowerment. *IDS Bulletin* 39(6): 18–27.

Sen, A. (1999) *Development as Freedom*. Anchor Books, New York.

Sen, G. and Grown, C. (1987) *Development, Crises, and Alternative Visions: Third World Women's Perspectives*. Monthly Review Press, New York.

Staudt, K., Rai, S.M. and Parpart, J.L. (2003) Concluding Thoughts on (Em)Powerment, Gender and Development. In Parpart, J.L. Rai, S.M. and Staudt, K. eds., *Rethinking Empowerment: Gender and Development in a Global/Local World*. Routledge, New York.

Tripp, A.M. (2010) Creating Collective Capabilities: Women, Agency and the Politics of Representation. *Columbia Journal of Gender and Law* 19(1): 219–248.

Young, I.M. (2000) *Inclusion and Democracy*. Oxford University Press, Oxford.

17

Agency

Expanding choice through democratic processes

Matthew R. G. Regan

In his 1949 inaugural address, U.S. President Harry Truman imagined a new era of (American-led) international assistance that would "create the conditions that will lead eventually to personal freedom and happiness for all mankind." Even in those early days, when the concept of international development was explicitly tied to the political dilemmas of the post-war world, the equation of the processes of development with the expansion of personal freedom and increased well-being was clearly and unequivocally presumed. The expression of this freedom may have differed in the halls of Washington, London, Moscow, and Beijing, but the concept that the "recognition of the inherent dignity and of the equal and inalienable rights of all members of the human family is the foundation of freedom, justice, and peace in the world" (Universal Declaration 1948) seemed unassailable. And yet, as the history of the development interventions of the intervening decades remind us, despite their noble intentions, development projects do not always live up to these lofty aspirations. Far too often, the life-altering decisions made by those undertaking development projects, even those explicitly framed as "participatory," are not made by robust means of collective decision-making, but through mechanisms which are

> comparatively weak, limited and vague, expressed in guidelines that could be satisfied by token consultation that accords no significant respect, voice, or bargaining power to stakeholders, including potential oustees, those that will be indirectly displaced and others who are socially non-advantaged.
>
> *(Penz et al. 2011, 112)*

The reasons for this failure are complex, of course. For one, personal freedom and empowerment are not the sort of the things that lend themselves to easy, incontrovertible, quantitative measurement. It is almost nonsensical to say that a certain project or policy intervention increased one's freedom or ability to act in the world by such-and-such percent, in the same way that it is relatively straightforward and easy to measure increases in income, nutrition, or any of the other quantitative data points that modern development agencies and implementers crave to demonstrate their "evidence-based" and "data-driven" successes. The recognition of this difficulty lies at the heart of the capability approach, pioneered by Amartya Sen and Martha Nussbaum, which aims to move development thinking "beyond the traditional view of development

DOI: 10.4324/9781315626796-21

in terms of 'the growth of output per head'" (Sen 1999, 291). But, in the two decades that have passed since the approach's early formulation, there has emerged a wide variety of emphases and interpretations of the approach's basic insight, namely "that the key question to ask, when comparing societies and assessing them for their basic decency of justice is, 'What is each person able to do and to be?'" (Nussbaum 2011, 18).

There is not enough space here to explore all the ongoing conversations within the capability literature, but there is one formulation, that of David Crocker's "agency-focused" capability approach, that deserves special attention when considering the role of democratic engagement within the processes of international development. As Crocker's appellation "agency-focused" suggests, the key to this formulation lies in the distinction between "agency" and "well-being" drawn by Amartya Sen (see, for example, Sen 1995). Following a favorite example of Sen's, Crocker (2008, 168–169) uses the difference between someone choosing not to eat (a Burmese hunger striker) and someone who cannot eat without choosing such a state (a starving North Korean infant) as an illustration of the basic concepts of well-being, functioning, and capability. Both the hunger striker and the starving infant are alike in terms of *functioning* – that is, there is a basic condition of their lives, being well-fed, that neither are actively enjoying. The difference between the two, then, comes in terms of *capability* – presumably, the hunger striker is not engaging in her form of protest because she does not have the opportunity to eat, but precisely because she does so. Despite being capable of eating – despite being able to transform the potential functioning of being well-fed into an actual functioning – the hunger striker is choosing not to do so because there is something else she values more. Presumably, at the end of her protest, she will happily tuck into a bowl of *san pyoke* (rice porridge), whereas the North Korean infant has no such luck. The protestor, who possesses the *capability* but temporarily not the functioning, is able to transform the former into the latter. Without a drastic intervention, however, the poor infant is unable to gain even the capability of being well-nourished. The provision of something else, in this case the material good of available nourishing food, is required for the infant to gain this capability, and hopefully, very soon thereafter, this functioning.

Although the hunger striker and the infant are clearly different in terms of capability, despite similar functioning, they also differ drastically in terms of agency. The hunger striker clearly has more freedom to choose among options than the starving infant, but to make the contours of agency clearer, let's examine the case of two other people who, like the hunger striker, are also not enjoying the functioning of being well-fed, despite holding the capability of being well-fed: a clever thief, who has snuck into a bank vault to steal a collection of precious jewels, but must stay in there for several days before her best opportunity to escape, and a poor man who believes he has fallen victim of a curse that will cause him to burst into flames if he eats a single morsel of food. Like the hunger striker, the thief and the cursed man have the capability of being well-fed, but they are currently not actualizing that potential, bringing them all to the same level of functioning as the starving baby. Whereas the baby's ability to achieve the functioning of being well-fed can be realized by providing him with milk powder, the other three require (or more properly insist upon) the provision of something else, something that is not necessarily a material good, but rather, something that satisfies their personally determined objectives. In the case of the hunger striker, this is the assurance that her political demands are being met. In the case of the thief, it is the perfect moment to escape with the jewels. And in the case of the cursed man, it is the provision of some remedy to break the curse, or perhaps even better, reassurance that he's not under a curse at all and able to safely eat. Sen uses the term agency to denote this process of choosing between different, and often competing, capabilities.

An agent, according to Sen (1999, 18–19, quoted in Crocker 2008, 158) is "someone who acts and brings about change, and whose achievements can be judged in terms of her own values and objectives, whether or not we assess them in terms of some extern criteria as well." The actions of the hunger striker and the thief certainly seem to fall under this definition, while those of the cursed man might be seen as a marginal case of agency – he does, indeed, have some agency, as he's choosing one course of action (not eating) over another (whatever he perceives the effects of curse will be), but because of the constraints placed upon him, he is not able to fully exercise his agency to the degree of his more empowered peers. The insight that people are endowed with different levels of both well-being (capability/functioning) and agency (freedom/achievement) forms the cornerstone of Crocker's agency-focused approach. Just as the capability approach asserts that it is not sufficient to look at some purely material criterion to assess people's well-being (looking, for example, at income without asking what people are able to buy), Crocker's agency-focused approach asserts that opportunities alone are not enough if they are not paired with the ability to make valuable choices. The Burmese hunger striker may have access to all sort of capabilities that the North Korean infant does not, but she is still constrained in her ability to actually choose by forces of intimidation, social pressure, and even her own self-perceptions. Agency, thus, can be viewed as the capability of choosing other choices – the ability to decide between options, to make determinations between outcomes, and to judge our preferred way of life, in terms of both ends and means.

So far, we have considered agency as a feature of an individual life, something people possess in greater or lesser degrees, but it is also important to consider it from a broader, social perspective. Our own freedom to act and change the world is always bounded by the freedoms of others. This is why the concept of agency plays such an important role in Crocker's thinking about the role of democratic consultation in international development, and more broadly, in society as a whole. Even in our simple illustration above, we encountered people with wildly different choices and motivations related to a single capability, that of being well-fed. Not only did we find some who lacked this basic capability, we found others who, despite possessing the capability of being well-fed, made choices based on a wide variety of motivations that subordinated being actually well-fed to other preferred outcomes. When we consider a real society composed of real people, people who have a dizzying array of capabilities, motivations, and desired outcomes, we begin to realize what a daunting task even simple provisions like "make sure everyone has enough to eat" might be to achieve. Not only will we need to consider cases like the starving infant, who have the desire to eat but not the means, but also those of our other three, who have the means but not the (immediate) desire, and whether or not all of those motivations are equally valuable. Should we, for example, respect the choices of the hunger striker and the jewel thief equally? After all, they are both sacrificing their immediate material well-being in pursuit of a larger goal. And yet, there seems something more praiseworthy about the hunger striker's self-imposed deprivation than that of the thief.

The question of when and which certain capabilities should be privileged over others has produced two broad categories of responses. The first, emblemized by Martha Nussbaum's famous list (see Nussbaum 2011, Chapter 2), attempts to provide a universal list of "central capabilities" that form a basic framework of the necessities of a good life. A life that has access to the central capabilities, however they are conceived, is not necessarily an ideal one, but an ideal life could not be considered so if it lacked access to one of the central capabilities. A second range of responses, however, is more skeptical of this approach. As Crocker (2013, 109) explains:

> There are four reasons [to be skeptical of universal lists of central capabilities.] First, Sen doubts whether there will be or could be theoretical agreement on principles of justice. Second, such agreement is not needed to identify and remedy particular injustices about which most can agree. Third, a fixed list of principles and given weights reduces the

> opportunity for citizens and groups to exercise their agency, to run their own lives by their own continued scrutiny. Finally, a universal list with given weights risks preventing groups in particular times and places from addressing local or changing conditions as well as closing off the possibility of new and better ideas from both far and near.

Yet, even if we agree with Crocker and Sen that there is something more elegant about a local, collectively determined arrangement of capabilities than universally derived ones, we should not be lulled into a false sense that relying on deliberation and agency is an easy method. In fact, Crocker (2008, 342–344) himself notes that real-world "participatory" bodies often fail to live up to their ideals, and lists eight different modes of participation, ranging from the thinnest form of nominal participation (people are consulted, but their input has no effect on the final decisions) to the thickest of true deliberation (where non-elites can meet and decide upon courses of actions that are genuinely considered and enacted). Participatory processes seem to emblemize everything we would hope to avoid in determining good allocations of social resources – they are messy, complicated, difficult to keep on track, and even more difficult to predict their outcomes. The underlying conditions of the processes, from time of day the meeting is convened to whether or not a snack break is allowed, can drastically alter their determinations, and even the same group of people, given the same problem, might very well reach a very different conclusion if tasked with a problem one day rather than another.

And yet, for proponents of democratic processes like Crocker, these are not bugs, but features of democracy. It is true that democratic procedures can be misdirected, tricked, and even hijacked, but the nature of democracy ensures that, while individual mistakes are commonly, if not likely, when taken over the longer term, democratic procedures are able to draw upon a pool of collective knowledge and experience that allow it to change, correct, and adapt in ways that more rationalist, structural approaches might not be able to accomplish. Josiah Ober (2008), who studies democracy in ancient Athens, for example, asserts that it is precisely because democracy is able to provide a more complete field of knowledge about a particular problem that it prevails over other forms of governance. Whereas a more command-and-control type governing structure might be expert at one particular thing, or perhaps even well-versed in a number of general things, it is incredibly unlikely for even the most well-meaning of philosopher-kings, or even technocratic oligarchs, to have the same level of knowledge about the problems within a given area than those who actually live there. Democratic procedures, when they function well, allow for information to flow from those with the power to enact decisions to those who are directly affected by them. And, unlike other forms of governance, part of the information that flows within a democracy is directly related to the health of the system itself. Healthy democracies tend to reinforce their democratic procedures, while unhealthy ones tend to slide into factionalism, or worse, abandon democratic means entirely. Like any dynamic system, the health of a democratic process is measured by its ability to give, receive, and incorporate feedback. And when a democratic system begins to falter, the solution, as Crocker (2008, 319) reminds us "is not some nondemocratic system, but more and better democracy."

This chapter began with the observation that, despite being acknowledged as an essential feature of international development from the very beginning, agency, participation, and democratic empowerment often plays second-fiddle to the more "pressing" needs of development, both in terms of actual project design and the wider theories of how development gets done. At first blush, this is not surprising. As Crocker (307) himself acknowledges – using a malapropism coined by former Chicago mayor William Daley – "Democracy is not . . . a 'pancreas.'" Participatory procedures do not, at the outset, provide anything but delay and complication. When out-of-the-box solutions are so readily available, why should one waste so much time and effort consulting with people, often poor, uneducated people, who do not have a clear grasp of the problem, let alone the solution? And perhaps, if we lived in a simple world of simple problems, where technical solutions could be abstracted away from social issues, where cultural mores and historical injustices could be distilled out of simple problems of resource allocation, our frustrations with democratic procedures would be justified. But instead, the world we live in is complicated, messy, and constantly changing. We live in a world of agents, each of whom are pursuing their own ends, making choices that impact not only their own lives, but the lives of countless others, near and far. In such a world, where information comes at a premium and certainty is often little more than a statistical assumption, we need to make sure that people, especially those most vulnerable, have the best chance possible to ensure that proposed changes enacted in the name of "development" not only produce the desired effects, but also minimize unintended consequences. Democratic empowerment and a focus on agency will not necessarily prevent mistakes from being made, from bad projects moving forward, from human lives and livelihoods falling victim to the negative consequences of well-meaning change, but it will, if committed to broadly and deeply, ensure that such negative consequences are identified, addressed, and corrected, and that future projects and strategies, growing on the lessons and mistakes of the past, are better and more beneficial than their predecessors. Democracy might not be the most efficient of systems, but there is a strong case to be made that democratic procedures ensure solutions that are more effective, robust, and humane than other approaches can offer.

References

Crocker, D.A. (2008) *The Ethics of Global Development: Agency, Capability, and Deliberative Democracy*. Cambridge University Press, Cambridge.

Crocker, D.A. (2013) Amartya Sen on Democracy and Justice. *Indigo* 8(Spring/Summer): 102–109.

Nussbaum, M.C. (2011) *Creating Capabilities: The Human Development Approach*. Harvard University Press, Cambridge MA.

Ober, J. (2008) *Democracy and Knowledge: Innovation and Learning in Classical Athens*. Princeton University Press, Princeton.

Penz, P., Drydyk, J. and Bose, P.S. (2011) *Displacement by Development: Ethics, Rights and Responsibilities*. Cambridge University Press, Cambridge.

Sen, A.K. (1995) Agency and Well-being: The Development Agenda. In Heyzer, N., Kapoor, S. and Sandler, J. eds., *A Commitment to the World's Women: Perspectives on Development for Beijing and Beyond*. UNIFEM, New York.

Sen, A.K. (1999) *Development as Freedom*. Anchor Books, New York.

Truman, H.S. (1949) Inaugural Address. Delivered at the US Capitol, Washington, DC, January 20. Transcript available from the Harry, S. Truman Presidential Library and Museum, public papers collection. www.trumanlibrary.org/publicpapers/index.php?pid=1030.

Universal Declaration of Human Rights (1948) Text available from the United Nations. www.un.org/en/universal-declaration-human-rights/.

18

Education

Worthwhile education for ethical human development

Alejandra Boni and Merridy Wilson-Strydom

Introduction

How development should be understood and defined is a major area of controversy. Implicit values assumptions and associated policy responses are linked to the nature of the definitions employed and theories of development proposed (Summer and Tribe 2008, 25). There is widespread agreement that education is important for development; but there is also considerable disagreement about why and how this is so. One of the central aims of development ethics is to identify development that is worthwhile and can be ethically defended. In this chapter we make a case for the human development and capabilities approach as worthwhile and ethically sound, particularly in the educational domain. We begin by briefly reviewing five approaches to development that have been relevant for the field of education and which, in different ways, respond to the questions of how and why education is valuable. Our aim is not to conduct a comprehensive overview of development theory, but instead to make clear the understanding of development put forward in those theories, their implicit and explicit values, and how development is linked with education. In doing this, we have followed McCowan's (2015) helpful classification of five paradigms of development theory: liberal capitalist, Marxist, liberal egalitarian, post-structural and radical humanist. This grouping is not intended as an exhaustive categorization but rather as a purposive selection to highlight the major approaches of particular relevance to education.

After setting out the five paradigms of development theory, we conceptualize worthwhile education using the human development and capability approaches. To illustrate our argument we then apply this conceptualization to the specific case of higher education and development at one university in the South African context. In so doing, we stress the potential of this approach to inform a deeply ethical way to understand and practice education.

Development theories and education

Liberal capitalist approaches

This approach foregrounds economic growth as the central policy driver for poverty eradication, beginning in the 1940s, with the disasters caused by the 1930s Great Depression and World

 DOI: 10.4324/9781315626796-22

War II in mind. As Streeten (2004, 68) explains, the idea was that economic growth is a benign force, and thus market forces (the demand for labour, rising productivity, rising wages, lower-priced consumer goods) would spread the benefits of economic growth 'widely and speedily'. It was assumed that any increase in the per-capita gross national product would reduce poverty and would raise the general level of well-being and living standards of the population. However, instead of being a means to reach development, economic growth began to be considered the end goal. Liberal capitalist approaches have also been aligned with modernization theory. The first development economists (such as Nurkse or Rostow) supported modernization theory and the implicit goal of their theories was to reproduce the experience of developed countries, to replicate these countries' industrialization process and labour utilization. Development was viewed as an ahistorical process, without conflicts, where modernity was always positive and tradition always negative (Bustelo 1998).

Also falling under this group of theories are the 'new growth theories' of the 1980s (Streeten 2004), in which the emphasis shifted from growth arising from productive factors and technological progress to the behaviour of people, with an emphasis on human capital and higher levels of education. Better-educated people were seen to be more productive, innovative and efficient. This approach had been anticipated by rising investments and expansion in higher education in the USA and the UK from the 1960s, driven partly by equity concerns, and by the conceptualization of 'human capital theory' in the 1960s by Becker (1964) as the basis for increased incomes. More education, it was argued, meant higher wages and economic growth.

The 1990s witnessed the emergence of a new neo-liberal orthodoxy in which development was understood to turn on economic liberalization unleashing market growth, accompanied by privatization, deregulation and reduced government spending on public services, with the state having to support or sustain markets but not replace them (Bustelo 1998). This neo-liberal orthodoxy goes hand in hand with globalization, a concept contested in terms of its meaning, form and implications (Kothari, Minogue and DeJong 2002; Harber 2014). For education, the globalization process has been extremely relevant. It has expressed itself through the privatization of educational systems, leading to the creation of quasi-markets and introduction of cost-sharing within public systems, together with the growth of private providers. In this model, education not only serves to form productive workers, but is also a source of profit making itself (McCowan 2015). Moreover, referring to the role of higher education, globalization has reinforced the importance of human capital specifically in the field of science, technology and innovation. Many development institutions have stressed the significance of links between science and industry because innovation requires more external and more multidisciplinary knowledge as technologies have become increasingly complex and specialized (OECD 2000).

Marxist

Modernization approaches were strongly criticized by dependency theory as ahistorical, technicist and only focused on an internal diagnosis of the problems of developing countries, ignoring how they become inserted into and are shaped by international economic dynamics. According to dependency theorists, who draw on Marxist ideas, developing countries are societies which are structured in a different way and which, after being colonized, are forced to take on the capitalist production mode to play a role that suits industrialized countries as suppliers of raw materials and importers of manufactured products. The proposed development solutions included changing the peripheral countries' insertion into world markets as a basic condition to break through the obstacles of the modernization and development process.

However, as Unceta (2001) highlights, there is little evidence that dependency approaches contributed new proposals to what had been the main dimensions in existing conceptions of development, those which linked it to economic growth, productive investment and industrialization. Nevertheless, there have been more direct applications of the theory to education. Some analyses highlighted the ways in which education systems in the South after independence continued to be dependent on the systems of the former colonial powers. These systems retained colonial languages within education, maintained similar curricula (focusing on Western subject matter) and continue to rely on Western publishing houses (Harber 2014). The implication was, as in the economy as a whole, that countries should delink and pursue their own educational course. Others showed that instead of providing an opportunity for social mobility, education systems merely reproduced existing social class inequalities (McCowan 2015; Bourdieu and Passeron 1977).

Post-colonial and post-development approaches

Post-colonialism and post-development constitute powerful critiques of 'development' and so present an important challenge to dominant ways of apprehending North–South relations (McEwan 2001). Post-colonial approaches problematize the ways in which the world is known, challenging the unacknowledged and unexamined assumptions at the heart of Western disciplines that are profoundly insensitive to the meanings, values and practices of other cultures. They challenge the meaning of 'development' as rooted in colonial discourse which depicts the North as advanced and progressive and the South as backward, degenerate and primitive (Said 1978). It is argued that one of the main failures of the development discourse is its limited historical analysis and its unreflective nature, partly engendered through the imperative to achieve development goals and targets (Kothari 2002). This ahistoricism is continually legitimated by the pervasive representation of development as Western philanthropy, as a humanitarian mission that bears no resemblance to the perceived inequalities and exploitations of empire. Thus, development can only be 'good' when set against colonialism which was 'bad'.

Escobar (2005, 19) stresses the importance of challenging this developmental vision in three ways. The first is through the ability to create different discourses and representations that are not mediated by the constructions of development (ideologies, metaphors, language, premises, etc.). The second is to change practices of knowing and doing and the 'political economy' of truth that defines the development regime. The third is the need to multiply production centres and agents of knowledge production to make visible forms of knowledge produced by those who are supposedly the 'objects' of development so that they can become subjects and agents. Educational applications of post-colonialism and post-development have been focusing on either recuperation of indigenous knowledge forms, or of a fusion of indigenous and Western perspectives (McCowan 2015). Decolonizing education is a process of learning to read the world through other eyes, of acknowledging the multiple perspectives on reality and refraining from imposing a single reading (Andreotti 2011). The global necessity of decolonization in the educational domain has been powerfully highlighted recently in several regions, including South Africa, UK, USA, Asia and others (Alvares and Faruqi 2014; Glazebrook 2015).

Liberal egalitarian paradigm

Liberal egalitarian theories do not take the eradication of capitalist modes of production and the free market as a starting point, but they do require a significant tempering of its workings and practice in accordance with principles of justice. In opposition to some versions of socialism, they also assert the primacy of individual liberty – guarding against the subordination of the individual to the collective; while in opposition to post-structuralist thought they retain faith in the possibility of a universal morality and the assumption that concrete steps towards improvements in practice can be made (McCowan 2015).

One version of this approach is the rights-based approach to development that redefines the nature of development problems, by shying away from a focus on passive 'beneficiaries' with needs towards considering people as rights-holders (Schmitz 2012; Belda et al. 2016). As part of that move, states and other actors are presented as bearers of responsibility in ensuring that rights are guaranteed (Nyamu-Musembi and Cornwall 2004). Other basic principles shared by different rights-based perspectives include framing poverty in the language of human rights and challenging the root causes of poverty and rights denial; focusing on development processes and not exclusively on outcomes; and redefining development as an entitlement, rather than as benevolence or charity (Gready 2009). Linked to rights-based approaches are participatory approaches to development, especially in the most recent versions, in which participation is linked to the idea of citizenship and participatory governance (Gaventa 2006). In this sense, participation is no longer understood as a tool to make development interventions more efficient but as a process for resolving social conflicts democratically (Frediani et al. 2016).

Another version is the human development and capability approach, to which we will refer in more detail in the next section. Capabilities are defined by Sen (1999) as the substantive freedoms to lead the kind of life that people value. Sen indicates that worthwhile development means that individuals have the freedom and the opportunity (capability) to lead the kind of lives they want to lead, to do what they want to do, and to be who they want to be. Once they actually have these substantive opportunities, they may choose to implement those options that they value most, whether or not this enhances their own well-being. Martha Nussbaum presents ten central capabilities for the functioning of human beings which she argues are fundamental requirements for a decent life, and which together, meet a minimum degree of justice in a given society. A society that does not guarantee these capabilities for all of its citizens, at an appropriate level, cannot be considered a just society, whatever its level of affluence (Nussbaum 2000).

Another key element of the capability approach is its explicit reference to development as the promotion of human development values. As a result, the development of society is a normative concept that differs from economic growth or social change. The standard definition of the dimensions of human development by the United Nations Programme for Development (UNDP) includes: 1) empowerment, understood as the expansion of the capabilities of people (real opportunities to achieve valuable ends) and the expansion of valuable functionings (valuable purposes achieved) and participation; 2) the equitable distribution of basic skills; 3) sustainability; and 4) the freedom of the people to enjoy their opportunities and achievements (Boni and Gasper 2012). As McCowan (2015) points out, these approaches to development have particular applications for education. Firstly, educational systems must distribute their benefits in an egalitarian manner; secondly, the aim of educational processes is to be a multiplier of capabilities and/or to empower the individual to understand, exercise and defend their rights; thirdly, educational practices should foster individual autonomy, the ability to choose between different life courses and enhance agency.

Radical humanism

The final approach cannot be considered a development theory as such, but it refers to the work of certain theorists and practitioners that place an emphasis on the role of education in development, considering education not a fruit of development, or even a driver, but development itself:

"the process of learning, understood as the fundamental experience of emancipation, and the necessary engagement in it of all members of society, is both the means and the end of development" (McCowan 2015, 46).

The best-known thinker is the Brazilian Paulo Freire, for whom education and politics are inextricably linked. Freire asserted that revolution needed to start with the transformation of the self and the emergence of critical consciousness. The collective development of understanding of the oppressed, and the consequent liberation from oppressors, would lead organically and sustainably to the transformation of societal structures (McCowan 2015). Central to this vision is dialogue – understood not just as conversation, but as a radical revisioning of the pedagogical relationship, through which teachers approach learners not as empty vessels to be filled with knowledge (the so-called banking education), but engage with them in a shared and horizontal process of critical reflection and learning leading to critical consciousness (Freire 1972). The work of Freire and other pedagogues such as Orlando Fals-Borda and Augusto Boal is linked to participatory understandings of development. Given that these structures of oppression are rooted in oppressed people's own beliefs, it is through participation that people become active subjects of knowledge and action, and begin to build their own history by engaging in processes of authentic development (Goulet 1989).

Finally, in this radical humanistic approach, we can also place (at least parts of) the critical pedagogy movement (with pedagogues such Aronwitz, Apple, McLaren, Giroux, Car and Kemmis), strongly influenced by the Frankfurt School of Critical Theory. Among other ideas, one of the main contributions of critical pedagogy is drawing attention to the importance of reflexive processes that critique the development of modern forms of knowledge where processes of critical debate tend to be subverted (Blake and Masschelein 2003).

Table 18.1 summarizes the main elements of these different development theories and their links to education.

An ethical approach to worthwhile education grounded in capabilities for human development

In this section we position ourselves within a specific approach to education, grounded in the human development and capabilities approach (Boni and Walker 2013, 2016; Wilson-Strydom 2015), thus rooted mainly in egalitarian theory but with elements of radical humanism and some thoughts from post-development approaches. It is beyond the scope of this chapter to go into detail about the strengths and weaknesses of each of the paradigms discussed or to argue in detail for why the capability approach has distinct advantages. (See Chapter 7.)

McCowan and Unterhalter (2013) suggest three main ways in which capabilities have a bearing on education (and ethical development): 1) relating to the *distributional aspect of education*, 2) its *substantive values and content* and 3) *democratic citizenship*.

Distributional aspects of education

With regard to *equality*, the general position taken by the capability approach can be applied to educational settings: 'Just as the approach rejects an emphasis on equality of initial resources or of preference satisfaction, so it rejects in education an approach of equal treatment or equal attainment regardless of individual or group differences' (McCowan and Unterhalter 2013, 143). Consequently, as Unterhalter points out, 'thinking in terms of capabilities raises a wider range of issues than simply looking at the amount of resources or commodities people have. Because of interpersonal diversity, people need a different amount of resources in order to transform these

Table 18.1 Development paradigms and their links to education

Paradigm	*Vision/Main Values*	*Strategy*	*Links to Education*
Liberal capitalist	Economic growth for 'catch-up' with developed countries	Modernizing economic activity and institutions, changing attitudes, and enhancing workers' skills and productivity	Schooling is instrumental in forming productive workers
(modernization, human capital, new-growth, neo-liberalism)	Modernity	Economic liberalization	Expanding higher education especially in the fields of science, technology and innovation
	Technological progress		Education as a productive good Privatization of educational sectors
Marxist (dependency)	Freedom from economic exploitation for peoples and countries subjected to international and local elites	De-linking from dependent relations with former colonial or neo-colonial powers	Education systems also dependent on the former colonial power and reproduce unequal relations
	Critique of representation as 'other' and assertion of authentic voice	Critique and deconstruction of dominant conceptions of development (ahistorical and unreflexive)	Education is an instrument for disparagement of indigenous cultures and for articulation of critical vision.
Post-colonial – Post-development	Reflexivity	Creation of alternative discourses not mediated by development	Multiple agents of knowledge production
	Power	Challenging how mainstream knowledge is produced	
	Historical perspectives		
Liberal egalitarian	Equality of opportunity and fundamental entitlements, with individual agency, well-being and liberty	Constitutional guarantees, global obligations and individuals holding state to account	Educational opportunities must be distributed fairly, and must equip individuals for full participation in society
(Basic needs;	Sustainability, participation, empowerment, diversity, human rights	Participatory governance	Fostering individual autonomy and agency
Human rights; participatory approaches	social justice		

(*Continued*)

Table 18.1 (Continued)

Paradigm	*Vision/Main Values*	*Strategy*	*Links to Education*
Human development / Capabilities)			
Radical humanist	Transformation of consciousness for the emancipation of the people and creation of a just society	Individual and collective empowerment through learning and action	Education is intrinsic to development; social transformation starts with learning; dialectic of reflection and action
(Freirean pedagogy;	Reflexivity		Education as a way to develop critical consciousness
Participatory learning and action, critical pedagogies)	Critical dialogue		

Adapted from McCowan 2015, 35

into the functioning of being educated' (Unterhalter 2009, 166). This explicit acknowledgment of heterogeneity and diversity is understood as a positive feature of our societies and, in that sense, special efforts should be made to challenge the homogenous strand of globalization. This perspective resonates, partially, with post-development approaches which also challenge an homogenizing development vision.

Substantive values and content

In the context of worthwhile education for ethical development, firstly, it is important to acknowledge the *capability multiplier* role of education. Education is valuable for its democratic contributions; it can teach us to reason and deliberate with others in an informed and critical way. In that sense, the capability approach is aligned with critical pedagogies. Education has interpersonal effects in opening up opportunities for others. For example, family members or people in our communities might come to see education as possible when they observe someone from their community or family pursuing education. Education can also have empowerment and distributive effects. For example, disadvantaged groups can increase their ability to overcome inequalities and get a fairer deal in and through education. Crucially, having a good education affects the development and expansion of other capabilities so that an education capability expands other important human freedoms. Education thus includes both market and non-market goods, and both need to be captured for a full account (Boni and Arias 2013; Walker 2006).

The capabilities approach also has implications for *curriculum and pedagogies*. In this aspect, the capability approach in education has strong links with radical humanism, having in common concerns with the voices of those who have to struggle to be heard and included in educational spaces. The approach is also concerned with human flourishing and how equality and social arrangements have to change to ensure flourishing for all within education (Wilson-Strydom and Walker 2015). When we teach about the capability approach, we therefore need to keep in mind that our pedagogy ought to be consistent with the core principles of the approach itself. It ought to be both a critical and humanizing pedagogy (Walker 2009).

The last contribution of the capability approach to education has to do with *values*. It is not just that education should promote particular political and moral values, but that it is always inescapably charged with values (McCowan and Unterhalter 2013). Further, values are formed through the education process (Vaughan and Walker 2012). As noted earlier, from a human development perspective four fundamental values ought to be at the core of any development process: efficiency, equity, participation and empowerment, and environmental sustainability. These values are equally relevant for education.

Education and democratic citizenship

The human development and capability approach to education also makes an important contribution to our understanding of the idea of *citizenship* and how citizenship is developed through education. This relates primarily to three aspects: *deliberation, the acknowledgement of heterogeneity and the emphasis on agency* (McCowan and Unterhalter 2013). In that sense, the capability approach is linked with other participatory approaches to development in considering a deeply democratic way of taking decisions, with adequate mechanisms that allow real participation of people, and paying special attention to the most marginalized groups who have fewer opportunities to participate in the decision-making process. The implications for education practice are illustrated in the next section.

Applying these ideas in practice

In order to illustrate the value of a capability approach to education we draw on a case study of participatory educational research being conducted at one university in South Africa, applying the human development and capability approach. South Africa is currently one of the most unequal countries globally (Oxfam 2014), and this inequality is mirrored in the higher education sector. A commitment to fostering equality and creating capabilities is thus critical for ethical development. The study is focused on inequalities of access into and through university for a group of 40 students who hail from marginalized backgrounds – poverty and/or poor quality public schooling. The longitudinal qualitative study has included a range of participatory research activities, such as river of life drawings, photo voice, and participatory video as well as in-depth interviews conducted annually. Importantly, students are positioned as active agents in the research and learning process. In reflecting on how this study demonstrates the principles of applying a human development and capability approach to education and development we draw on both research project, which became an informal educational experience for the participants, as well as emerging research findings of relevance to the formal educational enterprise of a university.

The project is firmly located in a human development agenda, and, for this reason, the participants (all of whom volunteered to join the project) were selected from groups typically marginalised in South African higher education. Recognition of diversity has been central, both with the group of participants and between the group and other students in order to better understand (and ultimately to act on) the complex range of factors that make it difficult for marginalized students to convert the resources available to them into the functioning of being educated. The results of the research have highlighted the importance of moving beyond assumptions of equality consisting of equality of resources, such as a place at university, or a student loan, and the influence of personal and social conversion factors – at the levels of family, school and community (Wilson-Strydom and Okkolin 2016).

In one participatory activity, students drew a 'success tree' to discuss and debate the factors (positive and negative) that influence their lives and success as students. Not only did the activity highlight important conversion factors that require action from the university to promote equality of educational opportunity, but students also reported that having an opportunity to share experiences with other students was empowering, as many did not realise that others were facing the same challenges that they were. In the words of one student: 'The best part was when we did the tree, because it brought us together, as we share a lot of things and have almost everything in common'. Through the regular participatory workshops students developed friendships across the usual disciplinary bounds. In this way, the approach has been building affiliation between students. As Nussbaum (2000) argues, affiliation is an architectonic capability which, like education, can act as a capability multiplier.

Further, each year the participating students receive a voucher for the academic book store on campus in recognition of their time and contribution to the research. This small gesture has in itself added to the distributional aspect of the study since for many of the students, this provides the means for them to purchase much needed textbooks which are too expensive for many. As one of the students remarked when asked why she decided to volunteer for the project: 'Honestly at first I was attracted by the book voucher because I really needed the money to buy my law textbook.' The importance of actively working to understand and address the complex distributional challenges faced daily by students which undermine their flourishing was clear, and the enormous challenge of learning under conditions of poverty was powerfully highlighted. As one student said: 'It [lack of funding] does affect my studies because, like, sometimes I can't study when I'm hungry. I'd rather just drink water and sleep and then see [what happens] the next day. . .'

Despite the difficulties many of the students in the project experienced during their educational journey, the opportunity to study at university (formal education) and to participate in the research project (informal education) also acted as capability multipliers for the students themselves as well as for their families and their communities. One student said:

> I wanted to get a feel of what it is really like to participate and not be an onlooker, this project allows me to be the person telling a story that can inspire and motivate others.
>
> In my bright future after university I would like to be helping people. Being, or making a difference to others people's lives. Actually, I don't want to be, like, rich, rich, rich, but I want to be, I want to have money so that I can help other people, so that I can bring a difference to other people's lives [as a teacher]. . . .

Further, the students decided that they wished to share what they have learnt through participating in the project with other young people in marginalized communities – so creating capability multipliers beyond the boundaries of the project and the university. Students are working on a participatory video project in which, in groups, they are producing a series of four videos for other marginalized high school students. The themes being addressed include: know what you want and then be the best you can; valuing learning and knowledge; the importance of reading; and building your confidence as a person and a student. During the interviews, several students also described how they had gone back to visit their schools to share information and application forms with other young people who wished to attend university. They also served as role models in their communities and worked hard to raise awareness about the opportunities created through higher learning.

Table 18.2 Capability dimensions for university access and success

Dimensions	*Capabilities*
Practical reason	Being able to make well-reasoned, informed, critical, independent and reflective choices about post-school study.
Knowledge and imagination	Having the academic grounding for chosen university subjects, being able to develop and apply methods of critical thinking and imagination to identify and comprehend multiple perspectives and complex problems.
Learning disposition	Having curiosity and a desire for learning, having the learning skills required for university study and being an active inquirer (questioning disposition).
Social relations and social networks	Being able to participate in groups for learning, working with diverse others to solve problems or complete tasks. Being able to form networks of friendships for learning support and leisure.
Respect, dignity and recognition	Having respect for oneself and for others, and receiving respect from others, being treated with dignity. Not being devalued, or devaluing others because of one's gender, social class, religion or race. Valuing diversity and being able to show empathy (understand and respect others' points of view). Having a voice to participate in learning.
Emotional health	Not being subject to anxiety or fear that diminishes learning. Having confidence in one's ability to learn.
Language competence and confidence	Being able to understand, read, write and speak confidently in the language of instruction.

Across the project, participatory research activities and the annual interviews provided spaces to explore students' experiences of curriculum and pedagogy, and to reflect on the enablers and constraints on their well-being as students as well as for success in their studies. Based on these analyses, together with earlier research in the same context (Wilson-Strydom 2015), and through active dialogue and discussion of emerging findings, the following set of capabilities dimensions was identified. For higher education to contribute towards worthwhile development in the South African context, these capabilities ought to be fostered for all students entering and learning at universities (see Table 18.2).

Conclusion

In this chapter we have sought to set out key approaches that have an implication for how we think about education and development, with a particular emphasis on what we think ought to count as worthwhile ethical human development. After setting out the dominant development theories as applied to education, we presented a case education conceived of as human development and capabilities expansion. Our argument was illustrated with a case study of a participatory research project being conducted at a South African university. With this case study we sought to demonstrate what a human development and capability approach to education might look like and what aspects are considered when we research education and development from this perspective. Key values such as equality, diversity and participation are essential to promote a worthwhile education that acts as capability multiplier, not only for the students themselves but also for their families and communities.

In the words of one of the students:

> I am of the view that everyone is capable and that, if given a chance [through worthwhile educational opportunities], especially those of my kind [from an impoverished background] can and are willing to make the most of their situations. All that has to be in place is purpose, impact and aspirations to conquer. . . . I am of the many that fought, and still fight to this day to maintain their dreams.

References

Alvares, C. and Faruqi, S.S. (2014, EPub) *Decolonising the University: The Emerging Quest for Non-Eurocentric Paradigms*. Penerbit Universiti Sains Malaysia (USM) and Citizens International, Pulau Pinang, Malaysia.

Andreotti, V. (2011) *Actionable Postcolonial Theory in Education*. Palgrave Macmillan, London.

Becker, G.S. (1964) *Human Capital: A Theoretical and Empirical Analysis*. University of Chicago Press, Chicago.

Belda, S., Boni, A., Cuesta, I. and Peris, J. (2016) Are rights-based approaches helping (re) politicise development NGOs? Exploring the Spanish Case. *International Development Planning Review* 38(2): 135–157

Blake, N. and Masschelein, J. (2003) Critical Theory and Critical Pedagogy, in Blake, N., Smeyers, P., Smith, R. and Standish, P. eds., *The Blackwell Guide to the Philosophy of Education*. Blackwell Publishing: Malden, MA, 38–56.

Boni, A. and Arias, M.B. (2013) People First: Rethinking Educational Policies in Times of Crisis Using the Capability Approach. *Scuola Democratica* 3: 797–816.

Boni, A. and Gasper, D. (2012) Rethinking the Quality of Universities – How Can Human Development Thinking Contribute? *Journal of Human Development and Capabilities* 13(3): 451–470.

Boni, A. and Walker, M. eds. (2013) *Universities and Human Development. A New Imaginary for the University of the XXI Century*. Routledge, London.

Boni, A. and Walker, M. (2016) *Universities and Global Human Development: Theoretical and Empirical Insights for Social Change*. Routledge Sustainability Series, London.

Bourdieu, P. and Passeron, J.C. (1977) *Reproduction in Education, Society and Culture*. Sage Publications, London.

Bustelo, P. (1998) *Teorías Contemporáneas del Desarrollo Económico*. Editorial Síntesis, Madrid.

Escobar, A. (2005) El "postdesarrollo" como concepto y práctica social. [Post-Development as Concept and Social Practice). In Mato D. ed., *Políticas de Economía, Ambiente y Sociedad en Tiempos de Globalización* [Policies of Economic, Environment and Society in Globalization Times]. Facultad de Ciencias Económicas y Sociales, Universidad Central de Venezuela, Caracas, 17–31.

Frediani, A., Peris, J. and Boni, A. (2016) Notions of Empowerment and Participation: The Contribution of the Capability Approach. In Clark, D., Biggeri, M. and Frediani, A. eds., *The Capability Approach, Empowerment and Participation*. Basingstoke, Palgrave (forthcoming).

Freire, P. (1972) *The Pedagogy of the Oppressed*. Herder and Herder, New York.

Gaventa, J. (2006) Triumph, Deficit or Contestation?: Deepening the "Deepening Democracy" Debate. *IDS Working Paper 264*, 29 April 2016. http://opendocs.ids.ac.uk/opendocs/handle/123456789/4064.

Glazebrook, D. (2015) Decolonizing Education: Rhodes Must Fall [WWW Document]. RT International. www.rt.com/op-edge/323094-decolonizing-education-cecil-rhodes/. Accessed 1 September 2016.

Goulet, D. (1989) Participation in Development: New Avenues. *World Development* 17(2): 165–178.

Gready, P. (2009) Reasons to Be Cautious about Evidence and Evaluation: Rights-based Approaches to Development and the Emerging Culture of Evaluation. *Journal of Human Rights Practice* 1(3): 380–401.

Harber, C. (2014) *Education and International Development. Theory, Practice and Issues*. Symposium Books, Southampton.

Kothari, U. (2002) Feminist and Postcolonial Challenges to Development. In Minogue, M. and Kothari, U. eds., *Development Theory and Practice: Critical Perspectives*. Basingstoke, Palgrave, 35–51.

Kothari, U., Minogue, M. and DeJong, J. (2002) "The Political Economy of Globalization" *Development Theory and Practice: Critical Perspectives* Basingstoke, Palgrave, 16–34.

McCowan, T. (2015) Theories of Development. In McCowan, T. and Unterhalter, E. eds., *Education and International Development: An Introduction*. Bloomsbury Academic, London, 31–48.

McCowan, T. and Unterhalter, E. (2013) Education, Citizenship and Deliberative Democracy: Sen's Capability Perspective. In Hedtke, R. and Zimenkova, T. eds., *Education for Civic and Political Participation: A Critical Approach*. Routledge, New York, 135–144.

McEwan, C. (2001) Postcolonialism, Feminism and Development: Intersections and Dilemmas. *Progress in Development Studies* 1(2): 93–111.

Nussbaum, M. (2000) *Women and Human Development*. Cambridge University Press, Cambridge.

Nyamu-Musembi, C. and Cornwall, A. (2004) What is the "rights-based approach" all about? Perspectives From International Development Agencies. *IDS Working Paper 234*, Institute of Development Studies, Brighton.

OECD (2000) Science, Technology and Innovation in the New Economy. *Policy Brief, OECD Observer* 12. www.oecd.org/publications/Pol_brief/. Accessed 29 April 2016.

Oxfam (2014) *Even It Up: Time to End Extreme Equality*. Oxfam, La Paz.

Said, E.W. (1978) *Orientalism*. Routledge, London.

Schmitz, H.P. (2012) A Human Rights-based Approach in Practice: Evaluating NGO Development Efforts. *Polity* 44(4): 523–541.

Sen, A. (1999) *Development as Freedom*. Oxford University Press, Oxford.

Streeten, P. (2004) Shifting Fashions in Development Dialogue. In Fukuda-Parr, S. and Shiva Kumar, A.K. eds., *Readings in Human Development: Concepts, Measures and Policies for a Development Paradigm*. Oxford University Press, New Delhi.

Summer, A. and Tribe, M. (2008) *International Development Studies: Theories and Methods in Research and Practice*. Sage, London.

Unceta, K. (2001) Perspectivas Para el Desarrollo Humano en la Era de la Globalización. In Unceta, K. and Guell, P.I. eds., *Ensayos Sobre el Desarrollo Humano*. Icaria Editorial, Barcelona, 401–426.

Unterhalter, E. (2009) What Is Equality in Education? Reflections from the Capability Approach. *Studies on Philosophy and Education* 28: 415–424.

Vaughan, R.P. and Walker, M. (2012) Capabilities, Values and Education Policy. *Journal of Human Development and Capabilities* 13(3): 495–512.

Walker, M. (2006) *Higher Education Pedagogies*. Society for Research into Higher Education and Open University Press, Berkshire and New York.

Walker, M. (2009) Appendix 1: Teaching the Human Development and Capability Approach: Some Pedagogical Implications. In Deneulin, S. and Shahani, L. eds., *An Introduction to the Human Development and Capability Approach*. Earthscan, London, 240–243.

Wilson-Strydom, M. (2015) *University Access and Success. Capabilities, Diversity and Social Justice*. Routledge, London.

Wilson-Strydom, M. and Okkolin, M-A (2016) Enabling Environments for Equity, Access and Quality Education Post-2015: Lessons from South African and Tanzania. *International Journal of Educational Development* 49: 233.

Wilson-Strydom, M. and Walker, M. (2015) A Capabilities-Friendly Conceptualisation of Flourishing in and through Education. *Journal of Moral Education* 44(3): 310–324.

19

Displacement

Land acquisition and disempowerment

Asmita Kabra and Jay Drydyk

Displacement by development occurs when a development project or process deprives individuals, families or communities of access to space on which they lived and/or which they used for livelihood, resources and activities. Mega-dam projects are the most vivid example of displacement, since they submerge large tracts of farm land, habitations, forests and even towns. Mining projects cause displacement by removing humans and non-human species from the land's surface to get at the minerals below. An estimated 10 million people were displaced each year from 1980 to 2000, and the numbers are estimated to have gone up to 15 million people per annum since 2001 (Scudder 2012; Cernea and Mathur 2008; Hoshour and Kalafut 2010). Justifications given for changing existing uses of land and curtailing access of current users often claim to be based on the common good, usually through economic growth, but sometimes they are based on *prevention* of economic activity (for instance, to create protected areas for biodiversity conservation).

This curtailment of access is referred to variously as 'development-induced displacement', 'development-forced displacement and resettlement', 'forced migration', 'dispossession' or 'land grabbing'. The precise meaning of these terms is the subject of several debates (Borras et al. 2011; Hall 2013). Displacement may or may not involve relocation of people from one place to another. If it does, it is referred to as 'physical displacement', and if it does not, it is called 'livelihood displacement'. Conversion of land to other uses may simply make that land and its resources off-limits for prior users, without requiring them to move. It is also important to make a distinction between people displaced for the purpose of carrying out a development project (direct displacement), and those displaced as an unforeseen after-effect (indirect displacement). The latter can include impacts on 'host' communities whose land and resource access is curtailed due to resettlement of physically displaced people in their vicinity (Penz et al. 2011; Cernea and Schmidt-Soltau 2006). Indirect displacement could require that responsibility for mitigating adverse impacts be exercised on a regional scale rather than by project, because it affects groups rather than identifiable individuals (Penz et al. 2011, 49–53, 236–240).

Policy response to displacement, resettlement and rehabilitation ranges from 'techno-managerial' to 'movementist' (Dwivedi 2002). The former focuses mainly on minimizing displacement and restoring or replacing the quantity of resources to which access is lost, and (to a lesser extent) the quality of lost resources, with the stated goal of livelihood restoration. Compensation is usually

DOI: 10.4324/9781315626796-23

decided on the basis of the quantum of loss, while some resettlement policies indicate that resources of equivalent quality should be made available at the resettlement site. The movementist/activist responses tend to focus on ethical and redistributive aspects of displacement, for instance on the validity of 'public purpose' of population displacing projects, and on the distribution of gains and losses across different social groups.

Displacement invariably involves involuntary loss of access, where access is defined as 'the ability to benefit from things' (Ribot and Peluso 2003, 153). Access is influenced by rights (legal or customary) and norms. It is also influenced by structural and relational mechanisms, including markets, social networks, technology, labour, identities etc. Access is linked intricately to power; those who have power control access to resources, while others obtain access through more roundabout ways like the mediation of the powerful (Milgroom et al. 2014). Displacement and resettlement reconfigure the rules, norms and practices of access, and this usually results in unequal outcomes for the resettlers, depending on their degree of powerlessness (Kabra and Mahalwal 2014; Milgroom 2015; Rantala et al. 2013; deWet 2015). Institutions (formal and informal) as well as laws and policy processes (sub-national, national and international) are critical to the way power proscribes the outcomes of displacement (Wolford et al. 2013; Borras and Franco 2013; Price 2009; Price 2015).

Displacement and the values of worthwhile development

While the editors have rightly classified displacement as an empowerment issue, well-being and equity are also central to it, and on occasion displacement also puts other values of worthwhile development at risk.

Well-being

Displacement inevitably imposes great social, political and economic risks of harm on the 'oustees' (Cernea 2000) and on host communities (Kabra and Mahalwal 2014). According to a review of World Bank funded projects globally, the actual impact of projects it has funded has been to convert these potential risks into actually negative livelihood outcomes for resettled people (World Bank 1996). A more recent internal audit by the bank showed that commitment to meet resettlement targets among its own staff is abysmally low, and the incentive structure of the organization is biased systemically against achieving positive resettlement outcomes (Diagne 2016).

Equity

If these risks are not mitigated, the gains of people who benefit from a project may contrast starkly with the impoverishment of those who have been displaced. Displacement can potentially create new inequalities and exacerbate others. Project proponents and funders cite the Kaldor-Hicks compensation criterion to argue that so long as project benefits are greater than costs, there is the possibility to compensate those who lose, and projects should be allowed to go ahead (Cernea and Kanbur 2005). The response, which has by and large prevailed, is that this is not the kind of development that nations should value. Marxist scholars like Harvey have theorized this as new imperialism and 'accumulation by dispossession', which benefits the rich at the cost of the poor (Harvey 2004; Chakrabarti and Dhar 2010).

National governments across the world, as well as international financial institutions (IFIs) like the World Bank, which provide financial support to population displacing projects, have put in place detailed and well-articulated 'safeguard policies', as well as a plethora of grievance redress and benefit-sharing mechanisms that are aimed at minimizing the inequitable effects of displacement (Penz et al. 2011, Chapter 5, 84–115). These govern land acquisition by public as well as private entities, and lay down detailed processes by which compensation, resettlement and rehabilitation should be governed (Smyth et al. 2015). The ethical core of these policies and guidelines is the principle of 'do no harm', which translates in the policy directive that resettlement should result, at the very least, in restoration of original livelihoods, and should be treated by land acquiring bodies as a development project aimed at improving the well-being of the 'oustees'.

Participation/empowerment

Free participation in development is endorsed universally – and most authoritatively in the Declaration on the Right to Development, which stipulates that people are entitled to development 'on the basis of active, free and meaningful participation' (United Nations General Assembly 1986). Does this freedom entail consent? Does it forbid resettling people without their free, informed, prior consent? If so, we face a dilemma: the right to veto resettlement may conflict with the rights of other stakeholders to share in the benefits of development. A series of policy responses have emerged. One is that *indigenous peoples* are owed free, prior and informed consent to displacement and use of their traditional lands (ILO 1989; UN General Assembly 2007; Penz et al. 2011, 108). A second calls for the extent of involuntary displacement to be minimized (Penz et al. 2011, 87–89). A third deems the right to adequate housing to include security of tenure, which has been interpreted in international law to entail that expropriation and eviction are permissible only for projects of 'compelling and overriding public interests' (Penz et al. 2011, 98).

Central issues today: empowerment and democratic deliberation

This legal gap is large enough to accommodate a great many construction vehicles. It creates an ethical blind spot that deserves foremost attention in development ethics. Values such as public interest, common good and development of the nation are typically invoked to placate dissatisfaction, but that dissatisfaction may be warranted if two further questions cannot be answered.

The first question is: Which public interests are being served, which interests of the oustees are blocked, and exactly why should the former override the latter? Theory can make valuable contributions on which advantages matter and on how disadvantages incurred weigh against advantages gained – for instance, whether disadvantages to the worst off should block or at least weigh against gains for others. Yet even if an idealized public reason could give us ideal rules about where public interests should prevail, something else would be needed to give these ideal rules political force over decisions on the ground. At ground level, all we can ask for is that outcomes are governed by the verdict of a fair public deliberation. Underlying all rights is a right to justification: state legitimacy hangs on whether the exercise of authority is justifiable to those over whom it is exercised (Forst 2012). It follows that state decisions about when people's security of tenure may be overridden by public interests must be subject to fair public deliberation.

The second question is: In cases where displacement and resettlement are justifiable, how should stakeholders including the oustees and their host communities participate in managing the process? One UN body has interpreted international law as requiring full and informed consent as to relocation sites, along with fully informed consultation and participation in resettlement decision-making (Penz et al. 2011, 99). The World Commission on Dams has proposed a project governance model that would empower displaced people and other stakeholders to ensure at each stage of development and resettlement that prior commitments to them have been honoured (World Commission on Dams 2000; Penz et al. 2011, 100–104). Governments and funding agencies, on the other hand, cling to vague expressions like 'meaningful consultation', leaving the details of how these are actualised largely to project proponents. (Penz et al. 2011, 89–90). Thus while national and international policy guidelines are firm and clear about unacceptable outcomes, they are slack and opaque about unacceptable exclusion of stakeholders from decision-making. This is especially problematic because mechanisms of recourse and grievance through which stakeholders can hold guideline violators accountable are unreliable (Clark et al. 2003). In 2016 the World Bank revised all of its environmental and social safeguards, including those on involuntary resettlement, and devolved responsibility for monitoring, enforcement, and grievance to the borrowers (World Bank 2016, 2017). Civil society organizations are concerned about the impact these changes will have in cases of displacement and involuntary resettlement, especially on social impact assessment and stakeholder engagement (Bank Information Center 2018).

Thus the central ethical issues in displacement by development at the present time are democratic deliberation and empowerment. Project proponents, governments and international donors have moral responsibilities to make such deliberation and empowerment happen. And almost all of them are oblivious to these responsibilities, merely pay lip service to them, or are in denial. One challenge arising from this is to examine why this is so. How can one explain the fact that despite several individuals within these institutions being champions of minimizing non-worthwhile displacement, the actual performance of legal and policy safeguards has been overwhelmingly inadequate (Modi 2011; ICIJ 2015; Cernea and Mathur 2008; World Bank 1996; Schmidt-Soltau 2003; Brockington and Igoe 2006; Lustig and Kingsbury 2006; Smyth et al. 2015).

It is here that the new literatures on political economy, political ecology and critical agrarian studies have made significant contributions. Political economy critiques focus on displacement as exclusionary development and land-grabbing, either by the state for its own projects or on behalf of the corporate sector. Displacement is viewed as a mechanism by which neo-imperialist resource grab and 'accumulation-by-dispossession' takes place (Harvey 2004; D. Hall 2013; Fairhead et al. 2012). In an interesting extension of this idea, Tania Li distinguishes between two kinds of dispossession – where the land is needed but the labour of the oustees is not, and one where both their land and labour is needed. She argues that the livelihood outcomes in the two cases will differ, with the latter likely to be less inequitable (Li 2010a, 2010b).

Several national and transnational anti-displacement social movements are deeply dissatisfied by 'techno-managerial' attempts at improving resettlement outcomes, rather than examining and eliminating the root causes of displacement and uneven development in the capitalist mode of production (Chakrabarti and Dhar 2010; Dwivedi 2006). However, the literature on anti-displacement movements and resistance has now become more nuanced, bringing in ideas of heterogeneity of the state as well as the local community and 'everyday politics' to complicate the straightforward narratives of elite capitalist land grab and poor people's resistance (Milgroom 2015; Mamonova 2015; Borras and Franco 2013; Hall et al. 2015; Wolford et al. 2013). An important new direction is to theorize the politics of dispossession in terms of 'regimes of dispossession' based on variations in 'state roles, economic logics tied to class interests and ideological articulations of the public good' (Levien 2013).

Ethical discussion of empowerment and democratic participation in displacement and resettlement must engage critically with these new literatures in order to push the boundaries of the current discourse and generate ethically sound prescriptions that are also grounded in the lived realities of those at the receiving end of unfair displacement.

References

Bank Information Center (2018) World Bank Safeguards Review. Bank Information Center, Washington, DC. www.bankinformationcenter.org/our-work/safeguards/. Accessed 29 January 2018.

Borras, S.M. and Franco, J.C. (2013) Global Land Grabbing and Political Reactions 'From Below'. *Third World Quarterly* 34(9): 1723–1747. doi:10.1080/01436597.2013.843845.

Borras, S.M., Hall, R., Scoones, I., White, B. and Wolford, W. (2011) Towards a Better Understanding of Global Land Grabbing: An Editorial Introduction. *Journal of Peasant Studies* 38(2): 209–216. doi:10.1080/03066150.2011.559005.

Brockington, D. and Igoe, J. (2006) Eviction for Conservation : A Global Overview. *Conservation and Society* 4(3): 424–470.

Cernea, M.M. (2000) Risks, Safeguards and Reconstruction: A Model for Population Displacement and Resettlement. *Economic and Political Weekly* 35: 3659–3678.

Cernea, M.M. and Kanbur, R. (2005) An Exchange on the Compensation Principle in Resettlement. , *Working Papers: 127327, 2005.* Cornell University, Department of Applied Economics and Management.

Cernea, M.M. and Mathur, H.M. (2008) *Can Compensation Prevent Impoverishment? Reforming Resettlement through Investments and Benefit-Sharing.* Oxford University Press, New Delhi.

Cernea, M.M. and Schmidt-Soltau, K. (2006) Poverty Risks and National Parks: Policy Issues in Conservation and Resettlement. *World Development* 34(10): 1808–1830. doi:10.1016/j.worlddev.2006.02.008.

Chakrabarti, A. and Dhar, A.K. (2010) *Dislocation and Resettlement in Development: From Third World to the World of the Third.* Routledge, Abingdon and New York.

Clark, D., Fox, J. and Treakle, K. eds. (2003) *Demanding Accountability: Civil-society Claims and the World Bank Inspection Panel.* Rowman & Littlefield, Lanham, MD.

deWet, C. (2015) Spatial- and Complexity-Based Perspectives on the Ethics of Development-Induced Displacement and Resettlement. In Satiroglu, I. and Choi, N. eds., *Development-Induced Displacement and Resettlement.* Oxford: Routledge, Abingdon and New York, 85–96.

Diagne, M. (2016) *Report on an Advisory Review of the Bank's Safeguard Risk Management.* World Bank, Washington, DC.

Dwivedi, R. (2002) Models and Methods in Development – Induced Displacement (Review Article). *Development and Change* 33(4): 709–732. doi.org/10.1111/1467-7660.00276.

Dwivedi, R. (2006) *Conflict and Collective Action: The Sardar Sarovar Project in India.* Routledge India, New Delhi.

Escobar, A., Rocheleau, D. and Kothari, S. (2002) "Environmental Social Movements and the Politics of Place." *Development.* doi:10.1057/palgrave.development.1110314.

Fairhead, J., Leach, M. and Scoones, I. (2012) "Green Grabbing : A New Appropriation of Nature?" *Journal of Peasant Studies,* May: 37–41.

Forst, R. (2012) *The Right to Justification; Elements of a Constructivist Theory of Justice.* Columbia University Press, New York.

Hall, D. (2013) Primitive Accumulation, Accumulation by Dispossession and the Global Land Grab. *Third World Quarterly* 34(9): 1582–1604. doi:10.1080/01436597.2013.843854.

Hall, R., Edelman, M., Borras, S.M., Scoones, I., White, B. and Wolford, W. (2015) Resistance, Acquiescence or Incorporation? An Introduction to Land Grabbing and Political Reactions "from Below." *The Journal of Peasant Studies* 42(3–4): 467–488. doi:10.1080/03066150.2015.1036746.

Harvey, D. (2004) The "new' Imperialism: Accumulation by Dispossession. *Socialist Register* 40: 63–87.

Hoshour, K. and Kalafut, J. (2010) *A Growing Global Crisis: Development-Induced Displacement & Resettlement. Issue Paper* International Accountability Project, San Francisco.

International Consortium of Investigative Journalists (ICIJ) (2015) Evicted and Abandoned: The World Bank's Broken Promise to the Poor. www.icij.org/project/world-bank.

International Labour Organization (ILO). (1989) *Convention (No. 169) Concerning Indigenous and Tribal Peoples in Independent Countries.* International Labour Organization, Geneva.

Kabra, A. and Mahalwal, S. (2014) Impact of Conservation-Induced Displacement on Host Community Livelihoods: Complicating the DIDR Narratives. *Land Use Policy* 41: 217–224. doi:10.1016/j.landusepol.2014.05.010.

Levien, M. (2013) Regimes of Dispossession: From Steel Towns to Special Economic Zones. *Development and Change* 44(2): 381–407. doi:10.1111/dech.12012.

Li, T.M. (2010a) Capitalism, and the Management of Dispossession. *Current Anthropology* 51(3): 385–414.

Li, T.M. (2010b) To Make Live or Let Die? Rural Dispossession and the Protection of Surplus Populations. *Antipode* 41(s1): 63.

Lustig, D. and Kingsbury, B. (2006) Displacement and Relocation from Protected Areas: International Law Perspectives on Rights, Risks and Resistance. *Conservation and Society* 4(3): 404–418.

Mamonova, N. (2015) Resistance or Adaptation? Ukrainian Peasants' Responses to Large-Scale Land Acquisitions. *The Journal of Peasant Studies* 42(3–4): 607–634 doi:10.1080/03066150.2014.993320.

Milgroom, J. (2015) Policy Processes of a Land Grab: At the Interface of Politics "in the Air" and Politics "on the Ground" in Massingir, Mozambique. *The Journal of Peasant Studies* 42(3–4): 585–606. doi:10.1080/03066150.2014.991721.

Milgroom, J., Giller, K.E. and Leeuwis, C. (2014) Three Interwoven Dimensions of Natural Resource Use: Quantity, Quality and Access in the Great Limpopo Transfrontier Conservation Area. *Human Ecology* 42(2): 199–215. doi:10.1007/s10745-013-9635-3.

Modi, R. (2011) The Best and the Worst of the World Bank: Involuntary Resettlement and the Mumbai Urban Transport Project (MUTP), India. *Development (Basingstoke)* 54: 400–406 doi:http://dx.doi.org/10.1057/dev.2011.69.

Penz, P., Drydyk, J. and Bose, P.S. (2011) *Displacement by Development: Ethics, Rights and Responsibilities.* Cambridge University Press, Cambridge.

Price, S. (2009) Prologue: Victims or Partners? The Social Perspective in Development-Induced Displacement and Resettlement. *The Asia Pacific Journal of Anthropology* 10(4): 266–282. doi:10.1080/14442210903305821.

Price, S. (2015) A No-Displacement Option? Rights, Risks and Negotiated Settlement in Development Displacement. *Development in Practice* 25(5): 673–685. doi:10.1080/09614524.2015.1051514.

Rantala, S., Vihemäki, H., Swallow, B. and Jambiya, G. (2013) Who Gains and Who Loses from Compensated Displacement from Protected Areas? The Case of the Derema Corridor, Tanzania. *Conservation and Society* 11(2): 97 doi:10.4103/0972–4923.115721.

Ribot, J. and Peluso, N.L. (2003) A Theory of Access. *Rural Sociology* 68(2): 153–181.

Schmidt-Soltau, K. (2003) "Conservation-Related Resettlement in Central Africa: Environmental and Social Risks." *Development and Change* 34: 525–551 doi:10.1111/1467–7660.00317.

Scudder, T. (2012) "Resettlement Outcomes of Large Dams" in Tortajada C, Altinbilek D, and Biswas AK eds., *Impacts of Large Dams: A Global Assessment* Springer, Berlin doi:10.1007/978-3-642-23571-9.

Smyth, E., Steyn, M., Esteves, A.M., Franks, D.M. and Vaz, K. (2015) Five "Big" Issues for Land Access, Resettlement and Livelihood Restoration Practice: Findings of an International Symposium. *Impact Assessment and Project Appraisal* 33(3): 220–225. doi:10.1080/14615517.2015.1037665.

United Nations General Assembly (1986) *Resolution 41/128 Declaration on the Right to Development.*

United Nations General Assembly (2007) *Declaration on the Rights of Indigenous Peoples.* United Nations, New York.

Wolford, W., Borras, S.M., Hall, R., Scoones, I. and White, B. (2013) Governing Global Land Deals: The Role of the State in the Rush for Land. *Development and Change* 44(2): 189–210. doi:10.1111/dech.12017.

World Bank (1996) *The Bankwide Review of Projects Involving Involuntary Resettlement 1986–1993* World Bank, Washington D.C.

World Bank (2016) World Bank Approves New Environmental and Social Framework. World Bank, Washington, DC. www.worldbank.org/en/news/press-release/2016/08/04/world-bank-board-approves-new-environmental-and-social-framework. Acessed 4 August 2016.

World Bank (2017) *Environmental and Social Safeguard Policies.* World Bank, Washington DC. www.worldbank.org/en/programs/environmental-and-social-policies-for-projects/brief/environmental-and-social-safeguards-policies. Accessed 5 April 2017.

World Commission on Dams (2000) *Report: Dams and Development; A New Framework for Decision-Making.* Earthscan, London and Sterling, VA.

Part V
Environmental sustainability

As the United Nations 2015 resolution "Transforming our World: The 2030 Agenda for Sustainable Development" recognizes through the *Sustainable Development Goals*, environmental sustainability is at the heart of ethical development. In the first chapter in this part concepts of environmental sustainability are discussed, while the other two chapters provide a closer look at two of the many issues related to sustainability: food, and the *buen vivir* movement that grounds the constitutionally enshrined rights of nature in Bolivia and Ecuador.

In Chapter 20, Andrew Crabtree discusses various concepts of environmental sustainability, including weak, strong, and very strong sustainability, natural capital, critical natural capital, greenhouse gas neutrality, and planetary boundaries. Crabtree considers the case of negative greenhouse gases as he advances a conceptualization of sustainable development as an increase in legitimate freedoms that cannot be reasonably rejected. Finally he discusses the principle of common but differentiated responsibilities, in the context of climate change mitigation, adaption, and ecological resilience, loss, and damage.

Paul Thompson draws on economists, philosophers, population ecologists, and development critics as he traces the evolution of discussions of the ethical issues surrounding food production from hunger and economic development to food security and food sovereignty. He explains nuances in current discussions over accessing and consuming adequate nutrition not only in terms of biophysical food requirements, but also in the context of social institutions and cultural norms of appropriateness, and the lack of political control that vulnerable and marginalized groups have over the structure of their food systems.

Finally, Johannes Waldmueller and Laura Rodríguez present the *buen vivir* (living well) movement in Latin America. Although the specifics vary, the indigenous insight of union between humans and nature is at the core of the broad epistemological, social, political, and ecological systems that identify as *buen vivir*. It is from these insights that the rights of nature have been derived and enshrined in the constitutions of Bolivia and Ecuador. The authors discuss some of the challenges of implementing *buen vivir* while recognizing its value for critically evaluating ethical dimensions of development theory and practice.

DOI: 10.4324/9781315626796-24

20

Sustainability and climate change

Human development and human responsibilities

Andrew Crabtree

In geological and evolutionary terms, the earth has been constantly changing. Ecosystems are dynamic. Indeed, an estimated 90% of all species that have ever lived are already extinct. In this timeframe, environmental sustainability is the exception rather than the rule. Our discussions on environmental sustainability are generally concerned with an undefined short term. The major difference of our present era is that we have now entered the Anthropocene in which humans are the major driving force behind environmental change not least climate change. Climate change is here and as some greenhouse gases (GHGs) take up to 200,000 years to break down, we are living for all intents and purposes in an irreversibly unsustainable world (Archer 2009; Crabtree 2016). This raises complex issues concerning ethics and development not least in relation to what kind of development is ethically acceptable and what kinds of responsibilities are involved. In this chapter I take a detailed look at climate change; it should be remembered that climate change is not an isolated concern, but it is one of many related, interlinked environmental and developmental issues.

I first outline the concept of environmental sustainability and the concepts of weak, strong and very strong sustainability; natural capital; critical natural capital; and planetary boundaries. Inspired by Sen's capability approach (see Sen 1999 and Chapter 7, this volume) and Scanlon's contractualist ethics, the chapter then goes on to discuss the notion of development as an increase in legitimate freedoms that cannot be reasonably rejected. It argues that GHG neutral and GHG negative development are ethically acceptable but that there are also intractable wicked problems which are exemplified by the case of India where the government has justified increased GHG emissions by arguing that they are necessary for reducing poverty. I then discuss the principle of common but differentiated responsibilities (CBDR), climate change mitigation, adaption, resilience and loss and damage. It concludes by indicating avenues for further research into the chapter's concerns.

Environmental sustainability

The idea of environmental sustainability was institutionalized at the 2005 United Nations World Summit on Social Development as one of the three pillars of sustainability, together with economic and social development. Approaches to sustainability are often divided into weak, strong

DOI: 10.4324/9781315626796-25

and very strong sustainability (Goodland 1995). Within economics, distinctions can be made between natural capital (for example, ecosystems such as woodlands, fish and the atmosphere), manufactured capital (such as buildings and roads), and human capital. Weak sustainability, the view held by mainstream economics and the World Bank, maintains that all forms of capital are substitutable and thus sustainability is a question of keeping total capital intact. The three pillars of sustainability merge into one. An example of this is the World Bank's measure of Adjusted Net Savings (ANS), (or genuine savings) which provides a composite indicator of sustainability (World Bank 2011).

The calculation of ANS starts with gross national savings, thereafter the depreciation of fixed capital (such as land, buildings and production equipment) is determined to arrive at net savings. Subsequently, changes in human capital are taken into consideration by adding education expenditure as a proxy measure for educational attainment. Having arrived at this figure, the depletion of natural resources (energy, mineral and net forest) and pollution damages (carbon dioxide and particulate emissions) are deducted to arrive at genuine savings. Monetary calculations are thus used for all measures.

A number of criticisms have been leveled against the approach both in terms of economics and in relation to the environment. Stiglitz et al. (2009) have argued that current prices are not a good indicator of the value of non-renewable resources as prices, which have strong influences on ANS, fluctuate considerably and thus sustainability can vary from year to year in both directions. Indeed, when natural resources are depleted their market prices increase, which can suggest that the use of such resources is more sustainable than it actually is (Fitoussi and Malik 2013). Furthermore, prices used for carbon emissions decrease the significance of CO_2 for sustainability and are thus a poor guide to sustainability this weakens the usefulness of ANS as a policy tool. An additional problem is that given the contents of the measure, natural resource exporting countries tend to be unsustainable whereas those countries that import the resources are not. In addition, education expenditure rates may not reflect the quality of education or attainment. Neither a pay raise for teachers nor expenditure on buildings automatically means improved education.

From an environmental perspective, we would expect any indicator of sustainability to include at the minimum major environmental problems that we know from natural science. This is not the case with ANS; although CO_2 emissions are included, the number of countries that would be counted as unsustainable would increase by two thirds if pollution damages included other GHGs such as methane and nitrous oxide (Crabtree 2016). Moreover, water depletion, over fishing, soil degradation and biodiversity loss are not considered. These substantial limitations reduce both the measure's value as an indicator and its force as a guide for policy.

The preceding arguments from an environmental perspective are arguments against the particular measure (ANS) rather than weak sustainability *per se* as one could broaden the number of factors taken into consideration. A more fundamental question is whether it makes sense at all to maintain that education expenditure can make up for deforestation given the completely different roles they play for maintaining life on earth. This is exactly what strong sustainability denies. For ecological economists "zero natural capital implies zero human welfare because it is not feasible to substitute, in total, purely 'non-natural' capital for natural capital. Natural capital can be loosely thought of as our natural environment, which ecological economists conceptualize as 'the stock of environmentally provided assets'" (Goodland and Daly 1996, 1005). Manufactured and human capital require natural capital for their construction" (Costanza et al. 1997, 254). We cannot construct the atmosphere out of manufacturing capital. Thus, strong sustainability is defined as the "maintenance of natural capital" (Goodland 1995, 10). This accords with the so-called input/output rule, which stipulates that on the input side the depletion of non-renewables such as oil should not be at a rate greater than that at which renewables, such as solar energy, can provide substitutes. Furthermore, renewables, such as forests, should not be harvested at a rate faster than they can be regenerated. On the output side, waste should remain within an environment's assimilative capacity (Goodland 1995). In other words, there are limits to carrying capacity. It should be noted that as soon as we introduce words such as "capital" and "asset" we are already implying that humans own the "natural environment." The change in terminology has normative consequences. (See Chapter 12 on Indigenous peoples and Chapter 22 on *buen vivir* and the rights of nature.)

The concept of natural capital is closely linked to that of ecosystem services. Natural capital can be thought of as a *stock* such as trees, fish and ecosystems. An ecosystem is defined as "a dynamic complex plant, animal and microorganism communities and the non-living environment interacting as a functional unit" (Millennium Ecosystem Assessment 2005, V). Ecosystem *services* are defined as "the benefits people obtain from ecosystems" or flows that produce human welfare (Costanza et al. 1997), and as such ecosystem services are the links between ecosystems on the one hand and human well-being on the other. If ecosystem services are defined in terms of the benefits people actually experience, then such services also differ from natural capital which exists whether it benefits people or not.

The concept of ecosystem services received greater public attention with the publication of the 2005 Millennium Ecosystem Assessment Report, which provided a synthesis of scientific knowledge of ecosystems at that time. The endeavor was comparable to that of the Intergovernmental Panel on Climate Change (IPCC) reports and involved some 1,360 experts from 95 countries. The Assessment identifies four types of ecosystem services, namely provisioning, regulating, supporting and cultural, which may interact and operate on different scales from ponds to oceans. These are considered as the bases for human well-being.

The report emphasizes four main findings. Firstly, the impact of human activity over the last fifty years has had a more profound effect on ecosystems than at any other time in human history largely due to increased demands for provisioning services. (The Anthropocene era is not solely linked to climate change.) Secondly, whilst the changes in ecosystems have played an important part in achieving gains in development, for certain groups there have been significant losses. Moreover, continued environmental degradation may lead to non-liner changes (tipping points will be reached), increase poverty and diminish future well-being. Thirdly, such changes might be a barrier to meeting the Millennium Development Goals (and now the SDGs). Fourthly, preventing degradation will require changes in policies, institutions and practices.

The fact that ecosystem services are seen in terms of benefits raises the question of how we are to understand the term 'benefits'. This has led to the criticism that it induces people to have an overly positive view of ecosystems (Schröter et al. 2014). Not surprisingly, ecosystems can be both beneficial and harmful (ecosystem *dis*services), for example the Ceratopogonid mosquito infects people through viruses, protozoa and filarial worms but they also pollinate cacao, which is essential for chocolate. On a general level, the eradication of mosquitos would be of great benefit to human health and only have a few negative consequences for the other parts of the ecosystems. Ecological economists are not averse to placing prices on ecosystem services. The Economics of Ecosystems and Biodiversity approach (2010) does so with the aim to make nature's value visible. For instance, it has been calculated that wild bees contribute $3,251 hectare $^{-1}$ for certain crops. However, as the authors point out, pricing ecosystem services can be problematic as endangered species often add little economic value, consequently economic value is an inadequate ground for arguing for biodiversity conservation (Kleijn et al. 2015).

The concept of critical natural capital (CNC) is employed to draw a distinction between the strong and very strong sustainability approaches. The latter holds that all capital can or should be sustained, but this is seemingly impossible if one wishes to sustain human life. A standard way of defining CNC is as the "part of the natural environment that performs important and irreplaceable functions" (Ekins 2003), but two immediate problems arise, namely who defines what is important and irreplaceable and secondly who knows what is important and irreplaceable? To highlight the second problem first, some of the first articles about natural capital expressed a worry about the depletion of oil reserves (e.g. Goodland 1995; Daly and Goodall), we are now, due to climate change, worried about using the oil reserves we can already exploit and rejecting the search for new reserves (UNEP 2014). In other words, what is argued to be critical at one time may be rejected as such later on.

There have been several attempts to answer the first question. Brand (2009) has usefully divided the "important and irreplaceable" aspects of the environment into six to some extent compatible categories, namely: social-cultural (highly significant for a particular social group), ecological (vital for, say, biodiversity), sustainability (fundamental for human well-being), ethical (animal and ecosystem rights for example), economic (capital loss would have high economic costs) or human survival. "Important and irreplaceable" for one approach is not necessarily so for another.

The planetary boundaries (PB) approach, which is now in its second edition depicted in Figure 20.1, may be considered as one prominent answer to the question of what the limits to

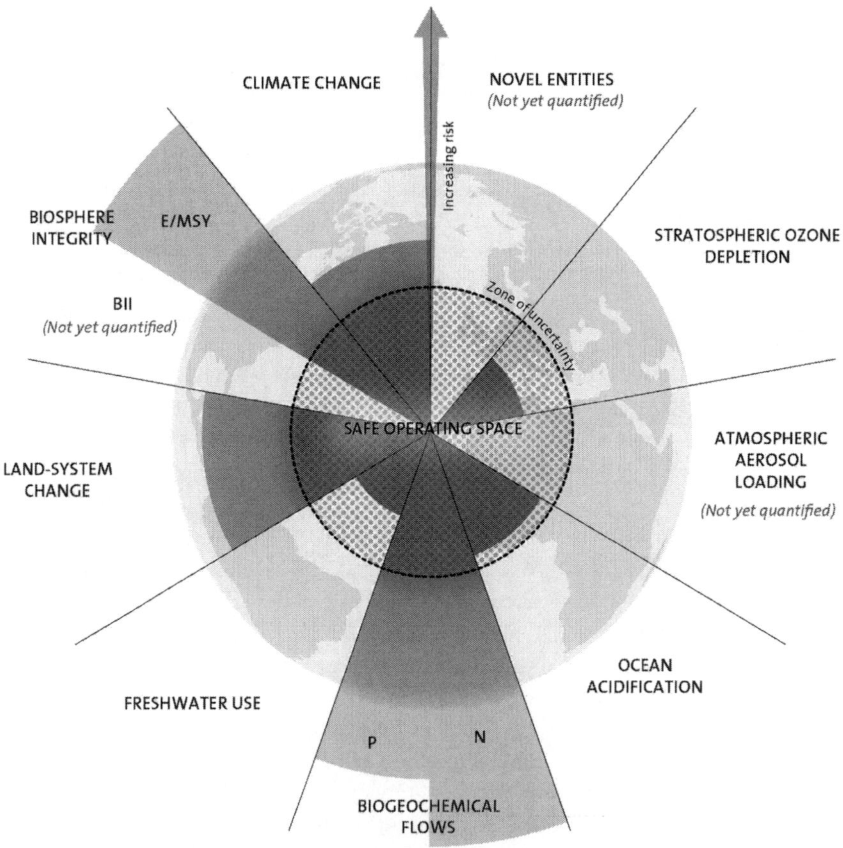

Figure 20.1 Planetary boundaries, second version

Source: Azote Images/Stockholm Resilience Centre. Adapted from the graphic published in Steffen et al. Planetary boundaries: guiding human development on a changing planet. *Science*, January 16, 2015.

human activity are (I shall refer to them as PB I and PB II, respectively). It seeks to establish a "safe operating space for humanity with respect to the Earth system" (Rockström et al. 2009, 472) which clearly has links to the concept of carrying capacity and limits to growth. Transgression of planetary boundaries "constitutes unacceptable human-induced global environmental change" (Rockström et al. 2009, 470).

The editorial of the issue of *Nature* in which the original article was published stated "The exercise requires many qualifications. For the most part, the exact values chosen as boundaries by Rockström and his colleagues are arbitrary. So too, in some cases, are the indicators of change" (*Nature*, September 2009, 447–448). Unusually, *Nature* simultaneously published comments on the paper by seven leading experts in relevant spheres. The responses from these commentators can be summarized as follows: (1) there was a universal rejection of the particular parameters chosen; (2) depending on the earth system process, there was a questioning of the value of developing planetary boundaries as opposed to regional or local boundaries; and (3) some authors questioned the value of establishing any boundaries at all. On the positive side, the importance of all of the earth system processes under discussion was not questioned.

Planetary boundaries: Guiding human development on a changing planet (Steffen et al. 2015 is an attempt by the PB team to meet criticisms and take newer research into consideration. The main differences between PB I and PB II are fourfold. Firstly, PB II introduced a two-tier approach for a number of the boundaries. This was aimed at capturing regional-level heterogeneity. Secondly, the quantification of the boundaries was updated to meet criticisms and reflect the latest scientific knowledge. Thirdly, two core boundaries were introduced and, fourthly, a regional boundary for biosphere integrity (previously biodiversity), biogeochemical flows (phosphorus and nitrogen cycles), land-system change, freshwater use, and atmospheric aerosol loading) were introduced.

Boundaries are set as a way of indicating, not least to policy makers, that transgressing them means we have moved from a safe operating space for humanity to a zone of uncertainty within this zone there may be a threshold or tipping point where abrupt (relatively speaking) and irreversible change takes place. The distance between the PB and the threshold is a buffer zone and is designed to take uncertainty about exact boundaries into consideration. Take the example of climate change: PB version I and II suggest two boundary levels of (i) 350 ppm CO_2 concentration and, compared with pre-industrial levels, a rise in top-of-atmosphere radiative forcing of $+1.0\,Wm^{-2}$ (the latter is more inclusive, than solely concentrating on CO_2 which means the measures are not directly equivalent), and an uncertainty zone of 350–450 ppm and $+1.0$–$1.5\,Wm^{-2}$. One fundamental problem with this is whether is it right to have one planetary boundary at all, for an average increase effects different parts of the world differently, and, if the IPCC is right in asserting that climate change is already here, it would make sense to say that both the boundaries and thresholds have already been crossed.

As the PB authors make clear, we are concerned with normative judgments as to what is safe, dangerous and unacceptable, and the limits have been contested on these grounds. For example, in relation to PB I, Bass (2009) found the boundary for land use as cropland at a maximum of 15% (compared with the present 12%) problematic, as there is no scientific consensus about the percentage. This being so, he argues that policy makers will ask why they should respect it and people, especially where there is an expanding population, will query why more land cannot be used. Similarly, Brewer (2009) argues that fertilizers have been central to maintaining people's existence. Setting limits without providing alternatives will be of little value in such circumstances, as food "is not an option" (Brewer 2009, 118). That is, in Brewer's opinion, there may be *acceptable* grounds for transgressing a boundary.

Returning to the definition of CNC, the PB approach can capture some of the approaches identified by Brand but not others. Biodiversity loss has consequences for animal rights, yet the BP approach is concerned with a safe operating space for humanity as a whole. The PB approach does not capture the significance of 'local' problems which might be of great importance to a specific group of people (Brook et al. 2013). It is possible that deforestation could take place within the boundary limits but destroy the safe operating space for some indigenous people. Nor are the religious, aesthetic and other cultural values of ecosystems taken into consideration. Yet for some people these ecosystems may be of central importance for their "safe operating space" i.e. different groups of people might have different safe operating spaces and thus "devastating for *humanity*" is the wrong limit. As the PB authors state, the boundaries are not just scientific; they are also normative. That is, they depend on our value judgments.

To summarize, firstly the debate tells us that environmental problems are of acute importance for human wellbeing. Secondly, as scientists themselves point out, decisions about which capital is critical and about planetary boundaries are ethical decisions. Thus, any approach to development, the capability approach included, is truncated if it does not take environmental and ethical issues into consideration.

Sustainable development as increasing legitimate freedoms

The legitimate freedom approach outlined here takes its point of departure in Sen's (1999) understanding of development as an increase in freedoms that people exercise to live "the lives they value and have reason to value" (Sen 1999, 291) rather than in income, or modernization or technological advance. The approach offered here differs in two substantial ways. Firstly, Sen has had relatively little to say about sustainable development, while here sustainability is central. Secondly, Sen's definition of development seem too open ended. Perhaps even more confusingly, at the start of *Development as Freedom* Sen defines development as "a process of expanding the real freedoms that people enjoy" (Sen 1999, 3) with no reference to values or reasons. As Nussbaum (2003; Crabtree 2013) and others have also argued such wording appears to suggest that freedoms *tout court* are acceptable. Even if such open-endedness is not Sen's intent, his definitions are surprisingly unclear (for an excellent discussion see Khader and Kosko 2018). Here, I introduce the notion of legitimacy to distinguish between those freedoms which are rejectable and those which are not. A schematic outline of Sen's capability approach is presented in Figure 20.2.

Figure 20.2 highlights, in light grey, that the evaluative space of Sen's capability approach is capabilities/real freedoms and, in some instances, our actual doings and beings (more technically called functionings). The rationale for this is that the once dominant income- and resource-based approach to development fails to capture important aspects of well-being. A well-known example of Sen's is that a person in a wheelchair needs to have more resources to undertake the same activities as someone who is able bodied. Conversion factors are those that affect the relationship between resources and a person's capabilities (e.g., a person's ability to spend money on a wheelchair may be affected by access to markets and supplies). A rejoinder to this argument would be that the example does not destroy a resource-based approach, but that it only makes things more complicated as more resources need to be taken into consideration. However other examples, such as discrimination, may require institutional change for people to live the lives they value (to achieve various functionings) rather than a change in the amount of resources available to individuals – having more money does not compensate for disenfranchisement (for an interesting discussion on Sen, Nussbaum and freedom expansion see Keleher 2014).

Figure 20.2 The evaluative space of the capability approach

However, if we only take people's actual doings and beings (achieved functionings) into consideration, we exclude important information. A supermodel and someone in a famine may have the same calorie intake but the former has a greater choice to so do in that she chooses her job. Hence, capabilities are the relevant space for evaluating well-being. Obviously, in certain situations, such as a famine, one might want to concentrate on actual functionings, such as calorie intake, rather than ask people whether or not they chose to be in the famine.

Sen's writings on sustainable development and environmental ethics are limited to one peer reviewed article together with Sudhir Anand (Anand and Sen 2000), a sub-section of Chapter 11 of *The Idea of Justice* (Sen 2009) which is mostly a reprint of *Why We Should Preserve the Spotted Owl* published in the *London Review of Books* (2004). There is also a very brief discussion of the environment in Drèze and Sen's 2013 book on India *An Uncertain Glory*. Several of the basic arguments are upheld throughout. In line with the preceding framework, there is a rejection of conceptualizations of sustainable development rooted in the standard of living (Solow) or basic needs as embraced by the Brundtland Report (Crabtree 2013), and an offer of a capabilities alternative in Sen's most recent formulation: "[T]he preservation, and whenever possible expansion, of the substantive freedoms and capabilities of people today 'without compromising the capability of future generations' to have similar – or more – freedom" (Sen 2009, 151–152). Interestingly, Sen seems to have dropped the view held in *Why We Should Preserve the Spotted Owl*, in which he concurs with the finding of the Royal Society's 2000 Report *Towards Sustainable Consumption* calling for "major changes in the lifestyles of the most developed countries – something that none of us will find easy." In *An Uncertain Glory*, Sen (together with Drèze) argues that as far as India is concerned, growth still plays a central role (Drèze and Sen 2013). However, if the Royal Society's conclusion is correct, sustainable development will involve *reducing* some of our freedoms we presently value.

The arguments for capabilities, or freedoms, being the correct evaluative space for understanding development is inadequate if we turn to sustainable development. In particular, the evaluative space needs to be extended. Firstly, drawing on the previous discussion, resources play a central role, and to answer the question 'Is development sustainable or not?', we need to include resources in the evaluative space. Not surprisingly, people working within the capability approach reject the notion of weak sustainability because of conversion problems. The Millennium Ecosystem Assessment Report provides a strong empirical and theoretical support for taking an ecosystems services approach to 'resources' and Lessmann (2011) and Pelenc and Ballet (2015) have argued that this concept and that of CNC might be integrated into the capability approach. As argued earlier, the shift from 'ecosystems' to 'ecosystem services' is problematic hence using the concept of 'ecosystems' leaving the extent to which the result in services or disservices or indeed whether or not they are for us open. This is an ethical question, some worldviews, such as the Maori's, would hold that we are an integral part of the environment. It is not just a service (Watene 2016).

At the other end of Figure 20.2, those working on sustainability within the capability approach are also concerned with the consequences of our doings and beings both for human beings and the environment more generally and placing limits on our freedoms (Holland 2008; Crabtree 2013; Pelenc and Ballet 2015; Schultz et al. 2013). In contrast, Sen's framework tends to be static (Robeyns 2005), ending with functionings. Thus, one has the capability x to do y, but there is comparatively little discussion about the consequences of doing y. This can also be seen in the Human Development Reports. The aim is for countries to be of very high human development though the consequences of doing so are not taken into account. This is also reflected by the fact that much work on justice within the capability approach concerns intragenerational justice and not intergenerational justice.

Thus, there are two normative problems relating to limits. Firstly, we need to establish the normative limits to environmental indicators and, secondly, we need to find the limits of our freedoms to live the lives we value. Consequently, I have defined sustainable development as *a process of expanding the real freedoms that people value which are in accordance with principles that cannot be reasonably rejected by others* (Crabtree 2010, 2012, 2013). The idea of reasonable rejection is taken from Thomas Scanlon who offers a contractualist approach to ethics (Scanlon 1998), which a number of other philosophers have also employed (Barry 1995; Parfit 2011; Forst 2002, 2007). For Scanlon, judgments of right and wrong center on justification to others and reasonable rejection: "they are judgments about what would be permitted by principles that could not reasonably be rejected, by people who were moved to find principles for the general regulation of behavior that others, similarly motivated, could not reasonably reject" (1998, 4).

The fundamental idea in Scanlon's approach is that an action is morally wrong if the actor cannot *justify* his or her action to others in accordance with principles that they could not reasonably reject. The Scanlonian formulation ensures impartiality by ensuring justifiability to all and all can reasonably reject a principle. For example, returning to the planetary boundaries approach, Rockström et al. (2009) define the boundaries in relation to what may be deleterious for *humanity* as a whole. This is clearly appealing for if deleterious to humanity isn't wrong, what is? But climate change is already here and people are already suffering the consequences, we do not have to reach a 1.5°C boundary to assert that the world is unsustainable. The question is whether or not GHG emissions are justifiable to any individual on grounds that they cannot reasonably reject.

There may be development with little or no effect on the environment, for instance at the very local level people's lives in retirement homes may go significantly better if they are visited by schoolchildren (Andersen and Bilfeldt 2016). Furthermore, eradicating many important unfreedoms and promoting aspects of well-being related to basic human dignity may in many cases be environmentally neutral. If we examine Nussbaum's list of Central Capabilities which are necessary to lead a dignified life (see Chapter 7 of this *Handbook*), we find that many of these are more or less carbon neutral: being secure against violent assault, freedom of expression, being able to engage in practical reason, being able to love and grieve, to be respected and not face discrimination, and certainly to live with concern for the environment. Conversely, there may be gains for the environment such as the IUCN defined strict nature reserves, such as Kevo in Finland and Torsa in Buhtan, where human activity is strictly controlled.

However, there are also complex wicked problems in which it seems that alternative options are reasonably rejectable. The most obvious case is climate change. Increasing human well-being, which may be considered a human right (Moellendorf 2013), appears to require an increase in GHG emissions which will have severe repercussions for human well-being. It is to this issue we now turn.

Climate change

Whilst we may question the PB for climate change, there is little scientific doubt that climate change can be catastrophic for humanity. Moreover, climate change brings the whole basis of modern society into question. If we meet the pledges made in Paris, we are heading for a 3.2°C world by 2100, when some people alive today will be alive then. We need to justify our actions to them (or ourselves) and not just to future generations. A '3.2°C world' is a term that reflects an average temperature increase, which may vary considerably from one region to the next (including within countries). The specific consequences for crop yields, fish stocks, water availability, the loss of livelihoods, food insecurity, the spread of diseases, migration, displacement, possible violent conflicts and the corresponding effects on health (both physical and mental) and social well-being vary considerably (Schellnhuber et al. 2013). Yet, the potential harms give good reasons for climate change mitigation defined by the IPCC as "human intervention to reduce the sources or enhance the *sinks* of greenhouse gases".

Clearly, societies can and do flourish under extreme weather conditions from the polar circle to desert areas. It would be a mistake to see societies as inactive victims of the impacts of climate change. Migration, for example, takes place within a context. For instance, there was no substantial migration from California during the 2011–2017 drought as California was able to deal with the threats it faced. There is a cluster of concepts that stress the ability of societies and the agency of individuals to respond to climate change. In IPCC terms, adaption refers to "the process of adjustment to actual or expected *climate* and its effects. In human systems, adaptation seeks to moderate or avoid harm or exploit beneficial opportunities. In some natural systems, human intervention may facilitate adjustment to expected *climate* and its effects." The idea of coping range refers to "the capacity of systems to accommodate variations in climatic conditions". *Resilience* is defined as "the capacity of social, economic and environmental systems to cope with a hazardous event or trend or disturbance, responding or reorganizing in ways that maintain their essential function, identity and structure, while also maintaining the capacity for *adaptation*, learning and *transformation*" (all quotes IPCC 2014). Such responses to climate change include growing climate smart crops, better water resource management and improved health services.

Each of these definitions are open to criticism (see Pelling 2011), but perhaps the most important criticism is that the definitions imply the maintenance of the status quo. The suggested adjustments are often technological fixes rather than the deep societal transformations which development requires (see e.g. World Bank 2011). It is unclear what exactly the 'capacity to transform' means but it clearly stops short of *requiring* actual transformation. This is not to deny that technology can clearly play a very significant positive role in responding to climate change as is the case with renewable energy, but as Cannon and Müller-Mahn have rightly argued, the emphasis on these concepts has taken the attention away from the vulnerability context in which climate change occurs. In many instances, the stress on adaption and resilience has led to a de-politicization of the debate, with issues related to power side-tracked (Cannon and Müller-Mahn 2010). The capability approach's emphasis on empowerment is potentially radical and so would demand the kind of changes that are ignored by technological fixes. Furthermore, there is the ethical question of who should pay for adaption costs, it is curious that people should put forward the idea microfinance schemes for poor farmers who will be adversely affected by climate change (e.g. Akter 2012). Why should poor farmers who add little in terms of GHG emissions pay for insurance to cover potential damage caused by others? Surely, such costs should be paid for by those who cause or fail to prevent climate change.

We now turn to examine the wicked problem of climate change more precisely by taking the case of India. India is interesting on several accounts. Firstly, it is now the world's third largest GHG emitter causing 6% of global emissions. Secondly, there are more poor people in India than the entire sub-Saharan Africa (Sumner 2012). Failure to improve the Indian population's well-being can also be reasonably rejected. Thirdly, improvements in well-being though measured in capability terms are argued to require rapid growth (Drèze and Sen 2013) necessitating increased GHG emissions. Fourthly, India will be severely hit by climate change not least in terms of droughts, water shortages, flooding, changing monsoon patterns, decreasing crop yields and the potential flooding of its coastal cities not least Mumbai its financial capital. In other words, it is in India's own interests to reduce GHG emissions. Fifthly, reducing vulnerability would seem to require growth (Drèze and Sen 2013). Sixthly, it is estimated that India will have the world's largest population by 2020, and that population will make demands on the environment. Furthermore, it is not clear that Indians will be satisfied if and when their basic needs are met. They will want to share prosperity and would reject an argument saying that they cannot do so because of climate change.

The United Nations Framework Convention on Climate Change (UNFCCC) was introduced at the Rio Earth Summit in 1992 and ratified in 1994 (it now has 195 signatories). Its main aim is "to stabilize greenhouse gas concentrations at a level that would prevent dangerous anthropogenic (human induced) interference with the climate system" (United Nations Framework Convention on Climate Change, Article 2 1992). The main principle within international environmental law relating to climate change is that of Common but Differentiated Responsibility (CBDR), which states:

> In view of the different contributions to global environmental degradation, States have common but differentiated responsibilities. The developed countries acknowledge the responsibility that they bear in the international pursuit of sustainable development in view of the pressures their societies place on the global environment and of the technologies and financial resources they command.

The concept of common responsibility relates to resources, such as the climate, that are not under the control of one state but are, in legal terms, of common interest. In this case, there is a commitment to equality in terms of the common use of the resource, i.e. developing countries have the right to use the climate in the same way as developed countries. Differentiated responsibility concerns the situation of developing countries, which should be allowed to develop and have different socio- and economic capabilities (understood in terms of income rather than Sen's freedom to do and be). The UNFCCC distinction between developed and developing countries was based on membership in the Organisation for Economic Co-operation and Development, with developed countries and countries in transition being referred to respectively as Annex I and II countries. Developing countries, which (still) include India and China, are referred to as non-Annex countries. It is important to note that the CBDR principle was brought into the UNFCCC in 1992 *before* the IPCC asserted that climate change is already present (2007). At the time, it was assumed that there was still room for emissions that would not cause loss and damage. As climate change is with us, this is no longer the case.

Most of the philosophical debate concerning the ethics of climate change has followed the line that the developed countries have the greatest ethical responsibility for climate change as, historically, their emissions have been the highest (see Caney 2009; Caney 2010; Gardiner 2006; Gardiner 2004; Scruton 2012; Moellendorf 2013). It is also the thinking that lies behind the arguments of many NGOs and the case brought by Dutch Urgenda foundation2 and 886 individual citizens against the Dutch government (Cox 2014).

By placing responsibility at country level, a number of ethical issues are put on hold. Firstly, individual people might claim that they should not take responsibility for climate change when they did not know of the consequences or were extremely sceptical of the climate scientists' pronouncements. Secondly, the assumption is that the polluters are able to pay; the fact that many of them, in terms of historical emissions, are dead and hence unable to pay raises the question of whether present generations should pay for the actions of past generations (and future generations for us). Thirdly, countries take responsibility for their area of jurisdiction in 1992, even if they did not have the same borders – and the same polluters – as they did previously (especially if one considers the substantial number of border changes since the start of the industrial revolution). For example, Germany took responsibility for East German GHG emissions prior to reunification in 1990. Arguably, former West Germans could claim that they should not be responsible for the pollution cause by former East Germans. Fourthly, countries acknowledged that they were aware of the possibility of dangerous climate change in 1992, at a time when *prevention* was still possible and there were no claims that climate change was already with us. Hence, even if present generations are only responsible for the GHG emissions they cause, they also have the ethical responsibility to prevent harms when they have the power to do so (Scanlon 1998; Moellendorf 2013). Given the UNFCCC framework it would appear that India has the right to develop and not pay for the consequences of climate change.

India has offered three lines of argument against taking more responsibility for its carbon emissions (Dröge and Wagner 2015). These should be considered as possible grounds for reasonably rejecting a principle that would require India to do so. The first maintains that while the nation's emissions are high, their historical emissions are low. The second is that its per capita emissions are low. The third is that growth is needed to reduce poverty and growth implies increased emissions.

Regarding the first argument, recent work suggests that in historical terms, developed countries have accounted for 52% of CO_2 emissions and developing countries for 48%; it is expected that developing countries' emissions will be greater than those of developed countries by 2020, i.e. in six years' time (den Elzen et al. 2013). China and India play major roles in this shift, with China's CO_2 emissions now being the largest in the world and India's being the fourth (following those of the USA and the EU 27). Historically, India has accounted for 4.1% of emissions, which is larger than many developed countries including Japan, Canada and Australia. Even in terms of per capita emissions, China's emissions are now on a par with the EU 27, although those in India remain much lower. Developing countries' emissions are now so great that even if developed countries' emissions were immediately cut to zero, India would still need to reduce its emissions in order for global emissions to meet the IPCC's demands (Raghunandan 2012). The changes in emissions discussed suggest a new scenario in terms of responsibility, as there is an emergence of a middle group of developing countries (namely China, India, Brazil and Indonesia) that are becoming major emitters.

Concerning the second, the per capita allocation principle is that there should be "equal access to the atmosphere for all individuals in the world" (Thaker and Leiserowitz 2014, 3) and hence no discrimination. The per capita argument claims that all individuals have the same rights to or restrictions on emissions. As India's per capita CO_2 emissions are on the same level as those of Gabon, it is not automatically clear why an individual Indian should face restrictions that a Gabonese individual does not.

Equality of emissions arguments can be reasonably rejected. The equality of per capita argument is problematic, as Caney (2012) rightly argues different people need different emissions to have the same levels of well-being. For example, we have different heating requirements depending on where we live. The argument fits in well with the capability approach, and from this perspective we should be more interested in capability equality and then work back to emission requirements. A related point concerns what alternatives are available, living in Iceland may be just as cold as living in some parts of Greenland but if geothermal power is available in Iceland and not in Greenland, there is no reason why Icelanders should have equality of emissions.

Furthermore, one might argue that discussions about per capita emissions are only advanced at country level for practical reasons relating to international negotiations (Margalioth and Rudich 2013). There is no reason why we should not examine CO_2 emission inequalities within countries, too. These inequalities are quite strong in India. In 1993, the top 10% of the country's urban population were responsible for 3,416 kg per capita per annum, while the bottom 10% were responsible for 141 kg. More recent data suggest that agricultural workers' emissions are approximately half of those of the urban elite, which reflects the consumption of lifestyle goods (Michael and Vakulabharanam 2015). Taking India as a whole hides these disparities.

Moreover, the per capita argument suggests that India's emissions can continue to grow as long as India's population expands at a sufficient rate. Current projections show that India's population will be the largest in the world by 2050; this is highly problematic, as according to the United Nations Environment Programme, the world needs to be carbon neutral by 2070 (United Nations Environment Programme 2014).

An attempt to justify potential harms relates to the third argument, namely that emission increases are needed in order to eradicate poverty. Shue (1993) in particular has argued that emissions should be sufficient to meet basic needs, defined as $1 a day (the arguments could be updated to $1.9 a day in line with the World Bank's redefinition of absolute poverty). India has been making a similar argument since the early 1990s (Thaker and Leiserowitz 2014). More recently, whilst Prime Minister Modi has announced his intention to emphasize renewable energy in relation to the provision of electricity to the poor, the Minister of the Environment, Prakash Javadekar, has stated that India will increase its CO_2 emissions, not least from coal. Amongst other things, he has noted that "India's first task is eradication of poverty" and "Twenty percent of our population doesn't have access to electricity, and that's our top priority. We will grow faster, and our emissions will rise" (quoted in *The New York Times*, Sept. 24, 2014). Clearly India has limited intent to make the reductions that are necessary in order to avoid dangerous climate change (Thaker and Leiserowitz 2014).

Drèze and Sen (2013) also use the capability deprivations of poor Indians as the basis for stating that rapid economic growth is required in India even if we do not have solutions concerning its environmental consequences. However, based on their own evidence it is questionable that providing essential capabilities such as health and education will necessitate rapid economic growth. In fact, in questioning India's current success these authors compare India's failures with the relative success of Bangladesh, despite India's lower rates of growth.

> Although India's per capita income is twice that of Bangladesh, during the 20 year period despite India's higher growth rate Bangladesh has *overtaken* India in terms of a wide range of basic social indicators, including life expectancy, child survival, enhanced immunization rates, reduced fertility rates, and even some (not all) schooling indicators.
>
> *(Drèze and Sen 2013, 54)*

Indeed, Drèze and Sen maintain that every South Asian country with the exception of Pakistan is doing better on many social indicators despite India having the highest growth rates of them all. If this is correct, then high rates of growth are not necessary to reduce basic capability deprivations.

Furthermore, vast increases in CO_2 emissions are not needed to supply electricity to the 400 million Indians who are currently without it. Pachauri (2014) calculates that 234 million tons of additional emissions have resulted from both the direct and indirect electricity use of more than 650 million Indians who connected during the period 1981–2011. This is the equivalent to 3% to 4% of India's growth in emissions over the same period (for a wider range of countries, Rao et al. (2014) reach the conclusion that basic needs can be met without large increases in emissions).

There is also an underlying, but false, understanding that the causes of poverty lie in the lack of economic growth rather than in socio-cultural and political factors. Fieldwork carried out in Gujarat by Aubron et al. (2015) highlights the problem. Whilst the state has high growth rates including the agricultural sector they found that the main determinants of poverty to be land and water ownership and dependency relationships. Findings that are reminiscent of the work undertaken by Wood (2003) in Bihar, which shows how dependency relationships lead to the poor discounting the future to ensure their present security. As Aubron, Lehoux and Lucas (2015) conclude, the hope that economic growth will trickle down and reduce poverty is 'highly unrealistic'. Thus the charge made by the Alliance of Small Island States that India (or more correctly, the Indian government) is 'hiding behind poverty' whilst the SIDS drown (Thaker and Leiserowitz 2014) seems substantiated, and a principle allowing high growth rates that lead to large-scale GHG emissions can be reasonably rejected by members of the alliance.

As stated earlier, those working on sustainability within the capability approach are deeply interested in the responsibilities people have related to their doings and beings. In the climate change debate this relates to issues of loss and damage. Again, the main debate has claimed that Annex I countries should pay for the loss and damage resulting from their emissions. There are three major problems with this line of argument. Firstly, developing countries historical emissions will soon overtake the historical emissions of Annex I countries. Secondly, some emissions have regional impacts. For example, the Asian Brown Cloud which affects glacial melt in the Himalayas is primarily the result of Chinese and Indian emissions (Gustafsson et al. 2009) and thus it is unclear why Annex I countries should pay for the related damages. Thirdly, there are no pure climate change disasters – this is also implied by the adaption literature – 40 years of disaster risk reduction literature, including Drèze and Sen's work on famines, has argued that there are two sets of factors contributing to disasters, namely the hazard and the society in which the disaster takes place (Hewitt 2012; Pelling 2011; Wisner et al. 2004). As Sen has repeatedly claimed, famines are relatively easy to stop (e.g. Sen 1999). This being so there are two sets of responsibility for climate change loss and damage, namely those who contribute to the hazard and those related to creating the vulnerability in which the disaster takes place. The matter is complex, but India, too, should take its responsibility here (Crabtree 2016).

Conclusion

Surprisingly, almost half a century after the United Nations Conference on the Human Environment in Stockholm (1972), work within the capability approach on sustainability is still in its infancy. The leading proponents of the approach – Amartya Sen and Martha Nussbaum – have had little to say on the matter. I have argued that we ought to conceptualize sustainable development as a process of increasing freedoms that cannot be reasonably rejected. In terms of environmental sustainability, the concept of ecosystems seems most fruitful as it has substantial scientific credibility and can be used on all scales from the very local to the global. Our understanding of the relationship between ecosystems and ecosystem services and disservices is a normative one and involves issues surrounding animal and ecosystem rights. Depending on conversion factors, ecosystems can produce services and disservices in relation to people's freedoms and doings and beings (bees help pollination, but for some people a bee sting can be fatal). Sustainable development is not merely a process of increasing freedoms but may require a reduction of freedoms, the consequences of our doings and beings, including those for future generations, become of uttermost importance as the case of climate change illustrates. In comparison with Sen's version of the capability approach the evaluative space of the legitimate freedom approach is extended to include not just capabilities and functionings but also ecosystems and the consequences of our functionings.

Given climate change, the world is already irreversibly unsustainable, but this does not mean that there is ample room for improvements in well-being as many aspects of well-being are environmentally neutral or positive. Work needs doing on all of these aspects and, not least, finding ways to a better world.

Acknowledgement

I would like to thank two insightful referees and two insightful editors for their thoughtful comments and support.

References

Akter, S. (2012) The Role of Microinsurance as a Safety Net Against Environmental Risks. *Bangladesh Journal of Environment and Development* 21(2): 263–280.

Anand, S. and Sen, A. (2000) Human Development and Economic Sustainability. *World Development* 28(12): 2029–2049.

Andersen J, and Bilfeldt, A. (2016) Action Research in Nursing Homes. *Action Research* 14(1): 19–35.

Archer, D. (2009) *The Long Thaw*. Princeton University Press, Princeton, NJ.

Assessment, M.E. (2005) *Ecosystems and Human Well-being: Wetlands and Water*. World Resources Institute, Washington, DC.

Aubron, C., Lehoux, H. and Lucas, C. (2015) Poverty and Inequality in Rural India. Reflections based on Two Agrarian System Analyses in the State of Gujarat. *EchoGéo 32*.

Barry, B. (1995) *Justice as Impartiality*. Clarendon Press, Oxford.

Bass, S. (2009) Planetary Boundaries: Keep Off the Grass. *Nature Reports Climate Change* 3(0910): 113–114.

Brand, F. (2009) Critical Natural Capital Revisited: Ecological Resilience and Sustainable Development. *Ecological Economics* 68(3): 605–612.

Brook, B.W., Ellis, E.C., Perring, M.P., Mackay, A.W. and Blomqvist, L. (2013) Does the Terrestrial Biosphere have Planetary Tipping Points? *Trends in Ecology & Evolution* 28(7): 396–401.

Brewer, P. (2009) Planetary Boundaries: Consider all Consequences. *Nature Reports Climate Change* 3(0910): 117–118.

Caney, S. (2009) Justice and the Distribution of Greenhouse Gas Emissions. *Journal of Global Ethics* 5(2) 125–146.

Caney, S. (2010) Climate Change, Human Rights, and Moral Thresholds. In Gardiner, S., Caney, S., Jamieson, D. and Shue, H. eds., *Climate Ethics: Essential Readings*. Oxford University Press, Oxford, 163–177.

Caney, S. (2012) Just Emissions. *Philosophy and Public Affairs* 40(4): 255–300.

Cannon, T. and Müller-Mahn, D. (2010) Vulnerability, Resilience and Development Discourses in Context of Climate Change. *Natural Hazards* 55: 621.

Costanza, R., D'Arge, R., De Groot, R., Farber, S., Grasso, M., Hannon, B. and Van den Belt, M. (1997) The Value of the World's Ecosystem Services and Natural Capital. *Nature* 387(6630): 253–260.

Cox, R. (2014) The Liability of European States for Climate Change. *Utrecht Journal of International and European Law* 30(78): 125–135.

Crabtree, A. (2010) Sustainable Development, Capabilities and the Missing Case of Mental Health. In Nielsen, K.A., Elling, B., Figueroa, M. and Jelsoe, E. eds., *A New Agenda for Sustainability*. Ashgate, Aldershot 159–176.

Crabtree, A. (2012) A Legitimate Freedom Approach to Sustainability: Sen, Scanlon and the Inadequacy of the Human Development Index. *International Journal of Social Quality* 2(1): 24–40.

Crabtree, A. (2013) Sustainable Development: Does the Capability Approach Have Anything to Offer? Outlining a Legitimate Freedom Approach. *Journal of Human Development and Capabilities* 14: 40–57.

Crabtree, A. (2016) *Sustainability and Unsustainability*. Roskilde University, Roskilde.

Den Elzen, M.G.J., Olivier, J.G.J., Höhne, N. and Janssens-Maenhout, G. (2013) Countries' Contributions to Climate Change: Effect of Accounting for All Greenhouse Gases, Recent Trends, Basic Needs and Technological Progress. *Climatic Change* 121(2): 397–412.

Drèze, J. and Sen, A. (2013) *An Uncertain Glory: The Contradictions of Modern India*. Allen Lane, London.

Dröge, S. and Wagner, C. (2015) India's Position in International Climate Negotiations. *Stiftung Wissenschaft und Politik*. www.swp-berlin.org/fileadmin/contents/products/comments/2015C14_dge_wgn.pdf. Accessed 23 September 2016.

Ekins, P. (2003) Identifying Critical Natural Capital: Conclusions about Critical Natural Capital. *Ecological Economics* 44(2–3): 277–292.

Fitoussi, J. and Malik, K. (2013) *Choices, Capabilities and Sustainability*. http://hdr.undp.org/sites/default/files/hdro_malik_fitoussi.pdf. Accessed 23 January 2018.

Forst, R. (2002) *Contexts of Justice*. University of California Press, Berkeley.

Forst, R. (2007) *The Right to Justification*. Columbia University Press, New York, NY.

Gardiner, S. (2004) Ethics and Global Climate Change. *Ethics* 114(April): 555–600.

Gardiner, S.M. (2006) A Perfect Moral Storm: Climate Change, Intergenerational Ethics and the Problem of Moral Corruption. *Environmental Values* 15(3): 397–413.

Goodland, R. (1995) The Concept of Environmental Sustainability. *Annual Review of Ecology and Systematics* 26(1): 1–24.

Goodland, R. and Daly, H. (1996) Environmental Sustainability: Universal and Non-Negotiable. *Ecological Applications* 6(4): 1002–1017.

Gustafsson, O., Kruså, M., Zencak, Z., Sheesley, R.J., Granat, L. Engström, E. Rodhe, H. (2009) Brown Clouds over South Asia: Biomass or Fossil Fuel Combustion? *Science* 323(5913): 495–498.

Hewitt, K. (2012) Environmental Disasters in Social Context: Toward a Preventive And Precautionary Approach. *Natural Hazards* 66(1): 3–14.

Holland, B. (2008) Ecology and the Limits of Justice: Establishing Capability Ceilings in Nussbaum's Capabilities Approach. *Journal of Human Development* 9(3): 401–425.

Intergovernmental Panel on Climate Change (2014) *Climate Change 2014 Synthesis Report Approved Summary for Policymakers*. www.ipcc.ch/pdf/assessmentreport/ar5/syr/SYR_AR5_SPMcorr2.pdf. Accessed 2 January 2016.

Khader, S. and Kosko, S. (2018) "Reason to Value," Perfectionism, and the Process Aspect of Freedom. In Keleher, L. and Kosko, S. eds., *Agency, Democracy, and Participation in Global Development*. Cambridge University Press, Cambridge.

Keleher, L. (2014) Sen and Nussbaum: Agency and Capability-Expansion. *Ethics and Economics* 11(2): 2014.

Kleijn, D., Winfree, R., Bartomeus, I., Carvalheiro, L.G., Henry, M., Isaacs, R., . . . and Ricketts, T.H. (2015) Delivery of Crop Pollination Services Is an Insufficient Argument for Wild Pollinator Conservation. *Nature Communications* 6.

Lessmann, O. (2011) Sustainability as a Challenge to the Capability Approach. In Lessmann, O., Omann, I., Frühmann, J. and Rauschmayer, F. eds., *Sustainable Development, Capabilities, Needs, and Well-being*. Routledge, London.

Margalioth, Y. and Rudich, Y. (2013) Close Examination of the Principle of Global Per-Capita Allocation of the Earth's Ability to Absorb Greenhouse Gas. *Theoretical Inquiries in Law* 14(1): 191–206.

Michael, K. and Vakulabharanam, V. (2015) Class and Climate Change in Post-Reform India. *Climate and Development*, 1–10.

Millennium Ecosystem Assessment (2005) *Ecosystems and Human Well-being: Synthesis*. Island Press, Washington, DC.

Moellendorf, D. (2013) *The Moral Challenge of Dangerous Climate Change*. Cambridge University Press, Cambridge.

The New York Times, Sept. 24, 2014 Indian Emissions Will Rise, Official Says

Nussbaum, M. (2003) Capabilities as Fundamental Entitlements: Sen and Social Justice. *Feminist Economics* 9(2–3): 33–59.

Pachauri, S. (2014) Household Electricity Access a Trivial Contributor to Co2 Emissions Growth in India. *Nature Climate Change* 4(12): 1073–1076.

Parfit, D. (2011) *On What Matters, Volumes 1 and 2*. Oxford University Press, Oxford.

Pelenc, J. and Ballet, J. (2015) Strong Sustainability, Critical Natural Capital and the Capability Approach. *Ecological Economics* 112: 36–44.

Pelling, M. (2011) *Adaptation to Climate Change*. Routledge, London.

Raghunandan, D. (2012) India's Climate Policy: Squaring the Circle. *IDS Bulletin* 43(s1): 122–129.

Rao, N.D., Riahi, K. and Grubler, A. (2014) Climate Impacts of Poverty Eradication. *Nature Climate Change* 4(9): 749–751.

Robeyns, I. (2005) The Capability Approach: A Theoretical Survey. *Journal of Human Development* 6(1) 93–117.

Rockström, J. and Noone, K. (2009) Planetary Boundaries: Exploring the Safe Operating Space for Humanity. *Ecology and Society* 14(2).

Rockström, J., Steffen, W., Noone, K., Persson, A., Chapin, F.S., Lambin, E.F. and Foley, J.A. (2009) A Safe Operating Space for Humanity. *Nature* 461: 472–475.

Scanlon, T.M. (1998) *What We Owe to Each Other*. Harvard University Press, Cambridge, MA.

Schellnhuber, H.J., Hare, W., Serdeczny, O., Adams, S., Coumou, D. and Frieler, K. (2013) *Turn Down the Heat: Why a 4 C Warmer World Must Be Avoided*. IBRD, World Bank, Washington, DC.

Schröter, M., Zanden, E.H., Oudenhoven, A.P., Remme, R.P., Serna-Chavez, H.M., Groot, R.S. and Opdam, P. (2014) Ecosystem Services as a Contested Concept: A Synthesis of Critique and Counter-Arguments. *Conservation Letters* 7(6): 514–523.

Schultz, E., Christen, M., Voget-Kleschin, L. and Burger, P. (2013) A Sustainability-Fitting Interpretation of the Capability Approach: Integrating the Natural Dimension by Employing Feedback Loops. *Journal of Human Development and Capabilities* 14(1): 115–133.

Scruton, R. (2012) *Green Philosophy*. Atlantic Books, London.

Secretariat of the Convention on Biological Diversity (2010) *Global Biodiversity Outlook 3*. Montréal. www.cbd.int/gbo3/. Accessed 15 November 2016.

Sen, A. (1999) *Development as Freedom*. Oxford University Press, London.

Sen, A. (2009) *The Idea of Justice*. Allen Lane, London.

Shue, H. (1993) Subsistence Emissions and Luxury Emissions. *Law & Policy* 15(1): 39–60.

Steffen, W., Richardson, K., Rockström, J., Cornell, S.E., Fetzer, I., Bennett, E.M., . . . and Folke, C. (2015) Planetary Boundaries: Guiding Human Development on a Changing Planet. *Science* 347(6223): 1259855.

Stiglitz, J.E., Sen, A. and Fitoussi, J.-P. (2009) *Report by the Commission on the Measurement of Economic Performance and Social Progress*. http://graphics8.nytimes.com/packages/pdf/business/Stiglitzreport.pdf. Accessed 12 November 2016.

Sumner, A. (2012) Where Do The Poor Live? *World Development* 40: 865–877.

Thaker, J. and Leiserowitz, A. (2014) Shifting Discourses of Climate Change in India. *Climatic Change* 123(January): 107–119.

UNEP (2014) *The Emissions Gap Report 2014*. United Nations Environment Programme (UNEP), Nairobi.

United Nations (1992) United Nations Framework Convention on Climate Change. https://unfccc.int/files/essential_background/background_publications_htmlpdf/application/pdf/conveng.pdf. Accessed 1 November 2017.

Watene, K. (2016) *Valuing Nature: Māori Philosophy and the Capability Approach*. Oxford Development Studies 44(3): 287–296.

Wisner, B., Blaikie, P., Cannon, T. and Davis, I. (2004) *At Risk: Natural Hazards, People's Vulnerability and Disasters*. Routledge, London.

Wood, G. (2003) Staying Secure, Staying Poor: The Faustian Bargain. *World Development* 31(3): 455–471.

World Bank (2011) *The Changing Wealth of Nations: Measuring Sustainable Development in the New Millennium*. http://siteresources.worldbank.org/ENVIRONMENT/Resources/ChangingWealthNations.pdf. Accessed 15 September 2012.

World Commission on Environment and Development (1987) *Our Common Future* 42/187: 8–9. www.un.org/documents/ga/res/42/ares42-187.htm. Accessed 7 March 2015.

21

Food production

Food security and agricultural development

Paul B. Thompson

Food is an ethical thicket. Recent work by philosophers has recognized moral arguments for vegetarianism, and virtually everyone acknowledges moral reasons to address hunger through shelters, food banks and other relief efforts. At the same time, new issues of fairness to workers in the food system, environmental impacts of agriculture and responsibility for rising rates of obesity and attendant health issues are being recognized (Thompson 2015a). This chapter provides an introductory discussion of food issues that is tuned to the global orientation of development ethics. A brief overview of global food ethics is followed by a discussion of how early philosophical work on food security is connected to food production. As reflected by its title, the chapter emphasizes *production* over equally important problems in the consumption of food, not the least of which is the rapid rise of Western-style supermarkets (Reardon and co-authors 2003) and the attendant growth of dietary disease among citizens of less industrially developed nations (Patel 2008). The third section of the chapter discusses agricultural development within development theory, followed by a section on Green Revolution approaches to food system development between 1960 and 2000. The final section is a forward-looking discussion of present day dilemmas in food production, especially in countries that continue to have more than 20% of their population whose livelihood depends on farming, animal husbandry, fishing or other forms of harvesting food resources.

Global food ethics

Though too infrequently a topic of ethical reflection, food is both fundamental and central to the human condition. It is fundamental because human beings must eat in order to live, and also because the distinctive metabolism of *homo sapiens* is crucial to the species ability to survive in and adapt to a wide variety of terrestrial ecosystems. In contrast to many animals, humans can consume a wide variety of different plants and animals allowing them to adapt their diet to different ecosystems. Furthermore, while most vertebrates succumb to disabling weakness after even a few days of food deprivation, humans can subsist on water alone (supplemented only with key minerals) for months and have endured periods of energy deficit (expending more energy than consumed) that extend over years. This adaptive flexibility notwithstanding, even relatively brief periods of food deprivation stimulate psychological distress, often leading to

DOI: 10.4324/9781315626796-26

social disruption, (Russell 2006). As a result, *food security* has been a key focus of national, international and non-governmental agencies undertaking programs of development (see Masters and coauthors 2013; Naylor 2014).

Humans' biological endowment has also allowed the human species to develop a wide variety of cultural forms keyed to the availability of radically different food sources within any given environment. Each culture exhibits distinct methods for *acquiring* nutrients from the natural environment, for *processing* plant and animal matter to suit storage, transport and preparation, for *distributing* edible products through a population, and for *consuming* food. Practices of acquisition may be structured around scavenging un-managed ecosystems (e.g. hunting, gathering and fishing), settled cultivation (e.g. farming) or herding animals across several distinct ecotones (e.g. pastoralism), each leading to a corresponding form of social organization. Consumption occurs in different institutional sites – the kitchen, the campfire, the table, the dining hall, the commercial food establishment – and reflects distinct foodways (e.g. recipes and cuisines, as well as food-related events and cultural practices). Attachment to and maintenance of foodways can be an important source of the values that drive alternative conceptions of appropriate or inappropriate social change (Harris 1987). It is through its role in the formation of these diverse and distinctive forms that food becomes central to human culture.

The tension between food security and other developmental goals associated with food systems undergirds many of the ethical issues involved in directed or policy-guided change in the production, distribution and consumption of food. Food security is a function of an individual or group's justified confidence in their ability to gain access for adequate supplies of food over the foreseeable future. There are a number of social, economic and environmental contingencies implied by this concept, including culturally based notions of what is and is not food, what constitutes appropriate patterns and venues for food consumption and an array of capabilities for finding, acquiring and securing access in a predictable manner. These contingencies imply that the comprehensive definition for food security is highly general, and that institutions and practices assuring secure food access in one situation may not be appropriate in another (Naylor 2014).

Nevertheless, development agencies have assigned a high priority to ensuring that minimal nutrient needs are met, especially for children who are susceptible to diseases of malnutrition and who may suffer lifelong health effects as a result of food deprivation. The ethical rationale for this prioritization will not be contested in this chapter, yet the emphasis on nutrition gives rise to situations in which nutritional needs might be satisfied through means that are not compatible with cultural foodways, that place recipients of food aid in positions of dependency and that undermine the viability of production systems that may have been contributing a significant (but perhaps inadequate) portion of the nutritional needs to a given population prior to the initiation of a development program or policy (Schanbacher 2010). The development ethics of food requires inquiry and elaboration into the ethical underpinnings of food security as well as a discussion of the many ways in which development specialists have attempted to address the tension between alleviation of hunger, on the one hand, and the broader cultural dimensions of food systems, on the other. In this chapter, however, these issues are de-emphasized in comparison to those that arise in connection with food production.

Famine ethics and food security

Philosophical work on food and development has tended be overly preoccupied with the problem of famines, on the one hand, or to presume that issues of global poverty subsume the ethical issues in food production, on the other. Peter Singer's 1972 article "Famine, Affluence and Morality," marks a heightening of awareness among philosophers about the ethical imperatives of development in general, and food deprivation in particular. Singer wrote at time when population ecologists, notably Garrett Hardin (1968) and Paul Ehrlich (1968), were predicting an uptick in food shortages associated with unrestrained growth in human population at the global scale. Recent famines in Northern Africa and East Bengal (Now Bangladesh) were presumed by many to have been indicated by these predictions. Singer's article produced an argument for coming to the aid of famine victims that has been subjected to several bouts of comment and analysis, arguably becoming a mainstay in the literature of development ethics. This literature exhibits a strong emphasis on obligations to give aid and devotes virtually no attention to the circumstances giving rise to famine or to the consequences that might follow from the various types of aid that might be given.

Importantly, Singer's analysis seemed to accept the population ecologists' claim that hunger was caused by food deficits, that is by a lack of available food, at least on a local basis. This lent support to an implicit assumption (not argued or explicitly endorsed by Singer) that the obligation at issue was for wealthy people to ensure that food is made available to the victims of famine. This obligation itself had a half-century history in the creation of food aid programming targeted initially to Europeans whose food system had been disrupted by World War I and World War II, and extended to less industrially developed countries with the creation of the U.S. "Food for Peace" program in 1954 (Veit 2013). Whether intended or not, many of Singer's readers assumed that food aid – assistance in the form of gifts of food – was what the victims of famine needed, and the specific target of the general obligation that Singer's argument was intended to defend.

Amartya Sen's 1981 book *Poverty and Famines: An Essay on Entitlement and Deprivation* had a transformative effect on the philosophical debate over hunger. Sen's analysis of African and Bengal famines showed that food had been available in both cases. In the African case, deficits due to crop failures could have been alleviated from supplies available on a regional basis, while in East Bengal food was literally available within the shops while people starved due to their inability to buy it. The East Bengal famine had been caused by a collapse of what Sen called an *income entitlement*: rapid inflation had undercut the buying power of local currency, placing poor people who depended on purchasing their food in a situation where their income was insufficient for doing so (Sen 1981). As I have argued elsewhere, subtler ethical lessons might have been drawn from Sen's study, but the message that many drew from it was that hunger is not a problem of food production, it is a problem of inadequate distribution (Thompson 2015b). The upshot is that (with a few important exceptions) food production has not been a focus of work in development ethics for some time: ethicists have presumed that food security could be subsumed under a more general rubric of poverty and deprivation.

This presumption neglects some important facts. First and foremost, many nations that rank low on the various scales of development have a high percentage of their population engaged in fishing, farming or some other form of food production. Development programming that fails to reach people engaged in such livelihoods is unlikely to achieve its objectives. More generally, estimates state that at least 50% and as much as 80% of those living in extreme poverty (less than one Euro per day) are engaged in some aspect of food production. Even if poverty (rather than food) is the focus of moral significance, food production and its role in livelihood will be critical for the majority of the world's poorest people. Finally, food really does matter for reasons stated at the beginning of this chapter. Yet there are forms of development that address the food needs of urban populations at the expense of the more numerous (and equally needy) food producers residing in less visible rural areas. As such, Denis Goulet's question – what *kinds* of development are ethically justified? – really cannot avoid food production, to the contrary of the "it's not production but distribution" nostrum.

Agricultural development

Today food production systems are acknowledged as important elements in development theory. Work on inland and coastal fisheries led to Elinor Ostrom's well-known work on institutions for governance of common pool resources, for example. However, early approaches to development often emphasized heavy industry and urban infrastructure on the assumption that investments manufacturing and services would promote rapid economic growth. The 1960s and 1970s saw a number of theoretical innovations that elevated the importance of agriculture within development thinking. These innovations include both technical economic arguments and ethically based claims. The arguments were bolstered by empirical data drawn from the Rockefeller Foundation's work on new seeds and management techniques that would help crop farmers and livestock managers increase the monetary return on the labor that they expend in food production.

On the technical side, John Mellor demonstrated that efforts to increase the productivity of farming and animal husbandry would have complex and beneficial implications for other sectors of a developing country's economy. Rather than attracting people *into* these trades, increased agricultural productivity would actually shrink the agricultural sector in comparison to other sectors of the economy. This was because with higher yields a smaller number of production units could meet the local demand for food, and because increased yields would lower the price of food. Lower food prices give people the flexibility to shift a portion of their budget to non-food consumption. This stimulates demand for non-food goods, in turn creating opportunities for investment beyond the food sector. Increased agricultural productivity thus has the dual effect of releasing people from agriculture for employment in other sectors, while boosting the opportunities for growth in other sectors of the economy (Mellor 1966). Mellor's work showed economists who were aiming to increase activity in manufacturing and services that investments in agriculture would abet this process.

Other arguments stressed points already noted earlier in this chapter: Agriculture is where the poor people actually are. If one hopes to stimulate economic or cultural growth, one should target the sectors of the population where development activities can actually reach the largest number of people, or where there is the greatest need. For many countries, a focus on food production serves both of these ends. Although rapid urbanization is changing development priorities in the 21st century, during this early era of development the vast majority of people in the countries that were the focus of 1960s and 1970s era development theory lived in rural areas and were engaged in some form of food production. Programs to improve their knowledge and skills, on the one hand, or their technology, on the other, would most faithfully implement the goals of "bottom-up" or people-centered development (Lappé et al. 1977; Cernea 1985). This combination of technical and moral argument has established a firm commitment to agricultural development within development theory and practice.

Yet the question remains, what *kind* of agricultural development? Here debates over the legacy of Rockefeller Foundation efforts rage. The agricultural development programs of the 1950s, 1960s and 1970s placed primary emphasis on genetic improvement of the plants and animals being used in food production. Within fisheries, technical means for increasing the "catch" were stressed. These efforts were called "the Green Revolution" in a 1968 speech delivered by William Gaud, the administrator of the U.S. Agency for International Development (USAID). Gaud's point was that efforts to help poor people were an effective means to combat the "red" revolutions being promulgated by socialists (Gaud 1968). Yet the Green Revolution has accumulated an impressive list of critics.

Critics of the green revolution

Work within development economics has long noted that while increasing yields through improved plant varieties and animal breeds did indeed stimulate growth as Mellor had argued, it also created new problems. Here, a few of those problems are summarized. First and foremost, new varieties encouraged monoculture – the emphasis upon a single crop. Prior to the Green Revolution food producers had typically distributed their efforts across a wide variety of plant and animal species available in their environment. Cultivated crops would be supplemented with products harvested from animals, trees and weedy species that required relatively little day-to-day management. The improved varieties introduced by development projects offered considerably greater opportunity for monetary gain, but they also required greater management and in many cases literally crowded other food sources out as land under cultivation was expanded to maximize economic return.

This had the further effect of making food producers more dependent on the sale of their crops for their own subsistence. Even today, producers in countries with a high percentage of their population involved in agriculture or fishing continue to produce some portion of what they eat, but as in industrialized agricultural systems, they increasingly depend on purchasing food (as well as other goods) from the monetary return they derive from their "cash crop". There is, in effect, a self-reinforcing feedback that can lock producers into ever increasing reliance on their most salable product. As they increase their effort to produce that product, they decrease efforts in other subsistence activities. This makes them even more dependent on the commodity product, inducing a new round of intensification in that activity and driving their overall effort toward monoculture (Falcon and Gotsch, 1968).

Monocultures reduce biodiversity because producers dedicate more and more of the locally available land and water to production of the commodity product. They may also create dependence on additional technologies that have problematic environmental and social impacts. Here, a focus on dwarf varieties – the work that won Norman Borlaug the Nobel Peace Prize – must be representative of larger critiques. Traditional varieties of wheat or rice do not respond well to fertilization: they just grow taller, which makes them vulnerable to lodging – they fall over when subject to wind or rain, and the edible grain is ruined. Dwarf varieties are literally shorter and put a relatively greater portion of the soil nutrients into the grain. When fertilized, they grow taller but not nearly as tall as a fertilized traditional variety. They thus yield significantly more total grain than traditional varieties, yet will be of no benefit to farmers unless fertilizer is also available. Although it is theoretically possible to obtain fertilizer through activities (such as feeding livestock) that complement crop production, in almost all cases fertilizers for improved varieties have been purchased inputs. This has drawn farmers into debt finance, as they borrow the money for buying fertilizer and repay it after the crop is harvested. In some instances, synthetic fertilizers have also polluted water and depleted soil microorganisms. Monocultures also set the table for devastating invasions of insect and fungal pests, leading to pesticide purchases and further environmental impacts.

Readers wishing to follow this literature of critique should consult Falcon (1970), Cleaver (1972), Griffin, (1974) and Dahlberg (1979) from the reference list. A careful assessment and partial defense of the Green Revolution was conducted by Michael Lipton and Longhurst (1989). Philosophers are almost certainly most familiar with criticism of the Green Revolution through the work of Vandana Shiva. Shiva's 1989 book *Staying Alive: Women Ecology and Development* resituated critiques of the Green Revolution within the literature of feminism and postcolonial scholarship. Shiva noticed facts that were known to previous critics of agricultural development, but that were not recognized to have significance: a majority of farmers in the developing world are women from racially oppressed groups. However, Shiva's failure to acknowledge the earlier body of criticism limits uptake of the feminist critique within development studies. Shiva has been perceived as at best rehearsing well-known problems in ignorance of the way that current theory and practice have already been reformed in response to criticisms, then reframing them in highly romantic terms (Shome 2015). At worst she is portrayed as a self-aggrandizing publicity seeker who has concealed her indebtedness to mainstream critics of agricultural development while making claims about present-day development efforts that are not supported by the facts (Spector 2014). Work by Bina Agarwal connects the poverty of women farmers to structural factors such as laws governing the ownership and heritability of land or access to credit, as well as informally enforced ways that men enjoy privileged positions in rural society (Agarwal 2001; Panda and Agarwal 2005). The linkages proposed by Shiva and demonstrated by Agarwal permit a richer articulation of the ethical critiques leveled against Green Revolution-style development in the 1970s.

Looking ahead

One might summarize the current debate over food production in countries that receive development assistance as a contest between those who continue to advocate Western-style production systems and those who advocate on behalf of peasant systems that still dominate in many parts of the world. Jeffery Sachs (2005, 137) and Paul Collier (2008) recommend the former view while Shiva may be the best known advocate of the latter. But there are more nuanced visions that reside in between these extremes. "Sustainable intensification" is a buzzword conveying the idea that social and ecological disruptions associated with the industrialization of agriculture are no longer acceptable, yet there is still a need to transform production practices of small scale farmers, especially among the poor (Pretty 1997; Garnett and coauthors 2013). Sustainable intensification has been acknowledged to require explicit attention to ethics (Stannard 2008). The complex interweaving of ethical imperatives – to minimize harm to health, to maintain fertility and productivity, to respect the rights of poor people who are food producers – combine to make sustainable intensification into a social as well as a technical challenge for technological interventions.

Theorists of agricultural development have also attempted to develop a more nuanced approach by emphasizing the "food-water-energy nexus." This line of thinking has challenged the assumption that attempts to transform food production should follow the Green Revolution model by incorporating recent work on the impact of developed world production into development theory (Cuéllar and coauthors 2014). At the same time, it emphasizes the fact that all forms of agricultural production depend on the availability of water, and that intensification of any kind (not to mention modernization of food distribution) requires energy (Burney 2014). What is more, this nexus of interlocking resources is now being dramatically affected by climate change, creating new sources of vulnerability for small-scale food producers in less developed economies (Lobell et al. 2014).

Yet while sustainable intensification and the nexus approach are frameworks that challenge the thinking behind mainstream Green Revolution thinking, they nevertheless reflect science-driven perspectives. They are forward-looking visions of change in food production that emanate from the CGIAR (an international consortium of research centers), FAO and elite U.S. and European universities. "Food sovereignty" is an alternative that has been promoted especially by Via Campesina, a coalition representing local peasant-based social movements. Food sovereignty is a somewhat flexible concept that has been adapted to support individuals and groups who oppose the control that corporations, governments and international organizations (such as the

World Bank or the International Monetary Fund) currently exert over the global food system. Via Campesina argues that control over *which* crops or livestock to produce and how food is produced and distributed should be maintained as close to the site of production as possible (Rosset 2008).

Food sovereignty can be understood as a challenge to the claim that food security is the leading ethical priority in developing country food systems. In an era of market-based policy, one politically acceptable approach to food security is to maintain prices that remain within the limited budgets of poor people. However, small farmers represented by Via Campesina have found themselves disadvantaged by these policies when the markets in which they must sell their products are flooded by cheap food produced in the industrialized world. As such, food sovereignty is advocated as an alternative to food security that assures greater autonomy to local food producers (Schanbacher 2010). Advocates of food sovereignty have resisted what they take to be efforts at expanding the reach of powerful actors. This includes the introduction of genetic engineering, which is often accompanied by the assertion of intellectual property rights that limit farmers' ability to replant seeds (Patel 2009).

In summary, a development ethics that still focuses on Peter Singer and Garrett Hardin's debates over famine relief overlooks many of the most enduring issues in food production. Nevertheless, future visions of the development ethics for food production remain rife with ethical issues. In key respects, they continue to reflect a long-standing rift between theorists who emphasize technology and who tend toward utilitarian or consequentialist orientation and an alternative vision that stresses power relations and is more comfortable with an ethic of rights or human development. In either case, a substantive and detailed understanding of how food is produced is needed. The opportunity for new work from the perspective of development ethics is rich.

References

Agarwal, B. (2001) Participatory Exclusions, Community Forestry, and Gender: An Analysis for South Asia and a Conceptual Framework. *World Development* 29: 1623–1648.

Burney, J. (2014) Creating Synergies between Water, Energy and Food Security for Smallholders. In Naylor, R. ed., *The Evolving Sphere of Food Security*. Oxford University Press, New York, 153–179.

Cernea, M. ed. (1985) *Putting People First: Sociological Variables in Rural Development*. Oxford University Press, New York.

Cleaver, H.M. (1972) The Contradictions of the Green Revolution. *American Economic Review* 62: 177–186.

Collier, P. (2008) The Politics of Hunger: How Illusion and Greed Fan the Food Crisis. *Foreign Affairs* 87(6): 67–79.

Cuéllar, M.F., Lazarus, D., Falcon, W.P. and Naylor, R. (2014) Institutions, Interests, and Incentives in American Food and Agriculture, Policy. In Naylor, R. ed., *The Evolving Sphere of Food Security*. Oxford University Press, New York, 87–121.

Dahlberg, K.A. (1979) *Beyond the Green Revolution: The Ecology and Politics of Global Agricultural Development*. Plenum Press, New York.

Ehrlich, P.R. (1968) *The Population Bomb*. Ballantine Books, New York.

Falcon, W.P. (1970) The Green Revolution: Generations of Problems. *American Journal of Agricultural Economics* 52: 698–710.

Falcon, W.P. and Gotsch, C.H. (1968) Lessons in Agricultural Development-Pakistan. *Development Policy – Theory and Practice*. Harvard University Press, Cambridge, 269–315.

Garnett, T. et al (2013) Sustainable Intensification in Agriculture: Premises and Policies. *Science* 341: 33–34.

Gaud, W. (1968) The Green Revolution: Accomplishments and Apprehensions, March 26, The Shoreham Hotel, Washington, DC. Republished in *AgBioWorld* http://agbioworld.org/biotech-info/topics/borlaug/borlaug-green.html.

Griffin, K. (1974) *The Political Economy of Agrarian Change: An Essay on the Green Revolution*. Macmillan, London.

Hardin, G. (1968) The Tragedy of the Commons. *Science* 162: 1243–1248.
Harris, M. (1987) Foodways: Historical Overview and Theoretical Prolegomenon. In Harris, M. and Ross, E.B. eds., *Food and Evolution: Toward a Theory of Human Food Habits* Temple University Press, Philadelphia, 57–90.
Lappé, F.M., Collins, J. and Fowler, C. (1977) *Food First: Beyond the Myth of Scarcity*. Houghton-Mifflin, New York.
Lipton, M. and Longhurst, R. (1989) *New Seeds for Poor People*. Johns Hopkins University Press, Baltimore.
Lobell, D.B., Naylor, R. and Field, C. (2014) Food, Energy and Climate Connections in a Global Economy. In Naylor, R. ed., *The Evolving Sphere of Food Security*. Oxford University Press, New York, 239–268.
Mellor, J. (1966) *The Economics of Agricultural Development*. Cornell University Press, Ithaca.
Masters, W. et al. (2013) Urbanization and Farm size in Asia and Africa: Implications for Food Security and Agricultural Research. *Global Food Security* 2: 156–165.
Naylor, R. (2014) The Many Faces of Food Security. In Naylor, R. ed., *The Evolving Sphere of Food Security* Oxford University Press, New York, 3–27.
Patel, R. (2008) *Stuffed and Starved: From Farm to Fork, the Hidden Battle for the World Food System*. Portobello Press, London.
Patel, R. (2009) Food Sovereignty. *The Journal of Peasant Studies* 36: 663–706.
Panda, P. and Agarwal, B. (2005) Marital Violence, Human Development and Women's Property Status in India. *World Development* 33: 823–850.
Pretty, J.N. (1997) The Sustainable Intensification of Agriculture. *Natural Resources Forum* 21: 247–256.
Reardon, T. et al (2003) The Rise of Supermarkets in Africa, Asia, and Latin America. *American Journal of Agricultural Economics* 85(5): 1140–1146.
Rosset, P. (2008) Food Sovereignty and the Contemporary Food Crisis. *Development* 51: 460–463.
Russell, S. (2006) *Hunger: An Unnatural History*. Penguin Books, New York.
Sachs, J. (2005) *The End of Poverty: Economic Possibilities for Our Time*. Penguin Books, New York.
Schanbacher, W. (2010) *The Politics of Food: The Global Conflict between Food Security and Food Sovereignty*. Praeger, Santa Barbara.
Sen, A. (1981) *Poverty and Famines: An Essay on Entitlement and Deprivation*. Oxford University Press, New York.
Shiva, V. (1989) *Staying Alive: Women Ecology and Development*. Zed Books, London.
Shome, S. (2015) The Social Vision of the Alternative Food Movement. In Herring, R. ed., *The Oxford Handbook of Food, Politics and Society*. Oxford University Press, New York, 523–542.
Singer, P. (1972) Famine, Affluence and Morality. *Public Affairs Quarterly* 1: 229–243.
Spector, M. (2014) Seeds of Doubt: An Activist's Controversial Crusade Against Genetically Engineered Crops. *The New Yorker* 25 August 2014 Issue. www.newyorker.com/magazine/2014/08/25/seeds-of-doubt. Accessed 20 June 2016.
Stannard, C. (2008) Doing Ethics in Food and Agriculture. In Thompson, P.B. ed., *The Ethics of Intensification: Agricultural Development and Cultural Change*. Springer, Dordrecht NL, 43–58.
Thompson, P. (2015a) *From Field to Fork: Food Ethics for Everyone*. Oxford University Press, New York.
Thompson, P. (2015b) From World Hunger to Food Sovereignty: Food Ethics and Human Development. *Journal of Global Ethics* 11: 336–350.
Veit, H. (2013) *Modern Food, Moral Food: Self-control, Science, and the Rise of Modern American Eating in the Early Twentieth Century*. UNC Press Books, Chapel Hill.

22

Buen vivir and the rights of nature

Alternative visions of development

Johannes M. Waldmueller and Laura Rodríguez

With the beginning of the 21st century Latin America witnessed important social, political and economic changes. Particularly in the Andes the previous decades of neoliberal politics had been characterized by austerity, a constant withdrawal of the state, mass migration, violence and politics along the Washington Consensus (Williamson 1993). With the progressive governments in Venezuela, Ecuador, Bolivia, Uruguay and, to a lesser extent, Argentina and Peru, this change led several authors to speak of a "post-neoliberal" (Grugel and Riggorizzi 2009; Bebbington and Bebbington-Humphreys 2011) turn, although controversy persists over its concrete meaning and the degree to which transformational politics have been advanced in different countries (Escobar 2010; Yates and Bakker 2014; Klein and Wahl 2015). Emanating from long-standing processes of resistance involving social, ecological, indigenous and peasant movements, two important yet elusive, and at the same time profoundly ethical, examples of this turn emerged in Bolivia and Ecuador.

Beginning around the year 2000, and following a series of consultations organized by the German Technical Development Cooperation (GIZ, then-GTZ) in Bolivia (Altmann 2013a), indigenous movements backed by international NGO support began to promote plurinationalism, interculturality and rights of nature, which culminated in *buen vivir* ("living well") inspired by the Amazonian indigenous concept of *sumak kawsay* ("living in completeness"), in Kichwa language. Although this concept was first described by the Ecuadorian anthropologist Carlos Viteri (1993, 2003), in the context of Bolivia it has been described as an "invention" by international actors together with indigenous intellectuals (Spedding 2010). In its original meaning, *sumak kawsay* refers to a subjectively coherent integration between cosmic cycles, spiritual understanding and animated, mutual relationships of humans and nature in community, which should lead to life in complementary plenitude (Macas 2010). Being in Bolivia called *vivir bien* or *suma qamaña* (derived from Aymara), and mythically connected to the Andean *ayllu* community life (Yampara 2001), both express a similar and distinctive "Latin American" vision as opposed to mainstream utilitarian development. The latter is based firstly on the modern Cartesian distinction (see Latour 1993) between *res cogitans* (animated matter) and *res extensa* (the environment, viewed as unanimated matter) and secondly, on a more or less constant material accumulation which should lead to progress and modernity. On the contrary, central to *buen vivir* is the questioning of traditional views of economic development by either pointing to non-Western pre-modern life philosophies in

 DOI: 10.4324/9781315626796-27

the Americas and/or by linking it to very modern debates of socio-ecological sustainability, post-growth or degrowth (Thomson 2011; Unceta 2013; Escobar 2015). In both versions, proponents of *buen vivir* typically draw a reference to interrelated concepts or pillars, such as moving beyond Western multiculturalism (Taylor 1992; Kymlicka 1995; Hale 2005) by recognizing interculturality, plurinationality (Altmann 2013b) and an extension of eco-social life in a somewhat biocentric sense, legally enshrined as rights of nature. In this sense, three major currents of *buen vivir* became classified by several authors: (1) indigenous-Pachamamist or culturalist *buen vivir*, (2) ecologist or post-developmentalist and (3) socialist-statist or eco-Marxist (Le Quang and Vercoutère 2013; Hidalgo-Capitán and Cubillo-Guevara 2014).

From a governance perspective, *buen vivir/vivir bien* were constitutionally enshrined in 2008 (Ecuador) and 2009 (Bolivia) together with rights of nature as pillars of cultural recognition. This process was also an integral component to the post-neoliberal project to strengthen state structures by consolidating the tax base, renegotiating national debts and nationalizing the extractive sectors. Both countries implemented binding supra-institutional *buen vivir* plans (for Ecuador, see SENPLADES 2009, 2013) that replaced former development plans, while adhering to a focus upon standardized bureaucratic procedures and measurable outcomes.

In a broader sense, however, *buen vivir* represents a plurality of more or less specific discursive and practice-related "platforms" (Gudynas 2011a) that intend to develop alternative visions to capitalist development. One common element for these efforts is the idea that an alternative development should stem from the lived subaltern experience in Latin America, or more specifically, the Andean region, i.e. in Bolivia, Ecuador, and Peru (while being virtually nonexistent in Chile, Venezuela and Colombia, where indigenous influence is lesser, though debates are growing). What is certain is that *buen vivir* was taken up by international actors and scholars and soon became promoted by civil societies in several other countries (particularly in Spain and Germany).

In Ecuador and Bolivia however, *buen vivir* has gradually shifted towards a program of increased dependency on the exploitation of natural resources for exports, the expansion of public expenditure as well as repression and control of civil society by way of gradually shutting down dissident space. This points to an inherent gap between far-reaching expectations and the reality of business-as-usual (Caria and Domínguez 2016). Whether or not *buen vivir* in its original meaning in fact still "exists" in the region (or rather in countries such as Germany), and what sort of practices, contents and priorities of the transition strategies would be required towards actual *buen vivir*, remain therefore broadly debated questions within academic and activists' circles (e.g. Walsh 2010; Radcliffe 2012; Farah and Vasapollo 2011; Artaraz and Calestani 2014; Waldmüller 2014).

In what follows we first trace the emergence, main components and contemporary threads of *buen vivir* as the most promising alternative framework to linear, accumulation-based, economic and modernizing development. In a next step, some influential references to historical and current movements are analyzed. This analysis leads to this chapter's focus on rights of nature in Ecuador and Bolivia, which is at the same time a crucial and controversial component of *buen vivir*. Ideally, the extension of natural rights toward nature provides an intriguing path for academics and practitioners for overcoming the utilitarian conception of nature and ecosystems as having merely instrumental value for humans.

What is *buen vivir*?

In very basic terms, *buen vivir* has been approached in the following way:

> In its most general sense, *buen vivir* denotes, organizes, and constructs a system of knowledge and living based on the communion of humans and nature and on the spatial-temporal-harmonious

> totality of existence. That is, on the necessary interrelation of beings, knowledges, logics, and rationalities of thought, action, existence, and living. This notion is part and parcel of the cosmovision, cosmology, or philosophy of the indigenous peoples of Abya Yala.
>
> *(Walsh 2010, 18)*

Ethical principles enshrined in the impressively declaratory constitutions of Bolivia and Ecuador have not always translated into according politics, for example with regard to preservation of nature and respect for plurinationality. Thus a discursive splitting of *buen vivir* and *sumak kawsay* has recently been discussed (Oviedo 2014a). It is, therefore, important to look closer at the underlying conceptions of *buen vivir* and *sumak kawsay*. Three (or more) main types of such conception have been differentiated within the vast field of discourses and practices (Hidalgo-Capitán et al. 2012). They remain however interrelated in several publications by scholars, governments and activists:

(1) *Buen vivir* as a political "socialism of the 21st century" (Ramírez 2010), led by a reinforced and centralized government; that is, a blending between neo-Aristotelian, Christian and Andean values (mainly with regard to ecologically conscious currents), linked to all sorts of claims from 'do-gooders', into a political state program. Conceived this way, *buen vivir* resides broadly within the framework of Western development, especially human development thinking following Amartya Sen and Martha Nussbaum (Sen 1999; Nussbaum 2011) who are also cited in the Ecuadorian National Buen Vivir Plans, which replaced traditional development plans (SENPLADES 2009, 2013).

(2) As a "utopia to be constructed" (Acosta 2010), in form of a post-modern collage combining viewpoints of various international movements of peasants, ecofeminists, socialists, ecologists, pacifists, theologians of liberation, unionists, etc. (Hidalgo-Capitán et al. 2014: 35–36). Important in such a conception is the desired reconstruction of the national economy toward local and eco-socially sustainable practices of production, transport and consumption – a common thread uncommonly discussed in *buen vivir* discourses of type (1) and (3).

(3) An "indigenist" form of living and thinking (as opposed to indigenous) that adds important spiritual and ontologically relational dimensions, based on individually and collectively acquiring a practice and lifestyle (in addition to knowledge) of all-connected consciousness. This form of relational being is seen as in constant exchange and reflection with the social and natural environment (Oviedo 2014b). In order to avoid essentialist accounts of indigenous being and living, a distinction is frequently drawn between *indigenist thinking* and *indígena thinking*. The discursive assumption here is that the first supports *indigenismo* (or *indianismo*), a "political ideology that defends indigenous claims within the framework of nation-states" (Hidalgo-Capitán et al. 2014, 30), based on a century-long endured suppression and attempts to extinction. One does not necessarily need to be indigenous to support it as *indigenista*, and in turn not all indigenous people are *indigenistas*, but both refer to distinctive values, (re)presented as "indigenous". It is questionable if such a distinction is really able to avoid essentialist elements, especially with regard to constant emphasizing of indigenous/non-indigenous providence of authors in collected works such as that of Hidalgo-Capitán et al. (2014): exploring "strategic essentialism" with regard to political ethnicity should certainly be considered in this respect (Lucero 2006; Altmann 2014).

However, the third account described here is commonly differentiated from *buen vivir* (as state program) and referred to as alternative *sumak kawsay*, typically linked to positions against extractive industries or deepened insertion of Andean countries within a highly speculative and unequal global system of capital accumulation by dispossession (Harvey 2003). Several contributions bear a forceful critique of '*buen vivir* politics' as the Ecuadorian and Bolivian state gradually co-opted the paradigms. In this sense, their politics are interchangeably regarded as either a postmodern mixture of everything, a naïve form of "pachamamismo", a distraction from tackling real political problems (Sánchez-Parga 2011), a Foucauldian type of control mechanism (over civil society and democracy, see Cortez 2015) or profoundly patriarchal biopolitics around the figure of the "permitted Indian" (Cusicanqui 2014). An example for such a critique can be read in the following:

> Buen Vivir in the political constitution of Ecuador and Vivir Bien in the political constitution of Bolivia are a mix or hybrid as it is currently in vogue by a postmodern thinking that likes to mix everything a bit. It's a combination of platonic Buen Vivir with certain Christian and Humanist postulates with concepts of the ecological and socialist paradigms as well as finally adding some general principles of sumakawsay, what becomes called 'Andean Buen Vivir', this way demonstrating a lack of respect and disregard for the ancient and wise Andean tradition.
>
> *(Hidalgo-Capitán et al. 2014, 276)*

While *buen vivir* had emerged as an eco-socialist political alternative to what became characterized as wrong or undesired global development (discussed as *maldesarrollo* in the Spanish-speaking hemispheres, see Tortosa 2009), it is thus associated in Latin America today with populism, authoritarian structures of political decision-making within centralized and vertical state structures, deepened dependency on so-called natural "resources", Chinese loans, corruption and clientelist structures, increased public spending as well as little respect for human rights and fundamental principles of deliberation and public participation.

Yet, as some sort of a "benign" populist hyper-presidential framework and state centralism, *buen vivir* politics in Ecuador and Bolivia have indeed succeeded (at least during the recent commodity boom) in reducing both extreme poverty and structural poverty rates, and in increasing investments in education, health and infrastructure. In Ecuador, the poverty rate decreased between 2006 and 2014 from 37.6 percent to 22.5 percent, and extreme poverty dropped from 16.9 percent to 7.6 percent. In the same period, the Gini coefficient decreased from 0.54 to 0.47, which was a quicker reduction than the regional average (Caria and Domínguez 2016, 25). Overall, both countries have seen tremendous modernization programs in virtually all aspects, broadly following the so-called South Korean development model (Domjahn 2013; Yi and Mkandawire 2014; Sosa 2016).

However, in terms of advancing institutionalism in a Weberian sense (Andrade 2015), deepening meritocracy, transparency, democracy and civil participation, *buen vivir* politics have broadly malfunctioned or not yet been realized. While Ecuador and Bolivia formally recognized collective and group rights (Jordan 2008) and national constitutions declared human rights as the *raison d'être* of the state, governments have largely fractioned from (or co-opted) the social, ecological and indigenous movements that constituted the strength of their political base and which led the constituent assemblies, resulting in a severe fragmentation and weakening of civil societies.

It is noteworthy, though, that civil society organizations and activists against official state politics – such as the *Yasunidos* popular movement against the oil extraction inside the Amazonian Yasuní national park following a decision taken by the Ecuadorian government in 2013 (Rival 2012), or the broad movement against the construction of a road across a protected biosphere park in Bolivia (Cusicanqui 2014) – also refer to *buen vivir*, or *sumak kawsay*, in the sense of a 'real' transition yet to come and therefore to be fought for. Central to their demands is reclaiming rights of nature, the adoption of eco-socially sustainable politics and thus the necessity to overcome export-oriented extractivism and clientelistic politics as well as an agroindustry which gradually displaces (typically indigenous) smallholder peasants in the Andean highlands (Dufumier 2014; Houtart 2014; Radcliffe 2015).

As some have argued (Acosta and Martínez 2009b), the question is therefore not simply to create an alternative development, but instead to conceive an alternative to development altogether in a dialogue with non-Western philosophical and practical underpinnings. This claim points to development as a mere extension of the (still persistent) colonial project in Latin America (Quijano and Ennis 2000; Quijano 2011), particularly with regard to the exploitation of natural resources for global markets. Post-developmental (Latouche 1993; Escobar 2015) demands in this sense are entangled with ecological concerns. These are particularly provoked by climate change and related catastrophes on the one hand (the Andes are a highly affected area, e.g., with regard to glacier meltdown and water shortage), and on the other with increased extraction and destruction of natural areas due to mining and oil exploration, including within national parks and protected areas (Orihuela and Thorp 2012; Bebbington and Bury 2013; Dávalos and Albuja 2014). It is therefore necessary to delve further into one of the most fundamental pillars of *buen vivir*: the rights of nature.

Rights of nature

In fact, rights of nature are neither new nor specifically Andean. Their constitutional and legal enshrinement in Ecuador and Bolivia in the context of *buen vivir* is indeed a global novelty – thus perhaps the most broadly discussed alternative to globalized development, which became widely recognized and debated.

The rights of nature draw upon a long-standing debate within Western sciences, law and philosophy that dates back to (at least) the 17th century and is somewhat in contrast to anthropocentric Humanism (Nash 1989; Zaffaroni 2011). For instance, Henry More (1614–1687), who taught at Cambridge University, asserted the existence of the soul of the world that he called *anima mundi*, and that was present in every part of nature. In addition, Gottfried Leibnitz (1646–1716) and Baruch Spinoza (1632–1677), organicists and philosophers, discussed the interconnectedness of everything thus anticipating both ecological consciousness and environmental ethics. Just like the British reformer Henry Salt (1851–1939), the English botanist John Ray (1627–1705) was "convinced that the idea that the whole natural world existed only for people's benefit was an unsupportable conceit" (Nash 1989, 20). In 1796, John Lawrence drew upon Roman *ius animalium* and natural law when he defended in his 700-pages *Philosophical Treatise on Horses and on the Moral Duties of Man towards the Brute Creation* that life, intelligence and feeling – characteristics all shared by animals – necessarily imply rights. Already in 1879, the American tax reformer Henry George challenged in his *Progress and Poverty* the private ownership of the Earth, owing to his perspective that capitalism victimized both nature and people. In addition to these currents in the Anglo-Saxon context, the Republic of Weimar in the 20th century made early contributions through its legislation on the protection and preservation of forests, although from a rather utilitarian-instrumental perspective (Zaffaroni 2011, 90–91).

Overall, these as well as other sources paved the way toward the emergence of the environmentalism of the 20th century and its related scholarship on ecology and environmental ethics. More holistic considerations of humans and nature as interwoven living beings emerged in Aldo Leopold's *Sand County Almanac* (1949), Albert Schweitzer's *The Teaching of Reverence for Life*

(1966), Peter Singer's *Animal Liberation* (1975) as well as the writings of Arne Næss on "deep ecology" (1989), to name a few paradigmatic contributions. Widely cited in Ecuador and Bolivia's debates is the Gaia hypothesis by James Lovelock and Lynn Margulis (1974), who argued that organisms interact with their inorganic surroundings to form a synergistic, self-regulating system for life on Earth. Less known but nevertheless influential in the Latin American debates about nature under capitalism in the 1970s are the works of the Bolivian writer Manuel Céspedes (1878–1932) and the Argentinian Rodolfo Kusch (1922–1979). While Céspedes developed a transcendental identification with nature in his literary books ("animals and plants are our siblings in the community of existence", Céspedes 1971, 35), Kusch emphasized the need to overcome the "myth of the transformation of nature" towards an understanding based on "geoculture", meaning that every culture is linked inextricably with nature (Kusch 1976). This concept conveyed for Kusch the possibility to recognize any cultural ethos as embedded in environment, a key intellectual movement to overcome the colonial gaze of territories as spaces to be conquered and used by humans.

In Bolivia and Ecuador, these and other references serve occasionally as academic corroboration of long-standing indigenous demands that build on a deeply engrained, animated relationship between humans and nature, expressed as mutual caring and learning beyond rational accounts (see e.g. Mujica 2014; Estermann 1999; Pacari 2009; Acosta and Martínez 2009a). Anthropologists have been particularly vociferous in defending indigenous human-nature relations, and contemporary debates refer either to plural ontologies, (e.g. Viveiros de Castro 1996; Blaser 2009; de la Cadena 2015); or to more structuralist assessments (e.g. Descola and Pálsson 1996; Descola 2013). For this reason, the legal enshrinement of rights of nature in Bolivia and Ecuador has at least three different sources of inspiration, which cannot easily be separated from each other:

1 Indigenous world views, especially from the Amazon and the highland Andes, claim human-nature to be of one, undividable, interrelated and animated ontology. Moreover, this ontology, while in principle extended globally, would lead to a radically different form of social and political organization in contrast to the mainstream colonial model of modern development (Dudgeon and Berkes 2003; Osco 2010; Mignolo 2011; Gudynas 2013). In principle, nature as a living being and source of all emanation – an idea known as Pachamama, from which even space and time emerge – is understood as having inherent, and thus never merely instrumental, value for humans. Instead, humans and nature are regarded as mutually constitutive. Furthermore, the principles of Andean philosophy – relationality, correspondence, complementarity and reciprocity (Estermann 1999, 2012a, 2012b, Sobrevilla 2008) – have also been influential in the articulation of the rights of nature and its legitimacy (Ávila 2011).
2 At least since the 1960s, ecologists sought a rapprochement with human rights defenders, most notably manifested by the United Nations Conference on the Human Environment (Stockholm 1971) as well as subsequent summits in Rio (1992 and 2012). The San Salvador Protocol (1988) of the Inter-American human rights framework includes the right to a healthy environment and the obligation of states to promote the protection, preservation and improvement of the environment. Both clauses have been used extensively by human rights defenders and environmentalists. A prime motivation for the links between ecologists and the human rights movement lies in the fact that the international human rights protection system guarantees certain access to legal protection mechanisms for ecological concerns (Picolotti and Taillant 2003; Shelton 2011). This origin gave rise to ideas and influences from the international development cooperation NGOs and foundations

active in the Andes, which certainly had an impact on the framing of indigenous demands (Greene and Muñoz 2013) – now as legal claims – during the past decades (Warren and Jackson 2002; Warren 2005; Becker 2012).

3 The works by renowned ecologists mentioned earlier also had repercussions within legal scholarship, for example in works by Godofredo Stutzin (1976, 1984) in Latin America. Stutzin first argued for the implementation of rights of nature recognized by governments. He was perhaps influenced by Christopher Stone (1972, 2010; Grear 2012), a US lawyer who already in the early 1970s contended the legal standing of nature, since its vital interests could be legally represented before courts similar to other non-human entities, such as companies. To do so, Stone proposed a system of guardians who should act as legal representatives of nature's concerns.

Overall, fundamental to the rights of nature is the claim of the environment and ecosystems to be of *inherent*, as opposed to instrumental, value. In its most radical sense, this amounts to an eco- or biocentric position (Agar 1997; Sterba 2011) that defends the inherent value of life as such. This perspective differs largely from the mainstream anthropocentric conception of not only the environment, but also Western conceptions of law, politics and even of sustainability, which share an anthropocentric bias to the extent that it seeks to preserve certain environments for later human generations. Biocentrism puts forward a recognition of *life as such*, which entails also the recognition of its natural cycles of arriving and passing. Especially natural passing would require to reflect politically and ethically about limits to human conduct and striving, not merely in terms of capping degrees because of climate change, but both in a broader historical reflection of human being and time (e.g. questioning prevalent paradigms of development) as well as with relation to daily practices of individuals and its aggregated effects (e.g. carbon footprints related to consumption habits, city ecological food prints, etc.).

Current issues of rights of nature in Ecuador and Bolivia

Ecuador was the first country in the world to constitutionally enshrine rights of nature, while Bolivia enacted a Law of Mother Earth in 2010 with eleven rights of nature. The 2008 Ecuadorian constitution refers without distinction to Nature and Pachamama and grants it (1) the right to be respected in its integral existence, (2) the right to preservation and regeneration of its structure, functions and evolutionary processes (Art. 71) and (3) the right to reparation (Art. 72). The state has the obligation to implement precaution and prevention measures to restrain activities impacting nature (Art. 73). Somewhat paradoxically, Article 74 establishes the right to enjoy nature and to benefit from its riches in order to achieve *buen vivir* (Asamblea Constituyente 2008). It is this article that complicates the legal application of these rights, as we discuss later. Overall, the referred norms are conceptualized as *principio in dubio pro natura*, a legal principle which prescribes that in case of doubt the application of the norm shall always be made in the most favorable sense of the protection of nature.

In Bolivia, the 2009 Constitution does not recognize rights of nature, but it includes a particular language regarding nature in its preamble: *Madre Tierra*, Mother Earth or Pachamama – referring to concepts derived from indigenous traditions that entail spiritual connotations – provided the foundations for secondary legal developments. Indeed, the Law of Mother Earth (2010) and later the Framework Law of Mother Earth and Integral Development to Live Well (2012) complemented and amplified the environmental precepts of the Constitution. The Framework Law sanctioned the following rights of nature: (1) continuation of vital life cycles and processes free from human alteration; (2) rights of maintenance of the integrity of life and natural processes; (3) pure water and clean air; (4) balance and equilibrium; (5) to be free of toxic and radioactive pollution; (6) to not be affected by mega-infrastructure and development projects that disturb the balance of ecosystems and local resident communities (Gregor Barié 2014). Furthermore, an ombudsman for Mother Earth was formally created by the legal framework though it has not been established yet.

The legal conception of rights now valid in both countries therefore ceases to be solely anthropocentric, yet the extent of desired biocentrism, and in particular biocentric consequentialism, remains unclear (see Attfield 2014, 42–45, 89–94). It constitutes, however, a notable deviation from Western positive law, which relegates nature below the right to property, thus objectifying and making it dependent on the owner's will. The Ecuadorian constitution presents a conceptual rupture to the extent that it guarantees protection to nature *in itself*, including its vital cycles, structure, functions and evolutionary processes. This "rights' utopia" represents a collective aspiration emerging from Ecuadorian social movements and civil society, as well as a starting point in terms of its implementation (Gudynas 2009; Ávila 2011). An interesting avenue for such realization lies in the "diatopic hermeneutics" proposed by Sousa Santos (2009) as the transcultural dialogue leading to the articulation of complex answers to remedy the incompleteness of Western cultural concepts:

> human rights are incomplete because they are unable to establish a link between the part (the individual) and the all (reality) . . . instead of focusing on the primordial imperative, the duty of people to find their place in the order of society and the cosmos.
>
> *(ibid., 519)*

Despite these important advancements, contemporary practices and debates on the rights of nature in Bolivia and Ecuador reveal a set of critical issues to be addressed. First, there is an important tension between the treatments of nature as subject of rights and as an object of appropriation and use, as expressed in Article 74 of the Ecuadorian Constitution. The ongoing governmental practices in the two countries point to a scenario of acute confrontations between indigenous and environmental rights and economic and political interests around development policies (Lalander 2014) in the context of neo-extractivist policies implemented in both countries (Gudynas 2011b; Veltmeyer and Petras 2014; Svampa 2015). In Bolivia, the TIPNIS (*Territorio Indígena y Parque Nacional Isiboro Secure*) conflict during 2011 and 2012 demonstrated the complexities of resource sovereignty claims made both by the government and Amazonian indigenous people, as well as these actors' use of indigenous identities coupled with varied interpretations of environmental harmony (Laing 2015).

The most paradigmatic example of the limits to development imposed by respecting rights of nature was the 2007 Yasuní-ITT oil moratorium proposal by Ecuador. It suggested to leave around 850 million barrels of oil underground in exchange for international compensation for Ecuador's environmental services paid into a dedicated UN funds (Fontaine 2008). The initiative was terminated in 2013 by the same government. While a popular referendum was initiated and rejected in the country, the government gave paltry excuses to file the moratorium. As of 2016, Ecuador has begun to extract oil in the Yasuní national park.

The second issue relates to the need of clarification with regard to the guardianship or stewardship for nature's interests, as awkwardly assessable, as they may be (Attfield 2014, 21–23; 30–33). The Ecuadorian framework permits in principle for everyone to legally claim rights of nature. Since 2008, individuals have successfully defended the rights of nature in legal processes in at least four cases (Bedón Garzón 2017). At the same time, this open conception permits its abuse by the government (see Whittemore 2011). At the moment of writing, about half of the pending litigations were initiated by the government, occasionally claiming rights of nature as a pretext for advancing large infrastructure and extractive projects.

What seems to be required therefore is an independent third party to invoke the rights of nature as legitimate defense in a situation of aggression against, or disturbance, of nature. The possibility of targeted criminalization of individuals or groups arises on the grounds of an instrumental use of the rights of nature. To prevent the political use of the rights of nature a doctrine of legal interpretation aligned with the spirit embedded in the constitutive sources of these novel rights is needed (Martinez 2014).

Up until 2016, the rights of nature have been invoked in eighteen legal cases in Ecuador (Greene 2016), about half of them brought forward by the government. The first judicial application took place in 2011 when two US citizens filed a lawsuit against the provincial government of the city of Loja in favor of the protection of the Vilcabamba river that suffered from works on a highway expansion (Rühs and Jones 2016). The court in charge declared the Provincial Government responsible for the damages yet it allowed for the continuation of the works but on the condition of no longer affecting the river (Suárez 2013). Rights of nature have been also invoked in international contexts. In 2010, a group of Ecuadorian and US nationals introduced a demand of protection in an Ecuadorian tribunal against the company British Petroleum after the oil spill in the Gulf of Mexico, arguing for the continuum of nature and thus the duty to protection beyond national frontiers. The demand was finally rejected due to the tribunal's lack of competence. In 2010, the Universal Declaration of the Rights of Mother Earth was adopted at the World People's Conference on Climate Change and the Rights of Nature. In Mexico there have been steps towards the recognition of the rights of nature with the amendment of the Environmental Law in 2013, later known as the "Earth Protection Law" (Garza Grimaldo 2015). As of 2016, around one hundred communities in the United States have included legal protection mechanisms for nature. These achievements of the conservationist agenda and its constitutional provisions hinge on the capacity for organized citizens on the one hand to effectively claim the exercise of the new rights, and on the other to resist instrumentalization by governments and extractive industries against their interests.

Finally, there is an ethical and legal debate required that would permit to go beyond stereotyping or essentializing accounts of both humans and nature and their constant interaction (Leff 2012). Eventually, neither unfettered anthropocentrism nor unlimited biocentrism (or ecocentrism) appear as viable ways forward (Watson 1983; Attfield 2014). As ample scholarship has demonstrated, the Amazon, for instance, is neither an untouched nor unspoiled ecosystem but in fact has been profoundly shaped by human impact during thousands of years (Raffles and Winkler-Prins 2003; Kohn 2013). Indeed, the precise structure of the interwoven dependency of "socionatures" (Castree and Braun 2001) still remains to be deciphered and transformed into detailed and useful legal language. It links to important further ethical questions of what counts as "desired" nature, worthy of legal protection, and what does not (for instance, should we protect malign forms of viruses or bacteria?). These issues are still unaddressed not only in Ecuador and Bolivia, where current transdisciplinary debates (see e.g. Raffles 2010; Attfield 2014, 89–96) only slowly trickle in, but also globally. Despite these shortcomings due to the gap mentioned earlier between aspirations and reality and the short time in which proposals of *buen vivir* and rights of nature are made, this framework offers a unique and valuable repertoire for critically and ethically engaging with development-induced processes.

References

Acosta, A. (2010) El Buen (con)Vivir, una utopía por (re)construir: Alcances de la Constitución de Montecristi. University of Cuenca. http://pydlos.ucuenca.edu.ec/index.php?option=com_remository&Itemid=57&func=startdown&id=51. Accessed 17 June 2017.

Acosta, A. and Martínez, E. eds. (2009a) *Derechos de la Naturaleza. El futuro es ahora.* Abya Yala, Quito.

Acosta, A. and Martínez, E. eds. (2009b) *El Buen Vivir. Una vía para el desarrollo.* Abya Yala, Quito.

Agar, N. (1997) Biocentrism and the Concept of Life. *Ethics* 108(1): 147–168.

Altmann, P. (2013a) Good Life as a Social Movement Proposal for Natural Resource Use: The Indigenous Movement in Ecuador. *Consilience: The Journal of Sustainable Development* 10(1): 59–71.

Altmann, P. (2013b) Plurinationality and Interculturality in Ecuador: The Indigenous Movement and the Development of Political Concepts. *Nordic Journal of Latin American and Caribbean Studies* XLIII(1–2): 47–66.

Altmann, P. (2014) Strategischer Essentialismus als Wiederaneignung von Geschichte. Die Ethnisierung der Indigenenbewegung in Ecuador als Prozess der Subjektwerdung. *Nebulosa* 4(5): 89–104.

Andrade, P. (2015) *Política de industrialización selectiva y nuevo modelo de desarrollo* Universidad Andina Simón Bolívar/Corporación Editora Nacional, Quito.

Artaraz, K. and Calestani, M. (2014) Suma Qamaña in Bolivia: Indigenous Understandings of Well-being and their Contribution to a Post-neoliberal Paradigm. *Latin American Perspectives* 204(42(5)): 216–233.

Asamblea Constituyente (2008) *Constitución Política de la República del Ecuador.* Montechristi. www.asambleanacional.gov.ec/documentos/Constitucion-2008.pdf. Accessed 17 June.

Attfield, R. (2014) *Environmental Ethics: An Overview For the Twenty-first Century.* Polity Press, Cambridge MA.

Ávila, R.S. (2011) El derecho de la naturaleza: fundamentos. In Acosta, A. and Martínez, E. eds., *La Naturaleza con Derechos* Abya Yala, Quito, 173–239.

Bebbington, A. and Bebbington-Humphreys, D. (2011) An Andean Avatar: Post-neoliberal and Neoliberal Strategies for Securing the Unobtainable. *New Political Economy* 15(4): 131–145.

Bebbington, A. and Bury, J. (2013) *Subterranean Struggles: New Dynamics of Mining, Oil, and Gas in Latin America.* University of Texas Press, Austin.

Becker, M. (2012) The Limits of Indigenismo in Ecuador. *Latin American Perspectives* 39/5(186): 45–62.

Bedón Garzón, R.P. (2017) Aplicación de los derechos de la naturaleza en Ecuador. *Veredas do Direito* 14(28): 13–32 doi: http://dx.doi.org/10.18623/rvd.v14i28.1038.

Blaser, M. (2009) The Threat of the Yrmo: The Political Ontology of a Sustainable Hunting Program. *American Anthropologist* 111(1): 10–20 doi: DOI: 10.1111/j.1548–1433.2009.01073.x.

De la Cadena, M. (2015) *Earth Beings. Ecologies of Practice across Andean Worlds.* Duke University Press, Durham NC and London.

Caria, S. and Domínguez, R. (2016) Ecuador's Buen vivir: A New Ideology for Development. *Latin American Perspectives* 206(43) doi: 10.1177/0094582X15611126.

Castree, N. and Braun, B. (2001) *Social Nature: Theory, Practice, and Politics.* Blackwell, Malden MA.

Céspedes, M. (1971) *Sol y Horizontes. Símbolos Profanos.* Editorial Juventud, La Paz.

Cortez, D. (2015) Genealogía del sumak kawsay y el buen vivir en Ecuador: un balance. In Endara, G. ed., *Post-Crecimiento y Buen Vivir: Propuestas globales para la construcción de sociedades equitativas y sustentables.* Friedrich Ebert Stiftung FES – ILDIS Ecuador, Quito, 315–353.

Cusicanqui, S. (2014) *Mito y desarrollo en Bolivia. El giro colonial del gobierno del MAS.* Plural Editores, La Paz.

Dávalos, P. and Albuja, V. (2014) Ecuador: Extractivist Dynamics, Politics and Discourse. In Veltmeyer, H. and Petras, J. eds., *The New Extractivism. A Post-Neoliberal Development Model or Imperialism of the Twenty-First Century.* Zed Books, New York, 144–172.

De Sousa Santos, B. (2009) *Sociología jurídica crítica. Para un nuevo sentido común en el derecho.* Taurus, Madrid.

Descola, P. (2013) *The Ecology of Others.* Trans G. Godbout and B. Luley. Prickly Paradigm, Chicago.

Descola, P. and Pálsson, G. eds. (1996) *Nature and Society: Anthropological Perspectives.* Routledge, London and New York.

Domjahn, T.M. (2013) What (if Anything) Can Developing Countries Learn from South Korea? *Asian Culture and History* 5(2): 16–24. doi: 10.5539/ach.v5n2p16.

Dudgeon, R.C. and Berkes, F. (2003) Local Understandings of the Land: Traditional Ecological Knowledge and Indigenous Knowledge. In Selin, H. ed., *Nature across Cultures*. Springer, Dordrecht, 76–96.

Dufumier, M. (2014) Agriculturas familiares, fertilidad de los suelos y sostenabilidad de los agroecosistemas. In Hidalgo, F.F., Houtart, F., and Lizárraga, P.A. eds., *Agriculturas campesinas en Latinoamérica*. IAEN, Quito, 35–55.

Escobar, A. (2010) Latin America at a Crossroads. *Cultural Studies* 24(1): 1–65. doi:10.1080/09502380903424208.

Escobar, A. (2015) Degrowth, Postdevelopment, and Transitions: A Preliminary Conversation. *Sustainability Science* 10(3): 451–462.

Estermann, J. (1999) *Andine Philosophie. Eine interkulturelle Studie zur autochthonen andinen Weisheit*. IKO (Denktraditionen im Dialog: Studien zur Befreiung und Interkulturalität), Frankfurt am Main.

Estermann, J. (2012a) *Apu Taytayku. Religion und Theologie im andinen Kontext Lateinamerikas*. Matthias Grünewald Verlag, Ostfildern.

Estermann, J. (2012b) Diatopische Hermeneutik am Beispiel der Andinen Philosophie. Ansätze zur Methodologie interkulturellen Philosophierens. *Polylog. Zeitschrift für interkulturelles Philosophieren* 27: 21–41.

Farah, I. and Vasapollo, L. (2011) *Vivir Bien: ¿paradigma no capitalista?*. CIDES-UMSA, Sapienza, OXFAM, La Paz.

Fontaine, G. (2008) ITT: un problema de gobernanza para el Ecuador. In *La guerra del fuego. Políticas petroleras y crisis energética en América Latina*. FLACSO, Ministerio de Cultura, Quito.

Garza Grimaldo, J.A. (2015) Los derechos de la naturaleza en México. *Revista Mexicana de Ciencias Agrícolas* 1: 181–190.

Grear, A. (2012) Should Trees Have Standing: 40 Years On. *Journal of Human Rights and the Environment* doi: 10.4337/jhre.2012.02.00.

Greene, N. (2016) *Los derechos de la naturaleza en Ecuador*. Quito.

Greene, N. and Muñoz, G. (2013) *Los derechos de la naturalzea son mis derechos. Manual para el tratamiento de los conflictos socioambientales bajo el nuevo marco de derechos constitucionales*. Plataforma de Acuerdos Socioambientales – PLASA, Colectivo Nacional por los Derechos de la Naturaleza, Programa de Pequeñas Donaciones del FMAM – PPD/ FMAM/PNUD, Quito. https://therightsofnature.org/wp-content/uploads/pdfs/Espanol/Greene_Munoz_Manual_DDN_2014.pdf. Accessed: 5 May 2014.

Gregor Barié, C. (2014) Nuevas narrativas constitucionales en Bolivia y Ecuador: el buen vivir y los derechos de la naturaleza. *Latino América* (2): 9–40.

Grugel, J. and Riggorizzi, P. (2009) *Governance after Neoliberalism in Latin America*. Palgrave MacMillan, New York.

Gudynas, E. (2009) *El mandato ecológico. Derechos de la Naturaleza y políticas ambientales en la nueva Constitución*. Abya Yala, Quito.

Gudynas, E. (2011a) Buen Vivir: Today's Tomorrow. *Development* 54(4): 441–447. doi: 10.1057/dev.2011.86.

Gudynas, E. (2011b) Neo-Extraktivismus und Ausgleichsmechanismen der progressiven südamerikanischen Regierungen. *kurswechsel*. Translated by J. Becker and J. Jäger, 3, 69–80.

Gudynas, E. (2013) Debates on Development and its Alternatives in Latin America: A Brief Heterodox Guide. In Land, M. and Mokrani, D. eds., *Beyond Development. Alternative Visions from Latin America*. TNI 15–39, Amsterdam.

Hale, C.R. (2005) Neoliberal Multiculturalism: The Remaking of Cultural Rights and Racial Dominance in Central America. *Political and Legal Anthropology Review* 28(1): 10–28.

Harvey, D. (2003) *The New Imperialism*. Oxford University Press, Oxford/New York.

Hidalgo-Capitán, A.L. and Cubillo-Guevara, A.P. (2014) Seis debates abiertos sobre el sumak kawsay. *Íconos* 48: 25–40.

Hidalgo-Capitán, A.L. et al. (2012) *El Buen Vivir. La (re)creación del pensamiento del PYDLOS*, PYDLOS Ediciones, Cuenca. http://pydlos.ucuenca.edu.ec/index.php?option=com_remository&Itemid=57&func=startdown&id=59. Accessed 3 May 2014.

Hidalgo-Capitán, A.-L., Arias, A. and Ávila, J. (2014) El pensamiento indigenista ecuatoriano sobre el Sumak Kawsay. In Hidalgo-Capitán, A.-L. et al. ed., *Antología del Pensamiento Indigenista Ecuatoriano sobre Sumak Kawsay*, FIUCUHU, Huelva & Cuenca, 25–75.

Houtart, F. (2014) El desafío de la agricultura ampesina para el Ecuador. *ALAI, América Latina en Movimiento*. http://alainet.org/active/78437. Accessed 3 July 2015.

Jordan, P. (2008) Group Rights. *Stanford Encyclopedia of Philosophy*, September. http://plato.stanford.edu/entries/rights-group/. Accessed: 4 August 2016.

Klein, D. and Wahl, J. (2015) *Progressive Transformationsprozesse in Lateinamerika. Auf der Suche nach produktiven Balancen*. Rosa-Luxemburg Stiftung, Berlin.

Kohn, E. (2013) *How Forests Think. Toward an Anthropology Beyond the Human*. University of California Press, Berkeley, Los Angeles and London.

Kusch, R. (1976) *Geocultura del Hombre Americano*. Fernando García Cambeiro, Buenos Aires.

Kymlicka, W. (1995) *Multicultural Citizenship: A Liberal Theory of Minority Rights*. Oxford University Press, Oxford.

Laing, A. (2015) Resource Sovereignties in Bolivia: Re-Conceptualising the Relationship between Indigenous Identities and the Environment during the TIPNIS Conflict. *Bulletin of Latin American Research* 34(2): 149–166.

Lalander, R. (2014) Rights of Nature and the Indigenous Peoples in Bolivia and Ecuador: A Straitjacket for Progressive Development Politics? *Iberoamerican Journal of Development Studies* 3(2): 148–173.

Latouche, S. (1993) *In the Wake of the Affluent Society: An Exploration of Post-Development*. Zed Books, London.

Latour, B. (1993) *We Have Never Been Modern*. Harvard University Press, Cambridge MA.

Le Quang, M. and Vercoutère, T. (2013) *Ecosocialismo y Buen Vivir. Diálogo entre dos alternativas al capitalismo*. IAEN, Quito.

Leff, E. (2012) Latin American Environmental Thinking: A Heritage of Knowledge for Sustainability. *Environmental Ethics* 34(4).

Leopold, A. (1949) *A Sand County Almanac and Sketches Here and There*. Oxford University Press, New York and Oxford.

Lovelock, J. and Margulis, L.E. (1974) Atmospheric Homeostasis by and for the Biosphere: The Gaia Hypothesis. *Tellus* 26(1–2): 2–10. doi: 10.1111/j.2153-3490.1974.tb01946.x.

Lucero, J.A. (2006) Representing "Real Indians". The Challenges of Authenticity and Strategic Constructivism in Ecuador and Bolivia. *Latin American Research Review* 42(2): 31–56.

Macas, L. (2010) Sumak kawsay: la vida en penitud. *América Latina en Movimiento* 452: 14–16.

Martinez, E. (2014) *La naturaleza entre la cultura, la biología y el derecho*. Instituto de Estudios Ecologistas del Tercer Mundo and Abya Yala, Quito.

Mignolo, W.D. (2011) *The Darker Side of Modernity. Global Futures, Decolonial Options*. Duke University Press, Durham NC and London.

Mujica, L. (2014) Conocimiento o riqsiy: apuntes para una epistemología en el mundo andino. In Ansion, J. and Villacorta, A.M. eds., *Qawastin ruwastin. Viendo y haciendo*. RIDEI-PUCP, Lima, 37–71.

Næss, A. (1989) *Ecology, Community and Lifestyle: Outline of an Ecosophy* (translated and edited by Rothenberg, D.). Cambridge University Press, Cambridge.

Nash, R.F. (1989) *The Rights of Nature. A History of Environmental Ethics*. University of Wisconsin Press, Madison.

Nussbaum, M. (2011) *Creating Capabilities: The Human Development Approach*. Belknap Press of Harvard University Press, Cambridge, MA.

Orihuela, J.C. and Thorp, R. (2012) The Political Economy of Managing Extractives in Bolivia, Ecuador and Peru. In Bebbington, A. ed., *Social Conflict, Economic Development and the Extractive Industry: Evidence from South America*. Routledge, London and New York, 27–46.

Osco, M.F. (2010) Ayllu: Decolonial Thinking and (An)other Autonomy. In Blaser, M. et al eds., *Indigenous Peoples and Autonomy: Insights for a Global Age*. UBC Press, Vancouver, 27–49.

Oviedo, A. ed. (2014a) *Bifurcación del Buen Vivir y el Sumak Kawsay*. Ediciones Yachay, Quito.

Oviedo, A. (2014b) El Buen Vivir posmoderno y el Sumakawsay ancestral. In Hidalgo-Capitán, A.-L., Guillén García, A., and Deleg Guazha, N. eds., *Antología del Pensamiento Indigenista Ecuatoriano sobre Sumak Kawsay*. FIUCUHU, Huelva and Cuenca, 267–297.

Pacari, N. (2009) Naturaleza y territorio desde la mirada de los pueblos indígenas. In Acosta, A. and Martínez, E. eds., *Derechos de la Naturaleza*. Abya Yala, Quito, 31–39.

Picolotti, R. and Taillant, J.D. eds. (2003) *Linking Human Rights and the Environment*. University of Arizona Press, Tucson.

Quijano, A. (2011) "Bien Vivir": Entre el "desarrollo" y la des/colonialidad del poder. *Ecuador Debate* 84: 77–88.

Quijano, A. and Ennis, M. (2000) Coloniality of Power, Eurocentrism, and Latin America. *Neplanta: Views from South* 1(3): 533–580.

Radcliffe, S.A. (2012) Development for a Postneoliberal Era? Sumak kawsay, Living Well and the Limits to Decolonisation in Ecuador. *Geoforum* 43: 240–249. doi: 10.1016/j.geoforum.2011.09.003.

Radcliffe, S.A. (2015) *Dilemmas of Difference. Indigenous Women and the Limits of Postcolonial Development Policy*. Duke University Press, Durham, NC.

Raffles, H. (2010) *Insectopedia*. Vintage Books, New York.

Raffles, H. and WinklerPrins, A.M.G.A. (2003) Further Reflections on Amazonian Environmental History: Transformations of Rivers and Streams. *Latin American Research Review* 38(3): 165–187. doi: 10.1353/lar.2003.0041.

Ramírez, R. (2010) Socialismo del sumak kawsay o biosocialismo republicano. In *Los nuevos retos de América Latina. Socialismo y sumak kawsay*. SENPLADES, Quito, 55–76.

Rival, L. (2012) Planning Development Futures in the Ecuadorian Amazon: The Expanding Oil Frontier and the Yasuní-ITT initiative. In Bebbington, A. ed., *Social Conflict, Economic Development and the Extractive Industry: Evidence from South America*. Routledge, London and New York, 153–172.

Rühs, N. and Jones, A. (2016) The Implementation of Earth Jurisprudence through substantive Constitutional Rights of Nature. *Sustainability* 8: 174. doi: 10.3390/su8020174.

Sánchez-Parga, J. (2011) Discursos retrovolucionarios: sumak kawsay, derechos de la naturaleza y otros pachamamismos. *Ecuador Debate* 84: 31–50.

Schweitzer, A. (1966) *The Teaching of Reverence for Life*. Peter Owen, London.

Sen, A. (1999) *Development as Freedom*. Oxford University Press, Oxford and New York.

SENPLADES (2013) *Buen Vivir Plan Nacional 2013–2017*. SENPLADES, Quito. www.buenvivir.gob.ec. Accessed 4 September 2013.

SENPLADES, S.N. de P. y D. (2009) *Plan Nacional de Desarrollo. Plan Nacional para el Buen Vivir 2009–2013. Construyendo un Estado plurinacional e intercultural (Version resumida)*. SENPLADES Quito.

Shelton, D.L. ed. (2011) *Human Rights and the Environment*. Edward Elgar, Cheltenham and Northampton, MA.

Singer, P. (1975) *Animal Liberation: A New Ethics for Our Treatment of Animals*. HarperCollins, New York.

Sobrevilla, D. (2008) La filosofía andina del P. Josef Estermann. *Solar* 4: 231–247.

Sosa, C. (2016) Cuando Ecuador perdió la brújula del modelo coreano. *El Comercio*, 21 February.

Spedding, A. (2010) "Suma qamaña" ¿kamsañ muni? (¿Qué quiere decir "vivir bien"?). www.iseatbolivia.org/vivirbien/index.php/articulos-y-documentos/doc_download/3-articulo-alison-speddingsuma-qamana. Accessed 5 October 2016.

Sterba, J. (2011) Biocentrism Defended. *Ethics, Policy and Environment* 14(2): 167–169 doi: 10.1080/21550085.2011.578376.

Stone, C.D. (1972) Should Trees Have Standing? Towards Legal Rights for Natural Objects. *Southern Californian Law Review* 45: 450–501.

Stone, C.D. (2010) *Should Trees have Standing? Law, Morality and the Environment* 3rd ed. Oxford University Press, New York.

Stutzin, G. (1976) Should we Recognize Nature's Claim to Legal Rights? *Environmental Policy and Law.*

Stutzin, G. (1984) Un imperativo ecológico: reconocer los derechos de la naturaleza. *Revista Ambiente y Desarrollo*, 1(1). www.cipma.cl/web/200.75.6.169/RAD/1984-1.html. Accessed 10 June 2017.

Suárez, S. (2013) *Defendiendo la naturaleza: Retos y obstáculos en la implementación de los derechos de la naturaleza. Caso río Vilcabamba*. http://library.fes.de/pdf-files/bueros/quito/10230.pdf. Accessed 5 May 2014.

Svampa, M. (2015) Commodities Consensus: Neoextractivism and Enclosure of the Commons in Latin America. *South Atlantic Quarterly* 114(1): 65–82. doi: 10.1215/00382876–2831290.

Taylor, C. (1992) The Politics of Recognition. In Gutmann, A. ed., *Multiculturalism and the 'The Politics of Recognition'*. Princeton University Press, Princeton, 25–75.

Thomson, B. (2011) Pachakuti: Indigenous Perspectives, Buen Vivir, Sumaq Kawsay and Degrowth. *Development* 54(4): 448.

Tortosa, J.M. (2009) Maldesarrollo como Mal Vivir. *America Latina en Movimiento* 455: 18–21.

Unceta, K. (2013) Post-crecimiento, Desmercantilización y Buen Vivir. *Revista de Economía Mundial* 35: 21–45.

Veltmeyer, H. and Petras, J. (2014) *The New Extractivism. A Post-Neoliberal Development Model or Imperialism of the Twenty-First Century*. Zed Books, New York.

Viteri, C. (1993) Mundos Míticos. Runa. In Paymal, N. and Sosa, C. eds., *Mundos Amazónicos. Pueblos y Culturas de la Amazonía Ecuatoriana*. Sinchi Sacha, Quito.

Viteri, C. (2003) *Súmak Káusai. Una respuesta viable al desarrollo*. Universidad Politécnica Salesiana (Master's Thesis) Quito.

Viveiros de Castro, E. (1996) Images of Nature and Society in Amazonian Ethnology. *Annual Review of Anthropology* 25: 179–200.

Waldmüller, J.M. (2014) Buen Vivir, Sumak Kawsay, "Good Living": An Introduction and Overview. *Alternautas* 1(1): 17–28.

Walsh, C. (2010) Development as Buen Vivir: Institutional Arrangements and (de) Colonial Entanglements. *Development* 53(1): 15–21.

Warren, K.B. (2005) Indigenous Movements in Latin America, 1992–2004: Controversies, Ironies, New Directions. *Annual Review of Anthropology* 34: 549–573.

Warren, K.B. and Jackson, J.E. (2002) *Indigenous Movements, Self-Representation, and the State in Latin America*. University of Texas Press, Austin.

Watson, R.A. (1983) A Critique of Anti-anthropocentric Biocentrism. *Environmental Ethics*, 5(3): 245–256.

Whittemore (2011) The Problem of Enforcing Nature's Rights under Ecuador's Constitution: Why the 2008 Environmental Amendments Have No Bite. *Pacific Rim Law Policy Journal* 20: 660–691.

Williamson, J. (1993) Development and the "Washington Consensus". *World Development* 21: 1239–1336.

Yampara, S. (2001) *El ayllu y la territorialidad en los Andes. Una aproximación a Chambi Grande*. CADA, La Paz.

Yates, J.S. and Bakker, K. (2014) Debating the "post-neoliberal" Turn in Latin America. *Progress in Human Geography* 38(1): 62–90.

Yi, I. and Mkandawire, T. (2014) *Learning from the South Korean Developmental Success. Effective Developmental Cooperation and Synergistic Institutions and Policies*. Palgrave MacMillan, Houndsmill and New York.

Zaffaroni, E.R. (2011) La Pachamama y el humano. In Acosta, A. and Martínez, E. eds., *La Naturaleza con Derechos*. Abya Yala, Quito, 25–139.

Part VI
Human rights

From time to time political figures have found it expedient to pit development against human rights. This can be done by claiming that development is more important than the niceties of human rights – which is a normative claim. Or the opposition can be framed as a matter of fact, a trade-off, claiming that human rights are an impediment to development. Among development policy makers, practitioners, researchers, and theorists alike, these claims are generally opposed. The consensus, in other words, is that worthwhile development and human rights are linked. While the debates are interesting, we are more interested in this *Handbook* in the positive linkages, both conceptual and empirical, between worthwhile development and human rights.

Polly Vizard identifies five types of linkage. While (1) ethical values that justify human rights have direct implications for worthwhile development, the international human rights framework is also a source of (2) pragmatic consensus on fundamental values which can have a directive influence on development policy; moreover, (3) as legal guarantees, human rights can be used as grounds for challenging maldevelopment. Beyond this, (4) "human rights–based development" has become well-known as a distinctive approach to development policy and practice, and, as Vizard shows, (5) human rights discourse can also be invoked in other ways by civic action groups and social movements.

Stephen Marks discusses an even more direct link between human rights and development. Remarkably, there is an accepted human rights instrument, the Declaration on the Right to Development, that directly addresses each of the seven values of worthwhile development discussed in this *Handbook*. Yet realization of those values through this right remains mired, according to Marks, in "political theatre," which, he finds, constitutes a glaring contradiction in human rights politics and practice.

Breakdowns of security jeopardize development and human rights alike. Stephen Esquith argues that security is not a condition but a dynamic process of peace building and political reconciliation, which is an active part of worthwhile development as much as any other basic right. This process is conceptualized, in most of the literature, either as transitional justice or as restorative justice. Esquith contrasts both with "localism," a third normative approach to peace building and reconciliation, and he calls for a reconsideration of transitional justice and restorative justice from a localist perspective.

DOI: 10.4324/9781315626796-28

23
Human rights
Shaping development ethics, pragmatics, law, policy and politics

Polly Vizard

In this chapter I examine the ways in which the idea of human rights can contribute to broader reflection on the ends and means of worthwhile development. The chapter considers the different ways in which development theorists, policy makers, practitioners and agitators appeal to the idea of human rights: as ethically justified claims; as a source of pragmatic international consensus on the values underpinning worthwhile development; as legal guarantees; as a policy framework for development policies, programmes and arrangements; and as elements of civic action mobilisation and broader social movements. I address the importance of the idea of human rights in thinking about the theoretical characterisation of worthwhile development and the practical action that can help to bring worthwhile development about.

Human rights can be conceptualised as a core set of freedoms that should be guaranteed to all people everywhere on the basis of non-discrimination and equality, regardless of country, nationality, and citizenship, gender, age, race, ethnicity, religion or belief, or other characteristics or status. Examples of human rights that are widely claimed and cited by development practitioners, policy makers, theorists and agitators include the right to life, the right to freedom from torture and cruel and unusual treatment and punishment, the right to participate in free and fair elections, the right to an adequate standard of living, the rights to education and health, and the right to work. Human rights are generally viewed as being related to a set of correlative responsibilities, obligations or duties on others not to violate or to uphold and secure human rights. Saying that someone has a human right to X is generally taken to imply that others (governments, international organisations, corporations, other individuals etc.) have correlative responsibilities, obligations or duties of this type. For example, appeals to the idea of the human right to life suggest that (1) the human right to life is a basic freedom that should be universally enjoyed and (2) that others have responsibilities, obligations and duties to uphold the human right to life. Similarly, appeals to the human right to an adequate standard of living, health or education, a development practitioner, policy maker, theorist or agitator suggest that (1) these human rights are universal basic freedoms and (2) that others have responsibilities, obligations or duties to ensure that these human rights are upheld.

My analysis in this chapter highlights how the idea of human rights can be important in bridging theory and practice within development ethics and in taking forward an interdisciplinary dialogue relating to the ends and means of worthwhile development. The analytical

DOI: 10.4324/9781315626796-29

framework I adopt builds on Sen's pivotal distinction between (1) the intrinsic importance of freedoms as ends of development and (2) the instrumental importance of freedoms as means to development (Sen 1999). I highlight both the intrinsic importance of human rights as freedom-focussed fundamental values, and the instrumental importance of human rights in terms of the mechanisms, institutions, arrangements and processes via which freedom-focussed development and social change can be promoted and achieved.

Following on from this introductory section, the chapter is organised as follows. First I consider human rights as *ethical claims*. In the following two sections section I consider the international human rights framework first as a source of *pragmatic consensus* on fundamental values and then as *legal guarantees* and as a basis for challenging maldevelopment within international, regional and national legal systems. *Human rights based development* policies, programmes, and arrangements are discussed next. This discussion is followed by a section on how civic action and social movements can appeal to human rights, drawing on the global human right to food movement as an illustration. In the concluding section I highlight priorities for future research.

Human rights as ethical claims

Human rights-based approaches to development suggest that the fulfilment of human rights such as the human right to life, to freedom from torture and cruel and unusual treatment or punishment, or an adequate standard of living, or to education, health or work, should be viewed as fundamental moral rights and as central objectives of national and global development processes, programmes and arrangements. Conversely, human rights-based approaches to development suggest that the nonfulfilment of human rights – and the nonfulfilment of the negative and positive obligations that flow from human rights – should be regarded as forms of maldevelopment and as a basis for moral condemnation and critique, as well as moral pressure and influence, within processes of social evaluation, social mobilisation and social change.

To what extent is it coherent and meaningful to discuss ethical claims concerning worthwhile development in this way, in terms of the ethical language of human rights? There is a vast literature in ethics on the feasibility, justification and content of human rights based ethical claims. At a foundational level, advocates of human rights based approaches to development must grapple with the pivotal question of how – amidst the diversity of moral practices, norms, principles and reasoning over centuries and societies with vastly different cultural, religious and philosophical traditions and periods of history – an objective, impartial or otherwise valid theory of human rights is possible. Another key issue relates to the critical question of whether, even if an objective, impartial or otherwise valid theory of human rights is possible, concerns such as global poverty and the nonfulfilment of basic needs and capabilities, as well as the importance of positive obligations and collective obligations, can be meaningfully accommodated and elucidated within a human rights based ethical framework.

In the past, many influential theories of human rights have been highly restrictive in these respects (Vizard 2006). For example, the libertarian position specifies the objects of fundamental rights in terms of negative liberties, with the obligations that correspond to fundamental rights being characterised as prohibitions on harmful interference with others, and the demands of justice viewed in terms of processes rather than outcomes Based on this approach, second generation economic and social rights, as well as positive obligations of assistance and aid, are viewed as beyond the realm of human rights based ethical claims (e.g. Nozick 1974, Hayek 1960). Within the liberal tradition, Rawl's (1999) treatment of human rights in the Law of Peoples is essentially concerned with the limits of international toleration rather than the specification of the demands of global justice. Other approaches, such as O'Neill (1986, 1996), take the development ethics agenda forward by providing strong support for positive moral obligations of assistance and aid – including for positive imperfect obligations to assist the poor, hungry and needy – within a global context. However, O'Neill argues that positive imperfect obligations are non-specific, discretionary and non-enforceable and cannot be meaningfully elucidated and claimed within a human rights based ethical framework. On this basis, she rejects the normative status of economic and social rights as universal and fundamental.

In contrast, increasing concern with the ethics of development is resulting in new and emerging theories that provide more secure normative foundations for human rights-based approaches to development and for linking the idea of human rights to concerns such as global poverty and the nonfulfilment of basic needs and capabilities, the harmful and adverse effects of maldevelopment, and international development obligations. Pogge's account of global poverty and human rights has been particularly influential in recent years and addresses how global poverty can be characterised as a human rights concern within a framework of negative duties. His theory focusses on the (causal) role of socio-economic arrangements including international development policies, programmes and arrangements, such as international trade agreements, property rights and patent rules, in generating and perpetuating global harm. Pogge argues that (1) strict and well defined duties to refrain from supporting policies, programmes and arrangements of this type can be elucidated and understood within a framework of negative obligations; and (2) that where global poverty and the nonfulfilment of other basic needs such as health result from harmful policies, programmes and arrangements these can be meaningfully characterised as violations of human rights (Pogge 2008;Vizard 2006).

Internationally, it is becoming increasingly common to challenge national and global development policies, processes and arrangements on the grounds of human rights, and Pogge's analysis highlights how a number of these challenges can be understood, elucidated and advanced within a framework of negative duties. For example, Fukuda-Parr highlights the importance of recent campaigns for the human right to health by medical networks in bringing about pressure to change international global rules that harmfully impact on global health. Specifically, the human right to health was invoked as a basis for challenging WTO rules on the production, export, patenting and licensing of pharmaceutical products during the Doha Development Round. The Doha Declaration on the TRIPS Agreement and Public Health, which was eventually agreed and negotiated in the context of this challenge, provided for exceptions and greater flexibility in relation to WTO rules in order to promote access to essential medicines. Campaigns for the human right to health by medical networks have also helped to deliver reductions in the cost of HIV retroviral medications in some developing countries (Fukuda Parr 2016). Pogge's analysis highlights how challenges to global rules and regulations of this type can be framed in terms of negative duties to refrain from supporting international policies, programmes and arrangements that undermine access to essential medicines within the least developed countries – and hence in terms of violations of the human right to health.

Penz et al (2011) and Drydyk (2013) set out a framework of rights and responsibilities for specifying the moral entitlements of individuals who experience displacement in the context of development policies, projects, programmes as well as broader processes such as climate change, including entitlements to compensation and aid for resilience or resettlement. Arguably, moral entitlements of this type can also be understood, elucidated and advanced within a framework of negative duties – in terms of the prohibition on harmful interferences with human rights such as property, food, livelihood and health.

Nevertheless, when development practitioners, policy makers, theorists and agitators appeal to the idea of human rights, they often make reference to the concept of positive obligation: for example, to the positive obligations of governments to guarantee and secure human rights; to international collective obligations in the context of development cooperation; and to the positive obligations of individuals in a position to help. Moreover, as the discussion in the next two sections will illustrate, the concept of positive obligation is firmly embedded within the evolved and expanded international human rights framework, and states parties to core international human rights treaties are required to take positive actions to protect and fulfil human rights, as well as to respect human rights by refraining from violating human rights, under widely accepted interpretations of international human rights law. There is a need to establish more secure normative foundations for authoritative international standards of this type.

An emerging body of literature in ethics addresses the need for a broader account of human rights that recognises economic and social rights and the notion of positive obligation. Campbell (2007) highlights the universal humanitarian obligation to participate in the relief of extreme suffering. Tasioulas (2007) emphasises the merits of interest-based accounts. Griffin rejects the "strong claimability" account of the existence of a human right and argues instead that human rights are grounded in human personhood or agency. These are viewed as requiring liberty, autonomy and certain minimum guarantees, including basic education "a human right to the minimum resources needed to live as a normative agent" (Griffin 2008: 33, 206). Note, however, that Griffin opposes what he views as the non-minimalist formulation of some contemporary international human rights standards, challenging the formulation of Article 25.1 of the Universal Declaration, which recognises a person's right to "a standard of living adequate for the health and wellbeing of himself and his family", as well as the formulation of the human right to the highest attainable standard of physical and mental health in international human rights treaties (on which, see below) (Griffin 2008: 33, 177–187, 206–208). Beitz (2009) highlights the importance of a political account of human rights informed by contemporary human rights ideas, language and practice - including the contemporary articulation of "anti-poverty rights".

The literature on the capability approach provides a distinctive point of departure in a number of important respects. Nussbaum provides an account of capabilities as universal entitlements based on human dignity (e.g. Nussbaum 2004, 2011). She argues that it is possible to arrive at cross-cultural agreement on capabilities as universal entitlements without requiring further agreement on underlying (and diverse) norms, principles and beliefs, taking forward discussions about the possibility of universal values in the face of the relativist, subjectivist and communitarian critiques. Nussbaum builds here on the Rawlsian idea of an "overlapping consensus". This in turn addresses how people with different normative perspectives and religious beliefs can arrive at common principles of justice through processes of moral reasoning.

Other contributions emphasise the importance of democratic deliberation and public reasoning in discussions about capabilities and human rights. Crocker's (2009) account of global ethics and development emphasises the importance of democratic practice and deliberative processes in arriving at value specifications. Drydyk (2011) suggests that arguments for human rights will be undermined if there is an over-reliance on purely theoretically derived principles of human dignity. He proposes that Nussbaum's emphasis on Rawlsian "reflective equilibrium" is replaced by constructive engagement with "all reliable moral discourses" and cross-cultural knowledge of principles of care and neglect. These, he contends, provide a basis for inter-cultural convergence on principles of equal dignity. Sen (2004b) highlights the constitutive role of democratic processes and public reasoning in arriving at lists of needs, capabilities and human rights, whilst drawing attention to antecedents of the idea of human rights in non-Western thought (Sen 1997).

The links between capabilities, second generation human rights and positive obligations are another important theme. Nussbaum notes that her theory of capabilities as universal entitlements is associated with fundamental (pre-institutional) negative and positive claims and has many similarities with a human rights approach that recognises the importance of second-generation human rights (e.g. Nussbaum 2004, 2011). Crocker's theory of capabilities and global ethics specifically addresses collective obligations in the context of development, with central emphasis on second generation human rights, and on positive global responsibilities to bring about their fulfilment (e.g. Crocker 2009). Drydyk (2011) maintains that inter-cultural convergence on principles of equal dignity provides a basis for agreeing on a set of human rights that should be respected, protected and fulfiled.

Sen's "Elements of a Theory of Human Rights" also puts emphasis on both second generation human rights and positive obligations. Sen proposes that the admissibility of human rights based claims depends on the importance and influenceability of the freedoms at hand (rather than on the specific formulation of corresponding duties) and that positive imperfect obligations can be incorporated into a human rights based ethical framework and understood in terms of obligations of "reasonable" assistance and aid on the part of others (individuals, governments, international organisations etc.) in a position to help. He argues that, in a human rights based ethical framework of this type, "opportunity freedoms" (such as the capability to be adequately nourished or to be educated), as well as "process freedoms" (such as due process), can be meaningfully viewed as human rights and are associated with both negative and positive claims on others, individually and collectively, including on governments, socio-economic arrangements, laws and public action (Sen 2004a, 2005, 2009, 2012; Vizard 2006; Vizard et al 2011; Vizard forthcoming).

These accounts differ in their emphasis and their precise characterisations of the relationship between capabilities and human rights. Collectively, however, they provide a potentially powerful basis for linking capabilities and human rights and for operationalising these concepts as a basis for practice orientated human rights and development paradigms.

Human rights as a source of "pragmatic consensus"

Whilst further ethical reflection on foundational issues relating to the existence, justification and content of human rights based claims constitutes an important priority for development ethics, it is important to recognise that appeals to human rights by development practitioners, policy makers, theorists and agitators are commonly articulated directly in terms of the standards embodied within the international human rights framework – rather than in terms of foundational ethical principles, positions and theories. Such appeals to the idea of human rights can play an important role in bridging theory and practice within development ethics and in establishing human rights as a practice orientated body of standards that can provide a basis for laws, public policy and broader civic and social action.

The international human rights framework is the set of internationally recognised human rights standards and norms that are set out in international instruments such as international declarations and treaties. The Universal Declaration of Human Rights (1948) is the cornerstone of the international human rights framework and specifies a basic set of civil, political, economic, social and cultural rights that should be enjoyed by all human beings on the basis of non-discrimination. A substantial body of international standards and norms has subsequently evolved from these foundations. To date, the provisions of the Universal Declaration have been translated into a set of nine core international treaties, including the Convention of the Elimination of All Forms of Racial Discrimination (1965); the International Convention on Civil and Political Rights (ICCPR) (1966); the International Convention on Economic, Social and Cultural Rights (ICESCR) (1966); the Convention on the Elimination of All Forms of Discrimination Against Women (1979); the Convention on the Rights of the Child (CRC) (1989); and the Convention on the Rights of People with Disabilities (2006). All States have ratified at least one, and 80% of States have ratified four or more, of the core human rights treaties. The ICCPR and the ICESCR have 168 and 164 state parties respectively, whilst the CRC has 196 (UN nd a, b).

The evolution and expansion of the international human rights framework in recent decades presents new possibilities for forging links between human rights, public policy and development. Whilst recognition of economic and social rights dates back to the Universal Declaration, for much of the second half of the twentieth century, the international human rights agenda was dominated by civil and political rights. Poverty and other aspects of multidimensional deprivation such as lack of access to food, water, shelter, housing, education or healthcare were not recognised as "legitimate" elements of the international human rights agenda. The World Conference on Human Rights convened in 1993 was a watershed in terms of new the evolution of new norms emphasising the "interdependence" and "indivisibility" of human rights and the "interdependent and mutually reinforcing" nature of human rights and development.

As noted above, the evolved and expanded international human rights framework recognises positive obligations on governments and other duty holders to take positive actions to secure and guarantee human rights. Authoritative international standard setting establishes that three discrete tiers of legal duty follow from international obligations in the field of human rights. The obligation to respect human rights means that states must refrain from interfering with or curtailing the enjoyment of human rights. The obligation to protect human rights requires states to protect individuals and groups against human rights violations. The obligation to fulfil human rights means that states must take positive action to facilitate the enjoyment of basic human rights. Violations of human rights occur where states fail to respect, protect or fulfil human rights (see for example, UN (nd), General Comments of the UN CESCR (OHCHR nd) and Maastricht Guidelines (1997); for overviews of links with the capability approach, see Vizard (2006), Fredman (2008) and Vizard et al. (2011).

Vizard (2006, 2007) proposed that, in an important sense, the evolved and expanded international human rights framework provides a source of pragmatic international consensus on the meaning and content of human rights. This proposal was set out in the context of broader debates about how the capability approach might be extended and combined with the idea of human rights as a basis for public policy, poverty elimination and development. The capability approach, in its broadest form, leaves open both the question of how to identify a list of basic and central capabilities, and the question of how to relate basic capabilities to obligations on individuals, governments, international organisations and other bodies. Vizard (2006, 2007) suggested that the international human rights framework can be an important source of pragmatic guidance in both of these respects.

Scholars of development ethics would be well-justified in objecting to this proposal on the grounds of the massive schism between the realities of the political negotiation of international human rights instruments on the one hand, and the conditions of a true "unforced consensus" on human rights on the other – including conditions relating to the demands of deliberative democracy and to the constitutive role of democratic processes and public reasoning in arriving at lists of needs, capabilities and human rights. Yet the international human rights framework reflects processes that are in part democratic and deliberative and is recognised as an authoritative international agreement on basic values. Development theorists, policy makers, practitioners and agitators might therefore reasonably appeal to these standards as a source of international pragmatic consensus in discussions about worthwhile development (and its converse, maldevelopment).

Human rights as legal guarantees

Going one step farther, appeals to the idea of human rights by development practitioners, policy makers, practitioners and agitators sometimes relate to the understanding of human rights as a legal guarantee. This legal understanding of human rights goes beyond the values perspective outlined above by providing a basis for the characterisation of worthwhile development in terms of a basic consistency with international, regional and national human rights laws. Conversely, development policies, programmes and arrangements that are inconsistent with these laws can be challenged by invoking legal standards that can be enforced through international, regional and domestic legal systems.

The legal understanding and potential of human rights reflects the ways in which many human rights standards are established elements of international, regional and domestic law. Some of the standards set out in the Universal Declaration on Human Rights, such as the prohibition of slavery, are established elements of international customary law, whilst international human rights treaties establish legally binding obligations on states parties that sign and ratify them. The core international human rights treaties establish both negative and positive obligations on states parties to uphold and secure human rights, both individually and collectively. For example, the ICESCR recognises the right to an adequate living and freedom from hunger (article 11); the right of everyone to the enjoyment of the highest attainable standard of physical and mental health (article 12); the right of everyone to education (article 13) and compulsory primary education, free of charge (article 14); the right to work (article 6); and the right to just and fair conditions of work (article 7) and the right to social security (article 9). By signing up to this treaty, states agree "to take steps, individually and through international assistance and co-operation, to the maximum of its available resources, with a view to achieving progressively the full realisation of these rights" and to guarantee non-discrimination (article 2). Authoritative international guidelines state that these provisions require immediate steps that are "deliberate, concrete and targeted" towards the fulfilment of economic and social rights (e.g. UNCESCR 1991). Moreover,

> any situation in which any significant number of individuals is deprived of essential foodstuffs, of essential primary health care, of basic shelter and housing, or of the most basic forms of education constitutes prima facie evidence that a State party is failing to discharge its obligations under the Covenant.
>
> *(Maastricht Guidelines 1997)*

International human rights standards are increasingly incorporated into regional and domestic legal systems within both the Global North and the Global South, providing increased potential for challenging the adverse effects of maldevelopment within regional and national courts. The South African model is widely cited as an international model for the domestic enforcement of economic and social rights as human rights. The Bill of Rights included within Chapter 2 of the Constitution of South Africa (1996) establishes that the state must respect, protect, promote and fulfil the rights in the Bill of Rights and enshrines a number of economic and social rights including housing (section 26), health care, food, water and social security (section 27) and education (section 29). The South African Constitutional Court has found that the South African Government and public authorities have violated constitutional obligations relating to economic and social rights in a series of landmark cases. The Court's reasoning establishes that whilst the state is not under an immediate obligation to fulfil economic and social rights because of limited resources, there is nevertheless an immediate obligation to take steps to promote the progressive realisation of economic and social rights over time. Moreover, in order to be "reasonable" and compatible with the principle of "progressive realisation", certain tests must be satisfied. For example, in the Treatment Action Campaign case, a roll out plan for extending the coverage of anti-retroviral treatment to combat mother-to child transmission of HIV was found to be insufficiently comprehensive and coordinated and incapable of providing universal access to the whole affected population over time. As a result, the plan was found to be "unreasonable" and inconsistent with the principle of "progressive realisation". A violation of the right to health under sections 27(1) and (2) of the Constitution was therefore upheld (Vizard 2006).

UN Special Rapporteur on the Human Right to Food (UNGA 2013) examines how legal recognition of the human right provides a basis for challenging policies, programmes and arrangements in the context of malnutrition, hunger and food security. This analysis suggests that the legal scope of the human right to food should be broadly conceived in terms of threats to sources of self-production (e.g. rights of access to broader resources such as land, forests, water and seeds that are essential to food production for direct consumption) and livelihood (e.g. income generating activities and work) as well as access to food. Moreover, all three of the tiers of obligation discussed above (that is, the obligations to respect, protect and fulfil the human rights) are legally justiciable. Hence illegal violations of the human right to food can result from the direct actions and programmes of public authorities that undermine the ability of individuals and communities to produce their own food; from the failure of the state to adequately protect individuals or groups from violations of the human right to food by third parties (for example, other individuals and private organisations or bodies) by ensuring that appropriate regulatory frameworks, institutions and accountability mechanisms are in place; and where the state has failed to take adequate positive action to fulfil the human right to food (including adequate legislative and public policy measures) (UNGA 2013, especially paras. 6–19).

The Special Rapporteur's Report cites a series of examples which illustrate how challenges can be made through legal and quasi-legal processes when food security is threated and undermined, or fails to be adequately protected, in different countries and contexts. For example, the Report notes how the African Commission on Human and Peoples' Rights found that Nigeria had violated the human rights of the Ogoni people by putting state military and legal state powers at the disposal of oil companies that severely damaged, contaminated and polluted the environmental and food resources on which the Ogoni people depend for their livelihoods and nutrition as well as adversely impacting on health (UNGA 2013, para. 12.). More broadly, marine resources are a critical source of livelihood and nutrition for poor small-scale fishers worldwide. However, traditional entitlements to marine resources can be threatened by processes of modernisation and development. The Special Rapporteur's Report highlights an important case in South Africa, where the High Court ordered a revision of the Marine Living Resources Act to take into account "international and national legal obligations and policy directives to accommodate the socioeconomic rights of [small-scale] fishers and to ensure equitable access to marine resources for those fishers". The Report suggests that this case was an important lever for broader social change, resulting in a new Small-Scale Fisheries Policy recognising "the importance of small-scale fisheries in contributing to food security" and as "a critical safety net against poverty" (UNGA 2013, para. 12; IDLO 2015, 13).

Other examples cited in UN Special Rapporteur on the Human Right to Food (UNGA 2013) highlight how public policy failure by the state and public authorities in relation to food security can be challenged through legal action. This is exemplified by a landmark legal case in India which addressed complaints that established policies and arrangements for preventing starvation deaths were being inadequately and inefficiently implemented – with incomplete coverage of the population at risk, inefficient delivery mechanisms, and inadequate provision for meeting minimum needs. This included uneven implementation of Famine Codes which should have provided protection from starvation deaths under officially recognised famine conditions; the failure of the public food distribution system (restricted to families below the poverty line) to meet minimum nutritional standards; and food-for-work programmes with "labour ceilings" and inadequate cash and food provision. In response, the Indian Supreme Court derived a right to food from the right to life in article 21 of the Constitution (read in conjunction with Constitutional "Directive Principles") and set out a series of requirements regarding how social programmes should be expanded and implemented in order to ensure that the population is guaranteed a basic nutritional floor (Mckay and Vizard 2005; Drèze 2004; COHRE 2003; UNGA 2013, 23).

Human rights based development policies, programmes and arrangements

As well as being viewed as a source of pragmatic consensus and agreement on a set of basic freedoms, and as basis for a set of legally enforceable guarantees, the international human rights framework is increasingly viewed by development policy makers, practitioners, theorists and agitators as an overarching framework for public action, including for the formulation and delivery of national and global development policies, programmes and arrangements.

At the international level, the evolution and expansion of the international human rights framework over the last three decades has been reflected within a number of UN bodies in a human rights "mainstreaming" agenda that emphasises the positive connections and synergies between human rights and development. A UN Statement of Common Understanding on Human Rights-Based Approach to Development (HRBA) was agreed across UN agencies in 2003. This set out the principle that human rights should guide all phases and sectors of development and that development cooperation and programming should further the realisation of human rights as an ultimate goal of development. This has been followed up by the adoption of human rights based approaches to policies, programmes and arrangements within a number of UN bodies.

For example, an agenda setting report on human rights and human development was published by UNDP in 2000. This noted that "[h]uman development and human rights are close enough in motivation and concern to be compatible and congruous, and they are different enough in strategy and design to supplement each other fruitfully" (UNDP 2000). UNDP has subsequently adopted a policy of integrating human rights and human development, with human rights emerging as a key concern within its development activities, for example, adopting a human rights approach to development programming and development cooperation, whereby development cooperation, policies and technical assistance should further the realisation of human rights.

UNICEF's Education for All initiative is explicitly based on the recognition of education as a basic human right. UNICEF's targets, programmes, strategies and assistance to promote universal primary education have been explicitly formulated and implemented within a human rights framework since the early 2000s (UNICEF 2007). UNICEF (2015) highlights some of the broader ways in which embedding international human rights standards into development programmes and policies can help to improve outcomes for children. There is an important link, for example, between a human rights approach and new and emerging models of social accountability in development including both soft law approaches (monitoring, budgeting, empowerment, participation) and hard law approaches (international, regional and domestic enforcement action).

Within other UN agencies, the Food and Agricultural Organisation (FAO) issued Right to Food Guidelines to support the progressive realisation of the right to adequate food in the context of food security in 2004 (FAO 2005). These Guidelines underpin recent progress in the formal recognition of the right to food and a wave of constitutional, legal and policy measures that aim to implement a rights-based approach to food security and nutrition in a number of different developing country contexts (on which, see section 6). The right to health is recognised within the Constitution of the World Health Organisation and WHO's ongoing global universal health initiative, together with related policies and strategies that promote universal health systems, financing and coverage, are explicitly based on the recognition of health as a fundamental human right (WHO nd).

ILO views its conventions that address exploitative, unsafe and unhealthy working conditions, child labour, migrant workers, domestic workers, forced labour, human trafficking, discrimination, freedom of association and the right to join a trade union and so forth as integral to the international human rights framework. ILO is also a key partner in a recent global imitative which aims to achieve universal social protection as a key component of the post-2015 development agenda (on which, see below). The initiative draws on 23 country experiences to show that universal social protection is feasible in developing countries. This includes experiences of universal pensions and old-age pensions in Botswana, Brazil, South Africa, Thailand, Zanzibar, Trinidad and Tobago, Azerbaijan, Bolivia and China; experiences of universal social protection for children in Argentina and Mongolia; experiences of disability support in Nepal Timor-Leste and Ukraine; and experiences of cash transfer programmes in sub-Saharan Africa (World Bank Group and ILO 2016).

UN Poverty Reduction Guidelines provide a framework for international poverty reduction based on the standards set out in international human rights law (OHCHR 2003). The Guidelines specify that human rights principles are relevant to the content of poverty reduction strategies, with the international human rights framework used to identifying the major elements of a strategy for realising a number of specific human rights and human rights obligations of particular relevance to poverty reduction. In addition, they specify that human rights principles should inform the process of formulating, implementing and monitoring poverty reduction strategies – including by establishing legal institutions for implementing human rights and by ensuring that the principles such as universality, non-discrimination, transparency, accountability, participation and empowerment are specifically built into the design of poverty reduction policies and strategies.

Arjun Sengupta's right to development framework (RTDF) is another key initiative. This framework provides a basis for implementing the UN Declaration on the Right to Development which was adopted in 1986, partly as a response to pressure by countries within the Global South. This framework has been important in highlighting the issue of accountability and puts central emphasis on correlative duties and the identification of duty-bearers. Further emphasis is put on international collective obligations, including development cooperation, and explicit linkages between human right fulfilments and global economic structures including global economic and trade arrangements, debt and the activities of transnational corporations.

Related and ongoing processes of norm development seek to further strengthen the human rights framework in the context of globalisation, for example, through clarification of the nature and scope of the extraterritorial obligations of states in the field of economic and social rights, responsibilities in the context of development co-operation and through more effective regulation of non-state actors including transnational corporations (Sengupta 2004a, 2004b; Salomon 2007, 2010; De Schutter et al. 2012; Marks, this volume, Chapter 24). Nevertheless, as Stiglitz notes, globalisation requires both a downscaling of responsibility (for example, to cover non-state actors such as private companies) and an up-scaling of responsibility (to the global arena – for example, with more emphasis on collective responsibilities). Multinational private companies, for example, should be held responsible for misuses of power and market manipulation and held responsible for human rights abuses under international law (Stiglitz 2013a, 2013b; Vizard 2015).

Moreover, whilst the human rights mainstreaming agenda has permeated a number of UN institutions, the relationship between human rights and the World Bank remains unclear. The Bank's "economic growth" first and trickle-down development agendas are increasingly superseded by an agenda that recognises the importance of poverty elimination, equity, inequality, institution-building, human capital and minimum standards in areas such as health and social protection (e.g. World Bank 2006). Nevertheless, as recently as 2015, the World Bank was still receiving extensive criticism for its human rights positioning, with the Bank characterised as a "human rights free zone" by the UN expert on extreme poverty. At the heart of this critique is the Bank's interpretation of its Articles of Agreement. These include an interference in the political affairs of states and have been viewed as a prohibition on engagement with human rights (UNGA 2015).

The Millennium Development Goals (MDGs), which provided an international agreement on reducing global poverty by 2015, also had a complex relationship with human rights. Official evaluations suggest that international public action was galvanised through the MDG system of outcome-orientated and time-bound targets and indicators. However, whilst the international human rights framework makes provision for the "progressive realisation" of economic and social rights, some have argued that the MDGs targets were a "betrayal" of international human rights standards – with only weak links to international law, minimalist targets specified in terms of halving rather than eliminating extreme poverty and hunger, rather than in terms of universal targets, and weak mechanisms for accountability and enforcement. The absence of adequate mechanisms for implementing collective obligations under MDG 8 ("building a global partnership for development") has also been highlighted (e.g. Fukuda Parr 2006).

Following and building on the MDGs, the new set of UN Sustainable Development Goals have been negotiated and agreed as an international framework for achieving social progress within the period to 2020. Whilst the SGGs are not explicitly formulated in the language of human rights, early indications are that the new system of national level indicators will put more emphasis on universalism and equality, for example, with universal targets relating to poverty elimination, health and social protection, and through increased emphasis on inequalities by characteristics such as income, gender, age, race, ethnicity, migratory status, disability and area.

Human rights, civic action and social movements

Finally, in this section I turn to the ways in which development theorists, policy makers, practitioners and agitators appeal to the idea of human rights as elements of civic action, mobilisation and broader social movements. International human rights standards, underpinned by human rights principles such as universalism, equality, participation and accountability, are increasingly cited as a basis for the work of development focussed NGOs such as Oxfam and Save the Children, as well as NGOs with a more traditional human rights focus, such as Amnesty International. In addition, appeals to the idea of human rights as elements of civic action, mobilisation and broader social movements go far beyond the agendas of international NGOs and increasingly provide a global language for civil society demands and claims relating to worthwhile development in many different countries and contexts within the Global South.

The emergence of the human right to food movement provides an illustration. The recent assessment by the UN Special Rapporteur on the Human Right to Food examined above (UNGA 2013) concluded that globally there has substantial progress in the legal recognition, protection and institutionalisation of the human right to food including substantial progress within a number of poor countries within the Global South. The assessment focusses attention on the range of different mechanisms and process that are relevant to processes of social change – civic, legal, political, policy based etc. – and how social change results from "the interplay of different actors, including courts, parliaments, governments, national human rights institutions, civil society and social movements" (UNGA 2013, para.8). Four insights from this analysis are particularly relevant.

First, the report by the UN Special Rapporteur on the Human Right to Food shows that a wave of constitutional reform has resulted in greater legal recognition of human right to food in a number of different countries and contexts, spearheaded by Latin American countries but with considerable progress in Africa. These parallel processes of constitutional reform have been coupled with judicial enforcement of the human right to food, with landmark cases establishing the justiciability of all three tiers of international obligation relating to the human right to food that are recognised within international standard-setting (on which, see "Human rights as legal guarantees" above). Overall, legal strategies and legal pressure were found to be instrumental in moving malnutrition and hunger up the political agenda; in recognising and establishing food security as a national and societal goal; in securing appropriate public policy responses; and in establishing and embedding processes of on-going legal accountability (UNGA 2013, especially paras. 9-19).

Second, the strengthening of the legal recognition and enforcement of the human right to food was coupled with broader public action including an expansion of social legislation and the adoption of food security and malnutrition national plans, strategies and policies grounded in a rights based approach, for example, in Argentina, Guatemala, Ecuador, Brazil, Venezuela, Colombia, Nicaragua and Honduras, Mexico, Indonesia, Thailand, Zanzibar, Malawi, Mozambique, Senegal and Uganda. The expansion of legal entitlements relating to government food security schemes and the institutionalisation of formal social protection was taken forward in a number of countries, helping to reduce dependence on charity and supporting the establishment of a new relationship between duty-bearers and rights-holders (UNGA 2013, especially paras. 34–46).

Third, the Special Rapporteur's assessment focusses attention on the instrumental role of civic action, social mobilisation and broader social movements in bringing about this greater legal recognition of the human right to food and in securing the introduction of new social and public policies. Bottom-up civil society activism and pressure are credited with moving the human right to food up political agendas, creating pressure for constitutional reform, securing the introduction of new social and public policies and initiating legal action in a number of different countries and contexts. For example, constitutional reform to insert the right to food into the Mexican Constitution followed 20 years of advocacy from civil society groups. In Haiti, civil society was a major driving force behind adoption of the 2010 national plan for food security and nutrition. In Nepal, a civil society group was instrumental in bringing a landmark right to food case before the Supreme Court.

Fourth, the Special Rapporteur's Report (together with supplementary analysis by Oxfam) puts the spotlight on broader civil society processes and mechanisms that can be instrumental in promoting transparency and accountability in relation to the implementation of the human right to food over time. The emergence and proliferation of a wide range of different human rights and civil society monitoring methods and new forms of civic activism are presented as embedding new forms of social accountability for the implementation of legal standards and social and public policies, including by combatting public policy failure, corruption and the diversion of funds. Examples cited include the monitoring of outcomes by National Human Rights Institutions, Special Rapporteurs and other independent bodies such as ombudsmen and the use of a range of social auditing methodologies such as village-level oversight to prevent misuse of funds in Rajasthan; public expenditure tracking surveys in Ghana, Uganda, Tanzania; citizen report cards and community score cards in India, Gambia, Kenya, Malawi; and participatory audits in Philippines and Indonesia. In a number of countries, including Brazil, Chile, India, Pakistan and Bangladesh, monitoring was facilitated and strengthened by Right to Information Acts. For example, the Indian Right to Food Campaign used social audits and right to information laws to assess compliance with Court-mandated decisions relating to the right to livelihood and food. Measures to promote the participation of civil society and those affected by hunger and malnutrition in decision-making and the design of policies for combatting hunger and malnutrition were also found to be important (UNGA 2013, especially paras. 28–32 and 53–56; Oxfam nd).

Priorities for future research

In this chapter I have examined the different ways in which development theorists, policy makers, practitioners and agitators appeal to the idea of human rights and how appeals of this type relate to broader reflection in development ethics about the ends and means of worthwhile development. Building on Sen's pivotal distinction between the intrinsic and instrumental importance of freedoms as ends and means of development, I have explored both the intrinsic importance of human rights as freedom-focussed fundamental values, and the instrumental importance of human rights in terms of the mechanisms, institutions, arrangements and processes via which freedom-focussed development and social change can be brought about.

Looking forward, the analysis points towards an exciting and engaging research agenda on human rights and development. There are multiple lines of inquiry to be pursued across several different disciplines spanning ethics, law, public policy and political economy. A key priority relates to the need for further consideration of the principles of "reasonableness" that can inform the development of broad theory of human rights. Another (related) priority is to develop new inter-disciplinary methodologies for evaluating the progressive realisation of economic and social rights and the fulfilment of the corresponding national and global obligations, including the fulfilment of negative and positive obligations in the context of development cooperation. The new SERF index (Fukuda Parr et al. 2015) provides a model. A third priority is to build up a body of theory and empirical evidence on the general importance of human rights as a means to worthwhile development. This research agenda is already underway. However, as Vizard (forthcoming) notes, there remains a need to build up a much more comprehensive and substantial body of theory and empirical evidence on the importance of human rights, including economic and social rights, as a means to freedom-focussed development and social change.

Scholars working within the field of development ethics, with its dual emphasis on the nature of worthwhile development and the practical action that can help to bring worthwhile development about, are well-positioned to make an important contribution to interdisciplinary dialogue and future thinking on this subject in the years to come.

References

Beitz C. (2009) *The Idea of Human Rights*, OUP, Oxford.

Campbell, T., in Pogge, T. (2007) *Freedom from Poverty as a Human Right*. OUP, Oxford.

COHRE (2003) Litigating Economic, Social and Cultural Rights: Achievements, Challenges and Strategies. http://globalinitiative-escr.org/wp-content/uploads/2012/06/Litigating-ESCR-Report.pdf.

Crocker, D. (2009) *Ethics of Global Development Agency, Capability and Deliberative Democracy*. Cambridge University Press, Cambridge.

De Schutter, O., Eide A., Khalfan A., Orellana M., Salomon M., Seiderman I. (2012) Commentary to the Maastricht Principles on Extraterritorial Obligations of States in the Area of Economic, Social and Cultural Rights. *Human Rights Quarterly* 34: 1084–1169

Drèze, J (2004) Democracy and the Right to Food. *Economic and Political Weekly* 24(April).
Drydyk, J. (2011) Responsible Pluralism, Capabilities, and Human Rights. *Journal of Human Development and Capabilities* 12(1).
Drydyk, J. (2013) Development Ethics and the Climate Migrants. *Ethics, Policy & Environment* 16(1): 43–55, DOI: 10.1080/21550085.2013.768398.
FAO (2005) Voluntary Guidelines to Support the Progressive Realization of the Right to Adequate Food. www.fao.org/3/a-y7937e.pdf. Accessed 2 January 2018.
Fukuda-Parr, S. (2006) Millennium Development Goal 8: Indicators for International Human Rights Obligations. *Human Rights Quarterly* 28(4: 966–997.
Fukuda-Parr, S. (2016) Human Rights Are Not Losing Traction in the Global South. www.opendemocracy.net/openglobalrights/sakiko-fukuda-parr/human-rights-are-not-losing-traction-in-global-south. Accessed 2 January 2018.
Fukuda-Parr, D., Lawson-Remer, T. and Randolph, S. (2015) *Fulfilling Economic and Social Rights*. OUP, Oxford.
Fredman, S. (2008) *Human Rights Transformed: Positive Rights and Positive Duties*. OUP, Oxford.
Griffin, J. (2008) *On Human Rights*. OUP, Oxford.
Hayek, F.A. (1960) *The Constitution of Liberty*. Routledge and Kegan Paul, London.
IDLO (2015) Realizing the Right to Food: Legal Strategies and Approaches. www.idlo.int/sites/default/files/pdfs/publications/Realizing%20the%20Right%20to%20Food_Legal%20Strategies%20and%20Approaches_full-report_0.pdf. Accessed 2 January 2018.
Maastricht Guidelines on Violations of Economic, Social and Cultural Rights (1997) http://hrlibrary.umn.edu/instree/Maastrichtguidelines_.html. Accessed 2 January 2018.
Mckay, A. and Vizard, P. (2005) Rights and Economic Growth: Inevitable Conflict or Common Ground? www.odi.org.uk/rights/Meeting%20Series/Growth&Rights.pdf. Accessed 2 January 2018.
Nozick, R. (1974) *Anarchy, State and Utopia*. Basil Blackwell, Oxford.
Nussbaum, M.C. (2004) Beyond the Social Contract: Capabilities and Global Justice. *Oxford Development Studies* 32(1): 3–18.
Nussbaum, M. (2011) Capabilities, Entitlements, Rights: Supplementation and Critique. *Journal of Human Development and Capabilities* 12(1): 23–37.
OHCHR (2003) Human Rights and Poverty Reduction: A Conceptual Framework. www.ohchr.org/Documents/Publications/PovertyReductionen.pdf. Accessed 2 January 2018.
O'Neill, O. (1986) *Faces of Hunger: An Essay on Poverty, Justice and Development*. Allen and Unwin, London.
O'Neill, O. (1996) *Towards Justice and Virtue: A Constructive Account of Practical Reasoning*. CUP, Cambridge.
Oxfam (nd) http://oxfamblogs.org/fp2p/impressive-progress-in-guaranteeing-the-right-to-food-in-poor-countries-as-olivier-de-schutter-bows-out/. Accessed 2 January 2018.
Penz, P., Drydyk, J. and Bose, P. (2011) *Displacement by Development: Ethics, Rights, and Responsibilities*. Cambridge University Press, Cambridge.
Pogge, T. (2008) *World Poverty and Human Rights*, Second Edition. Polity, Cambridge.
Rawls, J. (1999) *The Law of Peoples*. Harvard University Press, Cambridge.
Salomon, M. (2007) *Global Responsibility for Human Rights: World Poverty and the Development of International Law*. OUP, Oxford.
Salomon, M. (2010) International Human Rights Obligations in Context: Structural Obstacles and the Demands of Global Justice. In Andreassen, B. A. and Marks, S. eds., *Development as a Human Right: Legal, Political and Economic Dimensions* Second Edition. Intersentia, Antwerp.
Sen, A.K. (1997) Human Rights and Asian Values. *The New Republic* 33 July 14 and 21, 1997.
Sen, A.K. (1999) *Development as Freedom*. OUP, Oxford.
Sen, A.K. (2004a) Elements of a Theory of Human Rights. *Philosophy and Public Affairs* 23(4): 315–356.
Sen, A.K. (2004b) Capabilities, Lists and Public Reason: Continuing the Conversation. *Feminist Economics* 10(3): 77–80.
Sen, A.K. (2005) Human Rights and Capabilities. *Journal of Human Development* 6(2): 151–166.
Sen, A.K. (2009) *The Idea of Justice*. Penguin, London.

Sen, A.K. (2012) Foreword. In Elson, D., Fukuda Parr, S. and Vizard, P. eds., *Human Rights and the Capabilities Approach: An Inter-disciplinary Dialogue*. Routledge, London.

Sengupta, A. (2004a) The Human Right to Development. *Oxford Development Studies* 32(2).

Sengupta, A. (2004b) Conceptualizing the Right to Development for the Twenty-First Century. www.ohchr.org/Documents/Issues/Development/RTDBook/PartIChapter4.pdf. Accessed 2 January 2018.

Stiglitz, J. (2013a) Human Rights and Globalization: The Responsibility of States and Private Actors. *Journal of Catholic Social Thought* 10(1).

Stiglitz, J. (2013b) India's Patently Wise Decision. www.project-syndicate.org/commentary/the-impact-of-the-indian-supreme-court-s-patent-decision-by-joseph-e-stiglitz-and-arjun-jayadev. Accessed 2 January 2018.

Tasioulas, J. (2007) The Moral Reality of Human Rights. In Pogge, T. (ed), op. cit.

UN (nd a) What Are Human Rights? www.ohchr.org/EN/Issues/Pages/WhatareHumanRights.aspx. Accessed 2 January 2018.

UN (nd b) The Core International Human Rights Instruments and their Monitoring Bodies. www.ohchr.org/EN/ProfessionalInterest/Pages/CoreInstruments.aspx. Accessed 2 January 2018.

UNCESCR (1991) General Comment No. 3: The Nature of States Parties' Obligations (art. 2, para. 1, of the Covenant). http://tbinternet.ohchr.org/Treaties/CESCR/Shared%20Documents/1_Global/INT_CESCR_GEC_4758_E.doc. Accessed 2 January 2018.

UNDP (2000) Human Rights and Human Development. http://hdr.undp.org/sites/default/files/reports/261/hdr_2000_en.pdf. Accessed 2 January 2018.

UNGA (2013) Interim Report of the Special Rapporteur on the Right to Food A/68/288. www.srfood.org/images/stories/pdf/officialreports/20131025_rtf_en.pdf. Accessed 2 January 2018.

UNGA (2015) Report of the Special Rapporteur on Extreme Poverty and Human Rights. www.un.org/ga/search/view_doc.asp?symbol=A/70/274. Accessed 2 January 2018.

UNICEF (2007) A Human Rights Based Approach to Education For All. www.unicef.org/publications/files/A_Human_Rights_Based_Approach_to_Education_for_All.pdf. Accessed 2 January 2018.

UNICEF (2015) Accountability for Children's Rights. www.unicef.org/policyanalysis/rights/files/Accountability-for-Childrens-Rights-UNICEF.pdf. Accessed 2 January 2018.

Vizard, P. (2006) *Poverty and Human Rights: Sen's 'Capability Perspective' Examined*. OUP, Oxford.

Vizard, P. (2007) Selecting And Justifying A Basic Capability Set: Should The International Human Rights Framework Be Given A More Direct Role? *Oxford Development Studies* 35(3): 25–250.

Vizard, P. (2015) The Human Rights and Equality Agenda in Social Disadvantage. In Dean, H., and Platt. L. eds., *Social Advantage and Disadvantage*. OUP, Oxford.

Vizard, P. (forthcoming) The Capability Approach and Human Rights. Chapter Prepared for the Cambridge Handbook on the Capability Approach.

Vizard, P., Fukuda-Parr, S. and Elson, D. (2011) Introduction. *Journal of Human Development and Capabilities* 12(1).

World Bank Group and ILO (2016) A Shared Vision for Universal Social Protection. http://www.ilo.org/wcmsp5/groups/public/---dgreports/---dcomm/documents/genericdocument/wcms_378996.pdf. Accessed 2 January 2018

WHO (nd) Health Financing for Universal Health. www.who.int/health_financing/universal_coverage_definition/en/. Accessed 2 January 2018.

24

The right to development

Ethical development as a human right

Stephen P. Marks

One of the most salient contradictions of human rights in international development is the fact that there exists a human rights instrument that directly addresses all agreed-upon ethical principles of development, as defined in this *Handbook* (see Chapter 1) and yet implementation of that instrument is mired in 'political theatre' and consequently is inoperable. Indeed, the Declaration on the Right to Development (DRTD), which was adopted by UN General Assembly (GA) on 4 December 1986, addresses directly all seven values analyzed by this *Handbook* and efforts to clarify the meaning of its ten articles through expert inputs provided to the United Nations have been even more explicit on these ethical principles.

The starting point of ethical development is the proposition that there are value-based differences between worthwhile development and undesirable maldevelopment and that worthwhile development cannot be reduced to economic growth. The first *Human Development Report* (*HDR*), published in 1990, affirmed, 'we are rediscovering the essential truth that people must be at the centre of all development' (UNDP 1990, iii). Fourteen years earlier, the DRTD affirmed, 'The human person is the central subject of development and should be the active participant and beneficiary of the right to development' (Article 2.1). The text and its subsequent interpretation also address enhancement of well-being, equitable sharing, empowerment, environmental sustainability, human rights, cultural freedom and anti-corruption. It is a complete catalogue of ethical development, defined as a human right itself, and universal in character by virtue of its formal adoption by the highest institution representative of all states.

In this chapter I examine the ethical underpinnings of the DRTD, the expanding interpretation of its ethical content, and its political and legal significance.

While all the concerns of ethical development are found in the DRTD, the context for its adoption was not directly the result of the emergence of ethical thinking among economists. It was rather a diplomatic move by newly independent countries, belonging roughly to the Non-Aligned Movement (NAM) to assert their priority concerns in the context of the Cold War and failed efforts to establish a New International Economic Order (NIEO). The idea of a human right to development also builds on a number of principles of international cooperation, reaffirmed in UN documents since 1944. (Documents supporting these principles are reviewed in United Nations 1990 and summarized in Kunanayakam 2013, 17–48; the bibliography of the OHCHR publication *Realizing the Right to Development* covers some 30 pages, including nearly

DOI: 10.4324/9781315626796-30

150 entries on the historical context of the right, 505–510.) Frustrated with the East-West rivalry dominating debates, developing countries supported Senegal's initiative to have the UN declare development itself a human right. As declarations on NIEO were not affecting real power relations, NAM sought to use its majority in the General Assembly to establish the normative basis and the blueprint for the creation of a more just international economic order. Their intention was to use the human rights framework through the declaration on the right to development to oblige those countries that dominate the international economy to accept greater responsibility for eliminating the causes of poverty, to pay more for raw materials extracted from developing countries, to provide more aid, and to improve the terms of trade in favour of developing countries.

Senegalese Judge Kéba M'Baye was the first to propose, in a lecture he delivered in 1972, that development be defined as a human right (M'Baye 1972, 503). In 1977, with Senegal as chair, the Commission on Human Rights requested a study on 'the international dimensions of the right to development,' (UNCHR 1977) using the expression for the first time as though there were a recognized right to development. Pursuant to that request, the UN secretariat produced in 1979 a 161-page study (United Nations 1979; see Alston 2013 for summary) providing the basis for what became the UN Declaration on the Right to Development, adopted eight years later by the UN General Assembly. That study was written by Philip Alston, who went on to chair the Committee on Economic, Social and Cultural Rights, among other mandates for the UN, and to be a prominent human rights professor and scholar. His study covered a wide range of legal and political dimensions of the right and specifically addressed ethical aspects of the right to development, which are worth reproducing in full as they have lost none of their salience nearly 40 years later:

> Consideration of the ethical aspects of the human right to development raises a variety of issues which were referred to during the relevant debate at the thirty-third session of the Commission on Human Rights in 1977. These range from the relatively pragmatic view that it is in the best interests of all States to promote the universal realization of the right, to the view that there are fundamental philosophical values which can be said to underlie the right to development in its broadest sense. These issues encompass in particular the following arguments:
>
> (a) *The fundamental character of development:* the promotion of development is a fundamental concern of every human endeavour;
> (b) *The international duty of solidarity for development*: in international relations there exists a duty of solidarity which is solemnly recognized in the Charter;
> (c) *Moral interdependence*: the increasing interdependence of all peoples underlines the necessity of sharing responsibility for the promotion of development;
> (d) *Economic interdependence*: it is in the economic best interests of all States to promote universal realization of the right to development;
> (e) *The maintenance of world peace*: existing economic and other disparities are inconsistent with the maintenance of world peace and stability;
> (f) *The moral duty of reparation*: the industrialized countries, former colonial powers and some others have a moral duty of reparation to make up for past exploitation.
>
> These are a variety of ethical arguments which may be considered to support the existence, in ethical terms, of a right to development.
>
> *(Alston 2013, 9–10)*

The UN study also anticipated the major issues that remain contentious today. Thus, the drafters of the DRTD were presented with ethical aspects, which they considered along with their political and legal preferences. In the context of the Cold War in the late 1970s, the political climate was highly charged with ideological positioning on practically every issue. North American and European delegations to the drafting committee agreed only to accept a general moral (not legal) commitment to human development and rejected the idea of using the right to development to affirm a legal obligation to transfer resources from North to South or to codify any specifics regarding any of the issues contained in the declaration. This tension continues today.

Ethical grounding of the declaration on the right to development

The human right to development was finally proclaimed by the UN General Assembly on 4 December 1986 in the Declaration on the Right to Development, by a recorded vote of 146 in favour, 1 against (United States) and 8 abstentions (Denmark, Finland, the Federal Republic of Germany, Iceland, Israel, Japan, Sweden and the United Kingdom). Being a resolution of the General Assembly, the Declaration does not create any legal obligations, although it has the potential for carrying the weight of moral and political obligations (Marks 2010). It was a compromise document of 16 preambular paragraphs and ten articles setting out a core definition; an enumeration of rights and duties of individuals and states; a commitment to the elimination of massive human rights violations and to international peace and security; a reiteration of the principles of non-discrimination, interrelatedness of rights, and participation; and an enumeration of steps states should take at the national and international levels to realize this right. A considerable body of commentary has appeared in support of the Declaration, mainly in human rights publications, but critical and sceptical views have also emerged in legal and political writings (Donnelly 1984; Donnelly 1985; Alston 1985; Donnelly 1985 'Reply to Alston'; Shelton 1985; Marks 2004). The ethical dimensions are more rarely addressed.

All seven principles of development ethics figure prominently in the normative content of the right to development, as set out in the Declaration and subsequently interpreted by various expert bodies of the United Nations, especially the High-Level Task Force which functioned from 2004 to 2010. In its final proposal of criteria and sub-criteria for the RTD (United Nations 2010c), it provided detailed suggestions for a core norm, three attributes, 18 criteria, 69 sub-criteria and 150 indicators. It is thus in those references, as well as the text of the DRTD itself, that one may find a high degree of congruence with the seven principles of ethical development. The contribution of the RTD to each principle will be reviewed later in the chapter.

Enhancement of people's well-being

The dimension of ethical development that seeks to define development as enhancement of people's well-being correlates directly with the definition of the right to development. Indeed, the second preambular paragraph of the DRTD defines development as

> a comprehensive economic, social, cultural and political process, which aims at the constant *improvement of the well-being of the entire population and of all individuals* on the basis of their active, free and meaningful participation in development and in the fair distribution of the benefits resulting therefrom.
>
> *(DRTD 1986, preamble, emphasis added)*

Article 2 establishes the right and duty of states 'to formulate appropriate national development policies that aim at the constant *improvement of the well-being of the entire population and of all individuals* . . . ' (DRTD 1986, 2[3], emphasis added).

The language of well-being had become fairly common in UN standard-setting in the development field. The term appears in Article 55 of the UN Charter and in numerous development-related documents adopted in the decades preceding the DRTD. For example, Article 8 of the 1969 Declaration on Social Progress and Development defines the 'primary role and ultimate responsibility' of States as being to ensure 'the social progress and well-being of its people' (UNGA 1969).

In assessments of the right to development since the adoption of the DRTD, the centrality of well-being has been regularly highlighted. For example, the Independent Expert on the Right to Development, Dr. Arjun K. Sengupta, wrote that

> [t]he concept of well-being in this context extends well beyond the conventional notions of economic growth to include the expansion of opportunities and capabilities to enjoy those opportunities, captured in the indicators of social and human development, which in turn expand substantive freedoms.
>
> *(Sengupta 2013, 69)*

He further explains that 'the concept of well-being here is broader than the concept of "human development," as it incorporates social, political and cultural processes into the economic process of realizing rights and freedoms' (Sengupta 2013, 71).

Equitable sharing in benefits of development

'The fair distribution of benefits resulting therefrom' is part of the definition in the DRTD preamble. Article 8(1) stipulates that States 'shall ensure, inter alia, equality of opportunity for all in their access to basic resources, education, health services, food, housing, employment and the fair distribution of income.' Article 2(3) defines appropriate national development policies as those that are that 'aim at the constant improvement of the well-being of the entire population and of all individuals, on the basis of their active, free and meaningful participation in development and in the fair distribution of the benefits resulting therefrom.'

Former High-Level Task Force member Raymond Atuguba, in his study for the OHCHR, was very outspoken on fair distribution: 'To say that the benefits of development are unfairly distributed is a contradiction in terms. Development, in the real sense of the word, implies fair distribution of resources in an equitable manner' (Atuguba 2013, 112).

In her study on poverty in relation to the RTD, Irene I. Hadiprayitno identified fair distribution of the benefits of development as one of 'two novel features' of the right to development (the other being popular participation, to be discussed in the next section) (Hadiprayitno 2013, 137). She begins by analyzing what 'fair' means in the theory of justice according to John Rawls in terms of both formal equality and distributive justice (Hadiprayitno 2013, 140), and concludes, 'The concept of fair distribution of benefits should be interpreted in a holistic manner; this demands recognition that, in many cases, pursuing human-centred development requires the economic means for realizing many human rights entitlements' (Hadiprayitno 2013, 141) [and thus] 'underscores the potential of the right to development as a framework of processes for facilitating a fuller realization of other human rights' (Hadiprayitno 2013, 142).

Beyond the impact on the full range of human rights, 'the right to development . . . requires that the primary emphasis in designing development policies be placed on how to protect people from possible adverse consequences and, in particular, from the abuse of power at the initial and execution stages of development processes' (Hadiprayitno 2013, 142). Finally, she draws attention to the extension of fairness under the RTD to intergenerational fairness, noting that the 1993 Vienna Declaration and Programme of Action call for the RTD to be 'fulfilled so as to meet equitably the developmental and environmental needs of present and future generations' (Hadiprayitno 2013, 141 citing the Vienna Declaration and Programme of Action1993). Such developmental needs include, for example, employment, education, health, nutrition, housing facilities, crime prevention and the well-being of children and thus resources must be allocated in these areas so that the outcomes are shared equitably. Hadiprayitno identified two duties of States regarding fair distribution, 'first, measures to protect against damage caused by an unjust distribution of development benefits and, second, to ensure access to remedies for harm caused by or attributable to development programmes, policies or projects' (Hadiprayitno 2013, 142).

The High-Level Task Force addressed equitable distribution in Attribute 3 'Social justice in development') and devoted three criteria and nine sub-criteria to this issue. Criterion 3(a) calls on states to '[p]rovide for fair access to and sharing of the benefits of development' and gives content to this criterion through four sub-criteria:

3(a)(i) Equality of opportunity in education, health, housing, employment, and incomes
3(a)(ii) Equality of access to resources and public goods
3(a)(iii) Reducing marginalization of least developed and vulnerable countries
3(a)(iv) Ease of immigration for education, work and revenue transfers

Empowerment to participate freely in development

As mentioned in the previous section, popular participation was one of the 'two novel features' of the right, reiterated in the preamble ('free and meaningful participation in development'), as well as in Article 1 ('every human person and all peoples are entitled to participate in, contribute to, and enjoy economic, social, cultural and political development'), and Article 2(3) ('active, free and meaningful participation in development'). In addition, Article 8(2) calls on States to 'encourage popular participation in all spheres as an important factor in development and in the full realization of all human rights.'

Already in 1979, Alston described participation as 'a central factor in realization of the right to development' and noted that '[p]opular participation as an integral part of the development process has long been accepted as an ideal at the international level and is increasingly being incorporated into national development strategies' (Alston 2013, 14). Drawing on numerous older references he concludes that

> Participation should be viewed both as a means to an end and as an end in itself. As a prerequisite for realization of the right to development, it is required at all levels ranging from the local through the regional and national to the international.
>
> *(Alston 2013, 14)*

In 1990 the UN organized a Global Consultation on the Right to Development, which considered participation to be 'the right through which all other rights in the Declaration on the Right to Development are exercised and protected,' adding that

> the forms, quality, democratic nature and effectiveness of participatory processes, mechanisms

> and institutions are the central and essential indicators of progress in realizing the right to development [which also] ... applies to the equality and democratic character of intergovernmental bodies, including financial and trade institutions.
>
> *(United Nations 1990b; OHCHR 2013, 62)*

The Global Consultation even proposed criteria for participation, including

> the representativeness and accountability of decision-making bodies, the decentralization of decision-making, public access to information and responsiveness of decision makers to public opinion. . . [as well as] from a subjective perspective based on the opinions and attitudes of the people affected – in other words, their confidence in leaders, feeling of empowerment and belief that they are affecting decisions.
>
> *(OHCHR 2013, 62)*

The High-Level Task Force included 'a national and global enabling environment conducive to ... participatory ... development' as part of the core norm. Further, one of the three attributes of the RTD is on 'Participatory human rights processes' (Attribute 2), with a criterion 2 (c) on 'Establishment of a framework to facilitate participation' and two associated sub-criteria: 2(c)(ii) 'establishment of a framework to facilitate participation' and 2(c)(iii) 'Procedures facilitating participation in social and economic decision-making.' Under criterion 2(d) ('Promote good governance at the international level and effective participation of all countries in international decision-making') is a sub-criterion 2(d)(ii) on 'Genuine participation of all concerned in international consultation and decision-making.' All of these sub-criteria have associated indicators.

Flávia Piovesan, a former member of the High-Level Task Force, wrote a study for the OHCHR on 'Active, Free and Meaningful Participation in Development,' in which she explained that the DRTD

> is the only international instrument that makes the nature of participation in development so explicit, emphasizing that States should encourage, promote and ensure free, meaningful and active participation of all individuals and groups in the design, implementation and monitoring of development policies.
>
> *(Piovesan 2013, 105)*

She further clarifies 'active' as meaning that '[p]eople should be active participants in development and implementing developing projects rather than treated as passive beneficiaries'; and 'meaningful' and 'effective' as reflecting 'the people's ability to voice their opinions in institutions that enable the exercise of power [with] material capacities and the material conditions on which meaningful political participation depends' (Piovesan 2013, 105–106).

The High-Level Task Force drew on the OECD and the World Bank indicators for measuring empowerment, which take human rights into account (United Nations 2010a, para. 18). It assessed several international programs from the perspective of their contribution to empowerment and participation (United Nations 2010a, paras. 46, 48, 49, 59).

Hadiprayitno, in her paper on poverty for the OHCHR, noted that

> Meaningful participation and empowerment are reflected by the people's ability to voice their opinions, recognizing the citizenry as the origin of and the justification for public authority' and enumerated several procedural and substantive 'forms by which populations can participate in development through mechanisms such as public consultation, information

> and decision-making with special consideration given to the participation of vulnerable groups, in particular taking the gender, race and ethnicity perspectives, giving voice to the deprived and the vulnerable.
>
> *(Hadiprayitno 2013, 105)*

Environmental sustainability

Although the DRTD was drafted fourteen years after the 1972 Stockholm Declaration, which enunciated as Principle I that 'Man has the fundamental right to freedom, equality and adequate conditions of life, in an environment of a quality that permits a life of dignity and well-being, and he bears a solemn responsibility to protect and improve the environment for present and future generations,' (United Nations 1973) the DRTD contains no explicit concern over the environment or climate change. The issue was mentioned occasionally but did not figure prominently in the work of the various bodies dealing with RTD. For example, in 1989, the open-ended Working Group of Governmental Experts on the Right to Development, created in 1981, was told by its chair that 'the deterioration of the environment and the ecological balance,' was among the 'other threats' (along with many development and peace issues) that should be considered but this concern was not expressed in the working group's own deliberations, conclusions or recommendations (view submitted by Working Group Chairman Alioune Sène, United Nations 1989, 13).

By the time the High-Level Task Force began its work, there was no doubt that global climate issues would be an integral part of its work. In its examination of the Paris Declaration on Aid Effectiveness, the Task Force welcomed the provisions on environmental sustainability in the Accra Agenda for Action and the Busan Partnership for Effective Development Cooperation (High-level task force on the implementation of the right to development 2013, 473). It also commissioned a study by Marcos Orellana on 'Climate change, sustainable development and the clean development mechanism,' in which the author proposed to 'look into the future and identify a role for the right to development in addressing the climate change crisis' (Orellana 2013, 321). After examining the relationship between climate change and the Millennium Development Goals, the United Nations Framework Convention on Climate Change (UNFCCC) and its Kyoto Protocol, and the Clean Development Mechanism (CDM), he discusses how the right to development can effectively address the climate change crisis and specifically urged that the attributes of the RTD adequately reflect the need for a non-carbon, sustainable development path in a climate-constrained world. He concludes that the RTD 'is central to effectively addressing the climate change crisis,' and specifically to 'help unlock UNFCCC negotiations,' and 'provide the vital moral compass to guide the economic transformation required to effectively address climate change and achieve sustainable development through the integration of economic, environmental and human rights issues' (Orellana 2013, 338; see also United Nations 2010b, paras. 35–47).

In its final report, the Task Force introduced sustainable development into Attribute 1 ('Comprehensive and human-centred development policy') and its criterion 1(g) ('Promote and ensure access to benefits of science and technology') through a sub-criterion 1(g)(v) on 'Green energy technology.' The principal focus on sustainable development was in criterion 1(h) ('Promote and ensure environmental sustainability and sustainable use of natural resources'), with these three relevant sub-criteria:

1(h)(i) Prevent environmental degradation and resource depletion
1(h)(ii) Access to natural resources
1(h)(iii) Sustainable energy policies and practices

Under Attribute 3 ('Social justice in development') the Task Force included criterion 3(b) ('Provide for fair sharing of the burdens of development') and focused on climate change in sub-criterion 3(b)(i) ('Equitably sharing environmental burdens of development') and specifically through indicators on 'availability of climate change funds for developing countries, multilateral agreements to reduce negative environmental impacts, and distribution of contribution to climate change.'

Promotion of human rights

It is to be expected that a norm emerging from the UN's human rights institutions would build in promotion of human rights. Indeed, already the preamble to the DRTD reiterates

> that all human rights and fundamental freedoms are indivisible and interdependent and that, in order to promote development, equal attention and urgent consideration should be given to the implementation, promotion and protection of civil, political, economic, social and cultural rights and that, accordingly, the promotion of, respect for and enjoyment of certain human rights and fundamental freedoms cannot justify the denial of other human rights and fundamental freedoms.
>
> *(DRTD 1986)*

The promotion of human rights in the context of the RTD is further articulated in Article 1 of the DRTD, which qualifies the development to which all have a right as being 'development, in which all human rights and fundamental freedoms can be fully realized.' The DRTD further clarifies, in Article 9(2), that 'Nothing in the present Declaration shall be construed as . . . implying that any State, group or person has a right to engage in any activity or to perform any act aimed at the violation of the rights set forth in the Universal Declaration of Human Rights and in the International Covenants on Human Rights.' Thus, a country that invokes its development needs, presumably in pursuit of the objectives of the DRTD, to weaken its human rights promotion and protection would be in violation of the DRTD. Since the RTD emerged out of concern for the socio-economic conditions of low income counties, one might assume that the reference to 'violation of the rights' in the UDHR and the Covenants was aimed at economic, social and cultural rights. However, Article 6 lays this matter to rest by recalling that human rights 'are indivisible and interdependent' and that 'equal attention and urgent consideration should be given to the implementation, promotion and protection of civil, political, economic, social and cultural rights.' The final paragraph of Article 6 eliminates all ambiguity regarding respect for civil and political rights in the RTD context: 'States should take steps to eliminate obstacles to development resulting from failure to observe civil and political rights, as well as economic social and cultural rights.'

The proposition that development policies and practices to which all have a right must be human rights compliant is, however, a matter of some controversy. Most developing countries acknowledge that the RTD calls for human rights to be part of the development process but bristle at the interpretation of the RTD as a pretext for human rights conditionality on aid or trade or as a basis for questioning internal policies and practices. An official statement of the Non-Aligned Movement (NAM) expressed this concern by arguing that the RTD is not about a 'human rights-based approach to development' but rather 'requires a development approach to human rights' (OHCHR n.d.). The statement has merit as long as a development approach to human rights does not imply a sequential relation between development and human rights, such that human rights are a luxury that come after a certain level of development is achieved.

This interpretation would be contrary to development ethics and, as explained earlier, to the clear wording of the DRTD itself.

The Task Force was attentive to this potential misinterpretation and included in the core norm that the right to development aims at 'development respectful of all human rights.' In Attribute 2, on participatory human rights processes, the first criterion (2(a)) is to 'Establish legal framework supportive of sustainable human-centred development,' by which is meant, as the three related sub-criteria specify, ratification of relevant human rights treaties, responding to international human rights monitoring and review procedures, and providing national legal protection of human rights. Similarly, criterion 2(b) calls for states to 'Draw on relevant international human rights instruments in elaborating development strategies' by which is meant applying a human rights-based approach in national development strategies and in the policies of bilateral and multilateral institutions and agencies. Criterion 2(c), which relates to non-discrimination, access to information, participation, and effective remedies, also draws on the application of human rights by calling for remedies for violations of human rights, participation through respect for freedom of assembly and association, freedom of speech, and accountability of duty bearers. Other sub-criteria call for non-discrimination through constitutional or legal protections, specifically for women, and equal rights for citizens regardless of race or ethnicity, as well as measures to avoid marginalization of vulnerable groups.

Promotion of cultural freedom, consistent with human rights

Of the seven principles of ethical development, promotion of cultural freedom received the least attention in the elaboration of the RTD. Nevertheless, it appears in Article 1(1) of the DRTD, which defines the right as including 'economic, social, *cultural* and political development, in which all human rights and fundamental freedoms can be fully realized' (emphasis added). The references to all human rights and to the ICESCR incorporates by reference the four rights relating to culture in Article 15 of the ICESCR (participation in cultural life, intellectual property rights resulting from any scientific, literary or artistic production, intellectual freedom for creative activity, and international cooperation in the cultural field).

Cultural development is not the same as cultural freedom. Denis Goulet, in defining development ethics, noted 'development means, ultimately, the quality of life and the progress of diverse societies towards enhancement values expressed in their cultures' (Goulet 1997, 1168). His approach suggests a protective function of development ethics regarding culture: 'the task of development ethics is to assure that the painful changes launched under the banner of development do not result in antidevelopment, which destroys cultures' (Goulet 1997, 1169). He also notes that 'Development ethics pleads normatively for a certain reading of history, one in which human agents are makers of history even as they bear witness to values of transcendence' (Goulet 1997, 1169). Cultural freedom is the only principle of development ethics that is qualified in the Handbook by being 'consistent with human rights.' The purpose of this qualification is to avoid an interpretation of the concept that would justify practices consistent with local traditional practices but that run counter to universally accepted human rights, such as various form of corruption, honor killing or female genital mutilation. The RTD, being imbedded in a framework of promotion and protection of human rights, is explicit in requiring, as the previous section demonstrated, that it never be used as a pretext for violating human rights.

There are also occasional specific concerns with cultural values in the RTD. The 1990 Global Consultation pointed out that '[p]revailing models of development have been dominated by financial rather than human considerations. These models largely ignore the social, cultural and political aspects of human rights and human development, limiting the human dimension to questions of productivity' (Report of the Global Consultation 2013, 60). Specifically, 'all cultures and peoples form part of the common heritage of humankind and have a dignity and value that must be respected. Both environmental and cultural considerations should therefore be an integral part of national, regional and international development strategies' (Report of the Global Consultation 2013, 60). The Global Consultation considered that participation was 'the primary mechanism for identifying appropriate goals and criteria for the realization of the right to development and assuring the compatibility of development activities with basic human and cultural values' (Report of the Global Consultation 2013, 62). Interestingly, the 1990 Global Consultation included 'intellectual and cultural needs' among the issues that must be addressed in the criteria for measuring progress in the realization of the right to development (United Nations 1990b; OHCHR 2013, 62). The cultural dimension was also linked to participation: 'Participation is also the primary mechanism for identifying appropriate goals and criteria for the realization of the right to development and assuring the compatibility of development activities with basic human and cultural values.' In its recommendations for action to the UN system, the Global Consultation called for a program of assistance for each country that would meet 'specific requirements regarding all aspects of the right to development in an appropriate environmental and cultural framework' (United Nations 1990b; OHCHR 2013, 6).

In her report for the Global Consultation, Tamara Kunanayakam drew on several UN studies on self-determination to bring out the cultural dimension of development (United Nations 1990a). For example, in a 1980 study for the UN, Héctor Gros Espiell wrote:

> Every people . . . has the right to determine and establish the cultural regime or system under which it is to live; this implies recognition of its right to regain, enjoy and enrich its cultural heritage, and the affirmation of the right of all its members to education and culture.
> *(Gros Espiell 1980, para. 158, cited in OHCHR 2013, 41)*

She adds, still quoting from Gros Espiell, '[t]he cultural aspects are essential for effective participation "in order that a people may be aware of its rights and consequently be fully capable of fighting for their recognition and implementation"' (Gros Espiell 1980, para. 160; cited by OHCHR 2013, 41).

Cultural freedom is particularly important for indigenous peoples. Former Task Force member Nicolaas Schrijver contributed a paper on 'Self-determination of peoples and sovereignty over natural wealth and resources,' in which he noted that '[u]nder international human rights law, the rights of indigenous peoples with regard to their traditional lands and the natural resources are inextricably linked to the right to enjoy their culture and to preserve their identity and natural environment' (Schrijver 2013, 99). Another paper for the Task Force by Koen De Feyter on indigenous peoples notes that the DRTD does not mention indigenous peoples and '[n]owhere is the need for a specific indigenous peoples' development plan acknowledged' (De Feyter 2013, 161). However, the United Nations Declaration on the Rights of Indigenous Peoples, adopted by the General Assembly in 2007 (resolution 61/295), includes, according to De Feyter, 'a right to development that is specific to indigenous peoples and recognizes their distinctness as peoples with their own histories, territories and beliefs, as well as their notions of poverty, well-being and development' (De Feyter 2013, 163). He notes that '[t]he indigenous right to development appears in the Declaration as a purely collective right, held by indigenous peoples only' and that 'indigenous peoples have a right to say no to a project that is based on a concept of development that the group does not share' (De Feyter 2013, 163). He concludes that 'Indigenous rights have evolved to the extent that the concept of "people" in the Declaration on the Right to Development is to be understood today as including indigenous peoples' (De Feyter 2013, 168). Therefore, their cultural freedom is also integral to the right to development.

A final source of reflection on cultural freedom and the RTD is the paper by Susan Randolph and Maria Green on 'Theory into practice: a new framework and proposed assessment criteria.' The authors observe that 'Cultural preferences also shape development objectives, reflecting heterogeneous values, and preferences are also endogenous and so can change over time.' Applied to the task of RTD indicators, they conclude that a

> balance needs to be struck between universally relevant indicators and contextually or culturally specific indicators, especially when it comes to monitoring implementation of the right to development with regard to States acting individually with regard to domestic development (the individual-internal component of the right to development).
>
> *(Randolph and Green 2013, 414)*

In sum, while cultural freedom is not explicitly integrated into the DRTD as such, it is implied in the concepts of cultural development and cultural rights which do appear, and of cultural values, cultural heritage and cultural dimensions, which are part of the interpretation of the RTD.

Promotion of integrity over corruption

The principles of transparency and accountability have been constantly reiterated by the various working groups and independent experts on the RTD and were incorporated by the High-Level Task Force into its core norm and criteria. In enumerating obstacles to the implementation of the RTD, the Global Consultation of 1990 clearly stated 'Corruption is also an obstacle to the realization of the right to development' (United Nations 1990b; OHCHR 2013, 61). The Independent Expert argued that 'respecting the principles of . . . accountability and transparency' was essential to realizing the RTD (Sengupta 2013, 79). In proposing 'Elements for a programme to implement the right to development', he specified '[t]he exercise of implementing the overall plan and realizing individual rights must be carried out according to the human rights standards, that is, with transparency, accountability' (Sengupta 2013, 85).

Promotion of integrity over corruption was a salient feature of the work of the High-Level Task Force. In its 2005 report, it stressed 'the importance of implementing a vigorous anti-corruption programme that eliminates misuse of aid and ensures that it meets its human development objectives' (United Nations 2005, para. 58(c)). The attribute relating to the process of development (Attribute 2: Participatory Human rights processes) contains three criteria relevant to promotion of integrity over corruption: Criterion 2(c) 'Ensure non-discrimination, access to information, participation, and effective remedies' includes sub-criterion 2(c)(vii) on 'Mechanisms for transparency and accountability'; Criterion 2(d) 'Promote good governance at the international level and effective participation of all countries in international decision-making' contains sub-criteria on aid recipients' voice in aid programming and evaluation as well as in international decision-making; finally, criterion 2(e) 'Promote good governance and respect for rule of law at the national level' contains three sub-criteria on government effectiveness, control of corruption, and rule of law (2(e)(i), (ii) and (iii)), with relevant indicators.

In his report in 2016, the president of the OWEWG argued that the RTD 'requires a comprehensive and inclusive approach based on good, responsible governance' and thus 'an environment that promotes the rule of law at the national and international levels; equal access to justice; reduction of corruption; accountable and transparent institutions; and inclusive, participatory and representative decision-making at all levels' (United Nations 2016, paras. 30, 32). In its 2017 resolution on the RTD, the General Assembly emphasized 'the urgent need to take concrete and effective measures to prevent, combat and criminalize all forms of corruption at all levels' (United Nations General Assembly 2017, para. 41). Thus the concern over the anti-corruption principle of development ethics continues to occupy the attention of the UN body responsible for moving the RTD to the next stage. However, as the next section explains, the prospects for moving from the conceptualization of the RTD to its practical implementation seem dim.

Practical impact of the RTD on development

Beyond the power of an abstract concept of an international (moral or legal) obligation to pursue development that is comprehensive, human-centred and respectful of human rights, which is the essence of the right to development and of development ethics, the principal players in national and global development lack the incentive to take this right seriously. While it is a sign of their value that all seven principles of development ethics have been incorporated into official RTD documents, it is disappointing that the ideas articulated in the 1979 UN secretariat paper, the 1990 Global Consultation, the early 2000s reporting by the Independent Expert and the detailed Task Force proposals of 2010 have not inspired action. In spite of the Task Force urging the Working Group to consider applying the criteria through context-specific reporting templates and to collect evidence of the difference, if any, of pro-right to development actions (United Nations 2010c, para. 73) there is very little to show for nearly 40 years of effort. Since the consolidated findings of the Task Force, the Working Group has collected comments and views by governments, groups of governments and regional groups, as well as by others (United Nations 2012) and the Human Rights Council has called for the OEWG to 'further consider, revise and refine the draft criteria and operational sub-criteria' (United Nations Human Rights Council 2012, para. 8) and 'once considered, revised and endorsed by the Working Group,' they 'should be used, as appropriate, in the elaboration of a comprehensive and coherent set of standards for the implementation of the right to development' (United Nations Human Rights Council 2012, para. 9(b)). In 2016, the Chair-Rapporteur of the OEWG, Zamir Akram from Pakistan, submitted, at the request of OEWG, a set of four 'standards for the implementation of the right to development.' While acknowledging that the report of the Task Force was 'also relevant' to the preparation of standards, Ambassador Akram utilized a different methodology from the policy-process-outcome employed by the Task Force. His standards relate to 1) political will (United Nations 2016, para. 28), 2) States cooperation 'to create the political, economic and social environment necessary to allow the implementation of the right to development' (United Nations 2016, para. 29), 3) focus on the individual and national level 'comprehensive and inclusive approach based on good, responsible governance' (United Nations 2016, para. 30) and 4) 'the most basic or core human needs . . . poverty, the right to food, water and sanitation, health, education, housing and gender equality' United Nations 2016, para. 37). The General Assembly instructed the Working Group to 'finalize consideration of the criteria and operational subcriteria, preferably no later than the nineteenth session of the Working Group [2018],' and appointed a Special Rapporteur on the right to development (United Nations Human Rights Council 2016, paras. 13 and 14). The Council considered the Chair-Rapporteur's standards to be 'a useful basis for further deliberations on the implementation and realization of the right to development' (United Nations Human Rights Council 2017a, para. 10), although the General Assembly underscored in that context 'the importance of finalizing the criteria and subcriteria of the right to development' (United Nations General Assembly 2017, para. 8). NAM also proposed a 'set of Standards regarding the implementation and realization of the Right to Development'

(United Nations Human Rights Council 2017b). While these 'standards' reflect some concepts of development ethics, they fall short of a systematic effort to provide guidance for the practice of the RTD as an intergovernmental commitment to shift from growth-based development to one reflective of development ethics. The Chair-Rapporteur proposed in 2018 a list of fundamental areas where he felt there was consensus (United Nations Human Rights Council 2018a). A more rigorous paper was presented to the OEWG by Olivier De Schutter proposing 'a fresh start towards improving accountability' (United Nations Human Rights Council 2018b).

It is unclear whether the appointment of a new special rapporteur, the standards drafted by the Chair-Rapporteur and the work of the OEWG will advance the effort since 2010 to move the right to development from political rhetoric to development practice. The General Assembly referred to the need 'to strive for greater acceptance, operationalization and realization of the right to development at the international level' (United Nations General Assembly 2017, para. 10(b)). Should the political will be found to transform the core norm, attributes and criteria into a set of guidelines or framework instrument, it will enshrine all seven principles of development ethics into an internationally recognized human right.

References

Alston, P. (1985) The Shortcomings of a "Garfield the cat" Approach to the Right to Development. *California Western International Law Journal.* United Nations, New York and Geneva.

Alston, P. (2013) The Emergence of the Right to Development. In Office of the High Commissioner for Human Rights ed., *Realizing the Right to Development: Essays in Commemoration of 25 Years of the United Nations Declaration on the Right to Development.* United Nations, New York and Geneva, 7–16.

Atuguba, R.A. (2013) Equality, Non-discrimination and Fair Distribution of the Benefits of Development. In Office of the High Commissioner for Human Rights ed., *Realizing the Right to Development: Essays in Commemoration of 25 Years of the United Nations Declaration on the Right to Development.* United Nations, New York and Geneva, 109–116.

De Feyter, K. (2013) Indigenous Peoples. In Office of the High Commissioner for Human Rights ed., *Realizing the Right to Development: Essays in Commemoration of 25 Years of the United Nations Declaration on the Right to Development.* New York and Geneva, 159–168.

Donnelly, J. (1984) The 'right to development': How Not to Link Human Rights and Development. In Welch, C. and Meltzer, R. eds., *Human Rights and Development in Africa* State. University of New York Press, Albany.

Donnelly, J. (1985a) In Search of the Unicorn: The Jurisprudence and Politics of the Right to Development. *California Western International Law Journal* 15(3).

Donnelly, J. (1985b) Theology of the Right to Development: A Reply to Alston. *California Western International Law Journal* 15(3).

Gros Espiell, H. (1980) *The Right to Self-Determination: Implementation of United Nations Resolutions.* United Nations, New York.

Goulet, D. (1997) A New Discipline: Development Ethics. *The International Journal of Social Economics* 24(11): 1160–1171.

Hadiprayitno, I.I. (2013) Poverty. In Office of the High Commissioner for Human Rights ed., *Realizing the Right to Development: Essays in Commemoration of 25 Years of the United Nations Declaration on the Right to Development.* United Nations, New York and Geneva, 137–147.

High-level task force on the implementation of the right to development (2013) The Right to Development in Practice: Provisional Lessons Learned. In Office of the High Commissioner for Human Rights ed., *Realizing the Right to Development: Essays in Commemoration of 25 Years of the United Nations Declaration on the Right to Development.* United Nations, New York and Geneva, 469–484.

Kunanayakam, T. (2013) The Declaration on the Right to Development in the Context of United Nations Standard-setting. In Office of the High Commissioner for Human Rights ed., *Realizing the Right to Development: Essays in Commemoration of 25 Years of the United Nations Declaration on the Right to Development.* United Nations, New York and Geneva, 17–48.

Marks, S.P. (2004) The Human Right to Development: Between Rhetoric and Reality. *Harvard Human Rights Journal* 17: 137–168.

Marks, S.P. (2010) Obligations to Implement the Right to Development: Political, Legal, and Philosophical Rationales. In Andreassen, B.A. and Marks, S.P. eds., *Development as a Human Right: Legal, Political and Economic Dimensions*. Intersentia, Brussels, 73–100.

M'Baye, K. (1972) Le Droit au Développement Comme un Droit de L'Homme [The Right to Development as a Human Right], Leçon inaugurale de la Troisième Session d'enseignement de l'Institut International des droits de l'Homme [Inaugural Address of the Third Teaching Session of the International Institute of Human Rights] *Revue des droits de l'homme* 5.

Orellana, M. (2013) Climate Change, Sustainable Development and the Clean Development Mechanism. In Office of the High Commissioner for Human Rights ed., *Realizing the Right to Development: Essays in Commemoration of 25 Years of the United Nations Declaration on the Right to Development*. United Nations, New York and Geneva, 321–338.

Piovesan, F. (2013) Active, Free and Meaningful Participation in Development. In Office of the High Commissioner for Human Rights *Realizing the Right to Development: Essays in Commemoration of 25 Years of the United Nations Declaration on the Right to Development*. United Nations, New York and Geneva, 103–107.

Randolph, S. and Green, M. (2013) Theory Into Practice: A New Framework and Proposed Assessment Criteria. In Office of the High Commissioner for Human Rights ed., *Realizing the Right to Development: Essays in Commemoration of 25 Years of the United Nations Declaration on the Right to Development*. United Nations, New York and Geneva, 401–433.

Report of the Global Consultation on the Right to Development as a Human Right (2013) The Challenge of Implementing the Right to Development in the 1990s. In Office of the High Commissioner for Human Rights ed., *Realizing the Right to Development: Essays in Commemoration of 25 Years of the United Nations Declaration on the Right to Development*. United Nations, New York and Geneva, 49–65.

Schrijver, N. (2013) Self-determination of Peoples and Sovereignty Over Natural Wealth and Resources. In Office of the High Commissioner for Human Rights ed., *Realizing the Right to Development: Essays in Commemoration of 25 Years of the United Nations Declaration on the Right to Development*. United Nations, New York and Geneva, 95–102.

Sengupta, A.K. (2013) Conceptualizing the Right to Development for the Twenty-First Century. In Office of the High Commissioner for Human Rights *Realizing the Right to Development: Essays in Commemoration of 25 Years of the United Nations Declaration on the Right to Development*. United Nations, New York and Geneva, 67–87.

Shelton, D. (1985) Response to Donnelly and Alston. *California Western International Law Journal* 15(3).

United Nations (1973) Report of the United Nations Conference on the Human Environment, June 5–16, 1972, U.N. Doc. A/CONF. 48/Rev. 1, at 4.

United Nations (1979) *The International Dimensions of the Right to Development as a Human Right in Relation with Other Human Rights Based on International Cooperation, Including the Right to Peace, Taking Into Account the Requirement of the New International Economic Order and the Fundamental Human Needs: Report of the Secretary-General*, UN Doc E.CN.4/1334, 2 January 1979.

United Nations (1989) Report of the Open-Ended Working Group of Governmental Experts on the Right to Development, UN Doc. E/CN.4/1989/10, 13 February 1989, Annex II, p. 13.

United Nations (1990a) Annotations to the Declaration on the Right to Development and Related United Nations System Instruments, Resolutions and Reports, Background paper to Global Consultation of 1990 UN Doc. HR/RD/1990/CONF.l.

United Nations (1990b) *Report of the Global Consultation on the Right to Development as a Human Right*, UN Doc. E/CN.4/1990/9/Rev.1.

United Nations (2005) *Report of the High-level Task Force on the Implementation of the Right to Development on Its Second Meeting*, UN Doc. E/CN.4/2005/WG.18/TF/3, 8 December 2005, para. 58(c).

United Nations (2010a) *Consolidation of Findings of the High-level Task Force on the Implementation of the Right to Development*, UN doc. A/HRC/15/WG.2/TF/2/Add.1, 25 March 2010.

United Nations (2010b) *Report of the High-level Task Force on the Implementation of the Right to Development on Its Sixth Session (Geneva, 14–22 January 2010)*, A/HRC/15/WG.2/TF/2, 4 February 2010, paras. 35–47.

United Nations (2010c) *The Right to Development Criteria and Operational Sub-criteria*, UN Doc., A/HRC/15/WG.2/TF/2.Add.2, 2 February 2010, Annex.

United Nations (2012) *Views Expressed by Other Stakeholders on the Right to Development Criteria and Operational Sub-criteria*, UN Doc. A/HRC/WG.2/13/CRP.1 and 2.United Nations Commission on Human Rights (UNHCR) (1977) Resolution 4 (XXXIII), adopted 21 February 1977.

United Nations Development Programme (UNDP) (1990) *Human Development Report*. Oxford University Press, Oxford.

United Nations General Assembly (UNGA) (1969) Resolution 2542 (XXIV). Declaration on Social Progress and Development, adopted 11 December 1969, art. 8.

United Nations General Assembly (1986) Resolution 41/128 Declaration on the Right to Development, adopted 4 December 1986. [DRTD 1986]

United Nations General Assembly (2017) Resolution 72/167 The right to development, adopted 19 December 2017.

United Nations Human Rights Council (2012) Resolution 21/32, adopted 28 September 2012.

United Nations Human Rights Council (2016) Resolution 33/14, The Right to Development, adopted 29 September 2016.

United Nations Human Rights Council (2016) Standards for the Implementation of the Right to Development. Report of the Chair-Rapporteur of the Working Group on the Right to Development. Chair-Rapporteur: Zamir Akram (Pakistan), UN Doc. A/HRC/WG.2/17/2, 16 March 2016.

United Nations Human Rights Council (2017a) Resolution 36/9, The Right to Development, adopted 28 September 2017.

United Nations Human Rights Council (2017b) NAM Proposal on Set of Standards Regarding the Implementation and Realization of the Right to Development, A/HRC/WG.2/18/G/1, 5 April 2017.

United Nations Human Rights Council (2018a) The Right to Development: Finding a Way Forward, A/HRC/WG.2/19/CRP.2, 26 March 2018.

United Nations Human Rights Council (2018b) The International Dimensions of the Right to Development: A Fresh Start Towards Improving Accountability. Olivier De Schutter, A/HRC/WG.2/19/CRP.1, 22 January 2018.

United Nations Office of the High Commissioner for Human Rights (OHCHR) (nd) Submission in Follow-up to HRC Resolution 15/25 "The Right to development," submitted by Egypt on behalf of the Non-Aligned Movement (NAM). www.ohchr.org/Documents/Issues/Development/Session12/NAM.pdf.

United Nations Office of the High Commissioner for Human Rights (OHCHR) (2013) *Realizing the Right to Development: Essays in Commemoration of 25 Years of the United Nations Declaration on the Right to Development*. United Nations, New York and Geneva.

25

Security

Building security through peace and reconciliation

Stephen L. Esquith

The protection and fulfillment of human rights are an integral part of worthwhile development. These rights include, but are not limited to, rights to basic health care, food and nutrition, gender identity, education, meaningful work, political liberty and participation, freedom of religion, and freedom of movement. They are the rights of agents actively engaged in worthwhile development, not passive recipients of it. They constitute a normative historical practice, not a set of natural entitlements or hypothetical agreements. The concept of human rights is arguably one of the most contested in contemporary ethical and political theory. I follow Charles Beitz and assume that human rights are a complex normative practice that have raised legitimate concerns but nonetheless play a central part in global politics. "Human rights," he concludes, "operate at a middle level of practical reasoning, serving to consolidate and bring to bear several kinds of reasons for action. Their normative content is to some extent open-ended and their application is frequently contested" (Beitz 2009, 212).

Security is not a precondition for worthwhile development. That is, it is not a fixed set of fundamental rights. It is a process of peace building and political reconciliation. As such, it is as much an active part of worthwhile development as any other basic human right. Hence, we can speak of a right to human security in this dynamic sense. Like other human rights, the right to human security is not a natural or fundamental right, but rather part of a fabric of normative practical discourse.

How *should* this discursive practice of peace building and political reconciliation proceed in the face of continuing threats to security, particularly in transitional societies struggling to overcome the legacies of civil war, colonization, and authoritarian rule? I discuss two holistic approaches to this normative question: transitional justice and restorative justice. Restorative justice typically is contrasted with retributive justice within the larger category of transitional justice. Instead, I have chosen to treat transitional and restorative justice on a par as converging holistic theories of justice, contrasting them both with a third normative approach to peace building and reconciliation that I call localism. Then, I suggest how transitional and restorative justice can be modified by a localist approach.

This local turn may sound surprising at a time when leading scholars in the field (e.g., Teitel 2014) are reminding us of the need for globalizing transitional justice because of the proliferation of fragile states, the growing strength of transnational corporations, and the growth of

DOI: 10.4324/9781315626796-31

transnational criminal organizations. However, efforts to achieve transitional or restorative justice without a local approach to peace building and political reconciliation are likely to continue to falter.

The record is admittedly mixed, given the myriad efforts to achieve transitional justice. One worrying sign is the withdrawal from the International Criminal Court of some states that had previously signed and ratified the treaty establishing the ICC. (For more systematic assessments, for and against, see references in Pham et al. 2016.) The most well-known and arguably carefully studied effort to achieve political reconciliation, the South African Truth and Reconciliation Commission, also seems to have been losing popular support (Du Toit 2017).

Localism in this sense differs from conventional forms of subsidiarity in which there is a division of labor between international, regional, national, and local political bodies. Where subsidiarity assigns particular issues and problems to the most appropriate political level, favoring local institutions whenever possible, localism involves a different relationship between local and other perspectives. A local perspective serves as a prism through which events conducted at other levels are refracted. Localism does not override or take priority over other levels of conflict resolution. It refracts peace building and political reconciliation at these levels in such a way that their limitations and their unrealized promises are more transparent. This can be done through music, film, dramatic reenactment, fiction, poetry, or other multifaceted forms of interpretation.

I have chosen the West African country of Mali to illustrate the value of this local turn in development ethics. While not as well-known as South Africa, Rwanda, Bosnia-Herzegovina, and other countries that are typically used to assess competing approaches to peace building and political reconciliation, Mali affords certain insights into and opportunities for peace building and political reconciliation that the others do not.

Key terms

Unlike emergency humanitarian and military interventions designed to protect the innocent and separate warring parties (Weiss 2012), peace building and political reconciliation emphasize achieving justice in unsettled transitional societies through a wide range of longer-term mechanisms, including legal prosecution, reparations, local dialogue, memorials, and performance art (Minow 2002). They also differ from more modest short-term strategies designed to achieve peaceful coexistence rather than reconciliation (Chayes and Minow 2003).

In their detailed analysis of *Reconciliation in Divided Societies: Finding Common Ground*, Erin Daly and Jeremy Sarkin define the general concept of reconciliation as "the coming together (or re-coming together) of things that should be together" (5). However, they realize that at the national and international political levels, reconciliation raises more questions than it answers.

> But what does "reconciliation" mean in these different countries? Is it national unity? Is it peace? Is it healing? Is it empathy? Is it stability? Is it harmony? Is it developing a democracy that ensures the fullest sense of inclusivity and opportunity, as well as access to resources for those who reside in the country? Is it all of these? Or none? Is it just moving on?
>
> *(5)*

Increasingly, political reconciliation indeed has become "all of these," and the challenge is to demonstrate how they may cohere.

Where Daly and Sarkin propose a concept of political reconciliation that will allow parties to avoid "ongoing and future violence and conflict," international peace building organizations such as Interpeace draw a distinction between violent and non-violent conflict. Violence is to be avoided; conflict is often unavoidable and sometimes productive.

Peace building must engage citizens throughout civil society in a process in which they learn how to understand their different views and priorities better, but it also must "restore the legitimacy of state institutions." Reconciling different groups across civil society so that they trust one another is a necessary part of peace building, but it is not sufficient. Political institutions must be transformed so that they are worthy of trust, not just trusted (Interpeace).

The term 'transitional societies' refers to a widening range of post-civil war, post-colonial, and post-authoritarian societies that have emerged out of extended periods of systematic and structural violence. At the center of these transitions is "an interval of intense political uncertainty during which the shape of the new institutional dispensation is up for grabs by incumbent and opposition contenders" (Bratton and van de Walle 1997, 10). As uncertain as this period is, there are still elements of the former regime that are preserved or conserved in modified form as incumbents and opposition contenders vie for power.

During this interval how is justice to be understood? Whose laws – old and new – are to apply and to whom? What mechanisms should be used to enforce them? One cannot talk about reconciliation and peace building in transitional society without confronting these and other questions of transitional justice (Arthur 2009).

Holism

Theoretical arguments for peace building and political reconciliation that strive to weave together interpretations of these key terms are no longer as divided as they were ten years ago, when secular and religious approaches were openly at odds (Philpott 2007, 4–5). Now, both religious and secular thinkers claim to be holistic and share considerable common ground.

Transitional justice

The secular approach to development ethics, since the creation of the International Criminal Tribunal for Rwanda and the International Criminal Tribunal for the former Yugoslavia, has been dominated by the notion of transitional justice, although not exclusively. Initially, this was primarily a legal orientation, favoring criminal prosecutions of human rights violations over other quasi-legal and cultural responses to approaches, most notably the South African Truth and Reconciliation Commission, but by no means limited to it (Hayner 2011). This strong preference for punitive legal measures began to change with the publication of *Truth v. Justice: The Morality of Truth Commissions* (Rothberg and Thompson 2000). While criminal prosecutions still were considered the best way to determine legal guilt and innocence for human rights violations, several of the authors in this collection recognized that other forms of truth could be found and other forms of justice could be achieved through quasi-judicial hearings and outreach activities.

Writing in *Truth v. Justice*, David Crocker called these other truths "emotional truths" and "general truths" in contrast to the "forensic truths" and "hard facts" that a criminal trial could establish (Crocker 2000, 100–101). Truth commissions also were thought to have a better chance of achieving "restorative" as opposed to "retributive" justice. According to Elizabeth Kiss, "In privileging reconciliation and reparation over punishment, restorative justice requires a leap of faith, a belief in the possibility of moral transformation of both persons and institutions" (83). Despite the religious overtones of this formulation, Kiss suggests that restorative justice 'is not concerned with exclusively theological conceptions like the salvation of the soul, but with themes like human dignity, respect, and mercy that qualify for what Rawls has termed "public reason," in the sense that they are comprehensible to free and equal citizens in a pluralistic democracy' (86).

Not long afterwards in 2006, a second important collection, *Transitional Justice in the Twenty-First Century: Beyond Truth versus Justice*, edited by Naomi Roht-Arriaza and Javier Mariezcurrena, questioned the dichotomies between secular and religious approaches and between transitional and restorative justice. In her own contribution, "The New Landscape of Transitional Justice," Roht-Arriaza argued,

> The debate about truth versus justice seemed to be resolving in favor of an approach that recognized them as complementary. Even those who had argued strenuously in favor of a non-prosecutorial, "truth-centered" approach recognized exceptions for crimes against humanity, while advocates of prosecution recognized that a truth-seeking and truth-telling exercise could serve as a valuable precursor or complement, even if not a substitute, for prosecutions.
>
> *(8)*

The theoretical ground was clearly shifting, at least for secularists and advocates of transitional justice.

In 2006 the International Center for Transitional Justice (ICTJ) already was looking beyond the courtroom to other ways in which transitional justice could be advanced such as reparations and truth commissions. In the collection of essays *Transitional Justice and Development: Making Connections* (De Greiff and Duthie 2009), ICTJ recognized how land reform and other forms of reparation could advance transitional justice. In 2011 ICTJ took up the challenge of identity politics in *Identities in Transition: Challenges for Transitional Justice in Divided Societies* (Arthur 2011). The authors in this collection explored how different processes could affect political identities in a way that supported the goals of transitional justice. The ICTJ, once thought of as the most sophisticated advocate for a legalistic approach to transitional justice by religious scholars such as Philpott, was beginning to support restorative measures as part of an expanded notion of transitional justice. By 2014 ICTJ published a collection of essays, *Transitional Justice, Culture, and Society: Beyond Outreach*, stressing the indispensable role of education, theater, photography, and public media as complementary mechanisms for achieving the goals of transitional justice (Ramirez-Barat 2014).

What has not been clear in these edited collections, however, is the unifying goal of this more holistic conception of transitional justice. In 2012 in the book series *NOMOS*, the Director of Research at ICTJ Pablo De Greiff addressed this challenge. In "Theorizing Transitional Justice," he provides a clearer formulation of holistic transitional justice from a secular perspective.

> Transitional justice refers to the set of measures that can be implemented to redress the legacies of massive human rights abuses, where "redressing the legacies" means, primarily, giving force to human rights norms that were systematically violated. A non-exhaustive list of these measures includes criminal prosecutions, truth-telling, reparations, and institutional reform.
>
> *(De Greiff 2012, 40)*

Human rights, including the right to security, are still at the center of De Greiff's conception of transitional justice, but this centerpiece is supported by a set of measures that reinforce each other rather than compete for priority with one another.

This means that measures, from criminal trials to truth and reconciliation commissions, from reparations to lustration, in their own ways should contribute to recognition, trust, reconciliation, and democracy. This, at least, is what De Greiff proposes. Recognition and trust are more "mediate" goals, and it is easier to see how measures like criminal trials and truth commissions can plausibly contribute to them (De Greiff 2012, 42–48). The connections between the four mechanisms of transitional justice and the other "non-mediate" goals of reconciliation and democratization are more tenuous.

For example, in order to show that transitional justice can contribute to reconciliation, De Greiff defines "reconciled society" in terms of non-resentful trust. Resentment rises to a political level when individuals have suffered violations of human rights at the hands of the state (or the state has stood by passively in the face of human rights violations perpetrated by other groups) and this elicits angry feelings of "normative isolation." In other words, political resentment is a reactive attitude toward those who should have intervened but did not and as time goes by can no longer be trusted. In contrast,

> . . . reconciliation, minimally, is the condition under which citizens can trust one another as citizens again (or anew). That means that they are sufficiently committed to the norms and values that motivate their ruling institutions, sufficiently confident that those who operate those institutions do so also on the basis of those norms and values, and sufficiently secure about their fellow citizens' commitment to abide by and uphold these basic norms and values.
>
> *(De Greiff 2012, 50–51)*

When truth commissions foster non-resentful trust, they contribute to reconciliation "by responding to the anxieties of those whose confidence was shattered by experiences of violence and abuse, who are fearful that the past might repeat itself. Their specific fear might be that the political identity of (some) citizens has been shaped around values that made the abuses possible" (De Greiff 2012, 51).

Some philosophers have disagreed about the centrality of psychological resentment for a political theory of forgiveness (Murphy 2012), although not all (Mihai 2016). Jon Elster takes De Greiff to task for ignoring the many ways in which the truth-telling mechanisms of transitional justice may fail to contribute to reconciliation, peace, or security, let alone retributive justice. Truth commissions can just as easily shame and re-traumatize as they can rehabilitate. Reparations and apologies can backfire. Vasuki Nesiah (2016) makes a similar argument, supporting impunity as opposed to amnesty through truth commissions.

Other critics have questioned the very idea of a transitional society, no matter how holistic, arguing that even "established" democracies have much unfinished business they ought to be addressing. They too are still in transition in this normative sense (Henry 2015). Other critics have argued that if transitional justice simply means applying general theories of human rights, retributive justice, restorative justice, and distributive justice to societies during periods of transition, this may ignore the interests and values of local communities (Mutua 2015; Weinstein et al. 2010). We return to this last criticism later in the chapter.

Restorative justice

Just as transitional justice began with a secular focus on criminal prosecution and evolved into a more holistic approach to peace building, political reconciliation, and human security, a parallel story can be told about restorative justice. The early advocates of restorative justice argued that the proper approach to peace building and political reconciliation is one that emphasizes relationship building and moral imagination. Only gradually did restorative justice become a more inclusive and holistic approach to peace building and political reconciliation.

In *The Moral Imagination: "The Art and Soul of Building Peace"* (Lederach 2005), Jean Paul Lederach insisted that there is an unprecedented opportunity to use our moral imagination and creativity to break with past cyclical responses to violence. Lederach chose the painting *September 11* by the Tajik painter Akmal Mizshakarol for the cover of his book for its imaginative power (4). The "shared mutuality" and the "simple offer of mutuality and healing" in this painting represent the promise of restored social relationships that criminal prosecutions alone cannot deliver, according to Lederach. "The turning point of human history in this decade of the 200-year present," Lederach concludes, "lies with the capacity of the human community to generate and sustain the one thing uniquely gifted to our species, but which we have only on rare occasions understood or mobilized: our moral imagination" (23). It is this faculty that will be able to envision and sustain the social relationships necessary for peace building (35). In difficult, presumably violent or nearly violent conflicts, Lederach tells us that he's been able to negotiate peace by representing the conflict in a short poem or some other simple image. "When you capture the heart of complex experience, you have arrived at insight and often at ways forward" (71).

Lederach has been a prolific exponent of this kind of restorative justice, which makes moral and aesthetic judgment the secret to peace building. Damaged social relations, he tells us, must be mended, but beyond inspiration and imagination, he has had little else to offer as yet. A second group of thinkers has taken up the cause, and in their hands, restorative justice has become more practical. Daniel Philpott has been the leading figure in this second wave of restorative justice thinkers, but he has not been alone. In his 2012 book *Just and Unjust Peace*, Philpott began by observing that war and dictatorship wound a society as a whole. They not only destroy political institutions and tear at the social fabric but inflict internal emotional damage as well. The resulting feelings of envy, hatred, and vengeance then spawn new cycles of physical violence and destruction. To counter this kind of negative "holism," Philpott argues, we need an equally holistic approach to peace building (4).

Restorative justice understood in a more inclusive or "holistic" way promises not just the end of violence but the beginning of reconciliation (5). After laying out his matrix of reconciliation as restorative justice, Philpott turns to Judaic, Christian, and Islamic scriptures to defend his claim that this form of holism can be described in both religious and secular language. Two years later in 2014, he and Jennifer Llewellyn co-edited a collection of essays, *Restorative Justice, Reconciliation, and Peacebuilding*, in which this conception of holistic restorative justice is fleshed out in more detail and with greater scope.

In their lead essay in this collection, Llewellyn and Philpott claim that restorative justice and reconciliation serve as dual "frameworks" for peace building because of the emphasis that they place on social relationships rather than individual rights and responsibilities. They call this a "theory of restorative justice," although it is not really complete enough to count as a theory. Their main idea is that equality must be understood relationally.

> The equality that is sought is equality in the basic elements required for peaceful and productive human relationships – namely equality of respect, dignity, and mutual concern for one another. These elements (which a fuller theory would explain in much more detail) reflect the building blocks of peaceful coexistence and human flourishing.
>
> *(Llewellyn and Philpott 2014, 19)*

Llewellyn and Philpott acknowledge that there is a strong family resemblance between their argument and secular arguments that ground rights to equal concern and respect on values such as dignity and human flourishing.

Restorative justice is no longer strictly a religious alternative to transitional justice. It encompasses the goals of De Greiff's conception of transitional justice, with more room for religious practices such as mercy and forgiveness based on their potential contribution to healing damaged relationships.

> What makes relational theories distinctive is the wide array of actors and activities that they incorporate into their theoretical ambit, an overarching account of the moral logic of various peacebuilding activities, and a framework in which actors and activities are intentionally linked.
>
> *(Llewellyn and Philpott 2014, 33)*

Even as transitional and restorative theorists have expanded the scope of justice and made peace with each other, there is still no final verdict on the effectiveness of the practices that they have begun to agree upon. However, what we do know is somewhat sobering. According to one study, *Transitional Justice in Balance: Comparing Processes, Weighing Efficacy*, focusing on the effects that retributive justice and restorative justice practices have had on civil rights and political rights, the impacts of trials and amnesties on democracy and human rights are generally "inconclusive." In countries that have only instituted truth commissions, the impact in terms of these dependent variables has been negative (Olsen et al. 2010, 153). Other empirical studies have come to similar ambivalent conclusions (van der Merwe, et al. 2009).

Localism

Theorists of transitional and restorative justice now both stress the importance of attending to local variations when applying principles they believe are necessary for peace building and political reconciliation. According to De Greiff (2012), "we need principles both to guide our choices and to account for and react to the abiding claims for justice during and even after transitional justice measures have been implemented." At the same time, "we need principles that will guide action in a way that is sensitive to context" (63). Localism goes further than this. According to Rosalind Shaw and Lars Waldorf (2010), "The local now becomes the shifted center from which the rest of the world is viewed" (6). Instead of viewing the local context sensitively from an outsider perspective, localism requires that transitional and restorative measures emerge from resilient local traditions to form hybrid practices.

Consider violence against women. According to Fiona C. Ross, the South African TRC failed to put this form of violence in its local context, and therefore was unable to see its victims or hear their voices when they appeared before the Commission. They were looking at it from the wrong point of view:

> Understanding harm in terms of gross violations of human rights, the Commission misidentifies oppression as individual injury. Women experienced the violences of colonialism, capitalism, and apartheid and their aftermaths differently from men, but when they spoke in forms that the Commission was not legally enabled to hear, it assumed that women had not spoken, had not offered of their experience, had failed as witnesses, or had not been as affected by apartheid's violence as had men.
>
> *(Ross 2010, 74–75)*

The Commission was not standing too far away. Its myopia was a product of its constricted "temporal ambit" (1960–94). A longer time frame that encompassed a changing pattern of patriarchy would have allowed the Commission to understand what witnesses were saying locally and realize that transitional and restorative justice also will take time.

Another blind spot that a local point of view can illuminate is the "gray zone" that is erased by the dominant victim-perpetrator dichotomy. Truth and reconciliation commissions categorize persons as victims, perpetrators, or witnesses to the victim-perpetrator relationship. The ambiguous positions that we know all too well are occupied by many swept up by mass violence and tend to be overlooked or underplayed. Victims, for example, may be forced into committing atrocities (Mamdani 2002, 100), and "in constructing people as victims, these commissions may silence other relationships people have with their pasts" (Theidon 2010). The same failure to see beyond the victim-perpetrator dichotomy into the complexities of these "gray zones" is even more evident, of course, in criminal tribunals. Findings of legal guilt or innocence are no substitute for political judgments in cases such as these (Leebaw 2011). Similar problems occur when a rigid victim-perpetrator dichotomy is used in humanitarian and research projects (Meyers 2016).

A third example discussed by Shaw (2010) herself explores the value of a local standpoint when we think of testimony in a performative sense rather than a truth-telling sense. In some cases, apologies that do not display any admission of guilt and regret nonetheless are accepted because the applicant for amnesty exhibits an appropriate level of humility and deference to higher ranking officials or officials from elite lineages. Their request is not based on an apology in the conventional sense as much as a performance demonstrating an attitude appropriate for reintegration into the armed forces. In other words, apology means something quite different in some local contexts than in others (Shaw 2010, 123–127).

Each of these local standpoints brings to light a different dimension of the violence that theories of transitional and restorative justice are likely to miss when applying their principles to particular cases. Elizabeth Drexler's analysis of the long period of violence in East Timor from 1974–1999 reveals an especially troubling unintended consequence of holistic programs for transitional and restorative justice that fail to adopt a local standpoint.

> What is missing from the proceedings is the role of the Indonesian military in designing the system. Not only do its architects remain beyond the reach of the court for trials and sentencing, but the narrative that emerges from the tribunals concerns what militias did to their own people in particular incidents, stripped of the longer historical context and of the systematic TNI [Indonesian military] operations that created the conditions for these acts.
>
> *(Drexler 2011, 59)*

As Roger Duthie, an experienced advocate of holistic transitional justice acknowledges, when local context is ignored – as it was by the courts and commissions in East Timor – criminal prosecutions, reparations programs, and truth commissions can unintentionally make peace building and political reconciliation even more unlikely than they would have been otherwise (Duthie 2011, 249–256).

Hybridity

How can strategies for transitional and restorative justice, seen from local standpoints, contribute to human security at a time when terrorism and other forms of extreme violence seem to be overshadowing debates over peace building and political reconciliation?

One answer lies within "the everyday local" practices of acceptance, resistance, cooptation, diversion – together known as "hybridization" – which citizens create in response to international and national peace building and political reconciliation (Richmond and Mitchell 2012, 8). Through these mixtures of acquiescence and subversion, material for a more resilient democratic culture can be generated (Richmond and Mitchell 2012, 33).

This hybridization does not always result in political reconciliation or greater human security. Some international tribunals and truth commissions are intentionally structured in hybrid forms, for example with international and local officials sitting on these bodies. "As institutions specifically set up to be hybrid, they are a natural forum for interaction between international and national personnel, but they also act as a convergence point between international demands and local claims" (Martin-Ortega and Herman 2012, 75). The problem is that these hybrid structures can be captured by partisan interest groups and be just as ineffective as purely international bodies (84). Formal-legal hybridity such as this does not address the blind spots and unintentional consequences that holism is subject to.

Hybridization is more effective when it occurs in everyday life where otherwise apolitical activities can become acts of resistance or cooptation. Graffiti is one familiar way in which a new everyday political space for contestation can be created (Kelly and Mitchell 2012). Fabric arts can have the same subversive effect (Watson 2012). Through critical reenactments film, theatre, and other performance arts can play similar roles (Reddy 2012; Reimer et al. 2015; Rush and Simic 2014). These acts of hybridization can produce new capacities to sustain peace building and political reconciliation through fearful times that threaten the right to human security broadly defined. That, at any rate, is the theoretical claim (Esquith 2010). How effective these artistic interventions turn out to be is another matter (Cole 2010; Falola and Abidogun 2014). Another word for this kind of strengthening is resilience.

Resilience

Initially the idea of resilience in the literature on terrorism and extreme violence referred to a means to de-radicalize those most vulnerable to their appeals (Holmer 2013, 7). More recently, a new notion, "resilience for peace," has emerged as a preventive measure. At the center of this notion is the importance of "endogenous resilience – i.e. capacities that are already embedded within individuals, communities and societies and relationships among them, as opposed to capacities that are cultivated or 'built'" (18). These endogenous capacities are highly context specific. In the three pilot studies done in Timor-Leste, Liberia, and Guatemala that inform the *Framework for Assessing Resilience for Peace* the contextual variations in endogenous resilience are clearly evident (21).

Hybrid forms of transitional and restorative justice, when they attend to this kind of endogenous resilience, are in a better position to identify and respond to terrorism and extreme violence at the same time that they attend to other dimensions of human security. In order to prosecute past wrongdoers effectively, reintegrate many of them into society, and provide victims (and others in the "gray zone") with mechanisms for healing, reparations, and reintegration themselves, peace building and political reconciliation will need an inventory of endogenous resources and a local hybridization strategy that can be deployed within and even sometimes against international peace building, political reconciliation, and human security institutions and practices.

This is certainly a daunting task. Given the skepticism of Elster and others (Ignatieff 2004), is there any reason to believe this kind of localism can advance peace and reconciliation at the same time that it protects the full range of rights to human security?

A study in *Science* published on May 13, 2016, examined the effects of Sierra Leone's community-level forums on reconciliation. According to this study, the community-level forums did encourage forgiveness and contributions by villagers to public goods. On the other hand, however, villagers who participated in these forums showed more signs of "depression, anxiety, and post-traumatic stress disorder" (Cilliers et al. 2016, 787). These are not insurmountable obstacles to successful local transitional and restorative justice initiatives. However, they remind us that resiliency will require more than institutional reform. Reliving traumatic experiences through theatrical reenactments and other artistic practices must be done with care and the active participation of the most vulnerable. This is not a new idea; it dates back to Ancient Greece (Meineck and Konstan 2014). Efforts have been made to adapt these ancient texts to contemporary transitional situations (Doerr 2015), and similar dramatic techniques have been developed for civilian victims and bystanders, including children (Chong 2012).

Mali

Mali is a transitional society in several senses. It still labors under the legacy of French colonial rule that formally ended in 1960 but continues to be felt politically, economically, and culturally. Mali's shift from a one-party dictatorship to multi-party democracy began in the 1990s, but after a promising start it has struggled to decentralize political power and eliminate corruption. Throughout the 57 years since Independence Mali also has endured a series of rebellions led by ethnic minorities and most recently a coup d'état in 2012 that ushered in a period of foreign occupation, military intervention led by French armed forces, and the deployment of a UN stabilization and peace-keeping force.

During the three decades prior to the coup d'état in 2012, Mali had suffered from two severe droughts and a series of rebellions in its northern territories. At the time of the coup on March 22 it still was heavily dependent on donor aid and unable effectively to decentralize political power after replacing authoritarian one-party rule with a multi-party electoral system in 1992. This was only made worse by the demands for an independent separatist state of Azawad in its northern territories on April 6, 2012, and the presence of violent extremists, many of whom had returned from Libya in 2011 with the fall of Qaddafi hoping to exploit the absence of a stable political regime in Mali for their own illegal purposes.

Writing for the ICTJ two years later in July 2014, Virginie Ladisch cautioned international donors to "monitor the political and security situation in Mali before rushing to support transitional justice approaches, like a truth commission" (Ladisch 2014, 2). The total loss of civilian lives in Mali during the coup, insurgency, and subsequent intervention in 2012–13 was not large compared to what other West African states have experienced in recent years, even as a percentage of Mali's relatively small 16 million inhabitants. The number of displaced persons (approximately 400,000) does not compare to refugees and displaced persons from, say, Syria over the last five years of civil war there. However, the unexpected shock (Wing) to the Malian body politic from the events in 2012–13 left the Malian political system severely damaged (Freedom House 2016).

Human Rights Watch, in an open letter to newly elected Malian President Ibrahim Boubacar Keita on September 3, 2013, urged that both criminal prosecutions and truth-telling hearings be conducted, but also noted the need for greater transparency, the restoration of trust between civilians and the military, and the reform of government institutions to eliminate corruption in general (2013). While attempts to prosecute the leaders of the coup have faltered, some success has been made on the international front, most prominently the prosecution of insurgents through the International Criminal Court for the destruction of sacred sites in Timbuktu.

At the time Ladisch was writing her 2014 ICTJ report, Keita and his newly elected government had just created its second truth commission, Commission Vérité, Justice et Réconciliation (CVJR) with "a three-year mandate to establish the truth about crimes committed in the north from 1960–2013," not just to restore order after the 2012 coup. Where the first commission appointed by the interim government had been charged with fostering dialogue and creating reconciliation, the new commission's title reflected an additional responsibility to see that retributive justice also was done. That meant referring appropriate cases that came to their attention to the Malian Ministry of Justice for further investigation and possible prosecution. Malians would still be able publicly to tell their stories of displacement, desecration, humiliation, and victimization, but there also would be no "impunity" (i.e., no amnesty and forgiveness) for those who seriously violated Malian or international law.

Malian public opinion in 2013–14 was mixed. Strong majorities favored unification over secession, but also favored retribution over restorative justice (Bratton et al. 2014). At roughly the same time, a majority also considered government corruption a more serious problem than any insurgent threats to security (Bleck et al. 2016). Given these disparate opinions, it is not surprising that it took until June 2016 for the CVJR to create a timetable for hearings and investigations and to publish a still general programmatic "Stratégie d'Intervention." Also during this period, there was a steady increase in violence (*Human Rights Watch* 2016; *International Crisis Group* 2016; FIDH 2014, 2016) and an accompanying increase in international peacekeeping forces.

While The American Bar Association's Rule of Law Institute and the Fédération Internationale des ligues des droits de l'Homme continue to monitor adherence to the rule of law, other organizations have taken an active role in peace building and reconciliation at the local level. For example, the Institut Malien de Recherche Action pour la Paix (IMRAP) has been active throughout the country since 2014 surveying public opinion and organizing local dialogue forums. Its *Self-Portrait of Mali: On the Obstacles to Peace* released in 2015 provides an inventory of the capacities identified by the *Framework for Assessing Resilience*. At the end of this 180-page document, the authors reach three conclusions: (1) the Malian education system is inadequate to meet the needs of the growing youth population and there are insufficient employment opportunities available to the youth, (2) local government is dysfunctional and lacks transparency, and (3) there is deep distrust between civilians and the military that can only be remedied through local dialogue forums. These fault lines have only deepened over the past two years (Shurkin et al. 2017).

What sources of resilience can local groups create under these conditions? In the absence of a functioning CVJR, what adaptations and hybrid forms are possible? One innovative strategy IMRAP has used has been to organize and videotape small village discussions and then show them in similar meetings in other villages before different ethnic groups. These local dialogues then made it possible to convene cross-communal dialogues at regional and national levels. Where face-to-face dialogues about land ownership, for example, are not yet feasible, these step-wise exchanges have provided the foundation for further conversations. Similar preliminary conversations have been held between civilians and army officers in order to build trust and mutual understanding (Institut Malien de Recherche Action pour la Paix, 2016a, 2016b, 2016c).

While these local dialogue forums designed by IMRAP to cultivate resilience have gained some momentum, human security – food, military, political, economic, and health security – remains precarious. Violent separatists continue to attack international peacekeepers as well as Malian government installations. Some ethnic groups remain armed and distrustful of the Malian army and violent separatists, and this also sometimes results in violent attacks. As President Keita has shuffled his ministerial appointments, there is a fear that another coup is possible (Sahel

Research Group 2016). Mali remains balanced on the edge of a razor thin divider between transitional and restorative justice on one side and even more violent civil war on the other.

According to IMRAP, one source of endogenous resilience in this precarious situation is the tradition of local mediation in Mali (Institut Malien de Recherche Action pour la Paix 2015, 152). There is some evidence that even during the coup and occupation in 2012–13 when international negotiations in Algiers were proving ineffective and inspired little confidence at the local level in Mali, traditional mediation between the occupying militias and local ethnic groups was able to secure safe passage for some humanitarian relief (153). One study of customary justice systems in northern territories hard hit by the civil war and still subject to violent conflict suggests that there is substantial confidence in this system about local leaders. On the other hand, it is not clear that grievances held by women, youth, and other vulnerable groups have been addressed to their full satisfaction (Goff et al. 2017).

It is difficult to imagine how peace building and political reconciliation can proceed under current levels of insecurity unless the mechanisms of transitional and restorative justice are trusted. Hybrid forms that take advantage of existing sources of endogenous resilience may be able to improve the legitimacy of these mechanisms. The June 2016 CVJR strategy document recognized that this hybridity and resilience is desirable. One CVJR sub-committee was charged with facilitating inter- and intra-community dialogues in which arguments for reparations can be heard, plans for returning refugees and displaced persons can be made, and proposals can be made to develop literary and artistic productions (*Stratégie d'Intervention* 20–21). Unless the rich cultural traditions of Malian ethnic groups are integrated into standard transitional and restorative justice mechanisms it is unlikely that they will be able to withstand the forces of insecurity that Mali, like so many other transitional societies, are facing today. As of 2016, the United States Holocaust Museum Early Warning Project ranked Mali as the seventh most likely state to devolve into genocidal violence.

Malians occasionally have approached peace building and political reconciliation from this local perspective. Let me close by briefly mentioning two very different examples of this kind of hybrid peace building and political reconciliation. One example is the role that traditional griots – recently collectively organized – played in the aftermath of the 2012 coup d'état, mediating one dimension of the conflict between the Malian army and the newly elected government. "A rather large organization of casted artisans, the Association of Traditional Communicators for the Development of Mali . . . not only took on an important role in the preparations for the elections, but had also attempted to intervene with the government and the army during the 2012 crisis" (Hoffman 2017, 108).

A very different example is the film *Bamako* directed by Abderrahmane Sissako (2006). The film locates an international tribunal trying the World Bank for human rights violations in a small family courtyard in the capital city Bamako. The witnesses are a mixture of ordinary people (some of whom are played by well-known political and cultural figures) whose lives have been negatively affected by World Bank policies. The film does not debunk international criminal courts nor does it simply validate them. The point is to show how this form of transitional justice, when refracted through a local lens, can illuminate the limits as well as the need for such mechanisms.

Acknowledgments

I am grateful to John Staatz and Michael Bratton of Michigan State University; Jerry McCann, former Deputy Director-General of Interpeace; and Virginie Ladisch with the International Center for Transitional Justice for thoughtful comments and suggestions on an earlier draft of this chapter.

References

American Bar Association (2015) *Stratégie de Justice Transitionnelle au Mali*. Rule of Law Institute, Washington, DC.

Arthur, P. (2009) How "Transitions" Reshaped Human Rights: A Conceptual History of Transitional Justice. *Human Rights Quarterly*, 31(2): 321–367.

Arthur, P. ed. (2011) *Identities in Transition: Challenges for Transitional Justice in Divided Societies*. Cambridge University Press, New York.

Beitz, C. (2009) *The Idea of Human Rights*. Oxford University Press, New York.

Bleck, J., Dembele, A. and Sidiki, G. (2016) Malian Crisis and the Lingering Crisis of Good Governance. *Stability: International Journal of Stability and Development* 5(1): 1–18.

Bratton, M. (2016) Violence, Displacement and Democracy in Post-conflict Societies: Evidence from Mali. *Journal of Contemporary African Studies*. http://dx.doi.org/10.1080/02589001.2016.1269880. Accessed 29 December 2016.

Bratton, M., Coulibaly, M. and Dulani, B. (2014) Malians Want a United Country, Post-conflict Justice. Policy Paper 13, *Afrobarometer*. http://afrobarometer.org/publications/pp13-malians-want-united-country-post-conflict-justice. Accessed 7 July 2016.

Bratton, M. and van de Walle, N. (1997) *Democratic Experiments in Africa: Regime Transitions in Comparative Perspective*. Cambridge University Press, New York.

Brown, K. and Aolain, F.N. (2015) Through the Looking Glass: Transactional Justice Through the Lens of Nationalism, Feminism and Transformative Change. *International Journal of Transitional Justice* 9: 127–149.

Carranza, R., Correa, C. and Naughton, E. (2015) More than Words: Apologies as a Form of Reparation. International Center for Transitional Justice. www.ictj.org/publication/more-than-words-apologies-form-reparation. Accessed 7 July 2016.

Chayes, A. and Minow, M.L. eds. (2003) *Imagine Coexistence: Restoring Humanity After Violent Ethnic Conflict*, 1st ed. Jossey-Bass, San Francisco.

Chong, P. (2012) *Undesirable Elements: Real People, Real Lives, Real Theaters*. Theater. Communications Group, New York.

Cilliers, J., Dube, O. and Siddiqi, B. (2016) Reconciling After Civil Conflict Increases Social Capital But Decreases Individual Well-Being. *Science* 352(6287): 787–795.

Cole, C.M. (2010) *Performing South Africa's Truth Commission: Stages of Transition*. Indiana University Press, Bloomington, IN.

Commission Vérité, Justice et Réconciliation, "Stratégie d'Intervention," 2016–18.

Crocker, D.A. (2000) Truth Commission, Transitional Justice, and Civil Society. In Rothberg, R.I., and Thompson, D. eds., *Truth v. Justice: The Morality of Truth Commissions*. Princeton University Press, Princeton.

Daly, E. and Sarkin, J. (2007) *Reconciliation in Divided Societies: Finding Common Ground*. University of Pennsylvania Press, Philadelphia.

De Greiff, P. ed. (2006) *The Handbook of Reparations*. Oxford University Press, New York.

De Greiff, P. (2009) Articulating the Links Between Transitional Justice and Development: Justice and Social Integration. In De Greiff, P. and Duthie, R. eds., *Transitional Justice and Development: Making Connections*. Social Science Research Council, New York, 28–75.

De Greiff, P. (2012) Theorizing Transitional Justice. In Elster J., Nagy R. and Williams M.S. eds., *NOMOS: LI*. New York University Press, New York, 31–77.

De Greiff, P. and Duthie, R. eds. (2009) *Transitional Justice and Development: Making Connections*. Social Science Research Council, New York.

Doerr, B. (2015) *The Theater of War: What Ancient Greek Tragedies Can Teach Us Today*. Knopf, New York.

Drexler, E.F. (2011) The Failure of International Justice in East Timor and Indonesia. In Hinton, A.L. ed., *Transitional Justice*. Rutgers University Press, New Brunswick, 49–66.

Du Toit, F. (2017) A Broken Promise? Evaluating South Africa's Reconciliation Process Twenty Years on. *International Political Science Review* 38(2): 169–184.

Duthie, R. (2011) Afterword: The Consequences of Transitional Justice in Particular Contexts. In Hinton, A.L. ed., *Transitional Justice*, 249–256.

Elster, J. (2012) Justice, Truth, Peace. In Elster, J., Nagy, R. and Williams, M.S. eds., *NOMOS: LI*. New York University Press, New York, 78–97.

Esquith, S.L. (2010) *The Political Responsibilities of Everyday Bystanders*. University Park: Pennsylvania State University.

Falola, T. and Abidogun, J., eds. (2014) *Education, Creativity, and Economic Empowerment in Africa*. Palgrave Macmillan, New York.

Fédération Internationale des ligues des droits de l'Homme (FIDH) (2014) Mali: la Justice en Marche. www.fidh.org/fr/regions/afrique/mali/14985-mali-la-justice-en-marche. Accessed 7 July 2016.

Fédération Internationale des ligues des droits de l'Homme (FIDH) (2016) Mali : la paix à l'épreuve de l'insécurité, de l'impunité et de la lutte contre le terrorisme. www.fidh.org/fr/regions/afrique/mali/mali-la-paix-a-l-epreuve-de-l-insecurite-de-l-impunite-et-de-la-lutte. Accessed 7 July 2016.

Frames, P. (2010) Transitional Justice after September 11. In Shaw, R. and Waldorf, L. eds., *Localizing Transitional Justice: Interventions and Priorities After Mass Violence*. Stanford University Press, Stanford, 49–65.

Freedom House (2016) Mali: 2014 Scores. www.freedomhouse.org/report/freedom-world/2014/mali.

Goff, D., Diallo, M. and Ursu, A-E. (2017) *Under the Microscope: Customary Justice Systems in Northern Mali*. Netherlands Institute of International Relations 'Clingendael', CRU Report.

Hayner, P. (2011) *Unspeakable Truths: Facing the Challenges of Truth Commissions*, 2nd ed. Routledge, London.

Helmick, R.G. and Peterson, R.L. eds. (2001) *Forgiveness and Reconciliation: Religion, Public Policy, and Conflict Transformation*. Templeton Foundation Press, Philadelphia.

Henry, N. (2015) From Reconciliation to Transitional Justice: The Contours of Redress Politics in Established Democracies. *International Journal of Transitional Justice* 9: 199–218.

Hinton, A.L., ed. (2011) *Transitional Justice: Global Mechanisms and Local Realities after Genocide and Mass Violence*. Rutgers University Press, New Brunswick.

Hoffman Barbara, G. (2017) The Roles of the Griot in the Futures of Mali: A Twenty-First Century Institutionalization of a Thirteenth-Century Traditional Institution. *African Studies Review* 60(1): 101–122.

Holmer, G. (2013) Countering Violent Extremism: A Peacebuilding Perspective. Special Report, United States Institute of Peace. www.usip.org/publications/countering-violent-extremism-peacebuilding-perspective. Accessed 7 July 2016.

Human Rights Watch (2013) Mali: Open Letter to President Keita. www.hrw.org/news/2013/09/03/mali-letter-president-keita.

Human Rights Watch (2016) Mali: Abuses Spread South. www.hrw.org/news/2016/02/19/mali-abuses-spread-south. Accessed 7 July 2016.

Ignatieff, M. (2004) *The Lesser Evil: Political Ethics in an Age of Terror*. Princeton University Press, Princeton.

Institut Malien de Recherche Action pour la Paix (2015) Self-Portrait – Obstacles to Peace in Mali. www.interpeace.org/programme/mali/. Accessed 7 July 2016.

Institut Malien de Recherche Action pour la Paix (2016a) Evaluation de la première phase du programme 'Agenda pour la paix, la réconciliation et la cohésion sociale au Mali' mis en oeuvre conjointement. par l'Institut Malien de Recherche Action pour la Paix et Interpeace, mai 2013 – mai 2015. www.interpeace.org/programme/mali/. Accessed 7 July 2016.

Institut Malien de Recherche Action pour la Paix (2016b) Renforcement de la Confiance entre les Populations Civiles et les Forces de Défense et de Sécurité: Diagnostic et Solutions pour une Paix Durable au Mali. www.interpeace.org/programme/mali/. Accessed 7 July 2016.

Institut Malien de Recherche Action pour la Paix (2016c) Mutation des Valeurs Societales: Diagnostic et Solutions pour une Paix Durable au Mali. www.interpeace.org/programme/mali/. Accessed 11 July 2016.

International Criminal Court (2016) *The Prosecutor v. Ahmad Al Faqi Al Mahdi* ICC-01/12-01/15-T-2-Red-ENG WT 01–03–2016 1–100 NB PT. www.icc-cpi.int/Pages/record.aspx?docNo=ICC-01/12-01/15-T-2-Red-ENG.

International Crisis Group (2016) Mali central: la fabrique d'une insurrection? *Rapport Afrique* No. 238. www.crisisgroup.org/~/media/Files/africa/west-africa/mali/238-mali-central-la-fabrique-d-une-insurrection.pdf. Accessed 7 July 2016.

Interpeace. What is Peace Building. www.interpeace.org/what-we-do/what-is-peacebuilding/. Accessed 7 July 2016.

Kaldor, M. (2007) *Human Security: reflections on globalization and intervention*. Polity Press, Cambridge.

Kelly, L. and Mitchell, A. (2012) Walking in North Belfast with Michel de Certeau: Strategies of Peace Building, Everyday Tactics and Hybridization. In Richmond, O.P. and Mitchell, A. eds., *Hybrid Forms of Peace: From Everyday Agency to Post-Liberalism*, Palgrave Macmillan, New York, 277–292.

Kimenyi, M.S. (2013) Can the International Criminal Court Play Fair in Africa? *Brookings: Africa in Focus*. www.brookings.edu/blogs/africa-in-focus/posts/2013/10/17-africa-international-criminal-court-kimenyi. Accessed 7 July 2016.

Ladisch, V. (2014) Possibilities and Challenges for Transitional Justice in Mali: Assessment Report. *Briefing*, International Center for Transitional Justice. www.ictj.org/sites/default/files/ICTJ-Briefing-Mali-Assessment-2014.pdf. Accessed 7 July 2016.

Ladisch, V. and Ramirez-Barat, C. (2014) Between Protection and Participation: Involving Children and Youth in Transitional Justice Processes. In Ramirez-Barat, C. ed., *Transitional Justice, Culture, and Society: Beyond Outreach*. Social Science Research Council, New York, 173–210.

Lederach, J.P. (1997) *Building Peace: Sustainable Reconciliation in Divided Societies*. United States Institute of Peace Press, Washington, DC.

Lederach, J.P. (2005) *The Moral Imagination: The Art and Soul of Building Peace*. Oxford University Press, New York.

Leebaw, B. (2011) *Judging State-Sponsored Violence, Imagining Political Change*. Cambridge University Press, New York.

Llewellyn, J.J. and Philpott, D. eds. (2014) *Restorative Justice, Reconciliation and Peacebuilding*. Oxford University Press, New York.

Mahgreb and Sahel: Sand, Tea, and Guns (2016) https://maghrebandsahel.wordpress.com/2016/07/04/mali-aqim – and-security-related-incidents-in-june-2016/. Accessed 7 July 2016.

Mamdani, M. (2002) *When Victims Become Killers*, Princeton University Press, Princeton, NJ.

Martin-Ortega, O. and Herman, J. (2012) Hybrid Tribunals: Interaction and Resistance in Bosnia and Herzegovina and Cambodia. In Richmond, O.P. and Mitchell, A. eds., *Hybrid Forms of Peace: From Everyday Agency to Post-Liberalism*. Palgrave Macmillan, New York, 73–87.

Meineck, P. and Konstan, D. (2014) *Combat Trauma and the Ancient Greeks*. Palgrave MacMillan, New York.

Meyers, D.T. (2016) *Victims' Stories and the Advancement of Human Rights*. Oxford University Press, New York.

Mihai, M. (2016) *Negative Emotions and Transitional Justice*. Columbia University Press, New York.

Miller, Z. (2008) Effects of Invisibility: In Search of the 'Economic' in Transitional Justice. *International Journal of Transactional Justice* 2: 266–291.

Minow, M. (1998) *Between Vengeance and Forgiveness*. Beacon Press, Boston.

Minow, M. (2002) *Breaking the Cycles of Hatred: Memory, Law, and Repair*. Princeton University Press, Princeton.

Murphy, C. (2012) *A Moral Theory of Political Reconciliation*, Cambridge University Press, New York.

Mutua, M. (2015) What Is the Future of Transitional Justice? *International Journal of Transitional Justice* 9: 1–9.

Nesiah, V. (2016) Transitional Justice Practice: Looking Back, Moving Forward: Scoping Study. *Impunity Watch*. www.impunitywatch.org/docs/scoping_study_FINAL.pdf. Accessed 7 July 2016.

Olsen, T.D., Payne, L.A. and Reiter, A.G. eds. (2010) *Transitional Justice in Balance: Comparing Processes, Weighing Efficacy*, United States Institute of Peace Press, Washington, DC.

Pham, Phuong Ngoc, Vinck, Patrick, Marchesi, Bridget, Johnson, Doug, Dixon, Peter J. and Sikkink, Kathryn (2016) Evaluating Transitional Justice: The Role of Multi-Level Mixed Methods Datasets and the Colombia Reparation Program for War Victims. *Transitional Justice Review* 1(4), Article 3. doi: http://dx.doi.org/10.5206/tjr.2016.1.4.3. http://ir.lib.uwo.ca/tjreview/vol1/iss4/3. Accessed 25 November 2016.

Philpott, D. (2007) *Religion, Reconciliation, and Transitional Justice: The State of the Field*. Social Science Research Council Working Papers, New York.

Philpott, D. (2012) *Just and Unjust Peace: An Ethic of Political Reconciliation*. Oxford University Press, New York.

Ramirez-Barat, C. ed. (2014) *Transitional Justice, Culture, and Society*. Social Science Research Council, New York.

Ramirez-Barat, C. and Duthie, R. (2015) Education and Transitional Justice : Opportunities and Challenges for Peacebuilding. *International Center for Transitional Justice.* www.ictj.org/publication/education-transitional-justice-opportunities-challenges-peacebuilding. Accessed 7 July 2016.

Reddy, P. (2012) *Peace Operations and Restorative Justice: Groundwork for Post-conflict Regeneration.* Ashgate, Burlington.

Reimer, L.E., Schmitz, C.L., Janke, E.M., Askerov, A., Strahl, B.T. and Matyok, T.G. (2015) *Transformative Change: An Introduction to Peace and Conflict Studies*, Lexington, Lanham.

Richmond, O.P. and Mitchell, A. eds. (2012) *Hybrid Forms of Peace: From Everyday Agency to Post-Liberalism.* Palgrave Macmillan, New York.

Roht-Arriaza, N. and Mariezcurrena, J. eds. (2006) *Transitional Justice in the Twenty-First Century: Beyond Truth versus Justice.* Cambridge University Press, New York.

Ross, F.C. (2010) An Acknowledged Failure: Women, Voice, Violence, and the South African Truth and Reconciliation Commission. In Shaw, R. and Waldorf, L. eds. *Localizing Transitional Justice: Interventions and Priorities after Mass Violence.* Stanford University Press, Stanford, 69–91.

Rothberg, R.I. and Thompson, D. eds. (2000) *Truth v. Justice: The Morality of Truth Commissions.* Princeton University Press, Princeton.

Rush, P. and Simic, O. eds. (2014) *The Arts of Transitional Justice: Culture, Activism, and Memory After Atrocity.* Springer, New York.

Sahel Research Group (2016) http://sahelresearch.africa.ufl.edu/. Accessed 7 July 2016.

Shaw, R. (2010) Linking Justice with Reintegration? Ex-Combatants and the Sierra Leone Experiment. In Shaw, R. and Waldorf, L. eds., *Localizing Transitional Justice: Interventions and Priorities After Mass Violence.* Stanford University Press, Stanford.

Shaw, R. and Waldorf, L. eds. (2010) *Localizing Transitional Justice: Interventions and Priorities After Mass Violence.* Stanford University Press, Stanford.

Shurkin, Michael, Pezard, Stephanie, Zimmerman, S. Rebecca (2017) *Mali's Next Battle: Improving Counterterrorism Capabilities.* Rand Corporation, Santa Monica, CA. www.rand.org/pubs/research_reports/RR1241.html.

Teitel, R.G. (2000) *Transitional Justice.* Oxford University Press, New York.

Teitel, R.G. (2014) *Globalizing Transitional Justice.* Oxford University Press, New York.

Theidon, K. (2010) Histories of Innocence: Postwar Stories in Peru. Shaw, R. and Waldorf, L. eds., *Localizing Transitional Justice: Interventions and Priorities after Mass Violence.* Stanford University Press, Stanford, 92–110.

United States Holocaust Memorial Museum (2016) Early Warning Project. www.ushmm.org/confront-genocide/how-to-prevent-genocide/early-warning-project/results-2016.

van der Merwe, H., Baxter, V., Chapman, A.R. eds. (2009) United States Institute of Peace. Washington, DC.

Villa-Vicencio, C. (2009) *Walk with Us and Listen: Political Reconciliation in Africa.* Georgetown University Press, Washington, D.C.

Watson, A.M.S. (2012) Agency and Everyday Activist. In Richmond, O.P. and Mitchell, A. eds., *Hybrid Forms of Peace: From Everyday Agency to Post-Liberalism.* Palgrave Macmillan, New York, 39–57.

Weinstein, H.M., Fletcher, L.E., Vinck, P. and Pham, P.N. (2010) Stay the Hand of Justice: Whose Priorities Take Priority? In Richmond, O.P. and Mitchell, A. eds., *Hybrid Forms of Peace: From Everyday Agency to Post-Liberalism.* Palgrave Macmillan, New York, 27–48.

Weiss, T.G. (2012) *Humanitarian Intervention*, 2nd ed. Polity Press, Malden.

Part VII
Cultural freedom

Cultural freedom is the freedom of individuals or groups to practice aspects of their culture. The freedom to participate in a culture with which one identifies is a valuable part of human flourishing. Such participation might include speaking one's native language at school or in public spaces, dressing in a way prescribed by one's culture, observing religious holidays and practicing one's religion, or participating in meaningful social institutions like marriage in accordance with one's cultural traditions. Freedom *to* identify with one's culture is often at risk when a minority cultural group within a territory or larger cultural backdrop wants to observe cultural practices, for example religious celebrations, that are not observed or are even considered inconsistent with dominate culture norms. On the other hand, freedom *from* participating in a dominant or minority cultural practice can be valuable when the cultural practice is at odds with individual agency or respect for an individual's universal human rights. Thus, how to recognize cultural freedom and to protect and promote both freedom to and freedom from cultural practice is an important part of authentic development.

Stacy J. Kosko discusses both freedom to and freedom from cultural practice in her chapter on cultural freedom. Kosko considers current debates on how cultural freedom can and should be understood and protected in global development. She examines the tension between the universal-individual human rights model and other models that make space for minority and group rights, and the role of multiculturalism in policy-making, before detailing the response most closely associated with contemporary development ethics: the "cultural liberty" model. She then explores the compatibility of this model with the seven values of worthwhile human development that are central to this *Handbook*. She concludes by highlighting the problem of agency vulnerability and the recognition gap in human rights protection as areas for future research.

The other two chapters in this section concern specific aspects of culture: sexual identity and religion in development. Yuvraj Joshi notes that sexuality is often invisible in the context of development. Moreover, when development strategies do recognize sexuality, it is typically a purely heteronormative sexuality, and when LGBTI issues are recognized it is too often in an "add LGBTI and stir" fashion. Joshi argues that sexual minorities need the right kind of visibility, which requires consideration of intersections such as race and economic status as well as cultural context in order to protect LGBTI people from economic exclusion, social and

DOI: 10.4324/9781315626796-32

political exclusion, violence, oppression, poor health (including lack of treatment for HIV/AIDS, reproductive health, and more), and a host of nuanced issues related to bodily integrity and autonomy, including sex work. Exclusion of LGBTI people has an economic cost to the population as a whole.

Katherine Marshall's chapter on religion makes explicit some of the complex ways in which religious teachings, practices and institutions relate to development ideas and actions. Marshall argues that critical engagement of the diverse religious traditions and their interplay with other facets of social, economic, and political affairs is essential when assessing the role of perceptions and realities of religion within development ethics.

26

Cultural freedom

Worthwhile development for a diverse world

Stacy J. Kosko

The notion of "cultural freedom" is central to development ethics. Building inclusive, diverse societies requires achieving other worthy goals in areas like health, education, poverty reduction, and human security. But allowing people the opportunity to be who they wish to be, and to live as they wish to live, is a development end unto itself and is intrinsic also to the *right* to development (General Assembly of the United Nations 1986). Cultural freedom is especially relevant where ethno-cultural minorities are concerned, which is to say, nearly everywhere, always. Embedded in the static notion of cultural freedom is a big, gnarly question, which we might summarize this way: "What is the role of culture in human well-being and freedom, and how can – and ought – development practice or policy-making protect and promote culture in this role?"

The editors of this *Handbook* take the position that cultural freedom, consistent with human rights, is one of the seven key values, or goals, of worthwhile human development (Penz et al. 2011). But to understand what cultural freedom brings to the practice and evaluation of development, we must take it as an object of inquiry within development ethics, not merely as a feature of ethical development, a condition to which "good" development aspires. The view of cultural freedom from development ethics thus can, and should, be interpreted through the lens of these same seven values. For cultural freedom to be deployed in a way that enhances human freedom and well-being, rather than weaponized in a way that can limit individual opportunity and agency, or in a way that fetishizes culture as a primary social good independent of its value for real human beings, it must adhere to, or at least not get in the way of, the seven goals of worthwhile development that form the backbone of this *Handbook*.

In the first part of this chapter, I canvas several prominent debates on the role of cultural freedom in global development, or in the protection and promotion of human well-being and freedom more broadly. These include the tension between the universal-individual human rights model and ones that make space for minority and group rights, and the firestorm over the role of multiculturalism in policy-making. In this space I am not able to do justice to any of these topics with the depth and breadth each deserves, but I do direct the reader to sources that do. In part two, I detail the response most closely associated with development ethics – the "cultural liberty" model – and explore its compatibility with the seven values of worthwhile human development. In the final section, I suggest that two areas of future

DOI: 10.4324/9781315626796-33

research might include the invisible problem of agency vulnerability and the recognition gap in human rights protection.

Current debates

The Minorities at Risk project at the University of Maryland estimates that one in every seven people in the world is subject to some form of exclusion not faced by other groups in their state (UNDP 2004, 6). These exclusions range from ethnic cleansing to damaging restrictions on language use and religion. This limits people's choices in how they wish to live their lives; produces social, economic, and political exclusion; and results in profound material deprivation that threatens both livelihoods and lives.

"Multicultural policies" are creative social policies "designed to provide some level of public recognition, support or accommodation to non-dominant ethnocultural groups" (Kymlicka 2007, 16). Such policies are typically centered around language, worship, political participation, access to socio-economic opportunity, support of art and other cultural activities, and access to justice. Support for them is often formulated in human rights terms. While both are useful in thinking about cultural freedom, the concepts of multiculturalism and human rights are by no means coterminous and can, in fact, be in tension with one another. However, they share at least one fundamental interest: protecting vulnerable minorities.

Minority and group rights

One of the most prominent current debates around cultural freedom is the tension between individual, "universal" human rights and more narrowly targeted minority and group rights. The concept of group rights is highly contested and its defense can be political kryptonite. One reason is philosophical: Can groups really be rights-holders? And if so, are such rights justifiable? The other reason is practical: Are they even necessary, or can individual universal rights do the same work? The work of James W. Nickel (especially *Making Sense of Human Rights*, 2007) is helpful in clarifying the philosophical and practical importance of group rights; Brian Barry (2001) offers one of several scathing critiques of both kinds of group-differentiated rights discussed below; and Jack Donnelly (2003) mounts a vigorous defense of the adequacy of the individual-universal rights model.

When arguing against the idea that a group can be a rights-bearer, one might point out that groups are not moral analogs to people and thus cannot hold *human* rights. Barry and Nickel appear to agree on this question. "Cultures are simply not the kind of entity to which rights can be properly ascribed. Communities defined by some shared cultural characteristic ... may under some circumstances have valid claims, but the claims then arise from the legitimate interests of the members of the group" (Barry 2001, 67). Barry stops there since, for him, there is no sense in which a group can be a rights-holder (nor should be, at least in a liberal society). For Nickel, a group *is* a bearer of rights – against genocide, for example – but only in the sense that the rights *apply* to the group as a whole, not only to individuals within that group. They are *justified* not by reference to a group as a moral rights-holder (in the same way as an individual is such), but by reference to the rights of individual members whose identity and security may be bound up with the security of their groups. Protecting *the group* against wholesale destruction (physical, cultural, linguistic, or otherwise) is fundamental to protecting the freedom and security of *its individual members*.

Will Kymlicka makes a strong case for the role of group affiliation in human freedom, since "[d]eciding how to lead our lives is, in the first instance, a matter of exploring the possibilities made available by our culture" (Kymlicka 2006, 340). This idea is forcefully expressed in the UN Declaration on the Rights of Indigenous Peoples, who "have the collective right to live in freedom, peace and security *as distinct peoples*" (Article 7, emphasis mine) (General Assembly of the United Nations 2007). The emphasis on "as distinct peoples" lies at the heart of the case for group rights. It recognizes that many ethnocultural groups enjoy a distinct way of life – cultures, traditions, languages or dialects, religions – that is central to the identity of each individual within that group, and if these distinct group characteristics were destroyed, individuals who enjoyed them would – in some relevant sense – also be destroyed. Donnelly agrees, but insists that proper implementation and enforcement of universal, individual human rights, through a "liberal rights strategy" underpinned by principles of non-discrimination and freedom of association, can effectively protect marginalized or vulnerable groups (Donnelly 2003).

Nickel remains unpersuaded. "Group Rights are often used to protect people's "identity" or group membership. Many people care passionately about their ethnic, national, or cultural identity. It forms part of their self-conception, structures their lives and social relations, and is interwoven with their well-being. Harm to the group is harm to them" (Nickel 2007, 165). Special mechanisms are needed to protect the members' (universal, individual) human rights with which Donnelly is concerned. It is not that non-members do not enjoy the same basic rights, it is that their protection may not require the special mechanisms sometimes required for vulnerable minorities. Group rights acknowledge the social reality of the human condition (Jones 2009). (For supplemental arguments that appeal also to the value of a diverse world, see Kymlicka 2006, 388.)

None of this assumes that culture is or should be static and unchanging. Cultures, as societies, evolve through natural economic, political, social, and even geological processes. "Ideas of 'cultural authenticity' or 'cultural purity' are often anthropologically naïve. They are also politically dangerous . . . it is cultural hybridity, not cultural purity, which is the normal state of human affairs" (Kymlicka 2007, 101). Indigenous peoples should not have special cultural rights because their culture is somehow more "authentic" or "pure" than others, but because their culture is more vulnerable than others. Moreover, one rarely belongs only to a single culture, or experiences that culture in the same way as other members of the group. (For Amartya Sen on monoculturalism, rigid cultural identities, and "singular affiliation," see Sen 2006, 20–21.) The point is that individuals ought to have the *substantive freedom* to prioritize one of their multiple identities over others at different times. In some circumstances, this freedom requires targeted protections in the form of minority or group rights.

Minority rights – those held specifically by minority *individuals* – share some features with group rights. (See Nickel's typology of rights, 2007.) Nickel argues that *specific* rights are answers to specific threats. Minority rights and group rights are group-differentiated because their members and their culture require the same protection already afforded to non-members through basic human rights or through the default position that most dominant (non-threatened) cultures occupy in society. They apply to some and not all because they respond to threats faced by some and not all. (See Kymlicka 2018, on minority rights in international political theory.)

Barry takes up this question of group-differentiated rights in the context of multiculturalism. *Culture and Equality* is directed at professed liberals who reject the claim that multiculturalism should protect groups regardless of how they treat their members but who nevertheless support the "politics of difference," according to which special group-differentiated rights are appropriate. Barry argues that group-differentiated rights may be justified by appeal to equal treatment only in very special circumstances. He largely rejects the claim that unmodified liberal egalitarian principles may be detrimental to the independence or survival of the communities and associations that make up minority cultures. Deeper discussion of the relationships between human rights and cultural freedom can be found in Barry (2001), Kymlicka (1995, 2006, 2007), Jones (2009), Lyons and Mayall (2003), and Nickel (2007, 2008, 2014).

Multiculturalism

There is also much disagreement about the effectiveness of and justifications for "multiculturalism," a term for the policies that seek to protect and promote cultural freedom and also for the philosophy that underpins them. Charles Taylor explains the political incarnation of this philosophy simply as the demand many people make that public institutions recognize their identity or identities (Taylor 1994). Any attempt to operationalize such views into policy or codify them in rights invariably leads to questions about the *kind* of legal protections a government can and should give to minorities, particularly in the face of possible clashes between liberal democracy and illiberal or oppressive "traditional" practices within minority groups.

The philosophy of multiculturalism comes in several forms, though. One includes the "conservative" approach to multiculturalism, sometimes also called the "traditionalist" approach, and also certain forms of the "communitarian" approach. These closely related views hold that the purpose of cultural rights and multiculturalist policies is to protect and preserve "authentic" or "traditional" practices from pressures to change, pressures that are frequently assumed to be "outside" or external, but which might just as easily be internal pressures that are resisted by group elites, such as religious leaders (see Sen 1999). This view celebrates the primacy of the group over the individual and is the form of multiculturalism Susan Moller Okin has in mind when she asks: "Is Multiculturalism Bad for Women?" (1999).

Kymlicka argues that another concept of multiculturalism, which has recently gained traction within international organizations and domestic governments in liberal democratic societies, can help address this question. The trend has been toward protecting only those expressions of minority culture that conform to national (liberal democratic) standards for the protection of the individual. This is what he calls "liberal multiculturalism": "an umbrella term [for] a wide range of policies designed to provide some level of public recognition, support or accommodation to non-dominant ethnocultural groups [. . .] to maintain and express their distinct identities and practices" (Kymlicka 2007, 16–17). Kymlicka argues that Western Europe, the US, and Canada have begun to embrace such policies, but the rest of the world largely has not. Recently, though, even Western governments have come under pressure to curb immigration and roll back multicultural policies. Witness, for example, the political earthquakes of Brexit and Donald Trump's election as President of the United States.

The emergence of liberal multiculturalism is rooted in the acceptance and expansion of the human rights revolution. This formulation rules out policies that would accommodate in-group oppression, for example of women or LGBTQI persons. Kymlicka argues that the now widely accepted normative force of human rights helps to assure governments that "there is no fear that self-governing groups will use their powers to establish islands of tyranny or theocracy" (Kymlicka 2007, 94). Yet one need only to look at certain practices of some religious and ethnic minority communities to see that patriarchal social systems continue to constitute "islands of tyranny" where women are concerned, even within the confines of Western democracies. Kymlicka ultimately accepts that there are "illiberal strands" within some minority groups and believes that policies should have built-in safeguards to ensure that the human rights goals of liberal multiculturalism are not up-ended in the name of tradition. However, he also believes in the possibility of cultural (r)evolution (see his optimistic discussion, following Nancy Rossenblum, on the "liberal expectancy," 2007, 94).

Whichever form multiculturalism takes, there are many justifications for and critiques of this approach to accommodating cultural minorities. These can be roughly divided into a few clear strands. Justifications include arguments from communitarianism (e.g. Charles Taylor), liberal egalitarianism (e.g. Will Kymlicka), and postcolonialism (e.g. Duncan Ivison). Critiques include arguments from cultural cosmopolitanism (e.g. Jeremy Waldron), toleration as indifference rather than accommodation (e.g. Chandran Kukathas), egalitarianism (e.g. Brian Barry), the "politics of redistribution" (e.g. Fraser and Honneth 2003), and from feminist and other scholars concerned about the problem of "internal minorities" or "minorities within minorities," which emphasizes in-group inequality and discrimination (e.g. Eisenberg and Spinner-Halev 2005). (For overviews of each of these lines of argumentation, see Song 2016.) Feminist critics emphasize this tension between feminism and multiculturalism, pointing out the many in-group forms of oppression that accrue to women and sexual minorities (e.g. Okin 1999 and Shachar 1998). Multiculturalist policies are also challenging to enact in practice, especially in the current atmosphere of extreme hostility toward immigrant groups and religious minorities, particularly Muslims in the West. However, there are powerful reasons for pursuing policies that encourage cultural freedom among the seven goals of worthwhile development and seek ways to mitigate potential harms, particularly toward internal minorities.

Cultural liberty

If liberal multiculturalism is meant to "extend some level of public recognition and support for ethnocultural minorities to maintain and express their distinct identities and practices" (Kymlicka 2007, 16–17), consistent with international human rights norms and the commitments of liberal democracies, then the rationale for such policies is what has come to be called "cultural liberty." In order to meet the requirements of most liberal Western governments, multicultural and group rights policies need to be justified within the constraints of the "liberal" imperative of protecting individual rights. In order to meet the requirements of justice, policies must also protect the rights of *individual* minorities against the tyrannies of in-group coercion just as it protects the rights of minority *groups* against assimilation and marginalization. The notion of "cultural liberty" – "the capability of people to live and be what they choose, with adequate opportunity to consider other options" – might offer one such framework, able to meet both requirements (UNDP 2004, 4).

A brand of liberal multiculturalism, "cultural liberty," developed by Sakiko Fukuda-Parr, Will Kymlicka, Amartya Sen, and others, and promoted by the United Nations Development Programme, makes a strong case for ensuring the protections of group rights, including cultural rights, while maintaining the fundamental protections of individual human rights. The 2004 UNDP Human Development Report (HDR) *Cultural Liberty in Today's Diverse World* explains that "[c]ultural liberty is about expanding individual choices, not about preserving values and practices as an end in itself with blind allegiance to tradition" and it argues that it "is a vital part of human development because being able to choose one's identity – who one is – without losing the respect of others or being excluded from other choices is important in leading a full life" (UNDP 2004, 4, 1). But the promotion and protection of cultural freedom in development practice and policy-making, to be consistent with the vision of ethical development advanced by this volume, must adhere to the seven values of worthwhile human development explored in this *Handbook*. Here I explore the suitability of the "cultural liberty" model to this task, taking each value in turn.

First, like worthwhile human development itself, cultural liberty must *enhance people's well-being*. One way it can do this is by alleviating the burdens of social exclusion, including the economic marginalization that so often separates minority groups from the mainstream. At the state level, cultural liberty "respects and promotes diversity while keeping countries open to global flows of capital, goods and people" (UNDP 2004, 11), which can help raise standards of living by opening investment and migration opportunities and making some important commodities cheaper. But cultural liberty also requires us to investigate how one *experiences* income poverty. The absolute income of a poor Canadian might be significantly higher than that of a poor Bolivian, yet the Canadian's experience of poverty might be more acute. "Indeed, culture establishes an important relation between relative incomes and absolute capabilities . . . The very notion of economic poverty demands cultural investigation" (UNDP 2004, 14).

Second, cultural liberty must *allow for equitable sharing in the benefits of development.* Certain social groups can be socially or economically excluded when they are explicitly barred from holding certain jobs, or are implicitly prevented from applying because their particular needs are not recognized in labor policy (e.g. allowing breaks for prayer); likewise when cultural goods, such as indigenous knowledge of medicinal botanicals, are exploited and patented by private companies. The cultural liberty model aims to identify then eliminate these kinds of inequalities. The approach that this model requires for managing the relationships between extractive industries or pharmaceuticals and indigenous peoples is an instructive example. Cultural liberty demands respect for three principles: "recognizing indigenous people's rights over knowledge and land, ensuring that indigenous groups have a voice. . ., and developing strategies for sharing benefits" (UNDP 2004, 11). Strategies that respect these principles may include official recognition of community-based rights to biological resources and the traditional knowledge that accompanies them (Bangladesh); governments involving indigenous communities in mining decisions (Peru); corporations investing in human development projects in communities in which they have extractive activities (Papua New Guinea); or corporations and indigenous groups working together to design collaborative ventures that bring mutual economic benefit while protecting traditional lifestyles (North America) (UNDP 2004, 11).

Third, cultural liberty must *empower individuals to participate freely in the development process.* Just as individuals can be excluded from other social, economic, and political processes, they can be excluded from participating in the development process, including decision-making about the means and ends of human development. Multicultural democracy offers a few models that provide effective mechanisms for power sharing between culturally diverse groups. These include formal power sharing arrangements, which can be effective in reducing inter-group tensions. Such arrangements can be extended to decision-making about development. Also, the 2004 HDR distinguishes between two forms of cultural exclusion that limit freedom and deepen deprivation: participation exclusion and living mode exclusion. In participation exclusion, a person or group is prevented from participating in society in the way that others are permitted and encouraged to do, for example in education, employment, and political activity. Living mode exclusion occurs when a person or group is unable to live in the way they would choose because their way of living is not recognized as valid or valuable, or may be outright banned. Examples include curtailing of religious freedom or language use, pressure on recent immigrants or non-dominant ethnocultural groups to assimilate, and discrimination against LGBTQI persons often on the grounds that their living mode is a "lifestyle choice" that ought not be tolerated. Using data from the Minorities at Risk project, UNDP estimated that in 2004, 891 culturally identified groups experienced some form of participation exclusion, while 518 experienced living mode exclusion. Living mode exclusion has been extensively explored under the headings of the "politics of recognition," "politics of difference," and "identity politics." These "share a commitment to revaluing disrespected identities and changing dominant patterns of representation and communication that marginalize certain groups" (Song 2016, 140). (See also Young 1990; Taylor 1994; Gutmann 2003.)

Cultural liberty also requires recognizing power imbalances resulting from globalization, the cultural, political, and military domination of the West, and its relationship to the destruction of vulnerable (non-Western) cultural elements such as music, food, and dance, and to staggering material deprivation in much of the rest of the world. The cultural liberty model emphasizes democratic participation of all elements of global society not only in governing decisions, but in less political aspects of our collective efforts to shape the world in which we want to live. The HDR gives the example of the dominance of imported cultural goods such as music and foodstuffs, so dominant because wealthier and more powerful foreign powers control the airwaves and marketing. But the authors caution against the temptation to ban foreign "influences" outright and instead advocate for multicultural policies that use public resources to open and protect spaces for indigenous cultural expression and dissemination, such as radio stations (UNDP 2004, 20). (On the "democratic deficit" in global governance, see Frances Stuart, in Keleher and Kosko 2018.)

Fourth, cultural liberty must *promote environmental sustainability*. Daniel Nettle and Suzanne Romaine's groundbreaking work in *Vanishing Voices* (2000) revealed the powerful link between language and environmental sustainability, coining the term "biolinguistic diversity" to describe "the rich spectrum of life encompassing all the Earth's species of plants and animals along with human cultures and their languages." They demonstrate the ways in which language loss affects the environment as linguistically-embedded ways of understanding ecosystems are lost, with "striking correlations between areas of biodiversity and areas of highest linguistic diversity" (ix). Indigenous peoples represent around four percent of the world's population but speak at least 60 percent of its languages, and the lands they inhabit hold the greatest biolinguistic diversity (ix). To illustrate why this has such profound implications for environmental sustainability, take the example of native fishing cultures who "show how native perceptions and detailed knowledge of the environment have been encoded in patterns of naming of fish, fish behaviors, fishing practices, and technology" (75–77). It is no accident that a language that has different words for each stage of a popular eating fish's lifecycle is spoken by a people who have successfully managed their fisheries for generations, but whose language loss now coincides with a threat to this fish's population (75). "When these words are lost, it becomes increasingly difficult even to frame problems and solve them in any but the dominant culture's terms and scientific classification schemes, which are not always adequate to the task" (Nettle and Romaine 2000, 77). Policies that promote cultural liberty can help mitigate this risk.

Fifth, cultural liberty must *protect and promote human rights*. Cultural liberty is itself a human right. But respect for human rights is also an important aspect of cultural liberty. It roundly rejects cultural relativism or conservativism. Nobel Peace Laureate Shirin Ebadi argues that "cultural relativity should never be used as a pretext to violate human rights, since these rights embody the most fundamental values of human civilizations," and offers her take on what those values might be. "The Universal Declaration of Human Rights is needed universally, applicable to both East and West. It is compatible with every faith and religion. Failing to respect our human rights only undermines our humanity" (UNDP 2004, 23). Cultural liberty takes this stand strongly, offering justifications for human rights generally and minority and group rights specifically.

Sixth, and closely related, cultural liberty aims to *promote the freedom to enjoy one's culture in a way consistent with human rights*. It draws a bright line between respecting human rights and using "cultural rights" as a justification for violating them. For example, "a girl's right to her education will always trump her father's claim to a cultural right to forbid her schooling for religious or other reasons" (Brown, in UNDP 2004, v). The cultural liberty model emphasizes cultural *choices*. It rejects the fetishizing of "traditional cultures" or the rigid conservatism that locks individuals into cultural patterns that are not of their choosing. Like all aspects of human development, what is important here is the capability of people to be and do what they value (provided that doing so does not violate value five: protect and promote human rights).

Seventh and finally, cultural liberty must *promote integrity over corruption*. The link between culture and corruption is not as immediately evident as the link between, say, culture and wellbeing. But there are clear ways in which they interact. Cultural domination can give rise to nepotism by privileging certain identities over others in the allocation of power and influence. Even in states where employment discrimination is formally prohibited, cultural tropes can denigrate certain groups or make it hard for members of different groups to communicate comfortably with one another. This can result in arguably more qualified candidates being effectively barred from certain positions because of their gender identity or religion, for example, while less qualified candidates are hired or promoted on the basis of kin affiliation or cultural "comfort." This can happen very overtly or more subtly through forms of corruption that privilege identity and insider status over qualification or the desirability of hearing diverse voices. Cultural liberty can help curb some of the forces that encourage certain forms of corruption, like affirmative action policies or job training programs and access to credit for excluded groups. As with the first six values of worthwhile human development, the cultural liberty model is *compatible* with promoting integrity over corruption and is *necessary* for societies to do so effectively.

Let us be clear, the cultural liberty model is not a celebration of cultural diversity in all forms, at all costs. Diversity derives its value from the importance of cultural liberty and not the other way around. Cultural liberty offers "a freedom-based defence of cultural diversity," as well as other forms of social diversity including gender identity and sexual orientation (UNDP 2004, 23). If, through reasoned and informed decision-making and uninhibited by exclusion and discrimination, a number of individual choices to adapt to another culture or lifestyle (including the dominate one) amount to an overall reduction in cultural diversity, then this freedom-centered view is compatible with such an outcome. "[L]iberty has constitutive – and intrinsic – importance of its own in a way that diversity does not" (UNDP 2004, 23).

Similarly, cultural liberty demands a rejection, or at least a careful interrogation, of cultural conservativism, especially when it takes the form of insisting that people adhere to their ancestral culture, whatever those individuals might themselves prefer. "It is particularly important not to fall into the confusion of taking unexamined traditionalism to be part of the exercise of cultural liberty," especially when those traditions are detrimental to the wellbeing or opportunities of internal minorities or women (UNDP 2004, 24). (For multicultural policies in human development, see UNDP 2004, Chapter 2.)

Future research in agency and recognition

Here, I offer two areas for future research: the invisible problem of agency vulnerability and the persistence of a recognition gap in human rights protection, both of which are particularly acute for ethno-cultural minorities and pose particularly grave danger to cultural freedom.

Agency vulnerability

First, let us return to the central question of cultural freedom: "What is the role of culture in human well-being and freedom, and how can – and ought – development practice or policy-making protect and promote culture in this role?" This formulation assigns culture a role in an effort with a larger purpose – the pursuit of human well-being and freedom – rather than assigning it a status as a subject of protection unto itself. "Many countries give language rights or political autonomy to those who are members of vulnerable minority cultures, since these policies help rectify their particular disadvantage (i.e., their cultural vulnerability)" (Kymlicka 1992, 141). But invoking "cultural vulnerability" might miss the point. It is not culture *per se* that we're concerned about; it is the individuals or groups and their ability to control the forces of change that affect them, whether it is to preserve or evolve their culture or something else entirely. When we speak of cultural freedom, it should be shorthand for "the freedom of human beings to control the social and economic forces that affect them, including in their practice and expression of culture." This is the central point of the cultural liberty formulation, and is captured by what I have termed "agency vulnerability."

Agency vulnerability is the risk of being limited in our ability to control the social and economic forces that affect us (Kosko 2013). It can remain even as physical or economic vulnerability declines. Luis Camacho (2010) defines "vulnerability" simply as "susceptibility to harm." Both individuals and societies can be susceptible to harm (Goulet 1971). Development can help reduce both individual and societal vulnerability, but if individuals and groups have little or no control over these changes, then development can be a source of vulnerability as well. As we have seen, one area of acute vulnerability, in which individuals and groups often struggle to retain control in the face of rapid social, economic, and environmental change, is cultural freedom. The threat to their cultures, traditions, or ways of life is the "particular disadvantage" of ethno-cultural minorities (Kymlicka 1992, 141). The importance of agency vulnerability stems from the greater risk that maldevelopment will occur when (even otherwise well-off) individuals lack agency, but also from the recognition that agency can be an end in itself, to protect oneself and one's community against maldevelopment or other harms.

By naming this form of vulnerability, we make it visible. Vulnerabilities to poverty, ill-health, or environmental disaster are usually easy to spot. But agency vulnerability can go undetected, while being no less threatening to human well-being and freedom. Threats to cultural freedom are legion and severe, and successfully identifying agency vulnerability, then evaluating development policies on the basis of their effects on this risk, will be one important way to advance cultural freedom in human development.

The recognition gap in human rights protection

> If handled well, greater recognition of identities will bring greater cultural diversity in society, enriching people's lives. But there is also a great risk. These struggles over cultural identity, if left unmanaged or managed poorly, can quickly become one of the greatest sources of instability within states and between them – and in so doing trigger conflict that takes development backwards. . . . Struggles over identity can also lead to regressive and xenophobic policies that retard human development.
>
> *(UNDP 2004, 1–2)*

Substantive freedom and wellbeing – bedrocks of worthwhile human development – require effective and even-handed political recognition of our (many, varied) identities.

Elsewhere, I have made the case that there is a human rights protection gap that afflicts ethno-cultural minorities but is not clearly articulated in the literature (Kosko 2016). What I have termed "the recognition gap" arises from the system of categorizing different types of minorities as, for example, national minorities or indigenous peoples, formally recognizing groups within those categories, and applying different protections accordingly. Thus, the ways in which different minority groups are protected in international human rights law is not necessarily in response to their particular vulnerabilities. Rather, their protection is contingent upon the label that their government has applied to them. The result is that different groups with similar vulnerabilities may be protected differently by the same law in different places.

The recognition gap is different than the more commonly acknowledged gaps. It interposes the politics of recognition between the principles of justice that ground human rights laws and the application of existing human rights laws to some of society's most vulnerable groups. On the one hand, protecting cultural freedom requires political recognition of minority identities. On the other hand, that very recognition sorts people, and their rights, by identity group rather than lived vulnerability. Better understanding the ways the recognition gap manifests, and strategies for closing it, will enhance any effort to protect cultural freedom in worthwhile human development.

Acknowledgments

For this chapter I am indebted to my research assistants, Hannah Chi, Scott Jones, James Mott, and Davida Schiffer.

References

Barry, B. (2001) *Culture and Equality*. Harvard University Press, Cambridge, MA.

Camacho, L. (2010) Goulet on Vulnerability as a Key Concept in Development Ethics. In *New Directions in Development Ethics: Essays in Honor of Denis Goulet*. University of Notre Dame, Notre Dame, 142–154.

Donnelly, J. (2003) In Defense of the Universal Declaration Model. In Lyons, G. and Mayall, J. eds., *International Human Rights in the 21st Century*. Rowman and Littlefield, Lanham, 20–45.

Eisenberg, A. and Spinner-Halev, J. (2005) *Minorities Within Minorities: Equality, Rights, and Diversity*. Cambridge University Press, Cambridge.

Fraser, N. and Honneth, A. (2003) *Redistribution or Recognition? A Political-philosophical Exchange*. Verso, London.

General Assembly of the United Nations (1986) *Declaration on the Right to Development*. United Nations, New York.

General Assembly of the United Nations (2007) *Declaration on the Rights of Indigenous Peoples*. United Nations, New York.

Goulet, D. (1971) *The Cruel Choice: A New Concept in the Theory of Development*. McClelland and Stewart Ltd.

Gutmann, A. (2003) *Identity in Democracy*. Princeton University Press, Princeton.

Jones, P. (2009) Cultures, Group Rights, and Group-Differentiated Rights. In Dimova-Cookson, M. and Stirk, P. eds., *Multiculturalism and Moral Conflict*. Routledge, Oxon, 41–53.

Keleher, L.W. and Kosko, S.J. eds. (2018) *Agency and Democracy in Development Ethics*. Cambridge University Press, Cambridge.

Kosko, S.J. (2013) Agency Vulnerability, Self Determination, and the Participation of Indigenous Peoples. *Journal of Global Ethics* 9(3): 293–310.

Kosko, S.J. (2016) The Recognition Gap: Why Labels Matter in Human Rights Protection. In Watene, K. and Drydyk, J. eds., *Theorizing Justice: Critical Insights and Future Directions*. Rowman and Littlefield, London, 173–190.

Kymlicka, W. (1992) The Rights of Minority Cultures: Reply to Kukathas. *Political Theory*: 140–146.

Kymlicka, W. (1995) *Multicultural Citizenship: A Liberal Theory of Minority Rights*. Oxford University Press, Oxford.

Kymlicka, W. (2006) Justice and Minority Rights. In *Contemporary Political Philosophy*. Blackwell Publishing, Malden, 327–349.

Kymlicka, W. (2007) *Multicultural Odysseys: Navigating the New International Politics of Diversity*. Oxford University Press, New York.

Kymlicka, W. (2018) Minority Rights. In Eckersley, R. and Brown, C. eds., *Oxford Handbook of International Political Theory*. Oxford University Press, Oxford.

Lyons, G. and Mayall, J. eds. (2003) *International Human Rights in the 21st Century: Protecting the Rights of Groups*. Rowman and Littlefield, Lanham.

Nettle, D. and Romaine, S. (2000) *Vanishing Voices: The Extinction of the World's Languages*. Oxford University Press, Oxford.

Nickel, J.W. (2007) *Making Sense of Human Rights*, 2nd ed. Blackwell, Malden, MA.

Nickel, J.W. (2008) Rights and the Exceptionally Vulnerable. In *Genomics and Environmental Regulation: Science, Ethics, and Law*. John's Hopkins University Press, Baltimore, 258–266.

Nickel, J.W. (2014) *Human Rights*. https://plato.stanford.edu/entries/rights-human/. Accessed 6 January 2017

Okin, S.M. (1999) *Is Multiculturalism Bad for Women?* Princeton University Press, Princeton.

Penz, P., Drydyk, J. and Bose, P.S. (2011) *Displacement by Development: Ethics, Rights, and Responsibilities*. Cambridge University Press, Cambridge.

Sen, A. (1999) *Development as Freedom*. Anchor Books, New York.

Sen, A. (2006) *Identity and Violence: The Illusion of Destiny*. W.W. Norton & Company, Inc., New York.

Shachar, A. (1998) Group Identity and Women's Rights in Family Law: The Perils of Multicultural Accommodation. *Journal of Political Philosophy* 6(3): 285–305.

Song, S. (2016) Feminists Rethink Multiculturalism: Resisting Essentialism and Cross-Cultural Hypocrisy. In Davies, M. and Munro, V.E. eds., *The Ashgate Research Companion to Feminist Legal Theory*. Routledge, Abington, 139–156.

Taylor, C. (1994) The Politics of Recognition. In Gutmann, A. ed., *Multiculturalism: Examining the Politics of Recognition*. Prnceton University Press, Princeton.

United Nations Development Programme (2004) *Human Development Report 2004: Cultural Liberty in Today's Diverse World*. Oxford University Press, Oxford.

Young, I.M. (1990) *Justice and the Politics of Difference*. Princeton University Press, Princeton.

27

LGBTI people

"Being LGBTI" in international development

Yuvraj Joshi

Over the past decade, development actors have directed their attention to lives of people who are marginalized based on their sexual orientations, gender identities/expressions and/or sex characteristics, often under the rubric of "LGBTI" (lesbian, gay, bisexual, transgender, intersex) issues. "Global LGBTI human rights" have emerged as a subject of development, with agencies, coalitions, and experts dedicated to their realization. In this chapter, I introduce the academic literature and current programming on, as well as some of the ethical concerns that arise in, LGBTI international development. As the title alludes, I both invoke and critique the widespread and at times uncritical adoption of LGBTI and similar constructions in development efforts. The chapter begins to apply existing ethical principles (such as "do no harm") in the context of LGBTI development.

Academic literature

Even as LGBTI issues have appeared on development agendas, they have received little sustained and critical attention from development scholars outside of a core group. This core group has convincingly demonstrated the heteronormativity and gender normativity of development discourse and practice, and identified some of the ethical concerns that arise in the course of working with people who are marginalized based on their sex, sexual or gender difference. It is beyond the scope of this chapter to provide a comprehensive overview of this literature, which is discussed elsewhere (Lind 2010; Cornwall and Jolly 2016). Nevertheless, we can identify five propositions that distill the concerns animating this field.

First is the proposition that development discourse and practice is heteronormative and gender normative in its interpretations and impact. In other words, development imagines and responds to a world in which sexual relations take place only between men and women, and people's acts and expressions fit social and cultural expectations of what it means to be male or female, which are taken to be the only genders that exist.

Part of the concern is the invisibility of sexuality in development altogether. Cornwall, Corrêa, and Jolly (2008) observe that many development practitioners fail to draw connections between sexuality and development, taking sexuality to be a private or health, rather than development, issue. Jolly (2000) describes how the development industry has always addressed issues

 DOI: 10.4324/9781315626796-34

of sexuality, albeit implicitly and negatively, under the rubric of population control, violence, and disease, most notably HIV/AIDS.

Where sexuality does appear, it tends to be *hetero*sexuality. Lind (2010) identifies the "entrenched nature of heteronormativity in development narratives, policies, and practices" based on the assumption on heterosexual families, households, and communities (2). He (2016) agrees that "development assumes heterosexual norms" and in so doing "disadvantages poor, gay and disabled people on the margins even further" (562).

Furthermore, sexuality that does appear tends to be viewed through the lens of disease and victimization instead of desire and pleasure. As a counter-frame, Cornwall and Jolly (2016) propose "pleasure-based development" that "offers the prospect of restoring to all people the right to seek a pleasurable sexuality – including people whose sexualities are often denied, such as people living with HIV, people with disabilities, and older people" and opens "an unexpected entry-point for work on women's empowerment" (532).

A second claim is that development institutions and actors, through their acts and omissions, shape the lives of people who are marginalized based on their sexual orientations, gender identities/expressions and/or sex characteristics. Lind (2009) describes how "both invisibility and hypervisibility serve as mechanisms of control and governance," explaining that "when non-normative individuals or family units are left out of policies, their invisibility on paper translates into myriad forms of symbolic and material violence against them" (35).

Third and more recent is the claim that the development actors are paying increasing attention to people who are marginalized based on their sex, sexual or gender difference. Bergenfield and Miller (2014, 11) document this shift along four dimensions of change:

(1) "explicit, publicized statements from senior leaders of development agencies or countries linking development to circumstance of people of marginalized sexual orientations and/or gender expression/identity in aid recipient countries;
(2) policies or strategies at development agencies explicitly including sexual orientation and gender identity/expression;
(3) employees of development agencies being protected against employment discrimination on the basis of sexual orientation or gender identity/expression; and
(4) agencies requiring implementing partners not to discriminate against people of marginalized sexual orientations and/or gender expressions/identities in their programming and employment".

A fourth insight from the literature is that geopolitical histories and circumstances – including legacies of slavery, colonialism, and westernization – shape how development efforts are perceived locally. Bergenfield and Miller (2014) explain that "[t]he historical and/or current exploitation of aid recipient countries by aid donor countries and their constituents is [an] additional, key context in which the current policy changes are situated" including "colonial rule, enslavement, the social effects of structural adjustment, and human and environmental harm from natural resource extraction" (10). Lind (2010) observes that "the increasingly globalized backlash" against sexual and gender rights in several countries is the result of complex factors including "ongoing struggles concerning post-colonial nation building and the debates on the effects of westernization on non-Western and poor countries in the western hemisphere" and "critiques of the US as empire and the accompanying notion of our world as unipolar" (2).

Fifth is the recognition that new development efforts create new normativities that in some ways challenge and in other ways reinforce heteronormative assumptions. Thangarajah (2015) questions whether seeking to be "normal" through marriage should be a goal for the

Sri Lankan movement, and cautions that pursuit of normalcy comes "at the cost of exclusion – of people with disabilities, single women, sex workers, and the poor" (42). Writing in the Chinese context, He (2016) observes that while "[t]he appeal for same-sex marriage is a main agenda item in current LGBT movements in the West. . ., [d]evelopment needs to question the institution of marriage because of its inherent discrimination of those outside the institution" (570).

Current programs

Development efforts aimed at improving the life conditions of people who are marginalized based on their sexual orientations, gender identities/expressions and/or sex characteristics assume different forms and strategies, including mainstreaming and targeting.

Mainstreaming strategies are aimed at integrating lesbian, gay, bisexual, transgender, or intersex people into the status quo. Under President Obama, the US Agency for International Development (USAID) stated that "it is committed to the principles of inclusive development for all and champions LGBTI interests in its policies, practices, and initiatives" (USAID 2014). Under the rubric of "inclusive development," USAID claimed to seek "the integration of [LGBTI] rights and empowerment in policies and programming," citing policies concerning gender, youth, and climate change among "LGBTI-inclusive policies" (ibid.). At the time of writing, Donald Trump's anti-LGBTI administration had cast doubt on the United States' commitment to development policies that benefit LGBTI people.

Mainstreaming strategies can be productive where they challenge the heteronormativity of development narratives, policies, and practice and focus attention on their implications for vulnerable populations, but this is not necessarily or invariably the case. To the contrary, Bergenfield and Miller (2014) observe that "most changes to date have not addressed development policies and processes that are seemingly unrelated to 'LGBT' communities but may intentionally or unintentionally harm such populations" (20). Cornwall and Jolly (2009) welcome attention to non-normative sexual orientations and gender identities/expressions yet caution against a simplistic "add LGBT and stir" approach that incorporates marginalized groups into policy and programming without questioning existing economic and political arrangements that result in their marginalization (8).

In contrast to mainstreaming, targeting strategies are aimed at addressing the specific needs and circumstances of lesbian, gay, bisexual, transgender, or intersex people in particular programs. But without attending to the multiple and complex ways in which development efforts within and across sectors affect the lives of people marginalized based on their sex, sexual or gender difference, development policies focused on LGBTI people can fail to address their needs. Bergenfield and Miller (2014) contend that "current 'LGBT specific' efforts work in isolation of an assessment of overall programming, such that agencies have no sense of harms arising from general programs for people marginalized based on their sexual or gender difference" (5).

Examples of specific policies and statements include USAID's 2011 LGBT Vision of Action that describes the agency's commitment to the rights of "LGBT" people, and a joint statement in 2015 by 12 UN agencies, ranging from UNICEF to the World Food Programme, that calls on governments to end violence and discrimination based on gender identity and sexual orientation.

One strand of targeted strategies focuses on promoting awareness about LGBTI lives. UN Development Project's (UNDP) "Being LGBT in Asia" program aims in part to "foster a greater understanding of the marginalization and exclusion faced by LGBTI people in the [South East and East Asia] region" (UNDP 2017). In addition to producing national-level dialogues and research reports, the program aims to have an active social media presence on Facebook, Twitter, Instagram, and Weibo, a Chinese social media site (ibid.).

Another related strand focuses on researching the lived experiences of LGBTI people as well as the socio-economic consequences of their marginalization. As a part of the Being LGBT in Asia program, UNDP in 2015 published a report that summarized data generated through literature reviews and regional dialogues, and identified factors that enable and hinder "progress towards more widespread acceptance of LGBTI people and recognition of their needs and rights" (UNDP 2015). A 2014 World Bank report studied the effects of stigma and exclusion of LGBT people on the Indian economy, and concluded that exclusion of LGBT people could be associated with as much as $32 billion worth of lost economic output (Badgett 2014).

A third targeted approach is indexing or benchmarking to track progress of LGBTI issues. Building on existing ways of measuring inclusion in human development, UNDP in 2015 proposed an "LGBTI Inclusion Index" in order to "assist governments, civil society and other development partners in measuring LGBTI inclusion, identifying data trends and gaps, and in providing evidence to help advance good policy" (Cortez 2015).

Importantly, not all development efforts aimed at lesbian, gay, bisexual, transgender, or intersex people have emerged in the Global North. UHAI-EASHRI (East African Sexual Health and Rights Initiative) is one example; founded in Nairobi in 2008, it is identified as "Africa's first indigenous, activist-led and activist-managed fund supporting LGBTI and sex worker activism in Tanzania, Burundi, Uganda, Rwanda, and Kenya." Nor do all development efforts aim to target every letter of "LGBTI." For instance, the Multi-Country South Asia Global Fund HIV Programme aims to reduce the impact of and vulnerability to HIV among men who have sex with men (MSM), *hijras* (a social group recognized as a third gender in India) and transgender people in seven countries (Afghanistan, Bangladesh, Bhutan, India, Nepal, Pakistan, and Sri Lanka).

Ethical concerns

LGBTI international development has become a domain where some of the most difficult ethical debates in human rights and development converge – including debates about the treatment of difference, cultural relativism, and Western imperialism. While one chapter cannot capture this complexity, this section highlights some ethical concerns that arise in formulating and implementing LGBTI development programs.

Problems of identification

"No-one must be left behind" has been heralded as the underlying moral imperative of the new sustainable development agenda (UN 2016). Yet, the words and identities used to describe the subjects of international development can shape who is included and who is left behind. As Budhiraja, Fried, and Teixeira (2010) observe: "[I]dentity-based social movements, and the LGBT movement in particular, have struggled to negotiate the boundaries of inclusion and exclusion in order to construct politically viable fixed-identity categories" (136). Of particular concern is the uncritical reliance on LGBT/LGBTI and similar constructions to define people who are marginalized based on their sex, sexual or gender difference.

While some development actors choose between "LGBT" versus "LGBTI" versus "LGBTIQ" and so on to reflect their financial, political and programmatic commitments, others use them reflexively and interchangeably. Development programs framed as being LGBT/LGBTI-inclusive may not allocate funding for, or address the needs of, each of those populations, or they may privilege the needs of certain populations over others. Framing programs as LGBT/

LGBTI-inclusive regardless of whether they actually address the needs of those constituencies is not only misleading, it may even contribute to leaving the needs of particular populations unaddressed by creating the illusion that those needs are already being met. Furthermore, it may reveal, or at least give the impression, that segments of the LGBTI population remain marginal to the new development agenda – implying that the old "add LGBT and stir" approach has become the new "add LGB or T or I and stir."

There is no singular experience of being lesbian, gay, bisexual, transgender, or intersex in any country, let alone continent or hemisphere. The needs and concerns of the different constituencies comprising an imagined LGBTI community are likely to vary within and across contexts. Variations may be particularly pronounced in places where progress for "LGB" and "T" or "I" populations has been uneven, with one constituency making strides while another lags behind. In such contexts, development actors who privilege the concerns of one constituency over another without taking local discrepancies and divisions into account may contribute to exacerbating both.

In many places, particular sexual and gender minorities are more likely to be singled out for abuse and discrimination, including those who are poor, who engage in sex work, or who obviously do not adhere to rigid gender norms. Speaking in the language of LGBTI without considering how marginalization based on sex, gender and sexual differences intersects with other forms of marginalization as well as forms of privilege can obscure more than it reveals.

Taking intersections such as race and class into account does not only reveal a much more complex picture than the term LGBTI suggests. It also raises fundamental questions about whether LGBTI development is attuned to the diverse lived experiences of people who are marginalized based on their sex, sexual or gender difference. The intersection between LGBTI and sex workers' rights is a case in point. As Cornwall and Jolly (2016) rightly ask, "how does the Swedish International Development Agency combine its support for LGBT with its abolitionist stance on sex work when the reality is that transactional sex is an important livelihood strategy for many people who are marginalized on account of their sexuality (e.g., single women, LGBT people) in the global South and North?" (576).

Inclusion of LGBT/LGBTI identities in development policies and rhetoric, without more, may be more affirmative than transformative – aimed at addressing inequitable outcomes without disturbing the underlying frameworks that generate those inequitable outcomes (Fraser 1995; Joshi 2014). Bergenfield and Miller (2014) caution that the focus on identities

> may rob development agencies of engaging in a more transformational project that addresses the underlying factors that generate violence, oppression, thus encompassing a benefit for all people who differ from mainstream conceptions of sexual or gender normality in a particular community, not just LGBT-identified people.
>
> *(5)*

Nyanzi (2016) calls for a "radical revisioning" of development to address issues of power and inequity that "involves an engagement with, assessment of and outright overhaul of diverse structural, systematic and societal factors that cause, facilitate, maintain, circulate and reproduce asymmetries of power based on patriarchal, heterosexist and heteronormative ideologies" (547).

To sum up, despite their ascendancy in certain Western and international contexts, LGBT/LGBTI identity-based framings adopted by many international development and human rights organizations raise concerns. They can gloss over indigenous identities that are not rooted in Western conceptions of gender, sex and sexuality. They can overlook non-normative sexual practices, gender expressions and sex characteristics that defy the LGBTI label. And they can confuse and obscure the needs and concerns of those comprising an imagined LGBTI community.

The first step toward mitigating the risks attached to LGBT/LGBTI constructions is to acknowledge and account for their limitations. The Dignity Initiative, a collective of Canadian civil society organizations working on LGBTI human rights issues, does so by acknowledging:

> There is a spectrum of gender identity and sexual diversity both in Canada and around the world, and there are many other words in various languages to describe this diversity, reflecting the culturally- and historically-specific ways in which sexual and gender identities are recognized and expressed. . . . We use LGBTI because it is widely understood in the Canadian context and in international settings, but acknowledge its limitations.
>
> *(Kerr 2016, 35)*

Furthermore, development actors should aim to disaggregate LGBTI when making analytic claims and funding or programmatic decisions, but only after taking account of local discrepancies and divisions as well as needs and opportunities.

Development actors might even consider more inclusive and transformative ways of speaking about marginalization based on sex, sexual or gender difference. In 2015, the US mission to the UN declared that the US would begin using the term "sexual rights" in discussions of human rights and global development to include all individuals' "right to have control over and decide freely and responsibly on matters related to their sexuality, including sexual and reproductive health, free of coercion, discrimination, and violence" (Erdman 2015). The mission's articulated reason for adopting the language of sexual rights was "a critical expression of our support for the rights and dignity of all individuals regardless of their sex, sexual orientation, or gender identity" (ibid).

Such a rhetorical move could be part of a shift that Budhiraja, Fried and Teixeira (2010) propose toward a sexual rights framework rooted in rights of bodily integrity and sexual and gender autonomy and expression, one that "aims to reformulate political empowerment to be inclusive of, but not limited to, people who claim recognised identities based on their sexual orientation and/or gender expression." The authors conceive of sexual rights as "a broad, multi-issue framework that serves to acknowledge the fluidity of identities" and "frees people from the (often unarticulated) expectation that identity and practice must always be externally coherent" (141).

Problems of justifications

The justifications for LGBTI development programs – the reasons produced to explain why marginalization based on sex, sexual or gender difference matters and why development interventions are needed – can shape who is included and who is left behind. Several different reasons are invoked to justify LGBTI development with the belief (sometimes articulated, but often implicit) that different rationales are harmonious, or at least not in tension with one another.

Some rationales are primarily "people-centered," such as those that use the language of human rights. As a joint government and multilateral agency communique emerging from the 2014 Conference to Advance the Human Rights of and Promote Inclusive Development for LGBTI Persons in Washington, DC reads:

> We aim to integrate the human rights and development concerns of LGBTI persons in assistance and diplomacy efforts. In particular, we intend to continue to use an approach to development that respects human rights. As we work with partners in government and

> civil society, we seek to support access to services across sectors in a way that appropriately accounts for the needs of all persons without discrimination and with dignity.
>
> *(US Department of State and USAID 2014)*

Other rationales are primarily socio-economic, including the increasingly prominent concern with the "economic costs of homophobia" and "the benefits of inclusion" for emerging economies. A World Bank statement to mark the 2016 International Day Against Homophobia and Transphobia (IDAHOT) declared: "Stigmatization and discrimination often have a direct impact on the lives of LGBTI people, but also affect economies and societies at large: when entire groups are left behind – including due to sexual orientation or gender identity – everyone loses out on their skills and productivity" (Ijjasz-Vasquez 2016).

This is not to suggest that economic and human rights rationales for "LGBTI inclusion" are produced in isolation from one another. Increasingly, businesses speak in the register of LGBTI human rights, and human rights and development actors direct their LGBTI inclusion efforts towards businesses. In 2016, the Office of the United Nations High Commissioner for Human Rights (OHCHR) held consultations with Indian companies in order to "develop guidelines on the ways corporations can respect and promote the human rights of LGBT people within their walls, but equally important outside of them" (Ratnam 2016).

In the realm of LGBTI rights and development, much less common are approaches that scholars and activists have offered as ways to overcome the limitations of dominant "corporate social responsibility" and "business and human rights" frameworks as well as singular identity-based analyses, such as a sexual rights framework that links struggles for greater acceptance of sexual and gender diversity with struggles to challenge patriarchy. These justificatory choices are important because they shape understandings of which LGBTI lives matter, why they matter, and what LGBTI inclusion entails.

Problems of frames

The historical, political, and social conditions under which LGBTI development programs emerge influence how those programs are perceived locally and should inform how they are framed. Bergenfield and Miller (2014) argue that "[t]he current and historical context for intervention in aid recipient countries profoundly matters and should inform the approach and tactics that North American and European activists and agencies use when aiming to support the sexual and gender justice movements there" (21). Thus, critiques of LGBTI programs as interventionist "should not be written off as merely homophobic, instrumentalist reactions, but also understood as generated in reference to long histories of colonialism and/or exploitation, yielding understandable, if sometimes also disingenuous, protests about policy intervention" (ibid).

International development and human rights actors increasingly frame LGBTI issues in "global" or "universal" terms, provoking the ire of states that repudiate homosexuality and gender non-conformity as an affront to their social and cultural traditions. Much less common are claims to LGBTI rights and development that situate universal egalitarian principles in local histories and commitments. In contrast, local activists and courts frequently locate non-normative sexualities and genders as well as egalitarian principles in local texts and traditions.

In India, for instance, activists and scholars have presented evidence of homoerotic activity in pre-colonial Hindu and Muslim traditions to demonstrate that homosexuality is neither "new" to India, nor a "Western" import. These accounts do not depict pre-colonial Indian society as some kind of queer utopia, but they do challenge the construction of homosexuality in India as something "foreign" (Joshi 2010, 315). In 2009, the Delhi High Court amended section 377 of the Indian Penal Code, India's sodomy law, effectively decriminalizing consensual same-sex sexual relations, before the Indian Supreme Court reinstated the law in 2013. In declaring that section 377 violates the Indian Constitution, the court concluded that "[t]he notion of equality in the Indian Constitution flows from the 'Objective Resolution' moved by Pandit Jawaharlal Nehru on December 13, 1946." Nehru, India's first Prime Minister, in his speech moving the Resolution, had said: "(The Resolution) seeks very feebly to tell the world of what we have thought or dreamt of so long, and what we now hope to achieve in the near future." By invoking the memory of Nehru's speech, the court showed that the value of "inclusiveness" was "deeply ingrained in Indian society, nurtured over several generations" (Joshi 2010, 311).

Finding the universal through the local can mitigate perceived conflicts between universal egalitarian principles and local traditional values that are often pronounced in debates over LGBTI rights and development. It might also function to curb immodest claims by proponents of local "traditional" values as well as those international actors who, in David Kennedy's words, "[speak] a 'truth' far more universal than our plural world could ever recognize" (Joshi 2009).

Problems of visibility

Development actors are faced with the choice between more or less publicly visible ways of taking up LGBTI issues. Perhaps because public visibility played a central role in the emergence of gay and lesbian rights in donor countries like the US and Canada, people trained in LGBTI rights and development in those countries may be susceptible to a sort of 'visibility bias' – believing that public awareness and action around LGBTI issues is the only path to LGBTI inclusion.

Yet, increased visibility does not necessarily result in "progress" and may even have unintended adverse consequences, especially for those who cannot afford privacy or cannot adhere to strict rules about gender and sexuality. Bergenfield and Miller (2014) explain that "in some cases not making bold public statements or issuing formal policy changes might be a sensitive, strategic decision" (8). Rather than pursuing visibility for visibility's sake as a default path, development actors should ask searching questions about whether and what sort of visibility is desirable, for whom it is sought, and at whose expense.

Consider benchmarking for "LGBTI inclusion." There may be compelling reasons for tracking progress on LGBTI issues, but "naming and shaming" countries with the worst records may not be one of them. For one thing, political leaders in many countries do not consider faring poorly on LGBTI inclusion to be a source of shame; some who promote anti-LGBTI rhetoric for political gain might even wear it as a badge of honor. And even where the aim of benchmarking is not to name and shame, it enables sensationalist media coverage (often emerging in the West) declaring countries like Jamaica and Nigeria as the "worst places to be gay," which in turn fuels hostilities toward people in those countries who are most vulnerable to abuse based on their sex, sexual or gender difference.

Increased visibility around LGBTI issues sometimes carries significant risk of backlash, which may be exacerbated by Western interventions. In 2012, then UK Prime Minister David Cameron's publicly linking countries' LGBT human rights record to UK foreign aid conditions provoked one of the most prominent instances of such backlash. Alluding to this episode, a subsequent Junior Minister for International Development reflected: "Recent experience has shown that there are increasing risks from loud championing of LGBT issues by the global North, stimulating a backlash on wider rights issues. The first principle of UK engagement must be to do no harm" (Duffy 2015).

A more recent example comes from Indonesia. Until 2016, UNDP's Being LGBTI in Asia program had engaged significantly with Indonesian activists, convening a national dialogue in

2013 and publishing a country report in 2014. However, during a rise in anti-LGBT rhetoric in Indonesia in early 2016, UNDP maintained a low profile and later confirmed: "Following discussions with the Indonesian Government, and taking into account the prevailing security concerns, UNDP suspended activities of the regional [Being LGBTI in Asia] initiative in Indonesia at this time" (Knight 2016). As Knight, who interviewed Indonesian activists in the wake on the 2016 crisis, reflected: "It is particularly concerning that activists were left with the feeling that UNDP, which had encouraged LGBT visibility, was not there for them when anti-LGBT incidents intensified" (ibid).

For development actors committed to the "do no harm" principle, the prospect of LGBTI backlash poses a profound ethical challenge. Some actors, particularly those who are detached from local contexts and thus do not directly know the lives at stake or witness the consequences of their actions, can become susceptible to an illusion of inevitability – the belief that backlash resulting from their interventions is an unavoidable and tolerable price for "progress." The intractability of this issue does not relinquish development actors of the ethical responsibility to consult local activists and communities in framing strategies, to critically question their own course of action, to identify and mitigate any risks posed, and to rectify any harms done, particularly since those who bear the brunt of backlash are likely to be those already most vulnerable. Without satisfying these basic requirements, the do no harm principle loses all meaning.

While the concerns identified here are diverse, together they point to a larger problem with grand narratives. Nowadays, many international actors put forward accounts of "global" change and priorities as if there is a single trajectory for the advancement of LGBTI rights and development – from "LGBTI underdeveloped" to "LGBTI developing" to "LGBTI developed." These "global" LGBTI agendas are at times presented as responding to local concerns and demands without acknowledging the complexity of local views, and they become legitimized through "global" conferences attended by an international elite of LGBTI rights and development. While international advocacy and coalition building can be constructive, development and human rights actors committed to social change should allow space for a plurality of agendas shaped by the diverse communities which are affected, and remain mindful of the people and interests for whom they do not speak.

Conclusion

Goulet (1971) cautioned that "development" that increases human suffering could amount to "anti-development." Those committed to achieving equality through law and development may proceed from a sense of moral imperative. Yet, interventions that are uninformed by regional, national and local realities, unconcerned for the most vulnerable lives, or unfettered by strong ethical principles can be counterproductive. While these insights are not new, their implications for LGBTI development are now emerging. Development actors and ethicists should continue to examine the meaning and parameters of ethical intervention in aid of people who are marginalized based on their sex, sexual or gender difference. Being serious about ethical principles – rather than merely paying lip service to them – entails understanding their requirements and boundaries.

References

Badgett, M.V.L. (2014) *The Economic Cost of Stigma and the Exclusion of LGBT People: A Case Study of India.* World Bank Group, Washington, DC.

Bergenfield, R. and Miller, A.M. (2014) Queering International Development?: An Examination of New "LGBT Rights" Rhetoric, Policy, and Programming among International Development Agencies. *LGBTQ Policy Journal* 4: 7–21.

Budhiraja, S., Fried, S.T. and Teixeira, A. (2010) Spelling It Out: From Alphabet Soup to Sexual Rights and Gender Justice. In Lind, A. ed., *Development, Sexual Rights and Global Governance*. Routledge, New York.

Cornwall, A., Côrrea, S. and Jolly, S. eds. (2008) *Development with a Body: Sexuality, Human Rights and Development*. Zed Books, London.

Cornwall, A. and Jolly, S. (2009) Sexuality and the Development Industry. *Development* 52(1): 5–12.

Cornwall, A. and Jolly, S. (2016) Sexuality and the Development Industry. In *The Palgrave Handbook of Gender and Development*. Palgrave Macmillan, London, 525–536.

Cortez, C. (2015) *When People Are Counted, No One Is Left Behind*. United Nations Development Project, Washington, DC.

Duffy, N. (2015) Loudly Championing LGBT Rights Could Spark a Backlash, International Development Minister Warns. *PinkNews*.

Erdman, R. (2015) *Remarks at the UN Women Executive Board*. United States Mission to the United States, New York.

Fraser, N. (1995) From Redistribution to Recognition? Dilemmas of Justice in a "post-socialist" Age. *New Left Review* 212: 68.

Goulet, D. (1971) *The Cruel Choice: A New Concept in the Theory of Development*. Athenaeum, New York.

He, X. (2016) Pink Space and the Pleasure Approach to Sexuality and the Development Industry in China. In *The Palgrave Handbook of Gender and Development*. Palgrave Macmillan, London, 561–571.

Ijjasz-Vasquez, E. (2016) How Can the World Bank Support LGBTI Inclusion? *World Bank*, Washington, DC. http://blogs.worldbank.org/voices/how-can-world-bank-support-lgbti-inclusion.

Jolly, S. (2000) "Queering" Development: Exploring the Links Between Same-sex Sexualities, Gender, and Development. *Gender & Development* 8(1): 8–88.

Joshi, Y. (2009) What's Wrong with Human Rights? *The Guardian*.

Joshi, Y. (2010) The Case for Repeal of India's Sodomy Law. *South Asia: Journal of South Asian Studies* 33(2): 304–317.

Joshi, Y. (2014) The Trouble with Inclusion. *Virginia Journal of Social Policy & Law* 21(2): 207–265.

Knight, K. (2016) *"These Political Games Ruin Our Lives": Indonesia's LGBT Community Under Threat*. Human Rights Watch, New York.

Kerr, D. (2016) *Advancing Dignity: Assessing Canada's Global Action on Human Rights for LGBTI People*. Dignity Initiative, Toronto.

Lind, A. (2009) Governing Intimacy, Struggling for Sexual Rights: Challenging Heteronormativity in the Global Development Industry. *Development* 52(1): 34–42.

Lind, A. (2010) Introduction: Development, Global Governance, and Sexual Subjectivities. In *Development, Sexual Rights and Global Governance*. Routledge, New York, 1–20.

Nyanzi, S. (2016) Redressing the Silofication Between Sexuality and Development: A Radical Revisioning. In *The Palgrave Handbook of Gender and Development*. Palgrave Macmillan, London, 537–550.

Ratnam, D. (2016) UN Wants Companies to be LGBT-inclusive. *Live Mint*. www.livemint.com/Leisure/abZJvgvwP46s84FHnMa68O/UN-wants-companies-to-be-LGBTinclusive.html.

Thangarajah, P. (2015) Marriage Equality and Queer Struggles. *Options* 50: 40–42.

UN (2016) *No-one Left Behind' Is Ethical Imperative of New Development Agenda – UN Deputy Chief*. UN News Centre, New York.

UNDP (2015) *Leave no One Behind: Advancing Social, Economic, Cultural and Political Inclusion of LGBTI People in Asia and the Pacific*. UNDP, Bangkok.

UNDP (2017) *Being LGBT in Asia*. http://www.asia-pacific.undp.org/content/rbap/en/home/operations/projects/overview/being-lgbt-in-asia.html.

USAID (2014) *LGBT Vision for Action: Promoting and Supporting the Inclusion of Lesbian, Gay, Bisexual, and Transgender Individuals*. USAID, Washington, DC.

US Department of State and USAID (2014) *Conference to Advance the Human Rights of and Promote Inclusive Development for Lesbian, Gay, Bisexual, Transgender, and Intersex (LGBTI) Persons*. USAID, Washington, DC.

28

Religion

Religious contributions to development issues

Katherine Marshall

World Bank President James D. Wolfensohn in 1998 reached out to a select group of world religious leaders, seeking a purposeful dialogue about development issues. He advanced four main arguments for doing so. Religious institutions and development activities were obviously significant in many world regions in providing services like education and health but were largely ignored in development theory and in the practice of who was 'at the table' in framing development policies and programs. Second, lively tensions between religious and development actors (for example, about poor country debt and reproductive health) threatened to undermine the consensus and political will needed to achieve development goals. Third, religious institutions offered potentially different and useful insights into the behavior and motivations of the poorest and most vulnerable communities. And finally, the ethical insights and challenges that religious leaders advanced, although sometimes jarring for mainstream development assumptions, deserved attention, above all because religious institutions shared with development actors a powerful concern for the welfare of poor communities. Wolfensohn's goal was to promote both dialogue and action, ideally involving new forms of partnership that would promote work towards common ends.

Strong opposition to the initiative from most governments that governed the World Bank came as an unpleasant surprise to Wolfensohn and his colleagues (I was among them). Protracted discussions during 2000–2001 explored the nature of doubts among development actors about engaging directly with religious institutions but also highlighted the myriad ways in which various religious actors viewed development thinking and practice. This process tempered plans for dialogue and action; the World Faiths Development Dialogue (WFDD), the institutional instrument for the faith initiative, took a more modest form and visibility than originally planned but the World Bank itself proceeded with its engagement, primarily through a series of conferences and engagement on specific issues, notably HIV and AIDS (Marshall and Van Saanen 2007). In parallel, a quite elaborate dialogue process involving the World Council of Churches, the International Monetary Fund (IMF), and the World Bank brought into the open divergent views about both approach and process in relation to development policies.

Wolfensohn's initiative and the ensuing debates were harbingers of lively exchanges that continue to the present, turning around religious roles in development and specifically their ethical dimensions. This was particularly evident in the mobilization of communities about

DOI: 10.4324/9781315626796-35

poor country debt around the 'Jubilee' year 2000, which owed much to religious leadership and religious images and teachings. The prominent role that religious leaders played in raising the profile of the debt issue, translating what had been a highly technical issue into an understandable, moral issue, reframed the debate and had a significant impact in changing policy through the Highly Indebted Poor Country initiative (HIPC). Likewise the discussions about various public health issues, including HIV and AIDS and malaria, gave the religious and ethical issues a practical dimension that sharpened as the United Nations launched the Millennium Development Goals (MDGs) in 2000.

In the years that followed, the geopolitical landscape changed, notably with heightened concern about religious dimensions of terrorist attacks and violent conflicts in some world regions. A growing consensus emerged that the so-called 'secular hypothesis' (Norris and Inglehart, 2004), that holds that religious observance declines with modernization, was simply incorrect. While some parts of the world saw a decline in collective religious practice in daily life, for example regular church attendance by Protestants and Catholics, and individual religious practices, such as participation in daily prayer or meditation, the modern world, sociologist Peter Berger argued, is still 'ferociously religious' (Berger, 2015). Scholars and practitioners have paid sharper attention to religious factors and institutions across many fields. This is true within various United Nations entities (Stensvold 2017), other multilateral institutions, bilateral development institutions, and non-governmental organizations (Karam 2015).

The seismic effect of terrorist attacks and especially September 11, 2001, was a major turning point and has focused interest on religious influences in global affairs. One result is a strong focus on what were termed Muslim West relationships in bodies ranging from the United Nations (where the Alliance of Civilizations was established), the World Economic Forum (de Gioia and Schwab 2008), and other entities concerned with various aspects of development. The ethics of conflict and its changing nature, and debates about how conflict relates, or does not relate, to development approaches and strategies color many approaches to religion and ethics. The catch all term 'countering violent extremism' (CVE) is primarily concerned with security but questions about the nature of enticements to be involved in terrorism and extremist religious tendencies and about grievances often shape the way many see religion today.

Alongside the security impetus to religious engagement, though somewhat muted following the collapse of most communist systems after 1989, have come debates about economic and social models that involve both ethical and operational dimensions. Critics of capitalist models have included different parts of the Catholic Church, notably the Pope (Laudato Si! as the most well-known example) (Pope Francis 2015) and Liberation Theology, a broad-based framework that centers on a powerful call to a 'preferential option for the poor'. The World Council of Churches is among Christian groups focused on social justice and there are parallel efforts within other faith traditions. Wide-ranging religious groups, for example, are actively involved in advocating for environmental action and in debates about the effectiveness and future of the humanitarian system. Various coalitions of religious groups are influential in polarized debates about gender roles and family planning. On all these issues there is a wide spectrum of views within religious communities. On no topic, including one as controversial as abortion, is there a single, unanimous 'religious view'.

A factor, especially in Europe, has been growing unease about the obvious Christian focus of the many historic partnerships with faith-inspired organizations, like Caritas Internationalis, World Vision, and Tearfund. This contributes to pressures on a wider range of development actors to engage with religious actors beyond traditional parners or to favor interreligious coalitions. Partnerships include large operational faith-inspired organizations like the Aga Khan Development Network, Islamic Relief Worldwide, and Buddhist Tzu Chi that are directly involved in supporting development programs, but also interreligious and ecumenical bodies (Religions for Peace, World Council of Churches and ACT Alliance), religious institutions themselves (the Vatican, Anglican Communion), and local organizations with an explicitly or implicitly religious character (Marshall 2015). New foundation supported operational and academic programs have emerged, albeit slowly and piecemeal. Contacts and partnerships have broadened as interest in religious matters, positive and negative, increased. Even so, treatment of religious dimensions of development is frequently episodic, with a tendency to lump religious factors together in an unhelpful manner and to over-simplify the complex forces at work, including their ethical dimensions. Institutional interest can fade with changes in leadership (the World Bank after Wolfensohn is one example). Often unhelpful debates about religious factors in conflict and about family welfare policies are prime examples of the patchy landscape.

What's religion got to do with development?

Notwithstanding their frequent invisibility in development literature and practice, religious teachings and practices are interwoven through the broad development agenda in countless ways. Thus awareness of the significance of religious identities and institutions across world regions is an essential first step. As a rough rule of thumb a widely cited Pew study indicates that some 85 percent of the world's population identifies with a religious tradition (Pew 2012). Even so, a 'secular hypothesis' still has a significant hold; practitioners and scholars often assume that religious adherence declines with modernization. Many who work in international and bilateral agencies, non-governmental organizations, and governments were trained in disciplines and institutions largely devoid of consideration of religious history and its contemporary institutional forms and impact. Thus 'religious literacy' tends to be low.

A result has been rather simplistic approaches or outright prejudices and misunderstandings, for example a tendency to assume that all religious traditions oppose gender equality (many were leaders in movements for women's suffrage and empowerment). In parallel, many religious actors perceive an 'aggressive secularism' among development actors that can deter mutual understanding and cooperation. Sadly in some cases this applies to core understandings of human rights, which have a suspect odor in some religious communities as assuming a character as a 'secular religion'. These long-standing barriers to understanding are exacerbated when the focus is primarily on religious dimensions of violent conflict and CVE. Interest sparked by security concerns can open the way to dialogue and understanding but it can also distort the way religious issues and actors are perceived and approached. In addressing complex questions about root causes of conflict in Nigeria, for example, it is equally unhelpful to place all blame for tensions on religious identities or on purely economic and ethnic factors.

Addressing religious dimensions is rarely simple. The manifestations of religious beliefs and their impact on behavior and on policy vary widely; context matters, significantly. Critical approaches that recognize wide diversity among religious traditions and their interplay with other facets of social, economic, and political forces are essential in assessing how religious factors are important for development, including the question of how they relate to development ethics.

Ethics and religion?

In exploring the complex terrain of ethics, religion, and development, it is useful to explore the historical roots of religious beliefs and teachings in shaping ethical debates. Religious beliefs are deeply embedded in many development ideas and approaches (the importance of education or caring for the sick, for example). Virtually every religious tradition has teachings that are pertinent for development. However, it is equally important to appreciate that multiple factors, religious and non-religious, are involved in the ethics of any development issue, whether it is an economic policy matter like tariff policy, operational questions surrounding responsibilities for water provision in an urban center, design of programs to encourage girls to go to school, or incentives for family planning. These complex links are hardly surprising since historically, religious institutions were pervasive and often the dominant institutions in communities. The notion of distinguishing the religious from the non-religious is quite modern and even today in various societies a separation is sharply contested (this argument is frequently raised by Muslim scholars). Even supremely secular formulations of ethical principles often emerged in reaction to religious traditions or teachings (witness Communism, French laïcité).

Accounts of the debates that surrounded the drafting of the Universal Declaration of Human Rights (UDHR), approved by the United Nations General Assembly in 1948, highlight the intricate ways in which the heritage of religious teachings infuses core human rights principles (Glendon 2002). Referring to Aquinas and invoking the ancient notion of 'natural law', legal scholar Andrew Woodcock argues that what unites divergent interpretations of rights is a revelation of law 'beyond that defined by the institutional sources of law' (Woodcock 2006, 245). Philosopher Jacques Maritain who managed the UNESCO consultation on the UDHR, highlighted this religious legacy but also its complexity, noting that while there was broad agreement on UDHR principles (and thus the underlying values) there was considerable disagreement on their source and justification (UNESCO 1949).

An example: varied influences of religious teaching on family decision-making

Decisions about family planning (for example, to use contraceptives, to abstain from sex, to seek another child, to ignore the topic and let 'nature' take its course) are intimate choices made by couples and individuals. They reflect the individuals' expectations, values, hopes, and fears; these can be shaped largely or in different degrees by one or the other of a couple (a woman basically decides, or the man has the power and far more influence) or by the two together. Rarely is a single factor involved. Decisions are colored by a host of factors: culture, family circumstances (including marital status), economics, social milieu and pressures, religious beliefs, and perceptions of health risks.

Government policies and programs on family health and planning, which address both the supply and demand of family planning services, are also shaped by various factors, among them local politics, assessments of costs and priorities, evolving international norms, expectations, and available funding.

In this mix of decisions by couples and by those making government policy, explicit interventions by religious actors can be significant. Religious beliefs, communities, and leaders at both individual and society/government levels can encourage positive attitudes and actions or discourage various forms of intervention. They can exert an emotional response (deeply held beliefs or fear of retribution, for example), as well as a political calculation (a government's wish to avoid criticism from religious authorities or to bolster political support). Exactly how those roles play out, however, is difficult to pin down with precision. Overt explanations often blend with unspoken assumptions and myths about intentions and risks.

The nature and impact of religious teachings on family health and planning decisions vary widely from place to place and among different religious traditions, as well as by individuals. Influence may come directly and explicitly in the form of religious leader pronouncements or actions, but individual understandings of cultural and religious obligations ('correct' or otherwise) also play a part. There are situations where religious beliefs are central to a couple's decisions or to a government policy, and others where they may rank low. Sometimes the ethical dimensions of the decision will be colored primarily by religious beliefs. Sometimes these beliefs play marginal roles.

Given the influential and complex ways in which religious factors can affect both personal decisions and policies on family planning, they deserve careful attention in family planning policymaking. The links are rarely simple but it is wise not to ignore them, whether at the community level, in refining family planning policies at a national level, or at the United Nations (where religious influences on various government positions often shape official positions).

Religion and ethics: common or divergent values?

Three prominent and long-standing scholarly debates involving religion and ethics have had a significant impact in shaping approaches to the relationships among religion, ethics, and development: Max Weber's focus on Protestant religious beliefs, Samuel Huntington's theory of a 'Clash of Civilizations', and Hans Kung's formulation of a Global Ethic. Each has sparked wide-ranging debates and shaped attitudes that permeate debates about development policy.

Weber's theories suggested that some religious traditions were more favorable for the changes involved in modernization than others. Specifically he contrasted the disciplines he saw as linked to Protestantism with parallel beliefs linked to Catholicism; Protestant teachings, he argued, favored savings, careful management of investments, and other practices, whereas these 'virtues' were less prominent in Catholic dominated societies. Similar efforts seek to pinpoint specific practices (frugal versus lavish, for example) and attitudes (fatalism versus personal responsibility) and associate them with different religious traditions (for example Buddhist belief in predestination, Confucian emphasis on family). Recent scholarship about Pentecostal religious traditions indicates that some attributes echo Weber's arguments (Smith 2016) that the virtues promoted (frugality, an entrepreneurial spirit, and commitment to family) support positive behaviors that are important in the transition from traditional to modernizing societies.

Samuel Huntington's article that appeared in *Foreign Affairs* in 1993 (followed two years later by a full length book) is still widely cited today (Huntington). The hypothesis that different 'civilizations', by which most read religious traditions, involve different values and ethical approaches to fundamental life choices is still intensely debated and contested. His thesis raises questions as to whether there are indeed 'universal' human values and human rights. And if not, where do the fundamental differences among societies lie? Scholars and practitioners credit Huntington with important insights into forces shaping geopolitical competition but contest his notions of separate and distinct 'civilizations' as so oversimplified as to be of limited validity. An April 2015 senior seminar on 'Clash of Civilizations 2.0' at Georgetown University's Berkley Center explored these questions, concluding that they continue to an astonishing degree to shape many contemporary debates.

Hans Kung, Swiss theologian, has taken an opposite view from Huntington's notion of 'clashing' values among civilizations in his efforts to define and hone a 'global ethic' (Kung 1998). This formulation looks to the world's religious traditions to draw out common ethical values, ranging from the rather straightforward ('thou shalt not kill') to more complex notions, notably related to values that promote business. Kung's approach has been featured at such diverse settings as the World Economic Forum, the International Monetary Fund (IMF), and the Parliament of the World's Religions, all in efforts to emphasize that several universal values amount to a practical, widely shared common ethic. His ideas have played significant roles in grounding interreligious dialogue and action approaches that aim to soothe tensions and build cohesive societies amidst rich diversity. His goal and insight is to highlight, as a force for peace, the power of what is held in common, in contrast to what pulls people and communities apart.

The notion of universality is, of course, a critical element of the United Nations Universal Declaration of Human Rights (UDHR), reflecting the hypothesis that notwithstanding cultural, language, and religious diversity there are solid common values that can be translated into practice. Another effort that draws heavily both on religious teachings as a foundation and on religious alliances is the Earth Charter, formulated at the turn of the millennium in 2000. It included many of the human rights principles enunciated in the UNDR but added to them with a wide-ranging commitment to environmental justice and an affirmation of commitment to the global goals around ending poverty. The Common Word is another effort, this one originating in a group of leading Muslim scholars and religious leaders; as the name suggests, it affirms strong common values and commitments between Muslims and Christians, looking to their respective religious traditions as a way to bridge divides and differences (Common Word 2007).

The common values approach, when it focuses on bridging divides among religious teachings and practice and when employed as a way to mobilize common action, is both an analytic tool and a means to advance cooperative action. The UN Millennium Development Goals (MDGs), followed in 2015 by the Sustainable Development Goals (SDGs), aim to translate these understandings of common, shared values. The wide array of United Nations Conventions move towards greater specificity, for example in defining a right to water or children's rights. While religious communities tended to look somewhat askance at these efforts in the early years, there are increasingly active efforts to engage religious communities in advancing the various SDGs through a wide series of consultations and collaborative efforts. Harking back to Wolfensohn's 1998 outreach to religious communities, the underlying assumption (and hope) is that religious and development communities share a common ethically grounded commitment to work to improve the lot of poor and marginalized people across the world. This hope is reflected in a marked increase in UN agency interest in engaging with religious communities (Karam 2017).

A parallel set of efforts focus on humanitarian work and on peacebuilding (both areas increasingly seen as intricately linked to development). Michael Barnett and Janice Stein examine the rich history of humanitarianism through a religious lens, emphasizing the strong ethical foundations of humanitarian principles and their links to religious traditions and teachings (Barnett and Stein 2012). Likewise there are many efforts to address the religious and ethical dimensions not only of war (just war theory) but of approaches to peace. An example is an edited volume that explores the approaches of different religious traditions to just peace (Thistlethwaite 2011).

Notwithstanding common religious teachings to mobilize communities to work together, nagging questions persist about how far exhilarating commitments to peace, ending poverty, and protecting the environment paper over not only simple differences in understanding but also the complexities that are involved. The straightforward principle 'thou shalt not kill' masks millennia of debate over the circumstances in which killing is justified or not. Even discussions around corruption, grounded in truth telling and admonitions to refrain from stealing, encounter layers of differing interpretations and emphases that in practice make it difficult to mobilize common religious efforts to address an issue that seems to exemplify core common religious values (Marshall 2008).

Moving from theory towards practice

Context matters, always, but perhaps especially so where ethical principles encounter the complex realities of different places, cultures, and religion. Different religious traditions and frequently different communities within a single religious tradition can approach development issues very differently, rarely seeing precisely eye to eye on even very similar issues. The following comments explore six development issues where religious dimensions and different ethical approaches are prominent. There are instances where the discourse of different religious traditions is notably similar to that of non-religious actors, others where there are wide disparities both in language and in the witness of experience.

Human rights and religious freedom

Freedom of religion was one of the four freedoms that Franklin Roosevelt highlighted in 1940 (Zeitz 2015), and it is embedded as a fundamental human right in the UDHR. Various activists and scholars argue that there are significant links between religious freedom and success (or failure) in development (Grim 2014). Debates center on how far it is freedom to choose, practice, or change one's religion that is critical or whether freedom of belief should be viewed as a factor within a broader human rights context. Some (including Brian Grim 2014) argue that freedom of conscience is at the core of human freedom and dignity and thus trumps other values. These debates have policy relevance because religious freedom is an important foreign policy principle for the United States and several other countries, although it has rarely figured explicitly in development practice (Marshall 2013b).

Freedom of religion is specifically linked to development approaches through the controversial issue of proselytism associated with development programs: thus, the question for humanitarian relief and for longer term development programs (education, health, community development, for example) is whether there are quid pro quos for religious participation or conversion. For humanitarian work, explicit guidelines make clear that such approaches are unethical, since discrimination in favor of any group and conditionality attached to assistance to those in dire need run counter to humanitarian principles. However, particularly for complex development areas like education and health, norms are less clear and grey areas more pronounced. For example, how far do ethical values embedded in a school curriculum reflect the specific beliefs of a faith tradition?

Hunger and food

The SDG (#2) to achieve zero hunger by 2030 echoes the traditions of many religious communities that emphasize feeding the hungry. Thus there is a marked convergence of United Nations approaches (framed within the UDHR context) and religious teachings and ethical principles. Likewise the widespread work of religious communities through soup kitchens and other programs for the neediest in communities across the world are widely acknowledged and respected. The complexity comes when the specifics of translating a global goal into policies and actions are at issue: what are reasonable food security policies? What is the best way to support small farmers or to eliminate food waste? There the consensus is less than clear and firm. While faith leaders and communities can serve as powerful advocates vis à vis governments, and while their knowledge of communities offers important ways to identify those most in need, translating these important assets into practice is challenging. Advocacy can be a powerful tool: for example, in the United States during a tense budget struggle that threatened social programs, religious figures formed a 'Circle of Protection', fasting to highlight the importance of programs to help the hungry (Circle of Protection 2015). The ethical principle to feed the hungry tends to remain focused at the individual and community level rather than on the global stage.

Prosperity gospel and economic models

Lively if imprecisely defined ethical debates involving religious leaders relate to economic models. Concerns are expressed through religious teachings (notably in the context of Catholic Social Teaching), sermons and other preaching, and, sometimes, formal advocacy or protests. Perhaps the most vivid examples of an expression of religious, ethical teachings calling basic economic models into question are the 2015 Papal Encyclical, Laudato Si! (Laudato Si!) and the Jubilee 2000 Movement, which sought action to forgive poor country debt. In both cases the reasoning is clearly ethical: focused on supporting those in need and arguing for equitable treatment across communities. But can a meaningful debate about courses of action take place without clear understandings of alternatives, bridging the very different language of theology and economics?

Ethical debates also center on the prosperity gospel, an approach advanced notably by various evangelical and Pentecostal communities. Put somewhat simplistically, the argument is that God will reward virtue and good behavior with wealth. This tends to put a premium on financial dimensions of welfare that jar with the teachings of other traditions that hold frugality and even poverty as a virtue. Debates about the prosperity gospel can be a dividing wedge within Christian communities.

Reproductive health and sexual rights

Perhaps the most intensive and ethically framed debates in development work center on reproductive health and sexual rights, debates widely perceived as primarily linked to religious views and advocacy. This spills over into broader issues around women's and gender rights, including LGBT (lesbian, gay, bisexual, and transgender) issues. Explicit Catholic Church positions on 'artificial' contraceptives and on abortion, alongside similar views from other traditions expressed through national authorities, color debates in the UN setting. In practice religious influences on decisions around family planning and sexuality are complex, intertwined with culture, economics, and other factors that shape both individual and public policy decisions and behaviors. And there are wide ranging approaches to these matters among and within religious traditions. A recent UNFPA led meeting and review highlighted the dangers of oversimplifying assumptions about religious approaches to these matters and significant religious support for actions to support women's rights in many communities (UNFPA/Norad 2016).

Authority, governance, corruption

Governance, writ large, plays vital roles in development success and failure and it involves wide-ranging ethical dimensions. Not surprisingly religious approaches color many debates, including the roles and responsibilities of government, the significance of secular versus religious foundations for state authority, and the ethics of citizen relationships with their governments. Understandings of freedoms, including freedom of speech, are another example. Among governance issues, approaches to corruption have particular importance, as a common grievance and because it undermines effective governance in practice and by eroding trust. Thus religious teachings about corruption and direct involvement in integrity movements (for example, those led by the international non-governmental movement, Transparency International) are to be expected. Surprisingly, religious engagement on corruption issues is rather sporadic, reflected in some examples of courageous 'speaking truth to power' but also in notable instances of strategic silence. Reasons are complex; corruption is viewed often as less than straightforward, involving imbalances of power and grey areas of morality. Religious figures often depend on government support, financial and administratively. Thus outrage and advocacy to end corruption is often muted (Marshall 2008).

Gender roles, women's rights

Gender equality offers many examples of ways in which principles and lived realities around ethical principles can come into conflict. Many core religious teachings as well as the UDHR are unambiguous in their assertions of equal dignity of all human beings as well as equal rights and obligations. Some religious leaders actively advance women's roles and work to shatter barriers to their dignity and development, drawing on their understanding of universal principles. However, deeply embedded in many holy scriptures, parables and stories, and institutions are large inequalities that in practice, in many traditions and world regions, limit women's possibilities for development, trample on their dignity, subordinate their positions, and denigrate their gifts and contributions. The 'glass ceilings' that limit women's possibilities in many spheres, in religious and secular institutions and in the home and within families, are often bolstered by religious beliefs and practices. There are few more enduring ceilings than those that can be described as 'stained glass ceilings'. The tempting notion of 'complementarity' as an adjunct to 'equality' is an insidious and ultimately incompatible approach that in practice means subordination and separation more than equality and unity.

Reflections on the path ahead

Knowledge, evidence, and understanding play outsize roles where religious intersections with development are concerned. Research and 'literacy' efforts thus have particular significance. Despite considerable research on how different religious traditions shape development approaches and practice, gaps in knowledge are large. Solid evidence about how religious communities influence development is sparse and scattered. An example of both richness of knowledge and its limits can be found for religious involvement in health care; a WFDD review of existing research identified numerous studies, across various disciplines, but also many areas where data and analysis are weak (Aylward et al. 2012). There is thus considerable scope both to communicate knowledge and for further research.

Religious institutions are clearly vital development actors but unresolved tensions around religious beliefs and positions can represent important obstacles and distractions. Purposeful efforts to address them deserve a high priority. Elucidating the implicit values that underlie different approaches to many dimensions of development and highlighting practical examples, good and bad, could help unravel twisted and unproductive debates and contribute to better development processes and outcomes. Given the ubiquitous presence of religious communities and institutional forms, working in this direction makes eminent sense.

A trickier question involves what some term the 'religious DNA': are there significant differences in development outcomes shaped specifically by the nature or degree of religiosity of the actors concerned? My answer is no. The not uncommon argument that without religious foundations there can be no solid ethics and, by extension, that no leader can be ethical unless they are a religious believer leads one down a slippery and dangerous slope. Such suggestions over-simplify the complex derivations of ethical norms at community and individual levels and the way that even the most seemingly clear understandings of ethics and values work in practice. Such assertions denigrate those who fall outside religious communities. Blanket assertions that the primary source of ethical norms is religious obscure the complex territory of interpretation and application of ethical standards in law and society. Such oversimplifications are not useful and they can be pernicious. Efforts to demonstrate a distinctive religious 'marker' or indeed to attribute actions solely to religious beliefs are unlikely to yield meaningful results. A more productive focus is to enrich understandings about development choices and paths with a probing understanding of the religious dimensions involved.

It is arguable that human dignity, as the foundation for understandings of equality, is grounded in deeply held religious understandings of creation, and that peace is a deeply religious principle. For both core concepts, however, multiple sources and inspirations are at play. Geography, the presence or absence of natural resources, global and local social and economic disparities, and psychology, among many other factors, influence the practical reality of inequalities and conflict, as well as circumstances of harmony and good will. The religious roots of ethical principles may be the lodestar in many situations and for communities, central in explaining the history of ideas, but looking solely to religious principles is rarely sufficient.

One path to addressing tensions and establishing clearer common ground is to build on a strong common thread of core values, ideally linking and thus bringing different religious traditions into closer harmony. The 'Golden Rule': 'do unto others as you would have them do unto you' is cited often as exemplary in this regard. Core religious values distilled in the Golden Rule are seen to offer an actionable, readily grasped common teaching as versions of this notion are found in virtually every religious and cultural tradition (this website offers an example www.religioustolerance.org/reciproc.htm). The admonition to 'do unto others as you would have them do unto you,' underscores a profound ethic of reciprocity. A story is attributed to Rabbi Hillel: 'The sage Hillel summarized the entire Torah by saying, "That which is hateful to you, do not do to your fellow. That is the whole Torah; the rest is the explanation; go and learn it"' (Twerski 2013). The Charter of Compassion, a global movement inspired by the Ted prize awarded to scholar Karen Armstrong, builds on this basic principle as the foundation for a common effort to address conflict and tensions in the world. A not dissimilar teaching linked to African spirituality is the notion of *Ubuntu*, sometimes explained as the notion that 'you are, therefore I am.' The core idea also points to the suggestion that universal values unite humankind.

Efforts to inspire, shame, even jolt human beings to a humane and common vision can yield results. The Golden Rule and Ubuntu principles are unlikely, however, by themselves to transform selfish and warmongering human beings into kind neighbors and dutiful citizens nor to build equitable, prospering societies. Rule of law, constant leadership efforts, economic incentives and disincentives, robust education, and opportunities for individual and community development that bring out the best in people (their 'better angels') all play their part. They come alongside the values and ethical principles that, to varying degrees, people draw from their religious heritage, identity, and teachings and that they use to weigh their course of action. There is far to go in translating the universal values of equality and dignity, whether as expressed in the UDHR, in scriptures, in a global ethic, and in a notion of the Golden Rule or Ubuntu, into practice in ways that can liberate human possibilities and move from aspiration and inspiration to reality.

References

Aylward, L. et al. (2012) *Global Health and Africa: Assessing Faith Work and Research Priorities* WFDD. https://s3.amazonaws.com/berkleycenter/GlobalHealthandAfricaWFDDEdition.pdf.

Barnett, M. and Stein, J. (2012) *Sacred Aid: Faith and Humanitarianism*. Oxford University Press, Oxford.

Berger, P. (2015) A Discussion with Peter Berger. https://berkleycenter.georgetown.edu/interviews/a-discussion-with-peter-berger-professor-emeritus-at-boston-university-29053f12–02c5–4441-b467-a544da22e99c.

Circle of Protection (2015) http://circleofprotection.us/media-room/. Accessed 25 September 2016.
A Common Word between us and You (2007) www.acommonword.com/.
De Gioia, J. and Schwab, K. (2008) *Islam and the West: Annual Report on the State of Dialogue* World Economic Forum, Geneva. https://berkleycenter.georgetown.edu/publications/islam-and-the-west-annual-report-on-the-state-of-dialogue. Accessed 26 September 2016.
The Earth Charter (2000) http://earthcharter.org/.
Glendon, M.E. (2002) *A World Made New: Eleanor Roosevelt and the Universal Declaration of Human Rights*. Random House, London.
Grim, B. (2014) Growing Religion and Growing Religious Restrictions: A Global Overview. *International Area Studies Review* 17: 134–145.
Huntington, S. (1993) A Clash of Civilizations? *Foreign Affairs*.
Karam, A. (2015) Opinion: Religion and the SDGs – The 'New Normal' and Calls for Action. *IPS* www.ipsnews.net/2015/07/opinion-religion-and-the-sdgs-the-new-normal-and-calls-for-action/. Accessed 26 September 2016.
Karam, A. (2017) Is Religion the New Colonial Frontier in International Development? *IPS*. www.ipsnews.net/2017/07/religion-new-colonial-frontier-international-development/.
Kung, H. (1998) *A Global Ethic for Global Politics and Economics*. Oxford University Press, Oxford.
Marshall, K. (2008) Ancient and Contemporary Wisdom and Practice on Governance as Religious Leaders Engage in International Development. *Journal of Global Ethics* 4(3): 217–229.
Marshall, K. (2013a) *Global Institutions of Religion: Ancient Movers, Modern Shakers*. Routledge, New York.
Marshall, K. (2013b) Religious Freedom in US International Development Assistance and Humanitarian Relief: Ideas, Practice, and Issues. *The Review of Faith and International Affairs* II(1): 38–48.
Marshall, K. (2015) Complex Global Institutions: Religious Engagement in Development. In Tomalin, E. ed., *The Routledge Handbook of Religions and Global Development*, Routledge, Oxford.
Marshall, K. and Van Saanen, M. (2007) *Development and Faith: Where Mind, Heart, and Soul Work Together*. The World Bank, Washington, DC.
Norris, P. and Inglehard, R. (2004) *Sacred and Secular: Religion and Politics Worldwide*. Cambridge University Press, Cambridge.
Pew Research Center (2012) *The Global Religious Landscape*. www.pewforum.org/2012/12/18/global-religious-landscape-exec/. Accessed 25 September 2016.
Pope Francis (2015) *Encyclical letter, Laudato Si!*, The Vatican. http://w2.vatican.va/content/francesco/en/encyclicals/documents/papa-francesco_20150524_enciclica-laudato-si.html. Accessed 25 September 2016.
Smith, K. (2016) *Max Weber and Pentecostals in Latin America: The Protestant Ethic, Social Capital and Spiritual Capital*. Georgia State University, Thesis. http://scholarworks.gsu.edu/cgi/viewcontent.cgi?article=1067&context=political_science_theses. Accessed 25 September 2016.
Stensvold, A. (2017) *Religion, State and the United Nations: Value Politics*. Routledge. Oxford.
Thistlethwaite, S. ed. (2011) *Interfaith Just Peacemaking: Jewish, Christian, and Muslim Perspectives on the New Paradigm of Peace and War*. Palgrave MacMillan, London.
Twerski, A. (2013) *Messages from the Mishnah*. Shaar Press Mesonah Publications, Brooklyn.
UNESCO ed. (1949) *Human Rights: Comments and Interpretations*. London: Allan Wingate.
UNFPA/NORAD (2016) *Religion, Women's Health and Rights: Points of Contention and Paths of Opportunities*. www.unfpa.org/sites/default/files/pub-pdf/50424_UNFPA_White_Paper_NORAD_Web.pdf. Accessed 26 September 2016.
Woodcock, A. (2006) Jacques Maritain, Natural Law and the Universal Declaration of Human Rights. *Journal of the History of International Law* 8: 245–266.
Zeitz, J. (2015) How Roosevelt Invented the Four Freedoms. *Politico*. www.politico.com/magazine/story/2015/07/roosevelt-four-freedoms-119728.

Part VIII
Responsibility

This last broad value is different from the others in three ways. First, it refers specifically to the agents of development, including individuals of course but also organizations, governments, and institutions. What we are looking for in development processes and activities is that these actors all carry out their particular responsibilities. Second, it demands that no important responsibilities go unassigned, or are assigned to the wrong actors. For example, it is not responsible development if no one is assigned responsibility for environmental safeguards, or if this responsibility is assigned to people who are powerless to implement them. Finally, it includes the omnibus responsibility to act with integrity. Aristotle observed that in a general sense 'acting justly' means acting ethically in all dealings with others, and this too is implied by acting responsibly.

Three different aspects of responsible development are addressed here: (1) for states, responsible development entails identifying and carrying out responsibilities of aid; (2) for individual practitioners, it means navigating conflicting responsibilities with integrity; (3) finally, responsibility and integrity call upon all development actors to avoid and combat corruption.

Julian Culp maps philosophical debates about international responsibilities towards development. How are these responsibilities grounded? Are we called upon to support development in order to maximize human utility? Should development aid be understood rather as humanitarian response to human suffering? Or, finally, is it global justice that demands international cooperation for development? While the idea that unequal development is *unjust* is intuitively powerful, it raises further questions about the grounds of global justice.

Within the community of development and humanitarian relief practitioners, development ethics is relatively unknown and little discussed, according to Chloe Schwenke, who considers a number of possible explanations: negative attitudes towards "soft" topics, shunning of ethical terminology and argumentation, lack of work for development ethicists, and conflation of "ethics" with regulatory codes around transparency and corruption. Nevertheless there is interest (even excitement) about development ethics among some practitioners, and the challenge is to nurture and sustain it.

The integrity issue that has drawn the greatest attention in connection with development is corruption. Sirkku Hellsten unpacks three difficult problems that loom around corruption. The first is conceptual: it is surprisingly difficult to settle on a workable definition of "corruption." Second, it is difficult to assess the costs of corruption, depending on whether we measure politically, economically, or in relation to human rights. Third, the causes of corruption and successful means of combatting it are also unclear.

DOI: 10.4324/9781315626796-36

29

International responsibilities

From utility and humanitarianism to global justice

Julian Culp

In this chapter I lay out several conceptions of international responsibility for development practice, that is, for rule-governed development activities across national borders. The actors who take on such responsibility include individuals, governments, international organizations and transnational corporations. Examples of such actors are development ministries and the United Nations Development Program.

Thus, strictly speaking, this chapter does not only discuss *international* responsibility in the narrow sense that refers solely to relations of responsibility among states. Rather, it also deals with issues of *transnational* responsibility, since it engages with the responsibility of non-state actors such as individuals or transnational corporation. These are issues of *transnational* responsibility because the usual meaning of *transnational* in political science refers to the relations of and interactions among actors from different states, at least one of which is a non-state actor. I simply assume that collective entities such as states, governmental and intergovernmental agencies can be regarded as corporate agents who can make choices and thus are morally responsible subjects (List and Pettit 2011). By assuming that collective entities are morally responsible subjects I mean to stay they are worthy of a particular kind of reactive attitude, namely that of praise or blame (Strawson 1982).

Conceptions of international responsibility refer to the practical reasons as to why and in which ways such actors ought to engage themselves in development practice. In this chapter I distinguish between three major pillars of today's development practice.

The first one is *bilateral aid*, which is comprised of states that participate in the inter-state practice to give and receive official development assistance (ODA). The Organization for Economic Development and Cooperation (OECD 2011) defines ODA as follows:

> [ODA consists of] those flows to states and territories on the DAC List of ODA Recipients and to multilateral development institutions which are: i. *provided by official agencies*, including state and local governments, or by their executive agencies; and ii. each transaction of which: a) is administered with the promotion of the *economic development and welfare of developing countries* as its main objective; and b) is *concessional in character* and conveys a grant element of at least 25 per cent (calculated at a rate of discount of 10 per cent).
>
> *(OECD 2011)*

DOI: 10.4324/9781315626796-37

The second one is *multilateral aid* and consists of international organizations that receive and provide ODA. Influential international development organizations include the World Bank Group, the European Development Fund, the Asian and the African Development Banks, the UN Funds and Programs as well as the Global Fund to fight Aids, Tuberculosis and Malaria. The third pillar is *private aid* which gets channeled through philanthropic foundations and other non-governmental organizations like the *Bill and Melinda Gates Foundation* and *Oxfam*, respectively.

The conceptions of international responsibility for development practice that I discuss in this chapter are *normative* conceptions. These types of conceptions will not necessarily reflect the reasons that pertain to those conceptions of international responsibility that govern *actual* development practice. Therefore the kinds of development practice that the normative conceptions support can be recognizably different from the ones which have become prevalent today. Indeed, it has become commonplace to regard the behavior of such actors to be motivated by self-interest rather than a sense of responsibility, although many of the actors that take part in development practice explicitly mention such normative conceptions of international responsibility. For example, economists (McKinlay and Little 1977), development organizations (World Bank 1990, 127–128; 1998, 40–41) and civil society groups (Niggli 2008, ch. 7) hold that wealthy states engage in development practice in order to further their foreign-policy goals. They argue that the richer states give ODA to foster political alliances with the poorer states in international negotiations or to sustain transnational networks among elites that are economically beneficial. On top of this many scholars (McGillivray 1989, 2004; White and McGillivray 1992, 1995; Alesina and Dollar 2000; Birdsall et al. 2003; Berthélemy and Tichit 2004) claim to be able to verify empirically the dominance of such self-interested reasons when examining how states allocate ODA. In this chapter I do not study the empirical question why certain actors engage in development practice that actually exists, but I do present different *moral* rationales as to why certain actors should engage in certain kinds of development practice. Normative conceptions of international responsibility for development practice represent such rationales and thus fulfill the dual practical purpose of justifying and criticizing development practice.

The chapter unfolds as follows. First I reconstruct the utilitarian conception of international responsibility for development practice that is based on the utilitarian principle that human action and institutions should maximize average or overall utility. The utilitarian conception has been very effective in drawing attention to the importance of development but has struck most commentators as being overly demanding. Then I go on to present the humanitarian conception of international responsibility for development practice which relies on the more moderate duty of humanity according to which one should prevent great human suffering if one can do so at small personal cost. This conception is less demanding than the utilitarian one, but it has been criticized by theorists of global distributive justice because it falsely suggests that the global interpersonal distribution of holdings is morally acceptable. Following this, I discuss three different global distributive justice-based conceptions of international responsibility for development practice, all of which put into question the claim that the way in which holdings are distributed among individuals globally is morally acceptable. These three conceptions rely, respectively, on statist, globalist, and internationalist theories of global distributive justice that offer quite distinct views regarding of what global distributive justice consists. Nevertheless, all of these theories are capable of supporting the claim that the responsibility to engage in development practice is not just a matter of charity or humanity but is rather a concern of distributive justice. This is significant, because it implies that participating in a development practice so as to bring about a certain conception of global distributive justice is mandatory even if doing so involves more than just small personal costs to the actors involved.

The utilitarian conception of international responsibility

The utilitarian philosopher Peter Singer made an extremely influential contribution regarding the moral reasons for development activities across states. In his seminal essay "Famine, Affluence and Morality," he argued that individuals from richer states would have obligations to donate a substantial portion of their holdings to aid organizations even if doing so made themselves much worse off. He argued that donating to a philanthropic foundation or international development organization is morally required as long as the alternative use of such a potential donation would not be of "comparable moral importance" (Singer 1972, 231). A quite radical implication of such a moral requirement is that it demands giving away all of one's resources up to the point where by giving away more one would become just as badly off as the potential recipient of one's donation. The normative premise of Singer's argument is the utilitarian principle that human behavior ought to maximize total or average utility. In combination with the empirical premise that it would improve total or average utility if individuals from richer states gave away large amounts of their holdings, it follows that individuals have a moral duty of doing so. (See also Unger 1996.)

However, this utilitarian conception creates problems, because it does not conform well with the moral idea that individuals must not be constrained by moral demands to such an extent that it prevents them from leading lives of their own. By being required to donate almost all of their holdings, and by constantly having to check whether giving away more improved total or average utility, it seems as though such individuals could not conceive of themselves as being authors of their lives (Smart and Williams 1973, 116–117). In a similar vein, Rawls (1971, ch. 1) famously criticizes utilitarianism on the ground that it does not seriously take the 'separateness' of persons into account. Utilitarianism can require lowering the utility of some individuals to an extremely low degree of absolute utility if it serves to maximize total or average utility.

Singer (1972, 231) has recognized that many people find the practical implications of the utilitarian conception to be in fact overly demanding and counter-intuitive. He insisted, however, that the practical obligation to donate would also follow from a more moderate principle: "if it is in our power to prevent something very bad from happening, without thereby sacrificing anything morally significant, we morally ought to do it" (Singer 1972, 231). Relying on this principle, Singer argues that individuals of the richer states have a moral obligation of donating at least some of their holdings, because they can thereby avoid doing something very bad without sacrificing anything morally significant. But this argument is no longer a utilitarian one, since it does not call for the maximization of average or overall utility. So the more moderate principle is indeed more closely aligned to a so-called *duty of humanity*, according to which human beings must prevent human suffering if they can do so at a small cost to themselves. I assume that the 'duty of humanity' is similar to what Rawls (1971, 109) calls the 'principle of mutual aid.' However, I will use the term *duty of humanity* rather than *principle of mutual aid* in order to clarify that the duty of humanity can provide reasons for action even if there is no mutual practice of helping one another. In the next section I present in greater detail the humanitarian conception of international responsibility for development practice which is implicitly premised on such a moral duty.

The humanitarian conception of international responsibility

The humanitarian conception of international responsibility is based on the premise of a moral duty of humanity to reduce great human suffering whenever one can do so at relatively small costs. The moral philosopher Thomas Scanlon (1998, 224) articulates the rescue principle, which captures the core idea of the duty of humanity: "If you are presented with a situation in which you can prevent something very bad from happening, or alleviate someone's dire plight, by making only a slight (or even moderate) sacrifice, then it would be wrong not to do so." The duty of humanity is a natural duty, which means that its validity is neither conditional on consent nor on participation in institutional arrangements (Rawls 1971, 114–117). It is the mere capability of helping others who are in need at small costs that generates this duty. The duty of humanity is thus akin to the idea of *noblesse oblige* which is the idea that great power comes with great responsibility. The conception of international responsibility for development practice that can be articulated on the basis of this duty is called the *humanitarian* conception simply because of the way in which ethicists refer to this duty. So despite the adjective "humanitarian" this conception is not meant to refer to a conception of international responsibility for humanitarian aid in cases of emergency.

The humanitarian conception of an international responsibility for development practice has found considerable support among the development practitioners that are active in bi- and multilateral aid activities. A prominent example for development practitioners' reliance on the humanitarian conception is to be found in the World Bank president Robert McNamara's (1973, section 3) Nairobi Speech in which he stated that "the fundamental case for development assistance is the moral one. The whole of human history has recognized the principle – at least in the abstract – that the rich and the powerful have a moral obligation to assist the poor and the weak." Similarly, In his Four Point Speech US President Truman also insisted: "Only by helping the least fortunate of its members to help themselves can the human family achieve the decent, satisfying life that is the right of all people" (Truman 1949). So, in a nutshell, this conception says that individuals of the richer states around the world are to be held morally responsible for reducing human suffering abroad, because they are able to do so at small cost to themselves. This conception rests on the empirical claim that via the promotion of the development practice it is possible to reduce great human suffering at a small cost. This conception relies therefore on the idea that development practice institutionally *mediates* the duties of humanity that individuals in richer states have vis-à-vis individuals in poorer states (cf. Shue 1988).

Some political philosophers who theorize distributive justice will affirm *only* this humanitarian conception for development practice but do not advance any distributive justice-based conception for it. Thomas Nagel (2005) is a good case in point. He accepts the validity of the duty of humanity, and he also believes that development practice can be effective in reducing human suffering at small costs. But he denies that there are duties of distributive justice beyond the state that could ground a further, distributive-justice based conception of international responsibility for development practice. As a reason for this he claims that the grounds which trigger the demands of distributive justice exists only inside but not beyond the realm of states. Nagel (2005, 128) says that such a ground is coercion which is purportedly authorized in the name of the coerced. Since such a coercion exists only inside but not outside the state, Nagel holds that there are no duties of distributive justice that could give reason to a justice-based conception of international development. *Pace* Nagel, however, several other theorists of global distributive justice have argued that there are principles of distributive justice that apply beyond states and that an international responsibility for development practice would be one of the most obvious practical implications of such principles. The next section lays out their reasoning in greater detail.

Global distributive justice-based conceptions of international responsibility

Several theorists of global distributive justice have argued that considerations of *global distributive justice* justify the international responsibility to participate in development practice. More specifically, they claim that the validity of some egalitarian (Beitz 1979, 172–173; Pogge 1989, ch. 6, 1994; Moellendorf 2002, 61) or sufficientarian (Brock 2009, ch. 5) principle of distributive justice is global in scope and grounds a practice that can bring the actual distribution of holdings into closer conformity with that which global distributive justice requires. The point of recognizing that there is also such a distributive justice-based conception of international responsibility, however, is not to deny the validity of the humanitarian conception. Rather, the point is to insist that there is an additional kind of international responsibility for development practice. The existence of such responsibility means that there can be a responsibility to continue engaging in development practice even once the demands of the humanitarian conception have already been fulfilled. After all, global distributive injustices might continue to persist, even once great human suffering has been relieved, or once all agents have done everything that they could at small costs to prevent human suffering. Under such circumstances a global distributive justice-based conception of international responsibility could still require addressing certain injustices through development practice. This is because, as Beitz (1979, 127) argues, different from the "duty of mutual aid to help those who, without help, would surely perish [. . .], [o]bligations of justice might be thought to be more demanding than this, to require greater sacrifices on the part of the relatively well-off."

So if a particular form of development practice is justified on the basis of considerations of global distributive justice, then this justification should not be rejected on the ground that it requires some individuals to incur more than small personal costs. And if justice calls for a particular practice, then no one can plausibly object to this demand simply by pointing out that it would be very burdensome to participate in that practice. For example, one would not think that a slaveowner should not have been asked to participate in institutionally reforming his slaveholding society, simply because freeing the slaves would have imposed on him substantial economic costs. By contrast, as we explained earlier, considerations of humanity establish a duty to relieve human suffering only on the condition that this can be done at a small personal cost. Thus if one were to propose establishing a form of development practice that required of individuals more than what they could provide at small personal costs, then such a practice could not be justifiable on the basis of a purely humanitarian conception.

Additionally there are some theorists of global distributive justice who offer an account of international responsibility for development practice and who also criticize those, like Nagel, who endorse solely a humanitarian conception. They reason that by solely suggesting that individuals from richer states ought to donate some of *their* holdings, those who only accept a humanitarian conception also morally accept the existing global distribution of holdings. This is because moral considerations of humanity involve what one ought to do with one's *own* holdings in order to relieve human suffering. And therefore any claim owed as a matter of humanity presupposes an assumption about the just distribution of holdings. Barry powerfully expresses this view:

> We cannot sensibly talk about humanity unless we have a baseline set by justice. To talk about what I ought, as a matter of humanity, to do with what is mine makes no sense until we have established what is mine in the first place.
>
> *(Barry 2008, 206–207)*

Hence theorists of global distributive justice criticize those normative theorists who solely articulate a humanitarian conception for international development that this falsely suggests that the current distribution of holdings is just (cf. Forst 2012, Pogge 2004). They argue that it makes no sense to speak of "beneficently" giving away resources which one does not in fact rightly possess. Such discourse is an instance of what Paulo Freire (1970, 44) has aptly dubbed a "false generosity." Along similar lines Kant has put into question that those who have accrued their holdings unjustly can in any way use such holdings beneficently to further the well-being of someone else:

> Having the resources to practice such benevolence as depends on the goods of fortune is, for the most part, a result of certain human beings favored through the injustice of the government, which introduces an inequality of wealth that makes others need their beneficence. Under such circumstances, does a rich man's help to the needy, on which he so readily prides himself as something meritorious, really deserve to be called beneficence at all?
>
> *(Kant 1996[1797], 203)*

Hence the criticism claims that those who justify the international responsibility for development practice *only* in terms of a duty of humanity are incorrect in accepting the given global distribution of holdings as just. The critics argue that this constitutes a moral flaw. So as you would expect given that their conception of international responsibility for development practice relies on an account of global distributive justice that involves precisely the claim that the current global system decreeing what persons are entitled to is unjust.

In the following three sub-sections I outline three major ways in which it is possible to defend such a claim which rely on statist, globalist and internationalist theories of global distributive justice. Statist theorists (Blake 2001; Nussbaum 2006; Brock 2009) recognize that justice requires the sufficientarian principles of justice are in place everywhere. They require that all individuals globally should enjoy sufficient autonomy which gives them a decent range of choices (Blake 2001). But statists limit the validity of comparative, non-sufficientarian principles of justice to the relations among co-citizens inside the state, which are principles that determine the persons' rights to certain goods relative to how much others possess of these goods. Globalists and internationalists, by contrast, do not limit the scope of comparative, non-sufficientarian principles of justice in this manner. Globalists (Beitz 1979, Pogge 1989, Moellendorf 2002, Tan 2004, Caney 2005) hold that certain egalitarian principles of justice are valid among all individuals globally, and internationalists (Rawls 1999, Pettit 2010, Culp 2014) maintain that inter-state relations should be governed by comparative principles. However, whereas globalists believe that principles of global justice should regulate the arrangements of a global society of individuals, the internationalists hold that such principles should regulate a society of states.

Statist conceptions of international responsibility

Statist theorists such as Blake (2001), Brock (2009, ch. 3) and Nussbaum (2006, part II) limit the demands of global distributive justice to the realization of a fundamental conception of distributive justice within all states. These statists thus do not hold that the persisting inequalities among individuals from different states or among states would constitute a problem from the point of view of global distributive justice. These statist theorists agree that global distributive justice requires, if at all possible, the institutionalization of development practice that helps fulfill the fundamental principles of distributive justice which they accept as valid inside all states. Along these lines Brock (2009, 136, 122), for example, suggests that an international taxation scheme should be established that raises revenues for a "justice fund" which in turn would provide the "revenue that is badly needed in developing countries."

Nussbaum's theory of global distributive justice is statist, because she (2006, 2011) recognizes merely the global validity of certain fundamental principles of distributive justice inside all states and denies that comparative principles of justice would be valid either among all individuals globally or among all states. While Nussbaum (2006, 315–324) indeed mentions explicitly the need for redistributing economic resources among states, she regards this kind of redistribution as being merely derivative of the individuals' justice-based entitlements to the ten central capabilities. According to Nussbaum's conception the richer states have a global distributive-justice based international responsibility to help other states in realizing their citizens' claims to fundamental distributive justice. Nussbaum creates these fundamental claims in terms of a list of ten central capabilities. They are life; bodily health; bodily integrity; sense, imagination and thought; emotions; practical reason; affiliation; contact with other species; play; and control over one's environment (Nussbaum 2011, 33–34). She maintains that these capabilities represent necessary elements of a life worthy of human dignity which is an idea that she holds to be cross-culturally valid (2003, 40; 2006, 70, 75, 78, 159–160, 292; 2011, 31, 73 and 78). However, the ten central capabilities are understood as *political* demands in the way in which Rawls (1993) defends a distinctively *political* as opposed to a comprehensive understanding of his theory of justice as fairness.

The international responsibility for development practice asks all sufficiently powerful actors to assist insufficiently powerful states in the realization of their citizens' central capabilities. This implies that inside all states citizens should become able to co-determine their social and political environments, since this is one of Nussbaum's ten central capabilities. It is important to note that this specific demand would not exist if there was only a humanitarian conception of the international responsibility for development practice, because there is no great human suffering that derives from being deprived of this particular capability. In addition, Nussbaum's global distributive justice-based conception of international responsibility requires us to realize the central capability of enjoying bodily integrity within all countries. It demands sufficiently powerful actors to do something in that respect, although there also exists a humanitarian conception of international responsibility that leads to a similar practical conclusion. So the recognition of a global distributive justice-based conception of this statist kind adds many practical reasons for development practice. It offers such reasons not only in terms of the particular aims that this practice should pursue, but also in terms of the reasons for participating in development practice in the first place.

However, several other political philosophers have seriously criticized the statist conceptions of global distributive justice. One strand of the criticisms has focused on the reasons for limiting the validity of comparative principles to the relations among co-citizens inside the state. The statist philosopher Blake (2001), for example, holds that the reason for this limitation is that only domestic legal coercion is influential for the distribution of holdings among individuals. Pogge, however, has shown that there is a sense in which international law, especially international trade regulation, also affects the interpersonal distribution of holdings (Pogge 2004; cf. also Culp 2014, ch. 3). And also the so-called globalist theorists of global distributive justice argue that from the point of view of justice relations among all individuals globally are analogous to those among co-citizens within states. They argue that the grounds of comparative, egalitarian principles of distributive justice are global in scope. Beitz (1979, 131), for example, has argued that social institutions with pervasive impact are to be found not only domestically, but also globally, and that such institutions constitute the reasons for the validity of an egalitarian content of global justice. So the globalists have come to extrapolate to the world at large some egalitarian content of justice, like in Rawls's theory of justice as fairness, which the statist philosophers, like Rawls himself, view as being valid solely within the state context. (For Rawls's final formulation of the equal liberties, the fair equality of opportunity, and the difference principles, see Rawls, *Justice as Fairness* (Cambridge, MA: Harvard University Press, 2001), 42–43.)

Globalist conceptions of internationalist responsibility

Globalist theorists defend a global ideal of interpersonal distributive equality and argue on that basis for a distributive justice-based conception of international responsibility for development practice. They maintain that since development practice is effective in bringing the global distribution of holdings into closer conformity with their ideal, there is a global distributive justice-based international responsibility to participate in such practice. More specifically, most of these theorists (Beitz 1979, 172–173; Pogge 1989, ch. 6; 1994; Gosepath 2001; Moellendorf 2002, 61) who have defended such a conception have endorsed a Rawlsian understanding of global distributive justice, according to which interpersonal global inequalities in income and wealth would only be justifiable to the extent that they would maximally benefit the members of the least advantaged group. In order to further realize such an ideal of global distributive justice through development practice, Pogge (1989, 256n18, 264–265; 1994, 202), for one, proposes an international tax on the extraction of nonrenewable resources that should finance this practice.

The globalists' case for development practice differs quite substantially from that of the statists. Supporting the realization of a global interpersonal egalitarian ideal through development practice calls for much more expansive measures than those that are necessary for achieving a fundamental conception of distributive justice inside all states. Among other things, development practice would have to reform institutions of primary and secondary institutions of education around the world in order to realize globally the Rawlsian ideal of fair equality of opportunity. But of course development practice alone would not suffice for fully achieving the globalists' ideal of global distributive justice. One important reason for this seems to be that this would require establishing supranational institutions capable of effectively limiting states' sovereignties. Radical changes of this sort, however, are not foreseen in any way by the logic of development practice, which accepts the fundamental norms of the system of states.

Scholars like David Miller (2005) have criticized the globalist conception of global distributive justice on the ground that its ideal of global fair equality of opportunity is parochial. Plausibly, Miller argues that such an ideal has to rely on a globally valid notion of social success, which all those with equal talents and equal willingness to use these talents should have an equal chance of achieving. Yet, as Boxill (1987) has argued, it is unclear whether there is a globally shared or shareable notion of social success, which is why the use of any such notion could amount to parochialism. Some globalists have responded to this critique by arguing that they would be able to construe a cross-culturally valid notion of success. They could do so, they have claimed, either by relying on Nussbaum's ten central capabilities (Caney 2001), or by reconstructing such a notion on the basis of what is actually valued within global market relations (Moellendorf 2009, ch. 4).

Furthermore, so-called postdevelopment scholars that are critical of *economic* development have put into question the globalist theorists' normative concern regarding global interpersonal differentials in economic resources. They have thereby exposed a materialist bias in most of the globalists' distributive justice-based conceptions of international responsibility for development practice, as most of them identify global interpersonal inequalities in income and wealth as global distributive injustices (Beitz 1979, Pogge 1989, Moellendorf 2002, Tan 2004). Especially Vandana Shiva (1988), Majid Rahnema (2010), Gustavo Esteva (2010) and Arturo Escobar (2012) have criticized that the focus on economic resources is inadequate for determining who should count as least advantaged. Individuals and groups can lack other important goods – cultural recognition, for example – that might even be more decisive than income and wealth for identifying who the least advantaged are. Moreover, Escobar does not limit his critique solely to a problematic materialist bias, but argues that *in general* development practice tends to be insufficiently context sensitive and suffers from ethnocentrism. Along these lines he argues:

> Ethnocentrism influenced the form development took. Indigenous populations had to be 'modernized', where modernization meant the adoption of the 'right' values – namely, those held by the white minority or a mestizo majority and, in general, those embodied in the ideal of the cultivated European.
>
> *(Escobar 2012, 43)*

In the next sub-section I present yet another conception of international responsibility for development practice which deliberately attempts to avoid the kind of ethnocentrism or parochialism that Escobar find so problematic about development. This conception relies on Rawls' internationalist conception of global distributive justice and emphasizes the importance of tolerating what he calls "decent societies." These are societies whose internal legal and political orders do not satisfy liberal principles of justice but who nevertheless should enjoy moral standing within international society.

Internationalist conceptions of international responsibility

Internationalist conceptions of global distributive justice defend intranational principles of justice that apply inside all states and international principles of justice that apply between all states. Rawls's *The Law of Peoples* (1999) continues to represent the most prominent internationalist conception of global distributive justice. Its title, the "Law of Peoples," refers to the normative order that ought to regulate international political relations among internally well-ordered societies. For a society to count as well-ordered, it must either fulfill liberal-egalitarian principles of justice or at least be a "decent society." A decent society respects a certain list of human rights as well possesses a consultation hierarchy that ensures that all societal groups' members' interests are taken into account when societal decisions are made (cf. Rawls 1999, 65, 71–72).

In one part of his non-ideal theory of international justice Rawls discusses the question of how to address situations in which societies are burdened insofar as they possess internal structures that prevent them from becoming well-ordered. As Rawls (1999, 90) puts it, this part asks how to respond to "conditions of societies whose historical, social, and economic circumstances make their achieving a well-ordered regime, whether liberal or decent, difficult if not impossible." Rawls argues that the international community of well-ordered societies has a so-called duty of assistance to support burdened societies in a way that effectively helps them establishing morally decent or liberal structures. As Rawls (1999, 37) puts it, the "duty to assist other peoples living under unfavorable conditions that prevent their having a just or decent political and social regime."

Four features characterize the duty of assistance. The carriers of the duty as well as the corresponding right holders are societies. It is a genuine international duty, and thus distinct in its content from the responsibilities to engage in development practice that are grounded on weak statists' or globalists' conceptions of distributive justice. Secondly, the fulfillment of the duty of assistance requires merely the establishment of those conditions that societies need in order to establish a well-ordered societal structure. That does not imply, however, that all well-ordered societies would have to dispose over great economic wealth, simply because meeting the conditions of a liberal or decent society specified above does not presuppose this. So the promotion of economic growth should be merely a means for fulfilling these conditions. Furthermore,

Rawls (1999, 108) believes that a society's political culture is crucial for becoming well-ordered. Thus, development practice must concern itself with processes of cultural transformation for the sake of transforming a burdened society into a just or decent one. Finally, Rawls (1999, 111) warns of paternalistic forms of development practice that would undercut "the final aim of assistance: freedom and equality for the formerly burdened societies." Societies' equal political self-determination should be the aim of development practice and the practice itself must not undercut the realization of that aim.

Rawls does not, however, think of these seemingly practical suggestions of nonideal theory as blueprints for political action. Rawls denies that political philosophy ought to be action guiding in a narrow sense of the term that refers to prescribing specific types of policies and actions for certain political actors. Determining such policies and actions requires practical political wisdom and judgment that his political philosophy does not provide because it presupposes a "political assessment of the likely consequences of various policies" (93). Only the relevant political actors can plausibly carry out such an assessment on a case-by-case basis. There is no a priori algorithm for determining the right kind of public policies and action.

Pogge (2007, 30–31; 2004, 265), however, harshly criticized Rawls's conception of international responsibility for development practice. In particular, he problematized that Rawls adheres to a "Purely Domestic Poverty Thesis," according to which solely domestic explanations suffice for explaining a society's economic well-being. This thesis, Pogge (2002, 23, 50, and 197) argues, fails to recognize that international arrangements also contribute to the incidence of poverty that is prevalent within societies. In order to substantiate his point, he explains the important role that the WTO plays for the poorer states' high incidence of poverty as follows:

> [WTO law] permits the affluent countries to protect their markets against cheap imports (agricultural products, textiles and apparel, steel, and much else) through tariffs, anti-dumping duties, quotas, export credits, and huge subsidies to domestic producers. Such protectionist measures reduce the export opportunities from poor countries by constraining their exports into the affluent countries and also, in the case of subsidies, by allowing less efficient rich-country producers to undersell more efficient poor-country producers in world markets. In the absence of these constraints, poor countries would realize welfare gains in excess of $100 billion annually (comparable to current official development assistance or ODA) and reductions of several hundred million in the number of poor.
>
> *(Pogge 2010, 20)*

In this manner Pogge shows how the rules of an international institution affect the incidence of poverty within poorer states. By contrast, Rawls's duty of assistance suggests that the poorer states' high incidence of poverty would be purely domestic. For that reason Pogge criticizes Rawls' conception of international responsibility for development practice as fundamentally flawed. In light of Pogge's critique some theorists (Forst 2012, ch. 12; Culp 2014, ch. 7; Culp 2016) have provided an alternative internationalist conception of international responsibility for development practice that do not rely on the purely domestic poverty thesis. They (Crocker 2008, ch. 8; Culp 2016) argue that irrespective of the reasons that explain the existence of poverty in poorer states, development practice should enable all states to arrange their internal political structures in a democratic manner. In addition, such practice should also help all states to participate as actors that count politically equal in international affairs. This is because, they argue, only through such participation in international affairs can the representatives of states that are internally democratically structured contribute to properly determining politically further principles of global distributive justice.

Conclusion

This chapter presented utilitarian, humanitarian, and global distributive justice-based conceptions of international responsibility for development practice. The chapter has shown that these conceptions differ regarding the extent to which they impose burdens on those who bear such responsibility, the particular goals that they expect development practice to achieve and their underlying views as to whether the existing distribution of holdings among individuals is morally acceptable. And thereby depending on which of which of these conceptions of international responsibility one ultimately ends up endorsing, the practical stance and consequences as to how to engage in development practice will differ quite remarkably. However, as I have already pointed out in the introduction of this chapter, development scholars and political commentators question that such ethical concerns matter in the actual practice of development activities across borders. But when it comes to question as to whether certain actors truly act out of a sense of responsibility, it seems as though not even these actors themselves are able to give the correct answer. Among other things, this is because human beings like to view and portray themselves in a moral manner because of the particular kind of recognition and praise from others that such moral motivation tends to evoke. Thus human beings may be prone to betray themselves about their actual motivation for action, which might indeed be more self-interested rather than originating in a sense of responsibility. Indeed, this is a real possibility. However, even if human beings do not know for sure what their actual motivation for action is, their ignorance does not demonstrate that a sense of responsibility is never an effective reason for action. For that reason development ethicists' work on how to conceptualize an international responsibility for development is of practical relevance.

References

Alesina, A. and Dollar, D. (2000) Who Gives Foreign Aid to Whom and Why? *Journal of Economic Growth* 5(1): 33–63.

Barry, B. 2008 [1982]. Humanity and Justice in Global Perspective. In Pogge, T., and Moellendorf D. eds., 179–209. Orig. 1982. In Pennock, J.R., and Chapman, J.W. eds., *Nomos 24: Ethics, Economics and the Law*. New York: New York University Press, 219–252.

Berthélemy, J.-C. and Tichit, A. (2004) Bilateral Donors' Aid Allocation Decisions – A Three-Dimensional Panel Analysis. *International Review of Economics and Finance* 13(3): 253–274.

Birdsall, N., Claessens, S. and Diwan, I. (2003) Policy Selectivity Forgone: Debt and Donor Behavior in Africa. *The World Bank Economic Review* 17(3): 409–435.

Beitz, C. (1979) *Political Theory and International Relations*. Princeton University Press, Princeton.

Blake, M. (2001) Distributive Justice, State Coercion, and Autonomy. *Philosophy and Public Affairs* 30: 257–296.

Boxill, B. (1987) Global Equality of Opportunity and National Integrity. *Social Philosophy and Policy* 5: 143–168.

Brock, G. (2009) *Global Justice*. Oxford University Press, New York.

Caney, S. (2001) Cosmopolitan Justice and Equalizing Opportunities. *Metaphilosophy* 32: 113–134.

Caney, S. (2005) *Justice Beyond Borders*. Oxford University Press, Oxford.

Cardoso, F. and Faletto, E. (1979) *Dependency and Development in Latin America*. University of California Pres, Berkeley.

Crocker, D. (2008) *Ethics of Global Development: Agency, Capability and Deliberative Democracy*. Cambridge University Press, Cambridge.

Culp, J. (2014) *Global Justice and Development*. Palgrave Macmillan, Basingstoke and New York.

Culp, J. (2016) Toward Another Development Practice. In Barcelos, P. and de Angelis, G. eds., *International Development and Humanitarian Aid*. Edinburgh University Press, Edinburgh, 79–107.

Escobar, A. (2012) *Encountering Development*. Princeton University Press, Princeton.
Esteva, G. (2010) [1992] Development. In Sachs, W. ed., *The Development Dictionary*, 2nd ed. Zed Books, London, 1–23.
Forst, R. (2012) *The Right to Justification*. Columbia University Press, New York.
Freire, P. (1970) *Pedagogy of the Oppressed*. Continuum, New York.
Gosepath, S. (2001) The Global Scope of Justice. *Metaphilosophy* 32: 135–159.
Kant, Immanuel. 1996 [1797]. *The Metaphysics of Morals*. In Mary Gregor (ed.). Cambridge: Cambridge University Press.
List, C. and Pettit, P. (2011). *Group Agency*. Oxford University Press, Oxford.
McGillivray, M. (1989) The Allocation of Aid Among Developing Countries: A Multi-Donor Analysis Using a Per Capita Aid Index. *World Development* 17(4): 561–568.
McGillivray, M. (2004) Descriptive and Prescriptive Analyses of Aid Allocation: Approaches, Issues, and Consequences. *International Review of Economics and Finance* 13(3): 275–292.
McKinlay, R. and Little, R. (1977) A Foreign Policy Model of US Bilateral Aid Allocation. *World Politics* 30(1): 58–86.
McNamara, R. (1973) *Address to the Board of Governors*. World Bank, Washington, DC.
Miller, D. (2005) Against Global Egalitarianism. *Journal of Ethics* 9: 55–79.
Moellendorf, D. (2002) *Cosmopolitan Justice*. Westview Press, Boulder.
Moellendorf, D. (2009) *Global Inequality Matters*. Palgrave Macmillan, Basingstoke and New York.
Nagel, T. (2005) The Problem of Global Justice. *Philosophy and Public Affairs* 33(2): 113–147.
Niggli, P. (2008) Der Streit um die Entwicklungshilfe: Mehr tun – aber das Richtige! Zürich: Rotpunktverlag.
Nussbaum, M. (2003) Capabilities as Fundamental Entitlements: Sen and Social Justice. *Feminist Economics* 9: 33–59.
Nussbaum, M. (2006) *Frontiers of Justice*. Harvard University Press, Cambridge, MA.
Nussbaum, M. (2011) *Creating Capabilities*. Harvard University Press, Cambridge, MA.
Organisation for Economic Co-operation and Development (2011) *Official Development Assistance – Definition and Coverage*. www.oecd.org/document/4/0,3746,en_2649_34447_46181892_1_1_1_1,00.html.
Pettit, P. (2010) A Republican Law of Peoples. *European Journal of Political Theory* 9: 70–94.
Pogge, T. (1989) *Realizing Rawls*. Cornell University Press, Ithaca.
Pogge, T. (1994) An Egalitarian Law of Peoples. *Philosophy and Public Affairs* 23: 195–224.
Pogge, T. (2002) *World Poverty and Human Rights*. Polity Press, Cambridge.
Pogge, T. (2004) 'Assisting' the Global Poor. In Chatterjee, D. ed., *The Ethics of Assistance*. Cambridge University Press, Cambridge, 260–288.
Pogge, T. (2007) Severe Poverty as Human Rights Violation. In Pogge, T. ed., *Freedom from Poverty as a Human Right*. Oxford University Press, Oxford, 11–53.
Pogge, T. (2010) *Politics as Usual*. Polity Press, Cambridge.
Rahnema, M. (2010) Poverty. In Sachs, W. ed., *The Development Dictionary*, 2nd ed. Zed Books, London, 158–176.
Rawls, J. (1971) *A Theory of Justice*. Harvard University Press, Cambridge, MA.
Rawls, J. (1999) *The Law of Peoples*. Harvard University Press, Cambridge, MA.
Rawls, J. (2001) *Justice as Fairness*. Harvard University Press, Cambridge, MA.
Rawls, J. (1993) *Political Liberalism*. Columbia University Press, New York.
Scanlon, T. (1998) *What We Owe to Each Other*. Harvard University Press, Cambridge, MA.
Shiva, V. (1988) *Staying Alive: Women, Ecology, and Development*. Zed Books, London.
Shue, H. (1988) Mediating Duties. *Ethics* 98: 687–704.
Singer, P. (1972) Famine, Affluence, and Morality. *Philosophy & Public Affairs* 1: 229–243.
Smart, J.J.C. and Williams, B. (1973) *Utilitarianism and Beyond*. Cambridge University Press, Cambridge.
Strawson, P. (1982) Freedom and Resentment. In Watson, G. ed., *Free Will*. Oxford University Press, Oxford, 59–80.
Tan, K.C. (2004) *Justice Without Borders*. Cambridge University Press, Cambridge.
Truman, H. (1949) Inaugural Address. www.bartleby.com/124/pres53. Accessed 10 December 2011.
Unger, P. (1996) *Living High and Letting Die*. Oxford University Press, Oxford.

White, H. and MacGillivray, M. (1992) Descriptive Measures of the Allocation of Development Aid. *Working Paper Series* 125, 1–22. www.repub.eur.nl/res/pub/18825/wp125.pdf. Accessed December 2011.
White, H. and McGillivray M. (1995) How Well Is Aid Allocated? Descriptive Measures of Aid Allocation: A Survey of Methodology and Results. *Development and Change* 26(1): 163–183.
World, Bank. (1990) *World Development Report 1990.* Washington, DC, Oxford University Press.
World Bank. (1998) *Assessing Aid – What Works, What Doesn't, and Why.* Washington, DC, Oxford University Press.

30

Development practitioners

Absent in the deliberative discourse on development ethics

Chloe Schwenke

We gathered in the Reserve Officers Association's conference room, directly across Constitution Avenue from the U.S. Senate offices. It was March 16, 2017, and earlier that morning President Trump had released his new "Make America Great" budget. It was officially described as a skinny budget, lacking the detail and policy weight of a comprehensive federal budget document, but it had the attention of everyone in that room. The audience consisted almost entirely of development practitioners who are women, which aligned with the topic on the day's agenda: the plight of women and girls around the world. Still, the idealist might be excused if she or he presumed that the topic of women and girls – half the population of the world – might reasonably attract the attention and concern of men who are active in the international relief and development community, but no. As happens so often, we were nearly all women talking to women about women, ironically in a room whose décor is resplendent of the patriarchy, its walls festooned with somber portraits of distinguished (male) military icons staring down sternly at the impudent female speakers.

The weight of that just-published skinny budget set the mood, despite the stalwart efforts of many speakers to be upbeat and positive. To me, it felt that all of us were hunkered down in an attitude of resignation; self-made victims of a disempowering capitulation to "the way things are". Many speakers spoke in pragmatic and occasionally wistful tones about the usual obstacles and successes, and how we might best find a way ahead for facilitating types of relief and development that would truly address and engage women and girls as full human beings. But there was no fire in their bellies, only numbness and the sense of a pervasive, unshakable weight that had settled upon all of us.

Former Secretary of State Madeline Albright – a truly remarkable woman whose presence alone in any room is deeply inspirational – spoke on a panel with former Obama-era USAID Administrator Rajiv Shah (Shah 2013), who had recently been elevated to become president of the Rockefeller Foundation. Both disparaged Trump's proposed slashing of foreign aid, yet both were diplomatic and measured in their abhorrence of what this budget signified. Secretary Albright urged everyone to reframe the conversation so that Trump supporters would see how foreign aid is "in America's interest" and to return to the contextualizing of foreign aid as an integral component of national security, as has been done under previous Republican administrations. Dr. Shah pointed out the obvious logical flaws in a foreign aid approach that cut U.S.

 DOI: 10.4324/9781315626796-38

contributions to multilateral institutions – contributions that leveraged five or six times as much money from other foreign donors – and he decried the impact of the proposed deep cuts to humanitarian relief and peacekeeping.

In that room any language of "resistance" was muted or absent altogether. Most of us simply felt the uncomfortable weight of a new America that is suddenly inward-turning, focused on strength and hard power, and dismissive of anything "soft": compassion, care, and sensitivity to the suffering of the poor and vulnerable beyond our borders (and even within our borders). It was an uncomfortable recognition for a room filled with women who care. Where were the strong normative voices insisting that human dignity is universal; that human rights must be respected, protected, and promoted; that poverty and conflict are not inevitable; and that women and girls – and all human beings – deserve to have lives characterized by freedom, choice, influence, equity, health, and respect? Where was the clarion call to the barricades, to stand in solidarity with the powerless and the vulnerable around the world? Where were the demands that human rights matter, and that America must stand up to own its leadership role as a global champion of human rights? Where were the ennobling howls of protest, disgust, and shock at what that latest iteration of the Trump agenda meant for all of us engaged in international relief and development?

Perhaps more than any single gathering in my three-decade career as an international development practitioner, that day spoke most eloquently – and disturbingly – about the lack of normative deliberative space within the practitioner community. One common trait among nearly all who pursue international humanitarian relief and development as a career is a deep sense of shared mission, but it is seldom spoken about. That day was no exception.

No surprise then that within the very complex and multifaceted industry that implements international relief and development, there appears to be currently no designated institutional positions for development ethicists, and no structured institutional space for such deliberations to occur. Historically, two major multilateral development banks did once take specific values-based initiatives as described later in this chapter, but currently the reigning discourse of international development is the political-economy framework. There is scant room within that discourse for deliberations beyond the priorities of effectiveness and efficiency, power and money, and the iron-clad presumption that all human behavior and decision-making is essentially a function of the maximization of self-interest. A comment by Nobel laureate Professor Amartya Sen is illuminating in this context:

> It strikes me as absolutely extraordinary that people can dismiss any attitude as irrational other than that of the maximization of self-interest. Such a position necessarily implies that we reject the role of ethics in our real decision-making . . . Taking universal selfishness as read may well be delusional, but to turn it into a standard for rationality is utterly absurd.
>
> *(Sen 1993, 18)*

To a considerable extent, any deliberative discourse within the international relief and development industry is constrained by the reality that it is an industry – a source of livelihoods for a relatively small number of people who are largely self-defined as problem-solvers, and as global experts on "best practices". It is an industry committed to achieve effective and timely relief in the face of calamities (natural or man-made), and to set communities and nations on the path to sustainable development in response to egregious and widespread poverty affecting literally billions of human beings. Yet as an industry, it is incommensurate to the task.

And what a task it is. First, the "demand" for assistance is enormous, and in some geographic locations (e.g. currently Yemen, Somalia, South Sudan, and Nigeria) exceptionally intense (Diehl

2017). Approximately 80% of humanity survives on less than the equivalent of US$10 per day, and many get by on far less. Inequality between the poor and the much better-off is widening rapidly. As noted in a recent study by Oxfam, back in 2010 it would have taken the richest 388 individuals on the planet to match the combined wealth of the bottom half of humanity. Now only the 62 wealthiest are needed. Disparity in income is hardly the only indicator of a world beset by enormous moral challenges; UNICEF's sobering statistic of 29,000 children dying each and every day due to poverty and preventable causes ought to give more of us reason at least to pause and take note, if not to act (UNICEF n.d.). Economist Steven Radelet offers a far more positive view of the results of international development, as follows:

> Since the early 1990s, 1 billion people have been lifted out of extreme poverty. The average income for hundreds of millions of people in dozens of poor countries has more than doubled, 6 million fewer children die every year from disease, war and violence have declined significantly, average life expectancy has increased by six years, tens of millions more girls are in school, the share of people living in chronic hunger has been cut nearly in half, millions more people have access to clean water, and democracy – often fragile and imperfect – has become the norm rather than the exception in developing countries around the world.
>
> *(Radelet 2015, 4)*

Despite the large numbers and compelling statistics that authoritatively describe the overwhelming demand for intervention, decision-makers, policy experts, and all people who enjoy the luxury of disposable income are not yet motivated to reframe priorities. Formal official development assistance (ODA) rates are miniscule in comparison to the urgent and scale of global need. The largest donor in gross terms is the United States – yet relative to its wealth as a nation it is also among the stingiest. In recent years, the U.S. has allocated well under 1% of the federal budget to this purpose, even if the average American believes the amount to be far higher (Simmons 2017).

Given its highly competitive nature, the relative scarcity of resources made available, the rigor and complexity of tightly time-constrained procurement processes to engage their services, and the dominance of a relatively few larger firms and non-profit organizations, the implementer side of the development industry isn't ideally shaped to engender any deliberative, collegial discourse on values. Three reasons stand out as being particularly significant. First, the industry has been established to be almost entirely reactive. The donors (e.g. USAID, the World Bank, or philanthropic foundations) typically decide what program they wish to pursue, and the donors formulate the overall terms of reference for the project. This leaves the development industry to respond, with each competitor developing proposals describing how they – better than all their rivals – will achieve the satisfaction of this scope of work (methodologies, theory of change, monitoring and evaluation techniques to track results achieved, work plans, descriptions of capabilities of assigned staff and the institution or firm as a whole, and the proposed budget). Each competing firm or organization is exhorted by the donors to generate a response that is innovative, cost-effective, based on "best practices", and achievable within or better yet, under the budget. It is not within any competitor's interest to divulge to others in the industry what their own thinking is on solving the development challenges posed by the terms of reference, and there is scant opportunity for these implementers within the industry to offer their insights on how to improve (or radically re-envision) the goals of the proposed project and the terms of reference upon which the procurement is based. In many cases, there is very little evidence offered that demonstrates that the terms of reference have even had the benefit of much (or any) participation by the intended beneficiaries themselves – the governments and citizens of the less developed countries that are being targeted.

Second, the development industry is divided among implementers (versus those who work directly as staff for the donors) among quite differing areas of functional focus: humanitarian relief workers, development researchers and analysts, human rights activists/advocates, and development program implementers. And third, the industry is legally structured between firms that operate as for-profit enterprises providing quality services in fulfillment of the donor's priorities, and non-governmental organizations (NGOs) and community-based organizations (CBOs), the latter two categories operating as non-profit entities in pursuit of their own declared mission (in recent years the dividing lines between these two groupings has become more permeable). This level of fracturing among what is a relatively small industry, and the high-pressure, highly cost-sensitive (i.e. "time is money") proposals-based competitive culture that characterizes this industry, offers few opportunities for practitioners to gather and discuss secular moral issues associated with development. (Some exceptions are worth noting, such as the Society for International Development, especially the Washington DC chapter, and InterAction, although even these organizations infrequently discuss normative and ethical concerns.) While there appears as yet to be very little direct research to support this, it may be reasonable to assume that the recent consolidation of the development industry into fewer, larger, more cost-efficient firms and organizations has further constrained collegiality and discourse among the practitioner community.

Then there is the influence of the lawyers, and what that has meant for the common perception of ethics in development. A quick Google search of "USAID, ethics" will take you directly to the Automated Directive System's Chapter 109, "Ethics and Standards of Conduct (USAID 2015). There the reader will immediately be confronted with "Title I of the Ethics in Government Act" and descriptions of the Designated Agency Ethics Official (DAEO), the Alternate Designated Agency Ethics Official (ADAEO), and the Office of General Counsel, Ethics and Administration (GC/EA). While the regulation of human behavior through such constraining measures is arguably made necessary by certain self-interested and irresponsible human tendencies, it's all very dry stuff. Even the morally significant domain of human rights, captured so eloquently in the Universal Declaration of Human Rights, and the UNDP's Human Development Report 2000, is reconfigured into a body of legislation, treaties, and protocols (covering largely just civil and political rights, not economic, social, or cultural rights). As such, the responsibility for managing the international human rights obligations of the United States becomes a matter of international law, not development per se, and shifts from the 20 development agencies involved in foreign assistance to the diplomats at the U.S. Department of State. Diplomats serve an important and vital role in defending the self-interests of their respective countries, but this is not the stuff – or discourse – of development.

Semantics and a lack of clarity are also often an issue when the development practitioner conversation attempts to turns to morality and moral values. The presumption that this focus should be rooted in an assertion of universal, secular moral values isn't a given, and often isn't made explicit in many instances. Instead, moral values and systems of ethics become entangled with those who advocate for priority to be given to relativistic local or religious-based values. Where values that are argued to be universal are subjected to rigorous standards of debates on the basis of rationality and logic, religious and cultural values are held to be unassailable solely on the basis of belief or tradition, i.e. not to be questioned. The fact that many of the leading development practitioner organizations are themselves faith-based and motivated by religious convictions further complicates any effort to stay within a permissible deliberative space defined and defended by rationality.

The absence of the vast majority of those situated within the development practitioner community from the more abstract deliberative discourse of development ethics is an enormous loss. Such practitioners have extensive, on-the-ground experience in the realization of development goals, as well as multiple instances of pragmatic and occasionally inspired problem-solving that attends to the development endeavor. They often have a uniquely well-honed understanding of the differences between development insiders and outsiders, as so well captured in David Crocker's framing, made all the more significant as indigenous development practitioners from less developed countries increasingly play central roles within the development industry (Crocker 1991, 149–173). These practitioners – expatriate and indigenous – straddle the insider-outsider divide from both sides with a level of appreciation and wisdom quite different from what is found in academia and among policy-makers. As the development industry is currently structured, however, their normative insights are unsought, and have no obvious outlet in which to be shared and deliberated.

What is there to be discussed? What insights might the development practitioner community offer? The issues are legion, and the diversity of sectors addressed by the international development community requires not just comprehensive skills and knowledge per sector, but also an appreciation for the most meaningful and productive ways to embrace intersectionality and complexity. Philosopher Martha Nussbaum's articulation of development challenges as "unfreedoms" – in concert with the capability approach's centrality of freedom to the process of development – offers an agenda that development practitioners would have much to contribute to, starting with poverty itself (Sen 1999, xii). Poverty manifests itself in development problems that have long been at the heart of development programming: insufficiency of basic resources such as food, housing, and hygiene; inadequacy of access to public services including health care, education, environmental management, law and order health; dysfunctional (and often corrupt) systems of governance; scant economic opportunities; and the denial of human dignity and human rights. Development practitioners have in many cases worked over the span of decades on fundamentally normative endeavors to evaluate and enhance freedom, agency, and opportunities to overcome these unfreedoms, yet the openness of academics, policy-makers, and development donors to invite practitioner insights and recommendations is thin at best.

Two notable exceptions warrant some attention. From 1981 to 2006, a small but dedicated group of people met every Friday morning (excluding only Christmas week) at 8 a.m. for just one hour over a simple but delicious breakfast in a small seminar room at the World Bank headquarters in Washington, D.C. This group was founded by David Beckmann, Ramgopal Agarwala, Sven Burmester, and Ismail Serageldin. Known officially as the Values in Development Group but far more commonly as the Friday Morning Group, most in attendance were active or retired staff of the Bank, although visitors were warmly welcomed and many – such as this author – became regulars. There were few rules, but the intention was to create that elusive, collegial, safe and deliberative space for the explicit consideration of values – secular and religious (Marshall and Van Saanen 2007, 6–7). Often there was a guest speaker, in which capacity I served on several occasions, but even when no guest speaker was featured this was a group that knew the fine art of deliberation and reciprocity. Bank staff, consultants, and development practitioners from many backgrounds, generations, and nationalities joined with academics and others frequently to speak from the vantage point of people who had "been there", who had extensive direct experience around the world in international relief and development, research and advocacy. Their first-hand stories and anecdotes created a vibrant narrative; ranging from deeply humorous to poignantly tragic. There was even space for contemplation of spiritual traditions: Hindu, Buddhist, Christian, Humanist, and Muslim, among others. Those of us who attended regularly saw a gradual but irreversible decline in interest from potential new "recruits", which some of us attributed to a younger generation's abhorrence of getting to work so early on a Friday! I have never since encountered such an inspired and dependable source of conversation on development values, and the laying-down of this very special and long-lasting deliberative experiment was a sad day.

Finally, credit is due to the Inter-American Development Bank, at that time under the leadership of its president, the Uruguayan-Spanish economist Enrique Valentín Iglesias García. With direct institutional commitment from Dr. Iglesias, and with the benefit of generous funding from the government of Norway, on March 1, 2002, the IDB established the Inter-American Initiative on Social Capital, Ethics and Development (ISED). ISED was conceived as an ongoing institutional mechanism intended to raise the profile and improve the awareness of development ethics and social capital. Through the efforts of its small staff (including, for a one-year consulting assignment, this author) and its institutional presence within the IDB, and with strong support from Amartya Sen, David Crocker, and others, the ISED initiative sought specific opportunities to demonstrate ethics and social capital in practice, with rigorous applications that arguably would add value and improve effectiveness of development interventions. These included, but were not limited to improving leadership and strengthening ethical behavior and norms. ISED also worked with universities throughout Latin America and the Caribbean to strengthen awareness of development ethics in tangible ways, and took strategic action to foster discourse on values in education and in the media. Unfortunately, once Dr. Iglesias left the Bank, the ISED experiment was unable to attract the institutional support that it needed to continue, and it was shuttered early in 2008. To date, no other multilateral or bilateral development institution has established anything of a similar nature or purpose.

In the normative context, the development practitioner community remains a largely untapped resource for its wisdom, insights, experience, and commitment to humanitarian relief, international development, development research, and human rights advocacy making a difference in advancing freedoms and opportunities, expanding peoples' agency, and promoting workable solutions to nearly intractable development challenges. Until we amend our institutional structures to embrace a meaningful space and appropriately trained staff to foster the deliberation of values, engage in development discourse that is not allergic to the vocabulary of applied ethics, and design development programming that is truly responsive to human dignity, a critically important dimension of development remains largely theoretical and abstract, to the detriment of achieving lives of well-being and freedom for all.

References

BBC News (2016) Oxfam Says Wealth of Richest 1% Equal to Other 99%. www.bbc.com/news/business-35339475. Accessed 18 January 2016

Crocker, D. (1991) Insiders and Outsiders in International Development. *Ethics & International Affairs* 5(1).

Diehl, J. (2017) No One Is Paying Attention to the Worst Humanitarian Crisis Since World War II. *Washington Post.* www.washingtonpost.com/opinions/global-opinions/no-one-is-paying-attention-to-the-worst-humanitarian-crisis-since-world-war-ii/2017/06/25/70d055f8–5767–11e7-ba90-f5875b7d1876_story.html?utm_term=.aebcfcd0dee7. Accessed 22 October 2017.

Marshall, K. and Van Saanen, M.B. (2007) *Development and Faith: Where Mind, Heart, and Soul Work Together.* World Bank Publications, Washington, DC.

Radelet, S. (2015) *The Great Surge: The Ascent of the Developing World.* Simon & Schuster, New York.

Sen, A. (1993) *Éthique et économie.* Presse Universitaire de France, Paris.

Sen, A. (1999) *Development as Freedom.* Anchor Books, New York.

Shah, A. (2013) Poverty Facts and Stats. *Global Issues* 7 January 2013. www.globalissues.org/article/26/poverty-facts-and-stats.

Simmons, A. (2017) U.S. Foreign Aid: A Waste of Money or a Boost to World Stability? Here Are the Facts. *Los Angeles Times,* 10 May 2017. http://beta.latimes.com/world/la-fg-global-aid-true-false-20170501-htmlstory.html.

United Nations. UNICEF (nd) Millennium Development Goals 4. Reduce Child Mortality. www.unicef.org/mdg/childmortality.html.

United States Agency for International Development (USAID) (2015) ADS Chapter 109, "Ethics and Standards of Conduct", Partial Revision Date: 03/16/2015, Washington, DC.

31

Corruption

Concepts, costs, causes and challenges

Sirkku K. Hellsten

Corruption is a global problem and no country nor any politico-economic system in history has been free from it, despite all efforts to combat corruption. Today corruption is a serious challenge to development, particularly in poor countries and in transitional societies struggling for democratic governance. In the era of globalization, corrupt political and business networks seem to be increasing in size and numbers across the globe. From the point of view of *development ethics*, corruption is a complex and multidimensional issue with various ethical, social, economic and political aspects. In this chapter, I will give an overview of some of the main debates that appear in studies and discussions on corruption, development and ethics. First, I will introduce the problems in defining corruption. Second, I will take a brief look at the costs of corruption. Third, I will reflect on the relationship between corruption and culture, as well as between corruption and politico-economic systems. Fourth, I will discuss some of the challenges related to anti-corruption efforts.

What is corruption – and why it is so hard to define?

The most common use of the word 'corruption' refers to 'the abuse of entrusted power for private gain'. More precisely it can be said to be: the misuse of public authority for private gains, where an official (the agent) entrusted with carrying out a task by the public (the principal) engages in some sort of malfeasance for private enrichment which is difficult to monitor for the principal (see Transparency International 2016).

Corruption, however, is difficult to define precisely because the concept has both descriptive and prescriptive elements in it when it attempts to depict a wide range of (trans)actions considered undesirable, illegal and/or unethical, particularly in the professional practice of the public sector. Thus, the word 'corruption' brings together issues of values with social, ethical and economic practices.

As Bardhan (1997) notes, we cannot use the terms 'corrupt', 'immoral' and 'illicit' interchangeably when trying to find what is acceptable behaviour in public service, and in general in official relationships and transactions. Not all illegal transactions are corrupt, nor are all instances of corruption or bribery illegal. In other words, many illegal transactions, such as direct embezzlement or theft, do not necessarily fall under corruption in the strictest sense of the definition.

DOI: 10.4324/9781315626796-39

Similarly, while rules and regulations are gradually becoming more restrictive, not all gift-giving by lobbyists to political decision-makers, political campaign contributions, (some but not all) tipping practices, shady global business transactions or tax avoidance are illegal, even if many of us may think that there are unethical and corrupt elements in these actions.

According to a dictionary definition of the word, its ethical aspects are underlined. *Oxford Dictionaries* (2016) defines corruption as: a) dishonest or fraudulent conduct by those in power, typically involving bribery; b) the action or effect of making someone or something morally deprived; c) the process by which a word or expression is changed from its original state to one regarded as erroneous or debased. Overall, the term 'corruption' refers to the process of decay, moral or otherwise.

Under the definition of corruption, we identify various types of activities and transactions by different agents. *Transparency International* (2016), for example, distinguishes three main types of corruption depending on the actors and actions involved: a) grand corruption, consisting of acts committed at a high level of government that distort policies or the central functioning of the state, enabling leaders and other actors to benefit at the expense of the public good; b) petty corruption, referring to everyday abuse of entrusted power by low- and mid-level public officials in their interactions with ordinary citizens, who often are trying to access basic goods or services in places such as hospitals, schools, police departments and other agencies; and c) political corruption, such as manipulation of policies, institutions and rules of procedure in the allocation of resources and financing by political decision-makers, who abuse their position to sustain their power, status and wealth.

Still, it is not always obvious what is clearly 'corruption' and which illegal and unethical acts may fall under a different classification, despite their family resemblance. The most common acts of corruption are bribery and extortion, though nepotism and cronyism are also often included in corrupt practices. Whether clientelism, rent-seeking, taking kick-backs in public procurement, money laundering, land-grabbing, election fraud and unfair or coercive campaigning, vote buying, illicit money transfers and even tax evasion should be considered as corruption can be debated (Johnston 2005, 1–5, Nye 1989).

From these considerations we can see that the strictest definition of corruption includes only those working in public service. However, this can be misleading, as corruption is prevalent also in business, in sports, in arts, etc. Individuals in their different roles, whether in public or private sector, make corrupt deals together. Thus, we cannot single out public servants as the sole agents of corruption. This would leave out other actors whose role is central in the persistence of corruption (Burbidge 2015, 4–5; Heywood 1997, 417–423; Philp 1997, 436–462).

Corruption can also be classified according to the various interests and arrangements in corrupt transactions. Alatas (1990) makes a distinction between *transactive* and *extensive* corruption. Transactive corruption refers to a mutual arrangement between a donor and a recipient actively pursued by, and to the mutual advantage of, both parties. Extensive corruption is an attempt to avoid some form of harm being inflicted on the payer or those close to him. We can also identify *active* and *passive* bribery. Active bribery refers to the offence committed by a person who promises or offers a bribe; in contrast to passive bribery, which is the offence committed by the official who receives the bribe. According to this division active bribery occurs on the supply side and passive bribery on the demand side. However, the bribe receiver/taker also can be active in asking for payment. Another division could be made between taking a bribe to do what you are supposed to do anyway, and taking a bribe for what you are not supposed to do. Across countries, different words may be used to describe these elements depending whose point of view is in question. We can make a distinction in who initiates the bribe: the bribe is *coercive* when the 'client' has to pay for a service that should be provided without extra cost. On the other hand, if the client is the initiator, the public servant who takes the bribe may see this action as merely *submissive* (Hellsten 2003, 55–81, 2006, 1–25; Heywood 1997, 426).

The following two examples contain elements of all these different formulations. The same corrupt transaction can be looked at from various perspectives. Imagine first that a student of a driving school fails his test, but offers a bribe to the instructor if she agrees to award him a pass on the test and he gets a licence despite his incompetence. The instructor takes the bribe and gives the student his driver's licence on a false basis. Consider then a different case in which a driving instructor insists on an extra payment to process the student's licence, even though he has passed his test competently and deserves the licence. The student will pay to avoid further delay and to be able to start driving as soon as possible. Both cases have overlapping elements of active and passive bribery, transactive and extensive corruption, and submissive and coercive corruption; both cases have two parties engaged in the same transaction, but their motivations and the overall effects – on society – of each situation are different. In the first case, using a bribe someone gets a licence without being able to drive well enough endangering traffic safety. In the second case, not paying the bribe would mean someone being denied the licence he deserves and is fully competent to get, but being seriously inconvenienced if he does not agree to pay the bribe; it is extortion, but he pays the bribe to avoid further inconvenience (Bardhan 1997, 1, 323; Hellsten 2003, 55–81).

In multidisciplinary research practices on corruption we can detect further complexity. First, depending on the discipline, the focus of research varies. While this can bring together various complementary aspects of corruption, it sometimes also creates problems in terms of comparability. Second, due to a lack of accurate, reliable, and comprehensive information, some of the theories presented are difficult to prove or disprove as empirically valid. Third, while more empirical research is gradually emerging, it often employs statistics and subjective indices and on corruption produced for business-related purposes, which leave out other important ethical and social aspects of corruption (Rose-Ackerman 1978 and 1999; Ades and Di Tella 1997, 496; Johnston 2005, 1–15).

Corruption is studied, for example, in relation to economics of crime, agency-based theory, political theory, development economics and development ethics. In their research, philosophers and ethicists often focus on the normative elements of corruption, emphasizing values and individual morality, as well as social, professional and leadership ethics. Moreover, political philosophers study corruption in relation to global justice. Political scientists, for their part, focus more on the ideals of political institutions and political systems, and the failures of these. Legal research emphasizes the need for, and role and efficiency of laws and regulations, as well as of the justice system. Behavioural scientists examine individual motivations as well as group dynamics. Economists consider economic effectiveness and rational choice, often setting their focus more on the economic causes and effects of corruption (Banerjee and Sengupta 2008, 474–475; Della Porta and Vannucci 1997; Heywood 1997, 422–424; Johnston 2005). This creates new challenges for researchers and policymakers, as it suggests that we need to take an approach that focuses not only on social and public service ethics, but simultaneously also on business ethics, and even wider on professional ethics of all sectors.

Overall, mapping out the different aspects and uses of the definition of corruption is important, as it helps us to better understand the complexity of the different dimensions of the phenomenon. Only then can we consider what the best measures to take to combat corruption would be. If we focus only on public-sector reforms and leave private-sector actors out, we cannot deal effectively with all the problems. If we only focus on reforms of norms, laws and institutional structures, and leave out civic education as well as professional training, it is likely that the root causes of corruption are causes will not be tackled accurately, etc.

Corruption and development

Corruption, ethics and politics

In general, we think that corrupt individuals fail to follow certain desirable (universal) moral standards. It is also useful to make a difference between moral and legal standards of corruption. In some instances of corruption and bribery, motivations appear to matter. For example, we might apply a degree of leniency, if you pay a bribe to a police officer to stop him from torturing an innocent suspect, or if you divert resources from the 'public purse' to save your neighbourhood or village from serious epidemic of illness. We would consider your actions to be compassionate, since you did not do them out of pure self-interest. Instead, your motivation was to help others. Of course, the police officer not willing to help out without taking a bribe is still guilty of illegal, unethical and unprofessional action.

In relation to motivations of taking and giving a bribe, some have argued that there can be actions that can be described as 'benign corruption', particularly in Africa and elsewhere in developing countries (Heilman et al. 2000). An often-cited example is that of US president Abraham Lincoln who had to manipulate the political decision-making process by 'buying votes' in order to pass the 13th Amendment that abolished slavery in the US (Winston 1994, 42).

A related issue in political ethics is *the problem of dirty hands*. Political realists claim that sometimes leaders (and politicians in general) are forced to use unethical means to reach higher and more important ethical (utilitarian) goals of public interest; a more idealistic stand would claim that there can and should be universal moral standards that everyone is to follow no matter what position they held. After all, there are international public service codes of ethics as well as other professional ethics standards (such as medical ethics, for example) that call for unified commitment to globally shared ethical standards (Winston 1994, 42–45).

Banerjee and Sengupta (2008), Heywood (1997) and Philp (1997) observe that the very notion of *political corruption* would presuppose that there can be clean and uncorrupted politics. Political realists such as E.H. Carr (1962) and A. Schlesinger (1971) deny such a possibility. They argue that politics should be separated from morality. They support Niccolò Machiavelli's notion in *The Prince* (1532) that leaders need to learn not to be good to rule efficiently. Other political philosophers such as Michael Walzer (1973) and Laurie Calhoun (2004) look for a middle way that calls for an ethical evaluation of political performance. This means that the political agents involved in 'necessary evil' and 'unethical deeds' should feel 'guilty' for breaking the ethical norms. Only if they agonize over their need to break the shared moral codes and are ready to take personal responsibility, can they maintain their integrity. If so required by the laws and decided by the people, they also should be ready to face the appropriate punishment for their deeds (Walzer 1973, 160–180).

In political life, the most often-used ethical approach is a *pragmatic* one. The dirty hands argument does not seem to justify the separation of ordinary moral requirements from political decision-making. Instead, it emphasizes that agreed ethical rules and codes of conduct also apply to politics, but in certain individual cases we can make an exception to the rules if the motive is to protect or contribute to the common interests and the public good (Winston 1994).

A different argument can be made about politicians' with inherently conflicting interests: the interests of elected politicians, particularly in the highest public offices, are not always focusing on contributing to the public good. They (and their support groups) may have wanted to hold that office almost merely for selfish reasons; to gain power and wealth. In this context, research has brought to the discussion the concept of 'business politicians', who use their public office to enhance their own personal interests in other businesses they run. This makes their offices as 'profit maximization units' (Philp 1997, 437; Van Klaveren 1989).

Cost of corruption

To understand the cost of corruption to societies, we should first consider the concept or the ideal of *development*. The currently dominant model for development sets liberal democracy as an ideal, but entails a necessary adherence also to economic liberalism. This model has various problems in integrating the incommensurable value frameworks of political vs. economic liberalism. The direction for global development that the West promulgated after the Second World War as 'free markets and democracy' has these inherent value conflicts because it entails both idealist and realist aspects. On the one hand, the ideal of *political liberalism* calls for the realization of such universal humanistic values as moral and political agency, equality and individual rights, political participation, as well as a certain level of social justice. On the other hand, *economic liberalism* calls for more instrumental values such as realization of self-interest and rational profit maximization. In current Western development policies confusion between these two value frameworks has sometimes led into inconsistent development cooperation policies and 'double standards'.

This means that many Western countries maintain the transition to political liberalism, that is, liberal democracy and good governance, as conditions to their aid in many developing countries, while at the same time pushing for their structural change towards economic liberalism (Hellsten 2006; Heywood 1997; Johnston 2005). Sometimes it is not clear then, which values and goals get greater emphasis: humanistic values of political liberalism or instrumentalist values of economic liberalism.

In most instances a country may not be seen as 'well developed' if it is suffering from huge inequalities, treating certain groups of people with less respect and value, and letting big parts of its population live in poverty. This is despite its impressive economic growth, and its commercial development. Some other times this seems not to be the case. Regarding Apartheid South Africa, the West held back recognizing it as 'well developed', because the country did not meet the standard of political liberalism. Contradictions arise, however, if these conditions are not held consistent. For example, now in post-Apartheid South Africa economic liberalism is doing well, but still the standards of political liberalism are not applied quite stringently anymore, and the social inequality is still deep, and poverty levels remain high. Still, now the West tends to recognize South Africa as a country that has made the transition from authoritarian and unjust rule to democratic (enough) governance. Political, business and trade relations continue as normal. Similarly, post-genocide Rwanda has had impressive economic growth and holds elections regularly. However, its authoritarian president has limited civic space and does not let opposition voice its concerns. Despite these illiberal trends there, the Western countries, for the most part, continue with their development and business partnership in the country without many complaints. The case is similar with Ethiopia and several other 'transitional' or 'post-transition' countries, even if human rights and ethical norms are violated and there have been clear signs of organized grand and political corruption.

Whether we talk about the use of tax payers' money for development cooperation, or social development of the less affluent countries in general, the cost of corruption is high and multifaceted in economic and social terms. This creates double standards for public service ethics than those required in the West. In Kenya, for example, the local anti-corruption and human rights civil society organizations have complained about the leniency and double standards of the Western partners towards corrupt leaders and political actors.

If we hold on to the ideal of development that calls for democracy and social justice, then corruption is clearly a major obstacle to its realization. Not only high volumes of money are lost in private pockets and off-shore accounts, but democratic development becomes less stable and societies have serious security problems. Internal and external conflicts and competition over power and resources, terrorism, increasing crime and connections to international crime networks. While corruption is harmful also for political practice of established democracies, it is particularly challenging for transitional and poor societies (see also KNCHR 2006; Transparency International 2016).

Economically, corruption depletes national wealth in many ways. Besides all the money and resources lost, corruption hinders a fair market structure. On one hand, investors do not trust governments or companies in corrupt countries, and worry about high costs (of bribes) and/or unreliable business deals. On the other hand, corrupt agents invest scarce public resources in projects that will line their own pockets rather than benefit communities – often leading into poor quality results (collapsing buildings, deteriorating roads, etc.) (see also Wraith and Simkins 1963). In summary, corruption obstructs economic competitiveness. While there might be some short-term benefits, the overall business environment is unstable and transparent competition is not possible (Bardhan 1997, 1323; Mauro 1995; Myrdal 1968).

This suggests that even a free market economy needs to realize some non-economic, ethical values such as reliability, honesty and trust. However, in a society in which corruption is institutionalized, these values are often turned on their head. For a corrupt economy to work efficiently, the partners in crime – that is, the parties to corrupt transactions – must deliver what they have promised. They also need to be trustworthy and loyal to their partners in crime to keep everything 'in confidence'. Systematic corruption creates selective business and often dubious transactions that also interest international crime syndicates. Corrupt governments are often captured by mafia-type cartels, which are based on coercion, extortion, restricted competition, and blocking of new competitors. In addition, they often entail violent punishments for those who break their internal rules and norms. In summary, institutionalized and omnipresent corruption develops a system of 'reverse ethics' in which originally desirable values are used to keep the corrupt system going (see also Hellsten 2003).

This type of corruption is very difficult to combat, despite that everyone within and outside the system can see its overall devastating effects. 'Old boys' networks' remain untouchable due to the embedded requirements of international crime networks, leaders, colleagues, family, community or their ethnic groups. Society with 'reversed' social ethics tends to label those who fight against corruption and unethical practices as the 'bad guys' rather than 'good guys' as they break the 'circle of trust' among the partners in crime. Thus, not going along with corrupt practices may cost individuals their jobs, social 'respect' in their organization or community, their health, and in the worst case, their lives (Hellsten 2003). The social pressures in a society with pervasive corruption encourage the mentality that 'if you cannot beat them join them' (Burbidge 2015, 79). What is needed to break this cycle is a comprehensive attitude change and *the critical mass* of people to stand for their rights and call for accountability on the use of public resources.

In several countries, people consider corruption as a human rights issue. For example, the Kenyan National Commission of Human Rights has made the following connections between corruption and human rights:

> First, it (corruption) seriously inhibits the full realisation of economic, social, and cultural rights. Grand corruption particularly diverts resources from the intended public use in realisation of rights to decent livelihoods into private bank accounts. Besides creating sudden and extreme income inequalities, the diversion of these kinds of resources causes massive human deprivations. It also causes distortion of government expenditure by diverting public resources away from pro-poor expenditure, such as health and education, towards large capital projects where bribes are higher. In addition, when public contracting is conducted

> corruptly, it results in sub-standard and overpriced goods and services.... It is particularly harmful to the poor because the bribes they pay constitute a greater share of their income. The poor are also more dependent on public services. Corruption therefore worsens poverty and inequality within societies.
>
> Secondly, corruption perpetuates discrimination. . . . It confers a privileged status on those who bribe – such preferential treatment secured through the payment of a bribe constitutes discrimination. Corruption is particularly harmful and poses great dangers when it becomes pervasive in law courts. By tilting the scales of justice, corruption denies citizens their right to legal redress when their freedoms are violated. In this way, a person's rights to a fair trial and recognition as an equal person before the law are violated.
>
> Thirdly, corruption leads to the infringement of numerous civil and political rights. When corruption permeates politics, for example, and electoral outcomes are determined through vote buying and bribery, citizens are denied their right to political participation. Their rights to vote through universal and equal suffrage are, therefore, greatly watered down. The consequences include incapable and weak leaders, patronage and sycophancy and the erosion of democratic principles.
>
> *(KNCHR 2006)*

Affluent countries are often part of a scheme of global networks involved in dodgy economic practices, including tax avoidance and tax evasion. These are related to illicit financial flows from developing countries to tax havens. Africa, for example, according to the report by the UN High Level Panel (UNECA 2015) led by former South African president Thabo Mbeki shows that the illicit financial flows from Africa are running at over 60 billion dollars per year. This is probably just a fraction of the real amounts. The Paris-based Organization for Economic Cooperation (OECD) estimates that illicit financial flows, such as deliberate trade mispricing and tax evasion, out of Africa are running at three times the level of foreign aid coming in (UNECA 2015).

Causes of corruption

Corruption and culture

There has been persistent debate on the role that culture plays in preventing or enhancing corruption particularly in development cooperation. We can try to distinguish at least three partly overlapping elements that are related to the question of development cooperation conditions and whether some cultures are more prone to corruption than others. If culture is seen as a cause for corruption, this might affect also the donor countries' stand on corruption. First, whether the standards for good governance are the same everywhere is relevant to the conditions set on development assistance; or should there be some leniency due to cultural differences. Second, if corruption is not to be tolerated at home, but nevertheless persists in partner countries, the question arises whether these countries can continue to be involved with corrupt countries; whether we are talking about development cooperation or business collaboration. Third, if we agree that certain principles and standards for good governance should be universalized and globally adopted, how can we simultaneously respect the (also universalistic) call for national sovereignty and cultural diversity, ownership and equal partnership – with governments/countries which may not respect these standards.

The core dilemma seems to be whether Western development partners insist that all countries across the world adapt to the same international best practices, even when these have originated mostly within an individualistic European value framework for good governance and well-ordered liberal democracy. This debate takes us back to the timeless dispute over *ethical universalism* vs. *cultural relativism*. Indeed, such terms as 'corruption', 'abuse of power' and 'personal interest' may be interpreted differently in different cultural contexts. Altogether different concepts and words might be used to describe the same activities and patron–client relations. It is also evident that social as well as work ethics vary between cultures: what in one culture may be considered as an unethical bribe, in another may be considered as an inevitable cost or price for a given service, and in yet another might be socially required as an important gesture of respect or gratitude. What is acceptable in professional life in public service in one country may be objectionable in another country with different value frameworks, cultural beliefs systems, traditions and social practices. It is often assumed that in more collectivist cultures that are based on communitarian rather than individualist traditions the distinction between one's public and private roles is not so great; and thus, the distinction between professional and personal ethical commitments also becomes more blurred. Based on real or appealed cultural differences, there might be some difference in applying the ethical standards in different cultural contexts (see Rose-Ackerman 1999, 91).

For instance, many Asian and African societies seem to be based on more collectivist, communitarian traditions that accept certain practices that might be seen elsewhere as either corrupt or leading towards corruption. There are societies in which gift-giving is often seen as a part of social life, including in providing public services. To take two examples from Africa: *harambee* and *takrima*. *Harambee* ('pulling together') cooperation is indigenous to Kenya and is based on showing social responsibility by participating in communal self-help events in communities. It entails voluntary contributions in cash and kind (e.g. labour) to public goods and community projects, such as schools or health clinics. Originally, it could be seen as a traditional development strategy, and even today is still used to help family, friends and neighbours in need (e.g. to contribute to the costs of a wedding, illness or accident). However, in the context of multiparty 'democratic' elections, this tradition was turned into coercive extraction of campaigning funds. *Harambee* contributions were not just imposed on ordinary citizens by local administrations, but they became almost a prerequisite for businesspeople to win government contracts (e.g. by investing in a particular political candidate) (Burbidge 2015; Hellsten 2006). In Tanzania, traditional hospitality is called *takrima*. However, similarly and particularly in relation to election campaigning, political candidates started to use it to buy votes by offering gifts and meals to potential supporters, often with money taken from the public purse (Heilman et al. 2000; Hellsten 2006, 1–16). Both traditions are now banned by law in the context of political campaigning and fundraising. *The Tanzanian Elections Act* of 1985 had forbidden the feting of voters by electoral candidates on the campaign trail. However, the problems with the tradition of *takrima* came back in the 2000 elections, when Tanzanian politicians argued that it was un-African not to give friends 'something to eat'. It is often noted that in Asia and Africa, people traditionally have seemed to tolerate a wider range of behaviours by government and state officials as 'permissible' that would have been called corruption in many Western countries.

However, to make some sense of this rather ambiguous context, in many cases we can use individuals' ethical sense as a compass. In many countries with collectivist value systems, people still disapprove of corruption, particularly when it becomes rampant. Many Africans and Asians see corruption and bad governance as major problems in their societies. An overwhelming majority of people who live in countries with endemic corruption wish that something could be done to reduce it (Banerjee and Sengupta 2008, 474; Burbidge 2015, 79; see also Rose-Ackerman 1999, 91–110). Even if ordinary citizens in these countries may offer or pay bribes – as part of the 'normal practice', they still know it is wrong and wish the system would change. Many may feel like a hostage of corrupt systems and networks, and go along as they see no alternatives to this (see also Burbidge 2015, 79). Again, critical mass is needed to push for the change and to break the cycle.

Also, in relation to cultural practice, often the self-interested politicians use tradition as an 'excuse' to continue a 'corrupted' practice, or to reject international best practices as 'foreign to their culture'. However, the examples from Kenya and Tanzania show that once people recognize when an originally good tradition had turned into a corrupt practice, and that something can and has to be done to change the situation (see Burbidge 1017; Heilman et al. 2000; KNCHR 2006). Similarly, the recent uprisings in the Middle East and Africa (the so-called Arab Spring) give a good example of people's general discontent with bad governance and frustration with corruption. The question many ask is, from where to find genuinely committed leaders to replace the corrupt ones.

Another possible way to look at the question of why some countries appear more prone than others to corruption – in particular, political corruption – is to pay attention to cultural traditions and how they relate to institutional and political structures, as well as individuals' roles in these structures. Culture gives value frameworks and traditions influence over individuals' actions, but it does not determine them. Cultural values also change in changing circumstances, by internal or external pressures. Thus, rather than making an appeal to some conception of national or cultural character, the nature of social practices in a country could be seen as a reflection of the long-term development and organization of its social and political system. Traditional hierarchies and relations of patronage, as well as the system of rewards when integrated with new formal political processes (such as elections), can make certain societies more prone to different types of corrupt activities. This, however, is not about culture as such, but about the failure to fit new forms of governance with old social systems and hierarchies (see Heywood 1997, 426–427; Johnston 2005, 141–152; Philp 1997, 439).

Historically, it is easy to see how various embedded cultural elements have had different impacts in different countries. Even countries with similar value frameworks have different levels of corruption. If we look at the development of democracy in the Western countries, we can distinguish that northern and central European countries (Scandinavia, Germany, Netherlands) are perceived as fairly 'clean', topping the Transparency International Corruption Perception Index year after year. Southern European countries, for their part, show more tolerance to, and practice of, corruption. Countries in Asia and Africa, which have gone through maybe the most radical political and economic transitions throughout their history, have gone in different directions. On the one hand, Singapore, with its highly regulated policies, has managed to achieve a market economy with low corruption rates. On the other, in many parts of Africa failure to establish sufficiently strong state structures, efficient public services and enforceable accountability mechanisms have contributed to widespread corruption (Burbidge 2015, Heywood 1997, 427–428).

While it would be a sweeping generalization to claim that certain cultures are more corrupt than others, we can note that certain cultural contexts may be more susceptible to corrupt practices than others and thus, it is important to clarify their underlying cultural values. No one says, my culture has corruption as such as an important value – rather they defend corrupt practices in the name of cultural tradition.

Politico-economic context of corruption

Another debate on the causes of corruption has been between *need* vs. *greed*. This can also be misguiding: it is likely that low income levels tempt people to engage in corruption to fulfil their needs. However, since people with power, resources and extreme personal wealth also continue to be part of corrupt activities, the greed argument seems also valid. In reality, both need and greed cause people to slip from the ethical standards in various circumstances (see Johnston 2005, 1–14; Rose-Ackerman 1999).

These circumstances are tied to the politico-economic order of societies in question. Earlier it was argued that corruption was rampant in the Soviet Union and other socialist countries. Thus, the transition to a market economy and democratic governance was essential. However, the situation in many of these societies has not significantly improved after their turn towards economic liberalism. At the same time, it has become even more clear that corruption is a serious problem also in neo-liberal 'minimum states'. Currently in so-called emerging economies such as the BRICS (Brazil, Russia, India, China, and South Africa) countries, with various systems of governance but clear commitment to market economy, corruption appears to be rampant. Affluent countries and mature democracies are not immune to corruption either. For example, the European Union's (EU's) bureaucratic administration has proved to be a nest of careless use of public resources. In the United States, the media regularly reports about corruption scandals and bad governance in public administration and private business activities (Ades and Di Tella 1997; Banerjee and Sengupta 2008; Bardham 1997; Myrdal 1968). The public–private partnership and involvement of private business in government contracts have produced new avenues and means for corrupt transactions.

Thus, state bureaucracy alone cannot be the problem. Scandinavian welfare states are good examples of this, with their rather extensive state administration and low levels of corruption (Bardhan 1997, 1330–1331; Heywood 1997, 428–429; Hutchcroft 1997, 641; Moilanen et al. 2006).

In Africa, with current trends in economic globalization, there is a rise of business politicians who have set their personal interests above the public interest. Globalization with neo-liberal economics has also brought new partnerships, which are connected to international crime and activities such as money-laundering and illicit transfers of funds. Global networks of economic criminals reach deep into developing countries' governments, but even in the affluent countries influential multinational business can affect governments' decision-making and policies (UNECA 2015).

To further clarify the foregoing, let us take a closer look at the wider development trends in Africa. Since achieving independence African states have struggled to gain their full sovereignty and working political arrangements; during the Cold War, competing forces from the Western and Soviet blocs pulled them in politically different directions. After the fall of Soviet-backed communism and state socialism Bretton Woods institutions sponsored structural adjustment programmes (SAP) and pushed for privatized economies. State structures could not adapt to the needs of economic development, thus many African countries faced economic crisis in the 1980s. The weakened states could not deliver needed services or create jobs and employment opportunities. The governments, nevertheless, remained strong and used the money that was raised by selling off national industries and companies as part of privatization programmes and gained by cutting government investments in public services and salaries in the sector – to enrich themselves in the opened markets. People lost faith in their governments and the result was an explosion in informal and self-help economic and social activities (Heilman et al. 2000; Hellsten 2006, 1–25; Hutchcroft 1997, 639–658; Mauro 1995, 681–721; UNECA 2015).

African leaders adapted to the market economy, and liberal democracy only functioned on the surface: elections are often held not to realize the will of the people but to legitimate the rule of those who continued in the seats of power and influence. Business politicians captured state machinery and public resources. People are no longer loyal to the state they cannot trust.

African traditional support systems – as well as non-governmental organizations – are taking over state duties by offering services to communities and families. These are based on mutual assistance and local solidarity. While commendable as such, in the long run, this has led into 'biased solidarity' that easily fuels tribalism, nepotism, cronyism and favouritism in all its forms. Gradually this normalized corruption in many countries, and made it more difficult to combat (Hellsten 2006, 14; see also Burbidge 2015; Johnston 2005).

Combatting corruption

Research on corruption – its variations across different political and economic activities, and the diverse motivations of the agents involved – is challenging. It is difficult to obtain precise and accurate information due to the very nature of corruption: its secrecy and illegality. Without reliable and comparative baseline studies, it is also difficult to determine whether corruption has actually increased or decreased in particular societies during particular periods. Increased reporting of corrupt incidents may mean there have been more cases of corruption, but could also mean that people have been more actively engaged in reporting corruption because of more favourable circumstances: protection for whistle-blowers, new reporting mechanisms, better understanding of acceptable practices and so on.

In the end, how we combat corruption depends on what we determine to be its main causes. If *need* is seen to be the main problem, increasing financial incentives could be an efficient cure. If we believe corruption is mostly based on *greed*, then new stricter regulations and laws, and their serious enforcement with harsher punishments would be a better approach.

Philosophically, this has traditionally been seen from a perspective that relies on a certain view of human nature. If we consider, along the lines of Thomas Hobbes and later classical liberals, that humans are self-interested by nature, we either give up our attempts to control this, and instead accept it, or we set up restrictions – like Hobbes' social contract. If, however, we consider that humans have an inborn capacity for good, but are corrupted by the system – like Jean-Jacques Rousseau or Karl Marx – we will focus on cultivating virtue, emphasizing the role of example and preventive education, and aim to change the whole system.

In practice, human behaviour is probably a combination of nature and nurture. This means that we are better off to take a wider, multidimensional approach to anti-corruption measures. We need to limit the opportunities that 'make a thief', and reform administrative processes and update regulations; provide professional ethics training and reform institutional arrangements to reduce inefficiency and call for transparency. Punishment and rewards should be balanced and consistent. *An example* for others to follow should come from the top.

Studies and research on corruption will help to find the most effective measures in different contexts. However, studies on corruption still take rather narrow perspectives. This limits our understanding of how the different aspects of the phenomena fit together. It naturally reduces the possibility of finding the right remedies to combat corruption in various contexts and situations. In the fight against corruption there is no one-size-fits-all solution. The various aspects of corruption, its causes and costs, need to be considered, if significant results are to be achieved. Reforms and system changes work well in some societies; strict laws and regulations with mechanisms to ensure their enforcement work better in others. In some poor countries, financial incentives for public servants may encourage them to work professionally, but at the same time, some control measures are still needed to prevent need from turning into greed. The problem with anti-corruption programmes in development cooperation is that when a certain approach does not work in a particular context, it may be thought futile and abandoned altogether. However, it might be a very effective approach in a different context (Johnston 2005, 195–199).

In most societies, different remedies work hand in hand. What is needed is the right balance of different *preventive measures* and *corrective measures*. In Singapore, corruption is low. Some explain that this is because of the relatively high public service salaries. However, in addition there are strict regulations and punishments for those who break them. In other countries where at least upper-level civil servant and politicians are well paid, as in Kenya or Nigeria, and several other African countries, corruption has remained rampant. Despite anti-corruption laws and regulations, impunity prevails. The problem is a lack of control mechanisms that work well and already rampant corruption in the investigative and justice systems. These circumstances continue to feed greed. Parliamentarians, for example, tend to try to increase their own salaries and other benefits as soon as they get their seat.

In Scandinavian countries, meanwhile, where the public service salary levels are adequate but usually not extravagantly high, and where taxes and living costs are significant, corruption levels again have remained low. There are control mechanisms in place in these countries, but this may also be a result of strict 'peer observance'. In addition, professional ethics are somewhat respected, integrity applauded and in general it is more difficult to engage in suspicious activity due to access to information and enforced transparency (Moilanen et al. 2006). The Scandinavian model, however, cannot be directly exported elsewhere. Reforms that northern European governments support in many African countries have simply not worked due to differences in historical, cultural, and political settings, as well as in people's attitudes and needs. As Johnston (2005, 199) notes, political and economic participation should be open, vigorous and in balance.

Conclusion

No political system or form of governance has ever been immune to corruption; there is no vaccine to prevent it. Thus, the cure must be made to fit the circumstances and context. It is by no means evident that the problem of corruption can be solved by pressuring countries to make a transition towards market-based liberal democracy alone. In the end, whether capitalist or socialist, liberal or authoritarian, the politico-economic order is as corrupt as its leaders, public officials and ordinary citizens allow it to be. If authoritarian governments keep strict control over corruption, they can efficiently prevent it, but never fully eradicate it. Similarly, if people in countries with market capitalism make sure that election processes are well regulated, codes of conduct professionally followed, and social responsibility in business maintained, relatively low levels of corruption are possible. In today's world, we need to acknowledge that our political practice can never be like Plato's *Republic* and ruled by virtuous and wise philosopher kings.

From the point of view of development ethics, more specific research is needed on the different aspects of corruption, as well as for empirical research on its prevalence in various forms. Further analysis of the relationship between culture, political order and corruption would be useful, because it would give policymakers and development administrators a better understanding of how different societies have developed and what their specific problems are in relation to corruption. In addition, global networks of corruption, their functioning and methods have been studied relatively little but need more attention, even if this work is very difficult. Similarly, the use of new technology in corrupt transactions – particularly information and communications technology (ICT) – should be further explored. Both have provided new opportunities for corruption. Studying the changing global nature of corruption is essential. Collecting all this information will help to plan for better measures to combat corruption across the world.

References

Ades, A. and Di Tella, R. (1997) The New Economics of Corruption: A Survey and some New Results. *Political Studies* XLV: 496–515.

Alatas, S.A. (1990) *Corruption: Its Nature, Causes and Functions*. Avebury, Aldershot.

Banerjee, S. and Sengupta, P.K. (2008) Conceptualizing Political Corruption: Issues and Problems. *The Indian Journal of Political Science* 69(3): 473–482.

Bardhan, P. (1997) Corruption and Development: A Review of Issues. *Journal of Economic Literature* XXXV: 1320–1346.

Burbidge, D. (2015) *The Shadow of Kenyan Democracy. Widespread Expectation of Widespread Corruption*. Ashgate, Farnham.

Calhoun, L. (2004) The Problem of 'Dirty Hands' and Corrupt Leadership. *The Independent Review* VII(3): 363–385.

Carr, E.H. (1962) *The Twenty Years Crisis 1919–1939: An Introduction to the Study of International Relations*. Palgrave Macmillan, London.

Della Porta, D. and Vannucci, A. (1997) The "Perverse Effects" of Political Corruption. In Heywood, P. ed., *Political Corruption*. Blackwell, Oxford, 100–122.

Heidenheimer, A. ed. (1970) *Political Corruption, Readings in Comparative Analyses*. Transaction, New Brunswick, NJ.

Heidenheimer, A. ed. (1989) *Political Corruption: A Handbook*. Transaction, New Brunswick, NJ.

Heilman, B, Kamata, N. and Ndumbaro, L (2000) Corruption, Politics and Societal Values in Tanzania. *Social Philosophy* XXXI(4): 497–506.

Hellsten, S. (2003) Trust Me! My Hands Are Dirty Also: Institutionalized Corruption and the Vicious Cycle of the Competing Codes of Public and Private Ethics. *The Journal of Business and Professional Ethics* 11: 55–81.

Hellsten, S. (2006) Leadership Ethics and the Problem of Dirty Hands in the Political Economy of Contemporary Africa. *Ethics and Economics* 4(2): 1–25.

Heywood, P. (1997) Political Corruption: Problems and Perspective. *Political Studies* XLV: 417–435.

Hutchcroft, P. (1997) The Politics of Privilege: Assessing the Impact of Rents, Corruption, and Clientelism on Third World Development. *Political Studies* XLV: 639–658.

Johnston (2005) *Syndromes of Corruption. Wealth, Power, and Democracy*. Cambridge: Cambridge University Press.

Kenya National Commission of Human Rights (KNCHR) (2006) *Human Rights Dimension of Corruption*. Nairobi, Kenya. www.knchr.org/Portals/0/EcosocReports/Human%20Rights%20Dimensions%20of%20Corruption.pdf. Accessed 1 September 2017.

Leff, N (1964) "Economic Development Through Bureaucratic Corruption. *American Behavioural Scientists*: 8–14.

Machiavelli, N. (1984) *The Prince*. Bondanella., P. ed., Oxford University Press, Oxford. (Original work published in 1532).

Mauro, P. (1995) Corruption and Growth. *Quarterly Journal of Economics*: 681–721.

Moilanen, T. and Salminen, A. (2006) Comparative Study on the Public-service Ethics of the EU Member States. *A Report from the Human Resources Working Group*, EUPAN. http://unpan1.un.org/intradoc/groups/public/documents/un-dpadm/unpan047469.pdf Accessed 30 September 2017.

Myrdal, G. (1968) *Asian Drama: And Inquiry Into the Poverty of Nations, Vol. II*. Pantheon, New York.

Nye, J.S. (1989) Corruption and Political Development: A Cost – Benefit Analysis. In Heidenheimer, A. ed., *Political Corruption: A Handbook*. Transaction Books, New Brunswick NJ, 963–984.

Oxford Dictionaries (2016). Corruption. www.oxforddictionaries.com/definition/english/corruption. Accessed 1 July 2016.

Philp, M. (1997) Defining Political Corruption. *Political Studies* XLV: 436–462.

Rose-Ackerman, S. (1978) The Economics of Corruption. *Journal of Public Economics* 4(2): 187–203.

Rose-Ackerman, S. (1999) *Corruption and Government: Causes, Consequences and Reform*. Cambridge University Press, New York.

Schlesinger, Jr. A. (1971) The Necessary Amorality of Foreign Affairs. *Harper's Magazine*: 72–77.

Transparency International (TI) (2016) What Is Corruption? www.transparency.org/what-is-corruption/. Accessed 1 July 2016.

UNECA (2015) *Illicit Financial Flow. Report of the High Level Panel on Illicit Financial Flows from Africa*. www.uneca.org/sites/default/files/PublicationFiles/iff_main_report_26feb_en.pdf.Accessed 1 July 2016.

Van Klaveren,V.J. (1989) The Concept of Corruption. In Heidenheimer, A.J., Johnston, M. and LeVine,V.T. eds., *Political Corruption: A Handbook*. Transaction, New Brunswick. NJ, 89–91.

Walzer, M. (1973) Political Action: The Problem of Dirty Hands. *Philosophy and Public Affairs* 2(2): 160–180.

Wraith, R. and Simkins, E. (1963) *Corruption in Developing Countries*. Gower, London.

Winston, K. (1994) Choice in Political Ethics. In Wueste, D.D. ed., *Professional Ethics and Social Responsibility*. Roman and Littlefield, Lanham.

Part IX
Regional perspectives

The values of development ethics are not immune to criticism; if they do not stand up to criticism, then they do not reliably distinguish worthwhile development from maldevelopment. They have no other basis than public reason, open to all relevant arguments and points of view.

Earlier chapters in this *Handbook* have presented discussion and debate on how these values should be interpreted. The chapters that follow provide a check on the relevance of these values. They do so by considering how well the broad values – well-being, equity, empowerment, human rights, cultural freedom, environmental sustainability, integrity, and responsibility – highlight the most prominent concerns about development in different regions of the world. They also draw attention to important voices in regional discussions that deserve greater recognition in international discussions of development ethics.

In Latin America inequality stands out as the greatest issue, according to Mario Solís. Weaknesses in democratic governance and social cohesion are also of concern, along with a range of environmental issues. Important critical perspectives coming from Latin America include liberation models, intercultural perspectives, de-colonial thinking, and the *buen vivir* world view – all of which contribute to what Solís analyzes as *vindicatory critical thinking*.

Shashi Motilal and Prakriti Prajapati find that unsustainable and conflictual exploitation of resources has been the central cause of maldevelopment in South Asia, leading to environmental damage as well as wide inequalities in sharing the burdens and benefits of such development. Opposition to this trend often invokes rich South Asian traditions which integrate values of sharing in a good life with ideas of ecological integrity, as exemplified by thinkers like Gandhi or Vandana Shiva.

The preeminent issues of development ethics in East Asia concern political rights, according to Benedict Chan. In the Asian values debate it is held that civil and political rights are not binding in East Asian countries where they conflict with cultural perspectives such as Confucianism. Against this, Chan puts forward a minimal dignity-based rationale for human rights and shows that the West has no monopoly on the idea of dignity.

The Arab Spring expressed some severe ethical shortcomings of development in the Middle East and North Africa region. According to Alain Piveteau and Eric Rougier, the political economy of these countries centres on authoritarian-redistributive states dominated by families that straddle positions of political and economic decision-making. When economic prosperity

DOI: 10.4324/9781315626796-40

is absent and the population becomes aware of the dearth of economic opportunities, social frustration and discontent increase and must be resolved by redistribution and/or repression.

Jérôme Ballet, Kouamékan J.M. Koffi, and Alice Kouadio identify a pattern of maldevelopment in French-speaking sub-Saharan Africa that is characterized by inequality, corruption, and governance that disempowers the populations. After independence from France, these countries were propelled towards a model of development that was greatly influenced by the colonial period. The model, after being undermined in the 1980s, gave way to new aspirations amongst the people, who were no longer looking for economic development alone, but for political freedom and social protection as well.

Byaruhanga Rukooko Archangel argues that development ethics is not only relevant to African societies but should be recognized as a full member of post-colonial studies. At the same time, the rich African philosophical traditions have much to offer development ethics, and so it would make sense for Africans to grow their own perspectives on development ethics from these traditional roots and to contribute these to international discussion. Conventionalist approaches are discussed as well as African communalism and environmentalism, including Ubuntu.

Louise Haagh observes that the very concept of development, much less ethical development, seems foreign to many Europeans, who think it more applicable primarily to 'third-world' countries than their own. Underlying this she finds a trend towards gutting the role of democratic state leadership in development by European governments. Rather than leading development, the state's role is restricted to "building investor confidence." Short-term thinking, fragmented governance, and the austerity agenda are impediments to human development. Haagh suggests a number of steps that could be taken to "bring Europe back to the spirit of the postwar welfare commitment to humanism and inclusion" and more broadly "to generate a more politically conscious development path."

In the final chapter, Eric Palmer argues that cultural shifts and legislative decisions over the span of the past half-century have displaced the ethos of social responsibility that the USA shared with Canada in the past, replacing it with one of self-reliance that has led to missed opportunities, backsliding, and maldevelopment. Several development failures are highlighted: horizontal inequalities related especially to race and religion, low social mobility, rising within-nation inequality, declining educational access and achievement, inefficient and disparate health care access, and uneven health outcomes.

32

Latin America

Inequality provoking critical thought

Mario Solís

When it comes to the analyses of development ethics as it relates to specific regions, it seems appropriate to look at specific issues or concerns regarding the realization of worthwhile development. Also, to understand worthwhile development in particular regions, we might have to recognize some type of value pluralism or embrace a non-monistic approach to the *ethics* of development. Conceptions of the good and the right vary regionally and are conceptually circumscribed, and notions such as 'development' gain their meaning from within those variations. Latin America has given birth to several novel perspectives distinguishing good and bad development which are not well known internationally, and with which development thinkers in other regions should engage.

It is with this in mind, that I explore the basic content and rationale of development ethics in Latin America. First I delineate one of the main issues in development ethics, namely inequality. Second, I outline some of the most prominent contributions to development ethics from Latin America, such as the '*ética del buen vivir*', as well as key ideas from specific perspectives such as liberation philosophy and intercultural philosophy. Finally, I outline a normative framework that not only captures the rationale of these lines of thought but also gives a distinctive account of the field of development ethics. We may call this *vindicatory critical thinking*.

Inequality

According to Denis Goulet, development ethics consists in the examination of 'ethical and value questions posed by development theory, planning and practice' (Goulet, 1977, 5, cited in Gasper 2004). In order to do just that, we should first look at the current state of affairs in Latin America, based on which we may then deal with good practice and planning of development.

Here are some general facts about Latin America's political and socio-economic challenges. First, there is gross inequality, measured either by income or by access to basic goods and the comparative life standards of the population. Second, there is political instability, be it for internal or external reasons, and absence of good governance. Third, not unrelated to these, there are weaknesses in social cohesion, perhaps due to high illiteracy rates as well as *diverse yet non-pluralistic* ways of understanding citizenship and civility. Diversity without pluralism is a recipe for disaster. Diversity *and* pluralism, on the other hand, is the most promising way to deal with

DOI: 10.4324/9781315626796-41

what we may call 'the fact of hybridation', or in the words of García Canclini 'culturas híbridas' (Canclini 1990), describing Latin America as the result of a long process of cross-cultural mixing, composed of the European (mainly Iberian) heritage and the non-European – Indigenous, African, etc.

Let us focus first on inequality. According to the World Development Indicators compiled by the World Bank, between 2000 and 2012, Latin America stands out as one of the two most unequal regions of the world alongside sub-Saharan Africa. Compared to other regions, Latin America is characterized by a level of inequality which is both high and persistent (Lustig et al. 2013), and which has remained a major concern for policymakers in the last two decades. Although it is true that there have been some impressive growth rates, particularly in countries such as Brazil (now rapidly moving toward recession), approximately 50% of Brazil's population still lives in impoverished conditions. Even if there have been good results in economic growth and even if we do not take into consideration the economic crisis, the gap between the haves and have-nots remains an object of considerable concern.

The following statement by the Economic Commission for Latin America and the Caribbean (ECLAC) captures both the challenge and the causes of inequality:

> The social gaps that exist in the region are closely related to productive asymmetries that involve unequal levels of quality and productivity between jobs, which lead to larger wage differentials and unequal income distribution. Disparate levels of productivity are still persistent in the region and remain a major obstacle to the success of policies for eradicating poverty and reducing inequality.
>
> *(ECLAC 2015, 57)*

The empirical literature regarding the economically and socially harmful effects of income inequality is extensive. Income inequality concentrates political power in the hands of a few (Dabla-Norris et al. 2015 and Perry et al. 2006), hinders human development (Perry et al. 2006), and weakens the impacts of economic growth and poverty reduction (Bourguignon 2004; Ravallion 2005; Lopez and Serven 2010; Perry et al. 2006). (I am indebted to Suráyabi Ramirez for drawing my attention to these empirical studies on inequality.) In short, inequality in Latin America is bad and requires a response.

The call for worthwhile development in Latin America must thus be understood precisely as an economic and political effort to eliminate asymmetries in wages, income, and clusters of production differentiated by quality of and access to education and technology. All of these factors contribute to the maintenance and perpetuation of inequality. Unsurprisingly, economic inequality is closely related to well-known democratic deficits, lack of good governance, and institutional instability. Due to such internal instability and a lack of governance within an individual country, cooperation between countries, governmental and non-governmental institutions seems to be of fundamental importance in advancing towards worthwhile development practices.

Beyond concerns about inequality and given our current understanding of climate challenge, it seems clear that in order to achieve worthwhile development, we should also focus on environmental sustainability in the search for equality. This is precisely ECLAC's perspective:

> Latin America and the Caribbean must shift its development paradigm if it is to achieve equality and environmental sustainability in today's complex and ever-changing socioeconomic conditions. The environmental dimension of sustainable development is crucial to ensuring the well-being of future generations and therefore intergenerational equality.
>
> *(ECLAC 2015, 13)*

Critical thought in Latin America

Latin America has a particular tradition of *critical thinking* embracing a host of overlapping, complex social and philosophical movements: environmental ethics, feminist theories, deep ecology, animal rights movements, liberation theology and liberation philosophy, intercultural philosophy, de-colonial and/or post-colonial thought, and perhaps the closest to development ethics, the ethics of *buen vivir*. *Buen vivir* – which is the Spanish translation of the Aymaran expression *suma qamaña*, from the Qechua *Sumak Kawasay* – translates into English as 'living well'. I will now trace four of the previously mentioned trends of critical thinking in order to advance *buen vivir*, which may be regarded as the most appropriate approach to development ethics from the standpoint of Latin America.

Ricardo Salas-Astraín (2006) divides the whole terrain into two main lines, best captured in the work of Enrique Dussel (*Ética de la globalización en la edad de la globalización y la exclusión*, 1998) and Raúl Fornet-Betancourt (*Transformación cultural de la Filosofía*, 2003). Salas-Astraín refers to these two tendencies as the 'liberation model' – based on the principle of autonomy – and the 'intercultural model', whose basic principle has to do with the constitution of subjectivity.

The liberation model is indebted to a widely recognized Latin American intellectual cluster: *teología de la liberación* (Gutiérrez 1971, Boff 1978), *pedagogía del oprimido* (Freire 1970), and *filosofía de la liberación* (Ardiles et al. 1973). The whole line of thought amounts to a denunciation of the inhumane living conditions (material and non-material) experienced by the poor, illiterate, the malnourished, indigenous, women, etc. Arguably, this model comprises a type of contextualism as we may see from its underlying claim: namely, that a normative principle underlying any social movement or worthwhile policy necessarily comes from within a particular socio-political and historical context, from the needs people face and the values they share. The normative principle is something you have to hear from the suffering, the victims, and the excluded, and it is not just a matter of rectification (which could already be a lot to hope for in various places) but a demand for self-ownership and self-determination.

The intercultural model of Fornet-Betancourt, García Canclini, and Jorge Larraín proposes that we must base any ethical or political principle on cultural pluralism and group-differentiated rights. This model brings ideas of identity and subjectivity to the forefront insofar as it emphasizes robust formal and substantive communal membership (being part of particular communities with their customs, languages, values, and so forth).

Both the intercultural and liberation models offer ways to put flesh on the bones of the seven values of development ethics that are the subject of this *Handbook*, particularly with the idea of empowerment and the need to make development consistent with cultural freedom. Along these lines, Adela Cortina insists on recognizing the necessary link between any effort towards development with the need to come to grips with value pluralism and the importance of 'dialogically discovering those values [and the values of development] within vibrant cultural communities' (Cortina 2011, 17).

A third model of critical thought in Latin America, which is closely related to the liberation model, is the so-called de-colonial or post-colonial thought. Aníbal Quijano (2014) and Walter Mignolo (2007) are two of the most influential representatives of this model, which is a sub-genre of contemporary sociology and history. It responds to the cultural, political, and even epistemological practices of exploitation and domination. Among its various sources, this line of thinking finds its roots in so-called dependency theory (originally advanced by economists Raúl Prebisch and Hans Singer in 1949 and very prominent in the 1960s and 1970s) and is extended by the well-known world system theory (Wallerstein 1974).

Dependency theory was a very influential economic theory which focused attention on the conditions of dependency of the once 'underdeveloped' countries, and on the arguments to overcome such a condition. The diagnosis of dependency was that the structure of the interaction between industrialized countries and those on the periphery helps create and consolidate deficiency, inequality, low productivity, unemployment, foreign domination, and colonialism (Cardoso y Falleto 1979). The response then, in economic terms, was basically a defense of import-substitution industrialization. Admittedly, this diagnosis and the associated prescriptions have fallen from favour, yet the broader dependency perspective has continuing relevance to the current state of the global economy, and dependency theory's criticism of narrow hyper-economic conceptions of development remains valid and feeds the critique of development advanced by de-colonial/post-colonial thinking.

According to de-colonial and other forms of critical thinking in Latin America, the practical outcomes of dependency theory have been nothing but different forms of what Goulet called maldevelopment. Such a critique also contributes to the idea of worthwhile development by calling attention to the structural problems faced by the Global South. Walter Mignolo puts it as follows:

> Although dependence theory has been under attack from several fronts (Cardoso 1977), it is important not to lose sight of the fact that from the perspective of Latin America, it clearly and forcefully put in the agenda the problems involved in 'developing' Third World countries.
>
> *(2012, 54)*

The fourth model of critical thought is called *buen vivir*. That is the name of a social, cultural, and political trend, a philosophy or a world view mostly from countries in South America (particularly Ecuador, Bolivia, and Uruguay) (Gudynas 2011). It calls for an ethos of life; it is a comprehensive conception of the world embedded in ancient belief systems of many original peoples of America, such as the Aymara peoples of Bolivia, the Quechua of Ecuador and the Mapuche of Chile and Argentina. It is an ethical proposal informing the political, telling us that the way forward must be fundamentally community-centric, ecologically balanced, and culturally informed.

The recently revised constitution of Ecuador includes the concept of *buen vivir*: 'We . . . hereby decide to build a new form of public coexistence, in diversity and in harmony with nature, to achieve the good way of living.' The ideal of *buen vivir* is politically very powerful – what could be stronger than a political agreement in the form of a constitutional essential? (For an instructive analysis, see Fatheuer 2011). *Buen vivir* is perhaps the most complete model insofar as it puts nature at the center of any moral or political emancipatory drive. It is a candidate for best theoretical/practical endeavour, featuring most of the best traits of critical thought in Latin America – and unsurprisingly the closest expression of an ethics and politics of worthwhile development. (For more on *buen vivir* see Chapter 22 in this *Handbook*.)

Buen vivir addresses the many pervasive forms of colonialism, as well as the capitalist system of large-scale production and its corollary, dependence on indiscriminate consumption and profit (*buen vivir* depicts an alternative conception of development). Some people might feel at home with this critique of large-scale brute capitalism and the culture of consumption. Others might not think the same way. Nonetheless, the fact of the matter is that we need not endorse this critique in order to see the normative potential of such a call – which, arguably, can also be put in terms of fundamental liberal values like freedom and equality. This is admittedly a large and contested issue that cannot be expanded on here, but the reader is invited to consider the following thought: we need no religious or philosophical world view to see what is good in the idea of *buen vivir*, and in the politics and policies that spring from it. *Buen vivir* provides a promising way of restating the basics and building the best narrative for the betterment of the world we live in.

Although it may seem paradoxical, I submit that *buen vivir* and the other expressions of critical thinking just mentioned leave room for development ethics while simultaneously seeming to abandon the term altogether. Eduardo Gudynas says: 'the vision promoted by *Buen Vivir* strongly supports the need to explore alternatives to development beyond conventional Eurocentric knowledge' and yet he adds '*Buen Vivir* can be considered as a platform where critical views of development are shared' (2011, 445). It seems that, in the end, development ethics and *buen vivir* share the same commitment to the urgent need to engage in struggle over what that term 'development' stands for. In other words, *buen vivir* captures in many ways the features and properties of development ethics. Perhaps this common ground is good news for at least one aspect of the movement in favour of worthwhile global development ethics: namely, the pluralistic non-dogmatic dialogical production of ideas related to values of *well-being* and *empowerment* in the development ethics value framework.

Vindicatory critical thinking

As these reflections suggest, a particularly Latin American approach to development ethics must be critically eclectic. Most importantly, Latin American moral and political philosophy must be *vindicatory* if it does not want to end up either as an extension of the natural sciences or, on the other extreme, as the expression of a dogma. 'Vindicatory' should not be understood in the usual sense of 'revenge' (as in 'vindictive'). It should be understood in the more constructive dialogical sense of 'transition as improvement' by recognizing rights and wrongs in bringing up the new and getting the old behind, and by making sense of what we believe in by also making sense of what others believe. This is one possible use of the term suggested in part by Bernard Williams (2006, 188–192).

It is therefore my contention that the normative stance that best responds to what we are and what we have in Latin America (and perhaps also in other vulnerable societies of the Global South) combines the normativity of *buen vivir* and the other types of critical thinking reviewed above and results in vindicatory critical thinking.

One relevant feature of this normativity is a certain skepticism about Western ethical and political theories such as contractarianism, Kantian ethics, or the various consequentialist and utilitarian moral outlooks. There is more to the idea of the good and the right than that which is captured in the maximization of utility or to the subjugation to any absolute norm or rule.

The other relevant feature of this type of normativity is its practical approach. Normative claims are fundamentally practical claims, which means that the object of negation in any vindicatory normativity must be a state of affairs as well as what is absent in the state of affairs. This also means that such normativity can reject, or be agnostic with respect to, a positive good because it is focused on practical matters, on present day situations, and at the same time can conceive its own positive normativity for a plausible state of affairs sometime in the future. It can be understood as present-tense utopian rather than future or forward-looking utopian. (For an instructive discussion of this issue from the standpoint of Adorno's practical philosophy, see Freyenhagen 2013.)

What, then, is the relationship between vindicatory normativity and development ethics? Des Gasper says that we may think of development ethics as a 'field of professional ethics' adding, however, that it is a 'forum for serious reflection (including feeling), on a broader scale than implied in the traditional model of professional ethics' (Gasper 2004, 21). Vindicatory normativity goes farther than this in that it grants some normative authority to development ethics' normative-cum-practical framework in its own right, and makes such a framework dependent upon global public reason. This is perhaps what the combination of a negative-vindicatory type of normativity and the ethics of *buen vivir* try to achieve. This is what a Latin American approach to development ethics might look like.

Conclusion

The framework of values of worthwhile development serves as a theoretical-practical mechanism to deal with challenging issues such as socio-economic inequality. It is also consistent with the distinctive type of critical thinking found in the region. Development ethics responds to the rationale of critical thinking, which can be related to what Helio Gallardo (1981) called *pensar radical* (radical thinking). As the etymological meaning of the term suggests ('radical' comes from the Latin word *radix*, meaning 'root'), *radical thinking* is about the re-making – 'from within' – of the political-institutional structures of a cluster of societies whose history has been one of 'coloniality' and gross inequalities, and whose urgent task is one of self-constitution. It is the idea of fulfilling the values of empowerment, sustainability, and cultural freedom (3, 4, and 6 of the framework of worthwhile development). So understood, the moral and political philosophy captured in development ethics should not be thought of as purely a speculative *a priori* enterprise but as a political practice in and for such diverse, plural, and interconnected societies as those of Latin America and the so-called Global South.

References

Ardiles, O., Casalla, M., Cerruti Guldberg, H., Cullen, C., Dussel, E., Kusch, R., Roi, A. and De Zan, J. (1973) *Hacia una filosofía de la liberación latinoamericana*. Bonum, Buenos Aires.

Boff, L. (1978) *Teología del cautiverio y de la liberación*. Ediciones Paulinas, Madrid.

Bourguignon, F. (2004) *The Poverty – Growth – Inequality Triangle*. The World Bank, Mimeo.

Cardoso, E. and Falleto, E. (1979) *Dependency and Development in Latin America*. University of California Press, Berkeley.

Cortina, A. (2011) Una propuesta de ética del desarrollo. *Éthique et économique/Ethics and Economics*, 8(1): 8–24.

Dabla-Norris, M.E. Kochhar, M.K. Suphaphiphat, M.N. Ricka, M.F. and Tsounta, E. (2015) *Causes and Consequences of Income Inequality: A Global Perspective*. International Monetary Fund.

Fatheuer, T. (2011) *Buen Vivir a Brief Introduction to Latin America's New Concepts for the Good Life and the Rights of Nature* in Publication Series on Ecology, Böll H. ed., *Foundation* 17 (Translation: Hayduska J.).

Freire, P. (1970) *Pedagogía del oprimido*. Herder y Herder, New York.

Freyenhagen, F. (2013) *Adorno's Practical Philosophy: Living Less Wrongly*. Cambridge University Press, Cambridge.

Gallardo, H. (1981) *Pensar en América Latina*. EUNA, San José, Costa Rica.

Garcia Canclini, N. (1990) *Culturas híbridas. Estrategias para entrar y salir de la modernidad*. Grijalbo, México.

Gasper, D. (2004) *The Ethics of Development*. Edinburgh University Press, Edinburgh.

Goulet, D. (1977) *The Uncertain Promise: Value Conflict in Technology Transfers*. IDOC, New York.

Gudynas, E. (2011) Buen Vivir: Today's Tomorrow. *Development* 54(4): 441–447.

Gutiérrez, G. (1971) *Teología de la liberación-perspectivas*. Centro de Estudios y Publicaciones. Lima.

Lopez, H. and Serven, L. (2010) Too poor to grow. *Policy Research Working Paper Series* 5012. The World Bank, Mimeo.

Lustig, N., Lopez-Calva, L.F. and Ortiz-Juarez, E. (2013) Declining Inequality in Latin America in the 2000s: The Cases of Argentina, Brazil, and Mexico. *World Development* 44: 129–141.

Mignolo, W. (2012) *Local Histories/Global Designs: Coloniality, Subaltern Knowledge, and Border Thinking*. Princeton University Press, Princeton.

Penz, P., Drydyk, J. and Bose, P. (2011) *Displacement by Development: Ethics, Rights and Responsibilities*. Cambridge University Press, Cambridge.

Perry, G., Arias, O., Lopez, H., Maloney, W. and Serven, L. (2006) *Poverty Reduction and Growth: Virtuous and Vicious Circles*. The World Bank, Mimeo.

Quijano, A. (2014) *Cuestiones y horizontes: de la dependencia histórico-estructural a la colonialidad/descolonialidad del poder*. Selección a cargo de Danilo Assis Clímaco CLACSO, Ciudad Autónoma de Buenos Aires.

Ravallion, M. (2005) *Inequality Is Bad for the Poor*. Working Paper No. 2558, The World Bank, Washington DC.

Salas-Astraín, R. (2006) Aportes hermenéuticos a una perspectiva latinoamericana de la justicia. Sobre el debate entre la ética de la liberación y la ética intercultural. *Veritas, Revista de Filosofía y Teología* 1(15): 313–328.

United Nations, Economic Commission for Latin America and the Caribbean (ECLAC) (2015) Inclusive Social Development: The Next Generation of Policies for Overcoming Poverty and Reducing Inequality in Latin America and the Caribbean, 2015 Regional Conference on Social Development in Latin America and the Caribbean, Lima.

Wallerstein, I. (1974) The Modern World-System. In *Capitalist Agriculture and the Origins of the European World-Economy in the Sixteenth Century*. Academic Press, New York and London.

Williams, B. (2006) *Philosophy as a Humanistic Discipline*. Princeton University Press, Princeton.

33

South Asia

Environmental concerns and human rights violations

Shashi Motilal and Prakriti Prajapati

The people of South Asia live amidst immense diversity of ethnicities, religions and languages. In 2014, there were about three times more persons living per square kilometre in this region than in Europe (World Bank 2014). High population density acts as a breeding ground for intense conflicts as people compete over a limited pool of resources. With the advent of liberalization in the 1990s, South Asian economies began freeing up trade, aspiring to 'develop' at faster rates by widespread urbanization, chasing living standards of the West and pushing indigenous cultures away into corners. This process benefited from the pace of globalization, causing a marked increase in consumerism. While the middle- and high-income classes were placed such that they enjoyed the fruits of 'development', the lower income strata bore most of the burden. Unsustainable and conflictual exploitation of resources has been the central cause of maldevelopment in this region, leading to environmental damage as well as wide inequalities in sharing the burdens and benefits of such development. However, it is also remarkable that there have been numerous South Asian philosophical sources which have addressed issues of maldevelopment by integrating human and environmental values, a move necessary for any form of worthwhile development.

Resource-based maldevelopment

The current stage of development has largely been steered by fast-paced urbanization. As cities rapidly develop and attract migrants in search of livelihoods, they demand more resources. This appetite engulfs natural resources like freshwater, fertile land and fresh air from the surrounding 'less developed', peri-urban landscapes, thereby forcing inhabitants to bear a high risk of loss to health, property, livelihoods and culture.

Damming rivers has hitherto offered tremendous hope for the woes of water and power deficits in the urban aspirational mindset. But while a typical hydropower plant would generate power, store water and catalyse inter-basin water transfers, it would also displace indigenous communities living in the river valley, risking life and property by causing economic and ecological disturbance.

Among the largest earth and rock-filled structures in the world, the Tarbela Dam in Pakistan supplies 16 per cent of the nation's total electricity demand (The World Bank 2013). Built in

DOI: 10.4324/9781315626796-42

1974 as part of the world's largest irrigation system, its construction disrupted the natural ecosystem and displaced around one hundred thousand people without adequately compensating them (Hill 2006). In pursuit of obtaining this compensation, indigenous communities, local bodies and environmental justice organizations have long struggled to broaden the definition of 'affected' in the Land Acquisition Act of 1894, which has not been revised (Temper et al. 2015). Indigenous tribal communities in valleys continue to suffer from the trauma of displacement, including the hardships and treacheries of resettlement and the ongoing struggle for justice; international funding agencies support the expansion of projects that aim to provide for aspiring urban sections of society, regardless of the environmental and cultural cost to marginalized communities. A similar case of displacement in the Mahanadi basin in India awaits justice as full compensation eludes victims even after 68 years (D Souza et al. 1998).

These episodes bring home an understanding of the inequitable distribution of the fruits of development, and of government's role in determining how the economic climate and state policies decide winners and losers. In this context, Arundhati Roy ingenuously explains the role of dams:

> Big dams are to a nation's 'development' what nuclear bombs are to its military arsenal. They are both weapons of mass destruction. They're both weapons Governments use to control their own people. Both Twentieth Century emblems that mark a point in time when human intelligence has outstripped its own instinct for survival. They're both malignant indications of civilization turning upon itself. They represent the severing of the link, not just the link – the understanding – between human beings and the planet they live on. They scramble the intelligence that connects eggs to hens, milk to cows, food to forests, water to rivers, air to life and the earth to human existence.
>
> *(Roy 1999)*

While dams demonstrate a case of one's 'development' threatening the development of the *other*, empirical investigations reveal that conflicts most often end up being between seemingly 'green' goals like the pursuit of cleaner energy and the conservation of biodiversity. At the turn of the last century, the government of Himachal Pradesh, a small hilly state in northern India, announced its commitment to becoming a green state through 'progressive' policies. However, 'What on paper seemed like the ideal model turned out to be more of green-washing with an agenda for (economic) growth promotion' (Himdhara 2016). This is clear in the fact that most hydropower plant projects pose social and environmental concerns. Groundwater sources are depleted, often drying out completely, leaving entire villages without potable water. Moreover, road construction and landslides, seismic risk, diversion of forests, exploitation of migrant labour, poor working conditions and the disruption of local livelihoods are other key ingredients of the Himalayan hydro boom. The government, however, has continued undeterred, tapping the remaining hydro potential rapidly through large and small projects, partnering with the private sector (Dharmadhikary 2008).

Sri Lanka's Nuclear Energy programme (NEP) to diversify their energy mix shows another similar example of 'progressive' policies gone awry. Despite environmentalists' opposition, the government implemented NEP on the pretext of an overstated energy deficit that needed to be met. This argument was ignorant of the generation of a large mass of radioactive waste relative to the island's capacity, and negated the credibility of solar, wind and radioactive sources in combating excess demand (Withanage 2015). In order to loosen China's embrace on Sri Lankan economy, Sri Lanka sought India's assistance. Recognizing a diplomacy win, India has promised to train personnel and assist in building nuclear infrastructure (Government of Sri Lanka 2014).

Such outcomes are results of either an explicit governmental agenda or an apparent absence of it. For instance, illegal and indiscriminate collection of shrimp larvae in Bangladesh has sustained in spite of a law enactment in 2000. Large spreads of mangroves guarding against cyclones along with agricultural and fishing livelihoods have been endangered as a result. In Khulna district, the situation has been worse. A project worth USD 38 million has been proposed to increase saline water availability in shrimp enclosures. Moreover, rampant human rights violations such as child labour, health and safety violations, withheld payments, sexual harassment, poor working conditions and long workdays of over 12 to 16 hours add to the agony of the workers (Alam et al 2012). Workers employed in the ship-dismantling industry on the shores of Bangladesh, India and Pakistan face similar hardships (Kumar 2009).

These realities expose many unethical actions undertaken in the pursuit of self-interest without much regard to their far reaching consequences. Adversely affected communities have, in few cases, been able to come together and stall these practices with the support of anti-incumbency politics and strong justice organizations. In contrast with the aforementioned, some cases demonstrate successful political mobilization against large multinational corporations.

Soon after the ruling party announced an industrial subsidy to attract foreign investors, a cement plant worth an estimated INR 900 billion was proposed in Himachal Pradesh by Lafarge. Given the magnitude and extent of mining involved and the diversion of forest and private agricultural land in and around the project area, the project's future hung in balance as the local community took in its hands the responsibility to question its feasibility. They also launched a legal battle (Agarwal and Asher 2010).

Besides causing a socio-economic plight, some mining projects also conflict with the rights and values of indigenous people. In an effort to promote growth of economically laggard but resource-rich state of Odisha, the state government signed several MOUs with companies to set up mineral based industries. Vedanta, a large mining corporation, signed to set up an aluminum refinery and a bauxite mining plant in the most environmentally diverse region, the Niyamgiri hill. The hill is home to the Dongria Kondh tribe, known for their harmonious, sacred and symbiotic relationship with nature. It is believed to be the abode of their divine god, Niyam Raja, and therefore, holds tremendous importance. The tribe understands that the 70 million tons of bauxite reserves at the top of the hill act as a sponge which soak up monsoon rains and hold deposits of water throughout hot summer months. These reserves ensure the continuous flow of perennial streams across the hill which are vital to the survival of the tribe, providing water for drinking and irrigation purposes (Sahu 2008). Strong trans-local mobilization as an assemblage of resistance individuated out of interactions between Dongria Kondh, civil society organizations, corporations and government. This mobilization resulted in a landmark decision for tribes' rights in India. The Supreme Court rejected Vedanta's appeal on the mining ban and decreed that the Dongria Kondh would have a decisive say in giving the go-ahead to Vedanta's mining project (Kumar 2014).

Integrating human and environmental values

Scrutiny of these cases reveals that unsustainable patterns of economic development result in the violation of some basic human rights, like the right to life, livelihood, secure work environment, land, religion and culture of individuals directly affected by such development. Clearly, the distribution of the burdens and benefits of this sort of development is not equitable. Lack of participation of all stakeholders in the processes of development results in inequities of outcome for the vulnerable, marginalized and economically weaker sections of society. In fact, one can argue that such unsustainable development which merely focuses on positive change in GDP not only violates human rights of the affected generation but also causes irreparable damage to the ecosystem, thereby compromising the rights of future generations. Sustainable development is 'a strategy by which communities seek to accommodate within economic development, approaches that also benefit the local environment and quality of life' (Motilal and Nanda, 2006, 237). Where maldevelopment can lead to 'congestion, sprawl, pollution and resource overconsumption, sustainable development offers real, lasting solutions that will strengthen our future' (Motilal and Nanda 2006, 237).

This squarely puts the question of sustainable or worthwhile development within the framework of human rights, where the human right to development must coexist with environmental sustainability. Where does one draw the line? What kind of alternative development models can we support which are compatible with the equal rights of the present generation as well as the rights of the future generation while also protecting the environment? What are the values such development would seek besides economic growth and how should these be measured? In this context it is useful to reflect on the seven values that are identified in this *Handbook* as characterizing worthwhile development (see the Introduction to this *Handbook*; also Penz et al. 2011, Drydyk 2011): well-being, equity, empowerment, environmental sustainability, human rights, cultural freedom, responsibility and integrity.

We need to understand development in human terms: in terms of meeting human needs, expanding freedoms (capabilities) or increasing happiness while also protecting the environment in which such development takes place. All of the cases discussed before violate one or more of the preceding goals of sustainable development. Note that since 1971, Bhutan has rejected GDP as the only way to measure progress. In its place, it has inspired a new approach to development, which measures prosperity through formal principles of gross national happiness (GNH) and the spiritual, physical, social and environmental health of its citizens and natural environment.

The issue of sustainable development as opposed to maldevelopment nests in the broader context of the relation between humans and non-human nature as spelt out in the debate ranging between anthropocentrism and ecocentrism. Anthropocentrism states that nature is valued only in so far as it serves the purposes, needs and interests of humans. Notwithstanding the difficulty of clearly distinguishing between a 'need' and a 'want', some of the cases just cited clearly show that an anthropocentric view in meeting the development needs of the few results in environmental degradation which in turn violates the human rights of others. Ecocentrism, on the other hand, is the view that nature has intrinsic value and not merely instrumental value and must be protected for its own sake. Extreme forms of either theory would be detrimental to humans and/or the ecosystem. It appears that some middle ground between anthropocentrism and ecocentrism has to be sought because although development is always for humans, it needs to be sustainable since all human activity is ecologically embedded. The ecological embeddedness of the self is to be construed as relational constituted by both social and environmental relations (Robyn Eckersley 1992). Thus, sustainable development is to be understood as development that will exist harmoniously with the eco-system and promote 'ecological integrity' as a standard by which to assess models of sustainability, whereby the most desirable policies are those that protect the integrity of ecosystems (see Norton 1999, 2002).

A similar idea is to be found in the writings of Vandana Shiva, the renowned environmental philosopher activist. Shiva has emphasized the 'ecological path of living with justice and sustainability'. Citing ancient Indian philosophical sources, she maintains that 'right living' consists in following 'dharma' which can be construed as the bridge between resources (artha) and human needs (kama) and which secures the balance between the two. In her view, the global economy has created an 'ecological imbalance' due to a conflict between 'economic laws' on the one hand and 'ecological laws' and 'social laws' on the other. This imbalance has also led to a non-sustainable paradigm of equity where everyone has an equal right to pollute and deplete the earth's resources, whereas what we need is a sustainable paradigm of equity which recognizes the equal responsibility not to do that. Shiva also talks of 'Earth Democracy' wherein all beings and all people are equal, and all beings and all communities have rights to resources of the earth for their sustenance (as found in an excerpt from Shiva 2008, 19, 22). It is the belief in integrating human and environmental values that has led to intense and widespread movements against displacement like the Narmada Bachao Andolan and the Chipko movements in India (Bandyopadhyaya and Shiva 1987).

The concept of sustainable development as an ideology has been a part of native communities of the South Asian region. For example, in India, traditional knowledge and philosophy has always emphasized the value of being frugal and leaving enough for society expressed in the attitude of non-acquisitiveness (aparigraha). Historically, nature was both revered and feared and continues to be so in many regions of India inhabited by indigenous communities. Rooted in Gandhi's best known aphorism – the world has enough for everybody's need and not enough for everybody's greed – the Gandhian lifestyle evokes the code of voluntary simplicity as a sustainable alternative to the modern over consumerist lifestyle (Guha 2006). This does not in any way undermine the importance of the right to development or even the right to consume since one must have this basic right so that one's human capabilities are enhanced. When this happens, one realizes one's fullest potential and leads a life of dignity. What is decried is the unsustainable pattern of over consumerism.

The unequal distribution effects of development projects discussed previously, such as gross violations of human rights, biodiversity loss, displacement, illegal acquisition of land and conflicts over use of resources, have triggered grave conflicts among interest groups and threatened the very existence of marginalized indigenous communities. Although testimonials exist, development pathways need to be increasingly questioned at all scales especially since means of operationalizing them are not restricted to jurisdiction. Law and policy are moulded and the marriage of the state and the corporations fuel unabated extraction from the powerless. This presses towards an urgent need to think about alternative forms of development which are more conversant with everyone's perception of well-being. Fortunately, people's tribunals, social activists, academicians, writers and artists along with indigenous people continue to come together to oppose the conventional economic development model and raise the voice of alternative forms of worthwhile, sustainable development.

References

Agarwal, N. and Asher, M. (2010) La Farce? A report on Lafarge's proposed greenfield project. http://www.himdhara.org/wp-content/uploads/2012/03/Lafarge-Investigation-Report_ERAC.pdf.

Alam, T. Md S. and Lasker, S. (2012) Economic Prospects as well as Human Rights Violation at Shrimp Farming: A Study Based in South West Coastal Region of Bangladesh. *Journal of Humanities and Social Science* 11.

Bandyopadhyaya, J. and Shiva, V. (1987) The Chipko Movement. Seminar 338, February.

Dharmadhikary, S. (2008) Mountains of Concrete: Dam Building in the Himalayas (No. id: 1815).

Drydyk, J. (2011) Development Ethics. In *Encyclopedia of Global Justice*. Springer, Netherlands, 251–254.

D Souza, R., Mukhopadhyay, P. and Kothari, A. (1998) Re-evaluating Multi-purpose River Valley Projects: A Case Study of Hirakud, Ukai and IGNP. *Economic and Political Weekly* 297–302.

Eckersley, R. (1992) *Environmentalism and Political Theory: Toward an Ecocentric Approach*. SUNY Press, Albany.

Government of Sri Lanka (2014) *Country Programme Framework*. http://aeb.gov.lk/web/attachments/article/299/SRL_CPF2014-17_Master_Document_FINAL.pdf. Accessed 20 May 2016.

Guha, R. (2006) *How Much Should a Person Consume? Environmentalism in India and the United States*. University of California Press, Berkeley.

Hill, D. (2006) The Politics of Water in South Asia. *Transforming Cultures eJournal* 1(2).

Himdhara (2016) Mapping Environmental Conflicts in Himachal Pradesh. www.himdhara.org/2016/01/21/mapping-environmental-conflicts-in-himachal-pradesh/. Accessed 23 May 2016.

Kumar, R. (2009) Ship Dismantling: A Status Report on South Asia. *Euroconsult Mott MacDonald and WWF-India*. http://www.shipbreakingplatform.org/shipbrea_wp2011/wp-content/uploads/2013/07/ship_dismantling_en.pdf.

Kumar, K. (2014) The Sacred Mountain: Confronting Global Capital at Niyamgiri. *Geoforum* 54: 196–206.

Motilal, S. and Nanda, B. (2006) *Human Rights, Gender and Environment*. Allied Publishers, New Delhi.

Norton, B. (1999) Ecology and Opportunity: Intergenerational Equity and Sustainable Options. In Dobson, A. ed., *Fairness and Futurity: Essays on Environmental Sustainability and Social Justice*. Oxford University Press, Oxford, 118–150.

Norton, B. (2002) Sustainability, Human Welfare and Ecosystem Health. *Environmental Values* 1(2): 97–111.

Penz, P., Drydyk, J. and Bose, P.S. (2011) *Displacement by Development: Ethics, Rights and Responsibilities*. Cambridge University Press, Cambridge.

Roy, A. (1999) The Greater Common Good. Cover Essay. *Frontline* 16(11). http://web.cecs.pdx.edu/~sheard/course/Design&Society/Readings/Narmada/greatercommongood.pdf.

Sahu, G. (2008) Mining in the Niyamgiri Hills and Tribal Rights. *Economic and Political Weekly*: 19–21.

Shiva, V. (2008) *Soil Not Oil: Environmental Justice in an Age of Climate Crisis*. Cambridge, Massachusetts: South End Press. https://www.amherst.edu/media/view/184096/original/Soil-Not-Oil-Article-and-questions.pdf.

Temper, L., del Bene, D. and Martinez-Alier, J. (2015) Mapping the Frontiers and Front Lines of Global Environmental Justice: The EJAtlas. *Journal of Political Ecology* 22: 255–278.

Withanage, H. (2015) Don't Nuke Sri Lanka Please! (blog). Accessed 15 May 2016.

The World Bank (2013) Expanding the Power of Tarbela Dam, 6 February.

The World Bank, World Development Indicators (2014) Population Density. http://data.worldbank.org/indicator/EN.POP.DNST. Accessed 12 June 2017.

34

East Asia

Challenges to political rights

Benedict S. B. Chan

When we talk about development in East Asia, probably the first thing that comes to mind is economic growth. After World War II, the first East Asian region with seemingly miraculous economic growth was Japan, followed by the "Four Asian Tigers" (Hong Kong, Singapore, South Korea, and Taiwan), and now Mainland China. Nevertheless, development cannot be reduced solely to economic growth, and there are other issues related to the ethics of development in East Asia, such as equality and justice, environmental sustainability, human rights, and many others. Among these issues, this chapter focuses on the human rights debate in East Asia. Although people also discuss other development issues in East Asia, such as Confucian perspectives of social justice (e.g., Chan 2008) and the Dao (Tao) in environmental sustainability (e.g., Cheng 1986), the human rights debate is the most prominent example of development ethics in East Asia and attracts the most attention in the world.

East Asia has discussed the concepts of rights since the end of the nineteenth century (Angle 2002; Svensson 2002), but the most famous debate is the Asian values debate. The Asian values debate has stimulated political theorists and philosophers to have further debates on the cultural differences between the East and the West. In these debates, people share the view that some human rights are only "Western values". Particularly, they argue that authoritarianism and meritocracy are East Asian values and so political rights, such as political freedom and democratic rights, are not human rights in East Asian contexts.

In my 'minimal account of human rights' I argue against these East Asian challenges to human rights (Chan 2011, 2014, 2015). This ongoing project is related to ideas from Sen and Nussbaum, especially Sen's reply to the Asian values debate, and their ideas on dignity, capability, and human rights. For the rest of this chapter, I first summarize the Asian values debate and the East Asian challenge to human rights from Daniel Bell in detail. I then explain how the minimal account of human rights can reply to these challenges to political rights.

In this chapter, I use Bell's manipulative definition of "East Asia," which includes mainland China, Hong Kong, Taiwan, South Korea, Japan, and Singapore, even though the latter is located in Southeast Asia (Bell 2006a, 6n13; see also Langlois 2001; Wan 2008). Also, due to space restrictions on the chapter, I discuss only Confucianism as a prominent expression of East Asian cultures.

DOI: 10.4324/9781315626796-43

The Asian values debate and the East Asian challenge to human rights

The Asian values debate was one of the most famous human rights debates in the world in the early 1990s. Although it has become less popular after the economic crisis in 1998, similar ideas still exist in East Asia because the economy in China is growing rapidly and continuously. The Asian values debate starts with economic issues, but the major controversy is about the claim that some political rights violate East Asian values. Some politicians, such as Singapore's former Prime Minister Lee Kuan Yew and Malaysia's former Prime Minister Mahathir Mohamad, argued that East Asians should abandon some Western values (especially political freedom and democracy) because these values undermine the values and cultures in East Asia (Zakaria 1994).

Although the Asian values debate does not aim to construct any philosophical argument, it has caused many scholars to think about the East–West cultural differences on human rights (Bell 2006b, 266). Here I focus particularly on the East Asian challenge from Bell on political rights. Bell believes that not only should we discuss East Asian values, but we should also take these values seriously. This assertion invites us to ask how we ought to go about taking East Asian values seriously. By way of an answer, Bell elaborates that human rights 'are universal because they apply in all cultural contexts', but that the controversial part of this idea 'is [specifying] the content of universal human rights. Which rights are fundamental, universally valid human rights, and which ones are locally valid, "peripheral" rights?' (Bell 1999, 849). To address this issue, Bell argues that cultural factors are so important that rights can be considered universal only when they are accepted in all cultures, or at least most major cultures, in the world. If East Asian cultures really have a separate set of values or fundamental human goods, then the list of rights in East Asia will likely be different as well. Recognition of cultural difference in this manner offers us a way to take East Asian values seriously.

According to Bell, some human rights are universal in this sense. His list of universal human rights includes 'prohibitions against slavery, genocide, murder, torture, prolonged arbitrary detention, and systematic racial discrimination' (i.e., security rights) and he thinks that they are 'what Michael Walzer terms the "minimal and universal code"' (Bell 2006a, 79). He also discusses whether East Asian cultures can extend the list of human rights, especially some economic, social, and cultural rights (Bell 2000, 95–103; 2006a, 76–78; see also Chan 2015). On the other hand, Bell also thinks that some items, such as political freedom or democratic practices (i.e., political rights), are not universal. This is his challenge to political rights in East Asia – which are the focus of this chapter.

Even though the reasoning for such a challenge is mainly based on ideas from Bell, it is also common reasoning among scholars who are against political rights in East Asia; the only difference is that they usually focus on different contexts of East Asian cultures. For example, Jiang (2011) also has a similar reasoning but he focuses more on the context of the political Confucian tradition (Xunzi, Han Confucians, etc.) and uses that tradition to argue against the idea from Chang et al. ([1958] 1988) that Chinese culture and democracy are compatible.

A minimal account of human rights

To reply to these human rights debates in East Asia, I have examined the contexts of East Asian cultures and I provide an argument for justification. Due to the limit on length, here I only briefly sketch the major argument. Readers can read my other writings for further details (Chan 2011, 2014).

Bell and others argue that security rights are universal while political rights are not, because some aspects of political rights conflict with Confucianism. Nevertheless, some aspects of security rights conflict with Confucianism as well. For example, in East Asian history, torture and slavery were once legalized and were a part of the cultural tradition. Nevertheless, one may also argue that some Confucians opposed torture and slavery. In short, it is possible to find some contexts in Confucianism for the items in security rights and some other contexts against those items (Chan 2011, 65–75; 2014, 574–578). Political rights also face a comparable situation, i.e., some contexts in Confucianism support authoritarianism and tyranny while some other contexts oppose them. Sen also discusses a similar reasoning in his reply to the Asian values debate. In addition to his argument that economic growth and political freedom do not necessarily conflict (Sen 1997, 33–34; 1999, 15), Sen quotes *The Analects* 14:3 and 14:22 and argues that Confucius is against tyrants (Sen 1997, 36; Confucius 1992, 133, 141). For another example, in *Mencius* 1B8 and 7B14, Mencius says that killing a tyrant is morally acceptable and the people are always more important than the ruler (Mencius 2003, 43, 315). Fung believes that these ideas from Mencius 'have exercised a tremendous influence in Chinese history, even as late as the revolution of 1911, which led to the establishment of the Chinese Republic' (Fung 1948, 74). As Gasper mentions, this is also related to how the founding father of the Republic of China, Sun Yat-Sen, describes the development of China (Gasper 2004, 33). All these points show that it is problematic to claim that some rights are not universal simply because they conflict with some contexts in Confucianism (Chan 2014, 568–574).

Why are security rights universal? Bell suggests that it is because they are 'minimal and universal codes' ('minimal values', in short). Bell only mentions that this is an idea from Walzer and he does not elaborate further. By examining ideas from Walzer, we realize that minimal values are a minimal threshold of human life that no one should be allowed to sink below (Chan 2014, 579; see also Walzer 1987, 21–24; 1994, 6). For example, Walzer mentions that 'against the tyrants' is one such minimal value shared by both Western and Chinese cultures (Walzer 1994, 59–61). Some common international standards, such as protecting a dignified life, can easily fit into this idea of minimal threshold of human life. I call them 'essential necessities of dignity'. There are at least two advantages to claiming that essential necessities of dignity are minimal thresholds of human life. First, dignity as a value is widely accepted in international documents (such as *Universal Declaration of Human Rights*) and in many cultures, including Confucianism. For example, Bloom argues that based on the ideas in *The Analects* 4:5 and *Mencius* 6A10, 16 & 17, the Confucian notion of "nobility of heaven" is essentially an ancient Chinese version of dignity (Confucius 1992, 28–29; Bloom 1999, 104–111; Mencius 2003, 252–255, 258–261. For further discussion, see Ni 2014). This Confucian concept of dignity is also based on major Confucian thought. From Mencius to Song-Ming and Contemporary Confucians, they all believe that we should develop our compassion and other moral senses. For example, in *Mencius* 2A6, Mencius argues that we should develop our four beginnings to the four virtues and apply that to the world (Mencius 2003, 73; see also Chang et al. [1958] 1988). This argument shows that dignity is not only a Western concept. Second, aspects of security rights and political rights are usually considered essential necessities for a dignified life. For example, if a person is tortured by other people or is a slave of other people, it is harder to claim that this person is still living in a dignified life. Similarly, if a person does not have freedom of speech or the freedom to vote, it is harder to claim that this person has a dignified life as well (Chan 2014, 581–585).

This reasoning echoes ideas from Sen and Nussbaum on human rights, cultural diversity, and the Asian values debate (Nussbaum 1997, 2000, 2011; Sen 1997, 1999, 2004). As mentioned before, Sen has a reply to the Asian values debate. Although Nussbaum does not discuss the Asian values debate as much as Sen, she does discuss the cultural diversity issue in human rights debates more generally (e.g., Nussbaum 2000, 34–110; 2011, 101–122). Nussbaum also discusses the importance of dignity. She argues that her capability approach 'focuses on the protection of areas of freedom so central that their removal makes a life not worthy of human dignity'

(Nussbaum 2011, 31). She also writes: 'What does a life worthy of human dignity require? At a bare minimum, an ample threshold level of ten Central Capabilities is required' (Nussbaum 2011, 32). Nussbaum applies these ideas in her account of human rights and these ideas are parallel to my analysis in this section. The Confucian notion of dignity mentioned above is just like a further interpretation of why some central capabilities, such as emotion, practical reason, and affiliation are so important in East Asia. As I have also discussed previously, human rights are minimal moral demands, which is a minimal threshold of human life that no one should be allowed to sink below. In other words, they are essential necessities of dignity. In this sense, this is a moral foundation of the universality of human rights.

This reasoning can be summarized by the following argument:

(1) X is a human right if X is a minimal value.
(2) X is a minimal value if X is an essential necessity of dignity.
(3) Items in security rights and political rights are essential necessities of dignity.
(4) Therefore, security rights and political rights are human rights.

This argument is a valid argument and it reveals a jointly sufficient condition for rights to X being human rights. Also, this argument cannot be considered as a 'Western' argument. Even Walzer and Bell agree that minimal values are important and 'close to the bone' (Walzer 1994, 6). Although it is hard to define dignity precisely, dignity is not just a Western concept and there is also a Confucian notion of dignity. Moreover, my argument is not about the conflict between the East and the West. It is only about the conflict within East Asian cultures. I simply suggest a way to select some East Asian contexts over others. In a word, this is not a Western argument whatsoever. Therefore, I conclude that this argument is a successful reply to the East Asian challenge to human rights and the Asian values debate.

Conclusion and further research

In this chapter I have discussed a prominent issue in development ethics in East Asia: the human rights debate. At the beginning of this chapter, I described the contents of the Asian values debate and the East Asian challenge to human rights. I then discussed how one may reply to them by developing a normative account based on minimal values. This account shows that despite what some East Asian scholars believe, political rights are still important in East Asia. There are at least two future research directions to develop this minimal account further. The comparison of Aristotelian and Confucianism is a hot topic in the field of East–West comparative philosophy (e.g., Yu 2007). Since this minimal account is closely related to concepts such as dignity or even capabilities, one may discuss this account based on the comparison between Confucianism and Aristotelian, such as Nussbaum's early notion of capabilities (see Nussbaum 1988). Another possible research endeavor is that in addition to the ideas from Sen and Nussbaum, there are many discussions on the capability approach to human rights (e.g., Elson et al. 2014). One may develop a complete theory of human rights based on the capability approach and the minimal account, and use it to contribute to the East–West discourses. I look forward to seeing further research on this topic in the future.

References

Angle, S. (2002) *Human Rights and Chinese Thought: A Cross-Cultural Inquiry*. Cambridge University Press, New York.

Bell, D. (1999) Which Rights Are Universal? *Political Theory* 27(6): 849–856.

Bell, D. (2000) *East Meets West: Human Rights and Democracy in East Asia*. Princeton University Press, Princeton.

Bell, D. (2006a) *Beyond Liberal Democracy: Political Thinking for an East Asian Context*. Princeton University Press, Princeton.

Bell, D. (2006b) East Asia and the West: The Impact of Confucianism on Anglo-American Political Theory. In Dryzek, J., Bonnie Honig, B. and Phillips, A. eds., *Oxford Handbook of Political Theory*. Oxford University Press, Oxford, 262–280.

Bloom, I. (1999) Mencius and Human Rights. In de Bary, W. and Tu, W. eds., *Confucianism and Human Rights*. Columbia University Press, New York, 94–116.

Chan, B.S.B. (2011) *An East and West Debate on Human Rights,* PhD Dissertation, University of Maryland, College Park.

Chan, B.S.B. (2014) A Human Rights Debate on Physical Security, Political Liberty, and the Confucian Tradition. *Dao: A Journal of Comparative Philosophy* 13(4): 567–588.

Chan, B.S.B. (2015) Do Economic Rights Conflict with Political Rights? – An East and West Cultural Debate. In Creller, A. ed., *Conflict and Harmony in Comparative Philosophy*. Cambridge Scholars Publishing, New Castle, 139–147.

Chan, J. (2008) Is There a Confucian Perspective on Social Justice?. In Shogimen, T. and Nederman, C. eds., *Western Political Thought in Dialogue with Asia*. Rowman & Littlefield, Lanham, 261–277.

Chang, C., Hsieh, Y., Hsu, F., Mou, C. and T'ang, C. ([1958] 1988) A Manifesto on the Reappraisal of Chinese Culture. In T'ang, C. ed., *Essays on Chinese Philosophy and Culture*. Student Book Co., Ltd, Taiwan, 492–562.

Cheng, C. (1986) On the Environmental Ethics of the Tao and the ch'I. *Environmental Ethics* 8(4): 351–370.

Confucius (1992) *The Analects* trans. Lau, D.C. The Chinese University Press, Hong Kong.

Elson, D., Fukuda-Parr, S. and Vizard, P. eds. (2014) *Human Rights and the Capabilities Approach: An Interdisciplinary Dialogue*. Routledge, New York.

Fung, Y. (1948) *A Short History of Chinese Philosophy*. The Free Press, New York.

Gasper, D. (2004) *The Ethics of Development: From Economism to Human Development*. Edinburgh University Press, Edinburgh.

Jiang, Q. (2011) From Mind Confucianism to Political Confucianism. In Fan, R. ed., *The Renaissance of Confucianism in Contemporary China*. Springer, New York, 18–32.

Langlois, A. (2001) *The Politics of Justice and Human Rights*. Cambridge University Press, New York.

Mencius (2003) *Mencius*. trans. La, D.C. The Chinese University Press, Hong Kong.

Ni, P. (2014) Seek and You Will Find It; Let Go and You Will Lose It: Exploring a Confucian Approach to Human Dignity. *Dao: A Journal of Comparative Philosophy* 13(2): 173–198.

Nussbaum, M. (1988) Nature, Functioning and Capability: Aristotle on Political Distribution. *Oxford Studies in Ancient Philosophy* (Supplementary Volume 6): 145–184.

Nussbaum, M. (1997) Capabilities and Human Rights. *Fordham Law Review* 66(2): 273–300.

Nussbaum, M. (2000) *Women and Human Development: The Capabilities Approach*. Cambridge University Press, New York.

Nussbaum, M. (2011) *Creating Capabilities: The Human Development Approach*. Belknap Press of Harvard University Press, Cambridge, MA.

Sen, A. (1997) Human Rights and Asian Values. *The New Republic* 14(21): 33–40.

Sen, A. (1999) *Development as Freedom*. Knopf, New York.

Sen, A. (2004) Elements of a Theory of Human Rights. *Philosophy and Public Affairs* 32(4): 315–356.

Svensson, M. (2002) *Debating Human Rights in China: A Conceptual and Political History*. Rowman & Littlefield, Lanham.

Walzer, M. (1987) *Interpretation and Social Criticism: The Tanner Lectures on Human Values 1985*. Harvard University Press, Cambridge, MA.

Walzer, M. (1994) *Thick and Thin: Moral Argument at Home and Abroad*. University of Notre Dame Press, Notre Dame, IN.

Wan, M. (2008) *The Political Economy of East Asia*. CQ Press, Washington, DC.

Yu, J. (2007) *The Ethics of Confucius and Aristotle*. Routledge, New York.

Zakaria, F. (1994) Culture Is Destiny: A Conversation with Lee Kuan Yew. *Foreign Affairs* 73(2): 109–126.

35

Middle East and North Africa

The Arab Spring as a political expression of ethical issues

Alain Piveteau and Eric Rougier

In this chapter we identify various ethical issues raised by decades of socio-economic transformation in the Middle East and North Africa (MENA) region. We describe the region's productive-distributive system and evaluate it according to an ethical or normative political criterion: the capacity of the system to provide real socio-economic opportunities – corresponding to all levels of qualifications, personal aspirations, and projects – to a broad range of the population, not just the politically connected and urban groups. Although national variations exist and are described, a fairly similar productive-distributive pattern, as well as the political equilibrium underlying and stabilizing it, is observed everywhere in the region. This pattern must be analyzed from the point of view of the interest of the majority of the population which only marginally benefits from it.

The Arab world (despite its name, which tends to reduce the cultural and linguistic diversity of the region) shows high levels of heterogeneity from a socio-economic perspective. Rauch and Kostyshak (2009) distinguish three Arab worlds: the Arab-speaking sub-Saharan Africa, the fuel-endowed, and the Arab Mediterranean countries. They note that all three groups are well-known for poor socio-economic performance, albeit income per capita can be high for some of them. Although this division is meaningful, we will retain two groups, focusing mainly on the Arab Mediterranean (Algeria, Morocco, Tunisia, Egypt, Jordan, Palestine, Lebanon, and Syria), considering the Gulf oil-endowed countries (Saudi Arabia, Oman, the Qatar, Barhain, and the UAEs) only marginally in this chapter. Although the Gulf countries face common economic concerns with the Arab Mediterranean group, they are all labour importers and dispose of massive fiscal resources to sustain the livelihoods of their limited population. As such, they face ethical issues radically different from those of the resource-poor, labour-exporting countries of the Arab Mediterranean region. (We will not consider such sub-Saharan countries as Mauritania, Sudan, or Somalia that were considered by Rauch and Kostyshak (2009).)

For MENA countries, ethical issues related to economic development came to light during the social movements that erupted in the region since 2011, mainly affecting labour-intensive and resource-poor countries. These movements put the demands for political transparency and socio-economic inclusion on an equal footing. Thus the political and economic balance which had prevailed for decades, at the cost of a systematic repression of discontent, suddenly crumbled at the end of the 2000s.

DOI: 10.4324/9781315626796-44

The Arab Springs were national crises that revealed or pushed to their climax issues that have existed for a long time but which were previously mitigated by a variety of instruments, including repression, recovery, alliances, and redistribution (Bayart 2014). Although there may have been a regional dynamic such as a snowball or domino effect, there was no regional mechanism behind it; rather, it was national mechanisms that led to this crisis (and previous ones). Our goal in this chapter is therefore to unveil the associated ethical issues, highly typical to the region, which have emerged regularly for decades in various forms of protest.

Inequality issues

Rauch and Kostyshak (2009) compared a series of socio-economic indicators for the two Arab worlds, Mediterranean and fuel-endowed, versus their Latin American and Southern European counterparts. They concluded that life expectancies and average years of education in the Arab fuel-endowed and in the Arab Mediterranean economies were respectively higher than in the comparison country groups and in the remainder of the non-Arab world in the late 2000s, as these two regions had caught up with Latin America and Southern Europe within two decades. Likewise, in the MENA region, official levels of income inequality were generally low with respect to other developing regions' standards. Still, they probably underestimated the real inequalities felt by the population.

Alvaredo and Piketty (2014) recently warned that data sources at the national level were insufficient to derive reliable estimates of top income shares and consequently of the profile of the entire income distribution, as top income tended to be underestimated when using household survey analysis alone. They complained that reliable fiscal sources which could allow comparing the region with other emerging or developed countries were lacking in most of the region. The political stake attached to distributional issues is huge in the MENA region. As an illustration, only two countries in the zone (Morocco and Tunisia) displayed GINI on the World Bank (WB) World Development Indicators (WDI) site. The singularity of the region with respect to the politically sensitive data reflecting the reality of income inequality bred the perceptions of uneven economic systems that may have prompted social unrest in 2011.

Alvaredo and Piketty (2014) also pointed to extremely large income inequality for the Middle East, as a whole, driven by large cross-country income heterogeneity. According to their estimates, the share of regional income accruing to the top 10% of income receivers was currently 55%, with the presumption that it might rise to 60% under realistic assumptions, far higher than in the United States (48%) and Western Europe (36%), and like that of the highly unequal South African region (54%). The top 1% share might even exceed 25% (against 20% in the United States, 11% in Western Europe, and 17% in South Africa). High concentrations of ownership of large companies' capital in the hands of government officials, their families, and politically connected families were also documented for MENA countries (Omet 2005). According to other estimates using Forbes data on the net worth of billionaires across the world, a few billionaires control a significantly greater share of national wealth than those of other developing and developed regions, with a few individual families controlling respectively 30% and 24% of GDP in Lebanon and Egypt (Ianchovichina 2015).

Diwan et al. (2016) also pointed to a big issue having potentially raised discontent. By using a unique dataset for all 22 Arab countries, he showed that, compared to other regions, the Arab region featured relatively low returns of education. These low returns might be crucial drivers of discontent as evidenced by the fact that revolt and social unrest increase with the share of educated unemployed young adults in the population, as found by Campante and Chor (2012). Skill mismatch is a crucial challenge for all labour-rich MENA countries, since the pace of structural transformation is too slow to create modern job opportunities for their young and educated work force (Rougier 2016), and for the latter to transform into a driver of future growth (Nicet-Chenaf and Rougier 2016).

In fact, inequality is multidimensional in the region, and some dimensions are less visible than others as they undermine the individual and collective capacity to improve their situation (United Nations and League of Arab States 2013). By using data on consumption expenditures and income from 12 Arab countries' harmonized household surveys, Hassine (2015) reconstituted social and spatial inequality and found moderate aggregate inequality hiding strong spatial inequality and metropolitan divide. Her estimations illustrate the great diversity of inequality across the countries hit by the Arab Spring, with some countries being poor and relatively equal (Egypt), while some others feature medium income and inequality (Syria) or higher income and inequality (Tunisia). Interregional and rural–urban divides are pointed out as critical challenges to social cohesion, as was obvious when social unrest started in remote areas of various countries of the region. Hassine (2015) points to inequality in household endowment in human capital per head between urban and rural areas to explain growing welfare gaps for poor and middle-income households. Moreover, urban labour markets tended to reward education more than their rural counterparts. Numerous studies have also revealed intergenerational inequalities in the distribution of the benefits of growth between insiders (public sector employees, politically connected firms) and outsiders (Hibou 2011).

These disappointing outcomes result from a succession of development strategies that could not support the productive diversification and upgrading that could have provided the growing young and educated population with real opportunities of economic inclusion.

Intransigence of authoritarian-redistributive social contracts

Describing social contracts in the MENA region as 'authoritarian-redistributive', Rougier (2016) has shown how the slowness of economic modernization has hindered any evolution towards more democracy and inclusion in markets for the population. The notion of authoritarian-redistributive social contract is close to the idea of an 'authoritarian bargain' first coined by Desai et al. (2009) and used by Diwan (2012) to describe the political economy typical of the Arab region.

Basically, authoritarian-redistributive bargains all consist of trading political liberties away for collective stability and individual security, with personalized redistribution of assets. In most MENA countries the exercise of power has tended to be split between the official government and non-official groups who effectively govern, like the Makhzen in Morocco or the Ben Ali or Mubarak clans in pre-revolution Tunisia and Egypt. Under this authoritarian-redistributive social contract, clientelist political systems, promoted by heavy political control over the economy and the personalized distribution of economic advantages, have facilitated patterns of crony capitalism in which a firm's position with respect to political power determines its accumulation capacities. North et al. (2009) analyzed the foundations of these patterns as personalized rules of the game, repression of organizational innovation and limitation of the access to political and economic resources.

Although small institutional changes occurred during the last decades and 'bargains' were denounced during the Arab Spring, the risk of persistence of deep structures is still high as analyzed by Diwan (2012). In the context of increased vulnerability for the largest share of the population, which is jobless or under-employed, the patron–client pattern remains a popular base since it provides security to a large population. Acemoglu and Robinson (2012) identified similar patterns in various historical contexts as 'the iron law of oligarchy'; they explained these by the persistence of the rent extraction structures based on unequal distribution of resources, although official rules have been changed towards apparently more inclusive ones.

Throughout the region, the sustainability of authoritarianism not only relied on the use of coercive force by governments: it was also based on the consent of the different parties with common interests in the preservation of the political stability (Hibou 2006). The system started to erupt when one of the parties perceived a risk of diminishing the benefits it derived from the existing balance or an increase in the economic or political costs associated with it. As symbolized by Hirschman's Tunnel (Ray 2010), unequal opportunities raising deep relative frustration in the MENA region's population may have prompted this collective rejection.

An interesting symptom of ethical issues raised by the MENA pattern of economic development is related to the middle class. The middle class is supposed to increase as a result of increased inclusion in the developing economy, and to bring about increased demand for public goods like health, education, and infrastructure, transparent and efficient economic and political governance, as these various elements should, in turn, improve the capacity of socio-economic inclusion of the whole politico-economic system (Clément and Rougier 2015). According to recent estimates by Dang and Ianchovichina (2016), MENA countries' middle classes experienced various patterns of evolution during the 2000s: they have tended to collapse in Egypt and Yemen while stagnating in Jordan and increasing in Tunisia and Syria. During the same period, middle class discontent increased, notably with respect to perceived deterioration of living standards driven by the inferior quality of public services, high unemployment, and governance issues (Arampatzi et al. 2015).

Critical divisions in terms of political and social preferences therefore emerged throughout the region, disrupting the consensus politics generally prompted by middle-class expansion (Easterly 2001). According to Diwan (2012), the MENA middle classes have reversed their historic alliance with political elites because they have had to bear the cost of changing public policies over the past two decades. Somehow the Islamist parties have been instrumentalized by critical parts of the middle classes, against the elites, to communicate their dissatisfaction (Diwan 2012; Bayart 2014), as has been frequent in most Muslim countries over the course of history (Platteau 2011).

A role for development ethics in social and political transformations

Like previous protest moments, the Arab Spring expressed the deep contradictions of contemporary capitalism in the MENA region. Typically, the political economy of each nation has four main dimensions (although their combination is specific to each national history): an authoritarian social contract combining coercion and redistribution; a civil society organized through its relationship to the state; omnipresence of a national ideal; and the implementation of neo-liberal economic programs. Each of these dimensions places the state at the center of an authoritarian situation whose economic base relies on the straddling of positions of power and accumulation by a homogeneous dominant class (Bayart 2014). When economic prosperity is absent and the population becomes aware of the dearth of economic opportunities, social frustration and discontent increase and must be resolved by redistribution and/or repression.

Economic liberalization, privatization, and decentralization in the 1980s did not fundamentally change this reality. A redeployment of state powers and means of action took place under the cover of extra-state entities (large private companies, family holdings agencies, foundations, consultancies, etc.) and new technical devices. Still, in no case was there a state withdrawal (Catusse 2009; Hibou 1998). The deep state (Bayart 2014) has been maintained as a central agent of the economy and social regulation. Concerned about the presumed rules of globalization, the state has attempted to expel public policy choices from political debate by entrusting them to managerial approaches. The analysis by Piveteau and Rougier (2011) of the role of international experts and consultancies in the case of Morocco provides a good illustration of this trend. For some observers, though, such a trend towards depoliticization of economic policies (Catusse 2009) is part of a general deterioration in the quality of the region's political systems (United Nations 2014). These trends may have fed the population a feeling of dispossession of collective choices. The ethical dimensions, of such dispossession in relation to self and to others, to the social contract and to the environment, should not be underestimated.

Despite these trends, the stability of the state, at the same time strong and weak, has remained decisive in the economic, political, and social transformations of the region over the last three decades. Certain common practices of political power were, of course, denounced by the protest movements from the end of 2010 to the beginning of 2011. Starting with disadvantaged rural areas or urban middle class, as was the case in Egypt, and initially mobilizing young populations, the popular protest denounced injustice and indignity in support of very concrete political demands, such as 'improved access to public services, employment, subsidies, improved infrastructure' (Diaz Pedregal 2015, 437). In addition to the development model itself, protests targeted its inability to keep the promise of education and of jobs that is at the heart of the social contract and is mandated in most national constitutions in the region (Diaz Pedregal 2015, 432). More concretely, they protested the daily practices of power that subjected them to inequality and domination in their own realities and experiences (Bono et al. 2015).

Inequality as a social concern, which was standardly ignored during the neoliberal turn of the 1980s and 1990s (op. cit., 8), therefore regained its importance and policy relevance in the context of the Arab Spring, and its reactivation in the revolutionary moments (Hibou 2011) highlighted the crucial dimension of ethics denied by economic and political elites. Ethically, the exercise of power must be justifiable to those over whom it is exercised, through public reasoning; otherwise it lacks legitimacy. In the Arab Spring, ethical questioning and public reasoning about states and societies were once again activated. Local powers were then perceived in their corruptive and nepotic dimensions and suddenly lost their legitimacy. New feminist demands also reached the Maghreb and the Middle East during the Arab Spring and conquered the political scene (Gillot and Martinez 2016). Gender stereotypes and violence against women were denounced, and gender justice was placed on the development agenda, demanding access to citizenship, equal rights with men, both in public and private spaces, health, work, decision-making power and representation in the family and society.

Our methodological approach focuses on the singularity of each historical situation, even though the size of this chapter does not allow fully describing them. Rather than a deep normative analysis (Sen 1988), we have chosen to focus on particular political and ethical judgments that are appropriate to the political economy of each country. Beyond the common traits of different national capitalist political economies, the diversity of the long-term national processes of political construction are essential. Recent studies from all fields of social sciences show that the processes of construction, stabilization, and rupture do not correspond to the myth of Arab-Muslim exceptionalism, nor to the culturalist view of a curse of authoritarianism in the region. Current scenarios ranging from conservative responses to authoritarian restorations or attempts at conservative modernization open few new opportunities for social transformation, when they do not put countries at risk of sinking into civil war (Bayart 2014). Therefore development ethics should focus critically on how the old authoritarian-redistributive models were constructed and how consent for them was manufactured, based on people's actual values; then it can be shown how those models have actually served those values poorly and need to be transformed accordingly in each national community. The goal of finding a new model of economic development carrying a truth or a justice that could be imposed without doing violence to that social world and its structures of power is illusory and misguided.

References

Acemoglu, D. and Robinson, J.A. (2012) *Why Nations Fail? The Origins of Power Prosperity and Poverty*. Profile Books, New York.

Alvaredo, F. and Piketty, T. (2014) Measuring Top Incomes and Inequality in the Middle East: Data Limitations and Illustration with the Case of Egypt. *ERF working Paper N°382* Economic Research Forum.

Arampatzi, E., Burger, M.J., Ianchovichina, E. Röhricht, T. and Veenhoven, R. (2015) Unhappy Development: Dissatisfaction with Life on the Eve of the Arab Spring. *World Bank Policy Research Working Paper No. 7488*. The World Bank, Washington, DC.

Bayart, J.F. (2014) Retour sur les Printemps arabes. *Politique africaine* 33: 153–175.

Bono, I., Hibou, B., Meddeb, H. and Tozy, M. (2015) *L'Etat d'Injustice au Maghreb*. Editions Karthala, Paris.

Campante, F.R. and Chor, D. (2012) Why Was the Arab World Poised for Revolution? Schooling, Economic Opportunities, and the Arab Spring. *Journal of Economic Perspectives* 26(2): 167–188.

Catusse, M. (2009) Ambiguous Privatization and the Emerging Social Question. In Pioppi, D., and Guazzone, L. eds., *The Arab State and Neo-liberal Globalization: The Restructuring of State Power in the Middle East*. Ithaca Press, Reading, 185–216.

Clément, M. and Rougier, E. (2015) Émergence et classes moyennes en Asie de l'est: Mesures et enjeux. *Mondes en développement* 169.

Dang, H. and Ianchovichina, E. (2016) Welfare Dynamics with Synthetic Panels: The Case of the Arab World in Transition. *World Bank Policy Research Working Paper No. 7595*. The World Bank, Washington, DC.

Desai, R.J., Olofsgard, A. and Yousef, T.M. (2009) The Logic of Authoritarian Bargains. *Economics and Politics* 21(1): 93–125.

Diaz Pedregal, V. (2015) La crise d'un modèle de développement. In Bono, I., Hibou, B., Meddeb, H. and Tozy, M. eds., *L'Etat d'Injustice au Maghreb*. Editions Karthala, Paris, 429–442.

Diwan, I. (2012) A Rational Framework for the Understanding of the Arab Revolutions, Centre for International Development. *Working Paper N°237*, Harvard University.

Diwan, I., Tzannatos, z. and Ahad, J.A. (2016) Rates of Return to Education in Twenty-two Arab Countries: An Update and Comparison Between MENA and the Rest of the World. *ERF Working Papers 1007* Economic Research Forum, Cairo.

Easterly, W. (2001) The Middle Class Consensus and Economic Development. *Journal of Economic Growth* 6(4): 317–335.

Gillot, G. and Martinez, A. (2016) *Femmes, printemps arabes et revendications citoyennes*. IRD éditions, Paris.

Hassine, N.B. (2015) Economic Inequality in the Arab Region. *World Development* 66: 532–556.

Hibou, B. (1998) Retrait ou redéploiement de l'Etat? *Critique internationale* 1(4): 151–168.

Hibou, B. (2006) *La Force de l'obéissance. Économie politique de la répression en Tunisie*. La Découverte, Paris.

Hibou, B. (2011a) Le mouvement du 20 février, le *makhzen* et l'antipolitique : L'impensé des réformes au Maroc. CERI, Sciences Po Paris.

Hibou, B. (2011b) Tunisie. Économie politique et morale d'un mouvement social. *Politique africaine* 121: 5–22.

Ianchovichina, I. (2015) How Unequal Are Arab Countries?. *Brookings Institution Future Development series*. www.brookings.edu/blog/future-development/2015/02/04/how-unequal-are-arab-countries-2/. Accessed 4 February 2015.

Nicet-Chenaf, D. and Rougier, E. (2016) Is Middle-East and North-Africa Different? A Comparative Analysis of Growth and Structural Change in and Outside MENA. *Middle East Development Journal* 8(2): 177–197.

North, D.C., Wallis, J.J. and Weingast, B.R. (2009) *Violence and Social Order. A Conceptual Framework for Interpreting Human History*. Cambridge University Press, Cambridge.

Omet, G. (2005) Ownership Structures in MENA Countries: Listed Companies, State-Owned, Family Enterprises and Some Policy Implications. MENA Regional Corporate Governance Forum: Advancing the Corporate Governance Agenda in MENA. 14–15 September, 2005. http://www.oecd.org/dataoecd/26/2/35402110.pdf.

Piveteau, A. and Rougier, E. (2011) Le retour en trompe l'œil de la politique industrielle: L'expert, l'État et l'économie politique locale. *Revue Tiers Monde* 208(4): 177–192.

Platteau, J.-P. (2011) Political Instrumentalization of Islam and the Risk of Obscurantist Deadlock. *World Development* 39(2): 243–260.

Rauch, J.E. and Kostyshak, S. (2009) The Three Arab Worlds. *Journal of Economic Perspectives* 23(3): 165–188.

Ray, D. (2010) Uneven Growth: A Framework for Research in Development Economics. *Journal of Economic Perspectives* 24(3): 45–60.

Rougier, E. (2016) Fire in Cairo: Authoritarian-redistributive Social Contracts, Structural Change and the Arab Spring. *World Development* 78(1): 148–171.

Sen, A. (1988) *On Ethics and Economics*. Wiley-Blackwell, Oxford.

United Nations (2014) *Arab Middle Class. Measurement and Role in Driving Change*. Economic and Social Division for Western Asia, Beirut.

United Nations and League of Arab States (2013) Arab Millennium Development Goals Report. Beirut, ESCWA.

36

French-speaking sub-Saharan Africa

From buying and selling loyalty to demanding democracy

Jérôme Ballet, Kouamékan J. M. Koffi, and Alice Kouadio

'Achieving development is not a self-validating absolute goal but a relative good, desirable only with reference to a particular view of the meaning of life' (Goulet 1995, 37). Thus, to enquire about development is to enquire about its purpose. What is it for? Goulet (1995) stresses that this question can be formulated on two levels: the first level involves the direction of development; the second level involves the practical choices that have to be made. Although there is a continued polemic over the direction, there has been a more ready convergence on the practical choices. It is therefore conceivable that an agreement might be reached on how to meet the basic needs of the many rather than the whims of the few.

Here our aim is not to ask what development is for ultimately, or what the practical choices are but to examine the policies that have been put in place in French-speaking sub-Saharan Africa. So our interest lies in the means of development and, more specifically, in the ethical dimension of these means. To cite Goulet (1995, 24): 'In a word, development ethics must become a *means of the means*. [. . .] Ethics must somehow get inside the value dynamisms of the instruments utilized by development agents and itself become a *means of the means*'.

Of course, the means that are put in place must be linked to the final outcome. We need to grasp to what extent the costs of development have been offset by the reduction in costs associated with underdevelopment. This 'mathematics of suffering', an expression used by Goulet (1995, 174), sheds light on the effectiveness of the means in default of their ethics. From this standpoint, we can see that the French-speaking countries in Africa are all at the tail end of the Human Development Index (HDI). This applies in particular to the former colonies of French West Africa (Benin, Burkina Faso, Ivory Coast, Guinea, Mali, Mauritania, Niger, Senegal, Togo), along with the group of former colonies that made up French Equatorial Africa (Central African Republic, Chad). Exceptions include Gabon and Congo-Brazzaville, which are ranked in the middle of the HDI and show all the characteristics of oil-producing countries. This situation, which compares extremely badly with the emerging economies from English-speaking countries in Africa (Botswana, Ghana, Namibia, South Africa, etc.), is an invitation to examine the specificities. Following Goulet (1995), we underline the undesirable maldevelopment that

 DOI: 10.4324/9781315626796-45

characterizes French-speaking sub-Saharan Africa, and that is associated with continued inequality, corruption, and governance disempowering the populations.

A development model inherited from the colonial system

Goulet (1995) identifies four main pathways to development: growth, redistribution, basic human needs, and development from tradition. Similar to many other countries, the French-speaking countries of Africa, once they had gained independence, chose to subscribe to models of growth. We will delineate these models and highlight the precise nature of the key ethical issues for these countries. There is also little doubt that vestiges of the colonial period have survived for a considerable time in these countries, despite their independence, so we will discuss some of these vestiges later in the chapter. The model of growth as applied to French-speaking countries in Africa, along with the ensuing ethical issues, must be interpreted in the light of what has been bequeathed from this period.

The colonial system was a trade economy consisting of four major elements (Grellet 1982; Hugon 1993). Primarily, it featured a political–administrative system. The French administrative system differed significantly from the British system. Whilst the British system was based on indirect rule via the nomination of local leaders from amongst existing chiefs who had no choice but to swear allegiance to the British monarch, the French system was based on direct rule via the nomination of governors from France who were attached to the Ministry of Colonies. The legacy for French-speaking countries in Africa is first and foremost domination by a centralist, omnipotent state. This characteristic also applies to the rules governing public finance (Mahieu 1983). During the preparation of national budgets, a significant share of the capital expenditure budget is politically managed. This financial dichotomy offers discretionary power to heads of state who show no hesitation in instigating cronyism and corruption.

Next up in the workings of the colonial system comes the issue of land. Although the appropriation of land by colonists was minimal, French land laws left their mark on its management. For example, the colonial decree of July 4th, 1935, introduced procedures for bringing land under state ownership in French West Africa. The decree gave all power to state representatives at the expense of rural people (Lavigne Delville et al. 1996). According to a text from 1930, this also happened in Madagascar (Montagne and Ramamonjisoa 2006). In effect, the legislation handed the control of land and natural resources over to a bureaucratic state which ignored local communities. The methods for managing were repressive (Ribot 2001) and led to institutional violence (Ballet et al. 2009).

Colonial policy categorized users in an arbitrary fashion. Ribot (2001) notes that certain inhabitants from urban areas who were considered 'citizens' enjoyed a number of civil rights and were granted licences to exploit forest land. Conversely, those living in rural zones were considered 'natives', and these 'subjects' could only claim subsistence and usufruct rights. When pressure was exerted by conservationists, whole areas of land and whole species could be placed under protection to the immediate detriment of rural populations. At the same time, licences and concessions were being conferred to 'citizens', urban elites, and European businesses. Only fragile 'forest rights' were available to the 'natives' (hunting, gathering, grazing, sacred rituals, etc.). These rights could be removed at any moment: for example, when wooded areas were earmarked for commercial exploitation. Rural populations therefore lived precariously whilst urban populations had the lasting benefits of exploiting natural resources. Changes to this legislation were a long time coming, beginning only in the 1990s, and the post-colonial period was noted for its considerable inertia in the domain of natural resources (Ballet et al. 2009).

Numerous demands to have forests reclassified fell on deaf ears (Collas de Chatelperron 2000). This continued reliance on the former system meant that states could assign land to whomever they chose. In 1934, when France created six villages for the Mossi people (an ethnic group from the Upper Volta) to make up for the lack of workers in their Central West Ivory Coast colony (Ibo 2006), the arrangement was maintained after independence. Additional strong incentives were put in place to increase the number of migratory workers so that the production of coffee and cocoa could be intensified. This approach, common to both the colony and the independent state, was unpropitious for the traditional usage/access rights of indigenous populations and led to forest areas being damaged (Ballet et al. 2009).

Alongside the omnipotent state and bureaucratic land control sits a third feature of the colonial system: the enforcement of a dominant merchant capital model. A poll tax and crop exports were intrinsic to the colonial system. After independence, this feature helped maintain the cash crop economy, which largely relied on the export of primary commodities (plantation economy). The cash crop economy is also inextricably entwined with the rentier state which sets aside its resources for export earnings. Fundamental to this system are the corporations and their subsidiaries that held a monopoly on external trade during the period of colonization. These were replaced by publicly owned and semi-public companies post-independence. The omnipotence of the state is not only on the governing side; independence also brings an economic side. The independent state adopts what is referred to as 'politics of the belly' (Bayart 1989), an even more one-sided state capitalism which clears the way for state representatives to readily profit from their political status by using public finance regulations to access *ad libitum* investment opportunities in companies.

Finally, the fourth feature of the colonial system was the establishment of favourable trade relations between the colonizer and its colonies. Import–export companies, freight companies, and banks had a pivotal role to play in this arrangement (Capet 1958). The privileged positions persisted during the first two decades after independence (1960–1980), and then began to fade. In the grand scheme of things, France carries on as the major supplier for Africa. However, the proportion of exports from France to African countries, including the Maghreb, fell from 8.7% in 1970 to 5.6% in 2006 (Hugon 2007).

Two salient aspects in the model of development

There are two salient aspects in the model of development that was inherited from the colonial period.

Firstly, private investment was positively correlated with public investment (CNUCED 2014) until the beginning of the 1980s. The figures distinctly show the existence of a mechanism for growth and development. But behind this positive phenomenon lies a deep-rooted problem: corruption and intragenerational equity. Because public finance regulations leave room for decision-makers to gain all manner of discretionary powers, public investment also bolsters private investment according to the type of relations that exist between the elites in power and international executives. Moreover, public investment projects were initiated on the back of loans from developed countries, and when these loans were not fully repaid, African countries found themselves with a debt burden. Ultimately, these investments pandered to the needs of national and international elites; there was no trickle-down effect for the general population. Income inequality remained high. The average Gini coefficient of 50% in 1960 became 47% in the 1990s. Even this slight lowering of inequality amongst middle class and poorer citizens did not endure. The coefficient rose again in the 1990s at the expense of the middle class, and poorer citizens lost out (Guénard and Dubois 2001).

Secondly, as African countries are specialized in the production of raw materials, they were able to establish stabilization funds and price support funds. These funds ensured that the population's loyalty could be bought by guaranteeing an income, and that the elites had a means of amassing wealth. The Ivorian CAISTAB, which was set up in 1960 to manage the production of cotton, cocoa, and coffee on a national scale, is an excellent example. It was finally dissolved in 1999, doubtless because of the difficulties in handling the fluctuations in the world prices of raw materials, but also and perhaps especially because it represented access to discretionary resources for the elites in power, hence paving the way for corruption.

This model of development was jolted by the first structural adjustment programmes of the 1980s, but development aid helped keep African countries drip fed in a context where developed countries delayed loosening their grip on former colonies.

Development aid: privileged positions in transition

Is development aid simply a form of social imperialism, as suggested by Samir Amin (1976), or does it really contribute to a country's development? Development aid is also a victim of trends and markets. What stands out in the French-speaking countries of Africa is a dual market: an internal market between governments and populations on the one hand, and an external market between governments and international backers on the other (Mahieu 1994). In this context, the effectiveness, indeed the usefulness, of aid, has been questioned (Cassen 1986; White 1992).

In the specific case of Africa, Koulibaly (1998) notes that from the 1980s onwards, during the period of structural adjustment, not only did gross debt rise by over 100%, but at the same time, public development aid rose by almost 200%. Thus, older loans had not been repaid. Faced with the disappointment and caution of lenders and investors, European governments provided more aid in the form of assistance, which replaced loans. Aid took over from investment. Its share of GDP grew threefold between the 1970s and the 1980s (Cogneau and Mesplé-Somps 1999).

As Koulibaly (1998) points out, when structural adjustment programmes are assessed as having delivered positive effects, they allow governments to justify the need for more aid, and when they are assessed as having delivered negative effects, they allow governments to argue that the level of aid is insufficient. The Samaritans (developed countries) are faced with 'rotten kids' (African countries) who adapt their behaviour so that they can receive as much aid as possible. Governments of African countries have therefore acquired a tendency to adopt policies without worrying about their effectiveness, as long as these policies are clearly visible to international backers. Aid has become impoverishing, and the debt burden is being passed on to future generations.

The special relations that exist between France and its former colonies have largely been responsible for the substitution of development aid for investment in the French-speaking countries of Africa (Golan 1981). These special relations rely heavily on the personal ties between the African elites in power and the French governing elites (Smith and Glaser 1992). These ties were quasi-family until the 1990s (Chafer 2005). Aid from France was not intended to support the poorest countries; rather it was intended to support the most influential of the French-speaking countries in Africa. France, a country in the grip of the Fashoda syndrome (fear of British territorial aspirations since being defeated at Fashoda, Sudan in 1898), used aid as a means to maintain its foothold in Africa (Cumming 2001).

The 1990s saw a clear increase in multilateral aid, which encourages reflection on relations between France and Africa. The new international setting, especially the European setting, has changed France's privileged position with the French-speaking countries of Africa. Indeed, since the 1998 agreement at Saint Malo, competition between France and the UK over the control of

Africa has metamorphosed into cooperation (Chafer and Cumming 2010). This new scenario has not at all led France to abandon its sphere of influence. However, in the absence of any normalization, the new scenario has at least ushered relations into a period of transition. The personal ties between the respective elites have had to keep in step with the different worlds in which they both operate (Chafer 2002). Development aid for Africa nevertheless has a long way to go before it complies with the normative criteria established by Europe. The interests of donor countries remain largely to the fore (Bountagkidis et al. 2015).

Not only have the French-speaking countries in Africa assumed the mantle of the 'rotten kid' to receive aid, but the Samaritans have been guided by their own vested interests. This situation has without doubt contributed to the limited impact of aid on reducing poverty. However, the situation has been deflected, particularly since 1994 (Chafer 2002). France's place in a wider European Union and the lessening of its rivalry with the UK, alongside the collapse of the global economic model and its subsequent devastation of structural adjustment programmes, have probably contributed to a new political model in Africa.

A new model: from buying loyalty to demanding democracy

One of the major ethical issues faced by African nations at the time of their independence was the legitimacy of power. As we have highlighted, the political elites of the French-speaking countries in Africa were caught up in a network of personal ties with France. Development was hence reliant on a dual mechanism for buying loyalty: on the one side was the model whereby France sponsored new African leaders; on the other side was the patron–client model between African governments and its populations. The sponsorship model enables the sponsor (France) to influence the decisions of the beneficiary countries and maintain power over those countries. The patron–client model enables the patron (African government) to buy the political loyalty of its population via material benefits (Kurer 1996). We have already mentioned the role of stabilization funds in guaranteeing income to rural communities. But the patron–client model extends further by way of a redistributive mechanism for earnings gained by the state that are paid in part to urban elites, particularly through public investment and corruption. It is this model which crumbled in the 1990s. The demand for democracy seeped in with the end of the redistributive model (Conac 1993). The route towards democracy in these countries has followed different directions depending on the influence of institutional legacy (Gazibo 2005), the process of demilitarization (Thiriot 1999), and the population's perception of democratic institutions (Babo 2009).

After more than two decades of reforms designed to encourage democratization, it should be noted that many of the French-speaking countries in Africa are struggling to achieve significant progress towards stable democratic institutions (see Guèye 2009). For Lunumba-Kasongo et al. (2005), the individualism advocated by democracy and the collectivist ethos of African countries (clans, tribes, etc.) are incompatible. And it is this incompatibility which explains the sluggish progress of democracy. Yet, this notion does not appear to be robust, as the people of Africa remain massively in favour of democracy (Razafindrakoto and Roubaud 2005).

Conclusion

After independence, the French-speaking countries of Africa were propelled towards a model of development that was greatly influenced by the colonial period. This institutional legacy, which is evidenced by France's continued leverage, has left a trail of political cronyism and corruption. The model, after being undermined in the 1980s, created new aspirations amongst the populations, who were no longer looking for economic development but political freedom and social protection.

However, unlike the beginning of the post-independence era, development objectives are now defined on the international stage. The room for manoeuvre enjoyed by both the former colonizers and the beneficiaries of aid is now determined by these objectives. In these circumstances, the specific characteristics of French-speaking Africa may end up being absorbed by the universality of international objectives. Certain features of the mal-development of the French-speaking sub-Saharan Africa (such as corruption and disempowering governance) should be attenuated, if only France and the governments of those countries agree to let go of their old practices.

References

Amin, S. (1976) Interview. *Africa* 1: 35–37.

Babo, A. (2009) Perceptions du fonctionnement des institutions et démocratie en Côte d'Ivoire, une analyse dans une perspective institutionnaliste. *Journal des sciences sociales* 6: 7–20.

Ballet, J., Koffi, K.J.M., Komena, K.B. (2009) La soutenabilité des ressources forestières en Afrique Subsaharienne francophone: Quels enjeux pour la gestion en commun? *Mondes en développement* 4: 31–46.

Bayart J-F. (1989) *L'État en Afrique. La politique du ventre*. Fayart, Paris.

Bountagkidis, G.K., Fragkos, K.C., Frangos, C.C. (2015) EU Development Aid toward Sub-Saharan Africa: Exploring the Normative Principle. *Social Sciences* 4: 85–116.

Capet, M. (1958) *Traité d'économie tropicale : les économies d'AOF*. Pichon et Durand-Aujas, Paris.

Cassen, R. (1986) *Does Aid Work?* Oxford University Press, Oxford.

Chafer, T. (2002) Franco-African Relations: No Longer So Exceptional? *African Affairs* 101: 3043–3363.

Chafer, T. (2005) Chirac and 'la Françafrique': No Longer a Family Affair. *Modern and Contemporary France* 13(1): 7–23.

Chafer, T. and Cumming, G.D. (2010) La coopération entre la France et le Royaume-Uni en Afrique. Des capacités sous-utilisées. *Afrique contemporaine* 4(236): 130–132.

CNUCED (2014) Le développement en Afrique. Catalyser l'investissement pour une croissance transformatrice en Afrique. Report 2014. United Nations, New York.

Cogneau, D., Mesplé-Somps, S. (1999) *La Côte d'Ivoire peut-elle devenir un pays émergent?* OCDE, Paris.

Collas de Chatelperron Ph. (2000) Fondements de la démarche du projet en matière de classement des forêts. In *Gestion durable des forêts au Cameroun : vers une foresterie responsable, contributions du projet Forêts et Terroirs* Actes de l'atelier d'échanges 4–6 Juillet 2000. CIRAD, Yaoundé. Cumming, G. (2001) *Aid to Africa*. Ashgate, Aldershot.

Conac, G. (1993). *L'Afrique en transition vers le pluralisme politique*. Paris, Economica.

Gazibo, M. (2005) *Les paradoxes de la démocratisation en Afrique: analyse institutionnelle et stratégique*. Presses Universitaires de Montréal, Montréal.

Golan, T. (1981) A Certain Mystery: How Can France Do Everything That It Does in Africa-and Get Away With It. *African Affairs* 80(318).

Goulet, D. (1995) *Development Ethics. A Guide to Theory and Practice*. Zed Books, London and Apex Press, New York.

Grellet, G. (1982) *Les structures économiques de l'Afrique noire*. PUF, Paris.

Guénard, C. and Dubois, J.-L. (2001) Inégalités, croissance et pauvreté en Afrique subsaharienne. In Winter, G. coord, *Inégalités et politiques publiques en Afrique : Pluralité des normes et jeux d'acteurs*. Karthala-IRD, Paris, 41–56.

Guèye, B. (2009) La démocratie en Afrique: succès et résistances. *Pouvoir* 129(2): 5–26.

Hugon, P. (1993) *L'économie de l'Afrique*. La découverte, Paris.

Hugon, P. (2007) La politique économique de la France en Afrique. La fin des rentes coloniales ? *Politique africaine* 105(1): 54–69.

Ibo, G.J. (2006) Retraits des terres par les "jeunes" autochtones sur les anciens fronts pionniers de Côte d'Ivoire : expression d'une crise de transition intergénérationnelle, Paper presented at the international conference "Les frontières de la question foncière". Montpellier, France.

Koulibaly, M. (1998) Solidarité internationale, altruisme et sous-développement africain. In Mahieu, F-R. and Rapoport, H. eds., *Altruisme. Analyses économiques ?* Economica, Paris, 263–294.

Kurer, O. (1996) The Political Foundations of Economic Development Policies. *Journal of Development Studies* 32: 645–668.

Lavigne-Delville, P., Toulmin, C. and Traore, S. (1996) *Gérer le foncier rural en Afrique de l'Ouest : dynamiques foncières et interventions publiques*. Karthala – URED, Paris.

Lumumba-Kasongo, T. (2005) Liberal Democracy and Its Critics in Africa: Political Dysfunction and the Struggle for Progress. Zed Books, London.

Mahieu, F.R. (1983) *Introduction aux finances publiques de la Côte-d'Ivoire*. Nouvelles éditions africaines, Abidjan.

Mahieu, F.-R. (1994) Planification ou marché du développement? Des projets à l'approche nationale des programmes. *Tiers Monde* 35(140): 851–873.

Montagne, P. and Ramamonjisoa, B. (2006) Politiques forestières à Madagascar entre pression et autonomie des acteurs. *Economie Rural*, 294–295, 9–26.

Razafindrakoto, M. and Roubaud, F. (2005) Gouvernance, démocratie et lutte contre la pauvreté : Enseignements tirés des Enquêtes 1–2–3 en Afrique francophone. *STATECO* 99: 169–201.

Ribot, J.-C. (2001) Historique de la gestion forestière en Afrique de l'Ouest. Ou : comment la 'science' exclut les paysans, Les dossiers d'Haramata, les publications de l'IIED.

Smith, S. and Glaser, A. (1992) *Ces Messieurs Afrique. Le Paris-village du continent noir*. Calmann-Lévy, Paris.

Thiriot, C. (1999) Démocratisation et démilitarisation du pouvoir: étude comparative à partir du Burkina Faso, Congo, Ghana, Mali et Togo, Doctoral dissertation, University of Bordeaux 4.

White, H. (1992) The Macroeconomic Impact of Development Aid: a Critical Survey. *Journal of Development Studies* 28(2): 163–240.

37

Sub-Saharan Africa

Development ethics and post-colonial debate

Byaruhanga Rukooko Archangel

Drawing upon the post-colonial studies framework, this chapter outlines the status of development ethics in sub-Saharan Africa today. This is achieved by first defining the subject territory, followed first by demonstration of the relevance of development ethics to the region and then by consideration of the contribution of African thinkers to its growth. Later, I speculate on the future of development ethics in the region, concluding that, while development ethics is critical to African development, much work remains to be done.

Development ethics and post-colonial thought

Post-colonial debate is interested in analysing, understanding, and responding to the socio-cultural and political legacy of colonialism. Having been motivated partly by the Marxist school and postmodernist thinkers like Frantz Fanon and Michel Foucault, the debate has been embraced by several social sciences and humanities, including ethics (Sharp 2008). Yet, 'development ethics', founded by writers such as Denis Goulet and Anglo-American thinkers like Peter Singer, Garrett Hardin, and Paul Streeten among others, is an emerging discipline that concerns itself with ethical reflection on the nature, processes, ends, and consequences of development. Development ethics draws on the role of moral values as an 'ethical toolkit' for evaluation of any development agenda. These values may include integrity, human rights, equity, participation, peace building, enhancement of people's well-being, freedom, identity, environmental sustainability, care and compassion, common good, social justice, and many others. Development ethicists further contend that ethical dimensions of development are as essential as scientific and policy aspects – they are not extras (Schwenke 2009; Crocker 2004; Drydyk 2016). Schwenke thinks that theological reflection is also within the scope of development ethics (Schwenke 2009), and this makes sense in Africa because many Africans have a strong sense of religion. Although there may be some areas of disagreement on scope of the subject, the prevailing consensus on most issues is compelling (Drydyk 2016; Crocker 2004; Schwenke 2009). To the extent that development ethics responds to post-colonial intellectual endeavours, it is a full member of post-colonial studies. But if so, what is its relevance to sub-Saharan African development agenda?

DOI: 10.4324/9781315626796-46

Relevance of development ethics to sub-Saharan Africa

Although the scope of development ethics goes beyond developing countries because it is also concerned with a chain of responsibilities of various players at local and international levels including intended beneficiaries and victims, it still pertains closely to the interests of Africa. The questions development ethicists ask can include 'How just are these relationships between donors and recipients?', 'What means should be used to develop sub-Saharan Africa?', 'What types of obligations are involved?' and many other concerns about Africa (Crocker 2004; Schwenke 2009). If we take the example of development aid to sub-Sahara, development ethicists would be interested in how values such as equity, human dignity, participation, well-being, environmental sustainability, governance, and peace-building are affected.

Development ethics is also relevant because of its ownership of 'an ethical toolkit' to respond to the current extreme anxiety over management of natural resources and environment degradation across the continent, human rights, displacement, landlessness, emigration, conflict, and many other negative effects of so-called development (Chin-Yee 2016; Hattingh 2011). There is urgency for appropriate principled moral response to such overwhelming dilemmas which development ethicists are more leveraged to offer (Crocker 2004 and Schwenke 2009). Their 'ethical toolkit', among other toolkits, provides well-argued and articulated moral positions that can be used to offer good insights on how to proceed or how to recognise, understand, and promote genuine ethical development. Indeed, it helps if Africans keep the 'ethical toolkit' close to their chest in the face of such challenges of development.

As I have noted, development ethics is a new discipline fast expanding in the global North but only beginning to show in some parts of Africa. If such an 'ethical toolkit' should be used by others for the benefit of sub-Saharan Africa, then it is only sensible that Africa should play its part by supplementing what others are doing for them. That is to say, Africa should analyse and develop appropriate principles, and if necessary, be advocates for their own societies, and make their voices heard loud and clear.

Peter Kanyandago has strongly argued that development can only be endogenous rather than exogenous (Kanyandago 2009). It is also well-known that with development ethics by nature being a cultural enterprise and part of philosophy, it would make a lot of sense for Africans to exploit their own traditional cultural value repository to build more coherent world views and moral principles affecting their development (Schwenke 2009). In fact, I would argue that Africans should develop their characteristic brand of African development ethics.

Moreover, earlier on, J.S. Mill argued that citizens' participation in matters that affect them enhances their maturity and appreciation of social responsibility (Mill, in Thompson 1976). In other words, Africa's increased participation in development ethics debates enhances their agency, empowerment, and opportunity for fulfilment and well-being.

Inversely, if Africans are not involved in development ethics' endeavours, it would mean that in their absence someone else will have to do it for them, which is akin to development aid. In fact, it would imply that Africans are also encouraging another form of development aid called 'ethics aid', the negation of which has already been demonstrated. Against this backdrop, the relevance of development ethics to Africa cannot be over-emphasised. Now, if these arguments are valid, can we identify what Africans have done to shape development ethics?

Contributions from Africa

Thus, within the bounds of the current development ethics approach, the response to the development debacle from thinkers in Africa is twofold: one maintains a 'conventionalist' ethics approach which Anthony Appiah describes as being 'continuous' with European ancestors, and the second 'Africanist' approach relies on the African traditional value system to bring about worthwhile development (Appiah 1998). Whereas the first category includes philosophers like Hountondji, Wiredu, Gyekye, Towa, Kebede, and Hattingh, the second category includes Nyerere, Nkrumah, Mbih, Hellsten, many literary writers (like Ngugi wa thiongo, Chinua Achebe, Wole Soyinka), and many others. Whereas I shall only make brief consideration of the 'conventionalists' because they are few, I shall offer more space to the 'Africanists' because they dominate in terms of numbers. But even here, I will exclude the literary authors because of space limitations.

Of the conventionalist development ethicists that can be identified, Messay Kebede is clearly one. He goes at length to defend the view that development is a matter of ethics and he fully recognises the role of values like human dignity, freedom, and choice while rejecting the economic growth model of development like most development ethicists do. His thought is generally intended to be objective – while defending westernisation he also supports African thought (Kebede 2004). Unlike the Africanists, he believes that worthwhile development is possible in a liberal democratic dispensation if it is supported by 'a moral faith' (Kebede 1994).

J. Hattingh, who is also unmistakably steeped in the development ethics discourse, is mainly concerned with sustainable environment but he avoids reference to African metaphysics and communitarian ethics to justify his proposals. Using Gardiner, he argues that sustainable environment has become threatened with multifaceted challenges to the extent that using the usual human-centred ethics is no longer tenable. Instead, he proposes 'a radical ethics approach' to deal with overwhelming problems of sustainable environment (Hattingh 2004, 2011). Interestingly, although he does not deploy the traditional African cosmology (discussed later in the chapter) as many others do to deal with the problem of sustainable development, he comes close to their view when he recognises that the universe is a multi-layered complex that needed a multi-layered solidarity (Hattingh 2011). Both Hountoudji and Towa reject the Africanists' views, but unlike Kebede, a view of development ethicists is not clear.

Africanists

The earliest of Africanist thinkers were not development ethicists in the strict sense of the discipline, but their themes, claims, and argumentation were clearly within the post-colonial studies ambit, marked by critique of neo-colonialist models of development as well as trying to re-define and re-assert African identity. They were opposed to Western exploitation, disorientation, and displacement of their value system, which they believed was a better basis for development. Indeed, quite a number of Africanists supported socialism, contending that it was either a derivative of, or very similar to, African pre-colonial social-political-economic set up which they described as African communalism (Nyerere 1971 Nkrumah 1970; Kaunda 1974). These thinkers included nationalists like Nkrumah, Nyerere, Oginga-Odinga, Obote and literary personalities like Ngugi wa thiongo, Chinua Achebe, Wole Soyinka, and many others. But what exactly did African communalism mean and how could this be a channel of development?

African communalism meant that society placed a higher premium on the common good than on an individual. Thus, an action was good if it promoted the common good and bad if it diminished common good (Nkrumah 1970; Nyerere 1971. For instance, rights of property were held under extended family, village, and societal scope rather than individuals (Appiah 1998, Tosam and Mbih 2015). It was further claimed that the communitarian ethics was also humanistic in the sense that it promoted values like care, compassion, sharing, love, peacefulness, generosity, and honesty. This is reflective of personal integrity as a cardinal pillar of African communitarian ethics, as opposed to the Western individualistic tendencies or a beast which did not carry such values (Wiredu and Gyekye 1992; Appiah 1998; Tosam and Mbih 2015). In addition, communitarian ethics entailed promotion of human dignity, solidarity, sharing, participation, non-discrimination, empowerment, full agency, equity, egalitarianism, hard work, social responsibility, and promoting brotherhood (Tosam and Mbih 2015).

It is thus held that such a toolkit of values was more likely to shove Africans into worthwhile development compared to the Western development toolkit which carries competitive, profit-motivated, conflict-potent values and a greed for power which bred colonialism (Hellsten 2013; Tosam and Mbih 2015). It was added that, moreover, from the biblical context (Genesis) even their Judeo-Christian religion was overtly anthropocentric. Namely, all things were created for man's gratification which further undermined environmental sustainability (Murombedz 2003). Finally, it is argued that African elite have adopted the Western hypocrisy and rhetoric of worthwhile development without interest in pursuing it practically (Murombedz 2003; Hellsten 2013).

In the post-apartheid era, this communitarian ethics has been reincarnated as 'Ubuntu' or 'Obuntu' philosophy in Africa's development thought and policy agenda, especially in Southern Africa. As Thabo Mbeki and Desmond Tutu argued, this thinking should become a new flagship ideology that is authentic to Africans and reflective of 'African Renaissance' (Mbeki 2015). In fact, there is an attempt to benchmark it for South Africa's foreign policy (New World Encyclopedia 2016). Understood as 'the belief in a universal bond of sharing that connects all humanity' or simply 'being human', Ubuntu was meant to encourage racial and ethnic harmony and cooperation among former separate people in Southern Africa and beyond. It is also a repository of values like mutuality, respect, community, sharing, caring, trust, responsibility, equity, participation, and many other human values, and it is hoped that Ubuntu can provide a basis for consensus and well-being of the community (New World Encyclopedia 2016). To this end, research on the relevance of Ubuntu philosophy to Africa's development as a practical program is growing.

Yet, a seemingly more interesting but supportive argument of the communitarian ethics derives from another pervasive African cosmology, first elaborated by Placide Tempels: that the universe of Bantu, its contents and inhabitants were one, but a hierarchically interconnected continuum. All the past, the present and the future inhabitants and contexts, events, nature, and non-human beings are one but complex interrelated whole (Tempels 1952; Mbiti 1969). This implied interdependence and sustainability of the world by all aspects of nature as 'forces' or vital forces – which were traditionally respected and worshiped although these forces were unequal. God had the highest vital force and the inanimate had the lowest. Forests, rivers, lakes, the sun and the moon, caves, rapids, rain, and everything else was sacred (Tempels 1952; Mbiti 1969; Tosam and Mbih 2015; Hellsten 2013; Murombedz 2003). The individual is ontologically, spiritually, economically, and normatively connected to the rest of nature and was never an atomistic agent with private interests (Hellsten 2013). However, I find this position somehow contradictory to the communitarian ethics argument that Africans were egalitarian when the world in which they were living in was hierarchical. Moreover, the ancestors and elders were assigned stronger vital forces than children and women.

It was further claimed that African metaphysics was a lived experience which was easily appreciated by most Africans as compared to the Western approach which was abstract, non-liveable and seemingly inapplicable and inaccessible to many Africans. Yet, African knowledge of the universe can be mediated through African sages who have the ability to ably interpret and convey it to the policymakers and others who need it (Odera Oruka 1983, 1991). Accordingly, government and non-governmental organisation officials in African countries who are concerned with development strategies and plans should therefore consult and utilise the thoughts of sages, if they sincerely wish to attain any meaningful degree of success in their development endeavours (Odera Oruka 1991, 57–65; see also Ochieng'-Odhiamabo 1994).

Finally, when the international model of sustainable development is compared with the African metaphysical-religious world view, there is compelling consistency and I see no reason why African cosmology cannot provide a blueprint for the so highly cherished holistic approach for sustainable development today. However, this reasoning has been challenged by one of the African thinkers with the argument that this cosmology is no different from Asian societies – especially Japan, which has high emission rates (Kelbessa 2002). Before we conclude this section, it should be clarified that generally, most of the Africanists are not radical in defence of the African ethical systems; no one, for instance, is suggesting that Western values should be decimated from Africa. Instead, they propose a synthesis of the two value systems, or complementarity, or a search for alternative approaches to sustainable development (Nkrumah 1970; Kelbessa 2002; Ssozi 2012; Hellsten 2013; Murombedz 2003; Ngabirano 2008). Whether these values were indeed applicable now are issues that would need further discussion.

Prospects of development ethics

True, development ethics is a new academic discipline, but that does not diminish its relevance; its importance extends from the past through the present to the future. Fortunately, strong indications of appreciation of the discipline are beginning to show on a number of fronts, including institutions, universities, governments, agencies, and non-governmental organisations. Some universities like Makerere University, University of Stellenbosch, and University of Zambia are teaching and researching in their various programmes, while others have development studies and environmental studies programmes that could conveniently integrate development ethics. Yet many have environmental studies programmes where sustainable development could also be integrated, and those which have human rights programmes could introduce the right to development as well as environmental rights. Universities such as Rhodes, Cape Town, UNISE, Pretoria, University of Dar es salaam, University of Bostwana, and many others are potentially seedbeds of growing development ethics in sub-Saharan Africa.

To that end, the work of various professors in African universities and outside, including their students and partners, needs recognition and support. International agencies like UNDP and UNESCO and other non-profit organisations should be identified and collaboration networks initiated. Governments in Africa also need to be informed and encouraged to support this discourse in relation to policy and development. It is practically useful if non-governmental organisations would also take part in such debates in their programmes and projects. Nonetheless, much more remains to be done.

Conclusion

In view of the preceding discussion, it needs to be emphasised that development ethics discourse is an important part of post-colonial debate because it leverages evaluation of development thinking programmes based on values. It is also important to observe that development ethics is a critical intellectual endeavour relevant to an African development agenda because development is, after all, for and about Africa. A number of scholars in various universities and other individuals in institutions and organisations have already begun this conversation, but this is not enough. More needs to be done in terms of coordination and mobilisation of capacity and resources.

References

Appiah, K.A. (1998) Race, Pluralism, and Afrocentricity. *Journal of Blacks in Higher Education* 19: 116–118.

Chin-Yee, S. (2016) Briefing: Africa and the Paris Climate Change Agreement. *African Affairs* 115(459): 359–368.

Crocker, D. (2004) Development Ethics: Sources, Agreements, and Controversies, https://msu.edu/~phl/EandDWebsite/sources/Development_Ethics.pdf

Drydyk, J. (2016) Ethics in Development. In Grugel, J. and Hammett, D. eds., *Palgrave Handbook of International Development*. Springer, London, 55–76.

Hattingh, J. (2011) Towards a Shared Ethics of Global Climate. *Current Allergy and Criminology* 24(2).

Hattingh, J. (2004) On the Ethical Analysis of Value Issues in Public Decision-Making. *South African Journal of Philosophy* 23(3): 213–225

Hellsten, S. (2013) The End of Development? Reflections on the Unsustainability of the Current Paradigm and a Quest for an African Alternative. *Public Reason* 5(2): 79–94.

Kanyandago, P. (2009) Culture as a Basis for Promoting Prosperity for All, Uganda Martyrs University. Unpublished paper presented at Equatorial Hotel, 19th May.

Kaunda, K. (1974) *Humanism in Zambia and a Guide to Its Implementation, Part II*. Zambia Information Services, Lusaka

Kebede, M. (1994) *Meaning and Development*. Rodopi, Amsterdam.

Kebede, M. (2004) *Africa's Quest for a Philosophy of Decolonization*. Rodopi, Amsterdam.

Kelbessa, W. (2002) Indigenous and Modern Environmental Ethics: Toward Partnership. *Thought and Practice in African Philosophy* 47–61.

Mbeki, T. (2015) The Arab Reawakening: Africa Renaissance Perspective. In Villa-Vicensio, C. Doxtader, E. and Moosa, E. eds., *The African Renaissance and the Afro-Arab Spring*. Georgetown University Press, Washington, DC.

Mbiti, J. (1969) *African Religion and Philosophy*. Heinemann, London.

Murombedz, J. (2003) Pre-colonial and Colonial Conservation Practices in Southern Africa and Their Legacy. Unpublished IUCN Manuscript.

Ngabirano, E. (2008) *The Environment in Uganda: An Ethical and Theological Assessment of the Conservation-Preservation Controversy* (Masters thesis) VDM Verlag Dr. Muller, Saarbrücken.

Nkrumah, K. (1970) *Consciencism: Philosophy and Ideology for Decolonization*. Monthly Review Press, New York.

Nyerere, J. (1971) *Ujamaa – Essays on Socialism*. Oxford University Press, New York.

Ochieng'-Odhiambo, F. (1994) *The Significance of Philosophic Sagacity in African Philosophy* (PhD thesis) University of Nairobi, Nairobi.

Odera Oruka, H. (1983) Sagacity in African Philosophy. *International Philosophical Quarterly* 23: 383–393.

Odera Oruka, H. (1991) Sage Philosophy: The Basic Questions and Methodology. In Odera Oruka, H. ed., *Sage Philosophy: Indigenous Thinkers and Modern Debate on African Philosophy*. ACTS Press, Nairobi.

Schwenke, C. (2009) *Reclaiming Value in International Development*. Westport: Praeger.

Sharp, J. (2008) Chapter 6, "Can the Subaltern Speak?" In *Geographies of Post-colonialism*. Sage Publications, London.

Ssozi, K. (2012) Values and Participation: The Role of Culture in Nature Conservation and Environmental Education among the Baganda. *Journal of Sustainability Education* March 19. www.susted.com/wordpress/content/values-and-participation-the-role-of-culture-in-nature-preservation-and-environmental-education-among-the-baganda_2012_03/

Tempels, P. (1952) *Bantu Philosophy*. Presence Africaine, Paris.

Thompson, D. (1976) *John Stuart Mill and Representative Government*. Princeton University Press, Princeton. http://press.princeton.edu/titles/684.html. Accessed 9 July 2016.

Tosam M.J. and Mbih, R.A (2015) Climate change, health, and sustainable development in Africa. *Environment Development and Sustainability* 17(4): 787–800.

Towa, M. (1979) Cited in Mbih Jerome (2014) The Relevance of Kom Ethics to African Development. *International Journal of Philosophy* 2(3): 36–47.

Ubuntu New World Encyclopedia. www.newworldencyclopedia.org/entry/Ubuntu_(philosophy). Accessed 10 July 2016.

Wiredu, K. and Gykekye, K. (1992) *Persons and Community*. Council for Research in Values and Philosophy, Washington, DC.

38

Europe

European development ethics – past and present

Louise Haagh

The problem of development ethics in Europe is governed by a paradox: Both theorisation and practice of development ethics can be traced to European modernity. Yet, today, the idea of 'development' as a collective project is relatively unfamiliar to European elites. Opinions expressed by delegates at Nordic green party events (Alternativet 2017) reveal how even more ethically based publics are puzzled about the notion of 'development policy' – believed to be a challenge specific to developing countries. More likely to sell green policies today is a language of export competitiveness and market rationality (European Commission 2017; Fankhauser et al. 2012; Apak and Atay 2015).

Two earlier periods in which ethical discourse applied to development was more manifest in European thinking were the onset of industrialisation in the second half of the nineteenth century, and the postwar period of the formation of the European welfare state. An obvious prompt for reconsidering ethics in development was the economic crisis of 2008 and the Great Recession that followed. Yet, the present period is different from the other two, which were preceded by momentous change, in the form of rural modernisation and mass urbanisation, and two world wars.

Below, I first look at development ethics as previously understood in European history. I then discuss some ways we can view the contemporary crisis affecting Europe in terms of a gradual erosion of state regulatory powers. Third, I consider the ethical dimensions and significance of regulatory differences within Europe. I argue briefly for more positive criteria for evaluating human development opportunity as a social condition shaped by the form of regulatory policy and public sector capacity. This presents imagining the humanist state as a key contemporary ethical challenge.

Development ethics in European history

Characteristic of the eighteenth and nineteenth centuries debates about development as systems of innovation in Europe was a clash that persists until today. About a hundred years after Adam Smith's *The Wealth of Nations* in 1776, the German development economist Friedrich List began a charge against Smith's notion that two countries of unequal endowments both benefit from open trade. In his work, *The National System of Political Economy*, published in 1885, List argued

DOI: 10.4324/9781315626796-47

the whole politics of nations drives development, its content and rate. Against Smith's notion of progress as driven by trade and monetary exchange, he argued the capability of peoples is the real value in development: List defended Germany's right to protect its own manufacturers so that they could compete with Britain. He defined development as a political rather than an economic project:

> Let us compare Poland and England: both nations at one time were in the same stage of culture: and now what a difference. Manufactories and manufactures are the mothers and children of municipal liberty, of intelligence, of the arts and sciences, of internal and external commerce, of navigations and improvements in transport, in civilisation and political power.
> *(List 1885, 31)*

The accuracy or otherwise of List's description is less relevant than how he saw political development within and equality among countries as necessary for development.

In common with List, contemporary critical development economists underline how productive power, not market value, gives the notion of development substance. For Chang (2003, 2007), the erection of ostensibly neutral market rules globally – exemplified by the formation of the World Trade Organisation regime in 1995, and especially its enforcement in a way that cuts states' powers to promote and protect industrial development, is a moral issue, as it was for List. We might say both scholars recognised that the formation of institutions of incorporation, broadly speaking, is a necessary part, if not the essence, of human progress.

A notion of progress linked with reformist states advancing humanist goals accompanied a second defining period in European development ethics, the formation of the postwar welfare state in the late 1940s till the 1970s. T.H. Marshall (1950, 21) thought that the early period of liberalism had created *opportunity for*, but not *rights to* welfare. For Marshall, the state's regulatory role and provision of services would therefore be central to ensure collective welfare covered all but the mere "frill and luxuries" (1950, 34). The forces of competition and money economy would be beaten back to enable human development As he wrote, (op. cit., 47), "The unified civilization which makes social inequalities acceptable, and threatens to make them economically functionless, is achieved by a progressive divorce between real and money incomes", which Marshall saw could only be achieved by cross-class inclusive public welfare, and significant regulation to generate a sense of permanent human security, e.g. control of rents, and "security of tenure" in housing (ibid.).

The extent to which T.H. Marshall saw individual freedom as bound up with social equality, and vice versa, is further exemplified in how he envisaged progress for the working classes as attaining control of time and occupation. Ultimately, quoting Alfred Marshall (cited in Marshall 1950, 6) a man could be identified as a gentleman, not by his title, but as *not* belonging to the working class in the sense that we recognise "the effect that he produces on his work", rather than "the effect that his work produces on him". On this basis, he viewed the problem of generating a social foundation for individual welfare – citizenship as a "developing institution" (op. cit, 18) as a gradual and difficult democratic project.

Erosion of state regulatory powers

Fast-forward to the twenty-first century, how much of the sense of collectivism behind human development, as expressed in Marshall's thought, survives? The deep effect of economic depression in especially Southern parts of Europe, combined with fiscal austerity reinforced by the 2008 crisis aftermath, should invite the thought that Europe today needs a positive development programme. A plausible reason why the idea of a developmental ethics nevertheless seems foreign to political elites is that the language of market economics has exerted a heavy influence on perceptions even when policymakers (still) preside over complex welfare states.

The EU-level approach is exemplified in the December 2011 Fiscal Compact (FC) which formed part of several steps taken to address Europe's banking and sovereign debt crises. According to the FC, underwritten by the European Court of Justice, the 25 EU member signatories commit to ensure a cap of 0.5 per cent on the 'structural deficit' within the annual public budget (Radice 2013). As Martin and Rowthorn (2012) discuss, there is a problem with the production factor model, that is, that it does not reflect real economic capacity. In broad development terms, however, the problem goes deeper than capacity measurement problems. The development economist Amartya Sen's evaluation of Europe's approach is indicative, as reported in the *Financial Times* (2011): "To move from that frying pan of mismanagement to the fire of indiscriminate cuts to satisfy the creditors and to placate the rating agencies has not been helping . . . countries to move into a responsible forward-looking recovery programme". At stake in the FC approach is a view about which forces in the economy should be incentivised, which differs radically from the past. In the postwar period, states sought to build 'investor confidence', which entailed a series of measures to ensure the private sector invests in the productive economy. The state's role today is more passive, and beholden to systemic forces. Measures such as the FC have come to be viewed as necessary to ensure the banking sector's confidence in risk-taking, simply to avoid another crisis. Confidence in this sense is now not about steering the private sector to invest in productive change (necessarily). It is geared to ensure the financial sector trades – e.g. takes risks about allocating financial assets based on intuitions about speculative returns – with confidence, so that the rest of the economy is not destabilised. In short, rather than banking enabling society, society must enable banking. The public sector is caught up in a toxic relationship with the financial sector.

The issue at stake is then how public risk sharing is differently premised today. Examples of public sector crises in Britain illustrate how the short-term cost-accounting model within the public sector stands in tension with forging a developmental role of the state. Although in theory long-term planning is possible, short-term accounting is an enabling basis for programmes that fragment public power. For example, where the state adopts a non-interventionist approach, yet retains commitments to social housing, it may end up footing a rather large bill that it might have reduced by regulating to cap private rents. Comparing Britain's housing subsidy bill as a share of social spending, it is much larger than in regulatory welfare (Nordic) states (Haagh 2018a). Estimates based on government figures by the National Housing Federation point to a 42 per cent real increase in public housing benefit costs between 2005 and 2016 relating with a larger private rental sector share (Independent 2016), in what is the least formally regulated sector in the EU (European Commission 2014, 6; Shelter 2018).

Another case in point is the crisis in the British National Health Service (NHS) – in winter of 2017 causing queues of ambulances outside emergency wards – which experts blame on fragmented governance – such as cuts to care homes rather than (merely) lack of cash (Jenkins 2018; Care Quality Commission 2017, 7).

A wider problem is the way short-termism in public finances entails a costly lack of planning, symbolised in the chronic staff shortages that caused doctors to claim British hospitals offered 'third world' conditions in hospital corridors (Guardian 2018). Lack of occupational planning, a historic problem in Britain (Snow and Jones 2011), reinforced by short-term cost management today, has led, according to expert reviews, to growing and costly reliance on temporary agency staff (The King's Fund 2017, 6), whilst private sector suppliers to the NHS are increasingly going out of business due to unstable contracting (ibid., 3).

Austerity-led public service provision in a deregulatory framework also makes the public sector vulnerable to risk presented by overexposed, large private contractors. A case in point is the collapse in January 2018 of the largest private contractor to the UK government, Carillion, founded in 1999, following a series of industry mergers. The company supplied prisons, schools, hospitals, the military and the railway network. Government stepped in with a package of over £100 million to cover its debts to contractors and save jobs (BBC 2018). The Carillion case is indicative of the new structure of public risk and governance by default it entails. Soon after Carillion's collapse, in January 2018, the Public Administration and Constitutional Affairs Committee of the British parliament sat down an enquiry. Chairman of the Committee, Bernard Jenkin MP, justified this in writing: "Seeing what has happened to Carillion and given the concentration of outsourced public sector contracts into such a small number of large companies, we need to ask if the rules on oversight and accountability of public services need to change?" (UK Parliament 2018).

The implication is, capable government and public scrutiny mechanisms – routinely and well-employed in the UK, are doing the job other collective institutions and government used to do, but evidently not in a way that can be effective in forging systemic change, because the role of public enquiries and courts is not to govern in the forward-looking sense, but to raise questions after the fact. In all, it is plausible to find a range of examples of how a new governance model of *regulation without development policy* is deficient: the tail is wagging the dog.

Ethical aspects of regulatory differences within Europe

Despite the trend towards policy convergence that is an inevitable part of both globalisation and Europeanisation, significant regulatory differences among European states remain, which can be traced back in time in ways which put into context regulatory choices Europe faces today.

An early manifestation of the role of narrative and reform behind the egalitarian Nordic tradition is the inscription by Crown Prince Frederik on the so-called Liberty Column erected in Copenhagen in 1792 to mark the end by royal decree of feudal social relations, followed by comprehensive land redistribution. On one side, it reads, "The king recognizes that freedom for citizens given by just law generates public affection for the fatherland, courage to guard and care for it, desire for learning, motivation to work hard, faith in good fortune." It continues, on the other side, "The king ordered that the feudal bond be repealed, that land reform deliver order and power, that the free peasant can become enlightened and informed, hard-working and kind, honourable citizen, happy." It is signed, "King Frederik, the people's friend."

Extensive land redistribution and public support of the cooperative movement that followed (Chang 2009) laid the context in which across Nordic states the idea and practice of humanist and life-long education (as portrayed in Campbell 1928) took hold, as practiced in Sweden and Denmark in churches and communal halls, in city and countryside (Sandberg 1979). In relevant contrast, the enclosure that preceded land modernisation in Britain was not broadly redistributive (Kananen 2014). State education remained stratified, and skills systems underdeveloped (Finegold and Soskice 1988; Thelen 2004).

The back story to the Nordic land reforms described was a series of conflicts, revolving around the desire of some noblemen for the King to modernise, and especially tackle the power of the wealthy aristocracy by empowering a new middle class: a classic liberal revolution, led by a king. Two aspects of this tale are noteworthy for my argument, being the humanist narrative represented in the language that grounds the repeal act, and how that entailed a form of commitment to a thoroughgoing reform programme, which then followed (Jensen 1936).

Development and social policy in Nordic states have combined liberal and voluntarist elements in industrial relations and contributory insurance with state compulsion in activation, generating problematic stratifications. On the other hand, arguably, neither the spirit nor the practice of the broad egalitarian commitments laid down historically ever really ran dry. As example of this is the persistence of policies in Nordic states to suppress competition in state education in favour of delaying exams (Steinmo 2010) and promoting student choice through public support of a range of post-education occupational systems, including tri-partite-governed apprenticeship (Anker 1998). As a testimony to the role of the egalitarian ideal is how 'retaining a low level of inequality' is expressed as a manifest aim of the Danish finance ministry in annual yearbooks (Haagh 2001). A lasting difference in regulatory tradition between Denmark and Britain, despite similarities in the creation of national health services and income security systems after World War Two, gives rise to two different forms of capitalism, hierarchical and horizontal (Haagh 2012). The long-standing egalitarian tradition set forth by the public sector suggests egalitarian social policy is not a recent response to liberalisation, as portrayed in Thelen (2014), but has deeper and more complex institutional and political roots.

The importance about this in today's terms is twofold: long-term institutional legacies explain how Nordic states – especially Denmark – have been relatively less open, if not immune, to corrosion of state regulatory power and developmental commitments in public policy. For example, whereas in the 2000s all countries slightly increased spend on family policy, the UK sees a remarkable reduction in public spending on education and training. The public share of tertiary education falls from 68 to 36 per cent between 2000 and 2007, whereas in most Nordic states it hovers around 97 per cent (Sweden has the lowest share – it drops from 91 to 89 per cent). In Britain, spending on training for adults, focused on the unemployed in particular, falls from 0.37 per cent of GDP to 0.05 during liberalisation, between 2000 and 2014, where in Denmark it goes up from 1.58 to 1.91 per cent of GDP, with Sweden dropping slightly from 1.37 to 1.34 per cent (OECD 2017). In these items of human development spend, Denmark and Britain are at either end of the OECD spectrum. An important consideration when thinking in this context about development ethics as having foundation in public opinion is how welfare values are shaped by public experience. For example, publics across Europe have roughly similar levels of support for social justice (Svallfors 2012, 223). However in Britain there is more support for health and pensions, less for the unemployed, childcare and family policy. In Nordic states, support for all these are more consistent and higher (Brooks 2012, 208). Welfare values are more differentiated (Edlund 2007, 63–71), more accurately reflect social reality and are more coherent (Svallfors 2007, 215) in Nordic publics.

Development ethics in the European future

In the context of an EU framework under strain by threats of defection, a relevant question to ask is then what in the future might sustain the social bases of a publicly conscious development ethics? Two interacting trends in particular threaten to undermine public trust, to the extent – as evidenced earlier – this relies on broadly humanist and egalitarian policies succeeding.

First, a steady rise in cost of infrastructure, transport, housing and subsistence over two decades has outstripped the value of real wages (OECD 2017). Two countries that have enacted or faced severe austerity, namely Britain and Greece, are both at the bottom of a list of 29 OECD countries in real wage growth. In both countries the real value of wages fell by around 10 per cent between 2007 and 2015. Indicative of the vacuum in development policy are the record youth unemployment rates in Europe today. The link between unemployment and enforced austerity is evident, with the highest levels of youth unemployment in Greece officially at 20.7

per cent in October 2017, compared with Euro-area level of 16.1 per cent (European Commission 2017).

Second, alongside this relative economic decline, rights-duties enforcement has taken a punitive turn in European countries since the late 1990s. Across especially Northern Europe with more extensive benefit systems, sanctions have been applied to reinforce the effect of conditionalities exercised among disabled or unemployed persons reliant on benefits (OECD 2013, Venn 2012). Sanctions interpret implied threats of removal of support literally by taking real steps to remove that support, and – to implement this – raise the intensity and frequency of scrutiny of claimants' behavior or/and medical conditions. Countries like Denmark and Britain both had a sanction rate of about 24 per cent in the mid-2010s, counting all claimants. The form and implementation of threats to withdraw subsistence have been comparably more developmental in Denmark (Haagh 2018a, 2018b; Adler 2016). Yet, for social democratic publics like the Nordic countries and Holland, an implication of efforts to reinforce the cooperative ethic through sanctions is to put the tradition of respect for citizens' basic economic liberty (linked with public support of control of time, Goodin 2001, Goodin et al. 2008), at risk. In all countries, the justifiability of sanctions is called into question by the increasingly precarious nature of work at the lower end of the labour market (Standing 1999). The way application of sanctions nevertheless strongly *implies* personal responsibility then implicates government policy in a certain amount of truth distortion, which threatens to further undermine cohesive welfare values. We already know that more fractured (highly means-test-defined) assistance systems are associated with distrust among citizens. As an example, in Britain, 65 per cent of respondents to the European Social Survey think welfare makes people lazy, compared with 44 per cent in Denmark (Svallfors 2012, 208). On this basis, sanctions can be predicted to have further corrosive effects in intra-citizen trust.

The contemporary fracturing of welfare systems in Europe begs a rethink about what recreating universal welfare would look like, as distinct from the form it took in the postwar era. Postwar welfare state institutions had significant imperfections. For instance, they did not actually predistribute either housing or income support, but offered means-tested support in instances of need, which created poverty traps: people who had little in life in any case were asked to trade away state support for jobs they might lose, only then to face applying for state support all over. In this context, a modern universalism has two distinct foundations that jointly act as a condition for inclusion of all citizens in more diversified shared risk structures, represented in contribution and savings systems. The first is a genuinely universal form of predistribution of citizen access to public utilities, infrastructure, welfare services and basic income. Recent polemics (Portes et al. 2017) suggest European publics should choose between basic security in services or income. But this is mistaken, including by focus on imagined short-term cost trade-offs in place of institutional complementarity benefits (Haagh 2017a). Conversion in the form of access to transfers and services citizens already receive, so as to create a genuinely shared foundation, is a relevant alternative (Torry 216, Haagh 2017a, 2017b). This would bring Europe back to the spirit of the postwar welfare commitment to humanism and inclusion. Second, Europe needs a revived development policy, implicating public regulatory and planning commitments to enable a stable core of occupational streams in the economy. As noted, youth unemployment is at an all-time high. Yet, core social services face shortages of trained permanent staff – as in the case of NHS England (apparently short of 86,000 permanent staff in 2017, BBC 2017).

In all, generating foundations for human development in the institutional sense, of persons gaining command of core activities and social relations, entails the public ought to consider how to enable combined developmental choice. This is not exactly the same as capabilities, i.e. the idea we should be able to choose among certain human functions in liberty (Sen 1998; Nussbaum 2006).

The idea of combined developmental choices entails recognising how more built-up governing and incisive public regulation to stabilise and share work and care, constrain or enable us to live a life of integrity between core activities and social relations (Haagh 2012, 2015) giving added definition to the value of choosing. Public sector traditions in Europe – especially but not only Northern Europe – can be argued to have striven towards such an ideal. The sanctions pathway is a form of deviation.

Four steps forward

In summary, thinking about steps that can be taken to generate a more politically conscious development path begins simply with a reassessment of the rules within which what is already provided is given. First, European countries can make institutional adjustments to how they deliver welfare that would cost very little and solve current poverty traps that we know for certain are costly in both human development and economic terms. Second, the EU fiscal framework can be altered in a way that long-term budgeting and planning, and a certain level of public indebtedness for development, a return to tradition, in this respect, can be possible, with a view to strengthen stable public health and care occupations, and allow individual countries planning flexibility. Third, to that end, European countries need to reconsolidate fiscal powers, which entails tackling low-tax competition, which even the IMF recognizes has driven taxation down too far across mature states (IMF 2017). Intra-regional cooperation might evolve around this kind of long-term objective. The European Competition Commissioner Margrethe Vestager's more direct approach (Guardian 2017) to tackling tax avoidance of large companies and low tax havens in Europe that shield such behaviour shows steps that can be taken if the political will is there. Fourth, reclaiming of public ownership of vital utilities, that has become a trend among leading sub-national states, and some countries as a whole (Cumbers 2014), has an important role in addressing the pre-distribution deficits mentioned earlier, by giving the public control of infrastructure costs. Many public services across Europe lack staff, and young people are out of work. Recognizing that such intermediary institutions can only be viable through medium or long-term budget planning and occupational investment is the answer to stabilise European public sectors and the lives of new generations.

References

Adler, M. (2016) A New Leviathan: Benefit Sanctions in the Twenty-first Century. *Journal of Law and Society*, 43(2): 195–227.

Alternativet (2017) Annual Convention, Odense, May 2017.

Anker, N. (1998) *Eleverne, Virksomhederne og de nyudlærte*. Frederiskberg, Handelshøjskolen i København.

Apak, S. and Atay, E. (2015) Global Competitiveness in the EU through Green Innovation Technologies and Knowledge Production, Precedia. *Social and Behavioural Sciences* 181: 207–217.

British Broadcasting Corporation (BBC) (2017) More Than 86,000 NHS Posts Vacant, Says Report. *BBC News*, by Smitha Mundasad, 25 July 2017. www.bbc.co.uk/news/health-40715955.

British Broadcasting Corporation (BBC) (2018) Carillion Collapse: UK Puts up £100m to Back Carillion Contractor Loans. 3 February. www.bbc.co.uk/news/business-42925155.

Brooks, C. (2012) Framing Theory, Welfare Attitudes, and the United States' Case. In *Contested Welfare States – Welfare Attitudes in Europe and Beyond*. Stanford University Press, Stanford.

Campbell, O.D. (1928) *The Danish Folk School*. Palgrave Macmillan, New York.

Care Quality Commission (2017) The State of Health Care and Adult Social Care in England 2016/17. www.cqc.org.uk/sites/default/files/20171123_stateofcare1617_report.pdf.

Chang, H.-J. (2003) *Kicking Away the Ladder.* Anthem Press, London.

Chang, H.-J. (2007) *Bad Samaritans.* Random House, London.

Chang, H.-J. (2009) Under-explored Treasure Troves of Development Lessons – Lessons from the Histories of Small Rich European Countries (SRECs). In Kremer, M., van Lieshoust, P. and Went, R. eds., *Doing Good or Doing Better – Development Policies in a Globalising World.* Amsterdam University Press, Amsterdam.

Cumbers, A. (2014) Renewing Public Ownership – Constructing a Democratic Economy in the Twenty-First Century. Centre for Labour and Social Studies, Policy Paper, July. http://classonline.org.uk/docs/Renewing_Public_Ownership_-_Andrew_Cumbers_FINAL.pdf.

Edlund, J. (2007) Class Conflicts and Institutional Feedback Effects in Liberal and Social Democratic Welfare Regimes – Attitudes Toward State Redistribution and Welfare Policy in Six Western Countries. In Svallfors, S. ed., *The Political Sociology of the Welfare State.* Stanford University Press, Stanford.

European Commission (2014) Economic Papers 515 | April 2014 Economic and Financial Affairs ISSN 1725–3187 (online) ISSN 1016–8060 (print) Rental Market Regulation in the European Union Carlos Cuerpo, Sona Kalantaryan, Peter Pontuch.

European Commission (2017) ec.europa.eu/eurostat/statistics-explained/index.php/Unemployment_statistics.

European Social Survey (2017) http:// www.europeansocial survey.org.

European Commission (2017) The EU Regional Competitiveness Index 2016, Annoni, P, Dijkstra, L. and Gargano, N. (2017) Regional and Urban Policy Working Papers, 02/2017.

Fankhauser, F. et al. (2012) Who Will Govern the Green Race? In Search of Environmental Competitiveness and Innovation. Centre for Climate Change Economics and Policy, Working Paper No. 94.

Financial Times (2011) Nobel Economist blasts Europe's Austerity Plans. By James Lamont in Delhi, 14 December. www.ft.com/content/00a8b866-265c-11e1-85fb-00144feabdc0.

Finegold, D. and Soskice, D. (1988) The Failure of Training in Britain: Analysis and Prescription. *Oxford Economic Review* 4(3): 21–53.

Goodin, R.E. (2001) Work and Welfare: Towards a Post-Productivist Welfare Regime. *British Journal of Political Science* 31: 13–39.

Goodin, R.E, Rice, J.M., Parpo, A. and Eriksson, L.(2008) *Discretionary Time – A New Measure of Freedom.* Cambridge University Press, Cambridge.

Guardian (2017) www.theguardian.com/world/2017/sep/17/margrethe-vestager-people-feel-angry-about-tax-avoidance-european-competition-commissioner.

Guardian (2018) A&E Doctor Sorry for "Third World Conditions" as NHS Winter Crisis Bites. 2 January 2018. www.theguardian.com/society/2018/jan/02/ae-doctor-sorry-for-third-world-conditions-as-nhs-winter-crisis-bites.

Haagh, L. (2001) The Challenges of Labor Reform in Korea: A Review of Contrasting Approaches to Market Enhancement and Experiences from Chile and Denmark. In Park F-K, Park Y-B, Betcherman, G. and Dar, A. eds., *Labor Market Reforms in Korea: Policy Options for the Future.* The World Bank, Washington, DC.

Haagh, L. (2011a) Basic Income, Social Democracy and Control Over Time, Policy and Politics 39(1): 41–64.

Haagh, L. (2011b) Working Life, Well-Being and Welfare Reform: Motivation and Institutions Revisited. *World Development* 39(3): 450–573.

Haagh, L. (2012) Democracy, Public Finance, and Property Rights in Economic Stability: How More Horizontal Capitalism Upscales Freedom for All. *Polity* 44(4): 542–587.

Haagh, L. (2015) Alternative Social States and the Basic Income Debate: Institutions, Inequality and Human Development. In Basic Income Studies, Special Issue on Thomas Piketty's Capital in the Twenty-First Century, August, ISSN (Online) 1932–0183, ISSN (Print) 2194–6094. doi: 10.1515/bis-2015–0002, August 2015, www.degruyter.com/view/j/bis.ahead-of-print/bis-2015-0002/bis-2015-0002.xml.

Haagh, L. (2017a) Basic Income Should be Seen as a Democratic Right – Not a Solution to Unemployment. *Royal Society of Arts Journal* 4.

Haagh, L. (2017b) Basic Income as a Pivoting Reform. *Nature. Human Behaviour* (1), Article No. 0125, 12 June.

Haagh, L. (2018a) Public Ownership Within Varieties of Capitalism: Regulatory Foundations for Welfare and Freedom. In Public Ownership in the Twenty-First Century, Special Issue of the *International Journal of Public Policy*, guest edited by Angela Cummine and Stuart White, forthcoming.

Haagh, L. (2018b) *The Case for Basic Income*. Polity, Cambridge.

Independent (2016) Taxpayer Money Paid to Private Landlords Doubles Over 10 Years. By Ben Chu, 19 August. www.independent.co.uk/news/business/news/private-landlords-taxpayer-money-housing-benefits-rent-housing-crisis-low-income-families-a7199111.html.

International Monetary Fund (2017) Fiscal Monitor – Tackling Inequality, World Economic and Financial Surveys, October.

Jenkins, S. (2018) A Special Tax to Save the Struggling NHS Won't Work. Here's Why. *The Guardian*, 5 February, https://www.theguardian.com/commentisfree/2018/feb/05/special-nhs-tax-wont-work-why.

Jensen, H. (1936) *Dansk Jordpolitik* 1857–1919 (translated as Danish Agricultural Politics) Gyldendalske Boghandel – Nordisk Forlag, Copenhagen.

Kananen, J. (2014) *The Nordic Welfare State in Three Eras*. Ashgate, Surrey.

The King's Fund (2017) Written Submission to the House of Lords Select Committee: Long-term Sustainability of the NHS, 29 June, The King's Fund, London.

List, F. (1885) *The National System of Political Economy*. Cosimo Inc., New York

Marshall, A. (1873) The Future of the Working Classes, lecture to the Cambridge Reform Club, Cambridge.

Marshall, T.H. (1950) *Citizenship and Social Class*. Pluto Press, London.

Martin, B. and Rowthorn, B. (2012) *Is the British Economy Supply Constrained II? A Renewed Critique of Productivity Pessimism*, UK Innovation Research Centre/Centre for Business Research, University of Cambridge, May 2012. www.cbr.cam.ac.uk/pdf/BM_Report3.pdf.OECD (2013) Employment Outlook, Activating Jobseekers: Lessons from Seven OECD Countries. www.oecd.org/els/emp/Employment-Outlook-2013-chap3.pdf.

Nussbaum, M. (2006) *Frontiers of Justice*. Harvard University Press, Cambridge.

OECD (2017) Employment Outlook.

Portes, J., Reed, H. and Percy, A. (2017) Social Prosperity for the Future: A Proposal for Universal Basic Services. Institute for Global Prosperity, University College London.

Radice, H. (2013) Reshaping Fiscal Policies in Europe: Enforcing Austerity, Attacking Democracy. *Social Europe*. www.socialeurope.eu/reshaping-fiscal-policies-in-europe-enforcing-austerity-attacking-democracy.

Sandberg, L.G. (1979) The Case of the Impoverished Sophisticate: Human Capital and Swedish Economic Growth before World War I. *The Journal of Economic History*, 39(1) *The Tasks of Economic History*: 225–241.

Sen, A. (1998) *Development as Freedom*. Oxford University Press, Oxford.

Shelter (2018) License to Rent. http://england.shelter.org.uk/__data/assets/pdf_file/0004/206779/A_Licence_to_rent_Briefing.pdf.

Smith, A. ([1776, 1904] 1961) *An Inquiry into the Nature and Causes of the Wealth of Nations*. Methuen University Paperbacks, London.

Snow, S. and Jones, E. (2011) Immigration and the National Health Service: Putting History to the Forefront. History and Policy, Policy Papers, 8 March.

Standing, G. (1999) *Global Labour Flexibility*. Palgrave Macmillan, Basingstoke.

Steinmo, Sven (2010) *The Evolution of Modern States*. Cambridge University Press, Cambridge.

Svallfors, S. (2007) Class and Attitudes to Market Inequality. In Svallfors, S. ed., *The Political Sociology of the Welfare State*. Stanford University Press, Stanford.

Svallfors, S. (2012) Welfare Attitudes in Context. In Svallfors, S. ed., *Contested Welfare States – Welfare Attitudes in Europe and Beyond*. Stanford University Press, Stanford.

UK Parliament (2018) www.parliament.uk/business/committees/committees-a-z/commons-select/public-administration-and-constitutional-affairs-committee/news-parliament-2017/lessons-collapse-carillion-inquiry-launch-17-19/.

Thelen, K. (2004) *How Institutions Evolve: The Political Economy of Skills in Comparative-Historical Perspective*. Cambridge University Press, New York.

Thelen, K. (2014) *Varieties of Liberalisation and the New Politics of Social Solidarity*. Cambridge University Press, Cambridge.

Torry, M. (2016) *The Feasibility of Citizens' Income*. Palgrave Macmillan, London.

Venn, D. (2012) Eligibility Criteria for Unemployment Benefits: Quantitative Indicators for OECD and EU Countries. OECD Social, Employment and Migration Working Papers, No. 131, OECD Publishing, Paris. http://dx.doi.org/10.1787/5k9h43kgkvr4-en.

39

USA and Canada

High-income maldevelopment

Eric Palmer

The focus of this chapter is on development within the United States of America and Canada. Indigenous peoples and their nations are also featured. Canada and the USA are both characterized by the UN Development Programme as maintaining very high human development. The two countries are developing, nevertheless. Such a claim could be taken as a truism, but addressable weaknesses are evident when performance is compared, for example, with OECD member nations, a group that is dominated by European nations of a similar development profile. The USA and Canada have also expressed explicit development commitments to the UN Sustainable Development Goals (SDGs). All parties to the SDG agreement pledge to national improvements for 2015–2030, and so the USA and Canada have numerous targets that include the following:

> Reduce at least by half the proportion of men, women and children of all ages living in poverty in all its dimensions according to national dimensions . . . Implement nationally appropriate social protection systems and measures for all . . . end all forms of malnutrition . . . ensure inclusive and equitable quality education for all . . . Strengthen the prevention and treatment of substance abuse . . . reduce inequality . . . Significantly reduce all forms of violence and related death rates. . .
>
> *(UNICEF 2017)*

One or both nations show particular weakness in each of these targets.

In what follows I focus upon political institutions and attendant social inequality in the areas of social welfare, education and health. Due to space constraints I cannot also provide a comprehensive picture of development concerns that pertain to gender inequality, employment opportunities, racial prejudice, nutrition and food insecurity, environmental injustice and much more. The last section concludes that cultural shifts and legislative decisions over the span of the past half-century have displaced the ethos of social responsibility that the USA has shared with Canada in the past, replacing it with one of self-reliance that has led to missed opportunities, backsliding and maldevelopment. For the sake of simplicity, "America" and "American" are used here to refer to the USA, despite the fact that other nations of the continent may sensibly lay equal claim to these terms.

DOI: 10.4324/9781315626796-48

Development shortcomings and horizontal inequalities

Politicians of both nations acknowledge development successes and failings, and recent political rhetoric shows diverging plans for improvement. US President Donald Trump acknowledged losses to development in his 2017 inaugural address, referring to an "American carnage" of drug addiction, crime, poverty, superannuated factories, unemployment and failures of educational policy. Canadian Prime Minister Justin Trudeau, addressing the UN General Assembly several months earlier, acknowledged Canada's continuing gender inequality, marginalization of indigenous peoples and insufficient support of the elderly and youth. Trudeau articulated a vision to improve a "strong, diverse and resilient" country through acceptance of immigrant and refugee populations, engaging them to "build a strong middle class" and so reduce "citizens' anxiety" (Trudeau 2016). Trump indicated a different path, reinforcing border controls so that "every decision on trade, on taxes, on immigration, on foreign affairs will be made to benefit American workers and American families" (Trump 2017).

Immigration, both historic and ongoing, is central to both ethos and demographic within these nations. The USA has, in the past, presented the incorporation of cultures as an assimilatory process (a "fresh start" or a "melting pot"). That ideal has faded over the past half-century, perhaps because it contradicts persistent intergenerational group inequalities, particularly in the experiences of indigenous peoples and the descendants of captured and transported Africans, now 150 years after the abolition of slavery in 1865 (Stewart 2009; Coates 2014). African Americans, who represented about a tenth of the nation's population in the mid-20th century, pressed their continuing concerns in the civil rights and Black power protest movements. Their efforts produced the Civil Rights Act of 1964, the Voting Rights Act of 1965 and the formal removal of racial segregation where it had remained in business and governance institutions, primarily in Southern states. Group inequalities have persisted, however, across the whole of the national map in many dimensions that are indicated later in the chapter, particularly for indigenous, African American (henceforth also referred to by the census category "Black") and Hispanic populations, with recently increasing bias against those perceived to be of Muslim faith. The USA's official characterization of groups is a blend of racial and ethnic categories: White non-hispanic (henceforth "White") reflect 77% of the population; Hispanic 17%; Black 13%; Asian 7%; American Indian, Alaska Native and Pacific Islander (including Hawaii) 2%; and two or more races 3%. Immigrants born in another country account for 13% of the legally recognized population, as of 2016 (US Census 2017).

Canada's cultural ideal is of multiple non-assimilated cultures (multiculturalism) and its governance system is consequently more complex. Canadian thinkers continue to develop the ideal: Will Kymlicka argues for the embrace of "ambivalent identifications and contested commitments" to state and to sub-state national, ethnic and linguistic groups and he holds that "citizenship agendas must promote a distinctly multinational conception of citizenship if they are to be fair and effective" (Kymlicka 2011, 283). Nineteen percent of Canada's population characterize themselves as "visible minority," with South Asian (5%), Chinese (4%), Aboriginal (Indigenous) (4%) and Black (3%) the major groups, as of 2011. Twenty-one percent of Canada's population was born in another country; the majority of recent immigrants are from Asia (Statistics Canada 2016).

Multiculturalism makes for complexity in governance. Canada is a Westminster parliamentary democracy built upon plurinational political relations for three cultural groups. English Canada is the majority. French Canada, which reflects 24% of households, has a distinctive status, including official language status. The French majority province of Quebec has a distinctive civil law system, undertakes distinct cultural prerogatives and holds designated provincial representation on the Supreme Court of Canada. Indigenous and Métis peoples have "inherent right of self-government" in Canada with "aboriginal and treaty rights" explicitly recognized in 1982 amendments to the Constitution. Indigenous "First Nations" retain significant claims to land not subject to treaty, particularly within the region of British Columbia (Indigenous and Northern Affairs 2017).

Internal development policy, social welfare and financial poverty

The USA's national system for human financial security, or welfare, has origins in the mid-1930s as a response to the Great Depression (the "New Deal" of the Franklin Roosevelt administration). Canada's welfare and health systems were conceived in the same era from socialist political currents; they developed more slowly and they have remained more stable. In the final quarter of the 20th century, the USA and Canada began with similar poverty rates (if calculated as <50% of median income). After taxes and transfers, these rates would diverge by the mid-1980s: Canada's rate dropped by one-third, to 10%, and the USA's rose one-tenth, to 18%. Rates are currently at 13% and 17% (Zuberi 2006, 21; OECD 2017).

Political history illuminates American strategies for development. In 1965, late in the era of the Civil Rights Movement, US assistant secretary in the Department of Labor Daniel Patrick Moynihan authored *The Negro Family: The Case for National Action*. His report documented rising crime and unemployment within black communities and stated:

> [T]he Negro family in the urban ghettos is crumbling. A middle-class group has managed to save itself, but for vast numbers of the unskilled, poorly educated city working class the fabric of conventional social relationships has all but disintegrated. . . . So long as this situation persists, the cycle of poverty and disadvantage will continue to repeat itself. . . . Measures that have worked in the past, or would work for most groups in the present, will not work here. A national effort is required that will give a unity of purpose to the many activities of the Federal government in this area, directed to a new kind of national goal: the establishment of a stable Negro family structure.
>
> *(Moynihan 1965)*

The Moynihan report was intended as a progressive clarion call as part of the "War on Poverty" of President Johnson's administration. Anthropologist Susan Greenbaum reflects that, "although Moynihan did assert that joblessness was the major problem facing African Americans, his focus was not on measures to expand employment, but on the psychological effects of male unemployment" (Greenbaum 2015, 3; c.f. Coates 2015). Demographer William Julius Wilson suggests that the report effectively racialized American discussion of poverty reduction, stalled progressive programs and opened space for politically conservative accounts focused upon promotion of individual responsibility as a remedy for problems that were framed as a "culture of poverty" and welfare dependence (Wilson 2012, 6). Following the election of Ronald Reagan as President in 1981 conservative agendas consolidated within policy and in social analysis. Charles Murray argued that public assistance both fostered the creation of the "welfare mother" and encouraged men to avoid parental responsibilities (Murray 1984, 231).

The welfare system has since contracted. The Personal Responsibility and Work Opportunity Reconciliation Act (PRWORA) of 1996 reduced a previous focus on training within welfare-to-work programs of the late 1960s. Temporary Assistance for Needy Families (TANF), which limited assistance to low-income families to five years in a parent's lifetime, replaced traditional federally funded welfare. Welfare benefits are now comparable between the USA and Canada, with the following exceptions: Canada does not keep a clock for eligibility, part-time earnings are largely retained by the underemployed in Canada (three-quarters retained vs. one-quarter), Canada has more extensive opportunities for retraining and further training for the unemployed, Canada provides more systematically for language training and, though the USA provides small tax credits for the poorest that increase for families with dependent children, Canada's financial benefits expand greatly for families with children (Zuberi 2006, 87, 95–96).

In the USA, poverty is not in decline, but aid to families, especially to children, is in decline: TANF rolls have reduced greatly since 1996. Modest increases in median family income have been slight for poor families and near to zero for single-parent families (US Census 2016a, Table F-10). In 2015, children represented less than one-fourth of the population and yet were one-third of the population living below the national poverty line. Two-thirds of families with children in poverty were single-parent households (US Census 2016b, 14–18).

Philosopher Iris Marion Young argued that the US welfare policy shift of 1996 reflects a re-conception of responsibility within American culture that dates from the Reagan era. Rhetoric of "personal responsibility" and "independence," has been cast as "family values," replacing the New Deal era view that all members of society are responsible for the social conditions that affect everyone. Social responsibility has been transfigured to blaming the poor, regardless of differences in ability, cyclical failings such as recessions and continuing injustice reflected in horizontal inequalities. The shift has reduced the burden of social services provided by the state in "the triumph of a more individualist understanding of social relations that weakens or even destroys [the] idea of collective responsibility" (Young 2011, 7–10; c.f. Greenbaum 2015, 14–15, 112).

Education: horizontal inequalities and social mobility

Shortly following World War II, in 1950, the USA held the highest graduation rate among large, very high development nations, at about 50%. An 82% graduation rate for 2014 places the USA 3% lower than the average of OECD member nations. Canada exceeds that average by 4% (OECD 2016 Table A2.1). "Baseline competency" at age 15 for mathematics, science and reading as measured by the Programme for International Student Assessment (PISA survey) is about average among highest-performing nations for US students. Canadian students are among the best (UNICEF 2017, Figure 4.1).

Inequality of outcome by race and socioeconomic status contributes to continued horizontal inequality in the USA. Above 88% of both White and Asian students graduate; they lead the Hispanic group by 10% and further lead other assessed groups: economically disadvantaged (76%), Black (75%), Native American (72%), limited English proficiency (65%), and students with disabilities (65%) (USNCES 2016). For many of these groups, then, one-fourth or more of children will not graduate high school.

Comparison of university achievement of adult children to that of their own parents also indicates an unpromising future for social mobility in the USA and an especially promising one for Canada. Upward mobility reflected in education is meager in the USA: children with parents lacking high school degrees themselves graduate university at an 8% rate. This compares with 42% in Canada, which is a rate much higher than the average of 22% for OECD nations. Comparison of US children of foreign-born parents who lack a high school education with children of similarly educated parents born within the USA shows that the former group are twice as likely to themselves achieve college graduation as the latter group. At 9% and 5%, these figures lag greatly behind the OECD averages (23% and 22%). Canada is again a leader: similar groups rate at 51% and 33% respectively (OECD 2016, Tables A4.4, A4.1, A.4.3).

Elizabeth Anderson offers structural explanations for horizontal inequality perpetuated by the public education system of the USA, particularly for African American and disabled students (Anderson 2012). Higher suspension and expulsion rates for these groups indicate that "outcome"-based standards of distributive justice, rather than the prevalent "opportunity"-based standards, would be needed to produce a fair educational system. Though "fair opportunity" ideals resonate, especially with the US culture of individual responsibility noted in Young's writing, those ideals serve to privilege socially dominant White and Asian groups that subscribe to values largely shared by teachers. So, Anderson argues, "middle-class" values and cultural practices that these groups share serve as "cultural capital" that creates a less inclusive environment and curriculum. Lower-class values and styles of parenting yield reduced opportunity in this setting, even though these values and strategies are not obviously in themselves of less value for equipping children for life: the strategies may reflect sensible adaptation to insecure circumstances and may display these parents' unfamiliarity with an educational system that had not served them well (112, 115–116). Anderson argues that a system that does not achieve proportional success rates for all groups reproduces group inequalities and low mobility for the younger generation, and so, ultimately reproduces economic and social injustice.

Health outcomes

Health outcomes should be distinguished from provision of health care. Health care and genetics have substantial effects upon health outcomes, but "social determinants of health" – material, behavioral and psychosocial factors – may play even greater roles. Health outcomes are greatly influenced by home, social and working environment; exercise and sleep; diet, especially salt and saturated fat; smoking, drugs and alcohol; and social hierarchy and economic status that influence the physiological correlates of stress (Marmot 2015; Brunner and Marmot 2006).

Health care spending is a very large portion of expenditures within all developed countries. Expenditures have increased as a portion of GDP in the USA, from 10.5% to 17.5% over the period of 1987–2011 (Barr, 2014, Figure 1.1). Canada's current expenditure is in line with most European countries, at two-thirds the portion for the USA. Since the USA has perhaps 20% greater GDP per person, costs nearly double those within Canada. There is general consensus that expenses for administration of the hybrid private/public health system in the USA accounts for much of the extra expense: estimates for such costs reach as high as 30% (Zuberi 2006, 70). Canada produces superior outcomes across many indicators: for example, 20% lower infant mortality and two more years life expectancy, at 78 and 83 years, for men and women born in 2013 (Barr 2014, Table 1.1). Life expectancies are similar to Canada's for US populations that are Hispanic (79, 84) and White (76, 81); these expectancies greatly lead Black (72, 78) and Native American (73, combined measurement) (Kunitz and Pesis-Katz 2005, 7; Center for Disease Control 2017, Table 15; Indian Health Service 2017).

Health care access has been universal since the 1970s in Canada's Medicare/Assurance-Maladie national insurance and care system. It is administered at the level of territories and provinces. This produces some inequities in quality and access related to wealth and policy as well as regional inequities suffered by rural populations. Care for indigenous populations located on both ancestral lands and in urban areas produces inferior outcomes. Many, especially the elderly, express dissatisfaction with the physician's gatekeeping role and with lengthy queues for some procedures (Romanow 2002, 218–222; 16–20). The waits also unduly increase morbidity (disease, or long-term reduction in health). A few with resources may opt for private clinics; very few will visit the USA or other nations for care.

Access in the USA is varied (US Census 2015). About half the population receives private insurance through plans involving cost-sharing with employers on a multi-payer (multiple-insurer), multi-provider open market. Special government service providers exist for military veterans and for indigenous populations within reserve lands. Medicaid, a single-payer federal system administered and supplemented at the level of individual states, covers individuals with disabilities, some low-income adults and children not otherwise covered. Medicare, a single-payer federal system paying most costs, is available to all over age 65 who can document legal residency for the five years before application. Elderly assisted living services are largely assured through personal expenditure and private insurance, but many rely on a social safety net administered at the state level that is uneven and requires a prior reduction of the individual to indigence.

Legislation towards creating universal health coverage in the USA that is coordinated with open markets – "Obamacare," or the Patient Protection and Affordable Care Act – was enacted in 2010. Late in 2016, a tenth of Americans under age 65 went uninsured, a historic low that halved the percentage in 2010. Proposed changes would almost certainly lead to a rise in the rate of uninsured (Luhby 2017).

Socioeconomic status and race are especially significant factors in health outcomes worldwide (Kunitz and Pesis-Katz 2005; Marmot 2015; Barr 2014). The effects of both are complex in the USA, with universal coverage for those over age 65 and access to health care linked to employment status for about half the population. In a much-discussed paper of late 2015, Ann Case and Angus Deaton argued that both morbidity and mortality at midlife (ages 45–54) for White Americans had risen consistently since 1995, very nearly matching historically higher rates for African Americans (Case and Deaton 2015). They found the increase to be confined to the one specific racial and age grouping, though they have recently noted a similar rise over a shorter term among African Americans. These declines reverse and cancel improvements to be found over the previous 20 years in the US population generally; the reversal is not seen in similar populations in Canada and Western Europe. The authors account for these increases as the results of drug overdose, suicide, and alcohol poisoning: such "deaths of despair come from a long-standing process of cumulative disadvantage for those with less than a college degree." They find contributing factors to be increasing precarity for workers, a culture of disdain for economic safety nets, and decreasing social support in the forms found in traditional institutions of marriage and religion. Case and Deaton lay blame specifically upon an American culture of individual responsibility in which one's lack of success is perceived as an individual moral failing, producing a "Durkheim-like recipe for suicide" (Case and Deaton 2017).

Similar concerns arise for indigenous youth and adults globally and within both countries (King et al. 2009). Suicide rates in Canada among indigenous people are three or more times the national average, they are five or more times the average among youth, and are of overwhelming concern within some geographically isolated communities (Marmot 2015, Ch. 8; Canadian Press and Globe staff 2017). The government acknowledges that Indigenous child welfare programs are underfunded and "the legacy of colonialism in Canada" and its remedy were central to Prime Minister Trudeau's UN address for 2017 (Murphy 2016; Trudeau 2017). Similar concerns have garnered less attention in the USA recently, despite that President Obama had acknowledged long-standing inequity (McGreal 2010).

Conclusion: outcomes and amelioration

Several development failures have been highlighted in this chapter: horizontal inequalities related especially to race and religion, low social mobility, rising within-nation inequality, declining educational access and achievement, inefficient and disparate health care access and uneven health outcomes. Canada's superior language and settlement services for immigrants, its health care system and its superior education and social welfare programs may account for some aspects of development that compare well against conditions in the USA. Alongside policy, culture is important: the multicultural ethos that Canadian politicians continue to support may buffer it from the USA's turn to isolationism, to oppositional politics, and to a culture of individualism that hazards disregard for structural causes of inequality. A dwindling culture of social responsibility may have fueled the USA's increasing inequality within education and its reduction in social welfare programs since the 1980s. Though Canada's economic productivity is less, the nations nevertheless rank about equally on the Human Development Index. In the final analysis, then, it is not evident that the USA's high productivity has paid off well in terms of development. Canada is by many measures a more equal society, but it shares many development shortcomings with the USA: continued failings in development for aboriginal populations is one among these, as well as vulnerability and despair for that group and for others.

References

Anderson, E. (2012) Race, Culture and Educational Opportunity. *Theory and Research in Education* 10(2): 105–129.

Barr, D. (2014) *Health Disparities in the United States*, 2nd ed. Johns Hopkins University Press, Baltimore.

Brunner, E. and Marmot, M. (2006) Social Organization, Stress and Health. In Marmot, M. and Wilkinson, R.G. eds., *Social Determinants of Health,* 2nd ed. Oxford University Press, Oxford.

Canadian Press and Globe Staff (2017) Attawaapiskat: Four Things to Help Understand the Suicide Crisis. *The Globe and Mail* [Toronto][web], 5 January. www.theglobeandmail.com/news/national/attawapiskat-four-things-to-help-understand-the-suicidecrisis/article29583059/.

Case, A. and Deaton, A. (2015) Rising Morbidity and Mortality in Midlife Among White Non-Hispanic Americans in the 21st Century. *PNAS* 112(49). www.pnas.org/content/112/49/15078.full.pdf.

Case, A. and Deaton, A. (2017) Mortality and Morbidity in the 21st Century. Brookings Papers on Economic Activity Spring: 397–476. https://www.ncbi.nlm.nih.gov/pmc/articles/PMC5640267/.

Center for Disease Control [USA] (2017) *Health United States, 2016*. www.cdc.gov/nchs/data/hus/hus16.pdf.

Coates, T. (2015) The Black Family in the Age of Mass Incarceration. *The Atlantic*. www.theatlantic.com/magazine/archive/2015/10/the-black-family-in-the-age-of-mass-incarceration/403246/.

Coates, T. (2014) The Case for Reparations. *The Atlantic*. www.theatlantic.com/magazine/archive/2014/06/the-case-for-reparations/361631/.

Greenbaum, S. (2015) *Blaming the Poor: The Long Shadow of the Moynihan Report on Cruel Images About Poverty*. Rutgers University Press, New Brunswick.

Indian Health Service [USA] (2017) *Indian Health Disparities*. www.ihs.gov/newsroom/factsheets/disparities/.

Indigenous and Northern Affairs [Canada] (2017). The British Columbia Treaty Negotiations Process. https://www.aadnc-aandc.gc.ca/eng/1348230937078/1348231345065.

King, M., Smith, A. and Gracey, M. (2009) Indigenous Health Part 2: The Underlying Causes of the Health Gap. *The Lancet* 374(9683): 76–85.

Kunitz, S. and Pesis-Katz, I. (2005) Mortality of White Americans, African Americans, and Canadians: The Causes and Consequences for Health of Welfare State Institutions and Policies. *The Millbank Quarterly* 83(1): 5–39.

Kymlicka, W. (2011) Multicultural Citizenship Within Multination States. *Ethnicities* 11(3): 281–302.

Luhby, T. (2017) "The Truth About the Uninsured Rate in America. *CNN Money,* 14 March. http://money.cnn.com/2017/03/13/news/economy/uninsured-rate-obamacare/index.html.

Marmot, M. (2015) *The Health Gap*. Bloomsbury Academic, London.

McGreal, C. (2010) Obama's Indian Problem. *The Guardian*, 10 January. www.theguardian.com/global/2010/jan/11/native-americans-reservations-poverty-obama.

Moynihan, P. (1965) The Negro Family: The Case for National Action. US Department of Labor. www.dol.gov/oasam/programs/history/webid-meynihan.htm.

Murray, C. (1984) *Losing Ground: American Social Policy 1950-1980.* Basic Books, New York.

Murphy, J. (2016) Canada Pledge to Overhaul Broken Welfare Program for Indigenous Children. *The Guardian*, 26 January. www.theguardian.com/world/2016/jan/26/canada-discriminated-against-indigenous-children-welfare-services.

OECD (2016) Education at a Glance 2016. *OECD Indicators*. www.oecd.org/edu/education-at-a-glance-19991487.htm.

OECD (2017) Poverty Rate. *OECD Data*. https://data.oecd.org/inequality/poverty-rate.htm.

Romanow, R. (2002) *Building on Values: The Future of Health Care in Canada.* Commission on the Future of Health Care in Canada. http://qspace.library.queensu.ca/bitstream/handle/1974/6882/BuildingOnValues.pdf.

Statistics Canada (2016) Immigration and Ethnocultural Diversity in Canada. 15 September 2016. http://www12.statcan.gc.ca/nhs-enm/2011/as-sa/99-010-x/99-010-x2011001-eng.cfm.

Stewart, F. (2009) Horizontal Inequality: Two Types of Traps. *Journal of Human Development and Capabilities* 10(3): 315–340.

Trudeau, J. (2016) Prime Minister Justin Trudeau's Address to the 71st Session of the United Nations General Assembly. http://pm.gc.ca/eng/news/2016/09/20/prime-minister-justin-trudeaus-address-71st-session-united-nations-general-assembly.

Trudeau, J. (2017) Prime Minister Justin Trudeau's Address to the 72th Session of the United Nations General Assembly. http://pm.gc.ca/eng/news/2017/09/21/prime-minister-justin-trudeaus-address-72th-session-united-nations-general-assembly.

Trump, D. (2017) Inaugural Address. www.whitehouse.gov/inaugural-address.

UNICEF (2017) Building the Future: Children and the Sustainable Development Goals in Rich Countries (Innocenti report card 14). www.unicef-irc.org/publications/pdf/RC14_eng.pdf.

US Census Bureau (2015) HI-01 Health Insurance Coverage Status and Type of Coverage by Selected Characteristics. www.census.gov/data/tables/time-series/demo/income-poverty/cps-hi/hi-01.html.

US Census Bureau (2016a) Income and Poverty in the United States: 2015. www.census.gov/library/publications/2016/demo/p60-256.html.

US Census Bureau (2016b) Historical Income Tables: Families. www.census.gov/data/tables/time-series/demo/income-poverty/historical-income-families.html. Accessed 13 September 2016.

US Census Bureau (2017) Quick Facts. www.census.gov/quickfacts/. Accessed 1 July 2016.

US National Center for Education Statistics (2016) Common Core of Data, Table 1. https://nces.ed.gov/ccd/tables/ACGR_RE_and_characteristics_2014-15.asp.

Wilson, W.J. (2012) *The Truly Disadvantaged: The Inner City the Underclass, and Public Policy*, 2nd ed. University of Chicago Press, Chicago.

Young, I.M. (2011) *Responsibility for Justice.* Oxford University Press, Oxford.

Zuberi, D. (2006) *Differences that Matter: Social Policy and the Working Poor in the United States and Canada.* Cornell University Press, New York.

Index

For Product Safety Concerns and Information please contact our EU representative GPSR@taylorandfrancis.com Taylor & Francis Verlag GmbH, Kaufingerstraße 24, 80331 München, Germany

Printed and bound by CPI Group (UK) Ltd, Croydon, CR0 4YY
11/05/2025
01866595-0001